Global Political Economy

Global Political Economy

Edited by

John Ravenhill

OXFORD

UNIVERSITY PRESS

OXFORD

UNIVERSITY PRESS

Great Clarendon Street, Oxford OX2 6DP

Oxford University Press is a department of the University of Oxford.
It furthers the University's objective of excellence in research, scholarship,
and education by publishing worldwide in

Oxford New York

Auckland Bangkok Buenos Aires Cape Town Chennai
Dar es Salaam Delhi Hong Kong Istanbul Karachi Kolkata
Kuala Lumpur Madrid Melbourne Mexico City Mumbai Nairobi
São Paulo Shanghai Taipei Tokyo Toronto

Oxford is a registered trade mark of Oxford University Press
in the UK and in certain other countries

Published in the United States
by Oxford University Press Inc., New York

British Library Cataloguing in Publication Data

Data available

Library of Congress Cataloging in Publication Data

Data available

ISBN 0-19-926584-4

10 9 8 7 6 5 4 3 2 1

Typeset by Newgen Imaging Systems (P) Ltd., Chennai, India
Printed in Great Britain
on acid-free paper
by Antony Rowe Limited, Chippenham, Wilts.

Preface

I first taught a class on International Political Economy—at the University of Virginia—in 1982. At that time, the field was in its infancy and the literature relatively sparse. Over the two decades since then, it has blossomed as one of the most dynamic sub-fields of international relations. The study of International Political Economy has been enriched by and has itself contributed to the full range of theoretical approaches that characterize the contemporary study of international relations. Moreover, the empirical scope of the subject has broadened considerably over the years.

A substantial number of introductions to international political economy has appeared over the last two decades. In teaching courses on IPE each year—at universities in Australia, Japan, the UK, and the US—I have, however, found it difficult to select a text that provided an introduction suitable for use in upper level undergraduate courses that was comprehensive in its coverage of the various subject matter the field now embraces, and that also was sophisticated in its application of contemporary theorizing. Some books were too introductory; others assumed too much of students who may have little background in international relations or in economics before undertaking an IPE course; still others failed to incorporate recent theorizing, while very few incorporated the range of pedagogical aids that can enliven introductory texts.

From conversations with other researchers in the field and with various publishers, I know others shared this frustration. The response from publishers, of course, was to ask 'why not write your own book?' This was an invitation that I resisted not least because I would not have felt comfortable, given the vast expansion of the scope of the field, to write on all the subjects that a comprehensive text should cover. I was, however, very attracted to a proposal from OUP that I take responsibility for bringing together a group of leading researchers in the field to provide a new theoretically-informed and empirically-rich book suitable for semester-length courses in IPE. That so many leading researchers accepted my invitation to contribute reflects a widespread perception that such a book would be timely. The great advantages of having an edited book consisting of chapters written specifically for this collection are that it not only exposes students to a variety of theoretical approaches but also gives them access to an enormous wealth of expertise in the main sub-fields of international political economy.

In my experience, the question that students most frequently ask on enrolling in a course in international political economy is whether they need a background in economics to do well. My answer is always that IPE is a sub-field of international relations, that the course is in political science not in the discipline of economics: a background in economics is neither necessary nor sufficient for doing well in IPE. On the other hand, the subject matter of IPE inevitably has an economic dimension—whether it be international trade, debt crises, or transnational investment—so students who loathe everything to do with economics would be well advised to select an alternative course.

For students who wish to strengthen their knowledge of economics, the following books are useful introductions, written with the non-specialist in mind:

- James Gerber, *International Economics* (2nd Edition) (Addison-Wesley, 2002)
- Graham Bannock et al, *The Penguin Dictionary of Economics* (7th edition) (Penguin, 2003)

- D. Rutherford, *Routledge Dictionary of Economics* (Routledge, 2002)
- John Charles Pool and Ross M. Laroe, *The Instant Economist: All the Basic Principles of Economics in 100 Pages of Plain Talk* (Perseus, 1986)

For those who are comfortable with basic economic concepts, the following are the best introductory overviews of international trade theory:

- Paul Krugman and Maurice Obstfeld, *International Economics: Theory and Practice* (6th Edition) (Addison Wesley, 2002)
- Peter B. Kenen, *The International Economy* (4th Edition) (Cambridge University Press, 2000).

John Ravenhill
Canberra, September 2004

Acknowledgements

This project has been overseen by three editors at OUP, all of whom played crucial roles in bringing it to fruition. Angela Griffin, then Commissioning Editor for Politics and International Relations, first encouraged me in May 2001 to think seriously about putting forward a proposal to the Press for an edited book that would aim to be an equivalent for the global political economy field to the very successful Baylis and Smith volume that the Press had published on theories of international relations. Angela was closely involved in the development of the proposal but transferred to another position with the Press before the proposal went to reviewers and to the Press. Her successor as Commissioning Editor, Sue Dempsey, steered the proposal through an extensive review process culminating in the approval of the project by the OUP Delegates, and was very helpful in initial negotiations with the contributors. Last but by no means least, Helen Adams shepherded the final manuscript through the production process with remarkable patience and good humour. We have been very fortunate in that the contributors have kept the project on schedule, some of them doing so despite having to cope with particularly adverse personal circumstances.

The task of completing what turned into a very large project would have been much more difficult without the assistance of the Department of International Relations, Research School of Pacific and Asian Studies, Australian National University. I am grateful to the Head of Department, Chris Reus-Smit, for making research assistance and funding available. Mary-Lou Hickey formatted the manuscript to OUP's requirements. All of the contributors as well as the editor owe an enormous debt to Robin Ward who very carefully reviewed the chapters, chased up incomplete, inconsistent or missing references, and did a superb job in proof-reading and in preparing the index.

Peter Dauvergne thanks Sanushka Mudalia, and Alan Rugman thanks Cecilia Brain for research assistance. My principal debt, as always, is to my wife, Stefa Wirga, who provided encouragement and support throughout the project and tolerated my distraction at a time when we were immersed in the traumas of a move between continents.

We are grateful to those listed below for permission to reproduce copyrighted material:

Figure 4.1 from Department of Trade and Industry (UK), 'Average Industrial Tariffs in Developed Countries since 1947', *The Government's Expenditure Plans* (Her Majesty's Stationery Office, 2000) Chapter 8. Reprinted with the permission of Her Majesty's Stationery Office.

Figure 5.1 from World Trade Organization, 'Regionalism Facts and Figures' [http://www.wto.org/english/tratop_e/region_e/regfac_e.htm]. Reprinted with the permission of the World Trade Organization.

Figure 5.2 from World Trade Organization, Committee on Regional Trade Agreements, 'Mapping of Regional Trade Agreements: Note by the Secretariat', WT/REG/W/41, (Geneva: World Trade Organization, 2000). Reprinted with the permission of the World Trade Organization.

Figure 5.3 and *Table 5.4* from World Trade Organization *World Trade Report 2003* (Geneva: WTO, 2003). Reprinted with the permission of the World Trade Organization.

Figures 7.1, 7.2, and *7.6* from data in Barry Eichengreen and Michael Bordo 'Crises Now and Then: What Lessons form the Last Era of Financial Globalization', *NBER Working*

Paper No. w8716 (National Bureau of Economic Research, January 2002) Tables 5, 6, and 7. Reprinted with the permission of the authors.

Table 8.1 from P.H. Lindert and J.G. Williamson, 'Does Globalization Make the World More Unequal?', in M.D. Bordo, A.M. Taylor, and J.G. Williamson (eds.), *Globalization in Historical Perspective* (Chicago, IL: University of Chicago Press) Table 5.1. Reprinted with permission of the University of Chicago Press.

Tables 10.2 to 10.9 and *Appendix to Chapter 10* from Braintrust Research Group (2003), *The Regional Nature of Global Multinational Enterprises.* Reprinted with the permission of Cecilia Brain and Alan M. Rugman.

Figure 11.1 from B. Milanovich, 'True World Income Distribution, 1988 and 1993', *Economic Journal* Vol. 112(476) (2002) Figure 6. Reprinted with the permission of the publisher, Blackwell Publishing.

Figures 11.2 to 11.4 from Yuri Dikhanov and Michael Ward, 'Evolution of the Global Distribution of Income in 1970-99' (mimeo), Figures 1, 5, 6, 7. Reprinted with the permission of the authors.

Table 11.1 from Giovanni Arrighi, Beverly J. Silver, and Benjamin D. Brewer, 'Industrial Convergence, Globalization, and the Persistence of the North-South Divide', *Studies in Comparative International Development* 38/1 (2003) Table 1. Reprinted with the permission of the publishers, Transaction Publishers.

Figures 12.1 to *12.4* and *Table 12.2* from Oxfam International, *Rigged Rules and Double Standards: Trade, Globalisation and The Fight Against Poverty* (Oxford: Oxfam International, 2002) Figure 1.4, Figure 2.4, Figure 6.1, Figure 6.2 and Table 6.1. Reprinted with the permission of Oxfam International.

Table 12.1 from M. Gautam, *Debt Relief for the Poorest: An OED Review of the HIPC Initiative* (Washington, DC: Operations Evaluation Department, World Bank, 2003). Reprinted with the permission of the World Bank.

Figure 14.1 from 'Graph on World Population'. Reprinted with permission of the publisher, Population Reference Bureau, Washington, D.C.

Figure 14.4 from 'Graph on Global CO_2 Emissions from Fossil-Fuel Burning, Cement Manufacture, and Gas Flaring' in G. Marland, T.A. Boden, and R.J. Andres, 'Global, Regional, and National CO_2 Emissions', in *Trends: A Compendium of Data on Global Change* (Oak Ridge, TN: Carbon Dioxide Information Analysis Center, Oak Ridge National Laboratory, US Department of Energy, 2001). Reprinted with permission of the Carbon Dioxide Information Analysis Center.

John Ravenhill
Canberra, September 2004

Contents

Part One   Theoretical approaches to global political economy

Part Two   Global trade

Part Three   Global finance

Detailed contents

List of figures

List of boxes

List of tables

Abbreviations

ACP	Africa, the Caribbean and the Pacific
AFL-CIO	American Federation of Labor—Congress of Industrial Organizations
AFTA	ASEAN Free Trade Area
APEC	Asia-Pacific Economic Cooperation
ASEAN	Association of Southeast Asian Nations
BIS	Bank for International Settlements
CAP	Common Agricultural Policy
CARICOM	Caribbean Community and Common Market
CFA	Communauté Financière Africaine (African Financial Community)
CFCs	chlorofluorocarbons
COCOM	Coordinating Committee on Export Controls
COMECON	Council of Mutual Economic Assistance
COMESA	Common Market for Eastern and Southern Africa
CPR	Common pool resources
CSAs	country specific advantages
CUSFTA/CUSTA	Canada–US Free Trade Agreement
DAC	Development Assistance Committee
DDA	Doha Development Agenda
DSU	Dispute Settlement Understanding
ECOSOC	[United Nations] Economic and Social Council
ECSC	European Coal and Steel Community
EC	European Community
EEC	European Economic Community
EFTA	European Free Trade Association
EMS	electronic-manufacturing service providers
EMS	Environmental Management System
EMS	European Monetary System
EMU	European Monetary Union
EPA	Environmental Protection Agency
EPZs	Export Processing Zones
EU	European Union
FDI	foreign direct investment
FSA	firm-specific advantages
FSC	Forest Stewardship Council
FSF	Financial Stability Forum
GATS	General Agreement on Trade in Services
GATT	General Agreement on Tariffs and Trade
GCC	Gulf Cooperation Council
GDP	Gross Domestic Product
GEF	Global Environment Facility
GEIs	global economic institutions
GM	General Motors
GNP	Gross National Product
GPE	global political economy

HIPC	Heavily Indebted Poor Countries
IAIS	International Association of Insurance Supervisors
IBM	International Business Machines
IBRD	International Bank for Reconstruction and Development
ICSID	International Centre for Settlement of Investment Disputes
IDA	International Development Association
IFC	[World Bank] International Finance Corporation
IFI	international financial institution
ILO	International Labour Organization
IMF	International Monetary Fund
IOSCO	International Organization of Securities Commissions
IPCC	Intergovernmental Panel on Climate Change
IPE	international political economy
ISI	import substitution industrialization
ISO	International Organization for Standardization
ITA	Information Technology Products
ITO	International Trade Organization
ITTO	International Tropical Timber Organization
JFC	[World Bank-Civil Society] Joint Facilitation Committee
LDCs	less developed countries
LMU	Latin Monetary Union
MAI	[OECD] Multilateral Agreement on Investment
MDGs	Millennium Development Goals
MEOs	multilateral economic organizations
MERCOSUR	Southern Common Market
MFA	Multifibres Arrangement
MFN	most-favoured-nation
MIGA	[World Bank] Multilateral Investment Guarantee Agency
MNC	multinational corporation
MNE	multinational enterprise
NAFTA	North American Free Trade Agreement
NAM	non-aligned movement
NEC	Nippon Electric Company
NGOs	non-governmental organizations
NIEs	newly industrializing economies
NIEO	New International Economic Order
NTBs	non-tariff barriers
NTMs	non-tariff measures
OECD	Organization for Economic Cooperation and Development
OEMs	original equipment manufacturers
OPEC	Organization of Petroleum Exporting Countries
PC	personal computer
PGA	Peoples' Global Action
POPs	Persistent Organic Pollutants
PPP	purchasing power parity
PRSPs	Poverty Reduction Strategy Papers
PSIA	Poverty and Social Impact Analysis
PTA	preferential trade agreement

PWC	Post-Washington Consensus
R&D	research and development
RNGMA	Regional Nature of Global Multinational Activity Survey
RTAA	Reciprocal Trade Agreements Act
RTA	regional trade agreement
SADCC	Southern African Development Coordination Conference
SDR	Special Drawing Rights
SMU	Scandinavian Monetary Union
SSA	Sub-Saharan Africa
TNC	transnational corporation
TPRM	Trade Policy Review Mechanism
TRIMS	Trade-Related Investment Measures
TRIPS	Trade-Related [Aspects of] Intellectual Property [Rights]
UN	United Nations Organization
UNCED	United Nations Conference on the Environment and Development
UNCTAD	United Nations Conference on Trade and Development
UNEP	United Nations Environment Programme
UNIDO	United Nations Industrial Development Organization
WC	Washington Consensus
WEU	Western European Union
WIDER	[UN] World Institute for Development Economics Research
WTO	World Trade Organization

About the contributors

Vinod K. Aggarwal is Professor of Political Science, Affiliated Professor of Business and Director of the Berkeley APEC Study Center at the University of California, Berkeley. His publications include *Liberal Protectionism* (University of California Press) and *Debt Games* (Cambridge University Press).

Peter Dauvergne is Canada Research Chair in Global Environmental Politics at the University of British Columbia, and editor of the MIT Press journal, *Global Environmental Politics*. His publications include *Shadows in the Forest* (MIT Press) and *Loggers and Degradation in the Asia-Pacific* (Cambridge University Press).

Cédric Dupont is Associate Professor of Political Science at the Graduate Institute of International Studies, Geneva. He is also Director of the Center on Alpine Environment and Society at the Graduate Institute Kurt Bosch in Sion, Switzerland. He has published in journals including the *European Journal of International Relations* and the *International Political Science Review*.

Colin Hay is Professor of Political Analysis and Head of the Department of Political Science and International Studies at the University of Birmingham. His publications include *Re-stating Social and Political Change* (Open University Press), *Political Analysis* (Palgrave) and *Demystifying Globalization* (Palgrave).

Eric Helleiner is Canada Research Chair in International Political Economy at Trent University. His publications include *States and the Reemergence of Global Finance* and *The Making of National Money* (both from Cornell University Press).

Michael J. Hiscox is John L. Loeb Professor of the Social Sciences, Weatherhead Center for International Affairs, Harvard University. His publications include *International Trade and Political Conflict* (Princeton University Press).

Andrew McGrew is Professor of International Relations in the Department of Politics at the University of Southampton. His publications include *Globalization/Anti-Globalization* and *The Global Transformations Reader* (both from Polity Press), and *Empire: The United States in the Twentieth Century* (Hodder and Stoughton).

Louis W. Pauly is Director of the Centre for International Studies, University of Toronto. His publications include *Opening Financial Markets* and *Who Elected the Bankers?* (both from Cornell University Press).

John Ravenhill is Professor in the Department of International Relations, Research School of Pacific and Asian Studies, Australian National University. His publications include *APEC and the Construction of Pacific Rim Regionalism*, and *The Asian Financial Crisis and the Architecture of Global Finance* (both from Cambridge University Press).

Alan Rugman is L. Leslie Waters Chair in International Business, Indiana University, and Thames Water Fellow, Templeton College, Oxford University. His publications include *The End of Globalization* (Random House) and the *Oxford Handbook of International Business* (Oxford University Press).

Caroline Thomas is Professor of Global Politics at the University of Southampton. Her publications include *Global Governance, Development and Human Security* (Pluto) and *Globalization and the South* (St Martin's).

Robert Wade is Professor of Political Economy, Development Studies Institute, London School of Economics. His publications include *Governing the Market* (Princeton University Press) and *Village Republics* (Cambridge University Press).

Marc Williams is Professor and Head of the School of Politics and International Relations at the University of New South Wales. His publications include *Contesting Global Governance* (Cambridge University Press) and *International Economic Organizations and the Third World* (Harvester Wheatsheaf).

Gilbert R. Winham is Professor of Political Science at Dalhousie University. His publications include *International Trade and the Tokyo Round Negotiation* (Princeton University Press) and *The Evolution of International Trade Agreements* (University of Toronto Press).

Theoretical approaches to global political economy

1

The study of global political economy

John Ravenhill

READER'S GUIDE

The contemporary international economic system is more closely integrated than in any previous era. The East Asian financial crisis provides a clear illustration of the relationship between trade, finance, international institutions, and the problems that governments face in coping with the problems generated by complex interdependence.

Since the emergence of international political economy as a major subfield of the study of international relations in the early 1970s, most introductions have divided the theoretical approaches to the subject into three categories: liberalism, nationalism, and Marxism. This threefold typology is of limited utility today given the overlap between many of the approaches classified in different categories, and the wealth of theories and methodologies applied in the contemporary study of global political economy.

Prologue: Thailand and the East Asian financial crisis

When the government of Thailand in July 1997 was forced to break the long-standing fixed exchange rate between the local currency, the baht, and the US dollar, its action precipitated what soon became known as the Asian financial crisis. The Thai economy had enjoyed one of the highest rates of growth in the world over the previous decade: observers frequently referred to Thailand as one of the new Asian tigers, or 'second-tier' newly industrializing economies (NIEs). The record of the central bank, the Bank of Thailand, had been widely praised as a model of responsible economic management. Yet plaudits for the country's economic record afforded no protection when the sentiment of the financial markets turned against it. Local and foreign investors alike rushed to move their money out of the country, fearing that if they did not move quickly, the Bank of Thailand's foreign exchange reserves would be exhausted. The government had no alternative but to allow the market to determine the value of the currency, and to turn to the International Monetary Fund (IMF) and to other governments for loans of foreign exchange. By the end of the year, the value of the baht had collapsed to close to half its level at the end of June.

Other countries quickly became embroiled in the crisis. Korea, one of the original 'Gang of Four' newly industrializing economies, a country whose phenomenal economic success had seen its annual per capita income rise from around $50 in the 1950s to close to $10,000 in the mid-1990s, endured its worst recession since the country's civil war at the start of the 1950s: the value of its currency collapsed; living standards fell precipitously; and a significant number of the country's largest companies went bankrupt when financial institutions were unable to continue to provide them with loans. The effects of the crisis went far beyond the East Asian region itself. Instability in financial markets spread as far as Brazil and Russia even though the developments in Asia did not have a significant direct impact on these economies, and their underlying economic fundamentals were quite different to those in the crisis-hit countries of East Asia. Given East Asia's increasing prominence as the 'workshop of the world', the crisis was a significant factor in the decline in overall international trade in 1998, which grew at only 3.5 per cent compared with 10 per cent in the previous year (WTO 1999a). Reduced levels of economic activity in East Asia also caused a drop in the prices of raw materials for African and South American exporters (World Bank 1999b).

At a fundamental level, the origins of the crisis illustrate the close interrelationship between the trade and financial spheres. Thailand's economic success in the previous decade owed much to the relocation of manufacturing industry from North-East Asia to relatively low-cost South-East Asian countries. This move had been precipitated by the appreciation of the currencies of Japan, Korea, and Taiwan, following an agreement (the 'Plaza Accord', named after the New York hotel in which the 1985 meeting took place) on exchange-rate realignment among the Group of Seven industrialized countries (Box 1.1). Many of the exports of the three North-East Asian economies were already facing cost pressures as a consequence of the rising prices of labour and of land; these were intensified when the exchange-rate realignments raised the price of their goods in their export markets. These pressures prompted massive flows of foreign direct investment from North-East Asia into South-East Asia as Japanese, Korean, and Taiwanese manufacturers sought to take advantage of the relatively low costs in their Southern neighbours (Bernard and Ravenhill 1995). The structure of the Thai economy was transformed in the process: whereas in 1980, manufactures contributed only one-quarter of the total value of Thailand's exports, by 1990, this figure had reached 63 per cent.

In the first half of the 1990s, Thailand not only received substantial inflows of foreign direct investment (FDI—the acquisition abroad by companies of physical assets such as plant and equipment) but also very large volumes of bank lending (portfolio investment). Unlike FDI, these portfolio flows could easily be reversed through the non-renewal of loans (most

<hr>

Box 1.1 The Group of Seven

The Group of Seven (G7) industrialized countries was established in 1975, the first of a series of annual meetings where politicians and officials from the world's leading economies discussed issues relating to macroeconomic policy coordination, trade and financial policies, and relations with developing countries.

Six countries were present at the initial meeting in Rambouillet: Britain, France, (West) Germany, Italy, Japan, and the United States. Canada joined the group at its second meeting in the following year. In 1977, the group allowed participation by a representative of the European Community. From 1994 onwards, the G7 met with representatives of Russia at each of its meetings; at the Birmingham meeting in 1998, Russia was accorded full membership, transforming the G7 into the G8.

For more details on the G7/G8 see
www.g7.utoronto.ca/

<hr>

of which were short-term). The growth in portfolio lending reflected changes on both the supply and demand sides, and in technology. On the supply side, the principal development was the growth in Western industrialized countries of pension funds with enormous sums to invest; moreover, to meet the needs of their clients, existing and new financial institutions developed ever more complicated financial instruments. Satellite communications made it possible for financial institutions to move funds around the world instantaneously.

On the demand side, access to these new sources of lending appeared to offer economies such as that of Thailand a relatively low-cost source of funds to supplement domestic savings. Countries undergoing industrialization—whether the United States and Russia in the nineteenth century or Brazil today— have always used foreign borrowing to bridge the gap between actual domestic savings and desired levels of investment. And in the first half of the 1990s, foreign borrowing was particularly attractive because loans from international sources carried lower interest rates than money available domestically. Like many other developing countries seeking to attract foreign capital, Thailand in the late 1980s took steps to

liberalize and deregulate its financial sector. It soon became apparent, however, that a large portion of the loans flooding into Thailand were not being used for productive purposes: rather, they fuelled speculation in real estate and the stock market. Banks, largely freed from government oversight, were lending recklessly and incurring substantial volumes of non-performing loans. The domestic inflation that resulted from the speculative investments in turn reduced the competitiveness of Thailand's exports.

Had Thailand, like most industrialized countries from the early 1970s onwards, maintained a flexible exchange rate, then depreciation of its currency could have compensated in international markets for the rise in the domestic prices of its products. But Thailand, like a large number of less developed economies, had chosen to maintain a fixed exchange rate between its currency and that of its largest export market, the United States. The loss of competitiveness of Thailand's exports because of domestic inflation was compounded by a depreciation of the exchange rates of some of its competitors. The value of the Japanese yen fell against the US dollar (and consequently also the Thai baht, because of the fixed exchange rate between the dollar and the Thai currency) in the mid-1990s, thereby raising the cost to Thai subsidiaries of Japanese firms of importing components from Japan, and making their products more expensive in the Japanese market. Consequently, a number of Japanese firms shifted their production back to Japan. And China, emerging in the 1990s as a significant competitor to Thailand and other South-East Asian economies in the production of labour-intensive products, devalued its currency, the renminbi (or yuan), in 1994.

The combination of domestic inflation, a fixed exchange rate, the depreciation of the currencies of competitors, and massive inflows of short-term capital proved catastrophic for the Thai economy. By 1996, because of the loss of competitiveness of its exports, the country was running a large trade deficit. Investors began to fear that the government would be forced to devalue the baht—which would have led to foreign exchange losses for them. And here the sheer volume of short-term lending exacerbated the panic among investors: the volume of short-term loans exceeded the Central Bank's total holdings of foreign currencies so it was rational for individual investors to scramble to move their money out of Thailand before the Bank's foreign exchange holdings were exhausted. The withdrawal of funds forced the Thai government to float the baht and to seek loans from the IMF and foreign governments to stabilize the economy. Thailand negotiated a package that gave it access to $3.9 billion of IMF money, and a further $12.7 billion mainly from other governments, of which the Japanese government provided $4 billion. For further discussion of the Thai experience see Haggard and MacIntyre (2000) and Warr (1998).

The involvement of the International Monetary Fund in crisis-hit Asian economies proved particularly controversial. Many observers believed that the conditions that the IMF attached to its loans were unnecessarily intrusive, that the policies it prescribed were inappropriate for the particular problems the East Asian economies faced, and that the Fund was conspiring with the US Treasury and Wall Street to open up the East Asian economies to foreign influence (see, from a variety of perspectives, Eichengreen 2000; Stiglitz 2002; Wade and Veneroso 1998). Criticism of the policies of the international financial institutions' response to the East Asian crises caused both the IMF and the World Bank to review their policies, and in turn led to a significant increase in the transparency of their operations. But the unhappiness of East Asian governments at what they perceived to be an unsympathetic response to their difficulties not just by the international financial institutions but also by most Western governments, also prompted new efforts to provide regional mechanisms to support economies in crisis—even though an initial proposal from the Japanese government for an Asian Monetary Fund failed, in part because of opposition from the United States, this was followed up by agreement on a series of bilateral arrangements between the central banks of East Asian governments to loan foreign currencies to one another should they experience a foreign exchange crisis. The momentum established by these proposals carried over to foster the negotiation of new regional trade treaties among the East Asian economies.

The East Asian economic crises provide an excellent illustration of many of the themes of this book:

• the growing interdependence of countries in a globalizing economy;

• the speed with which developments in one part of the world economy are transmitted to others;

• the increased significance of private actors in the contemporary global economy, especially in the financial sector;

• the way in which crises prompt governments to seek collaboration at the regional and the global level to regulate international markets—but concurrently the difficulties that states have in coordinating their behaviours to take effective action;

• the vulnerability of the contemporary global financial system to periodic crises;

• the significant role of the international financial institutions (the World Bank and the International Monetary Fund) in responding to crises in less developed economies;

• the manner in which the increased severity of financial crises, and other developments in the trade and financial relationships between industrialized and less developed economies, have had an impact on poverty and inequality;

• the relationship between economy and environment (the crisis in Indonesia, for instance, that followed quickly on the heels of that in Thailand, and which led to the Indonesian currency, the rupiah, losing 80 per cent of its value, in the words of a report by the US Department of Energy (Energy Information Administration 2001) 'accelerated natural resource depletion as environmental regulations were set aside and people opted for less expensive and environmentally damaging production and harvesting methods'); and

• the growing significance of civic groups in articulating alternative approaches on many economic issues to those favoured by states and corporate actors.

Although, as will become evident in later chapters, contributors to this book disagree on the question of whether there is such a thing as a 'global' economy, all would accept that we live in a globalizing economy that differs in some fundamental ways from anything that the world has previously experienced. The following section briefly sketches how the world economy evolved to reach its present state.

The world economy pre-1914

The 'modern world economy', most historians agree, came into existence in the late fifteenth and sixteenth centuries. This was a period in which despotic monarchs in Western Europe, seeking to consolidate their power against internal and external foes, pushed to extend the boundaries of markets. In this era of mercantilism, power was equated with wealth, and wealth with power (Viner 1948). Wealth, in the form of bullion generated by trade surpluses or seized from foes, enabled monarchs to build the administrative apparatus of their states, and to finance the construction of military forces. The new concentration of military power could be projected, internally and externally, to extract further resources. The consolidation of the state went hand in hand with the extension of markets. Gradually, most parts of the world were enmeshed in a Eurocentric economy as suppliers of raw materials and 'luxury' goods. Britain adopted domestic reforms largely pioneered by the Netherlands (which had the world's highest per capita income in the seventeenth and eighteenth centuries) to supplant the Dutch in many world markets: armed conflict and the use of the Navigation Acts (1651–1849) enabled it to monopolize trade with its ever-expanding empire.

The era of mercantilism did not, however, bring a notable increase in overall global wealth. Before 1820, per capita incomes in most parts of the world were not significantly different than those of the previous eight *centuries* (they increased by less than an average of one-tenth of 1 per cent each year between 1700 and 1820). And despite the striking extension of the global market during the seventeenth and eighteenth centuries, the vast majority of commerce continued to be conducted within individual localities until the advent of the industrial revolution. The introduction of steam power revolutionized transportation both internally and internationally. And in the second half of the nineteenth century, further technological advances—the introduction of refrigerated ships, the laying of submarine telegraph cables—contributed to a 'shrinking' of the world and to a deepening of the international division of labour. The value of world exports grew tenfold (from a relatively small base)

between 1820 and 1870: from 1870 through 1913, world exports grew at an annual average rate of 3.4 per cent, substantially above the 2.1 annual increase in world GDP (Maddison 2001: Table B-19: 262, and Table F-4: 362).

Trade was becoming increasingly important to world welfare. Yet the pattern of international commerce in 1913—indeed, even in 1945—was not dramatically different from that of the eighteenth century. The industrialized countries of the world—essentially a Western European core to which had been added the United States and Japan by the turn of the twentieth century—exported primarily manufactured goods while the rest of the world supplied agricultural products and raw materials to feed the industrialized countries' workforces and to fuel their manufacturing plants (as a relative latecomer to industrialization, and an economy with significant comparative advantage in agricultural production, the United States was an exception to this generalization: cotton remained the single most important export for the United States in 1913, contributing nearly twice the value of exports of iron and steel and machinery combined; it was not until 1930 that machinery exports exceeded those of cotton, although by 1910 the USA had become a net exporter of manufactured goods (data from Mitchell 1993: Table E3: 504; and Irwin 2003)).

With the exception of the United States, trade amongst the industrialized countries in manufactured goods remained relatively unimportant. In 1913, agricultural products and other primary products constituted two-thirds of the total imports of the United Kingdom. To be sure, some changes had occurred in the composition of imports. Although the 'luxury' imports of the previous centuries—sugar, tea, coffee, and tobacco—had become staples in the diet of the new urban working and middle classes, their aggregate importance in European imports had shrunk relative to other commodities, notably wheat and flour, butter and vegetable oils, and meat (Offer 1989: Table 6.1: 82).

For the early European industrializers, trade with their colonies, dominions, or with the other lands of recent European settlement, such as Argentina, was more important than trade with other industrialized countries. For the United Kingdom, a larger share of imports was contributed by Argentina, Australia, Canada, and India together than by the United States, despite the latter's importance in British imports of cotton for its burgeoning textiles industry. These four countries also took five times the American share of British exports in 1913 (Mitchell 1992: Table E2: 644). Similarly, Algeria was a larger market for French exports in 1913 than was the United States.

Tariffs continued to constitute a significant barrier to international trade even in what is often termed the 'golden age' of liberalism before 1914. Most industrialized countries (the significant exceptions being the United Kingdom and the Netherlands) had actually raised the level of their tariffs in the last three decades of the nineteenth century to protect their domestic producers against increasing import competition that had been facilitated by lower transport costs. In 1913, the average tariff level in Germany and Japan was 12 per cent, in France 16 per cent, and in the United States 32.5 per cent (Maddison 1989: Table 4.4: 47). The post-1870 increase in tariffs offset some of the gains from lower transportation costs. Lindert and Williamson (2001) estimate that nearly three-quarters of the closer integration of markets that occurred in the century before the outbreak of the First World War is attributable to these lower transport costs (see Table 8.1 in McGrew, Chapter 8 in this volume).

Governments continued to erect barriers to the movement of goods in the second part of the nineteenth century but capital and people moved relatively freely across the globe, their mobility facilitated by developments in transportation and communication. From 1820 to 1913, 26 million people migrated from Europe to the United States, Canada, Australia, New Zealand, Argentina, and Brazil. Five million Indians followed the British flag in migrating to Burma, Malaya, Sri Lanka, and to Africa while an even larger number of Chinese are estimated to have migrated to other countries on the Western Pacific rim (Maddison 2001: 98). The opening up of the lands of 'new settlement' required massive capital investments—in railways in particular. By 1913, the United Kingdom, France, and Germany had investments abroad totalling over $33 billion: after the 1870s, Britain invested more than half its savings abroad and

---

Box 1.2 **Most-favoured-nation status**

Under the most-favoured-nation (MFN) principle, a government is obliged to grant to any trading partner with which it has signed an agreement treatment equivalent to the best ('most preferred') it offers to any of its partners. For instance, if France had a trade treaty with Germany in which it had reduced its tariffs on imports of German steel to 8 per cent, it would be obliged, under the most-favoured-nation principle, if it signed a trade treaty with the United States, to reduce its tariffs on imports of US steel also to 8 per cent. The MFN principle is the foundation for non-discrimination in international trade, and is often asserted to be the 'cornerstone' of the post-1945 trade regime (see Winham, Chapter 4 in this volume). The MFN principle makes a significant contribution to depoliticizing trade relations because (a) countries are obliged to give equivalent treatment to all trading partners, regardless of their economic power; and (b) countries cannot discriminate in their treatment of the trade of certain partners simply because they do not like the governments of these countries.

---

the income from its foreign investments in 1913 was equivalent to close to 10 per cent of all the goods and services produced domestically (Maddison 2001: 100).

The spectacular growth in international economic integration was not accompanied by any significant institutionalization of intergovernmental collaboration. Even though the Anglo-French Cobden–Chevalier Treaty of 1860 had introduced the principle of most-favoured-nation status into international trade agreements (see Box 1.2), governments conducted trade negotiations on a bilateral basis rather than under the auspices of an international institution.

The international financial system was similarly characterized by a lack of institutionalization. The rapid growth of economic integration was facilitated by the international adoption of the gold standard (Box 1.3). The origins of the nineteenth-century gold standard lay in action by the Bank of England in 1821 to make all its notes convertible into gold (although Britain had operated a de facto gold standard from as early as 1717). The United States, though formally on

Box 1.3 **The gold standard**

A gold standard exists when a country fixes the price of its domestic currency in terms of a specific amount of gold. National money (which may or may not consist of gold coins as other metallic coins and banknotes were also used in some countries) and bank deposits would be freely convertible into gold at the specified price.

Because the level of each country's economic activity is determined by its money supply, which in turn rested on its gold holdings, a disequilibrium in its balance of trade in principle would be self-correcting. Let us assume, for example, that Britain is running a trade deficit with the United States because inflation in Britain has made its exports relatively unattractive to US consumers. Because British exports do not cover the full costs of imports from the United States, British authorities would have to transfer gold to the US Treasury. This transfer would reduce the money supply and hence the level of economic activity in Britain, having a deflationary effect on the domestic economy, and depress its demand for imports. In the United States, the opposite would occur: an inflow of gold would boost the money supply, thereby generating additional economic activity in the United States and increasing inflationary pressures there. Higher levels of economic activity would increase the country's demand for imports. Changes in the money supplies in the two countries brought about by the transfer of gold therefore would bring their demand for goods back into balance and lead to a restoration of the ratio of the two countries' prices to that reflected in the exchange rate between their currencies.

In principle, the gold standard should act automatically to restore equilibrium in international payments. Central banks, however, were also expected to facilitate adjustment by raising their interest rates when countries were suffering a payments deficit (thereby further dampening domestic economic activities and making domestic investments more attractive to foreigners) and, conversely, to lower interest rates when countries were experiencing a payments surplus. For most of the period from 1870 to 1914, the Bank of England fairly consistently played by the rules of the game. Other central banks—including those of France and Belgium—did not. They frequently intervened to attempt to shield the domestic economy from the effects of gold flows ('sterilize' their effects) by buying or selling securities (thereby reducing or increasing the volume of gold circulating in the domestic economy).

The gold standard was vulnerable to shocks that were often quickly transmitted from one country to another. The discovery of gold in California in 1848, for instance, led to an increase in the US money supply, domestic inflation, an outflow of gold to its trade partners, which in turn raised their domestic price levels. Countries on the periphery were particularly vulnerable to shocks: interest-rate increases in the industrialized countries, for instance, often drew capital from the periphery, leaving the peripheral countries with the major burden of adjustment.

For further discussion see Officer (2001) and Eichengreen (1985).

---

a bimetallic (gold and silver) standard, switched to a de facto gold standard in 1834 and turned this into a de jure arrangement in 1900. Germany and other industrializing economies followed suit in the 1870s. Because every country fixed the value of its national currency in terms of gold, each currency had a fixed exchange rate against every other in the system (assume, for instance, that the United States sets the value of its currency as $100 per ounce of gold while the United Kingdom sets its value at £50 per ounce of gold: the exchange rate between the two currencies would be £1 = $2).

The great contribution of the gold standard to facilitating international commerce was that economic agents generally did not have to worry about foreign exchange risks: the possibility that the value of the currency of a foreign country would change vis-à-vis their domestic currency. British investors in American railways could be confident that the dollars that they had bought with their sterling investments would buy the same amount of sterling at the date their investment matured and that the US Treasury would actually convert the dollars back into gold at this time (and meanwhile, of course, they received interest on the sums invested). Confidence in the gold standard rested not on any international institution but on the commitment of individual governments to maintain the option for individuals to convert their domestic currencies into gold at a fixed exchange rate. Ultimately, the implementation of the gold standard rested on the assumption that governments had the capacity and will to impose economic pain on their domestic populations when deflation was needed in order to bring their economy back into equilibrium. These domestic costs became less acceptable with the rise of working-class political representation and with the growth of expectations that a fundamental responsibility of governments was to ensure domestic full employment.

Key points

- The modern world economy came into existence in the fifteenth and sixteenth centuries.

- Despite the significant changes that occurred in the three centuries before the outbreak of the First World War, the fundamental composition and direction of international trade remained unchanged.

- Neither in the field of trade nor that of finance was any significant international institution constructed in the years before 1914.

- Advances in technology were the main driving force behind the integration of markets, and also facilitated the enormous growth in investment and migration in the nineteenth century.

- The great merit of the gold standard was that it largely removed the risk of foreign exchange losses for international investors.

The world economy in the inter-war period

The outbreak of the First World War was a devastating blow to cosmopolitan liberalism: it destroyed the credibility of the argument that economic interdependence in itself would be sufficient to foster an era of peaceful coexistence among states. The war brought an end to an era of unprecedented economic interdependence among the leading industrial countries: as discussed in the section on globalization later in this book, many of the indicators of economic openness and interdependence did not regain their pre-First World War levels until the 1970s.

The war devastated the economies of Europe: political instability compounded economic disruptions. Economic reconstruction was further complicated by demands that Germany make reparations for its aggression, and that Britain and other European countries repay their wartime borrowings from the United States. The economic chaos of the inter-war years was a sorry reflection of the inability of governments to agree on measures to restore economic stability, and their resort to beggar-thy-neighbour policies in their efforts to alleviate domestic economic distress. Although the collapse of international trade in the 1930s is the feature of the inter-war economy that figures most prominently in stories of this era, the most fundamental problem of the period

was the inability of states to construct a viable international financial system.

The international gold standard broke down with the outbreak of war in August 1914 when a speculative attack on sterling caused the Bank of England to impose exchange controls—a refusal to convert sterling into gold and a de facto ban on gold exports. Other countries followed suit. Leading countries agreed to reinstate a modified version of the international gold standard in 1925. They failed to act consistently, however, in re-establishing the link between national currencies and gold. The United Kingdom restored the convertibility of sterling at the pre-war gold price despite the domestic inflation that had occurred in the intervening decade: the consequence was that sterling was generally reckoned to be overvalued by at least 10 per cent, making exports uncompetitive, and very difficult for the British government to establish an equilibrium in its balance of payments without imposing severe deflation domestically. Other countries—notably France, Belgium, and Italy—restored convertibility of their currencies at a much lower price of gold than had prevailed before 1914.

The resulting misalignment of currencies was compounded by higher trade barriers than existed before 1914, the absence of a country/central bank with the resources and will to provide leadership to the system, and by a failure of central banks to play by the 'rules of the game' of the gold standard. Their inclination to intervene to 'sterilize' the domestic impact of international gold flows was symptomatic of a more fundamental underlying problem: in an era when the working class had been fully enfranchised, when trade unions had become important players in political systems, especially in Western Europe, and when governments were expected to take responsibility for maintaining full employment and promoting domestic economic welfare, the subordination of the domestic economy to the dictates of global markets in the form of the international gold standard was no longer politically acceptable. Polanyi (1944) is the classic statement of this argument; on the misguided attempts by Britain to restore the convertibility of sterling at pre-1914 levels see Keynes (1925).

The abandonment of the international gold standard followed another speculative attack on sterling in the middle of 1931. The Bank of England lost much of its reserves in July and August of that year, and Britain abandoned the gold standard in September, a move that precipitated a sharp depreciation of the pound (testimony to its overvaluation in the brief period in which the gold standard was restored). Other countries again quickly followed in breaking the link between their currencies and gold. By then, the world economy was in depression, following the shocks to the world economy transmitted from the United States after the Wall Street collapse of October 1929. The gold standard almost certainly exacerbated the effects of the depression because government efforts to maintain the link between their currencies and gold constrained the use of expansionary (inflationary) policies to combat unemployment and low levels of domestic demand (Eichengreen 1992).

The world economy was already in depression before the US Congress, in response to concerns about the intensification of import competition for domestic farmers, passed the Smoot–Hawley Tariff of 1930. This raised US tariffs to historically high levels (an average *ad valorem* tariff of 41 per cent, although tariff rates were already very high as a result of the Tariff Act of 1922, the Fordney–McCumber Tariff). Retaliation from US trading partners quickly followed, with the European countries giving preferential tariff treatment to their colonies. The value of world trade declined by two-thirds between 1929 and 1934 and became increasingly concentrated in closed imperial blocks.

As in the pre-1914 period, international institutions played no significant role in the governance of international economic matters. The League of Nations had established an Economic and Financial Organization with subcommittees on the various areas of international economic relations. It enjoyed success in the early 1920s in coordinating a financial reconstruction package of £26 million for Austria. It also held various conferences aimed at facilitating trade by promoting common standards on customs procedures, compilation of economic statistics, etc. But the economic and political disarray of the inter-war period simply overwhelmed the League's limited resources and legitimacy: the move to restore international economic collaboration awaited effective action by the world's leading economy, the United States. This began with the passage by Congress in 1934 of the Reciprocal Trade Agreements Act (RTAA), which gave the president the authority to negotiate foreign trade agreements (without Congressional approval). The RTAA and the subsequent signature before 1939 of trade agreements with twenty of America's trading partners laid the foundations for the multilateral system that emerged after the Second World War (the reasons why US trade policy changed so dramatically between 1930 and 1934 have been a focus of significant recent work in international political economy: see Hiscox 1999; Irwin and Kroszner 1997).

Key points

- Misalignment of exchange rates contributed to the problems of economic adjustment in the 1920s.

- The world economy was already in recession before tariffs were raised in the early 1930s—but higher tariffs exacerbated the decline in international trade.

- States did not negotiate any significant institutionalization of international economic relations in the inter-war period.

The world economy post-1945

The world economy that emerged after the Second World War is qualitatively different from anything experienced before. John Ruggie, a leading contemporary theorist of political economy, has identified two fundamental principles that distinguish the post-war economy from its predecessors: the adoption of what Ruggie (1982), following Polanyi (1944) terms 'embedded liberalism', and a commitment to multilateralism (Ruggie 1992).

Embedded liberalism refers to the compromise that governments made after 1945 between safeguarding their domestic economic objectives, especially a commitment to maintaining full employment, and an opening up of the domestic economy to allow for the restoration of international trade and investment. The 'embedding' of the commitment to economic openness—the liberal element—within domestic economic and political objectives was attained through the writing into the rules of international trade and finance provisions that would allow governments to opt out, on a temporary basis, from their international commitments should these threaten fundamental domestic economic objectives. Moreover, an acknowledgement of the legitimacy of governments' pursuit of domestic economic objectives was also written into the rules of the game. The adoption of the principle of embedded liberalism was an acknowledgement by governments that international economic collaboration rested on their capacity to maintain domestic political consensus—and that international economic collaboration was, fundamentally, a political bargain. This recognition explains, for instance, why the agricultural sector was for many years excluded from trade liberalization: the domestic political costs for governments of negotiating freer trade in agricultural products were judged to be so high as to jeopardize otherwise politically feasible trade liberalization in other sectors.

The institutionalization of international economic cooperation is another fundamental change in international economic relations in the post-war period. In neither the period of relative stability of the pre-First World War gold standard era nor in the chaos of the 1930s did leading economies create significant international economic institutions. As Ruggie notes, a commitment to multilateralism is one of the defining characteristics of

the post-1945 order. For Ruggie (1992: 571), multilateralism is not merely a matters of numbers—it involves collaboration among three or more states—but it also has a qualitative element in that the coordination of relations is on 'the basis of "generalized" principles of conduct—that is, principles which specify appropriate conduct for a class of actions, without regard to the particularistic interests of the parties or the strategic exigencies that may exist in any specific occurrence'. A classic example is the most-favoured-nation principle, which specifies that products from all trading partners must be treated in the same manner, regardless of the characteristics of the countries involved. This principle for behaviour contrasts, for instance, with the largely bilateral trade agreements of the inter-war years, where governments rather than applying a generalized principle treated trading partners differently.

The commitment to multilateralism that developed in the late 1930s and during the Second World War bore immediate fruit in the founding of the 'Bretton Woods' multilateral financial institutions: the International Monetary Fund, and the World Bank (Box 1.4). Note, however, that these global or universal institutions, whose membership is open to all states in the international system, are but one form of multilateralism. For all of the period since 1945, but especially in the last decade, regional institutions have also played an important role in international economic, as well as security, affairs (Ravenhill, Chapter 5 in this volume). States have increasingly enmeshed themselves in a dense web of multilateral institutions.

The unprecedented rates of economic growth achieved in the years after 1945 attest to the success of the pursuit of multilateral economic collaboration in this period. Global Gross Domestic Product (GDP) grew at close to 5 per cent in the period 1950–73; although the recessions that followed the oil price rises of 1973–4 and 1979–80, and the debt crises that afflicted Latin America and Africa, contributed to a slowing of growth in the quarter-century after 1973, world GDP nonetheless grew at an average of 3 per cent per annum, a faster rate than any experienced before 1945 (Maddison 2001: Table 8–19: 262). Moreover, world trade grew more rapidly than world production: world exports expanded by close to 8 per

Box 1.4 **Bretton Woods**

In 1944, the Western allies brought together their principal economic advisers for a conference at the Mount Washington Hotel in the village of Bretton Woods, New Hampshire, to chart the future of the international economy in the post-war period. The forty-four governments represented at what was officially known as the United Nations Monetary and Financial Conference agreed on the principles that would govern international finance in the post-war years, and to create two major international institutions to assist in the management of these arrangements: the International Monetary Fund; and the World Bank (formally known as the International Bank for Reconstruction and Development). For details of the discussions at the conference see Dormael (1978) (excerpted at **www.imfsite.org/origins/confer.html**; see also **www.yale.edu/lawweb/avalon/decade/decad047.htm**).

These institutions and the rules for managing international finance that were agreed became known collectively as the Bretton Woods regimes. In 1947, a United Nations Conference on Trade and Employment in Havana, Cuba, drew up a charter (**www.globefield.com/havana.htm**) for an International Trade Organization (ITO), to complement the Bretton Woods financial institutions. The ITO never eventuated, however—see Winham, Chapter 4 in this volume.

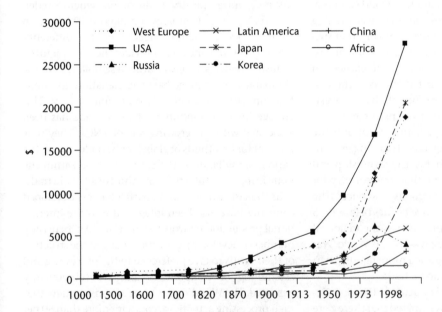

Fig. 1.1 Per capita income 1000–1998 ($US)

Source: Data in Maddison (1989, 2001).

cent per annum in the years 1950–73, and by 5 per cent annually in the subsequent twenty-five-year period. The internationalized sector grew in importance in most economies (Maddison 2001: Table F-4: 362).

Aggregate rates of growth, however, disguised substantial variations across different regions of the world economy. The gap between rich and poor widened substantially (Figure 1.1). In 1500, little difference had existed in per capita incomes across various regions of the world. Incomes per head in the United States did not exceed those of China until the second quarter of the eighteenth century. By the third quarter of the nineteenth century, however, a marked gap had devel-

oped between incomes per capita in the United States and Western Europe on the one hand, and those of the rest of the world. Per capita incomes in Africa and in most parts of Asia stagnated (and in China actually regressed for a century). Despite the economic turmoil and slower rates of growth of the inter-war years, the absolute gap between the industrialized economies and the rest of the world continued to widen: the divergence increased rapidly in the post-1945 era. Only a handful of previously less developed countries, mostly in East Asia, made significant progress in closing the gap. Africa, meanwhile, became increasingly detached from the globalizing economy: its exports, measured in constant prices, barely expanded in the years between 1973 and 1990. The poor export performance contributed to falls in per capita income that occurred in the majority of years between 1973 and 1998. By the latter date, the average per capita income in Africa was no more than Western Europe had experienced in 1820 (all data drawn from Maddison 2001). Growing international inequality has been a fundamental part of the modern globalizing economy (see Wade, Chapter 11 in this volume).

Another defining characteristic of the post-1945 international economy was the growth in the number of transnational corporations (TNCs—also referred to in some chapters of this volume as multinational enterprises). A growth of significant private economic enterprises with international operations had accompanied the emergence of the modern world economy in the fifteenth century. These, however, were trading companies, such as the East India Company, that specialized in moving goods between national markets. And when foreign investment took off in earnest, in the half-century before the First World War, the vast majority of it was portfolio investment, that is, investment in bonds and other financial instruments that did not give investors management control over the borrowing company. Companies that engaged in foreign direct investment, that is, the ownership and management of assets in more than one country for the purposes of production of goods or services (the definition of a TNC), were relative rarities before 1945 (with some notable exceptions such as the major oil companies and IBM). In the post-Second World War years, FDI took off, and has grown more rapidly than either production or international trade.

The TNC has become the key actor in the globalizing economy. By 2002, it was estimated that there were 64,000 TNCs in operation, which controlled more than 870,000 subsidiaries worldwide. The global stock of FDI amounted to $7 trillion, and the value added by TNC subsidiaries was equal to about 10 per cent of the world's GDP. Moreover, sales by the subsidiaries of TNCs were far in excess of the total value of world trade: an estimated $18 trillion compared to a figure of $8 trillion for all world exports (all data from UNCTAD 2003: xvi). Whereas in the period before 1960, the vast majority of FDI and TNCs came from the United States, in subsequent years the American presence has been supplemented by corporations with their headquarters in Europe, Japan, Korea, and, increasingly, in less developed countries such as Brazil and India (for further discussion see Dicken 2003).

The activities of TNCs in turn have fundamentally transformed the nature of international trade. In particular, the composition of world trade has changed dramatically since 1945. Whereas in the inter-war years the composition of trade differed little from that of the previous centuries, that is, it was based on the exchange of raw materials and agricultural products for manufactured goods, since the post-war reconstruction of Europe and Japan, the principal component of trade has been the international exchange of manufactured goods. At first, this trade was primarily among the industrialized countries and in many instances involved *intra-industry* trade, that is, the international exchange of products from the same industry. For instance, intra-industry trade occurs when Sweden exports Volvos to Germany and imports BMWs from Germany. As this example suggests, product differentiation by brand name often provides the basis for intra-industry trade, and bears little resemblance to the comparative advantage-based explanation for trade that underlies conventional economic theory. This change in the composition of world trade has been associated with the growing role of TNCs. They now account for two-thirds of global trade: trade among the various subsidiaries of TNCs, that is, trade within the same firm, constitutes fully one-third of all world trade.

In the last two decades in particular, less developed countries have also been integrated into the international production networks led by TNCs. An increasing number of developing countries changed the structure of their tariffs to give preference to the processing and assembling of components that are subsequently exported. The World Trade Organization estimates that such processing activities account for more than 80 per cent of the exports of the Dominican Republic, close to 60 per cent of the exports of China, and nearly 50 per cent of the exports of Mexico (WTO 2000*a*). This participation in global production networks is the most significant factor in a dramatic change in the commodity composition of the exports of less developing countries. Contrary to some popular impressions, by the end of the 1990s, manufactured exports constituted 70 per cent of the total exports from the developing world. The share of manufactures had increased threefold since the end of the 1970s (UNCTAD 2001: xviii).

Reference to these less developed economies provides a timely reminder of another dramatic change in international economic relations since 1945—a huge augmentation in the number of independent states in the system. As noted in Box 1.4, only forty-four countries were represented at the Bretton Woods conference, which was dominated by the industrialized countries of Europe and North America but also included a few of the long-independent countries of Central and South America. Within two decades, almost all of the colonies of the European countries had gained their independence. This development had profound implications for the international system. One was simply the consequence of an increase in both the number of states and in the diversity of the international community: the number of states in the system more than doubled. Collaboration in international economic relations and the management of various dimensions of this collaboration became increasingly complex, illustrated very clearly in the trade sphere by the difficulties in negotiating the Uruguay and Doha rounds of WTO talks (see Winham, Chapter 4 in this volume for details of these discussions, and Aggarwal and Dupont, Chapter 2, for discussion of the problems that larger numbers pose for collaboration). The growth in the number of less developed countries also brought institutional change, most notably in the foundation of the United Nations Conference on Trade and Development (UNCTAD) in 1964. And the new arithmetic in the international system generally, and particularly within the United Nations system, contributed to a change in international norms with the adoption first of decolonization (Jackson 1993), and then of development. Another defining characteristic of the contemporary system contributed to the enshrining of the development norm—the vast expansion in the number of non-governmental organizations, many of which were focused on the alleviation of poverty (for further discussion of this topic see the chapters by Wade, Thomas, and Williams in this volume). Relations between industrialized and less developed countries, and issues relating to global poverty and inequality, emerged as an important dimension of the study of international political economy, the evolution of which is discussed in the next section of this chapter.

Key points

The post-war international economy was qualitatively different from anything that preceded it on several dimensions:

- states made a commitment to multilateralism, reflected in the construction of institutions at the global and regional levels;
- the world economy grew at unprecedented rates after 1945—the internationalized component of economies became more significant as trade and foreign investment grew more rapidly than production;
- the TNC and FDI emerged as key agents in the process of internationalization;
- the composition and direction of international trade changed dramatically with intra-industry trade among industrialized economies constituting the vast majority of trade; and
- the number of countries in the international system rose substantially.

The study of global political economy

The emergence of international political economy as a distinct subfield

International political economy (IPE) developed as a significant subfield in the study of international relations in the 1970s. As has so often been the case in political science, the emergence of a new subject area was a response both to real world changes and to trends in theorizing within and outside the discipline (see Box 1.5).

In the early 1970s, the global economy entered a period of turbulence following an unprecedented period of stable economic growth. The 'long boom' from the early post-war years through to 1970 had benefited developed and less developed economies alike. Because of the comparative stability of this period, it was commonplace to regard international economic relations as a relatively uncontentious issue area that could be left to technocrats to manage. All of this changed in the late 1960s when the US economy encountered increasing problems because

---

Box 1.5 What's in a name? International versus global political economy

When IPE emerged as a major focus for students of international relations, it inherited the rather misleading adjective 'international' as the leading word in its title. Commentators have often pointed out that 'international' relations is a misnomer for its subject matter in that it confuses 'nation' with 'state', and fails to acknowledge the significance of private actors in global politics. But labels, like institutions, are often 'sticky'—once adopted, it is difficult to displace them even if a better alternative is available. The abbreviation IPE has become synonymous with the field of study. Even though we prefer 'Global Political Economy' for the title of the book because it more accurately reflects the contemporary subject matter of this field, many of the contributors follow conventional usage in employing the abbreviation IPE and in referring to 'International' Political Economy.

While the study of international political economy achieved a new prominence in the 1970s, a variety of work in what would now be recognized as the field of IPE was published much earlier than this. A prominent example is Albert Hirschman's (1945) study of Germany's economic relations with its East European neighbours. Much of the work in the field of development economics that blossomed in the post-war period included significant political and international components. And the Marxist tradition of political economy remained vibrant, particularly in Europe.

To confuse matters, the study of economics was known in the eighteenth and nineteenth centuries as political economy (see, for instance, John Stuart Mill's *The Principles of Political Economy*). The titles of some journals in the field of economics, for example, the *Journal of Political Economy*, first published in 1892, reflect this older usage.

---

its commitment to a fixed exchange rate constrained its policy options at a time when domestic inflation was being fuelled by high levels of government expenditure—domestically, on social programmes, and internationally on the pursuit of the Vietnam War. In August 1971, a new era of instability in the global economy was ushered in when the Nixon administration unilaterally changed the value of the dollar (expressed in terms of the price of gold—for further discussion see Helleiner, Chapter 6). In doing so, it set in train events that were to remove the system of fixed exchange rates, one of the pillars of the Bretton Woods financial regime.

The new instability in international finance reinforced perceptions that the global economy was about to enter an era of significant upheaval. Commodity prices had risen substantially in the early 1970s; Western concerns about the future availability and pricing of raw materials were compounded by the success of the Organization of the Petroleum Exporting Countries (OPEC) during the Arab–Israeli war of 1973 in substantially increasing the price of crude oil. Less developed countries believed that they could use their new-found 'commodity power' to engineer a dramatic restructuring of international economic regimes, a demand they made through calls at the United Nations for a New International Economic Order (NIEO—see Thomas, Chapter 12). Industrialized economies were already having difficulty in coping with a surge in imports of manufactured goods from Japan and the East Asian NIEs, causing them to revert to various measures to protect their domestic industries, in disregard of their obligations under the international trade regime. In trade and finance regimes alike, new pressures were causing governments to seek to rewrite the rules governing international economic interactions.

At this time of the greatest instability in international economic relations since the depression of the 1930s, the security realm, which had been the principal focus of the study of post-war international relations, appeared to be on the verge of a new era of collaboration. The United States was winding down its involvement in Indochina; Henry Kissinger was negotiating détente with the Soviet Union; and President Nixon's visit to China in 1972 appeared to presage a new epoch in which China would be integrated peacefully into the international system. For many scholars of international relations, the traditional agenda of the discipline was incomplete, and the preoccupation of the dominant, realist approach with security issues and military power seemed increasingly irrelevant to the new international environment (Keohane and Nye 1972; Morse 1976).

The new turbulence in international economic relations prompted political scientists to take an interest in a subject matter that had previously been left largely to economists. It was not, as some commentators have suggested, that international economic relations had suddenly become politicized. Politics and asymmetries in power had always underlain the structure of global economic relations, seen for instance, in the content of the various financial regimes negotiated at Bretton Woods. Rather, what was novel was that the turbulence of the early 1970s suggested that the fundamental rules of the game were suddenly renegotiable.

Political scientists' new interest in international economic relations also coincided with the abandonment by the economics profession of what had previously been taught and researched as institutional economics: as the discipline of economics aspired to more 'scientific' approaches through the application of statistical and mathematical models, so it increasingly abandoned the study of international economic institutions. Political scientists discovered a vacuum that they quickly filled: the field of international political economy was born.

What is IPE?

International political economy is a field of enquiry, a subject matter whose central focus is the interrelationship between public and private power in the allocation of scarce resources. It is not a specific approach or set of approaches to studying this subject matter (as we will see, the full range of theoretical and methodological approaches from international and comparative politics has been applied to the study of international political economy).

Like other branches of the discipline, IPE seeks to answer the classic questions posed in Harold D. Lasswell's (1936) definition of politics: *who gets what, when, and how?* This definition explicitly identifies questions of *distribution* as central to the study of politics. It also implicitly points to the importance of power—the concept that is central to the study of political science—in determining outcomes. Power, of course takes various forms: it is classically defined in terms of relationships—the capacity of one actor to change the behaviour of another (Dahl 1963). But

power is also exercised in the capacity of actors to set agendas (Bachrach and Baratz 1970; Lukes 1974), and to structure the rules in various areas of international economic relations so as to privilege some actors and to disadvantage others (Strange 1988).

Consider, for instance, the international financial regime. As the world's largest economy (and single most important market for many other countries in the global system), the United States has been able, over the years, to exercise relational power: to force changes in the behaviour of other countries, notably, to accept changes in their exchange rates (as, for instance, in the Nixon administration's breaking of the fixed exchange rate between the dollar and gold, and, as discussed at the beginning of this chapter, the forced appreciation of the North-East Asian currencies against the dollar following the Plaza Accord). The rules of the international financial regime have also been structured so that they privilege the more economically developed states in the system: not only do the wealthy industrialized economies enjoy more votes within the IMF and the World Bank under the weighted voting system employed in the two major international financial institutions (IFIs) (Box 1.6), but the industrialized economies also (in part because of arrangements that they have negotiated amongst themselves) largely escape the discipline imposed by the IMF on countries that run persistent balance of payments deficits. No industrialized country has sought assistance from the IMF since Britain and Italy did so in 1976. Despite running huge deficits in its balance of payments, the United States has not been subject to IMF discipline because it can take advantage of the international acceptability of the dollar and print more money to finance its trade deficits.

Besides a focus on questions of distribution and of power, two of the fundamental concerns of political science, students of international political economy have also been preoccupied with one of the central issues in the study of international relations: what conditions are more favourable for the evolution of cooperation among states in an environment in which no central enforcement agency is present? For many observers, this problem of 'cooperation under anarchy' is even more pertinent in the economic in contrast to the security realm. This is because greater potential exists in the economic sphere, particularly under conditions of interdependence, for

Box 1.6 **Voting in the international financial institutions**

When the allied powers decided at Bretton Woods to create two international financial institutions they agreed on a formula for voting rights that represented a compromise between the principle of sovereign equality and the realities of markedly unequal economic power. Members' voting power has two components: 'basic votes', assigned equally to all members, and (a much larger number offered) weighted votes that were linked directly to the money they subscribed to the two institutions. Quotas have been adjusted over the last half-century as the membership of the institutions has expanded but the G7 industrialized countries still control 45 per cent of the votes in the IMF while more than forty African countries combined have less than 5 per cent of the total votes.

Eight countries—China, France, Germany, Japan, Russia, Saudi Arabia, the United Kingdom, and the United States—have their own representative on the twenty-four-member IMF Executive Board, which is responsible for the day-to-day running of the institution. Others are arranged in various groups with a single executive director casting their collective votes. Five executive directors represent individual countries on the seventeen-member World Bank Executive Board: the United States, Japan, Germany, France, and the United Kingdom; the remaining twelve directors represent the Bank's other 179 member states.

In the IMF, 'Ordinary' Decisions require a simple majority whereas 'Special' Decisions require an 85 per cent 'supermajority'. The United States, with slightly over 17 per cent of the total votes at the IMF, can unilaterally block 'Special Decisions', such as changes in the IMF's Charter or use of its holdings of gold. Voting, however, is relatively rare, with most decisions being carried by consensus.

By convention, since the foundation of the two IFIs, the United States has nominated the president of the World Bank, and (West) European countries the managing director of the IMF. In an unusual move in 2000, the Clinton administration vetoed the German government's first-choice nominee for the post of managing director of the IMF. Although the appointment of the nominees is subject to a formal vote within the Fund and the Bank, other members only have the option of either voting for or against the nominated candidate rather than proposing alternative names.

The Washington DC location of the two IFIs enhances US influence over their operations. For more detailed discussion of the representativeness and accountability of the IFIs see Woods (2003).

A list of the members of the IMF and their voting rights can be found at **www.imf.org/external/np/sec/ memdir/members.htm**. (Unlike the IFIs, the World Trade Organization operates on the principle of one member, one vote but its members have never voted: decision making is by consensus, see Winham, Chapter 4 in this volume.)

---

cooperation on a win-win basis, but states have a considerable temptation to 'cheat' by attempting to exploit concessions made by others while not fully responding in kind (see Aggarwal and Dupont, Chapter 2 in this volume).

Much of the early IPE work in the 1970s and early 1980s, particularly in North America, married two of these central concerns—the distribution of power within the global economy and the potential for states to engage in collaboration. Conducted at a time when many perceived US economic power to be on the wane, this work focused on the link between hegemony and an open global economy (Box 1.7).

Approaches to the study of global political economy

Following the publication of Robert Gilpin's magisterial overview of the then emerging field of international political economy (1987), most introductions to the subject have identified three principal categories of theoretical approaches to IPE. In Gilpin's original terminology (he changed some of his labels in the updated version of his book (Gilpin 2001), these were liberalism, nationalism, and Marxism. Of these three labels, only liberalism has been used

Box 1.7 **Power and collaboration**

The 'theory of hegemonic stability' suggests that international economic collaboration in pursuit of an open (or liberal) economic order is most likely to occur when the global economy is dominated by a single power (because this country, the hegemon, will have both the desire and the means to support an open economic system). Theorists pointed to the experience of the mid-nineteenth century, when Britain was the dominant power, and to the period of US dominance from 1945 to 1971, as demonstrating the relationship between hegemony and an open world economy. In contrast, the interwar period, when no single country enjoyed equivalent pre-eminence, was characterized by a breakdown in international economic collaboration. The decline in the relative position of the US economy in the 1960s, following the rebuilding of the Western European and Japanese economies, appeared to coincide with renewed closure (a rise in protectionism in response to imports from Japan and the East Asian NIEs) and the general turbulence in global economic regimes noted above.

Subsequently, however, the hegemonic stability argument was undermined both by trends in the real world and by new theoretical work. In the 1990s, countries extended their collaboration on international economic matters, especially in trade, despite a relatively more even dispersion of economic power in the global system.

For statements of the hegemonic stability argument, see Kindleberger (1973) and Krasner (1976); for alternative theoretical perspectives see Keohane (1984, 1997) and Snidal (1985b). For further discussion see Aggarwal and Dupont, Chapter 2 in this volume.

universally in other categorizations. Other writers have substituted 'statism' or 'mercantilism' or 'realism' or 'economic nationalism' for nationalism. The approaches that Gilpin subsumed under the label Marxism have variously been identified as 'radical', 'critical', 'structuralist', 'dependency', 'underdevelopment', and 'world systems'.

In itself, the variety of labels applied points to one of the problems with the 'trichotomous' categorization of approaches to the study of IPE: the (sometimes misleading) lumping together of substantially different perspectives within a single category. Moreover, the trichotomous categorization does not capture the wealth of methodological and theoretical approaches used in the contemporary study of IPE, or provide an accurate signpost to the breadth of fascinating questions that currently preoccupies researchers in the field. For these reasons, we do not use this conventional categorization in this book. So common is the trichotomy in introductions to IPE, however, that it is worth investing a little time in understanding the underlying foundations of the categorization and why it has become of decreasing utility.

Gilpin's original conceptualization of the trichotomy is more sophisticated than those of many of his successors. He begins by asserting that these approaches should be viewed as *ideologies* rather than theories in a scientific sense. That is, they are worldviews or belief systems, which are as important for their prescriptive or normative elements (their laying out of what *should* be) as for their power in explaining what currently exists, especially given the level of generality at which they are cast.

Gilpin is conscious of the variety in the viewpoints that are represented within the individual categories. Nonetheless, he suggests that on key issues, the various writers within each perspective have sufficient in common with one another, and differ sufficiently from those in the other categories, to make the trichotomous classification useful. In the following discussion, we suggest various reasons why we have reservations about this argument.

Liberalism

Liberalism is arguably the most unified of the three commonly identified approaches to IPE, often equated today with mainstream academic (that is, neoclassical) economics. The essence of the liberal approach to IPE is usually traced back to Adam Smith's argument that the development of a division of labour within society generates a natural harmony of interests when the 'invisible hand' of market competition turns self-seeking individual behaviour into socially beneficial outcomes. Individuals strive to improve their own lot but the logic of competition in the market place ensures that the selfish motivations underlying their enterprise benefits society as a whole (reasoning that has its origins in literature earlier than Smith's work, see Barry 1982). The emphasis is on individual enterprise, on the virtues of market competition, and on restricting the role of the state to what is required to ensure that markets can operate successfully (providing not only, for instance, for national defence but also a system that establishes and enforces property rights—the legal right to ownership—so that individuals can benefit from their enterprise).

The notion that specialization and competition can maximize welfare was extended from the domestic to the international sphere through the development of the idea of production according to comparative advantage (Box 1.8). This somewhat counter-intuitive conception is so central to liberal theorizing, especially to arguments that international trade is fundamentally a win-win situation, that it is one of the concepts from economics that is essential for students of IPE to grasp.

The win-win situation that results from countries specializing and trading according to their comparative advantage creates a structure of international interactions that is referred to in game theory as 'harmony': this structure dictates that the natural outcome of these interactions will be cooperative (for further discussion see Aggarwal and Dupont, Chapter 2, Figure 2.7 in this volume). Nineteenth-century liberal theorists such as Cobden and Mill argued that an international system of free trade in which countries were able to pursue their comparative advantage would not only maximize international welfare but also guarantee peaceful relations among states. Warfare and colonialism would be seen as a waste of scarce resources; they disrupted trade and production, and gave governments an excuse for raising taxes. People would come to appreciate the benefits of free trade, and pressure governments to adopt this foreign commercial strategy. International commerce would make war obsolete—an argument discredited when an era of unprecedented economic openness and interdependence ended abruptly with the outbreak of the First World War (but one that has been resurrected with the growth of economic interdependence among industrialized countries since the 1960s).

Paul Samuelson, a Nobel laureate in economics, is reported, when he was once asked by a sceptic to identify a meaningful and non-trivial product of economic theorizing, to have nominated the concept of comparative advantage. But if the idea of comparative advantage remains central to liberal economic theorizing, one does not have to probe much beyond this concept to discover differences among various writers usually perceived as belonging firmly within the liberal camp. One source of disagreement is whether there are circumstances in which the standard prescription for free trade according to (current) comparative advantage does not apply—most notably on whether developing economies should protect their newly established industries until they are able to produce with sufficient efficiency to compete on world markets.

The case for 'infant industry' protection was accepted by one of the great nineteenth-century liberal writers, John Stuart Mill, in his *Principles of Political Economy* (Mill 1970) (although subsequently Mill retracted his support for the idea when he believed it had been abused by the then industrializing economies of Germany and the United States). While some economists in the liberal school continue to accept the validity of the infant industry argument, others believe that by establishing a principle for government intervention, it opens the door for states to abuse their power with the result that they will create inefficiencies in their national economies (see, for example, Irwin 1996). The somewhat broader question of whether less developed economies should be subject to the same disciplines as industrialized economies in international trade, or entitled to what has become known as 'special and differential' treatment, likewise is one that continues to divide 'liberal' economists (contrast, for example, Whalley 1999*a*; Srinivasan 1999; and Pangestu 2000).

Similarly, the liberal preference for market forces provides but the barest of bases of agreement from which liberal economists then depart in their prescriptions for reform of the international monetary regime. These range from Hayek's (1976) 'ultra-liberal' proposal that governments should cease to enjoy a

Box 1.8 The theory of comparative advantage

The case for free trade was stated succinctly by Adam Smith. In *The Wealth of Nations*, he wrote: 'If a foreign country can supply us with a commodity cheaper than we ourselves can make it, better buy it of them with some part of the produce of our own industry, employed in a way in which we have some advantage' (Book IV, Section ii: 12). The idea here is simple and intuitive. If a country can produce some set of goods at lower cost than can a foreign country, and if the foreign country can produce some other set of goods at a lower cost, then clearly it would be best for the country to trade its relatively cheaper goods for the foreign economy's relatively cheaper goods. In this way both countries can gain from trade. This is the theory of trade according to *absolute* advantage.

David Ricardo, working in the early part of the nineteenth century, realized that absolute advantage was a limited case of a more general basis for international trade (the idea was originally stated by another economist, Robert Torrens, in *Essay on the External Corn Trade* published in 1815, but most historians of economic thought believe that Ricardo reached his conclusions independently). Consider Table 1.1. Portugal can produce both cloth and wine more efficiently, that is, with less labour input than England (it has an absolute advantage in the production of both commodities). Ricardo argued that nonetheless it could still be mutually beneficial for both countries to specialize and trade.

The logic of comparative advantage rests on the *opportunity costs* of producing goods across countries, that is, the amount of one good that has to be given up to produce another good. In Table 1.1, producing a unit of wine in England requires the same amount of labour as required to produce two units of cloth. Production of an extra unit of wine means forgoing production of two units of cloth (that is, the opportunity cost of a unit of wine is two units of cloth). In Portugal, the labour required to produce a unit of wine would only produce 1.5 units of cloth (that is, the opportunity cost of a unit of wine is 1.5 units of cloth

in Portugal). To concentrate on wine production in Portugal requires giving up relatively less cloth output than would be the case in England. Similarly, if England produced only cloth, the amount of wine production forgone would be relatively smaller than if Portugal did so.

Portugal thus is relatively better at producing wine than is England: if Portugal concentrated on producing wine it would give up a smaller volume of cloth production than would England. Portugal is said to have a *comparative advantage* in the production of wine. England is relatively better at producing cloth than wine: so England is said to have a comparative advantage in the production of cloth.

Because relative or comparative costs differ, it can still be mutually advantageous for both countries to trade *even though Portugal has an absolute advantage in producing both commodities*. For international welfare to be maximized, Portugal should specialize in the product in which it is relatively most efficient; England in the commodity in which it is relatively least inefficient.

Table 1.2 shows how trade might be advantageous. Costs of production are as set out in Table 1.1. In this example, England is assumed to have 270 person hours available for production. Before trade takes place it produces and consumes eight units of cloth (requiring 120 person hours of labour input) and five units of wine (150 person hours). Portugal has fewer labour resources with a total of 180 person hours of labour available for production. Before trade takes place it produces and consumes nine units of cloth (requiring 90 person hours of labour input) and six units of wine (90 person hours). Total production for the two economies combined is seventeen units of cloth and eleven units of wine.

If both countries now specialize with Portugal producing only wine and England producing only cloth, and all their

Table 1.1 Comparative costs of production (cost per unit in person hours)

Country	Cloth	Wine
England	15	30
Portugal	10	15

Table 1.2 Production before and after trade

Country	Production before trade		Production after trade	
	Cloth	Wine	Cloth	Wine
England	8	5	18	0
Portugal	9	6	0	12
TOTAL	17	11	18	12

labour resources are devoted to the single product, England can produce (270 divided by fifteen) units of cloth and Portugal (180 divided by fifteen) units of wine. Total production by the two economies is eighteen units of cloth and twelve units of wine. Specialization according to comparative advantage and international trade, therefore, has enabled overall welfare to increase because total production has gone up by one unit of cloth and one unit of wine.

For trade to take place, the ratio of the price of the two goods must be lower than the domestic opportunity costs of production, that is, a bottle of wine will have to sell for somewhere between 1.5 and two bales of cloth. Note that the theory says nothing about distributional questions, that is, where in this range the price will settle and thus who will gain most from trade.

The simple theory of comparative advantage makes a number of important assumptions:

- There are no transport costs.

- Costs are constant and there are no economies of scale.

- There are only two economies producing two goods.

- Traded goods are homogeneous (that is, identical as far as the consumer is concerned).

- Factors of production (labour and capital) are perfectly mobile internally but not internationally.

- There is full employment in both economies.

- There are no tariffs or other trade barriers.

- There is perfect knowledge, so that all buyers and sellers know where the cheapest goods can be found internationally.

Despite the lack of correspondence between the contemporary globalized economy and these assumptions, most economists believe that the fundamental principle that Ricardo identified still holds.

---

monopoly over the issue of money within their territories, to arguments in favour of a return to the gold standard (under which the value of a currency would be linked to the price of gold, and the volume of money in circulation to a country's holdings of gold—for non-technical critical comments see Krugman 1996), to proposals for a system in which currencies fluctuate within broad bands against one another, to suggestions for a system of genuinely freely floating exchange rates (which, unlike today's 'dirty' floats, where governments intervene in foreign exchange markets to try to move the value of their currencies in a particular direction, would be determined strictly by financial markets).

Even within the relatively cohesive liberal approach, therefore, substantial differences are obvious among various writers once the focus shifts beyond generalities to specific policy prescriptions.

Nationalism

Compared with the range of approaches that have been lumped together under the label 'economic nationalism' or its variants, the category of 'liberalism' is a model of unity. Indeed, some have gone so far as to argue that economic nationalism has been applied to 'everything that did not fit in with the liberal definition of economy and development' (Koffman 1990, quoted in Helleiner 2002: 308).

A fundamental problem with the way in which the category of 'nationalism' has been used in the IPE literature is that it conflates the terms 'state' and 'nation'. The latter refers to a group of people unified around a shared identity; the former is used variously within political science generally and international relations in particular to refer both to a specific geographic territory, and to the apparatus of government within a territory. The geographical spread of nations, of course, is not necessarily coterminous with the boundaries of a particular state.

To interpret the terminology strictly, economic nationalism should be used in reference to measures that are intended to enhance the welfare of a *nation*, a particular group of people, rather than those that target economic development within a specific territory. And there is nothing in the term economic nationalism, contrary to the way it is conventionally employed, to suggest that adherents of this approach should necessarily choose 'statist' measures, that is, advocate state intervention to overcome perceived failures of domestic and international markets to allocate resources in a way that will realize economic goals. As Helleiner (2002) demonstrates, doctrines of economic nationalism historically have been compatible with a wide array of policy options. Some economic nationalists have advocated policies associated with classical liberalism, notably a greater reliance on market forces, than those then prevailing in the territories they inhabited. This preference for the market in the contemporary era often occurs where minority nationalities believe that state intervention has discriminated against their interests.

Defining economic nationalism in terms of its nationalist content rather than any specific set of policy prescriptions is to diverge from much of the conventional usage of the term in IPE (Levi-Faur 1997; Helleiner 2002). Much of the literature associates 'modern' economic nationalism (as opposed to that of the mercantilist writers of the sixteenth and seventeenth centuries) with a set of policies that build on the infant industry argument. This argument was first made systematically by Alexander Hamilton in his 1791 'Report on Manufactures' to the US Congress (Hamilton 1913), and developed by Friedrich List in his *The National System of Political Economy*, originally published in 1844 (List 1966). Strategic trade theory is a modern variant of the infant industry argument developed by economists in the 1980s (Brander 1987; Krugman 1986). Like other variants of mercantilist thought, strategic trade theory conceives of elements of the world economy in zero-sum terms, that is, gains by one economy inevitably must come at the expense of another. Strategic trade theory suggests that, in a world economy dominated by large corporations that distinguish their products by brand name, abnormal profits ('economic rents') can be sustained in the medium to long term by firms that succeed in getting their products to market first. Governments can assist their national firms to capture these rents by providing them with a protected domestic market, and by subsidizing their inputs or their exports.

Much of the secondary literature on Hamilton and List tends to caricature their argument in support of state intervention: a careful reading of their work indicates that they favoured only a *selective* and *conditional* application of tariffs and other protectionist policies (List, for instance, opposed protection for German agriculture); they also argued that these protectionist devices should be removed once an industry could compete internationally (Harlen 1999). They were, therefore, not as far removed from some liberal writers as is conventionally suggested. Similarly, a number of the economists who were significant participants in the development of strategic trade theory were also acutely aware of its limitations

(the possibility of retaliation by other countries, the danger that the state intervention they advocate will not be conducted rationally but be corrupted by special interests) so that the policy implications they drew were a very cautious and conditional departure from liberal prescriptions.

Marxist approaches

The unifying factor in the various approaches that are often lumped together under the category of Marxism (and the other labels noted at the beginning of this section) is a focus on distributional questions, on the constraining effects of domestic and international structures, and on social classes as a significant unit of analysis.

As with the other categories of approaches, authors within this third subdivision also frequently diverge on key theoretical and policy questions. One of these is whether capitalism should be regarded as a progressive force (and therefore supported because it paves the way for movement to a higher form of economic and social configuration). For classical Marxists (including those Marxist theorists of imperialism, such as Lenin, Hilferding, and Luxemburg, who wrote in the first two decades of the twentieth century), although capitalism was brutal and degrading in its impact, it nonetheless was progressive in that it undermined the economic and social structures that held back less developed societies. Only through external penetration by the forces of capitalism could the developmental potential of non-Western areas be realized. This theoretical stance, with its inevitable policy prescription that capitalism was a necessary phase through which all countries must progress, was increasingly challenged in the inter-war years by radical authors from less developed countries, especially from the communist party of India. Their argument—that imperialism could retard economic development in non-Western areas by forging an alliance with domestic feudal elements—was elaborated in the first two decades after the Second World War in what became known as underdevelopment theory (Baran 1976; Frank 1967). Capitalism, it was argued, had not only failed to develop non-Western economies: it had made them worse off by extracting their economic surplus through a process of 'unequal' trade (the exchange of raw materials, whose prices were in relative decline, for manufactured goods) and through the repatriation of profits by transnational corporations.

The underdevelopment approach was rejected not only by writers from the liberal camp but also by classical Marxists (Warren 1980), and by others within the radical tradition, particularly scholars from Latin America, the region which had been the focus of Baran's and Frank's work (Cardoso 1977; Cardoso and Faletto 1979; dos Santos 1970). The proposition that capitalism was causing less developed economies to regress economically became increasingly untenable (at the very least in terms of a *universal* process in which underdevelopment theorists cast it) when the newly industrializing countries enjoyed obvious success in sustaining rapid economic growth. A more nuanced approach was required to examine the manner in which integration into a globalizing economy not only constrained but also provided opportunities for less developed economies (Evans 1985, 1995), and to identify the forms of state apparatus and policy prescriptions that could capitalize on these opportunities (Amsden 1989; Wade 1990, 1992). Whether much of this newer writing is best classified as coming from a structuralist or an economic nationalist perspective is debatable.

In Europe in particular, some authors continued to write within the classical Marxist tradition. In the last two decades, however, challenges to the prevailing liberal orthodoxy have come from a variety of standpoints, prominent among which have been feminist and environmentalist perspectives. Feminist writers have rejected the Marxist emphasis on class in asserting that gender is the most important variable to focus on, and in researching IPE have done a great deal of work on the impact of globalization on women in less developed economies. Representative works from a feminist perspective include Enloe (1990), Pettman (1996), Steans (1998), Steans and Marchand (forthcoming), Marchand and Runyan (2000), and Ault and Sandberg (2002).

As Dauvergne discusses in Chapter 14, a rise in concern about the impact of global economic growth on the environment has sparked the development of another significant literature in the study of global political economy: environmental perspectives (see also Dryzek 1997).

Yet even if these relatively new approaches are unified in their focus on a particular variable or subject matter, little concord exists within feminist or environmental camps on key issues relating to their research. The distinguished feminist author, Jean Bethke Elshtain (1987: 232), described contemporary feminist writing as a 'polyphonic chorus of female voices'. A report of a workshop on feminist approaches to international relations, held by the British International Studies Association in 2000, documents ongoing differences among feminist writers in their approaches to theory and methodology (Elias and Kuttner 2001). Similar lack of unity is evident in the literature Dauvergne discusses in Chapter 14 of this book.

Contemporary approaches to IPE

This brief overview of the manner in which many introductions to IPE in the last quarter of a century have categorized theoretical approaches suggests significant flaws with the trichotomous typology. The commonalities across the approaches that are grouped together within a single category are often at such a high level of generality (for example, a primary focus on class as opposed to the state) that they afford little insight into how theorists address particular problems. To ask how an economic nationalist would view, for instance, investment in the local economy by a subsidiary of a foreign-based transnational corporation is largely a meaningless question that invites the response: 'it depends'. Similarly, only at the highest level of abstraction (for example, a preference for reliance on market forces rather than state intervention) can one find a unifying factor in the policy prescriptions of the various schools of thought.

Much of the best work in international political economy in recent years has been concerned less with prescription than with explanation—for instance, how differences in political institutions shape policy decisions, and why some sectors of the economy are more successful than others in seeking protection (see Hiscox, Chapter 3), why it is easier for states to collaborate on some issues rather than others (see Aggarwal and Dupont, Chapter 2), why states have increasingly pursued trade agreements at the regional instead of the global level (Ravenhill, Chapter 5), why states have been unable to agree to an effective regime for dealing with international debt (Pauly, Chapter 7), and why some global environments regimes are effective while others are not (Dauvergne, Chapter 14). Of course, policy prescriptions often follow from such theoretically informed analysis and they are far more specific than those of the 'get the state out of the market' variety. To abandon the trichotomous categorization is neither to abandon theory nor to eschew policy-relevant research.

In the past quarter of a century, the study of international political economy has been enriched by the application of a diverse array of theoretical and methodological approaches. Neither their subject-matter focus nor the methodologies employed allow easy categorization. Take, for instance, the role of ideas in shaping policy agendas, in helping states to reach agreement in various international negotiations, and in legitimating current economic, political, and social structures. Ideas have been the central focus of work firmly within the Marxist tradition, which builds on the arguments of the former Italian communist party leader, Antonio Gramsci, on how ideas help ruling classes to legitimate their domination (Cox 1987; Gill 1990). But ideas have also been pivotal to quite different approaches, drawing on the work of the German sociologist Max Weber, that examines the role they play in defining the range of policy options that governments consider, and in providing a focal point for agreement in international negotiations (Goldstein and Keohane 1993; Hall 1989; Garrett and Lange 1996). Also derived from Weberian analysis are constructivist approaches, which emphasize the significance of ideas in constituting actors' perceptions of their interests and identities, rather than taking these for granted—examples of the application of constructivist analysis to IPE include Colin Hay, Chapter 9 in this volume, Haas (1992), Hay and Rosamond (2002), and Burch and Denemark (1997). And, cross-fertilization has occurred across different approaches, for example, the Gramscian idea of hegemony has been used by writers from a non-Marxist perspective such as Ikenberry and Kupchan (1990), and finds resonance in Joseph Nye's (1990) concept of 'soft' power.

Likewise, turning to methodology, we find similar methods employed by scholars from dramatically different theoretical traditions. Consider rational choice approaches, for example. In the last decade, rational choice has dominated many areas of the study of political science, particularly in universities in the United States. Its origins lie in economic theory; the focus is primarily on individuals, the factors that lead them to choose preferred courses of action, and how strategic interaction generates uncertainty. In IPE, rational choice analysis has been prominent in the recent study of why international institutions, including the European Union, take particular forms, what the effects of institutions are, and why some institutions survive longer than others (Frey 1984; Martin 1992; Garrett and Weingast 1993). Vaubel (1986, 1991) has applied rational choice analysis in an examination of the behaviour of the officials of the IMF. Such work is very much in the mainstream of contemporary political science. But rational choice methods have also been applied by theorists working within the Marxist tradition, for example, Roemer (1988), and Carver and Thomas (1995).

Although rational choice methods have become dominant in some circles within American political science, a large number of scholars of IPE would find it difficult to accept the argument that IPE 'is today characterized by growing consensus on theories, methods, analytical frameworks, and important questions' (Martin 2002: 244). The discussion in the pages above has attempted to illuminate some of the diversity in contemporary work on international political economy. Many scholars find this rich mix of theories and methodologies a cause for celebration rather than concern. This is certainly the view of the contributors to this volume, which reflects much of the current lively debate in the study of IPE.

The first part of the volume looks at some of the approaches that have addressed the key concerns of theorists of IPE: what conditions are most conducive for the emergence of collaborative behaviour among states on economic issues, what are the determinants of the foreign economic policies of states? It then examines the evolution of trade relations first at the global and then at the regional level. Chapter 6 reviews the development of the global financial regime since 1944; the causes of financial crises and the reasons why international collaboration to date has been ineffective in devising strategies to combat them are addressed in the following chapter. Chapter 8 focuses on the growth of foreign investment in the post-war period. For many authors, the multinational enterprise (MNE) is the central actor in the process of globalization. Chapter 10 questions whether the contemporary behaviour of MNEs supports arguments that a global economy has come into existence.

In doing so, it provides a link with the chapters in the second half of the book that examine various aspects of the debate about globalization: whether in fact the contemporary economy is global and whether it differs, qualitatively or quantitatively from previous eras of economic interdependence; the consequences of enhanced globalization for the policy options available to states; the impact of globalization on world poverty and inequality; how globalization has changed the relations between industrialized and less developed economies; the impact of globalization on the environment; and the growth of transnational civil society in response to economic globalization.

Key points

• The field of international political economy emerged in the early 1970s in response to developments in the world economy, international security, and in the study of economics and international relations.

• IPE is a field of enquiry rather than a particular theory or method.

• IPE is best defined by its subject matter rather than as a particular theory or methodology.

• Approaches to the study of IPE have conventionally been divided into the three categories of liberalism, nationalism, and Marxism.

• This trichotomous division is of questionable contemporary utility because of the variation in approaches included within each of the three categories.

• The contemporary study of IPE is characterized by the application of a wealth of theories and methodologies.

QUESTIONS

1 What were the principal reasons why the Thai economy experienced a financial crisis in 1997?

2 What are the implications of the East Asian financial crisis for the contemporary world economy?

3 What were the principal features of the classical period of mercantilism?

4 What were the reasons for rapid economic growth in the nineteenth century?

5 How did the gold standard operate automatically to bring the payments position of countries into equilibrium?

6 What were the principal reasons for the breakdown of international economic relations in the inter-war period?

7 What are the defining characteristics of the post-1945 world economy?

8 What factors led to the emergence of IPE as a significant field of study?

9 What is IPE?

10 How does comparative advantage differ from absolute advantage?

11 What are the main weaknesses with the traditional threefold categorization of approaches to IPE?

FURTHER READING

Cohen, B. J. (1977), *Organizing the World's Money: The Political Economy of International Monetary Relations* (New York: Basic Books). The first major study from an IPE perspective of global financial relations.

Cooper, R. N. (1968), *The Economics of Interdependence* (New York: Columbia University Press). A pioneering work that laid the foundations for the emergence of IPE as a significant field of enquiry in the 1970s.

Crane, G. T., and Amawi, A. (eds.) (1997), *The Theoretical Evolution of International Political Economy: A Reader*, 2nd edn. (New York: Oxford University Press). An excellent compilation of selections from classical and contemporary writing on international political economy.

Gilpin, R. (1987), *The Political Economy of International Relations* (Princeton: Princeton University Press). The most theoretically sophisticated of the early introductory books on IPE.

Hirschman, A. O. (1945), *National Power and the Structure of Foreign Trade* (Berkeley and Los Angeles: University of California Press). A pioneering study of the relationship between power and the foreign economic relations of Nazi Germany.

Keohane, R. O. (1984), *After Hegemony: Cooperation and Discord in the World Political Economy* (Princeton: Princeton University Press). The most thorough assessment of the relationship between the distribution of power and collaboration among states on international economic matters.

Maddison, A. (2001), *The World Economy: A Millennial Perspective* (Paris: Development Centre of the Organization for Economic Cooperation and Development). Excellent source of historical statistics on the development of the world economy.

Palan, R. (ed.) (2000), *Global Political Economy: Contemporary Theories* (London: Routledge). The most comprehensive survey of contemporary theoretical approaches to global political economy.

Schwartz, H. M. (2000), *States Versus Markets: The Emergence of a Global Economy*, 2nd edn. (London: Macmillan). Provides an unusual historical perspective on the contemporary global economy by tracing its development since the 1500s, with emphasis placed on the links between the emergence of the modern state and the modern global economy.

Strange, S. (1971), *Sterling and British Policy: A Political Study of an International Currency in Decline* (London: Oxford University Press). A pioneering work on the relationship between politics and international financial policies.

Wallerstein, I. (1974), *The Modern World-System* (New York: Academic Press). The first volume of a multi-part work examining the emergence of the modern world economy.

WEB LINKS

www.stern.nyu.edu/globalmacro/   What Caused Asia's Economic and Currency Crisis and Its Global Contagion? Web pages maintained by Nouriel Roubini.

www.g7.utoronto.ca/   University of Toronto G8 Information Centre.

www.imf.org   International Monetary Fund.

www.worldbank.org/   World Bank.

www.unctad.org   United Nations Conference on Trade and Development (UNCTAD).

www.opec.org/   Organization of the Petroleum Exporting Countries.

www.eh.net/encyclopedia/officer.gold.standard.php   Gold Standard—EH.Net Encyclopedia.

www.amosweb.com/gls/   Glossary of Economic Terms.

Collaboration and coordination in the global political economy

Vinod K. Aggarwal and Cédric Dupont

READER'S GUIDE

How can one understand the problems of collaboration and coordination in the global political economy? In situations of global interdependence, individual action by states often does not yield the desired result. Many argue that the solution to the problem of interdependence is to create international institutions, but this approach itself raises the issue of how states might go about creating such institutions in the first place. This chapter examines the conditions under which joint action might be desired and provides an introduction to game theory as an approach to understanding interdependent decision making. It then discusses the conditions under which international institutions are likely to be developed and how they might facilitate the processes of collaboration and coordination of state actions. The chapter concludes by examining possible conflicts among institutions over their mandates to regulate an issue area.

Introduction

It is now commonplace to hear about the phenomenon of globalization. Much of this discussion concerns the increased movement of goods, services, ideas, people, and information across boundaries. Academics, policy makers, and the public actively discuss the pros and cons of globalization (see Part Four of this book). Much of the current debate on globalization has its roots in the international political economy literature on interdependence of the early 1970s (Cooper 1972; Keohane and Nye 1977). At that time, political scientists began to identify the characteristics of the changing global economy, including the increased flows of goods and money across national boundaries as well as the rise of non-state actors as a challenge to traditional conceptions of international politics.

While increasing interdependence among states was a relatively new phenomenon when considered against a baseline of the 1950s, high levels of interdependence had existed in earlier historical periods, including the period prior to the First World War (Bordo, Eichengreen, and Irwin 1999). This interdependence, however, was not matched by high levels of institutionalization in the form of the post-Second World War Bretton Woods organizations of the International Monetary Fund (IMF), the World Bank, and the General Agreement on Tariffs and Trade (GATT, and now the World Trade Organization). The debate on interdependence in the early 1970s was thus also driven by the problems that institutions such as the IMF faced with the breakdown of the Bretton Woods dollar-based standard in 1971, the movement toward trade protectionism that appeared to undermine the GATT, and instability in the oil market with the 1973–4 oil crisis.

In considering the implications of interdependence, a key issue revolves around the question of how to achieve collaboration and coordination among states. In particular, scholars have examined how states respond to perceived problems in the global economy that they cannot deal with solely on their own. Importantly, interdependence can be distinguished from interconnectedness based on the costs of interaction. 'Where interactions do not have significant costly effects, there is simply interconnectedness' (Keohane and Nye 1977: 9). With costly effects (and high benefits), however, we can consider countries as mutually dependent on each other, or interdependent.

This chapter considers the problem of collaboration by first characterizing the situations that might require states to work with each other to achieve a desired outcome (the problem of the nature of the goods involved). It then turns to an exposition of decision theory, with a focus on basic game theory as an analytical tool to tackle the nature of collaboration or coordination efforts. Finally, we consider how institutions might play a role in enhancing the prospects for cooperative behaviour.

Goods: the incentives and obstacles to collaboration

In examining the problem of collaboration, we begin by considering why actors might want to work together. We then turn to the obstacles that might impede such cooperation. To simplify the analysis, we first consider the domestic context of the production of goods, before turning to the international arena.

Four types of goods: production in the domestic context

Within countries, private firms and governments produce many different types of goods and services. Examples include goods like wheat, clothing, steel, and computers as well as the provision of financial, insurance, and other such services. Such goods are generally referred to as *private goods*, based on two characteristics: the goods are generally excludable and are not joint in production. The concept of *excludable* means that goods can be withheld from those who do not pay for them; *not joint in production* means that when a consumer utilizes the good, it is used up and cannot be used by others without additional production. In capitalist societies, private firms have generally produced such goods, but governments can also produce them. Indeed, in communist societies, the government produced most of these goods. Thus, the terms 'private good' refers to certain characteristics of a good, and *not* to the ownership of the entity that actually produces them.

In addition to private goods, communities may desire other goods such as national defence or parks. These goods, known as *public goods*, are characterized by the lack of ability to create exclusion (they are available to all regardless of whether people pay for them), and the jointness of production. Because anyone can have access to these goods, the private sector is unlikely to produce them, since producers cannot recover their investment and make a profit through their production. As a result, governments generally provide these goods. Of course, like firms, governments also face the problem that citizens may not be willing to pay for these goods. In the case of national defence, for example, if the government creates a nuclear deterrent through investment in submarines, missiles, and nuclear bombs, it is difficult if not impossible to exclude those who do not wish to pay for such goods. Thus, even those who might desire the good have an incentive to make it appear that they do not really care for the good, or to misrepresent their true preferences. Assuming the good is indeed produced, these actors will be able to consume the good without paying for it, engaging in what is known as *free riding* behaviour. For example, it is not a simple matter to specifically withhold the provision of a good such as a nuclear umbrella from citizens in various cities across the country that do not wish to pay for this good. At the same time, within limits, these goods can be extended to many users without the government accruing additional costs of production.

How do governments ensure that they will have the funds to provide such goods? Put differently, how can they overcome the problem of free riding? The obvious answer is taxation, which for the most part is mandatory and which citizens find difficult to avoid. In some cases, if some type of exclusion mechanism can be introduced (a high fence around a park, for example), even the private sector may have an incentive to produce such goods because consumers can be charged for using the park.

Beyond these two types of goods, we can also examine two other types. First, if a good is characterized by lack of exclusion and also lack of jointness of production, then such a good is referred to as a *common pool resource*. Examples of such goods include fish in the oceans, or even as a limiting case, a public park. If one overfishes the ocean, fish will cease to reproduce and die out. Similarly, although parks are often seen as public goods, too many users of the park create crowding, which impairs the enjoyment of the good for others. Private actors will be particularly reluctant to produce such goods, and even governments will be concerned about the problem of too many users. As we shall see, in the international context, countries often find themselves particularly at odds when they attempt to cooperate to provide common pool resources.

Another possibility is that the good may be excludable, and yet be joint in production. These goods, known as *inclusive club goods*, include software, music, literature, and a variety of other goods. In such cases, the private sector has a great incentive to produce the good, since once a unit of the good is produced, it can be distributed at either little or no cost. Firms may quickly develop a monopoly in the production of such goods if they are the first movers who make the good. Often, such goods are subject to regulation by governments, or in some cases, even produced by governments themselves. For example, consider a firm launching a satellite to beam television programming to consumers. Although the initial cost of securing a rocket to put the satellite in orbit will be very high, once the satellite is up and running, the programming can be disseminated to large numbers of consumers. In the case of software or music, there is often a great incentive to copy the materials, and governments may enforce property rights through regulations such as copyright laws to prevent such copying. Private firms will generally attempt to regulate consumption themselves if they can. In the case of satellite television, for example, they could encode

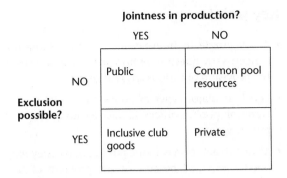

Jointness in production?

		YES	NO
Exclusion possible?	NO	Public	Common pool resources
	YES	Inclusive club goods	Private

Fig. 2.1 Types of goods

the transmission to prevent free riding. The Figure 2.1 summarizes the four types of goods.

Four types of goods: production in the international arena

How do the problems of providing various types of goods play out in the international arena, and what obstacles do states face in achieving cooperation? Consider the case of cooperation with respect to avoiding damage to the ozone layer. Chlorofluorocarbons (CFCs) and other chlorine and bromine containing compounds have many uses, including as coolants, aerosols, cleaning agents, and solvents. By the early 1970s, however, scientists began to argue that such compounds could damage the ozone layer that protects the earth against harmful ultraviolet radiation, leading to increased rates of skin cancer.

By the early 1980s, there was increasing scientific consensus that these products were indeed causing destruction of the ozone layer. Yet because CFCs have many valuable uses, the debate over how to reduce or eliminate these emissions became an internationally contentious issue. Protecting the ozone layer has characteristics of a public goods problem, and the temptation to free ride is high. With respect to crowding, at the extreme, protecting the ozone layer has common pool resource properties because jointness may be impaired if one country produces a huge amount of emissions that damages the ozone layer.

In response to demands from activists and governments for action to stop the destruction of the ozone layer, twenty countries signed a treaty in Vienna in 1985.

Soon thereafter the Montreal Protocol was negotiated in 1987 and ratified in 1989. The actual negotiations leading up to this agreement were complex, with sharply differing positions among the United States, European Union, and developing countries, among others. This agreement, though a step toward ozone layer protection, gave developing countries the right to continue production of CFCs for a significantly longer period than developed countries.

The public goods nature of the problem can be seen in the possibility of free riding by various countries who wish to benefit from the reduction in emissions of CFCs but who do not want to bear the costs of reducing their production. As some developing countries implied, actors such as the EU and the USA were actually such large producers of CFCs that the public good of ozone protection resembled a common pool resource—rather than simply a public good where any single actor's production would not impair 'consumption' of the benefits of having an ozone layer that protected against ultraviolet radiation. As we discuss below, both the problem of ensuring an adequate supply of public goods and of common pool resources can be analysed using game-theoretic tools and through an examination of the role that institutions can play in helping to enhance cooperation.

Turning next to inclusive club goods, the debate over intellectual property illustrates this problem well. At one level, greater knowledge is a classic public good, because my use of knowledge, say, to improve my health, will not generally impair your use of the same knowledge to improve your own. But some may argue that knowledge could potentially exhibit crowding or lack of jointness in a commercial setting. If I use knowledge to produce goods that can be sold on the open market, your use of the knowledge will crowd out my goods. Moreover, it may also be possible to create exclusion mechanisms to prevent others from using knowledge through the patent and copyright system.

These issues have been hotly debated in the international arena, and current negotiations in the World Trade Organization over the right to use generic versions of patented drugs illustrate the dispute over inclusive club goods. While developing countries often argue that they should have free access to drugs in view of their dire need for drugs to combat AIDS and other diseases, many firms in developed countries argue that access should be limited to those who are willing to pay because the drugs that have been developed are a product of an expensive research and development effort. The counter-argument that developing countries have used is that pharmaceutical companies often discover medicinal plants in their countries and fail to compensate these countries for the use of the basic material from which new drugs may be developed.

As we have seen, then, different types of goods generate different types of bargaining problems in both the domestic and international arena. How these problems might be analysed and whether or not the creation of institutions may alleviate potential conflict or facilitate cooperation are the topics to which we now turn.

Key points

- A key puzzle in international political economy concerns the question of how states negotiate over the provision of various kinds of goods.

- The four major types of goods are public goods, common pool resources, inclusive club goods, and private goods.

- Although actors may desire public goods, they may not be provided because of the problem of free riding.

- The provision of common pool resources is likely to lead to contested bargaining.

Games: modelling decision making

Our discussion of types of goods has shown us that in many situations, actors may wish to cooperate, but such cooperation is not a foregone conclusion because of the incentives to engage in free riding behaviour. To understand how actors might be able to provide different types of goods, we must consider how actors make decisions. In particular, our focus is on decision making in situations of interdependence, a problem that has been successfully analysed using tools from game theory. Before we turn to game theory, however, we first examine the broader problem of decision making (of which game theory is one part).

The branch of analysis known as *decision theory* focuses on how actors make decisions under various types of conditions (Luce and Raiffa 1957; Harsanyi 1977). The four most interesting types of conditions, in broad brush characterization, are *decision making under certainty, decision making under risk, decision making under uncertainty*, and *decision making under interdependence*. As we shall see, these various conditions call for different analytical approaches to examine likely outcomes.

Individual decision making

In the case of *decision making under certainty*, the state of the world is known prior to choosing an act. For example, if Country A invades Country B, Country B

will fight. The 'states of the world' in this scenario are 'Country B fights' and 'Country B surrenders'. More simply, when thinking about individual decision making, we can ask: Do you prefer Coke or Pepsi? To analyse such simple situations, we only need to know how actors evaluate their options in terms of the concept of 'utility'. Utility refers to an actor's subjective assessment of the benefits of a particular outcome or course of action (drinking Pepsi versus Coke). In this case, we can predict what an actor will do by simply examining how each actor evaluates his or her utility. We assume that actors will choose options that give them the highest utility.

Things become somewhat more complicated if actors cannot easily evaluate the exact utility of a particular action. In this case, we may find that they can only assign a certain probability to the event in question in evaluating utilities. Put differently, the environment in which they are operating will affect their preferred course of action, leading to a situation of *decision making under risk*. Here, each state of the world has a known probability of occurring, and these probabilities are based on known frequencies over many repetitions. The condition of risk occurs in most gambling games such as craps or roulette. In international relations, we can consider the somewhat unrealistic case where we might empirically observe that if Country A invades Country B, Country B will fight 90 per cent of the time, and surrender 10 per cent of

Box 2.1 Decision making under risk

If one is trying to decide whether to watch television tomorrow or to go on a picnic, one of the key factors will be the probability of rain (at least for most people!). Let us say that John has the following preferences, given in terms of utilities and based on possibility of rain. If John goes on a picnic, but it rains, he assigns this a utility of 1. If, on the other hand, he picnics and it doesn't rain, he will give this a utility of 10 (since John likes to be outdoors in the sunshine). If he does not go on a picnic but instead chooses to watch television and it rains, he will give this a utility of 7. And finally, if he decides to watch television but then it does not rain, he will give this a utility of 3. Note that we assume for simplicity that John cannot change his mind on the next day, but has to make a commitment on the day before as to his course of action. How then might we predict what John will do? The key factor here is the probability of rain. Let us assume that the

probability of rain based on the weather forecast is 50 per cent. Then, calculating the appropriate course of action is simply a matter of filling in the following table.

	0.5 probability of rain	0.5 probability of no rain	Outcomes
Watch television	$0.5 \times 7 = 3.5$	$0.5 \times 3 = 1.5$	5.0
Go on a picnic	$0.5 \times 1 = 0.5$	$0.5 \times 10 = 5$	5.5

As we can see from the calculations, because 5.5 is greater than 5, John will decide to go on a picnic, based on his utilities and on the probability of rain.

the time. An illustrative example of calculating how actors make decisions under risk is given in Box 2.1.

What if it is difficult to even assign probabilities to the likelihood of various outcomes? In this case, we are faced with what is known as *decision making under uncertainty*. In such cases, one can work to narrow down the range of probabilities. Two methods that can be used are the creation of scenarios and the Delphi Technique. In the first approach, one can take the existing information that is available and generate a number of hypothetical scenarios. This technique may allow decision makers to work through the potential consequences of different factors, with an eye to reducing the uncertainty about outcomes and possibly assigning a better evaluation of risk. In the second approach, the Delphi Technique, one can draw on experts who examine different options and comment on their likelihood (generally anonymously to prevent group pressure). Some method of aggregating their predictions to narrow down the range of likely outcomes might also be used in such cases.

Interdependent decision making

So far, we have operated under the assumption that in making decisions, actors are playing against 'nature' in the sense that in such situations, they need not

worry about how another actor might respond to their choice. Yet in most cases of international relations, actors—including individuals, governments, or other organizations—operate in a situation of interdependence. Put differently, one actor's choice depends on expectations regarding the choice another actor will make. Moreover, the types of interdependent situations also vary, thus further complicating the analysis of cooperation (Aggarwal and Dupont 1999; Cornes and Sandler 1996; Sandler 1992; Taylor 1987; Zürn 1992).

A game-theoretic perspective can help us understand likely behaviour in varying types of interdependent situations. Game theory provides a comprehensive toolbox that facilitates an in-depth exploration of actor's interactions. Game theory assumes actors' basic preferences and their strategic environment, and then helps us derive how actors rank the various policy options at their disposal and allows us to determine the likely outcome of the interplay among a variety of policy choices (see Box 2.2).

To keep this chapter's discussion of game theory as straightforward as possible, we focus on simple games with two persons and two strategies. Clearly, such modelling choices may appear to oversimplify real life examples, but as several authors have shown, simple models can clearly reveal the fundamental aspects of interdependence

Box 2.2 Game theory and its critics

Game theory has become a standard tool for analysis of situations of interdependence in social sciences. Aside from its predictive aim, game theory has a strong appeal for anyone engaged in explanation, investigation, or prescription. It often makes ostensibly puzzling processes intelligible, without attributing causality to factors such as the incompetence, irresponsibility, or lack of concern of decision makers.

Whatever its value, however, the use of game theory poses severe methodological problems that have prompted intense debates in the literature. Critics have traditionally emphasized (1) the overstretching of the concept of rationality and (2) the gap between abstract theoretical concepts and real phenomena. Regarding the notion of rationality, most applications of game theory assume that players, interacting under conditions of imperfect information, possess a very high computational ability. To make their decisions, players must evaluate a host of possible worlds on the basis of the knowledge commonly shared with others or privately known. This kind of situation often implies that players engage in counter-factual reasoning about a large set of possible worlds. Leeway in their interpretation often leads to a myriad of possible equilibria, which significantly decrease the predictive power of game theory. To avoid this indeterminacy, most game theorists have refined the concept of 'rationality' to allow the selection of one or very few equilibria among the vast initial array. For example, one might assume that people always choose to buy the cheapest product available (even though we know that

many people buy based on brand name, reputation, or other factors) because it makes the choices of actors easier to map. Most of these refinements to the concept of rationality thus lack empirical grounding.

A more recent controversy has focused on the empirical contribution of rational choice approaches to politics, including game-theoretic work. According to the most forceful critics (Green and Shapiro 1994), a variety of pathologies have prevented rational choice theory from improving our understanding of politics. In particular, rational choice theorists are, according to these critics, method driven rather than problem driven. In other words, instead of focusing on building models that accurately reflect decision making in the real world, game theorists (according to critics) are more concerned with constructing 'neat' but unrealistic models of decision making. As a consequence, game theorists neglect issues of empirical testing which allegedly undermines the scientific value of rational choice theory.

Although there clearly remain weaknesses in most game-theoretic analyses of international relations, the link between theory and empirics has clearly improved over the last decade. Users of game theory have employed different techniques to check the validity of their models based on a comparison with reality. The dominant approach has been indirect testing through the statistical analysis using either large-N data sets or a series of case studies. Another approach has been to use case studies to trace the behavioural attitude of actors and check it with specific predictions of models.

(Aggarwal and Dupont 1999; Cooper 1975; Snidal 1985*a*; Martin 1992). Furthermore, we do not attempt to provide comprehensive insight into the problems associated with measuring actors' preferences. Instead, we simply consider some ideal-type situations that reveal how actors might make decisions. Lastly, we use what is known as non-cooperative game theory, which assumes that actors cannot enter into a contract of some type that binds the other actors to play in a particular way. This approach helps set the stage for understanding the role that international institutions might play in fostering cooperation.

We begin with one of the best-known situations of interdependence, the Prisoners' Dilemma. We then focus on coordination games, assurance games, and the games of Chicken, Called Bluff, and Suasion (these last two are specific examples of asymmetric situations). For each of these games, we assume that actors have extensive knowledge of the other actor's preferences but that they cannot observe his or her actual choices. Obviously, in real life situations, actors may have less information about preferences and may be able to observe the other's behaviour. Still, these simplifying assumptions help reveal the essence of the problem of interdependent decision making.

The Prisoners' Dilemma

As we have seen from our discussion of goods, collective action is difficult because individuals have a tendency to seek gains but avoid costs. This problem of free riding or of shirking of one's obligations makes it difficult to produce desired goods. As the case of the Prisoners' Dilemma illustrates, even though actors may be better off cooperating, the structure of the bargaining situation may prevent them from achieving the collective gains that they desire.

The Prisoners' Dilemma is a story in which two individuals are involved in a robbery and are then caught near the scene of the crime. The District Attorney (the DA or prosecutor) does not have sufficient evidence to convict either of the suspects of robbery unless at least one of them reveals additional information to him but he has some evidence to convict both of them of a lesser crime (for instance, reckless driving or carrying a firearm). The DA wants more information to convict both suspects for a long period. The two prisoners are placed in separate interrogation rooms. The DA tells each prisoner that, if they confess and reveal the truth, they will get a much lighter sentence. If both prisoners confess, however (Strategy S2 in the game depicted in Figure 2.2 below) they each get a heavier sentence than if they both remain silent (Strategy S1 in Figure 2.2) and are charged with the lesser crime (when both confess, the DA has the evidence to convict both on the more serious offences). Confessing to the DA could bring the minimal sentence if the other one does not confess but could also lead to a lengthier sentence if the other turns him in. Remaining silent, on the other hand, may lead to either a moderate sanction if the other prisoner remains silent, or the maximum penalty if the other one speaks to the attorney. Facing this situation, and unable to communicate, the logical strategy for both prisoners is to choose to confess. They do so because confessing to the DA is individually always a safer strategy than remaining silent.

This story can be generalized using the game depicted in Figure 2.2. The numbers in the various cells indicate the preferences of players on an ordinal ranking scale, with four being the most preferred situation and one the least preferred. In the following figures, the first number in each box refers to Player Alpha's preference, while the second number refers to Player Beta's preference (thus '4, 1' is Alpha's most preferred outcome and Beta's least preferred outcome).

As Figure 2.2 shows, both players have a dominant strategy (to confess, that is, Strategy 2) that leads to what is called the *Nash Equilibrium* outcome, which is in the lower right cell of the matrix. A Nash Equilibrium is an outcome in which none of the players can improve his or her situation by changing their individual strategy. But if both switch to Strategy 1 (remain silent) together, both players will secure a better outcome (upper left cell). However, this collectively optimal situation is unstable because each actor can improve his or her own welfare by individually switching strategy to the cells in the upper right or lower left corners of the matrix.

The Prisoners' Dilemma has often been used to depict the problem of providing public goods. The problem of restricting access to these goods creates a temptation to use them without having to pay. Yet, this fact alone does not necessarily prevent the provision of such goods. Instead, restricting counsumption of public goods requires that the other actor gains nothing (at best) from providing the good alone. As we argue elsewhere (Aggarwal and Dupont 1999), the Prisoners' Dilemma best corresponds to the problem of CPR goods, or common goods under open access, a situation analysed by Hardin with his metaphor of the 'tragedy of the commons' (Hardin 1968). Free riding by some actors not only affects the *cost* to the actor who provides the good, but it also affects the *benefit* that each actor receives in view of the rivalry in consumption.

From an international political economic perspective, the Prisoners' Dilemma has been widely used to illustrate the problem of reciprocal trade liberalization (Grossman and Helpman 1995; Hoekman and Kostecki 1995; Maggi 1999). The difficulties in monitoring partners' trade policies and the potential political benefits to governments from open export

		Player Beta	
		S1	S2
Player Alpha	S1	3, 3	1, 4
	S2	4, 1	**2, 2**

Fig. 2.2 Prisoners' Dilemma game (ordinal form)

Note: Nash equilibrium in bold.

markets and closed domestic markets often push states to back out of their commitments to reciprocate trade liberalization measures. As Conybeare shows (1984), this tendency particularly applies to countries with large domestic markets, as these countries are less dependent on the success of trade liberalization (this makes the utilities of the lower right cell in Figure 2.2 relatively acceptable) and they can also positively affect world prices through their tariff policy (imposing a tariff on their imports, because they constitute such a large share of the overall world market, lowers the price that other countries will receive for their exports). For smaller countries, though, the Prisoners' Dilemma is not an adequate depiction of their situation. Rather, smaller countries tend to have preferences that reflect the game of chicken, a situation which we discuss below.

Another typical application of the Prisoners' Dilemma in international political economy has been on the collective management of resources. Whereas countries producing particular commodities traded on world markets would prefer a situation where they all manage production so as to keep prices sufficiently high, they also are tempted to increase extraction or production of those commodities so as to maximize individual profits. As a result, acting collectively to keep commodities prices stable (in commodities such as coffee, tin, oil for instance) has been a daunting task, particularly for developing countries.

Coordination games

A second class of games deals with the problems associated with choosing *among* Pareto efficient outcomes (Pareto efficient outcomes are defined as outcomes from which no actor could become better off without worsening the payoffs to another actor). Such cases are referred to as situations of *pure coordination* and are relatively easy to resolve when actors do not strongly prefer one outcome to another. But if actors have different preferences for various outcomes, the problem of cooperation quickly becomes more difficult. The game depicted in Figure 2.3 is a specific illustration of such a strategic interaction. Its name, 'Battle of the Sexes', comes from the story of a husband and wife who have to decide where to spend their evening after work. They either can go to the opera or go to watch a

Fig. 2.3 Coordination game (Battle of the Sexes) (ordinal form)

Note: Nash equilibrium in bold.

football match. Neither spouse derives much pleasure by being without the other one but they differ on the best choice for evening entertainment. The husband would prefer to watch football (Strategy S1 in Figure 2.3) whereas the wife prefers the opera (Strategy S2). In the scenario for this game, both are getting out of work and have to rush to either the stadium or opera. They cannot communicate to each other (say the batteries of their cell phones are dead!), and have to meet at one of the locations. If each of them follows their preferred solution, they end up at different locations, which both consider to be a bad outcome. If both of them want to please the other one by choosing the other's preferred entertainment, they also end up being separated. Thus, they have somehow implicitly to coordinate their behaviours, with one making a concession and the other getting his/her best choice. Figure 2.3 provides a generalization of that story.

In Figure 2.3, none of the players has a dominant strategy. Player Alpha prefers to play Strategy 1 when player Beta chooses Strategy 1 and prefers Strategy 2 when player Alpha chooses Strategy 2. With player Beta having the same preferences, the game has two equilibrium outcomes—the upper left and the lower right cells in Figure 2.3. These two outcomes are clearly preferable to the two other possible outcomes, but actors will disagree on which one to choose. Player Alpha prefers the upper left cell whereas player Beta prefers to end up in the lower right cell. Both players want to avoid being separated but each player prefers a different outcome. Accordingly, actors may fail to avoid this 'dilemma of common aversion' (Stein 1982) if they pay too much attention to the distributive tension between the two equilibrium outcomes.

In an international political economy perspective, efforts by developed countries to choose mutually compatible macro-economic policies typically reflect games of coordination (Putnam and Bayne 1987). For instance, when there is high volatility on financial and exchange-rate markets, coordinated responses by leading countries would often be best but each country would like to choose the policy mix that best fits its own domestic constraints. Another prominent example is the choice of international monetary system (Cooper 1975). Discussions between the United States and Great Britain during the Second World War regarding the architecture of the future international economic order reveal that although both countries agreed on the absolute need for coordination, they fought over the details of the new order, with each trying to impose its own plan. A more recent example, the debate within the European Union over the design of monetary union, saw Britain, France, and Germany proposing different collective solutions (Wolf and Zangl 1996).

Assurance games

A third category of situations deals with the possibility of being unable to seize an opportunity for co-operation that seems obvious. Players share one most preferred outcome but they do not have dominant strategies. As a result, in the game of 'Stag Hunt', there is a second, Pareto deficient, equilibrium outcome. The situation depicted in Figure 2.4 comes from the story of two hunters chasing a stag. They go out before dawn and take positions on different sides of an area where they think a stag is hiding. They have a mutual understanding to shoot only at the stag (Strategy S1 in the game depicted in Figure 2.4). Shooting at any other wild animal, say a hare (Strategy S2), would lead them to miss shooting the stag because the stag would be frightened by the noise and stay put in its hiding

place. As time goes by and as dawn arrives, however, both hunters start thinking that going back home with a hare might be better than continuing to wait for the stag to come out of hiding. If each of them thinks that the other one will eventually yield to the temptation to shoot at a hare, they will both end up killing a hare—a better outcome than not catching anything but clearly much less attractive than sharing a stag.

In such a game, reaching the Pareto efficient equilibrium is not a foregone conclusion. Doubts about the willingness of one's counterpart to choose Strategy S1 (shoot the stag) might push a player to choose Strategy S2 (shoot a hare), which guarantees the highest minimal gain. Yet, such an outcome is rather unlikely because of the attraction of the upper left cell.

Assurance games accurately reflect the problem of providing goods when a situation requires the so-called 'weakest link technology'. In this type of environment, each actor's contribution is needed for the good to be produced, and thus players do not have an incentive to free ride. In the international political economy, the provision of financial stability in a globalized financial world (with high mobility of capital), exhibits some features of an assurance game (at least among the major financial centres, which all must cooperate if the desired outcome is to be realized). Similarly, exchange-rate stability cannot simply rely on a hegemonic power but also requires the active participation of other states, as shown by the collapse of both the fixed exchange-rate systems of Bretton Woods and the European Monetary System (EMS) when other states failed to cooperate with the dominant actor (the USA and Germany, respectively).

Chicken, Called Bluff, and Suasion

We now turn to games that combine the three key essential dimensions of cooperation—actor preferences, actor capabilities, and communication between actors. The best example of this type of game is the game of Chicken, depicted in Figure 2.5. This game builds on the story of two cars, travelling in opposite directions, speeding down the middle of the road toward one another. Inside each car sits a driver who wants to impress his respective passenger that he is a tough person (that is, demonstrate resolve). The best way to do so is to continue driving straight down

Player Beta

		S1	S2
Player Alpha	S1	**4, 4**	1, 3
	S2	3, 1	**2, 2**

Fig. 2.4 Assurance game (Stag Hunt) (ordinal form)

Note: Nash equilibrium in bold.

		Player Beta	
		S1	S2
Player Alpha	S1	3, 3	**2, 4**
	S2	**4, 2**	1, 1

Fig. 2.5 Chicken game (ordinal form)

Note: Nash equilibrium in bold.

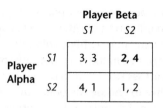

		Player Beta	
		S1	S2
Player Alpha	S1	3, 3	**2, 4**
	S2	**4, 1**	1, 2

Fig. 2.6 Called Bluff (ordinal form)

Note: Nash equilibrium in bold.

the middle of the road (Strategy S2 in the game depicted in Figure 2.5)—even when the car coming in the opposite direction comes dangerously close. Yet, if at least one driver does not swerve, the outcome will be disastrous and both cars will crash, killing everyone. To avoid this undesirable outcome, at least one driver will have to yield and swerve (Strategy S1 in Figure 2.5), but both would like the other one to be the 'Chicken' who swerves.

When it comes to games of coordination, players do not have dominant strategies and there are two equilibrium outcomes. There are two differences between these games and the game depicted in Figure 2.5. First, distributional tensions tend to be higher in Chicken; second, there is a Pareto efficient compromise solution (upper left cell) that is problematic because it is not an equilibrium outcome. Therefore, the Chicken game combines the problems of coordination games with the free riding difficulties of the Prisoners' Dilemma game (Stein 1982).

The Chicken game is a useful allegory for situations that deal with the provision of public goods, when each player has the resources and technology to provide the good and is anxious to avoid failures in the eventual provision of the good. Because the question of how the costs of production should be divided still remains, however, as each actor will want the other to carry the burden, there will be a resulting clash.

In the context of the global political economy, Chicken games are useful depictions of the complexity of burden sharing that occurs within a group of powerful players. For instance, when there is monetary and financial stability in the global economy, the United States and the European Union may tend to resist overcommitting internationally unless there is a clear sign that the other party will act similarly. Getting out of a trade negotiation stalemate or dispute can also be a Chicken-like situation in which

each actor is unwilling to agree to any asymmetric solutions.

To this point, we have only considered cases where actors have symmetrical preferences. We now examine two interesting *asymmetric* games, the first of which has one player with Prisoners' Dilemma preferences, and a second player with Chicken preferences. The resulting game, known as the game of 'Called Bluff', is depicted in Figure 2.6.

The predicted outcome is that player Beta gets her most preferred outcome, whereas player Alpha gets his second worse outcome. This scenario is often seen in situations where one player carries most of the burden of providing a good. This eventual outcome is caused from an asymmetry in the ability (resources) of both actors to provide the good or from a difference in sensitivity (vulnerability) to the good itself. The player with either weaker resources or less dependence on the benefits of the good (Beta in Figure 2.6) is able to free ride on the other player (Alpha in Figure 2.6).

The best illustration of this situation comes from Schelling's theory of the 'tyranny of weakness' (1960). As Schelling shows, by playing his dominant strategy (which is to 'defect' from the provision of a good), the weaker party forces the stronger player to carry the burden of providing the good. A real world example of this particular concept is the monetary policy of Germany and Japan in the 1960s, in the context of the Bretton Woods fixed exchange-rate system. The stronger player, the United States, asked these countries to revalue their currencies to help boost the competitiveness of US exports and relieve the pressure on the dollar. These countries, however, refused to implement any significant revaluation of their currencies, thereby placing an increasingly costly burden on the USA, and ultimately causing the downfall of the Bretton Woods system (see Helleiner, Chapter 6 in this volume).

Fig. 2.7 Harmony (ordinal form)

Note: Nash equilibrium in bold.

		Player Beta	
		S1	*S2*
Player Alpha	*S1*	4, 3	**3, 4**
	S2	2, 2	1, 1

Fig. 2.8 Suasion (ordinal form)

Note: Nash equilibrium in bold.

A second case of asymmetry is a game with one player having preferences oriented toward cooperation and the other one having Chicken preferences. In the game of 'Suasion', Player Beta has preferences similar to a player in a Chicken game but Player Alpha has preferences that are typical of another game, the game of Harmony. The basic feature of Harmony games (see Figure 2.7) is that both players not only dislike doing things differently (as in the case of coordination games) but they also do not differ on the best outcome. They both therefore have a dominant strategy to do the same thing. Cooperation is, so to speak, naturally guaranteed (as, for instance, in nineteenth-century liberal assumptions about international economic relations).

Combining a player with Chicken preferences and a player with Harmony preferences yields the game depicted in Figure 2.8, known as the game of 'Suasion' (Martin 1992).

The predicted outcome of the Suasion game shares some similarity with the game of Called Bluff illustrated in Figure 2.6 above. Both games feature a situation in which one player, Beta, gets her most preferred outcome. However, the difference between these two games is that in Suasion, the other player gets his second best outcome, which results from the choice of a dominant strategy by the stronger player (Beta) rather than the weaker one (the reverse of the Called Bluff

game). Put into the context of the provision of goods, this clearly reflects a group with an actor who values the good more than he values the costs associated with providing the good (what Olson 1965 labels the 'privileged' group). Because this actor (Alpha) absolutely wants to provide the good (always choosing S1), others actors (Beta) are in a situation whereby they will let him (Alpha) provide the good and thus enjoy it for free.

Even though one could also consider such a situation as one of the tyranny of the weak, the stronger player is not forced into an asymmetric outcome by the behaviour of the weak, but by his own preferences. From this perspective, the Suasion game features an opportunistic attitude by the weak rather than a deliberately tyrannical outlook. Martin (1992) argues that this game illustrates the Western world's restriction of technology exports to the Soviet Union during the Cold War. Control of technology sales to the Soviet bloc was done through the Coordinating Committee on Export Controls (COCOM). Within it, however, the United States had a dominant strategy to control technology whereas European states were more opportunistic. They could benefit from sales to the Soviet bloc without jeopardizing the overall balance of power between the two blocs. The USA was dissatisfied with this situation and had to persuade Europeans to participate fully with COCOM.

More generally, this type of game relates to situations where one actor (or group of actors) can provide a good that is immune (up to some degree) to the free riding behaviour of other countries. For example, tax havens in small countries have been 'tolerated' by bigger countries as long as the latter could use capital movement restrictions to secure financial stability. When capital restrictions were dismantled, there were significant increases in the efforts to circumvent the free riding behaviour of tax havens.

Key points

- The four key types of decision-making models are decision making under certainty, decision making under risk, decision making under uncertainty, and interdependent decision making.
- Game theory can help us analyse interdependent decision making.

- Cooperation can be expected to fail either due to actors' incentive to cheat, to actors' sensitivity to distribution issues, or to lack of confidence in the other actor's behaviour.

- Problems of distribution and free riding may be combined in some games.
- Strong countries may sometimes be exploited by weaker ones.

Self-help or institutions?

The discussion of collaboration problems in the global political economy highlights the varied nature of the challenges facing actors. We now turn to the question of how to address these challenges and focus on the key role international institutions can play in addressing collaboration problems. This analysis begins with situations where collaboration might be achieved without institutions and then turns to cases where institutions help the process of collaboration.

Self-help?

In most of the games that we have examined, individual actions by both players lead, or may lead, to an outcome that we can characterize as collectively optimal because there is no welfare loss. Yet, this notion of optimality tends to be short-sighted because the asymmetric outcomes of the Called Bluff, Suasion, Chicken, and even coordination games are optimal only in terms of a narrow view of *collective welfare*. Such a conception of welfare does not obviate the problems of the distribution of gains that may either make the road to an agreement difficult or plague the likelihood of collaboration. As we discuss below, institutions may play useful roles in addressing these problems, but collaboration may also occur through individual actions.

Individual action, though self-help in nature, can also be optimal in the thorny case of the Prisoners' Dilemma. In order for individual actions to produce a collectively beneficial outcome, players must have repeated interactions through time or across issues (Axelrod and Keohane 1986; Cornes and Sandler 1996; Sandler 1992; Taylor 1987). When players expect to meet again in the future, they may be more willing to cooperate. Yet even under such conditions of iteration, self-help may not be sufficient to ensure cooperation. For example, if the expected net value of cooperation is too low (for example, actors may overly discount the importance of future iterations owing to a dire economic or political situation at home for governments), defection may be likely. The Prisoners' Dilemma demonstrates that, if the cost of defection by one actor is too costly for the other actor (resulting in a lengthy prison sentence in Prisoners' Dilemma), or if actors cannot gather information easily, actors may not reach a Pareto optimal outcome.

Applied to the case of trade liberalization, self-help is difficult for governments that are under heavy domestic pressure, as the temptation to reap immediate gains through defection (offering protection to domestic constituencies) may simply be too big. Conversely, the cost of defection may be too high when actors invest heavily in cooperative efforts and value the outcome produced by cooperation. In such cases, they are significantly more reluctant to defect, even if others have defected.

Self-help is also not universally effective in securing the exchange of goods. As long as trading partners have access to other markets for their products, self-help can work in the context of global trade, since countries can simply turn to another market if a breach in the trading relationship occurs. However, if there is only one partner that is interested in the goods produced, or if it would be more costly to trade with other partners, such an option does not exist. If a country cannot threaten to 'defect' (sell the goods elsewhere), another country may take advantage of it. Another important qualification for successful self-help systems is if one (or both) of the parties have made relation-specific investments. In such case, these investments will discourage defection and may encourage cooperative behaviour.

What other factors might impede cooperation? Monitoring will be much more difficult if states only have limited information-gathering capability. If an actor has so little information that, for example, it is unsure whether the other actor 'defected' on the last go around, then the prospect of repeated interactions does not increase the chances of cooperation. Similarly, an expanding number of states, with an expanding range of trade products, that use increasingly sophisticated trade policies to intervene in markets makes monitoring trade policies increasingly difficult. It is therefore more difficult to detect non-compliance without the help of a third party.

The role of institutions

As our discussion above suggests, actors often need to go beyond individual choices if they want to achieve collectively optimal outcomes. One way that individuals might be able to coordinate their choices to achieve desired goals might be through the creation or use of international institutions or regimes. International regimes have been defined broadly as 'sets of principle, norms, rules and decision making procedures upon which actors' expectations converge' (Krasner 1983). To refine this definition, we can distinguish between the principles and norms—the 'meta-regime' (Aggarwal 1985)—and the regime itself defined as the rules and procedures, to allow us to distinguish between two very different types of constraints on the behaviour of states. In this case, we can use the term institution to refer to the combination of a meta-regime and a regime. Moreover, institutions may be characterized in terms of their strength (the degree to which they constrain state behaviour), nature (the objectives promoted by the institution), and scope (across both issues and actors). Issue scope refers to the breadth of coverage of the institution, while actor scope indicates the number of actors who are members of the institution. We structure our discussion below around three major functions of institutions.

First, institutions can help actors settle on a collectively optimal, but unstable, outcome. Institutions play the role of a third party that enforces cooperation. To successfully overcome the tendency of players to defect, institutions should be strong, and look more like binding contracts than conventions. Agreements that credibly restrain opportunism in trade and monetary policy, for instance, need to rely on some sort of enforcement mechanism. When self-enforcing agreements do not work (see our discussion above), actors may decide to delegate enforcement to an international institution. At its strongest expression, in the European Union or in the World Trade Organization, such a mechanism relies on an institutional entity (the EU has two such entities, the Commission and the Court of Justice) with supranational powers to monitor, evaluate, and sanction (if needed) the behaviour of its members (see Box 2.3).

Enforcement can also be enhanced through a different kind of centralization, one that ensures a prompt and undistorted dissemination of information. This type of facility helps identify the requirements of multilateral action and protects against possible defections. Enforcement can also be achieved through either positive incentives, as when the International Monetary Fund provides funds to countries that are following its policy recommendations, or through punitive action as when the World Trade Organization rules against a particular state policy (see Box 2.4).

Second, when actors face several optimal outcomes, institutions can help actors solve distributional problems. They may eliminate some sharply asymmetric outcomes and, through careful gathering of information about the preferences of actors, may help find or provide focal point solutions for both cost sharing and benefit splitting. Institutions with a firmly and widely established meta-regime tend to perform these tasks extremely well. Whereas there is some clear evidence that GATT, and its successor the WTO, have had a significant role in enforcing trade rules, the record of both institutions is less compelling when it comes to distributive issues. Deep disagreements among GATT members led in the 1960s to the creation of another forum on trade issues, the United Nations Conference on Trade and Development (UNCTAD), which less developed economies hoped would better serve their interests, and to serious hurdles in negotiations to extend the scope of GATT/WTO, as revealed in the difficulties in negotiating the Doha WTO round (see Winham, Chapter 4 and Thomas, Chapter 12 in this volume). Without a strong meta-regime, institutions may have difficulty generating potential solutions that are attractive to all members.

Box 2.3 **World Trade Organization (WTO)**

Established in 1995, the 146-member World Trade Organization aims to promote freer trade at the international level. Trade concessions are expected to be non-discriminatory (with concessions made equally to all members) and should not be subject to unexpected changes. From that perspective, the WTO is first a forum for the negotiation of liberalization agreements. Second, it seeks to ensure that members comply with agreements, which include both monitoring and technical help. Third, it provides a mechanism for solving trade disputes between members.

On the negotiation side, the WTO brings together different groups of countries for the negotiation of large packages of trade issues. Most of the negotiation happens on a daily basis between member delegations to the WTO headquarters in Geneva, Switzerland. The secretariat of the WTO, with a staff of 550, provides technical and logistical support for these negotiations. The highest authority of the WTO, biennial ministerial meetings, are supposed to give strategic impulse to the negotiations as well as conclude the process. Agreements are then further approved at the level of the General Council of the WTO, where all members are represented. Currently, there are three basic sets of substantive multilateral trade agreements: agreement on trade in goods (GATT), agreement on trade in services (GATS), and agreement on trade-related intellectual property rights (TRIPS).

On the monitoring side, the Trade Policy Review Mechanism produces an overall assessment of members'

trade policy (for the four biggest traders, the so-called Quad—USA, Canada, European Union, and Japan—this happens every two years) with the goal to promote transparency of policies and therefore make trade more predictable. But a big part of monitoring, decentralized and indirect, happens through disputes between members. Each member can raise some matter of concern and use the dispute settlement mechanism to have another member stop practices that breach WTO obligations. The WTO dispute settlement, which seeks to settle disputes rather than pass judgement, is thus not a court in the traditional sense. If members cannot independently settle their disputes, the Dispute Settlement Body intervenes and may produce a report on the case at stake. When a country is declared to be in violation of some WTO obligations, it must change its policy. If it does not do so, other members may be authorized to get compensation or to retaliate with trade sanctions.

The default decision-making mode is consensus in the WTO. But decisions may also be made at unanimity (suspension of MFN treatment), at 75 per cent majority (interpretation of an existing multilateral agreement, or a waiver of an obligation for a particular country), or at two-thirds majority (for admission of new members for instance).

For more information, **www.wto.org/english/thewto_e/ whatis_e/tif_e/understanding_e.pdf**

Third, institutions can ensure that actors do not miss the opportunity of a collectively optimal, and stable, outcome. Rather than enforcing a particular outcome, institutions should enable actors to reach it (by pooling resources, for example). To help the integration of developing countries into the global financial system, the International Monetary Fund provides cheap credit opportunities through the contributions subscribed by all members. The World Bank finances the development of basic infrastructure in developing countries to help them reduce poverty. At the European regional level, the EMS has relied on a decentralized system of very short lending facilities among members to help them defend the parity grid that tightened them together (see Box 2.5).

To address enforcement and distribution problems, institutions should establish property rights that either define mechanisms of exclusion or determine compensation schemes. In relation to our previous discussion of games and goods, careful institutional design can sometimes 'privatize' problematic goods such as public or CPR goods. The reduction of trade barriers almost always applies to countries that belong to particular clubs, be they regional (see Ravenhill, Chapter 5 in this volume) or global. Assigning property rights can also produce decentralized cooperation when institutions also provide information about the preferences of actors and reduce transaction costs to their minimum. When actors are more certain about who owns and is

Box 2.4 International Monetary Fund (IMF)

Conceived in July 1944 at a United Nations conference held at Bretton Woods, New Hampshire, USA, the IMF came into existence in December 1945. Its purposes, stated in Article I of its Articles of Agreement, have remained unchanged. First, and most generally, it seeks 'to promote international monetary cooperation through a permanent institution which provides the machinery for consultation and collaboration on international monetary problems' (Art. I, i). More specifically, the IMF has been a reaction against monetary disorder in the inter-war period and therefore its essential aim has been 'to promote exchange-rate stability, to maintain orderly exchange arrangements among members, and to avoid competitive exchange depreciation' (Art. I, iii). To help countries achieve exchange-rate stability, membership should 'give confidence to members by making the general resources of the Fund temporarily available to them under adequate safeguards' (Art. I, v).

As can be seen from its Articles of Agreement, the IMF should on the one hand monitor members' policies and on the other hand assist members in their efforts to achieve monetary and financial stability. On the monitoring side, the Fund conducts annual reviews of economic and financial developments in member countries. On that basis, it then gives policy advice to members. The assistance of the Fund is particularly important for members in times of difficulty. In addition to technical assistance, members can get financial assistance and lend reserves from the Fund's general pool of capital that comes from the quota subscriptions that members pay when they join the institution. Quota shares reflect countries' relative size in the world economy. Quotas have been regularly reviewed (eleven times since 1945) to reflect the evolution of the world economy and the needs of the Fund.

In terms of institutional structure, the Board of Governors is the highest authority governing the IMF, but the Executive Board carries the day-to-day work with the help of a large staff (about 2,800 people) under the leadership of a managing director. In contrast to the Board of Governors, where all members (currently 184) have a seat, the Executive Board consists of twenty-four executive directors representing directly or indirectly all members. The IMF's five largest shareholders—the United States, Japan, Germany, France, and the United Kingdom—along with China, Russia, and Saudi Arabia, have their own seats whereas the other sixteen executive directors are elected by groups of countries. For most, but not all, groups of countries, elections, each two years, may lead to rotation of directorship among countries.

An additional characteristic of the decision making in the Fund is weighted voting. Quota shares determine voting power. Hence the biggest contributor, the United States, has 17.6 per cent of the votes whereas Seychelles, the smallest, has 0.004 per cent of votes.

Although the normal decision-making mode is simple majority, all important issues are decided by qualified majority, either 70 per cent (suspension of one member's rights in case of non-respect of obligations) or by 85 per cent (for instance, modification of quotas, change in the seats of the Executive Board, provisions for general exchange arrangements). Qualified majority voting increases the power of the biggest contributors, in particular the United States, which has a veto power over issues requiring an 85 per cent majority.

A summary of the IMF's purposes, working, and recent development can be found at **www.imf.org./exteral/ pubs/ft/exrp/what.htm**

---

responsible for what (a result of the assignment of property rights), cooperation may result.

Under these conditions, as Coase (1960) suggests, actors do not need any centralized power to remedy the problem of negative externalities (Conybeare 1980; Keohane 1984) but should find a mutually satisfactory solution through financial compensation. The crucial aspect, in the Coasian framework, is to establish liability for externalities. The history of international monetary agreements provides several

examples of the difficulties associated with determining satisfactory schemes assigning responsibilities to the involved parties. For instance, the collapse of the fixed exchange-rate systems was largely due to the inability of IMF members to redistribute the burden of adjustment from the United States to Germany and Japan (see Helleiner, Chapter 6 in this volume). Difficulties in the so-called European Snake in the early 1970s led to a change in institutional design so that the European Monetary System was structured in

---

Box 2.5 **World Bank**

The 'World Bank' is the common name for the International Bank for Reconstruction and Development (IBRD) and the International Development Association (IDA). Both institutions aim at assisting developing countries by providing them with low-interest loans, interest-free credits, and grants. In addition to IBRD and IDA, three other organizations make up the World Bank Group: (*a*) the International Finance Corporation (IFC), promoting private investment in high-risk sectors and countries; (*b*) the Multilateral Investment Guarantee Agency (MIGA), providing political risk insurance to investors in developing countries; and (*c*) the International Centre for Settlement of Investment Disputes (ICSID), offering a forum for settling disputes between investors and host countries.

The general aim of the World Bank Group is to facilitate investment in order to promote growth and alleviate poverty in the world. Over the past years, the World Bank has put a particular emphasis on the provision of resources to activities with a potential global impact—named global goods—such as debt relief, HIV/AIDS programmes, water preservation and cleaning, or education. In the last decade, the Bank's main focus has been the reduction of poverty in the world.

Decision making within the institution closely resembles that of the IMF, both having been created during the 1944 Bretton Woods conference. Quota subscriptions determine voting (with slightly different shares by country, for instance 16.41 per cent for the United States) but they constitute a minor part of the Bank's resources, the bulk of them being raised by the Bank in the world's financial markets.

A summary of the World Bank's structure and activities can be found at **www.worldbank.org/wbsite/external/ extaboutus**

---

such a way as to push strong currency members (in particular Germany) to intervene as much as weak currency members in defending existing parities.

The solution of enforcement and distribution problems is more likely to occur when institutions have a large scope and connect different issues. When actors have broad interests, linkages across issues help deter defection on a single issue (Lohmann 1997; McGinnis 1986). For example, members of the WTO cannot subscribe to the agreement on goods (GATT) without also accepting the agreement on services (GATS) as well as the agreement on intellectual property rights (TRIPS), investment (TRIMs), and the dispute settlement mechanism (see Winham, Chapter 4 in this volume).

A diverse set of issues can also provide greater ground for compromise when players have different preferences and when they do not assign equal value to all of the issues. For instance, trade liberalization or monetary cooperation in the European Union has often been facilitated by the development of social or regional policies or packages. But, as the case of agriculture in the GATT/WTO shows, having different issues on the agenda is not helpful when countries exclude certain issues from consideration in making trade-offs.

Our discussion of the roles of institutions reveals the value associated with information gathering and dissemination. Long-term enforcement requires identifying the likelihood that actors will defect, finding a focal point based on the constellation of positions, and informing actors of the overall global context. Therefore, one of the most important roles of international institutions is to collect information about actors' behaviour, preferences, and the state of the international environment.

Key points

- Institutions are key instruments to solve enforcement, distribution, and insurance problems.

- Institutions help assign rights and obligations to benefactors of cooperation as well as define those benefactors.

- Institutions help make the international scene an information-rich environment.

The formation and evolution of institutions

We have seen that in many cases institutions can facilitate cooperation. But how might institutions be formed in the first place? In examining institutions, five different approaches in international relations have been brought to bear on this problem: Neo-realism, Neo-realist Institutionalism, Neo-liberal Institutionalism, Cognitivism, and Radical Constructivism (Haas 1992).

Neo-realists assume that in an anarchic international system, states must engage in self-help behaviour in order to ensure security. For neo-realist scholars, regimes, and international institutions have no significant role in international relations because power considerations are predominant in an anarchic world (Waltz 1979; Mearsheimer 1990). In this view, the only safe bet to ensure collaboration is on a self-help basis, and institutions have little role in fostering cooperation.

Within a power-based tradition, some scholars have examined changes in and the effects of international institutions. In this literature, labelled Neo-realist Institutionalism, the central concern is on how regimes affect the distribution of costs and benefits of state interaction. For analysts in this school (Krasner 1983; Aggarwal 1985; Krasner 1991; Knight 1992), institutions have distributional consequences (in other words, the benefits of cooperation may be unequal). Regimes, from this perspective, play a useful role as a device by which central decision makers control actors' behaviour, both that of other countries and/or that of domestic pressure groups (Aggarwal 1985). For example, from a domestic perspective, participation in regimes enables state elites to argue that their hands are tied and thus attempt to circumvent pressure for particular actions from domestic actors. Examples of this include the Mexican government signing onto the North American Free Trade Agreement (tying the hands of the Mexican government to a more open market posture in the face of domestic protectionist groups) or the American use of the Multifibres Arrangement (an agreement within the GATT that sets country quotas for exports from less developed to industrialized economies) to prevent textile and apparel interests from pressing for excessive protection.

With respect to the creation of regimes, a central theme in this literature has been the role of hegemonic powers in fostering the development of institutions through both positive and negative incentives (Kindleberger 1973; Gilpin 1975; Krasner 1985). Benevolent hegemons, for example, may provide public goods because their large size makes it worthwhile for them to take action on their own to overcome collective action problems. But while suggesting that regimes may form when powerful states desire them, this approach does not tell us much about the nature of regimes, and its focus on tactical, power-based linkages does not adequately account for new issue packaging. Moreover, scholars in this school overemphasize relative gains at the expense of understanding cooperative efforts that might lead to joint gains for all parties. And finally, this approach has little to say about actors' desire to pursue multilateral versus bilateral solutions to accomplish their ends.

Building on this critique, neo-liberal institutionalists have examined the specific incentives for states to create institutions—as opposed to simply engaging in ad hoc bargaining. This body of work, which builds on seminal research by Oliver Williamson (1975), examines the role of institutions in lowering transaction costs (the costs involved in choosing, organizing, negotiating, and entering into a social contract), and has garnered a considerable following (Keohane 1984). As we have seen, institutions provide many useful functions in helping actors to coordinate their actions or achieve collaboration. This theoretical approach assumes that action is primarily demand driven—that is, actors will create institutions because they are useful—but does not really specify a mechanism for how they would go about actually creating them.

An important theme of this work has been the implications of existing institutions in constraining future institutional developments (Keohane and Nye 1977; Keohane 1984). One aspect of this constraint is the possibility that existing institutions in broader areas will affect the negotiation of more specific institutions, leading to the 'nesting' of regimes within a hierarchy (Aggarwal 1985). Thus, while the notion of transaction costs and sunk costs are central elements in this thinking, the role of regimes in providing states with information and reducing organizational costs can be distinguished from the role of existing institutions in constraining future actions.

A fourth approach to examining institutional innovation and change places emphasis on the role of expert consensus and the interplay of experts and politicians (Haas 1980; Haas 1992). New knowledge and cognitive understandings may lead decision makers to calculate their interests differently. For example, work by Ernst Haas focused on the efforts of politicians in international negotiations to use linkages to create new issue packages to form international regimes (Haas 1980).

Lastly, 'Radical Constructivists', while focusing on the role of ideas, argue that reality is in fact constructed in the minds of decision makers. These scholars, drawing from Ernst Haas's work, go much further than Haas in suggesting 'power and interest do not have effects apart from the shared knowledge that constitutes them as such' (Wendt 1995). Analysts in this school see norms and values as being dominant causal forces and ascribe considerable power to institutions in not only constraining actors, but in fundamentally altering their basic interests. In summarizing their view, Peter Haas notes that this school argues that 'there is no "objective" basis for identifying material reality and all claims for objectivity are therefore suspect' (Haas 1992). This makes it more difficult to objectively evaluate the role that institutions might play or how they might be constructed.

Reconciling new and old institutions

When actors create new institutions, they generally do not do so in a vacuum. Thus, when new institutions are developed, they often must be reconciled with existing ones. One approach to achieving such reconciliation is by nesting broader and narrower institutions in hierarchical fashion. Another means of achieving harmony among institutions is through an institutional division of labour, or 'parallel' linkages. The challenge of institutional reconciliation is not, however, unique to the creation of new ones. In

lieu of creating new institutions, policy makers might also modify existing institutions for new purposes. When doing so, they must also focus on issues of institutional compatibility. Moreover, bargaining over institutional modification is likely to be strongly influenced by existing institutions.

A few examples will illustrate these ideas. One can think about the problem of reconciling institutions from both an issue-area and a regional perspective (Oye 1992; Gamble and Payne 1996; Lawrence 1996a). Nested institutions in an issue-area are nicely illustrated by the relationship between the international regime for textile and apparel trade—the Long Term Arrangement on Cotton Textiles and it successor arrangement, the Multifibres Arrangement (MFA)—with respect to the broader regime in which it is nested, the GATT. When the Executive Branch in the United States faced pressure from domestic protectionist interests simultaneously with international pressures to keep its market open, the USA promoted the formation of a sector-specific international regime under GATT auspices. This 'nesting' of the MFA within the GATT ensured a high degree of conformity with both the GATT's principles and norms as well as with its rules and procedures (Aggarwal 1985, 1994). Although the textile regime deviated from some of the GATT's norms in permitting the discriminatory treatment of developing countries, it did adopt and adapt the most-favoured-nation norm, which called for developed countries to treat all developing countries alike (for further discussion of this norm, see Winham, Chapter 4 in this volume).

The Asia-Pacific Economic Cooperation grouping (APEC), created in 1989, illustrates the concept of regional nesting. APEC's founding members were extremely worried about undermining the GATT, and sought to reconcile these two institutions by focusing on the notion of 'open regionalism'—that is, the creation of APEC would not bar others from benefiting from any ensuing liberalization in the region. APEC members saw this as a better alternative to using Article 24 of the GATT, which permits the formation of free trade areas and customs unions, to justify this accord. Rather than forming an institution that could conflict with the promotion of GATT initiatives, therefore, APEC founding members attempted to construct an institution that would complement the GATT (Aggarwal 1994; Ravenhill 2001).

An alternative mode of reconciling institutions would be to simply create 'parallel' institutions to deal with separate but related activities, as exemplified by the GATT and Bretton Woods monetary system. In creating institutions for the post-Second World War era, policy makers were concerned about a return to the 1930s era of competitive devaluations, marked by an inward turn among states and the use of protectionist measures. These 'beggar-thy-neighbour' policies were found across economic issue areas, and individual action by each state worked to the detriment of all. As a consequence, the founders of the Bretton Woods monetary system also turned their focus to creating institutions that would help to encourage trade liberalization. By promoting fixed exchange rates through the International Monetary Fund and liberalization of trade through the General Agreement on Tariffs and Trade, policy makers hoped that this parallel institutional division of labour would lead to freer trade. Finally, on a regional basis, one can see the development of the European Economic Coal and Steel Community and the Western European Union as parallel organizations. The first was oriented toward strengthening European cooperation in economic matters (with, of course, important security implications), while the WEU sought to develop a coordinated European defence effort.

Conclusion

This chapter has sought to provide a systematic analysis of the problem of collaboration in global political economy through the lenses of goods, games, and institutions. We have seen that states may need to collaborate or to coordinate their actions to provide various kinds of public goods and common pool resources that the private sector will not produce. Yet the central problem of dealing with free riders (actors who will benefit from the provision of goods, but who may attempt to avoid paying for them) remains a difficult issue and one that may impede the provision of goods—despite the desires of states to produce them.

The problem of free riding or the difficulty of finding a coordination equilibrium is a common one in a number of issues, including trade, monetary cooperation, the environment, human rights, and the like. Despite some limitations, game theory provides useful insight into the diverse set of problems that states may face in collaborating or in coordinating their actions. One of the most popularly used games, the Prisoners' Dilemma, has been used to show that in many issue areas, actors have a strong incentive not to cooperate despite the potential joint gains that they may receive from doing so. Yet as we have shown, the structure of many problems in international political economy is not that of the Prisoners' Dilemma game, but instead may be better characterized as chicken, assurance, suasion, or even harmony games. By carefully examining the types of goods involved in the issue area in which actors may wish to collaborate or coordinate their actions, game theory provides a way of differentiating the various sets of problems involved.

It is worth keeping in mind that the preferences that go into creating games are often assumed as given by many analysts—particularly those in the neo-realist institutionalist and neo-liberal institutionalist camps. Where do preferences come from and are such preferences amenable to change? It is on this dimension that constructivist arguments focusing on the role of experts, changing knowledge, and possible shifts in preferences through learning may provide significant insight that can help us to create more logically compelling games.

Once we can establish the basic game structure that actors face, we can better examine what role institutions might play in ensuring more favourable outcomes. In some cases, contrary to the perspective often taken by neo-institutionalists, institutions may not really be necessary for ensuring cooperative state action. Hence, we differentiated between cases where self-help might lead to a positive outcome versus those in which institutions might play a genuinely useful role in overcoming collective action problems.

The role of institutions in fostering collaboration itself raises two puzzles: first, how might states collaborate in the first place to create institutions? This in itself raises an analytical problem that various theories have attempted to address. As we have seen, hegemons may have strong incentives to create institutions to constrain the behaviour of other actors and possibly their own domestic lobbies. Other approaches such as neoliberal institutionalism focus on the strong incentives that major states may have in creating institutions and suggest that small numbers of actors may be able to overcome the usual collective action problems that may lead to free riding behaviour.

Second, the creation of institutions rarely takes place in a vacuum. An important issue is thus the question of how new institutions might be reconciled with old ones. This problem has arisen in the context of the Asian crisis, where efforts to create an Asian Monetary Fund faltered in the face of International Monetary Fund and United States opposition. In trade, the problems of the Doha Round have been followed by a renewed push to shift away from broad multilateral institutions to bilateral free trade agreements and regional accords. The extent to which such arrangements will further undermine the World Trade Organization remains an open question.

QUESTIONS

1 What is the most frequent problem of collaboration in global political economy?

2 How does the nature of different types of goods affect the prospects for collaboration?

3 Which good(s) are the most difficult to produce in international politics?

4 What is the thorniest situation of collaboration in global political economy?

5 Under what conditions do individual decision-making models make sense? When might one need to use game-theoretic approaches?

6 Is a lack of information always problematic for reaching cooperation?

7 Can problems of information make collaboration easier?

8 What are the conditions for decentralized, self-help, cooperation to work?

9 How do institutions facilitate collaboration?

10 Can enforcement really be carried out in international political economy?

11 Under what conditions might old and new institutions work together? When might they be in conflict?

FURTHER READING

Aggarwal, V. K. (ed.) (1998), *Institutional Designs for a Complex World: Bargaining, Linkages and Nesting* (Ithaca, NY: Cornell University Press). A collective volume that focuses on the relationships between institutions and the stability of dense institutional settings.

—— and Dupont, C. (1999), 'Goods, Games and Institutions', *International Political Science Review*, 20/4: 393–409. The original and technical presentation of our theory that links goods, games and institutions.

Cooper, R. N. (ed.) (1989), *Can Nations Agree* (Washington DC: Brookings Institution). An insightful collection of work on coordination attempts of economic policies among nations outside of institutional settings.

Hasenclever, A., Mayer, P., and Rittberger, V. (1997), *Theories of International Regimes* (Cambridge: Cambridge University Press). A collective volume on recent developments on theories of international regimes with application to all domains of international politics.

Kaul, I., Grunberg, I., and Stern, M. A. (eds.) (1999), *Global Public Goods: International Cooperation in the 21st Century* (New York: Oxford University Press). A collective volume with a range of examples of global public goods in economics, politics, environment with interesting lessons for the future provision of such goods.

Keohane, R. O. (1984), *After Hegemony: Cooperation and Discord in the World Political Economy* (Princeton: Princeton University Press). The classic work on the links between regime change and change in power distribution.

Koromenos, B., Lipson, C., and Snidal, D. (2001), 'The Rational Design of International Institutions', *International Organization*, 55/4: 761–99. Introductory article to the latest collective work on institutional design, using insights from game theory and considering various facets of institutions.

Krasner, S. D. (ed.) (1983), *International Regimes* (Ithaca, NY: Cornell University Press). The seminal collective volume on international regimes that includes the classic definition of regimes as well as a range of examples in various domains of international politics.

Olson, M. (1965), *The Logic of Collective Action: Public Goods and the Theory of Groups* (Cambridge, Mass.: Harvard University Press). Classic work on collective action and the conditions under which groups of actors may produce public goods.

Sandler, T. (1992), *Collective Action: Theory and Applications* (Ann Arbor: University of Michigan Press).

WEB LINKS

Game Theory

www.gametheory.net/

http://william-king.www.drexel.edu/top/eco/game/game.html

3

The domestic sources of foreign economic policies

Michael J. Hiscox

READER'S GUIDE

How should a nation manage its economic ties with the rest of the world? How should the government regulate the flow of goods, people, and investment to and from foreign nations? Debates over foreign economic policies are a recurring, often volatile feature of national politics in all countries. Indeed, how governments should now be dealing with the multiple facets of 'globalization' is perhaps the single most pressing political issue of our time. It is an issue that has been debated in international institutions, national legislatures, and lecture halls across the world; it has mobilized nationalist populist movements at one end of the political spectrum, and transnational environmental and human rights organizations at the other; and it has led to violent protests and demonstrations in the streets of Seattle, Melbourne, Washington, Genoa, and New York. What are the battle lines in these political debates? How are policies decided in different countries? How do differences in political institutions shape these policy decisions? And how do new ideas and information about policy options filter into politics? This chapter examines each of these questions, focusing on the domestic politics of trade, immigration, investment, and exchange rates.

Introduction

Each government must make choices about how best to manage the way its own economy is linked to the global economy. It must choose whether to open the national market to international trade, whether to liberalize trade with some nations more than with others, and whether to allow more trade in some sectors of the economy than in other sectors. Each government must also decide whether to restrict international flows of investment in different sectors and whether to regulate immigration and emigration by different types of workers. And it must either fix the exchange rate for the national currency or allow the rate to fluctuate to some degree in response to supply and demand in international financial markets.

Of course, if every government always made the same choices in all these areas of policy, things would be very simple for us as scholars (and much more predictable for us as citizens of the world). But governments in different countries, and at different moments in history, have often chosen radically different foreign economic policies. Some have closed off their national economies almost completely from the rest of the world, imposing strict limits on trade, immigration, and investment—an example is China in the 1960s, which kept itself almost entirely isolated from the rest of the world's economies. In other instances, governments have adopted the very opposite approach, allowing virtually unfettered economic exchange between their citizens and foreigners—ironically, Hong Kong in the 1960s may be the best example of this type of extreme openness. Most governments today adopt a mixture of policies that fall somewhere in the middle, imposing selective controls on activities that affect some sectors of their economy and restricting exchange with some foreign countries more than with others. Understanding why governments make the particular choices they do requires careful attention to the political pressures they face from different domestic groups and the political institutions that regulate the way collective decisions are made and implemented.

Politics, we know, is all about who gets what, when, and how. Different individuals and groups in every society typically have very different views about what

their government should do when it comes to setting the policies that regulate international trade, immigration, investment, and exchange rates. These competing demands must be reconciled in some way by the political institutions that govern policy making. To really understand the domestic origins of foreign economic policies we thus need to perform two critical tasks:

1 Identify or map the policy preferences of different groups in the domestic economy.

2 Specify how political institutions determine the way these preferences are aggregated or converted into actual government decisions.

The first step will require some economic analysis. How people are affected by their nation's ties with the global economy, and thus what types of policies they prefer to manage those ties, depends primarily on how they make their living. Steelworkers typically have very different views about most foreign economic policies from wheat farmers, for instance, because such policies rarely affect the steel and wheat industries in similar fashion. Of critical importance here are the types of assets that individuals own and how the income earned from those assets is affected by different policy choices. The second step calls for political analysis. How political representatives are elected, how groups organize to lobby or otherwise influence politicians, and how policies are proposed, debated, amended, and passed in legislatures, and then implemented by government agencies, all depend on the structure of political institutions. Democratically elected leaders face very different institutional constraints from military dictators, of course, and even among our democracies there is quite a wide range of institutional variation that can have a large impact on the behaviour of policy makers.

These two analytical steps put together like this, combining both economic and political analysis in tandem, are generally referred to as the *political economy* approach to the study of policy outcomes. In the next two sections we will consider each of the two analytical steps in some detail, examining the domestic sources of policies in the areas of trade, immigration, investment, and exchange rates. Then we will shift gears a little, and consider the ways in which ideas and information might affect policy making. We will also discuss linkages between the different policy dimensions and non-economic issues, focusing on environmental and human rights concerns and how they feature in debates over foreign economic policies. Finally, to link all this to the chapter that follows, in the conclusion we will briefly consider the impact of domestic politics on bargaining over economic issues between governments at the international level.

Policy preferences

The guiding assumption here is that, when it comes to taking positions on how to regulate ties with the global economy, individuals and groups are fundamentally concerned with how different policy choices affect their incomes. Of course people may also have important non-material concerns that affect their attitudes toward foreign economic policies. Many people are concerned about the cultural implications of globalization, for instance, and its impact on the world's environment and on human rights, and these concerns may have an impact on their views about the regulation of international trade, immigration, and investment. We will discuss some of these important considerations in more detail later in the chapter. But we begin here with the simplest possible framework in which economic policies are evaluated only in terms of their economic effects. Given that organized producer groups have almost always been the most vocal participants in domestic debates about foreign economic policies, and the debates themselves have been couched mainly in economic terms, this seems like an appropriate way to begin.

Trade

The dramatic growth in international trade over the last few decades has intensified political debate over the costs and benefits of trade openness. In the United States, the controversy surrounding the creation of the North American Free Trade Agreement (NAFTA) in 1993 was especially intense, and similar arguments have arisen in Europe over the issue of enlargement of the European Union and over attempts to reform the Common Agricultural Policy.

Rapid trade policy reforms have also generated a significant political backlash in many developing nations. And recent years have witnessed violent protests and demonstrations by groups from a variety of countries that hope to disrupt meetings of the World Trade Organization (WTO). Political leaders around the world frequently voice concerns about the negative effects of trade and the need to protect their firms and workers from foreign competition.

What is behind all of this political fuss and bother? At first glance it may seem puzzling that there is so much conflict over trade. After all, the most famous insight from all of international economics is the proof that trade provides mutual gains: that is, when countries exchange goods and services they are all generally better off. Trade allows each country to specialize in producing those goods and services in which it has a comparative advantage, and in doing so world welfare is improved (see Chapter 1, Box 1.8).

While there are gains from trade for all countries in the aggregate, what makes trade so controversial is that, among individuals within each country, trade creates winners and losers. How trade affects different individuals depends upon how they earn their living. To flesh out this story, economists have traditionally relied upon a very simple theory of trade devised by two Swedish economists, Eli Heckscher and Bertil Ohlin. In the Heckscher–Ohlin model of trade, each nation's comparative advantage is traced to its particular endowments of different factors of production: that is, basic inputs such as land, labour, and capital that are used in different proportions in the production of different goods and services. Since the costs of these inputs in each country will depend on their availability, differences in factor endowments across countries will create differences in comparative advantage. Each country will tend to export items whose production requires intensive use of the factors with which it is abundantly endowed relative to other nations; conversely, each country will import goods whose production requires intensive use of factors that are relatively scarce. Countries well endowed with land, like Australia and Canada, are expected to export agricultural products (for example, wheat and wool), while importing products that require the intensive use of labour (for example, textiles and footwear) from more labour-abundant economies like China and India. The advanced economies of Europe, Japan, and the United States, well endowed with capital relative to the rest of the world, should export capital-intensive products (for example, automobiles and pharmaceuticals), while importing labour-intensive goods from less developed trading partners where supplies of capital are scarce compared to supplies of labour.

Building on this simple model of trade, Wolfgang Stolper and Paul Samuelson derived a famous theorem in 1941 that outlined the likely effects of trade on the real incomes of different sets of individuals within any economy. According to the Stolper–Samuelson theorem, trade benefits those who own the factors of production with which the economy is relatively well endowed and trade hurts owners of scarce factors. The reasoning is straightforward: by encouraging specialization in each economy in export-oriented types of production, trade increases the demand for locally abundant factors (and bids up the earnings of those who own those factors), while reducing demand for locally scarce factors (and lowering the earnings of owners of such factors). In Australia and Canada, the theorem tells us that landowners should benefit most from trade, while workers can expect lower real wages as a consequence of increased imports of labour-intensive goods. In Europe, Japan, and the United States, the theorem predicts a fairly simple class division over trade: the trade issue should benefit owners of capital at the expense of workers. The converse should hold in relatively labour-abundant (and capital-scarce) developing economies like China and India, where trade will raise the wages of workers relative to the profits earned by local owners of capital.

By revealing how trade benefits some people while making others worse off, the Stolper–Samuelson theorem thus accounts for why trade is such a divisive political issue. The theorem also provides a neat way to map the policy preferences of individuals in each economy. In each nation, owners of locally abundant factors should support greater trade openness, while owners of locally scarce factors should be protectionist. There is a good deal of evidence in the histories of political conflict over trade in a variety of nations that fits with this simple prediction (see Rogowski 1989). In Australia, for instance, the first national elections in 1901 were actually fought between a Free Trade party, representing predominantly rural voters, and a Protectionist party that was supported overwhelmingly by urban owners of capital and labour. A very similar kind of political division characterized most debates over trade policy in Canada in the late nineteenth century, with support for trade openness emanating mostly from farmers in the vast western provinces. In Europe and Japan, in contrast, much of the opposition to trade over the last century or so has come from agricultural interests, anxious to block cheap imports of farm products from abroad. In the United States and Europe, at least since the 1960s, labour unions have voiced some of the loudest opposition to trade openness and have called for import restrictions aimed at protecting jobs in labour-intensive industries threatened by foreign competition.

On the other hand, political divisions and coalitions in trade politics often appear to contradict this simple model of preferences. It is quite common to see workers and owners in the same industry banding together to lobby for protective import barriers, for instance, in contemporary debates about policy in Europe and the United States, even though the Stolper–Samuelson theorem tells us that capital and labour are supposed to have directly opposing views. So what is going on here? The critical problem seems to be that the theorem is derived by assuming that factors of production are highly mobile between different industries in each economy. An alternative approach to mapping the effects of trade on incomes, often referred to as the 'specific factors' model, allows instead that it can be quite costly to move some factors of production between different sectors in the economy. That is, different types of land, labour skills, and capital equipment often have a very limited or specific use (or range of uses) to which they can be put when it comes to making products. The plant and machinery used in modern manufacturing industries

Box 3.1 The repeal of the Corn Laws

The story of the repeal of Britain's protectionist Corn Laws in 1846 is perhaps still the best-known example of a political clash over trade policy that fits nicely with the Stolper–Samuelson theorem. With the revival of foreign trade after the Napoleonic Wars, policy debates in Britain began to focus on the protectionist Corn Laws that restricted importation of various grains (wheat, rye, barley, and oats, as well as peas and beans), defended resolutely by the landowning elite. Pressure for reform came most strongly from manufacturers, and especially textile producers in Leicester and Manchester, anxious to reduce labour costs (see McCord 1958). It was these manufacturers who formed the leadership of the Anti-Corn Law League in 1838, and a cotton manufacturer, Richard Cobden, became the League's most famous advocate. The push for reform soon drew a larger following among both the urban middle and working classes, and attracted support from the working-class Chartist reform movement, which organized the 'bigger loaf' campaign in the 1840s (Magnus 1964: 65–6). The effects were soon felt in Parliament, transformed by the Great Reform Act of 1832 and the enfranchisement of voters in the large industrial centres of the West Riding. Cobden himself entered Parliament in 1841, campaigning with the cry 'You must untax the people's bread!' and the League stepped up its campaign with a storm of pamphlets, petition drives, public meetings, and addresses to labour unions. The widespread economic distress of the early 1840s had a great impact on the Tory prime minister, Robert Peel. He introduced a sliding scale for grain duties in 1841 and then reduced those rates slightly in 1842 and 1844, in an attempt to ease the food crisis, but this aroused fierce opposition from landed interests and from within Conservative ranks. The failure of the potato crop in 1845, and the ensuing crisis, gave Peel the pretext to act. Amid reports of widespread starvation, the prime minister pushed through a bill to repeal the Corn Laws altogether, with support from Liberals and Radicals. The conflict over repeal split the Conservatives irrevocably. Once 'purified' of their Peelite faction, the Tories (known for years as the Protectionists) were increasingly isolated on the trade issue in Parliament. Peel's supporters, including Gladstone, gravitated to the Liberals, and their free-trade platform drew on an immense base of support among urban industrialists, the middles classes, and workers. Gladstone's first budget as prime minister in 1860 effectively eliminated all remaining protectionist duties in Britain.

is very specialized: the presses used to stamp out automobile bodies are only designed for that purpose, for instance, and cannot be adapted easily or quickly to perform other tasks. Steel factories cannot easily be converted into pharmaceutical factories or software design houses. Nor can steelworkers quickly adapt their skills and become chemical engineers or computer programmers.

In the specific factors model, the real incomes of different individuals are tied very closely to the fortunes of the particular industries in which they make their living. Individuals employed or invested in export industries benefit from trade according to this model, while those who are attached to import-competing industries are harmed (see Jones 1971; Mussa 1974). In the advanced economies of Europe and the United States, the implication is that owners and employees in export-oriented industries like aerospace, pharmaceuticals, computer software, construction equipment, and financial services, should be much more supportive of trade than their counterparts in, say, the steel, textiles, and footwear industries, which face intense pressure from import competition. There is much evidence supporting these predictions in the real world of trade politics, especially in the debates over trade in the most advanced economies where technologies (and the skills that complement them) have become increasingly specialized in many different manufacturing and service industries, and even in various areas of agriculture and mining production (see Hiscox 2002; Magee 1980). In the recent debates over regional and multilateral trade agreements in the United States, for instance, some of the most vociferous opposition to removing barriers to trade has come from owners and workers aligned together in the steel and textile industries.

The leading research on the political economy of trade now routinely assumes that the specific factors approach is the most appropriate way to think about trade policy preferences, at least in the contemporary context in the advanced economies (see Grossman and Helpman 1994; Rodrik 1995), so we will rely upon it for the most part in the discussions below. This model, it is worth noting, is still nested within the broader Heckscher–Ohlin theory that explains trade according to differences in factor endowments. Newer theories of trade, motivated by some clear evidence that not all trade seems to fit well with this simple endowments-based theory (for example, Europe, Japan, and the United States all importing automobiles from each other), have made some significant departures from the standard Heckscher–Ohlin framework. One innovation is to allow that technologies of production and tastes among consumers may vary substantially across countries. Such differences might affect the types of products an economy will be likely to export and import, but the predictions about trade policy preferences derived from the specific factors approach are not otherwise affected: individuals engaged in export industries favour trade, while those in import-competing industries oppose trade. A more complicated innovation in trade theory allows for the possibility of economies of scale. In some industries requiring large investments of capital, the largest firms may enjoy such a dramatic cost advantage over smaller firms that those markets tend to be dominated by only a few, very large corporations. In such cases, in which firms compete with one another and with foreign rivals for different market niches, trade may have different effects for firms in the same industry. These types of complexities are difficult to incorporate into a broadly applicable model of trade, however, so we will not pursue them here. Although it might be pointed out that large firms that enjoy economies of scale in production also tend to engage in foreign investment, locating parts of their enterprise in different nations. Below we will discuss the political implications of this type of multinational investment in more detail.

Immigration

Of course globalization is not simply a matter of the amount of trade in goods and services, it also involves international flows of the factors of production themselves—the migration of workers between nations and international investment and lending that transfers capital across borders. There is not a radical difference between how we analyse these phenomena and how we examined trade, but neither is the analysis identical in terms of the economic effects and the policy preferences that we anticipate for different sets of individuals within each nation.

Political debates about immigration policy have been rising in volume and intensity in recent years in almost all Western economies. On the one hand, immigration is seen by many as an economic and cultural lifeline that can supply firms in key industries with skilled workers while also injecting new artistic and intellectual life into the nation. On the other hand, many people are concerned that immigrants take jobs away from local workers and create ethnic enclaves that can balkanize a nation and lead to more crime and other social ills. These latter concerns have encouraged the recent imposition of much tighter immigration controls in many countries, while also nurturing the growth of extremist anti-immigrant political movements in several European countries and increasing the incidence of hate crimes directed toward immigrants. The debate seems certain to continue in the years ahead, and grow fiercer.

Historically, immigration has almost always been a more politically controversial topic than trade or investment. The issue is so sensitive that tight restrictions on immigration are nearly universal. Again, this makes little sense if we look only at the aggregate welfare effects of international labour flows. It is easy to demonstrate that when labour is free to migrate to countries where it can be more productive (and earn correspondingly higher wages), there will be an increase in total world output of goods and services. And total output must also increase in any economy that allows more immigrants to enter. This expansion in production makes it possible, in principle, for everyone to enjoy higher standards of living. Migration flows can actually serve the same economic purpose as trade flows. Indeed, in the standard Heckscher–Ohlin model of trade described above, trade is simply a function of country differences in endowments of labour and other factors, and so international movements of goods and international movements of factors are actually substitutes for one another. Countries that are abundantly endowed with labour, like China and India, and in which wages are thus quite low compared to wages paid elsewhere, are not only natural suppliers of labour-intensive exports for the world market, they are also natural suppliers of emigrants.

As we already know, however, what matters most for politics is not that aggregate welfare gains are possible from exchanges (of goods or factors) between economies; what matters most is that some people gain and other people lose. Which individuals are most likely to oppose immigration? Again, the standard economic analysis emphasizes the importance of the different types of productive factors—including land and capital, as above, with an additional distinction made between high-skilled labour (or 'human capital') and low-skilled or blue-collar labour. What is critical, as you will have already guessed, is the impact that immigration can have on relative supplies of factors of production in the local economy. If immigrants have low skill levels, as is typically assumed when discussing the effects of immigration in the advanced economies of Europe and North America, allowing more immigration will increase the local supply of low-skilled labour relative to other factors. The effect is to lower the real wages of all low-skilled workers, as the new arrivals price themselves into employment by accepting lower pay, while raising the real earnings for local owners of land, capital, and skills, as demand for these other factors increases. Of course, if a nation only allows *high-skilled* workers to immigrate, the effect will be lower real wages for high-skilled workers, but higher real earnings for low-skilled workers and owners of land and capital.

The basic results from this simple model of the impact of immigration—often referred to as 'factor-proportions' analysis (see Borjas, Freeman, and Katz 1996; Borjas 1999)—are widely applicable. Immigration always harms local workers with similar skill levels to those of the arriving workers, while benefiting local owners of other factors. Even if we allow for high levels of trade, which can partially offset the impact of immigration as economies adjust to the change in factor supplies by importing less of some goods that can now be produced locally at a lower cost, the effects are always in the same direction—although they may become very small in size, and even disappear altogether, if the local economy is very small relative to other economies and if the inflow of immigrants is very small in magnitude (Leamer and Levinsohn 1995). The effects are even generally the same if we allow that the skills of workers can be highly 'specific' to particular industries, though the impact of immigration on earnings will be larger for high-skilled (specific) workers in some industries than in others. Any inflow of unskilled labour will be especially valuable for high-skilled workers in sectors that use unskilled labour more intensively, for example, but it will still benefit all high-skilled workers since output (and demand for their skills) will rise in each industry. On the flip side, an inflow of any type of high-skilled labour will generate the largest decline in earnings for high-skilled workers in the same industry (those who own the very same specific skills as the immigrants). But it will also hurt high-skilled workers in other industries in the local economy whose earnings will suffer, albeit in a relatively minor way, as demand for their types of specific skills falls in response to the expansion taking place in the industry into which the skilled immigrants have moved.

So again, we have a very simple and generally applicable way of identifying the policy preferences of individuals. Individuals can be expected to oppose any policy that would permit immigration of foreign workers with similar skill levels, but they will support other types of immigration. Individuals who make their living from ownership of land and capital are likely to be the strongest supporters of more open immigration laws. If we look at the actual political debates over immigration laws in particular countries, the general alignment of interests seems to fit rather well with these expectations. Typically, the most vocal opposition to changes in immigration laws that would permit more low-skilled immigration comes from labour unions representing blue-collar workers. In the United States, for instance, the AFL-CIO has traditionally taken a very tough stance in favour of restrictive immigration laws and border control measures aimed at stemming illegal immigration into the country from Mexico (Tichenor 2002: 209). American business and farm associations have taken a very different position, often lobbying for more lenient treatment of illegal immigrants and for larger quotas in various non-immigrant working visa categories. In similar fashion, trade union federations in Britain, France, and Germany have raised protests about enlargement of the European Union and the possible influx of low-skilled workers into their economies from new member countries in Southern and Eastern Europe. High-skilled workers have not shied away from immigration politics either, often lobbying to restrict inflows of immigrants with skills that match their own and would thus pose a competitive threat in the local labour market—the American Medical Association, for instance, the organization which represents doctors in the United States, has pushed hard in recent years to limit the number of foreign doctors granted visa status while also making it more difficult for them to obtain licences to practice.

This simple approach to the political economy of immigration restrictions is very useful, at least as a first step toward understanding the political forces that are likely to shape policy outcomes. It is extremely difficult, however, to analyse the politics of immigration without examining non-economic concerns among individuals having to do with questions of culture and identity. Immigration policy, after all, has a profound impact on who makes up the nation itself. In this way it is quite different from trade policy. A great deal of recent research suggests that divisions among individuals over immigration policy are most strongly related to fundamental differences in cultural values associated with ethnic and racial tolerance and cosmopolitanism (for example, Espenshade and Calhoun 1993; Citrin et al. 1997; McLaren 2001). This question of whether preferences related to non-economic issues have a profound effect on attitudes toward foreign economic policies is one that we will return to below.

Foreign investment

Capital can also move from one country to another. These movements usually do not take the form of a physical relocation of some existing buildings and machinery from a site in one nation to another site abroad (the equivalent to worker migration). Instead, they take the form of financial transactions between citizens of different nations that transfer ownership rights over assets: a firm in one country buys facilities abroad that it can operate as a subsidiary, for instance, or individuals in one country buy shares of foreign companies, or a bank in one country lends money to foreign firms. All such transactions increase the stock of capital available for productive use in one country, and decrease the stock of capital in another country.

The dramatic increase in the volume of international capital flows over the past forty years, outstripping the increase in trade, has had a profound impact on the international economy. Short-term flows of capital in the form of 'portfolio' investment (purchases of company shares and other forms of securities including government bonds), which can

---

Box 3.2 The 'new world' closes its door to immigrants

Beginning in the 1840s and 1850s, there was a huge surge in emigration from England, Ireland, and other parts of Europe and Asia to the 'New World' economies in North and South America and Australasia where labour was relatively scarce and wage rates were comparatively high. The rudimentary border controls and open policy toward immigrants in these frontier economies meant that labour flows responded quite quickly to economic events—and in particular, to gold rushes and other 'booms' associated with the construction of railways and the birth of new industries. Over time, however, as labour unions became more organized and politically influential in the New World economies, greater restrictions on immigration were imposed. The political pressure for limits on immigration became especially strong during economic recessions, when local rates of unemployment often rose swiftly and labour groups blamed new immigrants for taking jobs away from 'native' workers (see Goldin 1994). Between the 1880s and the 1920s, all the new world economies gradually closed themselves off to immigration (see O'Rourke and Williamson 2000). In the United States, the first bans were imposed on Chinese immigrants in 1882 and then immigrants from all Asia in 1917, when a tough literacy test was also introduced as a way of limiting inflows of low-skilled workers. In 1921 the Emergency Quota Act placed severe restrictions on all new arrivals. The strongest political support for these measures came from north-eastern states with highly urbanized populations working in manufacturing industries, where labour unions were particularly well organized and vocal.

change direction quite rapidly in response to news and speculation about changing macro-economic conditions and possible adjustments in exchange rates, have had a major impact on the choices governments can make when it comes to monetary and exchange-rate policies. Longer-term capital flows in the form of 'direct foreign investment' (where the purchase of foreign assets by a firm based in one country gives it ownership control of a firm located on foreign soil), have perhaps been even more politically controversial since the activities of these multinational firms can have a major impact on economic conditions in the host nations in which they manage affiliates. Many critics of multinational corporations fear that the economic leverage enjoyed by these firms, especially in small developing nations, can undermine national policies aimed at improving environment standards and human rights. The political debate over direct foreign investment is thus highly charged.

Tight restrictions on both short- and long-term investment by foreigners have been quite common historically, although the controls have been much less strict than those typically imposed on immigration. Clearly these controls cannot be motivated by a desire for economic efficiency. If such controls are removed and capital is allowed to move freely to those locations in which it is used most productively (and where it will be rewarded, as a result, with higher earnings), it is easy to show that the total output of goods and services will be increased in both the country to which the capital is flowing and in the world economy as a whole. Again, this expansion in aggregate production makes it possible, in principle, to raise the standard of living for people everywhere. International investment, just like the migration of workers examined above, can serve the same economic purpose that is otherwise served by trade. International flows of capital substitute for the exports of capital-intensive goods and services in the benchmark Heckscher–Ohlin model. In general, then, we can expect that the advanced industrial economies of Europe and the United States, which have abundant local supplies of capital for investment and in which rates of return on capital are thus quite low compared with earnings elsewhere, are the natural suppliers of capital (as well as capital-intensive goods) to poorer nations in which capital is in relatively scarce supply.

One point worth making here about the likely direction of capital flows concerns the distinction between lending and portfolio flows of capital and direct foreign investment (see Ravenhill, Chapter 1 in this volume). It is reasonable to imagine that the former types of international investment are driven purely by the quest to maximize (risk-adjusted) rates of return on capital, in line with the Heckscher–Ohlin model. With the small caveat that capital-poor developing countries are often politically unstable, and high levels of risk can deter investors, we should nevertheless expect large flows of capital from the industrial nations to the developing world. It is much less clear that economy-wide differences in rates of return are critical for explaining patterns in direct foreign investment. There is certainly a considerable amount of direct investment by European, American, and Japanese firms in developing nations, with many firms setting up a 'vertical' multinational structure of enterprises that locates land or labour-intensive parts of the production process in developing nations. But the vast bulk of direct foreign investment in the modern world economy actually takes the form of capital flows between the industrial economies themselves, with firms creating 'horizontal' structures in which similar functions are performed in facilities in different locations (see Graham and Krugman 1995: 36). This type of investment does not fit well with the standard Heckscher–Ohlin predictions based upon factor endowments, and is best explained instead by the special advantages that firms in some industries gain by jumping borders (and trade barriers) and by internalizing transactions within the firm itself. Firms that rely heavily upon specialized technologies and management and marketing expertise may have a hard time selling these kinds of intangible assets to foreign companies it would like to contract with as suppliers or distributors; instead, it may make far more sense to keep all these relationships within the firm (see Hymer 1976; Caves 1982). Many of these types of horizontal multinational firms also appear to have been established to secure access to foreign markets into which they might not otherwise be able to sell because they faced trade barriers. This 'tariff-jumping' motive was a big factor in motivating Japanese auto firms to set up manufacturing facilities in both Europe and North America beginning in the 1980s. The implication is that there is often a strong connection between the effects of trade policies and investment (and investment restrictions), a topic we will return to in the final section of the chapter.

Now, putting aside the aggregate welfare gains that international movements of capital make possible, which individuals are likely to benefit from such capital flows and which individuals will lose out? Here we can simply apply the logic of the same 'factor proportions' approach we used above to outline the effects of immigration. We might distinguish between different types of capital, in the same way we distinguished between low- and high-skilled labour above, and set apart lending and short-term or portfolio investment flows from direct foreign investment. But to keep things simple here we will just consider them all as a single form of capital. What is critical here, of course, is the impact that inflows of any foreign capital have on relative supplies of factors of production in the local economy. Allowing more inflows of capital from abroad will increase the local supply of capital relative to other factors and thus lower real returns for local owners of capital. At the same time, inflows of investment will raise the real earnings of local owners of land and labour by increasing demand for these other factors of production.

Again, even allowing for the fact that trade flows can partially offset the impact of international movements of factors of production—economies that get inflows of capital from abroad may adjust by importing fewer capital-intensive goods and producing more of them at home, since they are now less costly to make locally—the direction of the effects on the incomes of different groups is always the same. Local owners of capital are disadvantaged by inflows of foreign capital; local landowners and workers (in all categories) are better off. These effects may diminish in size in cases in which the local economy is very small relative to others and the inflow of capital is very small in magnitude, as we noted above when discussing the income effects of immigration, but they are always working in the same direction. And again, parallel with the analysis of immigration flows, these income effects are not drastically affected by allowing that capital can take forms that are highly 'specific' to use in particular industries, though the effects may be larger for owners of some types of capital than others. This is especially relevant when we think about direct foreign investment, which typically involves the relocation of a particular set of manufacturing or marketing activities that require very specific types of technologies in one particular industry. An inflow of any type of specific capital will of course result in a decline in earnings for local owners of capital in the same industry; it will also hurt all others who own specific types of capital used in different industries, in a more marginal way of course, as demand for their assets will fall in response to the expansion taking place in the industry favoured by foreign investment.

We can thus expect that policies allowing greater inflows of foreign capital will be strongly opposed by individuals who own capital in the local economy, but such policies will be supported by local landowners and workers. There is some evidence that does fit well with these basic predictions. Perhaps the best example involves the way European and American auto companies have supported restrictions on the operations of local affiliates of their Japanese rivals since the 1980s. In Europe, auto firms pushed hard for an agreement with Japan that included in the limits set on the total Japanese market share of the European auto market, cars produced in Japanese affiliates. In the United States, after some initial hesitation (perhaps reflecting the fact that they had themselves set up numerous foreign transplant firms around the world) the US auto firms supported a variety of proposals for 'domestic content' laws that would have placed local affiliates of Japanese auto makers at a considerable disadvantage by disrupting their relationships with parts suppliers at home (Crystal 2003). The 'big three' American firms (Ford, General Motors, and Chrysler) also seized the opportunity to demand high local content requirements in the 'rules of origin' for autos in the negotiations over the 1993 North American Free Trade Agreement, ensuring that they would have a major advantage over Japanese transplants producing cars in Mexico for the North American market. Interestingly, the workers that we would expect to be strongly supportive of incoming Japanese investment in the auto industry, represented by the United Auto Workers union, were actually quite lukewarm—perhaps because they had long advocated that tough domestic content rules be applied to American firms, to prevent them from transplanting their parts manufacturing facilities to Canada and Mexico, and perhaps also in response to concerns that the foreign transplants setting up in southern

American states like Tennessee (Nissan) and Kentucky (Toyota) were not employing union members.

Foreign investment tends to be even more politically controversial in developing nations, where the behaviour of large foreign corporations can have profound effects on the local economy and on local politics. One particular concern among critics of multinational firms has been the role that several large corporations have apparently played in supporting authoritarian governments that have restricted political organization among labour groups, limited growth in wage rates, and permitted firms to mistreat workers and pollute the environment (see Evans 1979; Klein 2002). While the evidence is not very clear, local owners of capital may well have muted their opposition to investments by foreign firms in order to support authoritarian policies adopted by military regimes in some cases: in Nigeria, for instance, where Shell (the European oil company) has long been the major foreign investor, or more recently in Myanmar, where Unocal (an American oil and gas firm) is the key foreign player. But the basic competitive tension between local capitalists and foreign firms (whose entry into the economy bids down local profits) is typically very obvious even in these unstable and non-democratic environments, as local firms have often encouraged their governments to impose severe restrictions on foreign investments, including onerous regulations stipulating that foreign firms use local rather than imported inputs, exclusion from key sectors of the economy, and even nationalization (seizure) of firms' assets (Jenkins 1987: 172). Newer evidence suggests that, as we might expect given the preferences of labour in capital-poor developing nations, left-wing governments backed by organized labour have made the strongest efforts to lure foreign firms to make investments (Pinto 2003).

So far we have considered only the issue of whether governments relax restrictions on *inflows* of foreign capital. Of course, governments can and often do take actions that influence how much investment flows *out* of their economies. And the same holds for labour flows, as governments often try to affect *emigration* as well as immigration—many governments, in countries as diverse as Australia, Canada, and India, are worried about a 'brain drain' of skilled workers and professionals, for instance, and have adopted a range of policies to discourage or tax such labour flows. But the issue of outward direct investment, often involving the 'outsourcing' of jobs by multinational firms to their affiliates in labour-abundant (low-wage) nations, has become an especially salient political issue recently in Europe and the United States. The political divisions over the issue are largely what we expect from the factor proportions theory: those who own capital are strongly opposed to any restrictions on their ability to invest it abroad in order to earn higher profits, but restrictions on outward investment are strongly supported by local workers who understand that capital outflows will reduce their real earnings. In the United States, for instance, the most ardent advocates of legislation that would raise the tax burden on profits earned abroad by American corporations has been the AFL-CIO and those workers among its membership that have been hit hardest by outsourcing (for example, labour unions in the textile and auto industries). Interestingly, these labour unions have often had support from environmental and human rights groups concerned that competition among developing countries to attract new investments from multinational firms may produce a 'race to the bottom' in environmental and labour standards. Coalitions of labour unions and human rights groups have waged campaigns to try to force US corporations to adhere to strict codes of conduct abroad. We will discuss these types of multi-issue political coalitions below.

Exchange rates

Of course a critical difference between transactions that take place between individuals living in the same country and transactions between people in different countries is that the latter require that people can convert one national currency into another. If a firm in Australia wants to import DVDs from a film studio in the United States, for example, it will need to exchange its Australian dollars for US dollars to pay the American company. The rate at which this conversion takes place will obviously affect the transaction: the more Australian dollars it takes to buy the number of US dollars required (the price of the DVDs), the more costly are the imports for movie-loving Australian buyers. All the trade and investment transactions taking place every day in the world

Box 3.3 Investment, imperialism, and the 'race for Africa'

Beginning in the 1870s, vast quantities of investment capital flowed from the centres of finance in Western Europe to the rest of the world, providing the capital necessary to develop railroads and telegraph networks, ports, and new mining industries in eastern and central Europe, the Americas, and much of Asia. Beginning in the 1880s, the political context in which these foreign investments were made began to change drastically as an intense race developed among the major powers for political control of territories in Africa and Eastern Asia. Governments in Britain, France, Germany, and Belgium made imperial expansion in these regions their most urgent foreign policy priority. Seizing political control of territories in which there was often no clear or stable governing authority, or at least not one capable of defending the area from conquest by outside force, was a way to safeguard the

investments that were being made in these territories (mostly in the production of raw materials, such as cotton, silk, rubber, vegetable oils, and other products of tropical climates, as well as railways and ports, that were all very vulnerable to seizure). These imperial policies were supported most strongly by financial interests and conservative parties, typically backed by commercial and shipping industries as well, and by military leaders anxious about the security implications of falling behind rivals in the control of strategic territories and ports. Indeed, British economist, J. A. Hobson (1902), and following him, Lenin (1916), famously interpreted the imperial expansion of this time as the natural consequence of owners of capital needing access to new investment opportunities overseas; imperialism was, in Hobson's terms, 'excessive capital in search of investment'.

economy are affected by the rates at which currencies are exchanged.

Prior to the First World War, almost all governments fixed the value of their currency in terms of gold, thereby creating an international monetary system in which all rates of conversion between individual currencies were held constant (for further discussion of this international gold standard, see Chapter 1, Box 1.3). Between the Second World War and 1973, most currencies were fixed in value to the US dollar, the most important currency in the post-war world economy. In this system, often referred to as the 'Bretton Woods' system (see Chapter 1, Box 1.4), the United States agreed to guarantee the value of the dollar by committing to exchange dollars for gold at a set price of $35 per ounce. Since 1973, when the Nixon administration officially abandoned the fixed rate between the dollar and gold, all the major currencies have essentially been allowed to fluctuate freely in value in world financial markets. Among developing nations, however, many governments continue to fix the value of their currency in terms of dollars or another of the major currencies (see Frieden, Ghezzi, and Stein 2001). And groups of nations in different regions of the world, including the members of the European Union, have made separate efforts to stabilize exchange rates at the regional level, even progressing to the adoption of a common regional currency.

The fundamental choice each government must make involves whether to allow the value of the national currency to fluctuate freely in response to market demand and supply, or instead fix the value of the currency in terms of some other currency or external standard—typically, the currency of a major trading partner or, as was common in the past, gold (a precious metal valued highly in most societies throughout history). When a government chooses to fix the value of the national currency, it sets the official rate of exchange and commits itself to buy the currency at that fixed rate when requested to by private actors or foreign governments. Between a 'pure float' and a fixed exchange rate there are intermediate options: a government can choose a target value for the exchange rate and only allow the currency to fluctuate in value within some range around the target rate. The wider this range, of course, the more policy approximates floating the currency.

When it comes to trade, immigration, and investment, economists agree almost universally on the policy choice that is best for maximizing national (and world) output and, hence, general standards of living: removing barriers to all types of international exchange is optimal because it allows resources to be allocated in the most productive way. There is no similar consensus, however, on the best approach to currency policy. Fixing the exchange rate has pros and cons, and it is not always clear which are larger. By eliminating fluctuations in the exchange rate, fixing makes international trade and investment less costly for firms and individuals, since they will not need to worry that the benefits from these international transactions will be adversely affected by some sudden, unexpected shift in exchange rates. By doing away with exchange-rate risk, fixing allows the economy to benefit more fully from international trade and investment. But what is the downside? What does the government give up by pledging to buy or sell its own currency on request at the official rate of exchange? The answer, in short, is control over monetary policy.

A nation's monetary policy regulates the supply of money (and the associated cost of credit) in order to manage aggregate levels of economic activity and hence levels of inflation and unemployment. Governments typically use monetary policy to counter economic cycles: they expand the supply of money and lower the cost of credit during recessions to increase economic activity and promote job creation, and they restrict the supply of money and raise the cost of borrowing during 'booms' to slow economic activity and control inflation. When a government commits to fixing the exchange rate, it effectively gives up the ability to tailor monetary policy to manage domestic economic conditions. To see why, just imagine what happens to money supply if, at the given exchange rate, the nation's residents spend more on foreign goods and services and assets in any given period than foreigners buy from firms and individuals in that nation: the country's 'balance of payments', which registers the value of all transactions with the rest of the world, will be in deficit. This means that that there is less overall demand for the country's currency than for the currencies of other countries (needed for residents to buy foreign products and assets). To satisfy this excess demand for foreign currencies and maintain the exchange rate at the fixed level, the government will be a net buyer of its own currency, selling off its reserves of foreign currencies (or gold). The automatic effect of maintaining the fixed exchange rate in these conditions then, is to reduce the total supply of the nation's money in circulation and slow domestic economic activity. Just the opposite should occur when the nation runs a balance of payments surplus: excess demand for its currency compared to other currencies will require that

the government increase the supply of its money in circulation, stimulating economic activity.

In effect, then, fixing the value of the currency makes monetary policy a hostage to exchange-rate policy. Even if a government sets the exchange rate at a level that it hopes will generate *no* balance of payments deficits or surpluses, since the balance of international transactions in any period will depend heavily upon external economic conditions and events in foreign countries, it has very little control. A recession abroad, for instance, will reduce purchases of a nation's products by foreigners and lead to a deficit on the balance of payments and so, if currency values are firmly fixed, this recession will be 'transmitted' to the home nation by the subsequent reduction in its money supply.

The crux of the choice between fixed and floating exchange rates is the choice between stability and policy control: a stable exchange rate will increase the economic benefits attainable from international trade and investment, but this requires giving up the ability to adjust monetary policy to suit domestic economic conditions. Governments in the most advanced economies have generally decided that policy control is more important to them than exchange-rate stability, at least since the early 1970s. Governments in smaller, developing nations have mostly chosen exchange-rate stability over policy control. In part this is because these countries tend to rely more heavily upon trade and foreign investment as sources of economic growth. This choice is also more attractive for governments in smaller countries trying to defeat chronic inflation. Government promises to deal with runaway inflation in these countries may not be regarded as credible by private actors if governments in the past have shown a tendency to act irresponsibly (for example, by printing and spending large amounts of money) when facing electoral challenges. Since the expectations that private actors have about government policy feed directly into the prices (and wages) set, inflationary expectations can have devastating effects. In such circumstances, fixing the nation's currency in terms of the currency of a major trading partner which has a comparatively low rate of inflation can serve an important function, providing a way for the government to commit itself more credibly to a low-inflation monetary policy. In essence, by committing to keep the exchange rate fixed, the government is ceding control of monetary policy in a very clear and visible way, and anchoring inflation at home to the inflation rate in the partner country (see Broz and Frieden 2001; Giavazzi and Pagano 1988).

In terms of the effects on aggregate welfare, the wisdom of fixing exchange rates is thus not always crystal clear. The best or most preferred policy for different sets of individuals within each country can be similarly difficult to identify. Consider first the case in which we assume that factors of production are mobile between sectors in the domestic economy (they are not 'specific' to particular sectors) and so we can apply the logic of the Stolper–Samuelson theorem and the factor-proportions analysis. Since exchange-rate volatility serves, in effect, as an added barrier or cost to international trade and investment flows, we have a place to begin when trying to map the policy preferences of individuals: in each economy, owners of locally abundant factors are more likely to support a fixed exchange rate, while owners of locally scarce factors are more likely to prefer a floating rate. In the capital-abundant, labour-scarce advanced economies of Europe and the United States, we might thus expect a simple class division over exchange-rate policy: fixed rates benefit owners of capital at the expense of workers. We could expect the reverse alignment of class interests in the labour-abundant, capital-scarce economies of, say, China and India. In such countries, greater exchange-rate certainty should encourage more trade and greater inflows of foreign investment, and both types of international flows will benefit workers at the expense of local owners of capital.

But here we cannot think about exchange-rate stability without thinking also about monetary policy control. In general, workers might be expected to oppose fixed exchange rates in most circumstances, since they are likely to bear greater costs than others when monetary policy can no longer be used to avert economic downturns that result in higher levels of unemployment. Owners of capital, on the other hand, care less about unemployment rates than they do about keeping inflation in check, which is typically much easier for the government to achieve (as noted above) when monetary policy is committed to keeping the exchange rate fixed. Just as in the case for the nation as whole then, owners of labour and owners of capital may have to make a difficult choice about

where they stand in terms of the trade-off between the effects of greater currency stability and less monetary policy control. In contemporary, labour-scarce Europe, for instance, workers would seem to be better off along both dimensions if exchange rates were more flexible, while owners of capital should prefer fixed rates. There is some evidence that fits with this interpretation. Labour unions in Western European countries generally provided the most vocal opposition to government policies aimed at fixing or stabilizing exchange rates in the 1970s and 1980s, particularly in France and Italy. But the record is mixed. While the labour-backed Socialist government that came to power in France in 1981 initially abandoned exchange-rate stability as a goal, by 1983 it was committed to a fixed currency peg (see Oatley 1997). In fact, during the inter-war period in Europe, *left*-wing governments tended to keep their currencies fixed to the gold standard longer than other governments (Simmons 1994). And looking across a broader range of countries, in which labour is the locally abundant factor and capital is scarce, the preferences of these broad classes of individuals when it comes to exchange rates becomes even more difficult to predict.

Perhaps one major reason why it is difficult to find compelling evidence to support simple class-based interpretations of exchange-rate politics is that individuals tend to see things very differently depending on the industries in which they are employed and invested. If we allow, as in previous discussions above, that factors of production are typically very specific to particular industries, we get a very different picture of the alignment of individual preferences on the exchange-rate issue. And the picture is also much clearer. Individuals employed or invested in sectors that invest or sell in foreign markets are likely to favour exchange-rate stability, since fluctuations in rates impose costs on their international transactions and because they have a relatively small economic stake in domestic (versus foreign) macro-economic conditions. Those individuals associated with firms and banks that invest heavily in foreign markets, for instance, and export-oriented sectors that sell a large proportion of their output abroad, should thus tend to support fixed exchange rates. On the other hand, owners and employees in import-competing industries and those producing non-traded services (for example, building, transportation, sales) whose incomes depend overwhelmingly on domestic economic conditions, are likely to favour flexible exchange rates that allow the government more control over monetary policy. There is some compelling evidence supporting these predictions, especially in the debates over exchange-rate policy in the most advanced economies. In Europe in recent decades, for instance, the strongest support for fixing exchange rates (and ultimately, for creating a common European currency) has come from the international banks, multinational firms in a diverse range of industries (including auto firms such as BMW and Mercedes), and from export-oriented sectors. The strongest opposition to fixed rates has tended to come from owners and labour unions associated with import-competing industries such as coal, steel, and textiles, especially in nations like France and Italy that have battled relatively high rates of inflation (see Frieden 1994). In developing nations, recent studies have indicated that governments are more likely to float their currency when the import-competing manufacturing sector accounts for a large proportion of the local economy (Frieden, Ghezzi, and Stein 2001).

Finally, when a government does decide to fix or stabilize its currency it must also decide the *level* at which to set the exchange rate. Whether the currency should be 'stronger' (that is, take a higher value versus other currencies) or 'weaker' (a lower value) is a second, important dimension of exchange-rate policy. Even when the currency is floating, in fact, if it happens to move strongly in one direction or another, the issue can become a salient one, since the government may be called upon to intervene in an effort to raise or lower the exchange rate toward some new target. What is interesting in this regard is that the alignment of the various groups in terms of preferences for fixing versus floating the currency are not quite the same as the way they are positioned on the issue of the actual rate that should be set or targeted. A stronger currency will harm those in both export-oriented *and* import-competing industries, since it will make their products less attractive to consumers relative to the foreign alternatives. Individuals in these sectors should prefer a weaker currency. But a weaker currency will harm all others in the local economy by eroding their purchasing power when it comes to buying foreign goods and services. Owners and employees in non-traded sectors should prefer a

stronger currency, as should any multinational firms or international banks that are investing abroad and purchasing foreign assets (Frieden 1994). In the real world of politics, in instances in which the level of a nation's exchange rate has in fact become a salient political issue, these types of coalitions do appear to emerge. Devaluation of the US dollar became a major election issue in the 1890s, for instance, with the rise of the Populist movement, supported predominantly by export-oriented farmers who demanded a break from the gold standard in order to reset the dollar exchange rate at a lower level. The Populists were opposed most strongly by banking and commercial interests in the north-eastern states who favoured a strong dollar (see Frieden 1997).

Key points

- According to the Stolper–Samuelson theorem, trade benefits those who own the factors of production with which the economy is relatively well endowed and trade hurts owners of scarce factors.

- In the alternative 'specific factors' model, individuals employed or invested in export industries are the ones who benefit from trade while those who are attached to import-competing industries are disadvantaged.

- The leading research assumes that the specific factors approach is the most appropriate way to think about the effects of trade in the contemporary advanced economies.

- Immigration harms the real earnings of local workers with similar skill levels to those of the arriving workers, while benefiting everyone else in the host country.

- Inflows of foreign capital will hurt individuals who own capital in the local economy, while benefiting all local landowners and workers.

- Individuals attached to firms and banks that invest abroad or export a large proportion of their output are likely to favour a fixed exchange rate. On the other hand, owners and employees in import-competing industries and those producing non-traded services are likely to favour a flexible exchange rate.

- A stronger currency will harm those in both export-oriented *and* import-competing industries, while benefiting all others in the local economy.

Box 3.4 **The politics of the rising dollar**

Between 1980 and 1985 the US dollar rose by approximately 50 per cent in value against the Japanese yen and by roughly similar amounts against the German deutschmark and the British pound. The rapid dollar appreciation placed immense strain on US producers of traded goods and services and by 1985 the Reagan government was being lobbied strenuously by a large variety of groups asking for some kind of action to halt the rise (see Destler and Henning 1989). The strongest pressure came from groups in a broad collection of export-oriented sectors, including grain farmers, firms like IBM and Motorola in the computer industry, and Caterpillar, a large exporter of construction equipment and machinery. The voices of these exporters were swelled by protests coming from firms in import-competing industries, including the major auto companies and the steel makers. The initial reaction from the Reagan administration was to sit tight, and characterize the rise of the dollar as a sign that the rest of the world held the United States and its economy in high esteem. The government had set a course to restrain inflation when entering office in 1981, and had raised US interest rates considerably. Taking action to devalue the dollar would have thrown into substantial doubt this commitment to defeat inflation. After their initial pleas were rebuffed by the White House, however, many groups from the steel, autos, and textile industries began demanding new forms of trade protection instead, bombarding Congress with calls for trade barriers that would make up for the competitive effects of the dollar appreciation. It was this threat of runaway protectionism in Congress that finally prompted the government to take action on the dollar. In 1985, the White House reached an agreement with the governments of Japan, Germany, Britain, and France, which became known as the Plaza Accord (a reference to the lavish New York hotel in which it was negotiated). This deal provided for a cooperative effort to manage a gradual depreciation of the dollar against the other currencies, with each government agreeing to alter its macro-economic policies in such a way as to ease demand for the dollar compared with other currencies (for example, the Reagan government agreed to lower interest rates and to make a new effort to reduce the size of the US budget deficit). By giving up some control over macro-economic policy, in coordination with other governments, the White House was able to reverse the rise in the dollar and ease the strain imposed on US producers of traded goods and services.

Institutions

Once we have specified the preferences of different individuals and groups on any particular issue we need to think about how much influence they will have over policy outcomes. This is where political institutions come in. Political institutions establish the rules by which policy is made, and thus how the policy preferences of different groups are weighed in the process that determines the policy outcome. It is appropriate here to start with the broadest types of rules first, and consider the formal mechanisms by which governments and representatives in legislative bodies are elected (or otherwise come to power). These broad features of the institutional environment have large effects on all types of policies. But then we can move on to discuss more specific aspects of the legislative process and administrative agencies that have implications for the formulation and implementation of trade, immigration, investment, and exchange-rate policies.

Elections and representation

Perhaps it is best to start with the observation that the general relationship between democratization and foreign economic policy making is a matter that is still open to considerable theoretical and empirical doubt. Part of the puzzle is that there is a great deal of variation in the levels of economic openness we have observed among autocratic nations. In autocratic regimes, the orientation of policy will depend upon the particular desires and motivations of the (non-elected) leadership, and there are different theoretical approaches to this issue. Non-elected governments could pursue trade and investment liberalization in an effort to maximize tax returns over the long term by increasing aggregate economic output. Such policies may be easier to adopt because autocratic leaders are more insulated than democratic counterparts from the political demands made by any organized domestic groups that favour trade protection and limits on foreign investment (Haggard 1990). Perhaps this is an apt description of the state of affairs in China as it has been gradually opening its economy to trade and investment over the past two decades, and non-democratic governments in Taiwan and South Korea pursued trade liberalization even more rapidly in the 1960s. On the other hand, autocratic governments may draw political support from small, powerful groups in the system that favour protection. Many such governments appear to have used trade and investment barriers in ways aimed at consolidating their rule (Wintrobe 1998). The experience in Sub-Saharan African nations since the 1960s, and in Pakistan and Myanmar, seems to fit this mould. Without a detailed assessment of the particular groups upon which a particular authoritarian regime depends for political backing, it is quite difficult to make predictions about likely policy outcomes under non-democratic rule.

In formal democracies that hold real elections, the most fundamental set of political rules is the set that defines which individuals get to vote. If the franchise law gives more weight to one side in a policy contest compared to others, it can obviously have a large impact on policy outcomes. Where only those who own land can vote, for instance, agricultural interests will be privileged in the policy-making process. If this landowning elite favours trade protection, as it did in Britain in the years before the Great Reform Act of 1832, then such a policy is almost sure to be held firmly in place. By shifting political power away from landowners and towards urban owners of capital and labour, extensions of the franchise had a major impact on all forms of economic policy during the late nineteenth and early twentieth centuries in Europe, America, and elsewhere. In England, the extension of voting power to the middle and working classes, achieved in the reforms of 1832 and 1867, had the effect of making free trade politically invincible— with a huge block of workers along with the urban business class supporting trade openness, and only a tiny fraction of the electorate (the traditional rural elites) against it, a government that endorsed tariffs or restrictions on investment would have been committing electoral suicide. In the United States and Australia, on the other hand, where labour and capital were in relatively scarce supply, the elimination of property qualifications for voting and the extension of suffrage had exactly the opposite effect, empowering a larger block of urban voters who favoured high tariffs. In general, extensions of the franchise to urban classes tend to produce more open policies toward trade, immigration, and investment in labour and capital-abundant countries, and more closed or protectionist policies in labour and capital-scarce economies.

The precise rules by which representatives are elected to national legislatures are the next critical feature of the institutional environment. Scholars have suggested that in parliamentary systems in which legislative seats are apportioned among parties according to the proportion of votes they receive ('proportional representation'), narrowly organized groups have far less impact on policy making in general than they do in electoral systems in which individual seats are decided by plurality rule (see Rogowski 1987). Parliamentary systems with proportional representation tend to encourage the formation of strong, cohesive political parties, which appeal to a national constituency and have less to gain in electoral terms by responding to localized and particularistic demands (McGillivray 1997). Other types of systems, in contrast, tend to encourage intra-party competition among individual politicians and the development of a 'personal vote' in particular electoral districts and thus are more conducive to interest group lobbying. The implications for foreign economic policies are usually spelled out in very clear terms: we expect that proportional representation systems with strong political parties (e.g. Sweden) will typically produce lower levels of trade protection and other restrictions than alternative types of electoral systems (e.g. Britain, the United States) in which particular local and regional interests have a greater influence.

Box 3.5 **The institutional foundations of the gold standard**

Why was the gold standard, the system of fixed exchange rates that appeared to work so well in bringing order and stability to the global economy between the 1880s and 1914, so difficult to re-establish in the 1920s? One very important reason has to do with the major changes in political institutions that took place in Western nations around the time of the First World War. The gold standard required that governments give up control of monetary policy in order to keep the value of their currencies fixed in terms of gold (and one another). In essence, macro-economic policy was held hostage to exchange-rate policy, so that currency values were stable. This was especially difficult for small economies that happened to run large balance of payments deficits at the set rates of exchange. To maintain their exchange rates they were forced to reduce the supply of their money in circulation and raise interest rates, thereby reducing economic activity at home and increasing unemployment. If they were already in the midst of an economic recession, this meant making the downturn even worse. Governments could only follow through with this type of commitment to a fixed exchange rate if the economic costs of recession—which fell predominantly upon workers who lost jobs and

income and small businesses and farmers driven into debt—did not have direct political consequences in terms of their ability to remain in office. This changed in many nations around the turn of the century when electoral laws were reformed, extending the franchise to larger proportions of the population (including workers who had previously been denied the right to vote in many places). Around this same time labour organizations, including both trade unions and labour parties, grew in political strength in almost all the Western economies, using strikes to push for political reforms while gaining significant electoral representation for the first time. Given these profound changes in the lie of the political land, the attempts to recreate the gold standard in the inter-war period appear to have been doomed from the outset. Governments elected by much broader segments of the population were increasingly unwilling give up their ability to manage domestic economic conditions, especially during recessions, just in order to maintain the gold parity. Eventually, after weathering several smaller crises, the system collapsed when governments began abandoning the gold standard altogether after 1929 in response to the onset of the Great Depression.

These conclusions about the impact of particularistic groups in different types of electoral systems rest upon a critical insight derived from theoretical work on collective action in trade politics: that there is a fundamental asymmetry between the lobbying pressure generated from groups seeking protectionist policies and the lobbying pressure that comes from groups who oppose such restrictions. The main reason for this is that restrictions on imports and other types of exchange, when imposed one at a time, tend to have very lopsided effects. As we know from the analysis of the specific factors model above, the benefits of a tariff on a particular good are concentrated on the owners of capital and labour engaged in that particular industry. If the tariff is substantial, these benefits are likely to be quite large as a share of the incomes of those individuals, and thus they will typically be willing to spend a good deal of their time and energy (and savings) lobbying to ensure they get the tariff they want. The stakes are very high for them. By contrast, the costs of

the tariff are shared among all the owners of other types of specific factors in the economy; they are dispersed so broadly, in fact, that they tend to be quite small as fraction of the incomes of these individuals. Thus it is unlikely that those hurt by the new tariff will be prepared to devote resources to lobbying against the policy proposal. Collective political action will always be much easier to organize in the relatively small groups that benefit from a particular trade restriction than in the much larger groups (the rest of the economy) that are hurt by the restriction (see Olson 1965). Perhaps the best example of this logic is the extraordinary political power that has been demonstrated by the small, highly organized agricultural groups in Europe, the United States, and Japan over the past fifty years. These groups, which together represent a tiny fraction of the population in each political system, have been able to win extremely high (if not prohibitive) rates of protection from imports and lavish subsidies (see Tyers and Anderson 1992).

Other aspects of electoral institutions may also play a role in shaping policy outcomes. In general, smaller electoral districts in plurality systems may be expected to increase the influence of sectoral or particularistic groups over elected representatives and thus lead to higher levels of protection (Rogoswki 1987; Alt and Gilligan 1994). In larger districts, political representatives will be forced to balance the interests of a greater variety of industry groups when making decisions about policies and will be less affected by the demands of any one industry lobby, and a larger share of the costs of any tariff or restriction will be 'internalized' among voters within the district. From this perspective, upper chambers of parliaments, which typically allocate seats among representatives of much larger electoral districts than those in lower chambers, tend to be less inclined toward trade protection and other types of restrictive foreign economic policies. Meanwhile, in legislative chambers in which seats are defined along political-geographic lines without regard for population (for example, in the United States Senate, where each state receives two seats), agricultural, forestry, and mining interests in underpopulated areas typically gain a great deal more influence over policy making than they can wield in chambers (e.g. the United States House of Representatives) where legislative seats are defined based upon the number of voters in each district.

We have generally been focusing on trade policies, since most of the past research on the effects of institutions has tended to concentrate on tariff levels. But recent studies also suggest that differences in electoral institutions can have a significant impact on exchange-rate policies. In particular, in plurality systems in which elections are all-or-nothing contests between the major parties, governments appear to be far less likely to fix exchange rates and give up control over monetary policy than governments in proportional representation systems (see Clark and Hallerberg 2000). It appears that the costs of having ceded control over monetary policy in plurality systems, should the government face an election contest during an economic slump, are much higher than elsewhere. This difference also appears to be more pronounced for governments in plurality systems in which the timing of elections is predetermined by law (Bernhard and Leblang 1999).

Legislatures and policy-making rules

The rules that govern the way national legislatures go about making laws can have profound effects on the way the preferences of individuals and groups are aggregated into different types of foreign economic policies. These rules determine the way new policies are proposed, considered, amended, and voted upon. They structure the interactions among different legislative and executive bodies and they establish which branches have what types of agenda setting and veto power over policy.

Most of the recent research on the impact of legislative institutions on foreign economic policies has been focused on American trade policy, but the implications from this work are quite general and so it is worth close scrutiny. The point of departure for many studies is the infamous Smoot–Hawley Tariff Act of 1930, which was such a disaster that it helped inspire a fairly radical change in the rules by which the Congress has dealt with trade policy ever since. The core of the legislative problem, as many see it, is the possibility for 'log rolling' or vote trading between protectionist interests. The benefits of a tariff or trade restriction can often go to an import-competing industry located almost entirely in one electoral district, with the costs born generally by individuals in the rest of the economy. In such cases, lobbying pressure by these industries can generate a protectionist log roll when tariffs are being set by voting among members of a legislature: each member of the legislature will propose generous protective measures for industries in his or her own district without accounting for the costs they impose on individuals elsewhere. To gain support for these measures, each member will vote in favour of similar measures proposed by other legislators. If members can vote indefinitely on a sequence of such proposals, a policy that includes every new tariff can be the equilibrium outcome (supported by each legislator's belief that a vote against another's proposal would induce others to retaliate by offering an amendment to withdraw protection from the defector's district). The result of such unchecked log rolling is a vast array of protective measures, such that all individuals are far worse off than they were before the bill was passed (see Weingast, Shepsle, and Johnsen 1981).

Box 3.6 **The Reciprocal Trade Agreements Act of 1934**

In 1930 the US Congress passed the infamous Smoot–Hawley Tariff Act, which raised import duties on a vast array of manufactured and agricultural goods (some to over 200 per cent), and was quickly dubbed the 'worst tariff bill in the nation's history' even before it was passed. Retaliation from other countries, in the form of higher tariffs, was swift and substantial, and the subsequent sharp decline in world trade and the collapse of the fragile international monetary system increased the depth and scope of the Great Depression. The 1930 tariff bill was widely regarded as a case of protectionist log rolling run wild. The Senate alone made 1,253 amendments to the original House bill, and duties on over 20,000 items were altered (Pastor 1980: 77–8). When the Democrats won control of the White House, and majorities in Congress, in 1932, they looked for a way to make a change. Rural interests still made up a large part of the Democrats' electoral base, especially in the south, and still strongly favoured trade and the party's traditional anti-tariff platform. Unilateral tariff reductions were politically sensitive in the midst of a recession, however, and were not popular at all among workers, who had thrown their support to the Democrats in the 1932 campaign. Roosevelt's secretary of state, Cordell Hull, a long-time advocate of free trade, instead designed new legislation that would permit the president to negotiate bilateral treaties with trading partners to restart trade by making reciprocal reductions in import duties. Passed as the Reciprocal Trade Agreements Act in 1934, the legislation granted the president authority (for three years) to negotiate alterations of up to 50 per cent in the existing import duties. When that initial authority expired in 1937, Congress renewed it and continued to do so in the decades that followed. Beginning in 1974, the president's authority was expanded to cover negotiations over a range of non-tariff barriers to trade, although various procedural and monitoring provisions were also introduced to constrain executive behaviour, and the Congress maintained the power to approve or reject any trade agreement by vote (under the so-called 'fast-track' provision that prohibited amendments and set a firm time limit for a ratifying vote). The delegation of policy-making power to the executive branch, which can aggregate the costs and benefits of protection across the entire nation and bargain for reciprocal changes in the policies of other governments to open foreign markets to American exports, is credited with reorienting US trade policy away from protectionism in the decades since 1934 (see Destler 1995; Gilligan 1997; Lohman and O'Halloran 1994; Bailey, Goldstein, and Weingast 1997).

According to conventional wisdom, the Smoot–Hawley tariff was just such a log-rolling disaster, and Congress reacted to it in a remarkably sensible way by redesigning the rules governing the way trade policy was made. Specifically, Congress delegated to the executive branch the authority to alter US trade policy by negotiating reciprocal trade agreements with other countries. This practice of delegating negotiating authority to the president has been continued since 1934. By delegating authority over policy to the president, who would presumably set trade policy to benefit all individuals within the one, *national* electoral district, this innovation eliminated the spectre of protectionist log rolling altogether and ensured that all the costs of trade protection were fully 'internalized' by a decision maker accountable to all voters. In addition, by empowering the president to negotiate trade agreements that elicited reciprocal tariff reductions from other countries, the change helped to mobilize support for trade liberalization among export interests who could now expect improved sales abroad as a result of tariff reductions at home.

The lessons drawn from this case are almost certainly overdrawn, and the conventional account has some gaping inconsistencies. In particular, there appears to have been no learning at all on the part of members of Congress between 1930 and 1934: the congressional voting records indicate that, amongst the members voting on both bills, almost all those who voted for Smoot–Hawley in 1930 voted against the RTAA in 1934 (see Schnietz 1994). Moreover, it is not at all clear that protectionist log rolls have been an otherwise unsolvable problem for tariff legislation in the US Congress (or elsewhere)—what of all the cases in which *liberalizing* bills were passed by legislatures in the absence of delegation? In the US Congress itself, the major acts passed by the Democrats when in control of government before the 1930s (the Wilson

Tariff of 1894 and the Underwood Tariff of 1913) stand out in this regard. Examples also abound in the legislative histories of other Western democracies. It should not be a mystery as to why. In parliamentary systems, political parties play critical roles in controlling the legislative agenda. In proportional representation systems these parties compete for a share of the national vote, and so legislation designed to appease district-specific interests holds little appeal. Even in plurality rule systems, however, the majority party that forms a government typically imposes strict control over the policy agenda in a way that prevents such self-defeating log rolls. Finally, the notion that presidents, simply by dint of having a large (national) constituency, must be champions of freer trade, is hopelessly ahistorical. Here again, we cannot ignore the critical role played by political parties. In the US case, the Republican base of support between the 1840s and 1940s was concentrated among manufacturing interests in the north-east and midwest states and was staunchly protectionist, and a long list of Republican presidents championed high tariffs in election campaigns and backed the most protectionist of Republican tariff bills in Congress (see Hiscox 1999). More generally, in all the Western democracies, political parties typically have very distinct core constituencies among the electorate, defined in regional or class terms, to whom they are principally accountable when designing policies. Whether a government allows protectionist amendments during legislative deliberations of policy, and whether a president supports trade liberalization, will depend on their partisan affiliation and the preferences of their party's core electoral base.

Despite the distortions, the story of the RTAA does still hold some valuable lessons for thinking about ways in which legislative rules can affect foreign economic policies. The explicit institutional connection that the RTAA forged between tariff reductions at home and reciprocal reductions in tariffs abroad, surely played a role in generating increased support for trade policy reform among export-oriented industries and thus made it easier for all policy makers to support trade liberalization. This same link is now more or less routine, of course, for policy making in most Western governments as a consequence of their membership commitments in the WTO. For nations outside the WTO, however, most of them developing countries, where attempts to liberalize trade policy have a poor political track record, this does suggest that governments are more likely to succeed with trade reform if they can do so as part of a bilateral or regional free trade agreement with major trading partners.

The RTAA also offers a lesson about group access to lawmakers that is often overlooked. Up until 1934, congressional committee hearings were pivotal in shaping the trade legislation voted upon in the US House and Senate. The hearings format, which assigned particular days for receiving testimony on the duties to be levied on different commodities, was especially convenient for industry group lobbying. This system was changed completely in 1934. After the RTAA, hearings were typically limited to general discussions about whether to extend the president's negotiating authority and, after 1974, whether to implement previously negotiated agreements (under 'fast-track' provisions that prohibited amendment). Closing off this very direct channel by which groups had been able for years to lobby for changes in duties on particular items, may have had the most profound effect on trade policy-making in the United States. In general, *any* type of policy-making rules which provide routine access for organized groups to exert lobbying pressure to change particular features of legislation will make trade protection and other forms of restriction more likely—including open legislative hearings and 'commissions' or industry advisory panels set up within government agencies to gather opinions from producer and labour groups (see Alt and Gilligan 1994; Verdier 1994).

Legislative institutions can influence other types of foreign economic policies too. One line of work by scholars has been focusing on the general differences between multi-party coalition governments and single-party majority governments. Coalition governments appear to have less incentive than majority governments to alter their monetary policy prior to elections to try to boost economic activity in an 'opportunistic' fashion, since voters find it difficult to assign blame or credit to any single party within the coalition. An implication seems to be that coalition governments are also much more likely than other types of government to adopt fixed exchange rates and give up control over monetary policy (see Bernhard and Leblang 1999).

Bureaucratic agencies

Lastly, there is the issue of how foreign economic policies are implemented or administered by the bureaucratic agencies of each government. The rules that are established to regulate these agencies and the way they make decisions can play a powerful role in shaping policy outcomes. Legislatures delegate the responsibility for implementing their laws to these agencies, establishing the rules by which they are to operate, the ways in which their performance is monitored and evaluated, and so on. Built into these relationships between the legislature and the bureaucracy, however, there is always some measure of 'slack'—that is, some room for bureaucrats to manoeuvre free from legislative interference. This bureaucratic independence can have important effects in terms of foreign economic policies.

When it comes to the implementation of trade policies, for example, there is often a real fear that the bureaucratic agencies that administer various aspects of trade laws may develop a far too cozy relationship with the sectors of the home economy that they are supposed to be regulating. This danger of bureaucratic 'capture' appears to be very real. In the US case, the Departments of Commerce and Agriculture are both regarded as unapologetic advocates of protection for their 'clients'—American business firms and farmers. Indeed, the International Trade Administration, located within the Department of Commerce, is renowned for having 'gone native'. Charged with making rulings on petitions from US companies claiming that foreign firms are dumping products below cost in the American market, the ITA finds in favour of local firms in approximately 99 per cent of cases (see Bovard 1991).

This problem is by no means unique to the American system. In Japan, the Ministry for International Trade and Industry (MITI), and the Ministry for Agriculture, Forestry, and Fisheries (MAFF), have long been known for their extremely close ties with Japanese industry and the farming and fishing communities (see Okimoto 1988: 310). While MITI was for many years heralded by Western observers as the model for a new kind of autonomous state bureaucracy, capable of expertly targeting subsidies to particular manufacturing industries that would excel in competition with foreign producers

(Johnson 1982), comprehensive evidence from recent studies indicates that MITI actually allocated support to favoured industries in a highly political and ineffective way, much like captured bureaucracies elsewhere (see Beason and Weinstein 1993).

In general, extreme cases aside, the interplay between bureaucratic independence and accountability is a complex thing. In some issue areas, greater independence is generally regarded as desirable. Central banking is perhaps the most important case. The general problem, which we have discussed briefly above, is often referred to as the time inconsistency of monetary policy. Governments have an incentive to allow an unexpected rise in inflation that boosts economic activity, especially when facing an upcoming election. But since private actors know this, any promises a government may make to keep inflation in check may not be considered credible. Even if the government has all the best intentions, private actors might nevertheless keep inflation expectations high. By delegating control over monetary policy to an independent central bank that is insulated from any political temptations to alter monetary policy, the government can beat the problem. Moreover, independent central banks also appear to play an important role in shaping currency policies. Recent studies have indicated that governments in countries with independent central banks are less likely to engage in electorally motivated manipulations of exchange rates (Clark and Reichert 1998). And a related claim is that governments that can commit credibly to low inflation by establishing an independent central bank are less likely to need to fix their exchange rate in order to gain anti-inflationary credibility. Central bank independence and fixed exchange rates, in other words, can function as policy substitutes (see Clark and Hallerberg 2000).

Key points

- Restrictions on the franchise can give more weight to one side relative to others in contests over foreign economic policies. Extensions of the franchise to urban classes tend to produce more open policies toward trade and investment in labour and capital-abundant countries, and more closed or protectionist policies in labour and capital-scarce economies.

- Collective action is easier to organize in the relatively small groups that benefit from a particular trade restriction than in the much larger groups that are hurt by the restriction, so the strongest lobbying pressure tends to come from protectionist groups.

- Proportional representation systems with strong political parties typically generate lower levels of trade protection and other restrictions than plurality rule systems in which particular local and regional interests have a greater influence.

- Small electoral districts in plurality rule systems tend to increase the influence of sectoral or particularistic groups over elected representatives when compared to larger districts, and thus lead to higher levels of protection.

- In plurality rule systems in which elections are all-or-nothing contests between the major parties, governments are less likely to fix exchange rates than governments in proportional representation systems.

- Whether a government allows protectionist log rolling in a legislature, and whether a president supports trade liberalization, will depend on their partisan affiliation and the policy preferences of their party's core electoral constituency.

- An explicit institutional connection that links tariff reductions at home with reciprocal reductions in tariffs abroad (e.g. a free trade agreement), can generate much stronger support for trade policy reform among export-oriented industries.

- Rules that provide access for organized groups to exert lobbying pressure to change particular features of legislation make trade protection and other forms of restriction more likely.

- The delegation of policy-making authority to bureaucratic agencies or bodies independent from national legislatures may not produce policies less affected by lobbying from protectionist interests, since groups may gain privileged access to decision makers in such agencies.

- The existence of an independent central bank makes it less likely that a government will choose to fix the exchange rate.

Conclusions, extensions, and complications

There is really no such thing as the 'national interest' when it comes to foreign economic policy—or, rather there is no *one* national interest, there are many. Different individuals have very different conceptions of what is best for the nation and, not coincidentally, best for themselves, when it comes to setting foreign economic policies. This chapter has attempted to outline the principal divisions that usually characterize domestic political battles over trade, immigration, investment, and exchange rates. These divisions, as we have seen, tend to fall along either class or industry lines. Owners of capital and workers are typically pitted against one another when it comes to restrictions on inflows of labour or capital, for example, but they tend to take the same position in each industry on trade and exchange-rate issues since the effects of policy can be very different for different sectors of the economy.

Once we know who wants what, the next task involves figuring out who gets what they want from the political process. This second step involves understanding how policies are decided in different countries and thus how differences in political institutions affect economic policy choices. Our ultimate goal is to figure out why governments in different countries often choose very different types of trade, immigration, investment, and exchange-rate policies. We might also hope to form some reasonably accurate predictions about what our governments are likely to do in the future. Understanding why governments make the choices they make, and predicting what they will do next, requires careful attention to the political pressures they face from domestic groups and to the ways in which the preferences of these groups are aggregated into collective decisions by political institutions. But there are at least three additional complications to this simple analytical picture that we should discuss briefly here: the first has to do with the knowledge or information that individuals have about the effects of different policies and about the preferences of others; the second extension involves allowing for linkages between the various policy issues and between these issues and other non-economic policy concerns; and the third complication involves international bargaining and the ways in which we might think about the connection between domestic politics and international politics.

Information and the role of ideas

Who gains and who loses? And who wins the political contest between those who gain and lose? Answering those questions in each issue area is the heart of the standard political economy approach that we have outlined above. In keeping with traditional assumptions, we have been taking it for granted that individuals know what they want, know what others want too, and know what types of policies will have what kinds of effects. These are heroic assumptions. A great deal of the most recent research in both economics and political science, in fact, has tried to depart from this notion that people have full or complete information about their world, examining the effects of uncertainty, asymmetry in information among actors, and changes in knowledge that might be attributable to learning and the impact of new ideas. It is useful in this respect to distinguish between two basic types of information that individuals may be missing: people may be lacking knowledge about the effects of different policies on economic outcomes, or they may not have full knowledge about other people (including government leaders) and their preferences. We can discuss each of these informational problems separately.

What if we allow that individuals are not sure about the effects of different types of policies? It took us quite a while to disentangle the various effects of trade, immigration, investment, and exchange-rate policies above, with the help of several simplifying assumptions, so this does seem an important question to pose. It clearly provides a large window through which new ideas, in the form of new beliefs about cause-and-effect relationships between policies and outcomes, might have a large impact on

policy making. Indeed, this is the view espoused by John Maynard Keynes (1936: 383) in his famous contention that 'the ideas of economists and political philosophers, both when they are right and when they are wrong, are more powerful than is commonly understood. Indeed the world is ruled by little else.'

Several prominent scholars have indeed argued that foreign economic policies have changed markedly in response to new ideas about policies and their effects. The abandonment of mercantilist restrictions on trade and investment by most European governments in the nineteenth century has been attributed, in some large measure, to the ideas of Adam Smith and David Ricardo and the development of classical trade theory (Kindleberger 1975; Bhagwati 1988). The multilateral liberalization of trade and investment among Western economies in the post-Second World War era, allowing governments considerable scope for managing their domestic economies to avoid recessions, has similarly been traced to the refinement of classical and neoclassical economic theories and the ideas of Keynes himself (Ruggie 1982; Goldstein 1993). More recently, the rush to liberalize trade by governments in developing nations has been attributed to a learning process and the discrediting of the idea that rapid development could be achieved by import-substitution policies (see Krueger 1995). Competing ideas about cause-and-effect relationships often appear in policy debates, and dominant ideas are frequently embedded within policy-making institutions as the foundations for rules followed by bureaucratic agencies (Goldstein 1993). Yet there remains much debate about the degree to which these types of ideas are independent of the interests that might be served by them. Weber's famous analogy compared ideas to 'switchmen' who determine the tracks along which human behaviour, pushed by interests, travel (Weber 1913). From a more sceptical perspective, one might suggest that the individuals who gain and lose the most from any economic policy, such as tariffs on trade, have all the knowledge they need about its effects and need no new ideas from economists to help them out; the policies just reflect the wishes of those interested actors who have the most political clout, and the ideas that attract our attention are just the ones sprinkled like holy water over the new legislation

Box 3.7 **The rise of free trade in Europe**

The publication of *The Wealth of Nations* by Adam Smith in 1776 stands out as an intellectual landmark in the history of thinking about international trade, pointing out the critical role that trade plays in encouraging specialization and the resulting gains in efficiency and wealth. Smith adroitly punctured the old doctrine of mercantilism, which favoured expanding exports while restricting imports and hoarding gold, making it clear that national wealth is defined not by stocks of gold but by how much citizens can consume with the resources they have at their disposal. But the modern theory of international trade really began with the arrival of David Ricardo's *Principles of Political Economy and Taxation* in 1817. Ricardo demonstrated that trade is mutually beneficial for all countries, even a country that cannot produce anything more efficiently than other nations in terms of the costs of its inputs. As long as the costs of production are different in different nations, Ricardo's analysis showed that it must be true that, in terms of the opportunity costs of production (the

value of other things that might have been produced with the inputs used to make a given item), each nation will be better at producing some things than others and thus there is a basis for specialization and exchange that will leave both countries better off. This 'law of comparative advantage', which Paul Samuelson has called the most beautiful law in economics, has had a profound impact on all scholarly and political debates about trade ever since. That the cause of free trade was taken up enthusiastically by the leading English political economists, including John Stuart Mill, all inspired by Ricardian theory, and that these ideas also spread rapidly throughout Europe during the nineteenth century, has led many scholars to suggest that the broad shift away from trade protectionism in Europe (which began in 1846 with the repeal of the Corn Laws that Ricardo himself had attacked) was due in large measure to a profound change in the way leaders understood the economic effects of trade (see Kindleberger 1975; Bhagwati 1988).

(to borrow an equally memorable metaphor from Kindleberger). The relationship between ideas and interests is still very murky, and will remain so until we have a better understanding of where new ideas about policy come from, and what explains which ideas catch on and spread.

But by focusing just on the role of new ideas and how they might change knowledge about policies, we may actually be missing the bulk of the iceberg here when it comes to the impact of incomplete information. We noted in the discussions above that while foreign economic policies such as tariffs on imported goods generate real costs for a large set of owners and workers in all the other (non-protected) sectors of the economy, these costs are dispersed across such a large number of individuals that the per-person losses can be extremely small. Not only will it not pay for those affected to take political action to oppose the tariff in these cases, it may not even pay for them to spend any time or resources acquiring accurate information about the policy and its effects. Public opinion experts typically regard foreign economic policies as a particularly complex set of issues about which survey respondents have very low levels of information

(see Bauer, Pool, and Dexter 1972: 81–4). Survey responses to questions about these issues tend to vary drastically with simple changes in question wording, making it very difficult to pinpoint where the public stands on any policy question at any particular point in time (see Destler 1995: 180). One implication is that voters may be very susceptible to issue framing or manipulation by political leaders and organized lobby groups whenever these issues become more prominent. Recent research on political communication and public opinion has highlighted this possibility (for example, Manheim 1991; Zaller 1992: 95). To the extent that this type of influence can be exercised, the politics of globalization may be regarded, at least to some degree, as a competition in issue framing among organized interests on different sides of the debate trying to sway public opinion to their side. This did appear to be an important dimension of the intense debate over NAFTA in the United States in 1993 (Holsti 1996: 52).

Another interesting implication of incomplete information among voters is that it may provide an explanation for why governments so often seem to do very inefficient things when setting foreign economic policies. Economists are fond of pointing out that if a government really wanted to redistribute income to particular groups of owners and employees, using restrictions on trade is a very inefficient way to go about it. It would be far better just to make a direct, lump sum payment to these groups that stand to benefit from protection, and thus avoid the inefficiencies generated by the allocation of resources to such uncompetitive industries. But if the costs of such direct payments to taxpayers are more visible (because they must appear, say, in the government's annual budget), they are more likely to generate a backlash among the voters on whom the burden falls. If this is true, it may make sense for a government to use trade policies to redistribute income to favoured groups because these policies provide an effective disguise in a low-information environment (see Tullock 1983). From this perspective, the use of trade protection can be characterized as 'optimal obfuscation' (Magee, Brock, and Young 1989).

Finally, what happens if we allow that individuals, even if they are fully informed about the effects of foreign economic policies, may nevertheless be uncertain about the motivations or intentions of the government managing them. One circumstance in which this type of incomplete information can become important is when setting exchange-rate policy, as we have discussed above. Since governments have an incentive to print money and allow a burst of inflation when facing an election, any promises they make to keep inflation in check may not be considered credible by private actors who understand that the government has an incentive to bluff and portray itself as 'tougher' on inflation than it really is. The problem is that no one can be sure that the government values its low-inflation reputation enough (relative to how much it wants to win re-election) to keep its pledge; even if the government would have followed through with its promises, private actors might nevertheless keep inflation expectations high. If there is no independent central bank to which control of monetary policy can be ceded, governments in these circumstances are likely to be drawn more to fixing the exchange rate, especially in countries that have a history of chronic inflation. Fixing the value of the currency is a way for the government to signal to private actors that it is committed to keeping inflation

under control by raising the potential costs to itself should it fail.

Another important context in which incomplete information about the government may play a key role in shaping policies is the case in which a government is attempting to reform trade policy in the face of stiff opposition from groups in import-competing industries. In such cases, since the government may indeed have an incentive to back down if it encounters a major political revolt, any promises it makes in advance to hold fast to the reforms may not be considered credible by the groups (who know full well that the government could just be trying to bluff its way through the painful reforms). Thus, even if the government does fully intend to stick with the reforms, it may have to weather a long and costly (and perhaps even violent) political protest. Again, tying its own hands in some clear and visible way can be an especially attractive policy option for a government in this situation, and by signing an international trade treaty with a major regional partner, it might be able to do the trick. This desire to make a credible commitment to trade reform is widely held to have been a large reason why the Mexican government initiated the negotiations that produced the NAFTA agreement in 1993, after two decades of failed efforts to lower trade barriers unilaterally (see Whalley 1999b).

Combinations of policies and issue linkages

Up to this point we have been examining one type of foreign economic policy at a time. It is clear, however, that the effects of different policy instruments often depend upon how *other* policies are set. In the basic Heckscher–Ohlin model, trade and factor movements are *substitutes* for one another—more of one type of international flow will generally mean less of another and vice versa. If exports of labour-intensive products can move easily across a border between a labour-abundant economy (where wages are low) and a labour-scarce economy (where wages are high), this will tend to equalize labour costs over time, reducing the incentives for workers themselves to try to migrate between countries. If exports between the countries are blocked or impeded, more workers are likely to try to cross the border into the country that pays higher wages. When a dam is placed in front of flows in one channel it tends to divert flows into other channels.

This interaction among policies can become very interesting because we know that while trade and factor flows are substitutable in general terms, they actually have different types of effects on individuals. Individuals may thus have preferences over different combinations of policies. Perhaps the best example concerns the relationship between trade flows (and trade barriers) and direct investment. There is a great deal of evidence that firms engage in direct investment in markets as a way of 'jumping' trade barriers that would inhibit exports, and they even seem to reduce exports and invest more to stave off anticipated pressure for tariffs among local firms—a phenomenon known as 'quid pro quo foreign investment' (Bhagwati et al. 1987; Blonigen and Feenstra 1996). Local firms may be able to raise trade barriers, since they should have the lobbying support of their workers whose jobs are endangered by high levels of imports, but they are less likely to win restrictions on inward direct investment by foreign firms since workers in the industry will benefit from any new inflows of capital. Indeed, the best *policy combination* for local workers in an industry facing competition from a (relocatable) foreign producer is a high tariff *and* no restrictions on inward foreign investment. Local firms would prefer restrictions of *both* types of exchange, but would accept any restrictions rather than none at all if those are the politically feasible options. This political logic helps explain the common pattern in policies toward the automobile industry in Europe and North America, where restrictions on imports were negotiated with Japanese auto firms but no restrictions were imposed to block the same firms from investing heavily in production facilities within both markets.

Exchange-rate policy can also be 'in play' at the same time as trade policy. Trade policy and exchange-rate policy are partially substitutable: a 1 per cent depreciation of the currency is equivalent to a 1 per cent across-the-board tariff on imports and a 1 per cent subsidy for all exports. But clearly the coalition that supports depreciation—those invested and employed in both import-competing and exporting

industries—is different from the coalition that would support higher tariffs (import-competing interests). Exchange-rate policies tend to be more rigid than trade policies, in general, mainly because the credibility of monetary policy commitments is undermined by frequent shifts in policy. But when there is an opportunity for the government to alter the exchange rate, intense lobbying for protection by import-competing groups (or even just the threat of it), may induce export interests to help persuade the government to weaken the currency—an outcome that would ease the competitive pressure on producers threatened by imports, while not harming (benefiting, in fact) those engaged in export industries. This seems to have been the case in the United States in the early 1980s, as the value of the US dollar rose dramatically. While the White House appeared to prefer to leave both its currency and trade policies unchanged, fearing a spate of protectionist legislation from Congress in response to lobbying by firms and unions in import sensitive sectors, and hearing support for depreciation from export interests as well, it moved in 1985 to weaken the value of the dollar. Similarly, in many Latin American nations in the 1980s and 1990s, governments attempting reforms aimed at lowering barriers to trade were able to render these changes more politically palatable to threatened sectors by devaluing exchange rates at the same time (see De Gregorio 2001).

Perhaps even more important, in some ways, than these connections between different foreign economic policies are the linkages that have been made with increasing frequency in recent policy debates between these policies and a variety of *non-economic* issues. Some of these linkages are not new. Trade and investment policies have always been connected in various ways to the issue of national security. Most governments place tight controls on trade in weapons and dangerous chemicals, for instance, and restrictions on foreign investment in strategically important industries (for example, energy, airlines, and broadcasting) are also common. And governments have strong incentives to lower barriers to trade and investment more rapidly among alliance partners than with other nations in the international system, as the post-Second World War experience in Europe, and among the industrialized democracies more generally, makes clear (see Gowa 1994). All individuals within an economy tend to share similar concerns about national security, so this form of issue linkage tends to affect policy making in a fairly straightforward way, generating more support among all citizens for policy options that contribute most clearly to national security. But foreign economic policies are now linked more regularly with a range of other non-economic issues about which individuals tend to have more varied opinions. Most importantly, trade and investment are now frequently linked to discussions of environmental policy and to human rights issues in the political debates about globalization in Western democracies.

How do these issue linkages affect the analysis of the politics of trade and investment? The clearest impact is the involvement of a variety of organized environmental and human rights groups in recent debates over regional trade agreements and the WTO (see Destler and Balint 1999). The members of these groups care deeply about addressing environmental and human rights problems in their own countries and in other countries around the world, and they either believe that globalization is making these problems worse and thus should be restrained in some way, or they argue that trade and investment provide economic leverage which can and should be used to persuade governments in developing nations to improve environmental and labour standards and democratic institutions. The position taken by many of these groups is that all trade agreements, including the WTO itself, should include provisions for minimum environmental and labour standards that would be enforced (if necessary) by the imposition of trade sanctions. Many environmental groups have also lobbied for changing the existing rules of the WTO, so that laws that discriminated against foreign products on environmental grounds (for example, import bans on tuna caught using nets that also endanger dolphins) would be permissible. But environmentalists and human rights activists have also expressed grave concerns about the behaviour of multinational firms in developing nations, with much of the focus being on whether these large corporations are moving production to areas in which they can pollute and otherwise damage the environment, or run 'sweatshop' factories in which they mistreat and underpay workers, avoiding the regulatory supervision that would prevent such behaviour in

their home countries. The policies recommended by these groups, and especially by human rights organizations worried by the lack of democratic institutions in countries such as China, typically involve a more proactive use of economic sanctions—that is, Western governments cutting off trade with, and investment to, such 'problem' nations until their leaders make significant political reforms. Consumer boycotts aimed at particular corporations that are investing in such nations are usually warmly recommended too (although these types of consumer actions represent private, market behaviour and are thus not a question of public policy).

One important general development has been the formation of what might be called 'Baptist and bootlegger' coalitions between some of these issue groups and the business and labour organizations that have an economic stake in restricting international trade and/or investment. This type of coalition gets its name from American politics in the era of Prohibition, when strong support for the ban on alcohol sales came from Baptists, on moral grounds, and from bootleggers, who made large fortunes selling alcohol on the black market (see Yandle 1984). In recent debates over the NAFTA in the United States, for instance, environmental groups such as the Sierra Club, joined with labour unions in lobbying against the agreement on the grounds that it did not contain provisions that would ensure a substantial improvement in environmental and labour standards in Mexico (see Destler and Balint 1999: 42–5). And recent 'anti-sweatshop' campaigns, organized by human rights groups and student activists, and targeting foreign investment and outsourcing by US apparel manufacturers to nations such as Vietnam and China, have been backed financially and supported enthusiastically by American textile unions and firms producing locally.

The concern among many analysts, especially among those who generally support international economic integration for its ability to raise living standards in all countries, is that these types of political coalitions may be hijacked by their protectionist members who support restrictions on international trade and investment *regardless* of whether they have any positive (or negative) long-term effects on environmental conditions or human rights standards. It would be far better, many argue, to pursue improvements in environmental and human rights standards by working towards separate international treaties dealing with those precise issues in a more direct way, perhaps by compensating developing nations for making costly improvements to their environmental and labour laws. Sanctions could severely limit economic growth in the very poorest developing countries where governments are likely to resist making political concessions (especially democratic reforms that increase the risk that they will be toppled from power). The issues are complex, however, and the political problems are difficult. The 'Baptists' are drawn to supporting economic sanctions rather than other policy instruments (for example, new international treaties, or foreign aid grants to nations that improve their environmental standards) because they have calculated that these alternatives are politically infeasible. With the support of the 'bootleggers' for restrictions on trade and investment, however, they might stand a greater chance of getting something done that will have beneficial effects.

The general point here is that our simple, one-issue-at-a-time approach to the analysis of foreign economic policies becomes much more complicated when we allow that different policy instruments are often up for grabs at the same time and have partially substitutable effects, and if we account for the fact that a variety of groups are often interested in using the tools of foreign economic policy to advance non-economic types of goals. Often it is the institutional context in which government decisions are made (many of the features of which we have discussed above) that determines which types of policy instruments are more adjustable than others and which types of political coalitions are more viable than others. The most comprehensive and persuasive accounts of economic policy making will take all these complexities into account.

International bargaining and domestic politics

Finally, in anticipation of the chapter that follows, it is worth pausing here briefly to consider the ways in which the domestic politics of foreign economic policies may be translated into international-level bargaining over these same issues. What we really require here is a theoretical model of the policy-making process that takes into account all of the incentives and constraints operating among actors at both the domestic and international levels. This is the type of model Putnam (1988) famously envisioned using the metaphor of the 'two-level game'. A government engaged in international economic negotiations actually plays two different political 'games' at the same time, he suggested, with its actions constituting 'moves' that must be seen not only in the context of the demands made by individuals and groups in *domestic* politics, but in view of the bargaining power that it has when negotiating *international* agreements with other governments. Government leaders negotiate with other leaders at the international level over the terms of economic agreements, and in those negotiations the relative size and strength of the economy can make a tremendous difference to the terms that can be demanded. But the leaders must be attuned to the preferences of the domestic groups whose support they need to remain in office and the set of international deals that would actually be ratified or supported by these groups at home.

To date, theoretical work along these lines has focused mainly on differences between the preferences of legislative and executive branches of government, and their different agenda-setting and vetoing powers, and how these features of domestic politics affect the outcomes of international negotiations and agreements (see Evans, Jacobson, and Putnam 1993; Milner 1997a). Much of the attention has been directed to the so-called 'Schelling conjecture', which holds that a hawkish domestic constituency—represented in the simplest models as a legislature that prefers very little international cooperation—can actually improve the bargaining power of the executive branch in its dealings with foreign counterparts (Schelling 1960: 28–9). Recent work has also focused on how executive-legislative divisions affect the credibility of governments during international negotiations (for example, Martin 2000) and whether international agreements are negotiated to allow for greater flexibility in cases when future changes in domestic political coalitions might lead to substantial shifts in the types of policies a government can implement (Downs and Rocke 1995).

While full of insights about the effects of domestic political institutions on the prospects for international cooperation, this line of work has so far paid very little attention to the roles played by organized interests and voters in shaping legislative and executive preferences on particular policy issues. In fact, to date, standard political economy models of trade politics, emphasizing the role played by organized lobby groups in the formulation of policy, have not been linked at all to two-level game models of negotiations over trade and other economic agreements. Moreover, the existing work on two-level games tends to concentrate overwhelmingly on parameters that operate only on one level—domestic politics in the home nation. Features of the strategic relationship between nations, such as the economic and military asymmetries that might affect relative bargaining power, or common ties to alliances or international institutions that might affect incentives to cooperate, are largely ignored. We clearly need a better two-level mouse trap: a model that incorporates a fuller representation of organized interests and lobbying at the domestic level, while also allowing for the ways in which incentives and constraints are generated at the international level.

In practice, most international political economists work with partial theories that focus on one set of causal variables operating at one level. Some argue that the features of the international system, such as the distribution of economic power, and any specific nation's position within it, impose broad but important constraints upon what governments can and cannot do when setting policies. Others, in keeping with the orientation of this chapter, argue that the prime focus of our attention should be placed on what is going on within nations—their particular sets of political institutions and the preferences and lobbying activities of different group of individuals—since it is these things that primarily determine the policies chosen by governments. But in principal, almost all scholars recognize that politics at both the domestic and international levels should be a feature of any complete analysis of foreign economic policy.

Integrating theoretical insights about politics at these two levels is an extremely complex and challenging task that still remains, to a very large extent, undone.

Key points

- To understand the domestic origins of foreign economic policies we need to perform two main tasks: first, map the policy preferences of different groups in the domestic economy, and then specify how political institutions affect the way these preferences are aggregated into actual government decisions.

- Policy preferences depend mainly on the types of assets people own, and how the income earned from those assets is affected by different policies.

- Political institutions affect policy outcomes by defining who gets to vote, how political representatives are elected, and how policy making takes place in legislatures and is delegated to presidents and government agencies.

- New ideas about cause-and-effect relationships appear to have had a large impact on foreign economic policies in different eras. The relationship between ideas and interests is far from clear, however, and we need a better understanding of where new ideas about policy come from and what explains which ideas catch on and spread.

- Foreign economic policies involve a complex set of issues about which most voters have very low levels of information. As a result, the politics of globalization may be regarded to some degree as a competition in issue framing among organized interests.

- If private actors have incomplete information about the degree to which the government is committed to policy reforms, the government may have an incentive to tie its own hands in some visible way (e.g. by fixing the exchange rate, or signing a trade treaty) to signal its intentions in a credible way.

- Since the effects of a change in one type of foreign economic policy may depend upon choices made about other types of policy, individuals may have preferences over different combinations of policies that are closely related (e.g. tariffs and restrictions on inward investment induced by tariffs).

- Trade and investment policies are also linked to discussions of *non-economic* issues. One important development has been the formation of 'Baptist and bootlegger' coalitions between environmental and human rights groups concerned about globalization and business and labour organizations that have an economic stake in restricting international trade and investment.
- Governments may be thought of as playing political games at two levels, their actions constituting moves that are both responses to demands made by groups in *domestic* politics and responses to offers made by other governments in *international* negotiations.
- We need a better theory of two-level games that incorporates fuller representations of both domestic and international politics. In practice, most international political economists employ partial theories that focus only on variables operating at one level.

QUESTIONS

1 If the economic case for trade liberalization is so strong, why is it that governments continue to impose barriers to trade and are so frequently engaged in trade disputes?

2 Trade theory does not imply that every individual within each nation will benefit from the lowering of trade barriers, just that aggregate benefits will exceed aggregate losses. Who stands to benefit most from trade liberalization in the advanced economies of Europe, Japan, and the United States and who is most likely to be disadvantaged? What about in developing nations with different types of factor endowments?

3 Can these different groups of individuals reach some kind of agreement so that trade liberalization can benefit everyone? What are the political obstacles to this type of agreement?

4 Is it inappropriate to think only, or primarily, in terms of economic gains and losses when evaluating the effects of increased international trade? How important are other types of concerns (for example, national security, income inequality, environmental hazards, human rights abuses) in the political debates that determine policy outcomes?

5 What types of electoral and policy-making institutions tend to mitigate the effects of lobbying by protectionist groups when it comes to the determination of trade policy? Are electoral systems based upon proportional representation likely to generate less protection than plurality systems?

6 Do the economic effects of immigration shape the political struggles over changes in immigration law? Or do the politics of immigration reflect other types of cultural and social divisions within host countries?

7 What are the economic effects of foreign investment for the source country and for the host country? Does foreign investment generate a 'race to the bottom' in labour and environmental standards in developing countries? Does it inhibit democratic reform?

8 What economic and political changes during the twentieth century led to the abandonment of fixed exchange rates among the advanced economies? Why do many developing countries continue to fix their exchange rates?

FURTHER READING

Trade

Destler, I. M. (1995), *American Trade Politics*, 3rd edn. (Washington DC: Institute for International Economics). This is required reading for anyone interested in how US trade policy is made. It provides a comprehensive analysis of American political institutions and policy making

Hayes, J. P. (1993), *Making Trade Policy in the European Community* (London: Macmillan). This book provides a thorough discussion of the processes of trade policy making in the European Community.

Hiscox, M. J. (2002), *International Trade and Political Conflict* (Princeton: Princeton University Press). An analysis of historical changes in levels of factor specificity in several Western nations, relating these changes to shifts in political alignments in trade politics.

Krueger, A. O. (1995), *Trade Policies and Developing Nations* (Washington DC: Brookings Institution). An engaging discussion of trade liberalization in developing nations in recent years.

Rogowski, R. (1989), *Commerce and Coalitions* (Princeton: Princeton University Press). A sweeping analysis of coalitions in trade politics in a variety of historical contexts, based upon an application of the Stolper–Samuelson theorem.

Immigration

Borjas, G. J. (1999), *Heaven's Door: Immigration Policy and the American Economy* (Princeton: Princeton University Press). A provocative analysis of the effects of immigration in the United States in recent decades.

Fetzer, J. S. (2000), *Public Attitudes toward Immigration in the United States, France, and Germany* (Cambridge: Cambridge University Press). This book uses available survey data to compare public attitudes toward immigration in the United States, France, and Germany and the determinants of anti-immigrant sentiments.

Tichenor, D. J. (2002), *Dividing Lines: The Politics of Immigration Control in America* (Princeton: Princeton University Press). A very impressive history of immigration politics in the United States.

Investment

Crystal, J. (2003), *Unwanted Company: Foreign Investment in American Industries* (Ithaca, NY: Cornell University Press). An excellent study of political debates about inward direct foreign investment in the United States

Graham, E., and Krugman, P. R. (1995), *Foreign Direct Investment in the United States* (Washington DC: Institute for International Economics). This book provides a comprehensive analysis of the economic and political effects of inward foreign investment.

Moran, T. (1998), *Foreign Direct Investment and Development* (Washington DC: Institute for International Economics). An excellent study of the effects of direct foreign investment in developing nations.

Exchange Rates

Frieden, J., Ghezzi, P., and Stein, E. (eds.) (2001), *The Currency Game: Exchange Rate Politics in Latin America* (New York: Inter-American Development Bank). A very interesting collection of research on the politics of exchange rate policies in Latin America.

Henning, R. C. (1994), *Currencies and Politics in the United States, Germany, and Japan* (Washington DC: Institute for International Economics). This book provides a clear and detailed discussion of exchange-rate policy making in the United States, Germany, and Japan.

Simmons, B. A. (1994), *Who Adjusts? Domestic Sources of Foreign Economic Policy During the Interwar Years* (Princeton: Princeton University Press). An impressive analysis of the political determinants of exchange-rate policies adopted by Western nations in the inter-war period.

Institutions

Gilligan, M. (1997), *Empowering Exporters: Reciprocity and Collective Action in Twentieth Century American Trade Policy* (Ann Arbor: University of Michigan Press). A fine study of the importance of institutionalizing reciprocity in trade policy making.

Hiscox, M. J. (1999), 'The Magic Bullet? The RTAA, Institutional Reform, and Trade Liberalization', *International Organization*, 53/4: 669–98. A critical review of research on the RTAA that emphasizes the role of political parties and their core constituencies in the politics institutional change.

Rogowski, R. (1987), 'Trade and the Variety of Democratic Institutions', *International Organization*, 41/2: 203–23. A classic analysis of the ways in which different types of electoral institutions affect trade policy outcomes in democracies.

Wintrobe, R. (1998), *The Political Economy of Dictatorship* (Cambridge: Cambridge University Press). An excellent analysis of policy making in non-democratic regimes.

Extensions and complications

Elliott, K. Ann, and Freeman, R. (2003), *Can Labor Standards Improve under Globalization?* (Washington DC: Institute for International Economics). This book provides a comprehensive review of the debates about whether trade and investment policies should be linked to agreements about improving labour standards in developing nations.

Goldstein, J., and Keohane, R. O. (eds.) (1993), *Ideas and Foreign Policy: Beliefs, Institutions, and Political Change* (Ithaca, NY: Cornell University Press). An important collection of essays discussing the impact of new ideas on foreign policy outcomes.

Graham, E. (2000), *Fighting the Wrong Enemy: Anti-Global Activists and Multinational Enterprises* (Washington DC: Institute for International Economics). A compelling analysis of the effects of direct foreign investment in developing nations that argues that criticisms made by environmental and human rights groups are misguided.

Irwin, D. (1996), *Against the Tide: An Intellectual History of Free Trade* (Princeton: Princeton University Press). A sweeping account of theoretical developments in economics that support the case for trade liberalization.

WEB LINKS

For regular research reports and briefs on policy issues:

www.iie.com/   Institute for International Economics.

For theoretical background on international economics and helpful beginner guides:

www.internationalecon.com/   International Economics Study Center.

www.amosweb.com/gls/   Amos World Economics Glossary.

For data and analysis of public opinion on international economic issues:

http://people-press.org/pgap/   The PEW Global Attitudes Project.

www.pipa.org/   The Program on International Policy Attitudes (PIPA).

For data on world trade, migration, and investment:

www.wto.org/english/res_e/statis_e/its2003_e/its03_toc_e.htm   WTO's International Trade Statistics.

www.migrationinformation.org/Profiles/   ILO's International Labour Migration Database.

http://r0.unctad.org/en/subsites/dite/fdistats_files/WID3.htm   UNCTAD's World Investment Directory.

For information and statistics on trade, immigration, investment, and exchange-rate policies:

http://cs.usm.my/untrains/trains.html   UNCTAD's TRAINS Database of Trade Control Measures.

www.wto.org/english/tratop_e/dda_e/tnc_e.htm   WTO's Negotiations Committee.

www.ustr.gov   United States Trade Representative (USTR).

http://europa.eu.int/comm/trade/   European Union Trade Policy.

www.meti.go.jp/english/index.html   Japanese Trade Policy.

www.migrationpolicy.org/   The Migration Policy Institute.

www.imf.org/external/np/tre/tad/exfin1.cfm   IMF's Country Finances and Exchange Rates.

www.federalreserve.gov/   Federal Reserve Board.

www.bankofengland.co.uk/   Bank of England.

www.ecb.int/   European Union Central Bank.

www.boj.or.jp/en/   Bank of Japan.

Part Two

Global trade

4 The evolution of the global trade regime

Gilbert R. Winham

READER'S GUIDE

The twentieth century witnessed a remarkable growth in international institutions, and nowhere was this growth greater than in the international trade system. Out of the ashes of a world economy torn by war and depression, a world trading regime was initiated at mid-century with the creation of the General Agreement on Tariffs and Trade (GATT) in 1947, which began with a few simple procedures and rules designed to promote the idea that if someone in one country can produce something that people in another country want to buy, they should have the right to sell it to them. From this simple beginning, the world trade regime developed by the end of the century into the most prominent example of cooperation between countries in the entire international system. This chapter reviews the history of this extraordinary development.

Introduction

Today, the global trade regime is a rules-based political system where the rules flowing from international agreements that seek to promote and stabilize economic exchanges between countries are ranged against the regulations of national governments that often seek to restrict those exchanges. The purpose of the international rules is to reduce the protectionism of national regulations, but even more to reduce the uncertainty and unpredictability of international trade relations, and to promote stability. The task of this chapter will be to show how the global trade regime has been established through the actions of trading countries over the past 150 years, and how it became institutionalized in the World Trade Organization (WTO).

The global trade regime of the late twentieth and early twenty-first centuries is based on three components: trade, national regulations, and international agreements. Trade and national regulations have been a theme and counterpoint throughout much of history, in the sense that when national regulations receded, trade flourished; and when those regulations intensified, trade languished. To this combination can be added the third factor of international agreements, by which countries attempt to establish international rules that would restrict their own (and other countries') capacity to interrupt international trade through national regulation. Rules and regulations appear to be inherent in our highly ordered lives, and the irony is that in order to reduce regulation of one kind, it requires the intercession of rules of another kind. The important issue is where the rules or regulations come from, and whether their purpose is to reduce or expand the scope of our economic activity.

Trade, which is a staple of our modern global political economy, is also a historic and even prehistoric phenomenon. It was important to many ancient and medieval powers. Trade lay at the centre of state revenue and state power in ancient Athens, Ptolemaic Egypt, the Italian city states of Venice, Florence, and Genoa, and the German Hanseatic League. Nowhere was this clearer than in ancient Athens, which developed through commercial activities and at its height was totally dependent on trade. Athens exported silver and olive oil, and the boundaries of its trade have been charted over time by the shards of pottery urns that have been discovered throughout the Mediterranean region. In return, the Athenians were dependent on the import of grain, which was essential to maintain the population of Athens in an arid region.

In examining the global trade regime, trade is by necessity the starting point, but government is equally part of the story. This point has been observed by many writers, but perhaps was expressed most effectively by John Condliffe (1950: 27) as follows: 'The beginnings of trade are to be found in the enterprise of groups and individuals, but regulation and taxation of trade are almost as old as trade itself. In tracking history, if enterprise is the theme, regulation is the counterpoint. As soon as the track begins to be beaten out, established authority intervenes to control and levy tolls upon the traders.'

Early trade was a primitive exercise in economic enterprise. The means of regulating trade were equally primitive. The earliest means were tolls, which were exacted by local leaders for the permission to pass through territory, or to trade, or simply for protection. From the earliest time, tolls were an expression of military control and political sovereignty, and if one controlled territory, one could exact tribute through tolls at will. This resulted in a great hindrance to trade, especially in Europe, which was divided into many small jurisdictions during the Middle Ages.

A more modern method of regulation than tolls was the tariff, or customs duty, which we now recognize as a percentage tax added to the price of imported goods. Tariffs are still with us today, but they are among the oldest functions of government. The purpose of early tariffs, whether on imports or exports, was to raise revenue. Tariffs were effective for this purpose, for by the beginning of the eighteenth century duties on imported goods had come to be the chief source of revenue in European countries. A further function of the tariff was to protect domestic producers from foreign competition.

Today, protectionism is the main purpose of the tariff. The revenue function is less important in developed countries as governments have found other more effective means to raise revenues, although the tariff is still an important source of revenue in some developing countries. However, as if to demonstrate the ingenuity of government regulators, new forms of protection have arisen which are collectively known as non-tariff measures (NTMs). These measures have now become more important than tariffs, the latter having been greatly reduced (again, mainly between developed countries) by successive trade agreements under the General Agreement on Tariffs and Trade (GATT).

The regulations that have restricted trade in recent decades have been the work of national governments. But those same governments have also reached international agreements with other governments attempting to constrain the extent to which domestic policies would restrict the free flow of international trade. These agreements started as simple undertakings between peoples as to how their commercial relations would be conducted, and trade agreements are almost as old as trade itself. For example, commercial treaties have been discovered between the kings of ancient Egypt and Babylonia giving the parties the right to exact duties on the merchandise of traders or travellers. In more modern times, such treaties have been instrumental in establishing the rules whereby trade could be carried on between different political jurisdictions.

There has been a close relationship between trade and commercial treaties down through history, to the extent that it accounts for much of the diplomatic practice between countries. An important watershed in this relationship occurred in the mid-nineteenth century with the Cobden–Chevalier (or Anglo-French) Treaty of 1860. This treaty initiated a brief period of liberalized trade between the United Kingdom and the Continent, which ended with the world depression of 1873–96. However, the treaty demonstrated that trade agreements could serve as an effective means of trade liberalization by alleviating some of the worst effects of competitive national regulation, and it set the stage for the deployment of trade negotiation in the twentieth century.

Key points

- The international trade regime is based on three components: trade, national regulations, and international agreements.

Historical antecedents: 1860 to 1945

War and depression

The impact of government regulation on trade was well understood by the nineteenth century from the writings of Adam Smith and other political economists. Smith noted that in addition to raising revenue, tariffs also had the effect of protecting domestic producers from foreign competition, something Smith and other reformers generally viewed with disfavour. As a political movement, however, the effort to curtail protectionist regulation did not begin until the Reform Act of 1932 in England. A campaign for free trade had begun among British merchants in the second quarter of the nineteenth century. The campaign was part of a broader effort of political reform in British society, and its eventual success resulted in part from the political realignment introduced by the Reform Act. The campaign was led by Richard Cobden, who demonstrated the importance of pragmatic leadership in promoting the ideal of free trade. In 1848 Britain repealed the Corn Laws, which provided high protection in agricultural products, and followed up this action with a series of administrative and diplomatic measures over the next two decades that put free trade into practice. Meanwhile, on the Continent the French free trade movement had sought to convince the government of Louis Napoleon to reciprocate the British move toward free trade that was initiated by the repeal of the Corn Laws. No action was taken until the opportunity arose to incorporate a tariff negotiation in a commercial and political treaty with Great Britain. The Cobden-Chevalier treaty of 1860 resulted, which later helped to open the French market to British manufacturers (Rosecrance 1986).

The European system enjoyed a brief period of liberal commercial exchange that started in the 1830s and lasted until the 1870s. This period was economically dominated by Great Britain. The Napoleonic Wars of the early 1800s had left British manufacturing capabilities unscathed, and following the wars Britain's economic strength allowed it to become the leading creditor country in the world. Britain provided aid and loans to European nations and had large exports of foreign investment, mostly to the United States and British colonies in Asia. In sum, the mid-century period of free trade essentially originated in the domestic politics of Great Britain and spread to the nations of Europe through the mechanism of international commercial treaties. The European commitment to free trade was considerably less enduring than the British, and it turned around quickly in the face of depression after 1870. For the British, however, free trade was the principal commercial policy of the nation until well after the First World War.

Protectionism reasserted itself in Europe as a straightforward response to hard times. Owing to a series of rapid technological improvements in the mid-1850s, the comparative advantage in grain growing shifted decisively to the New World, with the result that grain prices fell sharply in European markets. At the same time, a slump occurred in industrial production, which continued for over two decades in the form of low prices and low return on capital for manufactured products. International competition became severe, and in all countries there were strong pressures for protection against imports. One by one, national governments succumbed to the pressures, and reversed the period of relatively free trade that had been established prior to mid-century. Austria-Hungary raised tariffs in 1876, and Italy followed in 1878. In 1879, Germany shifted to a protectionist policy and so, because of its size in the European economy and its philosophy of nationalism and mercantilism, set a protectionist tone for the overall system. France responded to German protectionism with restrictions of its own, and for its part, the United States continued the protectionism it had pursued throughout the nineteenth century. The United Kingdom, the Low Countries, and Switzerland, however, resisted the move toward higher tariffs, but by the end of the century, the UK was the only major nation practising free trade (Kindleberger 1951).

The depression that began in the 1870s also ushered in a lengthy period of protectionism that never really turned around until after the Second World War. In the early part of the twentieth century, growing nationalism, and then war in 1914, exacerbated the protectionist trend that was already well established in response to the economic conditions of the late 1800s. The war broke up an imperfect but workable equilibrium between internal economic policies, trade, and payments that had existed under the gold standard of the nineteenth century. The war produced enormous dislocation that was even more serious in economic terms than the destruction that had occurred. The results were maladjustments to the free flow of labour, capital, and goods, which created impediments to economic activity that lasted well into the 1920s. But continued war planning also played an important role in the European mentality after 1919. In the realm of economic policy, war planning took the form of mercantilism, and later a bilateralism (that is, a focus on negotiating agreements with individual trade partners rather than through an international organization) inspired by Nazi Germany but copied by many other countries. Both mercantilism and bilateralism were designed to place the interests of the nation ahead of the wider community, and they inevitably took their toll on the economic performance of the overall system. The practice of both mercantilism and bilateralism, like war itself, was an expression of nationalism in economic policy.

The breakdown of the international economic system from war undoubtedly deepened the depression within national economies, and nations made efforts at the international level to repair the damage. Two such efforts stand out. The first was the World Economic Conference of 1927, and the associated Conference on Import and Export Prohibitions and Restrictions (Shonfield 1976). These meetings were aimed at countering the trend toward increased tariffs that was occurring in all countries during the 1920s. Countries initially agreed on a tariff truce and an agreement that would regulate quotas and other restrictions. However, the agreement failed to receive sufficient signatures to become binding, and the tariff truce was later discarded by individual country actions. The second effort was the World Economic Conference of 1933, at which time countries tried to achieve an international currency-stabilization agreement amid wildly fluctuating exchange rates that were perceived to cause significant disruptions to international trade. This plan failed to attract the Americans, and in the wake of the collapsed conference countries engaged in a period of competitive exchange-rate devaluations through the mid-1930s.

Reciprocal Trade Agreements Act of 1934

The United States had emerged from the First World War as the largest trading nation in the world; hence it was likely that domestic events affecting US trade capabilities would have a wide impact on commercial relations in the international system. This was the case with two events of the early 1930s: the Smoot–Hawley tariff of 1930, and the Reciprocal Trade Agreements Act of 1934 (Tasca 1938). The former was the culmination of a trend toward protectionism that had begun in the late nineteenth century. The latter was the beginning of a trend toward liberalism which was interrupted by the Second World War but then continued into the present. These two events were major watersheds in commercial policy, and probably more important than the Second World War because they were economic events originating in the world economic system, rather than being the economic results of upheaval in the international political system.

The Smoot–Hawley Act of 1930 raised US duties to historic levels and increased the scope of tariff coverage as well. The Act was not a dramatic turnabout in protectionism, since US tariffs were already high and all major trading nations were protectionist at that time. Rather, it represented a new level in the long movement by nations toward closing off their economies to foreign imports. In the wake of the Smoot–Hawley tariff and the retaliation by foreign countries that it precipitated, world trade fell by about two-thirds by the mid-1930s. The breakdown of trade after 1930 was alarming to Western governments, but even more alarming was the process that had led to that breakdown. The Smoot–Hawley Act was written in congressional committees that were essentially unable to master the detail that had become inherent in any major tariff legislation. Because of this economic illiteracy, and because of the general sympathy toward protectionism that had been created by the

depression, Congress essentially extended protection to all those groups that demanded it. The spectacle was that of a gross excess of the democratic process and a loss of control over the economy by both the US president and the congressional leadership.

The breakdown of trade took its toll on public sympathy toward protectionism. The tariff became an issue in the presidential election of 1932, and was attacked by Democratic candidate Franklin D. Roosevelt as contributing to the depression. Following his election, Roosevelt appointed Cordell Hull as Secretary of State, a man who was committed to the view that free trade was an essential ingredient in world prosperity and an even more important ingredient in international peace and stability. Hull and his officials began working with Congress to prepare new tariff legislation, and two years later the legislation was enacted under the title Reciprocal Trade Agreements Act (RTAA) of 1934.

The RTAA produced a revolution in US and even international trade policy. The central element of the RTAA was that it empowered the president to lower (or raise) tariffs up to 50 per cent from Smoot–Hawley levels in the course of trade negotiations with other countries. From the standpoint of American politics, the RTAA transferred tariff-setting policy to the presidency, which could organize itself bureaucratically for the task, and away from the Congress, which had ultimately proven incapable of managing the tariff or of discriminating between the many appeals brought by constituents for protection. This transfer substantially increased the control the government exercised over trade policy, and it has been an essential part of the US trade policy structure ever since 1934. From the standpoint of international politics, the RTAA was revolutionary in that it implicitly accepted that setting tariff rates could no longer be exclusively a unilateral policy by a nation state, but was rather a bilateral matter to be settled through negotiation. This action was reminiscent of the efforts by Michel Chevalier in the previous century to use commercial and political negotiation to reduce trade restrictions between France and Britain, and it commenced the changeover from a protectionist trade policy that had existed since the 1870s.

The US government pursued reciprocal trade agreements with other countries as far as economic circumstances after 1934 would allow. By 1939, the United States had concluded twenty-one agreements

Box 4.1 Most-favoured-nation principle (MFN)

The most-favoured-nation principle was introduced into the trade agreements of the 1930s and was incorporated as Article I of the General Agreement on Tariffs and Trade in 1947. It required GATT Contracting Parties to extend to all signatories the benefits of any agreement that it might reach with any other country (that is, the 'most favoured nation') in the GATT. The GATT provided a forum, and a legal regime, within which countries were encouraged to negotiate and to reach agreements to lower tariffs on a reciprocal basis. Normally a country (for example, Great Britain) would conclude such an agreement on a bilateral basis with the principal supplier of a good (for example, an agreement with Canada to lower the tariff on winter boots), but the resulting lowered tariff would be accorded to all countries exporting winter boots to Great Britain. In this example, it would be assumed that Canada might reciprocate by lowering its tariff on another good on which Great Britain was the principal supplier to Canada.

The effect of the MFN principle was to eliminate discrimination between trade partners, for countries in principle were obliged to have one MFN tariff that applied to all other countries, and therefore were prohibited from applying different tariffs on the same product coming from different countries. Non-discrimination introduced the problem of 'free riding' where a country might take unreciprocated benefits from a lowering of tariffs by other countries, but this was regarded as a lesser problem than that caused by overtly discriminatory tariff policies. The overall purpose of MFN and non-discrimination was to create a unified multilateral trading system, and to prevent the international trade system from degenerating into a balkanized system of regional preferences.

which made reductions in about a thousand duties. All agreements were made on a most-favoured-nation (MFN) or non-discriminatory basis, which slowed the negotiation because it engaged more parties, but also for the same reason extended more widely the impact of the agreements. The RTAA agreements were successful in increasing the flow of international trade, but the greatest value of the programme was that it provided a corpus of experience in trade liberalization that became integrated after the Second World War. The act of reaching bilateral agreements gave governments the opportunity to create mechanisms for liberalizing trade, which was demonstrated by the fact that most of the GATT articles drawn up in 1947 were taken from various agreements reached during the previous decade under the RTAA system. For example, the escape clause that became written into Article XIX of the GATT was drawn from an agreement the United States reached with Mexico in 1942.

The reciprocal trade programme was concurrent with a sea change in US and world public opinion regarding protectionism and free trade. In 1930, the passage of the Smoot–Hawley tariff took place in an environment favourable to protectionism, and within a legislative system that encouraged protectionist pressure groups to press their demands vigorously. This can be contrasted with the climate that existed in 1953–4 when the Republican Party under Dwight Eisenhower

reversed its historic policy of protectionism by extending the RTAA of 1934. In the second case, public opinion was much more supportive of free trade, and there was relatively little effective protectionist pressure on the legislators, particularly from the more important economic interest groups in the country (Bauer, Pool, and Dexter 1972). What appeared to have changed, not only in the United States but also elsewhere, was the principle of free trade versus protectionism, or more precisely, the expectations that people held as to which principle was just and would ordinarily prevail as a general rule. This change created a more favourable economic context for the major changes in the world trade regime that occurred after the Second World War.

Key points

- Organized efforts to establish freer trade in Europe began in the middle of the nineteenth century.

- A lengthy period of protectionism was initiated by the world depression that began in the 1870s, and then continued as a result of the world wars and depression of the first half of the twentieth century.

- Efforts to establish a liberal international trading system were begun with the US Reciprocal Trade Agreements Act of 1934.

The ITO and the GATT: 1947 to 1948

Post-war economic situation

The ascendancy of the United States in the early post-war period was immediately evident in the play of international policy making. In terms of security policy, the United States took over the leadership of the Western alliance. The United States enjoyed a preponderant position in the formation of the United Nations and other post-war international organizations. Reconstruction aid to Europe through the Marshall Plan further demonstrated the primacy of the United States in the Western system. In addition, US economic hegemony could be demonstrated by figures representing three important areas of the international economic system, namely international monetary payments, trade, and foreign investment. In 1947, the United States held about 70 per cent of the monetary gold stock of the world. Even a decade later, this figure had not dropped below 59 per cent of the world's stock (Cooper 1968). There was an acute shortage of US dollars over this period, and the dollar itself began to serve as a reserve currency for international payments. Regarding trade, by 1950 the United States accounted for nearly 17 per cent of world trade, and its share was about one and one-half times the share of Great Britain, the next leading nation (Krasner 1976). Through the decade of the 1950s the United States increased its preponderance in world trade. By 1960, US trade was 20 per cent of overall world trade, over twice as large as that of the next leading nation (Great Britain), and roughly equal to the combined total of the three leading European economies, namely Great Britain, France, and West Germany. Finally, with regard to foreign investment, the United States went from an initial accumulated stock of foreign investment of $7 billion in 1946 to over $100 billion in 1973. The latter figure represented 51 per cent of total world foreign investment in that year (*Transnational Corporations* 1978). The second ranking nation in foreign investment in 1973 was the United Kingdom with 13.5 per cent, or about one-quarter of the US total. In sum, all of the major indicators of international economic performance demonstrate that the United States was in a unique position of leadership in the first two decades of the post-war period.

United States leadership rested relatively easily on other Western nations because the security concerns of the Cold War with the Soviets encouraged those nations to be more willing to follow than they might otherwise have been. However, any system in which one nation is dominant is likely to reflect the values of that nation, which was the case of the trade regime set up under the GATT after 1947. One American value that was carried forward to the international system was a relatively liberal pro-business anti-government approach to international trade, which to the Europeans was problematic due to the uncertain circumstances facing European economies after the war and their emphasis on maintaining low levels of unemployment. For the Americans, however, trade liberalization was an attractive goal in ideological terms, and it was also consistent with US national interest, since the United States was favourably positioned to benefit from freer trade.

A second American value was that of multilateralism, which was intended to guarantee non-discrimination between all countries participating in the trade regime. The Americans blamed the 'closed' imperial trading blocs the Europeans created in the inter-war years for the collapse of international trade in that period, and saw in multilateralism a means to remove trade restrictions. However, the Europeans were much more guarded, fearing that their weaker economies would be unable to withstand the strain of multilateral trade liberalization. In the place of multilateralism, the Europeans promoted the virtues of regionalism, which later came to fruition in the forming of the institutions that led to the present-day European Union (EU). Yet another American value was a legal approach to international trade relations, complete with the conception of a code of international trade law backed up by a mechanism for settling disputes between parties. For their part the Europeans were wary of a code approach to international trade relations and sought instead to preserve their right to administrative discretion. They preferred to build a post-war trading system on practice rather than formal legal commitments (Gardner 1969).

The result of the different approaches taken by the United States and its allies is that the trade regime was and has always been based on compromise in the face of policy disagreements. Because of its predominant position, the US approach prevailed in the main on most issues, but the rules that were negotiated were often riven with exceptions that weakened the legitimacy and effectiveness of the regime. It is important when assessing the trade regime to recall that it has always been based on a negotiated consensus, and that in the real world consensus is often only achieved through compromises that are unpalatable to the purists.

The rules of GATT

Led by the United States, the Second World War allies attempted to create a new structure for the international system following the war. An essential part of this attempt was the Bretton Woods Conference of 1944, which established the International Bank for Reconstruction and Development (World Bank) and the International Monetary Fund (IMF). Along with these efforts in the development and monetary fields, the allies met in several conferences to establish the architecture of an international trade regime. To that end, countries concluded and signed an agreement to establish an International Trade Organization (ITO) in 1948, which was to complete the triad of functional organizations in the area of international economic relations. However, the US Congress failed to ratify the agreement, and without US involvement the ITO would have been irrelevant. In place of the ITO, countries relied on the General Agreement on Tariffs and Trade (GATT), which had been established in 1947, to provide structure for the rapidly expanding trade system. The GATT itself was simply a contract embodying trade rules that were negotiated during a multilateral tariff negotiation in 1947. The GATT rules were partly a mechanism to ensure that countries that reduced protection by lowering tariffs did not reinstitute that protection through other measures. The GATT was never intended to function as an international organization. The fact that the GATT came to look and function like an international organization is the result of a largely unplanned and incremental accretion of political and legal powers. It was institution building by accident.

The GATT rules are contained in the thirty-five articles of the General Agreement (Jackson 1969). Perhaps the most important rule was that of non-discrimination, which is found in Articles I and III of the GATT. Article I is known as most-favoured-nation principle (Box 4.1). It required that any advantage—such as a lowered tariff—granted to another contracting party would be immediately accorded to all other contracting parties. This obligation attacked the practice of bilateral tariff preferences, which were commonly employed for political reasons prior to the Second World War, and which compartmentalized and therefore reduced the flow of trade between nations. Another aspect of non-discrimination was found in Article III, which obliged nations to treat foreign products—once they had been imported and duty paid—no less favourably than domestic products in respect to taxes and other requirements. In general, Article I ensured a country could not discriminate externally, and Article III ensured it could not discriminate internally.

The principles of external and internal non-discrimination were not easy to establish in international trade. For example, in the 1930s Article I non-discrimination, or most-favoured-nation treatment, would have required a country like Great Britain to give another country (even Nazi Germany) that did not discriminate against British trade the same tariff preferences it might have negotiated with a third country. This principle had the effect of elevating economics over politics in international relations, and it was the subject of internal debate in Western countries in the years leading up to the Second World War. Similarly, Article III non-discrimination was also difficult for nations to accept because it removed a whole range of policy tools (such as internal taxes or distribution requirements) that governments traditionally used to extend preferential treatment to domestic products.

Non-discrimination continues to be the cornerstone of the international trade system. Article I remains a basic building block of the GATT, and even though it has been somewhat compromised by preferential free trade agreements, nations negotiating those agreements have been careful to ensure that preference arrangements did not introduce new protectionism into the broader system. As for Article III, its relevance is demonstrated by the frequency with which it has been tested in GATT and now World Trade Organization dispute settlement panels. An early example is the 1988 case on Canadian Liquor Board practices, where a panel found that discriminatory mark-up and listing practices by Canadian provincial liquor boards were inconsistent with Canada's obligations to its trading partners under Article III. This decision created pressure for reform of the Canadian practices.

A second important GATT rule was the prohibition in Article XI against quantitative and other non-tariff restrictions to trade (Dam 1970). The theory of the GATT was to delegitimize the use of protectionist measures other than tariffs, hence Article XI contained the stark obligation that 'no restrictions other than duties (that is, tariffs)' shall be maintained on the importation of any product. Article XI is increasingly regarded by trade lawyers as a key constraint on governments. For example, confrontations between trade and environmental concerns are a staple of contemporary trade policy, and Article XI obligations are the crux of this debate, as was illustrated in a 1991 GATT panel decision on tuna. At issue was environmental legislation in the United States which prevented the sale of tuna caught by methods that also kill dolphins, which served as the rationale for a ban on imports of tuna from Mexico. The United States lost the case when the GATT panel determined that the US restrictions violated that nation's obligations to Mexico under Article XI.

A third GATT rule deals with the methodology adopted by the GATT for reducing trade restrictions. This methodology was the sponsorship from time to time of tariff negotiations to be conducted 'on a reciprocal and mutually advantageous basis' and 'directed to the substantial reduction of tariffs' (Article XXVIII bis). The concept of reciprocity is the most interesting aspect of this methodology. Reciprocity can be seen as a normal aspect of negotiation in general, which in international trade has been promoted as a political imperative where nations give tariff reductions in order to get similar benefits from their partners, although economists often deride this concept arguing that it is countries offering tariff reductions that make their economies more efficient and hence realize the benefit. Nevertheless, in the GATT's early history of trade negotiations reciprocity was a guiding beacon as countries began the process of dismantling

tariff protectionism. However, reciprocity as a concept ran into difficulties when developing countries acceded to the GATT. Because it is questionable whether equal treatment of unequal partners in trade negotiations could be considered reciprocal, numerous exceptions from full reciprocity were granted by industrialized GATT partners in favour of developing countries. For example, in various negotiations an attempt was made to mitigate the obligations of GATT membership for developing countries through the concept of 'special and differential treatment'. In the end, the efforts to water down GATT reciprocity for developing countries have produced fairly little in concrete terms, which demonstrates how difficult it is in international trade to depart from the notion of 'equal treatment under the law'. Nevertheless, demands for special treatment are a continuing aspect of the trade regime, as evidenced in the Doha trade negotiations discussed later in this chapter.

Two other basic norms of the GATT are safeguards and the concept of 'commercial considerations'. Safeguards were based on the operational plan of the GATT framers that restrictive measures on trade would be converted to tariff protection, and then tariffs would be reduced through multilateral negotiations. In a situation where tariff reductions created an especially difficult political problem in any contracting party, the GATT also allowed (in Article XIX) for nations to backtrack on their commitments (that is, to raise tariffs) for a period of time to permit orderly adjustment of domestic markets. The intent was to ensure that problems in specific industries did not compromise the general process of liberalization. The fact that the GATT has accommodated itself to protectionist pressures over the years has often been viewed positively by governments and commentators as an example of pragmatism and resilience.

The other rule of 'commercial considerations', or support for the values of the free market versus government interventionism, is implicit in the entire framework of the GATT. The term is mentioned specifically in Article XVII, where state-controlled enterprises are enjoined to act according to 'commercial considerations', and it is implicit in Article XVI, where the harmful effect of subsidies on efficient production is mentioned. Because the GATT represents commercial, free market values, it has been a successful organization in a world that has recently moved in the same direction, and that continues to move in that direction following the dissolution of international communism in the early 1990s.

In sum, the rules of the GATT provided a basis for governance in a narrow, but fundamentally important sector of international relations. In any regime, or even government, the test of the regime is that the rules are understood and that they guide behaviour. Without doubt, the rules of the GATT were known in the main, and they were usually followed by the contracting parties to the Agreement (Hudec 1975).

Key points

- Following the Second World War, the United States was a preponderant presence in the world economy, and took a leadership role in post-war planning.

- Trading nations established the General Agreement on Tariffs and Trade (GATT) in 1947, and attempted in 1948 to create an International Trade Organization (ITO), which failed to receive ratification by the US Congress.

- The GATT obliged importing countries not to discriminate in favour of products coming from one country over another, or in favour of domestic products over foreign products, once the latter had paid any duties required and entered the importing country.

- The principles and rules of the GATT provided a rudimentary basis for the regulation of international trade.

Multilateral trade negotiations: 1950s to 1980s

Post-war negotiations and the Kennedy Round

The main role of the GATT was to liberalize trade, and most decisions to that end were initiated in trade negotiations. The GATT was established to support the trade negotiations in 1947, and following that date the GATT sponsored multilateral negotiations in 1949 (Annecy), 1951 (Torquay), 1956 (Geneva), 1960–1 (the Dillon Round), and in 1963–7 (the Kennedy Round). Further negotiations were the Tokyo Round (1973–9), the Uruguay Round (1986–93), and the WTO Doha 'Round', which was initiated in January 2002, and continues at this writing. Of these nine negotiations in total, the first four after 1947 took up some important institutional matters, such as the accession of new members, but they did not make significant progress in liberalizing trade. One reason is that the European countries relied heavily on non-tariff measures through the mid-1950s and hence any tariff concessions given during GATT negotiations were not meaningful in trade terms. Furthermore, European recovery from the war did not occur as quickly as expected, as evidenced by the fact that European currencies were not made fully convertible until 1958, which made it difficult for these countries to increase their exposure to international competition. In practice, the United States was the preponderant actor in the early negotiations and offered most of the tariff concessions.

The GATT incorporated the bilateral negotiation process established by the RTAA, and simply multilateralized it (Diebold 1952). However, this change was not accomplished in one stroke. The early GATT tariff negotiations were multilateral in name, but in fact the real action occurred bilaterally between nations that served as principal suppliers and principal consumers of each other's products. Bilateral agreements were then multilateralized automatically through the most-favoured-nation principle. If a country were to, say, halve its tariff of 10 per cent on Country A's widgets following bilateral negotiations with A, it would be obliged to extend the new tariff of 5 per cent on all imports of widgets from any other GATT contracting party. Nations could, and often did, remain aloof from the bilateral negotiating process, while nevertheless taking advantage—as free riders—of reductions concluded by other nations. Over time, the emphasis in the GATT shifted from the negotiation of tariff reductions to the negotiation of legal codes of behaviour. The latter negotiations are more fully multilateral, and are carried out in a process reminiscent of domestic parliamentary legislation, with a structured committee process leading to decisions in broader forums.

The Kennedy Round of 1963–7 emerged as the first significant negotiation in GATT after the initial negotiation in 1947 (Preeg 1970). It led to an average tariff reduction among the participants of about 35 per cent, in sharp contrast to the reduction of less than 10 per cent on a much smaller volume of trade in the Dillon Round that preceded it, or even the 20 per cent reduction achieved in the negotiation of 1947. The negotiation also produced an anti-dumping code designed to help standardize national policies in this difficult and contentious area, and as well an international grain agreement that established price ranges for wheat and provided for multilateral sharing of food aid to developing countries. The Kennedy Round was, moreover, the first GATT negotiation at which the nations of the European Community (EC) participated as a single unit, which was the first time Europe and America engaged in a major negotiation across the Atlantic on an apparent basis of equality and reciprocity. It is interesting to note the historical correlation between a successful outcome in trade negotiation and the increasing equality of the major actors in those negotiations, for it is a trend that continued through the Kennedy Round and on into the Tokyo Round of the 1970s.

Apart from the economic results of the Kennedy Round, there were important political results that flowed from the successful completion of this major negotiation. The negotiation of trade liberalization in GATT was always a continuing struggle between liberalizing and protectionist forces. Those governments favouring liberalization have used negotiation, especially multilateral negotiation, as the principal means to free trade from protectionist restrictions. Those favouring protectionism have been more ascendant, and more effective, between major trade negotiations. This increased the salience and importance of any given negotiation over time because there would be an increasing number of policy issues riding on the outcome. Thus, the pressure at the Kennedy Round to reach an acceptable settlement was increased, and ensured that any deadlock would constitute a failure that would go beyond the issues at the table.

Box 4.2 Dumping and anti-dumping duties

Dumping in international trade is generally understood as selling a product into another country less than it sells for in the exporting country. Dumping is more precisely defined in Article VI of the GATT as exporting below the 'normal value' of a product, meaning the price the product would fetch in the exporter's market, or alternatively the costs of producing the product. Dumping is 'condemned' by the GATT if it causes injury to a domestic industry producing a 'like product' in the importing country. In the event a product is dumped and causes injury, as determined by an anti-dumping investigation conducted by the government of the importing country, the importing country can impose an 'anti-dumping duty' (that is, an additional tariff) equal to the margin of dumping, that is, the difference between the normal value of the product and its export price.

In plain terms, dumping amounts to underselling, which is acceptable competitive behaviour within countries, but which in the politically sensitive terrain of international commerce is generally considered objectionable. Anti-dumping actions are widely sought after by import-competing industries as a convenient means of protection against foreign competitors, especially since trade laws in most countries make it relatively easy to establish a case against foreign dumping. As a result, there has been a sharp increase in the incidence of anti-dumping actions by GATT and WTO Members since the 1980s. However, anti-dumping duties themselves can be viewed as a harassing and objectionable impediment on legitimate trade, and consequently countries have negotiated Anti-Dumping Codes in the Kennedy, Tokyo, and Uruguay Rounds designed to discipline the actions governments can take to protect domestic industries from foreign dumping. To sum up, national legislation and international treaties on dumping and anti-dumping duties can be traced back to the beginning of the twentieth century, and these practices have been perhaps the most highly litigious and politicized area of the trade regime since its inception.

The upshot was that the Kennedy Round took on enormous importance as a symbol as it went along. It became a test of the national will of the major participants to continue the post-war trend toward trade liberalization. Even more important, it was a test of the willingness of nations to avoid a breakdown that would lead to increased protectionism. The main reason the Kennedy Round succeeded is that governments feared what the implications of failure might mean for the international economic system, and because they wanted to avoid blame for causing such implications. In a strict sense, of course, it is clear that a deadlock in the Kennedy Round would have meant only that nations did not agree to reduce tariffs or other restrictions; this would have had no necessary consequences for increased protectionism. However, the situation did not get framed in such terms. The political reality was that nations felt under great pressure to avoid a breakdown of a dialogue that had extended for five years and of a settlement that would help structure trading relations in the foreseeable future. Among these general concerns, the positions delegations took on individual tariffs or products ultimately became less important. Thus the main political result of the Kennedy Round was the achievement of the agreement itself, especially since the agreement was significant in trade terms.

Tokyo Round

At the close of the Kennedy Round in 1967, the GATT secretariat led by Director-General Sir Eric Wyndham-White sought to convince the major trading nations to extend liberalization into the area of non-tariff barriers to trade (NTBs) (Evans 1971). This early effort was unsuccessful, but by the early 1970s chaos in the international monetary system and increasing use of non-tariff barriers in response to the surge of exports from Japan and the newly industrializing economies (NIEs) resurrected fears of trade protectionism and convinced national governments to commence a new negotiation in the GATT. This negotiation, named after the city in which it was initiated, started slowly because of the need to gather and classify enormous amounts of trade data respecting NTBs. The negotiation was further delayed by the need for the United States to pass legislation authorizing the president to negotiate, an event which was not completed until January 1975, and as well by the US election of 1976. The negotiation effectively got under way in 1977, and comprehensive offers from delegations were in place by early 1978. Serious bargaining took place during the following year, and in April of 1979 the final agreements were signed, subject to later ratification.

The agreements reached at the Tokyo Round were the most comprehensive and far-reaching results achieved in trade negotiations since the creation of the GATT in 1947 (Winham 1986). The results fell in three categories: six legal codes (plus a sectoral code for trade in aircraft) that dealt with NTBs; tariff reductions; and a series of revisions of GATT articles primarily of interest to developing countries. The six codes updated and expanded aspects of the trade law of the GATT, and were the most important part of the Tokyo Round accords. These covered respectively customs valuation procedures, import licensing, technical standards for products, subsidies and countervailing duty measures, government procurement, and anti-dumping duty procedures. However, negotiations on a safeguards code failed.

The general thrust of the code negotiations was to effect a 'constitutional reform' of GATT law, and as well to improve the openness, certainty, and non-arbitrariness of the rules governing international trade. In some areas this was accomplished without appreciable controversy. In codes on customs valuation, import licensing, and technical barriers, nations proceeded from the widely shared philosophy that government regulations in those areas should not be used to provide protection for domestic producers, either through design or otherwise. In other areas, agreement was more problematic. The attempted code on Article XIX safeguards encountered a determined insistence by the European Commission on the right to apply safeguards selectively on a targeted basis, rather than non-discriminatorily or across the board. Selectivity was especially resisted by the developing countries, which would be the primary targets of this tactic. Also, the code on subsidies and countervailing duties triggered deeply held disagreements between the United States and the Commission over the appropriateness of agricultural export subsidies in modern government practice, but in the end this disagreement was reconciled by limiting the actions taken on agriculture and the code was signed.

The second category of results from the Tokyo Round was tariff reductions. To put these results in perspective, tariff negotiations were the main item of business in the six multilateral negotiations that were held under GATT auspices through the Kennedy Round of 1967. Tariffs were not the major focus of the Tokyo Round, yet the average reductions of about 35 per cent of industrial nations' tariffs achieved in this negotiation were very comparable to the reductions of the Kennedy Round. The reductions covered more than $100 billion of imports, and were phased in over an eight-year period which began in 1980 (Cline 1983).

A major controversy in the tariff negotiation was to arrive at a tariff-cutting formula for manufactured products. A similar controversy had occurred in the Kennedy Round, at which time nations settled on a linear approach (50 per cent cut across the board, less exceptions) supported mainly by the United States. In the Tokyo Round, proponents of a tariff-harmonizing formula carried the day, and nations agreed to table offers according to a compromise 'Swiss' formula that generally required tariff cuts to be proportional to the size of the tariff. The final bargaining produced a number of exceptions to the general formula, particularly in industries where imports were already high and 'sensitive' domestic interests were threatened. For example, in the United States, where the average tariff cut was 31 per cent, the duties for leather imports were reduced by only 4 per cent; for apparel, 15 per cent; for automobiles, 16 per cent; and tariffs for footwear and colour televisions were exempted from any cuts whatsoever. Similar exceptions were made by other trading nations as well.

The third category of Tokyo Round results was a proposed series of revisions to GATT Articles known as the 'framework' agreements. Negotiations on this subject were initiated by Brazil, and were intended to clarify GATT obligations and ease those obligations for developing countries. The framework agreements covered subjects such as safeguard actions for development purposes (or infant industry measures), trade measures taken to correct payments deficits, export controls, and deviations from most-favoured-nation procedures for developing countries. One important accord in the framework package was the Understanding regarding Notification, Consultation, Dispute Settlement, and Surveillance, which required GATT members to notify trading partners of the trade measures they adopt, and thus to provide early warning for all countries of actions that might adversely affect their interests. The framework agreements did not substantially rewrite GATT law to advantage developing countries, and as a result many of those countries felt the results were 'frustrating and incomplete' (*Multilateral Trade* 1979: 34). However, the agreements did improve GATT language on matters related to developing countries, and therefore probably improved the capacity of the GATT legal machinery to mediate and reduce trade disputes.

The Tokyo Round underscored the extent to which multilateral negotiation had become a point of departure for managing the international trade system. In contrast with past GATT negotiations, which were largely limited to the reduction of tariffs, the Tokyo Round was a rule-making exercise of major proportions. Furthermore, the agreements of the Tokyo Round constituted legal rules that reached further into the nation state and impacted more deeply on individual human behaviour than usually occurred with most international agreements. The process of negotiating these rules was extraordinarily complex, and arguably the code negotiations of the Tokyo Round were the most advanced, in terms of bureaucratic complexity, of any multilateral negotiations occurring at that time. The greatest complexity lay in attempting to integrate the conflicting trade legislation of many nations into a coordinated set of international rules. In their efforts to mesh the rule-making apparatus of different countries into a single structure, the Tokyo Round negotiators faced problems that became commonplace a decade later as nations coped with the implications of an increasingly interdependent world.

Key points

- Multilateral trade negotiations were conducted in the GATT to reduce tariff protectionism on a reciprocal basis.

- In the Tokyo Round (1973–9), countries focused on the more difficult task of reducing non-tariff measures that afforded protection in international trade. These measures were regulated through the negotiation of international codes of behaviour.

- The Tokyo Round demonstrated the importance of multilateral negotiation to the management of the international trade system.

The Uruguay Round and the WTO: 1986 to 1994

Background

The next major effort to further establish the world trade regime was the Uruguay Round negotiation, which was launched at a GATT ministerial meeting in Punta del Este, Uruguay, in September 1986 (Croome 1995). The path to the Uruguay Round was difficult indeed. The previous GATT multilateral negotiation had made considerable progress in reducing protectionism from non-tariff barriers. Pressure began to build shortly after 1979 to expand the GATT regime to include new issues, such as services, investment, and intellectual property, in addition to the old issues which dealt with trade in goods. Especially the United States argued that a new negotiation was necessary to make the GATT relevant to a changing world economy, and in 1982 a GATT ministerial meeting was convened to consider this possibility. The idea met sharp resistance, particularly from developing countries that were overwhelmed by the global debt crisis and mainly concerned to expand traditional exports to developed countries to service debt obligations to the International Monetary Fund, Western governments, and private banks. Led by India and Brazil, the developing countries insisted that they were not sufficiently developed to negotiate the new issues such as services, on an equal footing with the developed countries. Moreover, developing countries held that the developed countries had evaded their obligations in some of the traditional goods, such as textiles or agricultural products, which were of particular importance to developing countries, and they demanded further liberalization in these areas as a precondition to any new negotiations. The result was that the 1982 ministerial meeting was a failure for the proponents of new negotiations, although the meeting did establish important work programmes that generated the data needed for future negotiation.

The most dramatic part of the lead-up to the Uruguay Round negotiation came in the week-long special ministerial session at Punta del Este in September 1986 (Winham 1998a). At the eleventh hour, it was agreed between the Americans and the Indians that the session would launch negotiations on a range of issues, including services, but that negotiations on services would be undertaken in a separate structure from those on goods, which presumably would lessen the prospects that developed countries could force trade-offs between services and the traditional subjects in the negotiation. Once the breakthrough on services occurred, it was clear that the remaining issues were not worth holding up the prospect for a new negotiation, and settlement quickly followed on investment and intellectual property, which had also been major sticking points between the developed and developing countries.

New issues

The agenda of the Uruguay Round comprised fifteen negotiating groups arranged initially in four principal categories: market access (including the critical areas of agriculture and textiles); reform of GATT rules; measures to strengthen the GATT as an institution; and the new issues, specifically services, investment, and intellectual property (Preeg 1995). The new issues were included in the negotiation in order to make the GATT more relevant to the developments occurring in the world economy. By the late 1980s, services had come to account for well over half of the Gross Domestic Product of developed countries, and they were beginning to account for an increasing proportion of international trade. For the GATT, the incorporation of services was not a straightforward matter. Services are not goods, which had always been the focus of GATT rules, but rather are processes in which skills and knowledge are exchanged in order to meet a particular consumer need. They can include processes as widely differentiated as engineering consulting, financial intermediation, tourism, or legal advice. Services often require the movement of the factors of production (for example, the establishment of a bank branch on a foreign country to sell financial services), a condition which is constantly affected by changes in technology that decrease the barrier separating non-traded from traded services. For its part, the GATT had identified many services as 'non-traded goods', although this

Box 4.3 **Uruguay Round Agreements**

The GATT Multilateral Trade Negotiation known as the Uruguay Round began in September 1986, effectively concluded in December 1993, and formally concluded with official signatures at the Marrakesh (Morocco) Ministerial Meeting in April 1994. The Uruguay Round produced a wide range of agreements integrated under a common legal system. What is usually thought of as the 'WTO system' is contained in the Marrakesh Agreement Establishing the World Trade Organization and the Dispute Settlement Understanding. The WTO Agreement established the WTO as an international organization, and ensured that all the agreements negotiated at the Uruguay Round were accepted as a single undertaking, thus increasing the legal integration of the WTO trade regime. The dispute settlement system established by the DSU was also intended to apply to all areas of the Uruguay Round Agreements, hence it is an integral part of the architecture of the new WTO system.

The Uruguay Round Agreements comprise about sixty agreements totalling some 550 pages, covering subjects as widely diversified as agriculture, safeguards, trade in intellectual property, rules of origin, textiles and clothing, and technical barriers to trade. These agreements can be accessed on the WTO website **www.wto.org** under the title 'Legal Texts of the WTO Agreements'. In addition, the Uruguay Round Agreements also included the General Agreement on Tariffs and Trade 1994, which effectively incorporated the GATT of 1947 into the WTO system. There were some additional agreements interpreting various provisions of the GATT, such as the meaning of 'other duties and charges' in Article II which covers tariff schedules, but there is historical and legal continuity from the basic rules and provisions of the GATT to the modern WTO trade regime.

characterization was dropped and services became recognized as an integral part of the international economy. There are many obstacles that can prevent a free exchange of services between countries, but a main one is the reluctance of domestic authorities to grant foreign firms the right to establish and do business in their markets. Such a refusal may be motivated by protectionist impulses, but it may also be inspired, for example in the case of prudential banking legislation, by a desire to protect the consumer who is often viewed as being at a disadvantage with respect to the foreign service provider.

Because countries have different regulatory objectives and standards, the result is that the global services market is essentially protectionist. GATT principles required non-discrimination among trade partners, national treatment of foreign suppliers and transparency in the process by which domestic rules are developed, but the provision of services often requires the opposite behaviour if the consumer is to be protected and provided with a reliable and quality service. Governments generally seek to provide consistent regulation over their own markets; again, arguably this may require discrimination against trade partners that apply different standards to trade in services. Because services are processes, defining them is difficult unless a strict functional definition is

employed. The stricter the definition, however, the greater the chances that discrimination will occur. Yet, without strict definitions, domestic regulation may be more easily circumvented.

The tasks for the negotiators at the Uruguay Round were to incorporate GATT principles of transparency, national treatment and reciprocity, as well as newer principles such as market access, into an area of trade that was conceptually dissimilar from trade in goods, which was the normal milieu of GATT principles and practice (Arup 2000). Given the paucity of information on trade in services, the first task was to develop a common data base on which substantive decisions could later be made. Second, a code of principles (which later became known as the General Agreement on Trade in Services—GATS) would have to be negotiated that provided for a standard of treatment between countries of trade in services. Finally, the code of principles would have to be applied to specific sectors of services trade. To do this, negotiators needed to analyse existing measures that restricted trade in services in order to propose measures that would liberalize trade in specific services sectors.

The two other new issues on the Uruguay Round agenda were investment and intellectual property. Investment was included because by the 1980s it had become apparent that investment was interchangeable with trade, and, more important, that trade liberalization may be less valuable in stimulating international economic exchanges unless it is accompanied by liberalization of investment regimes. However, investment has always attracted considerable regulation in importing countries because of the risk to sovereignty associated with high levels of foreign investment in sensitive industries. In the Uruguay Round, the negotiation of a multilateral investment agreement eventually proved an unreachable goal, and the agreement that was reached on Trade-Related Investment Measures (TRIMS) dealt only with a small proportion of the issues raised in the negotiation.

Trade-Related Intellectual Property, better known as TRIPS, was the third of the new issues. Intellectual property rights grant state protection to producers of new ideas, but this protection was not well established in the international economy (Maskus 2000). Negotiations in the Uruguay Round began by addressing the problem of counterfeit goods in international trade, but developed countries—which asserted that inadequate protection of intellectual property rights was a serious non-tariff barrier to trade—quickly pressed for a broader negotiation over patents and copyrights. Developing countries, led by India and Brazil, viewed TRIPS protection as a potential barrier to trade in its own right, but they were more concerned over the monopolies effectively granted in developed countries for products like pharmaceuticals which they considered crucial to the public interest. The developing countries acquiesced on this issue because they felt their losses were compensated by gains elsewhere in the overall accord, and an agreement was concluded that set international standards for certain protections dealing with copyrights and patents (Winham 1998*a*). However, the controversy over the TRIPS Agreement continued as a mainstay of WTO politics, as developing countries saw intellectual property rights as a mechanism by which developed countries could maintain a competitive edge relative to countries that lacked a sophisticated technological infrastructure.

Developing countries

For most of the history of the GATT, the developing countries have been marginal players. The GATT itself was mainly a creation of the United States and its Western allies, and it mainly focused on trade rather than economic development, which was the central concern of the poorer countries of Africa, Asia, and South America. In terms of trade policy, most developing countries pursued a policy of import substitution industrialization (ISI), which called for high protective tariffs to force consumers to purchase domestic-made products at the expense of imports. These policies encouraged developing country governments to pursue trade policies of self-sufficiency, and to seek 'special and differential' benefits in GATT negotiations in lieu of accepting the multilateral rules of the GATT based on reciprocity. The upshot was that as the GATT system matured, it became clear that one of the major threats to that system was its inability to be relevant to traders and governments in countries representing over two-thirds of the world's population. This threat was largely overcome in the Uruguay Round negotiation, for one of the results of the negotiation was that for the first time developing countries became fully integrated into the world trade regime.

The developing countries did not support the initiation of the Uruguay Round. Led by India and Brazil, they insisted they were not sufficiently developed to negotiate the new issues such as services on an equal footing with the developed countries. Also, they argued that developed countries had not honoured their past commitment in traditional goods such as textiles or agriculture, and that further liberalization in these areas would be a precondition to any new negotiation. However, once developing countries relented and agreed to negotiate, they quickly engaged in all issues before the negotiation. As the negotiation wore on, it became clear that the capacity to determine the outcome of the Uruguay Round fell mainly to the two major trading powers, the United States and the European Union. At this point, a curious change took place: the major powers that had been so insistent on a new negotiation reached a deadlock largely over agriculture, while the developing countries that had fought so hard against a new negotiation for most of the 1980s became the greatest advocates for its successful conclusion in the early 1990s. From 1991 until the conclusion in December 1993, the developing countries kept the pressure on the majors to settle their differences, which was an important element in the multilateral agreement that was eventually reached.

The turnabout in the developing countries' position was one of the most interesting stories of the Uruguay Round (Winham 1998*a*). It occurred, first, because developing countries were advantaged by two negotiating principles that underlay the Uruguay Round, namely, consensus and the single undertaking. Single undertaking meant that all issues of the negotiation were treated as a single package with no exceptions, unlike the Tokyo Round where agreements were signed on a plurilateral (or pick and choose) basis with the result that countries were subject to differing rights and obligations. Consensus—which was a traditional GATT principle—meant that multilateral agreement required the passive support (that is, no formal opposition) of all participants. These principles combined to increase the power of small and middle powers at the Uruguay Round, which was dramatically demonstrated at the 1988 ministerial meeting in Montreal when five Latin American countries withheld consensus from an interim package agreement because their concerns over agriculture were not being met by the major countries. This action emboldened the developing countries, and led them to take greater interest in the overall negotiation.

Second, despite the reality that developing countries continued to be economically disadvantaged in comparison to developed countries, the agreements reached at the Uruguay Round were favourable to the interests of the former. Developing countries as a group benefited from agreements on agriculture, textiles, and clothing and probably services, while they likely lost on intellectual property and anti-dumping practices. Most important, however, developing countries were advantaged by the institutional arrangements resulting from the Uruguay Round Agreements, namely the strong dispute settlement mechanism and the creation of the World Trade Organization itself. On balance, these advantages encouraged the developing countries to support the Round.

Finally, and most important, the market-based economic reforms that took place in many developing countries in the 1980s encouraged their governments to look more favourably on the market-based principles and objectives of the GATT. That these changes were concurrent with pressures to liberalize economies from Western countries and international financial institutions is undeniable, but in the end the fall of communism and the obvious success of certain free market countries like Singapore or Taiwan led to an internal policy revolution in many countries. For example, India suffered a severe financial crisis in 1991, following which it took reforms designed to

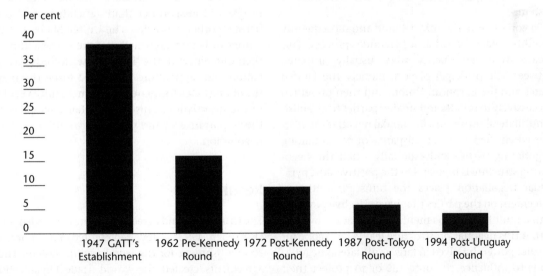

Fig. 4.1 Average industrial tariffs in developed countries since 1947

Source: Department of Trade and Industry, UK, **www.dti.gov.uk/expenditure/pdf/chapter_8.pdf**

deregulate the national economy and increase its economic efficiency. In the wake of these domestic reforms, India revised its negotiating strategy at the Uruguay Round from opposition to support for a multilateral agreement. In India and in many other developing countries, the impact of internal reform was to increase the congruence between domestic policies and the principles of the international trade regime (see Figure 4.1).

The United States and the European Union

The structure of the contemporary international trade regime is mainly centred around the US–EU bilateral relationship (Bergsten 1999). However, this was not always the case. Until the early 1960s, the United States held preponderant position in relation to other members of the GATT, and in multilateral negotiations it offered most of the concessions and expected little in return from other countries. This situation began to change in the Kennedy Round when the six European Common Market countries negotiated as a single bloc. The change was largely completed by the Tokyo Round, when the European Community (now the European Union) had expanded to include the United Kingdom, making the EC the largest trading entity in the international system.

Negotiations in the Tokyo Round and subsequently could be characterized as a pyramidal process. This means that agreements were usually initiated between the principal players, namely the United States and the European Union, and then presented successively to middle and smaller parties to establish a multilateral consensus. Pyramidal negotiation operates when there is a wide disparity of power among negotiating parties and especially when the negotiating structure is bipolar. On the positive side, pyramidal negotiation places the onus for initiating agreement on the parties that have effective power to veto a multilateral agreement. A drawback, however, is that this negotiation structure leaves less scope for smaller powers involved in large multilateral negotiations to influence the outcome or to protect their particular interests. As a result, criticism from smaller actors, including especially developing countries, is endemic in multilateral trade negotiations.

The negotiation over agriculture in the Uruguay Round offered a good example of pyramidal negotiation. At the outset of the negotiation, a group of approximately fourteen agricultural exporters from among the developed and developing countries formed under Australian leadership to promote the liberalization of global agricultural markets. Known as the Cairns Group, these countries played an important role in the early stages of the negotiation in bridging the differences between the United States and European Union over agricultural trade. However, by January 1992 it became clear that the Uruguay Round was blocked, and that the reason was the agricultural negotiation between the majors. Agricultural trade had long been a difficult problem for many countries in the GATT system, but in the Uruguay Round the inherent problems of agriculture became compounded because this issue pitted the interests of the United States and European Union against one another. The US–EU differences stemmed mainly from the fact that since the 1960s Europe had established a protectionist policy under the Common Agricultural Policy (CAP), while the United States was moving toward a comparative advantage in agricultural exports. The Uruguay Round thus turned into a politicized contest between the majors, and for eighteen months the main activity of the multilateral negotiation was a series of bilateral encounters between US and EU officials. This blockage halted progress in areas other than agriculture, and even between other countries. The United States and the European Union eventually reached a resolution of their differences in the 'Blair House' accords on agriculture, but agriculture continued to be the major stumbling block to a general agreement until very late in the negotiation. This whole affair re-emphasized the importance of the majors in multilateral trade negotiation.

Results

The Uruguay Round agreements were concluded on 15 December 1993. They represented an enormous accomplishment for the world trading system. These agreements created the World Trade Organization, which represented institutional progress in that the WTO is a formally constituted international organization and not—as the GATT was—mainly a contract over trade rules between countries. The WTO had enormous symbolic importance for the world trade regime, but it also had practical significance as well. Internally, the WTO and the Uruguay Round agreements provided for clearer rules on trade, and reduced the fragmentation and inconsistency that had existed between various GATT-sponsored agreements. Externally, the WTO reinforced the role of trade in international economic relations, and it permitted trade concerns to be more fully represented in relations with the World Bank and the International Monetary Fund.

Second, the various agreements reached at the Uruguay Round greatly expanded the rules of the international trade system. New issues like services were brought under multilateral rules for the first time, while old issues like agriculture and textiles which long had been essentially outside GATT disciplines were brought under multilateral rules, thereby beginning the lengthy process of reducing protectionism in two sectors that had long resisted the progression toward a more liberal world trade regime (Paarlberg 1997). Third, the Uruguay Round agreements were accepted by the developing countries engaged in the negotiation, and they represented the most far-reaching commitments those countries had made in the international trade regime. Effectively, they brought the developing countries into that regime. The Uruguay Round concluded at a time when many developing countries were undergoing

substantial liberalization, and the confluence of change in the developing world and the deepening of the multilateral regime will engage trade more fully in the progress toward international development.

Finally, the Uruguay Round agreements represented a further step toward a system based on rules instead of power in international trade. The agreements advanced the rules-based nature of trade relations between countries, and thereby increased the economic security of smaller and middle countries in their relations with larger powers. In particular, the agreements established a formal, integrated dispute settlement system to replace the largely ad hoc mechanism that had evolved under the GATT. The agreements created an obligation for countries to adjudicate an issue if a trading partner seeks this recourse. Conversely, countries are obligated not to use unilateral trade sanctions as an alternative to multilateral dispute settlement actions under the WTO. Both provisions were intended to increase the prospects that countries regardless of their size and power would be equal before the law in trade disputes.

Key points

- Developing countries resisted efforts by developed countries to establish a new GATT negotiation following the Tokyo Round.

Table 4.1 Results of GATT negotiations: 1960–94

Negotiation	No. of countries	Results
Dillon Round 1960–1	26	• Average tariff cut of 10% on $4.9 bn of trade
Kennedy Round 1963–7	62	• Average tariff cut of 35% on $40 bn of trade • Anti-dumping code
Tokyo Round 1973–9	102	• Average tariff cut of 35% on more than $100 bn of trade • Six codes dealing with non-tariff measures, plus aircraft code • Revision of GATT articles for developing countries
Uruguay Round 1986–94	128	• Average tariff cut of 39% on $3.7 tr of trade • 12 Agreements (including Agriculture, Textiles, Subsidies, Safeguards) • New issues: Agreements on Trade in Services (GATS) and Trade Related Intellectual Property (TRIPS) • Dispute Settlement Understanding • Numerous other agreements

- The Uruguay Round (1986–93) comprised a lengthy negotiating agenda, including new issues such as trade in services and trade-related intellectual property (TRIPS).
- The most difficult issue in the Uruguay Round was trade in agriculture, particularly between the major parties, the European Union and the United States.

- The Uruguay Round was an enormous accomplishment for the international trade system. International rules were established in most important areas of international trade, the World Trade Organization (WTO) was created, and a more effective dispute settlement system was established. The developing countries became full participants in the WTO system.

The WTO in action: 1995 and beyond

The structure of the WTO

The WTO was created as part of the results of the Uruguay Round negotiations that concluded on 15 December 1993, and it came into existence on 1 January 1995. Also included in the Uruguay Round results were a series of agreements that established rules dealing with agriculture, services, textiles and clothing, intellectual property, as well as a number of other issues related to trade. These agreements advanced substantially the rules-based nature of the trade regime originally established under the GATT. As the late Professor Raymond Vernon (1995: 330) observed shortly after the conclusion of the Uruguay Round, 'The agreements, if taken at their face value, show promise of reshaping trade relationships throughout the world.' This statement surely reflects the stunning accomplishment of the negotiation, which was all the more remarkable given the low expectations held at the start of the round.

The WTO portion of the Uruguay Round agreements created an unusual international organization. Most international organizations have specified procedures for making decisions in the name of the collectivity, but instead the WTO continued many of the consensual practices of the GATT. Essentially the WTO represented a contract between its members, the purpose of which was to establish trade rules and then to back up those rules with a powerful dispute settlement system. To understand the WTO, it is necessary to examine important legal elements drawn from the WTO Agreement and the Dispute Settlement Understanding (DSU).

At the outset, the WTO Agreement explicitly established a new international organization which was to provide symbolic visibility and permanence for international trade policy in the international system (Jackson 1998). The WTO was vested with legal personality, which the GATT did not have, and which placed the WTO on the same footing as other organizations like the IMF or World Bank. The WTO Agreement further stated the WTO should be the 'common institutional framework' for trade relations among its members, and that it should 'facilitate the implementation' of the various Uruguay Round Agreements. These provisions were important in that they centralized the governance of the trade system far more than had existed under the GATT. By comparison, the GATT in the 1990s was rapidly becoming a pot-pourri of decentralized separate agreements, which risked creating a watering down of the central obligations of the trade regime.

Second, the WTO Agreement provided that members would accept the WTO and the various other Agreements as a single piece, and would be obliged to bring their domestic laws into conformity with those Agreements. This commitment incorporated the well-known concept of 'single undertaking' that crystallized during the Uruguay Round negotiation. The single undertaking meant that countries were not free to pick and choose among the various agreements as in the Tokyo Round, but were required to accept and implement the agreements as a package deal. This stratagem insured that negotiators would make trade-offs in arriving at their final offers in the negotiation, and it also helped to clarify the obligations of members in the implementation stage that followed.

Third, the WTO Agreement provided for institutional structure and decision-making procedures for the new organization, which was more complex than the GATT had been to take account of the greater complexity of the subject matter in the Uruguay Round Agreements. On one point however the WTO continued the practice of the GATT, namely in the provision of decision making by consensus. The WTO Agreement in Article IX defined consensus as existing 'if no Member, present at the meeting when the decision is taken, formally objects to the proposed decision'. This procedure meant that the WTO would continue mainly as a contract organization that would not create obligations for individual countries beyond those it had accepted under the consensual decision-making practices of the WTO.

As for the Dispute Settlement Understanding, it is first necessary to note that the Uruguay Round negotiators were aware they were creating a vast addition to international trade laws, and they further recognized a legal system needed to be backed up with judicial procedures in order for the laws to have any practical impact. In practical terms, this meant that WTO members embroiled in a dispute with another member should have a right to proceed to a judicial process, and that the result of that process should be (legally) binding on the parties. The DSU provided for this basic right, and its significance can be appreciated by the fact that similar rights are practically non-existent in international law.

The practice of dispute settlement was begun on a customary basis under the GATT, and certain procedures, such as the establishment of adjudicatory panels to hear cases, were well in place prior to the creation of the WTO. The WTO's DSU improved the system in a number of particulars. First, whereas the GATT had required the consent of both parties for a panel to be established (thereby allowing the party complained against to quash the panel procedure), the DSU provides in Article 6 that: 'If the complaining party so requests, a panel shall be established . . .'. Furthermore, for the panel decision to become legally binding (or 'adopted' by the Council, the plenary body of the GATT's Contracting Parties), the GATT required consensus of all parties, meaning that the party that lost the case would have to acquiesce if the report were to be adopted. This procedure was not as meaningless as it might seem for dispute settlement was a valued concept

under the GATT, and consensual adoptions were the normal outcome of disputed cases. Nevertheless, GATT practice was an example of weak law, which was strengthened under the DSU by the requirement that a panel report would be adopted unless members decided by consensus *not* to adopt the report. This meant that a winning party would have to oppose adoption if the report was to be rejected, which is unlikely; hence the DSU rules virtually provide that panel reports are automatically binding (Palmeter and Mavroidis 1999).

Second, the DSU strengthened the scope and mechanics of dispute settlement in the WTO. An Appellate Body was established to improve the consistency of legal decision making. The coverage of dispute settlement was extended to all areas of the Uruguay Round Agreements, which provides for an integrated legal system and removes the competition that previously existed between differing dispute settlement mechanisms. Finally, the DSU makes it obligatory for Members engaged in a dispute to use the WTO system and not resort to unilateral measures as done in the past to settle the matter themselves. Taken in sum, the DSU represented an extraordinary step forward in the application of legal principles and methods in international law. That it would happen in the trade regime is an indicator of how much that regime has become governed by rules established in multilateral negotiations.

The WTO as an organization

The WTO is most accurately described as a formally contracted body of rules backed up by a judicial system and a minimum of political structure (Winham 1998b). The GATT, which was mainly a contract between parties, had provided for the possibility of joint organizational action by the 'Contracting Parties', but such actions were not emphasized in the General Agreement. By contrast, the WTO Agreement outlines a number of specific functions to be taken by the WTO as a collective body. These include: the implementation and administration of the Uruguay Round Agreements; maintenance of a forum for further negotiations; administration of the dispute settlement system; administration of the Trade Policy Review Mechanism (TPRM); and liaison with the World Bank and the IMF. With the exception of liaison with international financial institutions, these functions had been first established under the GATT on a customary basis.

The principal structures established to carry out the functions of the WTO are a Ministerial Conference meeting every two years; a General Council, which is a continuation of the Council of the GATT, and which can also meet as a Dispute Settlement Body and TPRM Review Body; and three councils in the area of goods, services, and intellectual property. Various other organs are mandated in the WTO Agreement, such as the Committee on Trade and Development, and additional bodies can be created by the Ministerial Conference as it deems necessary.

The WTO Agreement provided for a secretariat, which in the GATT had developed on an informal and customary basis. The WTO secretariat is small compared to the tasks it is expected to perform, and it is certainly small in relation to other international economic organizations. For example, in 1996, the complete staff of the WTO numbered 513, whereas comparable figures for the World Bank and the International Monetary Fund were 6,781 and 2,577 respectively (Blackhurst 1998). This same research showed that the WTO personnel numbers were exceeded by some fifteen international organizations, including some, such as the UN Industrial Development Organization (1,758 individuals) and the World Intellectual Property Organization (630 individuals), that have a much lower profile than the WTO.

As noted previously, decision making in the WTO is based on consensus, which is the same practice that had developed by custom in the GATT. Consensus is not the same as unanimity, and it is clear that the legal definition in Article IX of the WTO Agreement, as well as past and contemporary practice, permits countries to abstain and therefore to allow decisions to go forward in cases where not all members are in agreement with the issue under consideration. Consistent with the requirement for consensus, most organs of the WTO are plenary and all members are able to participate.

The tasks of the WTO are carried out by its professional staff, and also by the vigorous involvement of the Geneva delegations of the WTO members, which permits the WTO to function with a small secretariat. The WTO is usually described as a 'member-driven' organization, meaning that the members and not the secretariat are mainly responsible for setting the agenda and carrying out the functions of the organization. In the important routine tasks of the organization—including judgements on waivers of obligations, initiation of disputes or complaints, accession of new members, or working parties on free trade areas—action can only be taken by officials from member governments. Research from 1997 indicates that to cover this workload, there were some 97 members with representation in Geneva, with an average of about five professional officers per delegation (Blackhurst 1998). These officials, plus their back-up support in home capitals, exceeded slightly the manpower available in the WTO secretariat in the same year.

In addition to the principal structures of the WTO mentioned previously, there are over twenty-five committees and working groups, and a fluctuating number of working parties on accessions of new members, all of which in principle are plenary bodies. In addition, there are organs with limited membership, including the Textiles Monitoring Body, plurilateral committees, dispute settlement panels, and the Appellate Body. Additionally, multilateral trade negotiations occasionally create further structure and tasks, and during the Tokyo and Uruguay Rounds a parallel structure under a Trade Negotiations Committee was struck to service those negotiations. Finally, there is an informal and fluid structure of consultation groups designed to bring 'like-minded' members together to discuss issues of common concern. The work associated with the various organs of the WTO is carried out mainly by the Geneva delegations of the members, with assistance from the WTO secretariat. The frequency of meetings is large and growing, and countries with small delegations are hard pressed to monitor, let alone direct, the activities of the organization. Indeed, many of the least developed countries have no representation in Geneva, and have little capacity to pursue their own interests independent of the positions taken by developing countries as a bloc.

One of the important tasks of the WTO is to monitor and research the trade policies of the members. An important element in this task is the Trade Policy Review Mechanism which was begun by the GATT in 1989, roughly midway through the negotiation of the Uruguay Round. The TPRM is simply a review of a member's trade policy regime, conducted in part by the member itself and by officials of the GATT/WTO secretariat. Major trading countries such as the United States can expect a review once every two years, but for smaller countries the rotation will be less frequent. The main purpose of a TPRM review is information dissemination and transparency, but the reviews are also a valuable tool to evaluate whether members are in full compliance with their obligations under various WTO Agreements. The TPRM reviews are an example of collective executive action in an organization that has very much played down the executive function in comparison to the rule making and rule adjudication functions. Depending on the development of the international trade system and the politics conducted within that regime, the executive function of the WTO could become a much more important factor in the future.

The politics of the WTO

It is common to describe the WTO as a 'rules-based' system. Like the GATT before it, the WTO mainly consists of a set of rules intended to promote trade between member countries, and especially to provide for non-discrimination in trading relations. In any system of rules, a mechanism for handling disputes is a natural and logical extension of that system. In the GATT, a dispute settlement system developed by customary practice, but in the WTO it was mandated by international agreement in the form of the DSU, and included in the Uruguay Round Agreements. The DSU is a particularly powerful form of international dispute settlement, and the management of this system has created political controversy among the members of the WTO.

At the outset it should be noted that dispute settlement procedures have been frequently used in the WTO. World Trade Organization statistics (WTO 2000c) indicated that in slightly more than five years of operation, there had been some 193 member complaints to the WTO on 151 distinct trade issues. By October 2003, total complaints numbered over 300. Approximately half of the complaints are settled or dropped in the consultation phase that precedes formal dispute settlement (Davey 2000). Once a case

is formally engaged, it proceeds to a three-person panel comprising trade experts for a legal decision, and then if requested, it will continue to the Appellate Body on appeal. Once a decision has been reached, the next issue is implementation. This is a problem the WTO accepted in moving to a legally binding dispute settlement system compared to the more diplomatic and political system that existed previously in the GATT, where countries could avoid a legal decision they could not live with. In the WTO, countries are legally obliged to accept and implement a negative dispute settlement decision, and it is possible for an injured country to take retaliatory action, even though such an action is counter-productive from the standpoint of liberalizing the trade regime in that it erects further barriers to trade. But for the largest WTO members, it is usually impossible to oblige a powerful country—even through retaliatory sanctions—to implement an adverse decision that it is determined to ignore. This was particularly the situation with the *Hormones* and *Bananas* cases, two disputes that divided the United States and the European Union. The problem is that if major powers are able to circumvent the obligation to implement adverse panel decisions, the WTO dispute settlement system will quickly lose the moral authority to secure implementation from any countries. This could be a fatal blow to the WTO rules-based regime.

There are other problems with dispute settlement that have been raised by developing countries. One is the costs of litigation before WTO panels and the Appellate Body. There has been a tendency for disputes to grow in legal complexity, a problem that was already evident in the GATT in the late 1980s. There are now more agreements to consider, and the prospect of appeal to the WTO Appellate Body has increased the importance of factual evidence and precise legal argument. The complexity and costs are especially hard to manage for developing countries, which generally have small delegations in Geneva and therefore may be forced to choose between hiring expensive counsel or simply forgoing the opportunity to pursue a dispute settlement case. These difficulties can impel developing countries toward a defensive rather than offensive posture in dispute settlement, and may reduce the market-opening possibilities that the dispute settlement system may hold for more affluent WTO members.

A second problem is what some countries have called the 'politicization' of the dispute settlement system. One issue is the tendency in some countries that have lost WTO cases for governments to come under political criticism for permitting unwarranted foreign interference in domestic policies. Such criticism inevitably forces government officials to take political acceptability (as well as WTO law) into account when deciding how to implement dispute settlement decisions. A second issue is the decision of the Appellate Body to accept *amicus curiae* briefs from environmental non-governmental organizations (NGOs) in the *Shrimp–Turtle* case between the United States and a number of developing countries. The Appellate Body took this action to address criticisms that by refusing to accept inputs from NGOs (such as, for example, the World Wildlife Fund or Greenpeace), the WTO dispute settlement system was undemocratic and not inclusive. However, the action of accepting legal briefs from NGOs undercut the concept of the WTO as an organization having nation states as members, especially when some poorer WTO members might not have the capability or financial resources to submit *amicus curiae* briefs themselves, even if they had the legal right to do it. Thus, in attempting to increase the democratic inclusiveness between developed country governments and the NGOs which are their domestic constituents, the democratic inclusiveness and juridical equality of the developing country members of the WTO is called into question.

In spite of such problems, dispute settlement is functioning reasonably well in the WTO and indeed it is the cornerstone of the regime. Any system of rules requires a judicial function to interpret and apply the rules to specific cases, and the WTO system continues to serve the interests of the members. However, the rules are not always clear, and some judicial interpretation will be necessary to apply the rules to specific cases. As a result, panels and the Appellate Body will continue to face difficult decisions in which criticism is inevitable but outright condemnation is unlikely.

Negotiations

One of the major tasks of the WTO is to promote trade negotiations. This task is mandated in the WTO Agreement, which calls on the organization 'to pro-

vide a forum for negotiation' on matters arising under the Uruguay Round Agreements, and on further issues concerning the multilateral trade relations of the members. This mandate is more precise than that which existed under the GATT. However, the sponsorship of negotiations did arise by customary practice under the GATT, and in time those negotiations proved their value in terms of forwarding the agenda of trade liberalization. Hence, the WTO Agreement effectively codified GATT customary practice, and built negotiation of new issues into the organizational mission of the WTO.

The WTO moved quickly after 1995 to carry out its mandate to sponsor negotiations. In the area of trade in services, the Uruguay Round had concluded without commitments forthcoming from members in financial or telecommunications services. These became subjects of new negotiations, and by 1997 the WTO was able to announce major new agreements in both areas. The telecom agreement produced new liberalizing commitments from sixty-nine governments covering 90 per cent of global telecom revenues, while the financial services agreement included fifty-six scheduled offers from seventy countries (counting the EU as fifteen countries). Most important, the United States participated in both agreements, and dropped its previous refusal to apply concessions to all other participating countries on the basis of the most-favoured-nation principle.

Further, in 1997, another negotiation concluded that was novel and not a continuation of the Uruguay Round. In March of that year, some forty governments concluded the WTO Ministerial Declaration on Trade in Information Technology Products (ITA) that freed trade on computer and telecommunications equipment. This agreement was concluded very quickly and it is significant because, together with the telecom agreement, it covers trade of a value equal to that of agriculture, automobiles, and textiles combined. These agreements represent the new economy in terms of commerce between nations, and it is clear that that commerce is more liberalized than the commerce of the old economy.

In the areas of agriculture and trade in services, the Uruguay Round agreements had included a 'built-in agenda' that called for new multilateral negotiations to start in 2000. These negotiations got under way despite the failure of the Seattle Ministerial Meeting in

December 1999, which attempted to establish a mandate for a new round of negotiations in all areas. Thus, even allowing for the setback of Seattle, the WTO demonstrated it was capable of sponsoring new negotiations on a sectoral basis following the conclusion of the Uruguay Round. Over time, it appears that negotiation has become less an exceptional part of the GATT/WTO regime and more part of the normal business of multilateral trade relations. The WTO is moving toward a regime of 'permanent negotiation', in which the organization begins to look more like a typical national legislature and less like the occasional diplomatic encounters of international relations.

The WTO Agreement calls for a ministerial meeting every two years, and the Seattle meeting of December 1999 provided an opportunity for some members to press for the commencement of a major new round of trade negotiations. As had been the case with the Uruguay Round, calls for a new negotiation occasioned a major rift in the multilateral trade regime. The European Union enthusiastically supported a new negotiation, and proposed a set of new issues including the controversial subjects of investment and competition policy. It was, however, less forthcoming on agricultural subsidies. For its part the United States also favoured a new negotiation and proposed reductions in trade barriers in industrial goods, but it insisted on introducing trade sanctions to protect domestic policies related to labour and the environment. Developing countries feared these would be directed mainly at them. The United States also resisted tariff concessions on textiles and was lukewarm toward negotiations on investment and competition policy. On agriculture, Washington carried on its long-standing policy of making maximum demands on the European Union. Japan also supported a new negotiation, especially on new issues, but it was prepared to stonewall discussions on agriculture. Finally, the fifteen-nation Cairns group of agricultural exporters, including both developed and developing countries, continued the strong position they had initiated in the Uruguay Round against export subsidies on agricultural trade.

The developing countries were generally hostile to the idea of a new negotiation, largely on the grounds that there was unfinished business from the Uruguay Round, such as agricultural liberalization and implementation of the Uruguay Round Agreements; they argued that these had to be settled before the international trade community should undertake new initiatives. India took the lead in enunciating these concerns, and elaborated what became known as the implementation issue. A central argument was that the Uruguay Round Agreements had been unfair to developing countries, in that those agreements obliged governments to carry out costly administrative reforms, or to participate in subsequent negotiations they were unprepared to tackle. Arguably, these obligations were more easily borne by developed countries that were more affluent, or already had more elaborate government or administrative structures. Another argument in the implementation debate was that developed countries had drawn up, and then implemented, the Uruguay Round Agreements in a way that denied to developing countries the benefits supposedly forthcoming from those agreements. This argument was buoyed by the belief in developing countries that they had accepted greater liberalization of their own markets than was the case in developed countries, with the result that they did not receive the export access for their products, especially agriculture and textiles, that they had bargained for. In sum, India made the case that the developing countries had received a bad deal from the Uruguay Round, and that before any new negotiation could begin some effort should be made to redress the inequities of the previous negotiation.

The Seattle Ministerial Meeting was thus compromised by conflicting positions of the various WTO members (Odell 2002). To this was added a bitter fight over the selection of the WTO director-general, which took place over the six months prior to Seattle and compromised the preparations normally required for success in any major ministerial meeting. The meeting itself in Seattle was also compromised by street protests by groups opposed to the WTO and to globalization, and even by mismanagement of the negotiating agenda at the meeting itself. These factors combined to make the Seattle Ministerial Meeting a spectacular failure. Ministers left Seattle without agreeing to launch a new round, and the collapse was so complete that no communiqué was produced promising the usual efforts at cooperation in the future.

Members were alarmed at the failure at Seattle, and recognized it as a test of the success of the WTO itself. Following the Seattle meeting, work continued at the technical level to bridge the many gaps between WTO members. It was recognized the two-year cycle of ministerial meetings provides a stern test for the political viability of the organization, and members were determined to resolve as many problems as possible before the next meeting in the autumn of 2001.

Gradually, the major participants introduced concessions into their negotiating positions. The European Union reduced its expectations for new rules on investment and competition policy, and the US dropped its contentious demands on labour rights and the environment. There was also some promise for movement in agriculture, which traditionally has been the sticking point in GATT negotiations. Coupled with the increased flexibility shown by the participants, the WTO secretariat itself was better organized to mediate political differences and to manage the enormous detail associated with a large multilateral trade negotiation.

By September 2001 the most extreme positions had been modified and the parties had achieved a single negotiating text, which is the *sine qua non* for success in multilateral negotiation. By this time it was clear that the major issues for the WTO membership were those of the developing countries, including especially implementation, agriculture, as well as a concern that had suddenly risen on the world stage, the access to medicines needed to combat disease in poorer countries. Developing countries were fearful that the Intellectual Property Agreement would prevent access to cheaper generic drugs to fight AIDS and other diseases that preyed on poorer societies, and they demanded a modification of the TRIPS Agreement to permit discretion to override drug patents in the event of a national health emergency. Developed countries were generally unwilling to forgo concessions that had been achieved in the Uruguay Round, and the issue festered for several years while the AIDS epidemic gathered momentum, particularly in Africa. The severity of the AIDS crisis brought moral pressure to bear on developed country governments and the pharmaceutical industry which had supported strong patent rights in the Uruguay Round.

The ministerial meeting was held in Doha, Qatar, in November 2001. The conference agenda was pre-negotiated and well prepared, for in comparison to the Seattle draft declaration that had 402 pairs of square brackets in the text (which indicate disagreement), the draft declaration for the Doha

meeting had only thirteen pairs of brackets remaining for ministerial decisions (Odell 2002). The Doha draft reflected the continuing effort at compromise that had characterized the discussions since September. However, the TRIPS/health issue remained outstanding, and it was important enough that it threatened to cause the meeting to break down in disagreement. The stakes were high: for the developed countries, the TRIPS agreement represented an important security against the misappropriation and even theft of intellectual property, but for the developing countries, access to lower-cost generic medicines could be easily translated into lives saved or lost in the fight against AIDS and other diseases. An end to this impasse was eventually reached through an agreement to extend the date by ten years, until 2016, for least developed countries to provide patents on pharmaceuticals, and by a formal affirmation that 'the TRIPS agreement does not and should not prevent Members from taking measures to protect public health'. The latter statement only reiterated rights that were already contained in the TRIPS agreement itself, but it was accepted by developing countries because it created a presumption that WTO members would be able to exercise their rights to procure generic medicines, and more important, that other members (particularly the USA) would be unlikely to take dispute settlement actions against members that exercised those rights.

The resolution of the TRIPS/health issue insured success of the Doha meeting, although it would take another twenty-one months to eliminate the final obstacles to cheaper drug imports (WTO 2003b). Other issues were settled at Doha, particularly the question of implementation where the parties agreed to roll much of this agenda into the forthcoming negotiation. With the success of the Doha meeting, the WTO members formally initiated a new multilateral negotiation with a deadline of December 2004. The agenda comprised twelve wide-ranging issues, the focus of the negotiation was development, and in keeping with this focus the members eschewed the term 'round' in favour of the title Doha Development Agenda (DDA). The DDA commenced in January of 2002.

In its short history, the WTO suffered a serious setback in the Seattle Ministerial Meeting, and then it rebounded to launch a new multilateral negotiation in the Doha Ministerial Meeting. The latter meeting laid out an agenda for the negotiation, and the negotiation proceeded, but it was met with frequent delays and progress was slow. The first major deadline for the DDA was the ministerial meeting in Cancun, Mexico, in September 2003, at which time the Declaration from the Meeting was to take the form of an updated agenda and progress report on the DDA. In Cancun, the WTO members were unable to find consensus on a Ministerial Declaration. Once again, the WTO met with failure.

The goal at Cancun was to reach an interim agreement on the outstanding problems of the negotiation sufficient to advance the work of the DDA. This goal ended when the Mexican foreign minister chairing the conference exercised his discretion and abruptly called a halt to the negotiation. The issues on which the negotiation broke were investment and competition policy, which were pressed by the European Union and Japan but vigorously opposed by a group of mainly African developing countries. However, behind these issues was the far greater problem of agriculture, where again developing countries were intent to register their displeasure at the agricultural subsidy practices of the United States and the European Union. For example, four West African producers of cotton demanded a sectoral initiative to eliminate cotton subsidies in countries such as the USA, EU, and China, but they received a response suggesting African countries should diversify their production, a message which they interpreted as telling them to stop growing cotton. This response inflamed the Africans, and it added to the antipathy that threatened to spiral out of control at the conference.

Beneath the acrimony of the Cancun conference lay a subtle change in the politics of the WTO. The GATT was the creation of developed countries, and up to the Uruguay Round the developing countries were largely passive bystanders in the development of the international trade regime. This changed with the creation of the WTO, and the change has since accelerated, particularly with the accession of China to full WTO membership (WTO 2001*b*). At the Cancun Ministerial

Meeting, a group of developing countries formed a coalition known as the G21 + countries that succeeded in polarizing much of the debate into a North–South struggle. The basis for this polarization was the firm belief of the G21 + that the benefits of the trade regime have not been equitably proportioned between developed and developing countries. This is a belief that is increasingly given some credence by observers of international economics, and will have to be addressed by the organization in the future if progress is to be achieved in the international trade regime ('Special Report', *Economist*, 20 September 2003).

Key points

- The WTO is a rules-based international organization that operates on the basis of consensus. Members are legally bound to act consistent with the rules they have negotiated as interpreted by the dispute settlement mechanism.

- The work of the WTO is carried out by a series of committees supported by a small international secretariat. The dispute settlement mechanism has been especially active.

- The WTO has promoted further negotiated agreements in financial and telecommunications services, and in trade in Information Technology Products.

- The WTO Agreement calls for a Ministerial Meeting every two years. In December 1999, in Seattle, Washington, some members sought support to commence a new multilateral negotiation, but the meeting concluded without agreement. In November 2001, in Doha, Qatar, following lengthy pre-negotiations between developed and developing countries, WTO Ministers agreed to initiate a new negotiation with a deadline of December 2004.

Conclusion

The start of the Doha negotiation was a reaffirmation of the direction the world trade regime has taken since the middle of the past century. The focus of the regime has been to create rules whereby countries can exchange goods and services with a minimum of

interference from national governments, and the means to accomplish that task has been to reach international agreements through international negotiation. Such agreements are an important form of regulation, or system management, in the international economy. Trade has always been regulated, but in the past that regulation mainly has been done unilaterally by national governments, and that regulation always has posed a potential threat to trade and the stability of the international economy, as the 1930s amply demonstrated. Today, the regulation of trade is carried out as much through the negotiation of trade agreements as through the actions of domestic agencies, and the purpose is to replace inward-looking national regulation with a broader conception of international rules. The purpose is to keep the trade system moving in a liberal direction consistent with an open international society, because the alternatives to an open society—which were witnessed in the inter-war period in the last century—were so damaging to the interests of all countries.

The GATT and now the WTO are central features of the international trade system. Through negotiations in these institutions, which are analogous to law-making in domestic parliaments, countries have been able to establish a rules-based regime for regulating international trade. The negotiation process is critically important to the success of the WTO, but it is a fickle and sometimes fragile process. When it is successful, the rules of the regime are advanced and all countries can be said to benefit from the greater stability and predictability that comes from a regime based on rules rather than on the play of power politics. But the negotiation process is not always successful, and just as an absence of consensus occasionally paralyses the legislative agenda in domestic parliaments, the absence of consensus also stops the WTO from dealing with problems that many members think need to be addressed. If there is a major difference between domestic parliaments and the WTO, it is that an impasse in the former rarely calls into question the survival of the institution, whereas when an impasse occurs in the WTO, there is always the fear that the organization will be eclipsed and that countries will use other means, including unilateral actions, to resolve the problems they face in the trade system. Thus an analogy is often made between the WTO and a bicycle: both need to maintain forward momentum in order to remain stable.

As it looks to the future, the greatest challenge facing the WTO will be to fully incorporate the developing countries into a liberal international trade regime. Included in the Preamble to the WTO Agreement is a statement expressing the need that developing countries should 'secure a share in the growth in international trade commensurate with the needs of their economic development'. The Cancun Meeting was a political wake-up call that the developing countries will use their negotiating power to realize their aspirations in the Doha negotiation and beyond. In the past half-century the GATT and WTO have endured through many challenges, but the task of implementing a global and inclusive trade regime will be the most imposing test of all.

Key points

- A Ministerial Meeting in September 2003, in Cancun, Mexico, failed to find consensus on a Declaration designed to advance the work of the Doha negotiation.

- The greatest future challenge to the WTO is to find consensus between the developed and developing members of the organization.

QUESTIONS

1 What are the basic components of the international trade regime? Give examples.

2 What was the effect of the US Reciprocal Trade Agreements Act of 1934?

3 What does non-discrimination mean in international trade, and how is it put into effect by the rules of the GATT?

4 Compare the results of the Kennedy and Tokyo Rounds of GATT multilateral trade negotiations.

5 What was the role of the developing countries in the Uruguay Round negotiation, and why was it historically significant?

6 What were the challenges encountered in negotiating rules for trade in services in the Uruguay Round negotiation?

7 How does the WTO differ from the GATT?

8 What is the WTO Dispute Settlement Understanding (DSU), why is it necessary, and what are some of the difficulties with its operations?

9 What are the challenges for the WTO in conducting the multilateral trade negotiation known as the Doha Development Agenda?

FURTHER READING

Bhagwati, J. (1988), *Protectionism* (Cambridge, Mass.: MIT Press). A short but incisive review of the history, ideology and practice of the trade policy of protectionism.

—— (1991), *The World Trading System at Risk* (Princeton: Princeton University Press). An analysis of the challenges to the trading system that the Uruguay Round negotiation was intended to counter.

Condliffe, J. B. (1950), *The Commerce of Nations* (New York, NY: W. W. Norton). A penetrating history of international trade that makes use of the memorable concept of the contest between enterprise and regulation.

Croome, J. (1995), *Reshaping the World Trading System: A History of the Uruguay Round* (Geneva: World Trade Organization). An official history of the Uruguay Round noted for its detail and accuracy.

From GATT to the WTO: The Multilateral Trading System in the New Millennium (2000, WTO Secretariat) (Geneva: World Trade Organization). A collection of authoritative papers by noted experts on international trade and trade policy.

Jackson, J. H. (1998), *The World Trade Organization: Constitution and Jurisprudence* (London: Pinter). An analysis of the WTO legal regime by a foremost scholar of international trade law.

Ostry, S. (1997), *The Post-Cold War Trading System: Who's on First* (Chicago: University of Chicago Press). A masterful history of international trade from 1945 onward that blends economics, politics, and law into a rounded analysis of the subject.

Preeg, E. H. (1995), *Traders in a Brave New World: The Uruguay Round and the Future of the International Trading System* (Chicago: University of Chicago Press). A well-organized review of the major events of the negotiation that created the current international trade regime.

Rosecrance, R. (1986), *The Rise of the Trading State: Commerce and Conquest in the Modern World* (New York, NY: Basic Books). A comprehensive treatment of the history of trading relations.

Winham, G. R. (1992), *The Evolution of International Trade Agreements* (Toronto: University of Toronto Press). A review of trade agreements from antiquity to the mid-Uruguay Round, based on the 1991 Bissell Lectures at the University of Toronto.

WEB LINKS

The main link for international trade is the WTO link, i.e. **www.wto.org**. Other useful links are national ministries of international trade that can be found on Google, such as **www.ustr.gov** (United States) or **www.itcan-cican.gc.ca** (Canada).

5 Regionalism

John Ravenhill

READER'S GUIDE

The number of regional trade agreements has grown rapidly since the World Trade Organization (WTO) came into existence in 1995. More than 40 per cent of world trade is now conducted within these preferential trade arrangements, the most significant exception to the WTO's principle of non-discrimination. Governments have often entered regional economic agreements primarily motivated by political rather than economic considerations. Nonetheless, they may prefer trade liberalization on a regional rather than a global basis for several economic reasons. This chapter reviews the political economy of regionalism: why regional trade agreements are established, which actors are likely to support regional rather than global trade liberalization, the effects that regionalism has had on the trade and welfare of members and non-members, and the relationship between liberalization at the regional and global levels.

Introduction

When the Japanese prime minister, Junichiro Koizumi, and his Singaporean counterpart, Goh Chok Tong, signed a bilateral trade agreement in January 2002, Japan departed from the rapidly depleting ranks of WTO members that were not parties to a discriminatory trade arrangement. By the middle of 2003, only Macau and Mongolia among the WTO's 146 members were not parties to one or more regional trading agreements (RTAs). These take various forms ranging, in scope of cooperation, from free trade areas to economic unions (Box 5.1).

RTAs are the most important exception that the WTO permits to the principle that countries should not discriminate in their treatment of other members. Parties to regional arrangements are obliged to notify the WTO of the details of their agreements; the Committee on Regional Trade Agreements has responsibility for ensuring that the agreements comply with the WTO's provisions. World Trade Organization data reflect the explosion in the number of regional arrangements that has occurred since the early 1990s. Throughout its entire existence from 1948 to 1994, the General Agreement on Tariffs and Trade (GATT) received 124 notifications of regional trade agreements, of which only sixty-five were still in force when it was replaced by the WTO. Between 1995 and the beginning of 2003, the WTO received notification of a further 130 agreements. In addition, the WTO estimated that at the latter date a further seventy RTAs were operational but had yet to be notified to it. This growth in regionalism has led to a marked increase in the share of world trade conducted on a discriminatory basis. Trade within discriminatory regional agreements in 2000 accounted for 43 per cent of total world trade; the WTO expects this share to exceed 50 per cent by 2005 (WTO 2003c: 48, Table 1B10).

Three sets of rules in the WTO permit the creation of RTAs:

- Article XXIV of the GATT lays down conditions for the establishment and operation of free trade agreements and customs unions covering trade in goods.
- the 'Enabling Clause', formally the 1979 Decision on Differential and More Favourable Treatment, Reciprocity and Fuller Participation of Developing Countries, permits regional agreements among developing countries on trade in goods.
- Article V of the General Agreement on Trade in Services (GATS) establishes conditions that permit liberalization of trade in services among regional partners.

At the beginning of 2003, of the 179 RTAs in effect, 135 came under the auspices of Article XXIV, twenty-five were under GATS Article V, and nineteen under the Enabling Clause.

Why do governments choose to pursue their foreign economic policy objectives through regionalism rather than through other strategies? What explains the recent growth in regionalism? Which political interests are driving integration at the regional level? What impact do regional agreements have on the economies and on the political systems of participants? And what are the consequences of the growth of regionalism for the global trading system? These are the principal questions that this chapter addresses (our focus is on trade rather than the recent growth in regional collaboration on finance). But first, we turn to matters of definition: what do we mean by regionalism?

Regionalism refers to a formal process of intergovernmental collaboration between two or more states. It should be distinguished from *regionalization*, which refers to the growth of economic interdependence within a given geographical area.

One of the few issues on which writers on regionalism agree is that there is no such thing as a 'natural' region. Regions are social constructions whose members define their boundaries. Consider, for instance, the European Union: in its successive incarnations—European Economic Community, European Community, and, now, the European Union—its membership has risen from its six founders to the current total of twenty-five. And debates over EU membership for Turkey show that no consensus exists on either geographic or cultural criteria that could be used to distinguish the 'European' from the 'non-European'.

Box 5.1 A hierarchy of regional economic arrangements

Regional integration arrangements are usually perceived as a hierarchy that runs from free trade areas through customs unions and common markets to economic unions. The terminology of 'hierarchy' is used because each level incorporates all the provisions of the lower level of integration. This does not imply that particular regional arrangements will necessarily progress from a lower to a higher level of integration. Nor is it the case that regional partnerships inevitably begin at the lowest level and then move to 'deeper' integration: some arrangements, for instance, have been established as customs unions.

A *free trade area* exists when countries remove tariffs and non-tariff barriers to the free movement of goods and services between them. Governments meanwhile are free to choose how they treat goods and services imported from non-regional-partner states. Membership in one free trade area therefore does not prevent a country from establishing or joining other free trade areas: Mexico, for example, is a party to agreements with more than thirty countries. Because free trade areas impose relatively few constraints on national decision-making autonomy, they are the easiest of the regional arrangements to negotiate. More than 90 per cent of regional partnerships take the form of free trade areas. Examples include NAFTA, the Japan–Singapore Economic Partnership Agreement, and the Baltic Free Trade Area.

A *customs union* goes beyond the removal of barriers to trade within the region to adopt a common set of policies towards imports from countries outside the region. This includes agreement on a common level of tariffs (often referred to as a common external tariff) on all extra-regional imports. Such agreements cost governments autonomy in their foreign economic policies (joint institutions are usually required to negotiate and administer the common external trade policies). They will also have distributive effects, depending on the level at which the common external tariff is set for various items. Consequently, customs unions are usually more difficult

to negotiate than are free trade areas. The relatively small number of customs unions includes the Andean Community, CARICOM, MERCOSUR, and the Southern African Customs Union. Many have experienced difficulties in negotiating a common external tariff. Even in the European Union individual states maintained different tariffs on some products for more than thirty years after its formation. MERCOSUR's negotiation of a common external tariff took fifteen years longer than anticipated, it applied to only three-quarters of total products, and even then was not accepted by two of its members, Bolivia and Peru.

A *common market* includes a customs union and also allows for free movement of labour and capital within the regional partnership. Such free flows of factors of production inevitably require governments to collaborate in additional policy areas to ensure comparable treatment in all countries within the common market. Few governments historically have been willing to accept the loss of policy-making autonomy that occurs in a common market. The Andean Community, CARICOM, the COMESA (Common Market for Eastern and Southern Africa) grouping, and MERCOSUR have committed themselves to work for the establishment of a common market but it is too early to judge whether their aspirations will be realized.

An *economic union* includes a common market plus the adoption of a common currency and/or the harmonization of monetary, fiscal, and social policies. Only the European Union has reached this level of economic integration.

Many of the free trade agreements signed in recent years also include provisions for 'deeper' integration, the most common of which relate to the removal of restrictions on investment flows. But even though these are elements often found in common markets, these free trade areas do not aspire to the creation of a common external tariff or to the free flow of labour within the regional grouping.

For most of the post-war period, the concept of regional economic integration has usually been associated with an arrangement between three or more geographically contiguous states. Again, the EU provides an excellent example but consider also East African Cooperation (Kenya, Tanzania, and Uganda), and the Andean Pact (Bolivia, Colombia, Ecuador, Peru, Venezuela). In recent years, however, a large number of preferential trade agreements have been signed that involve only two parties (for example,

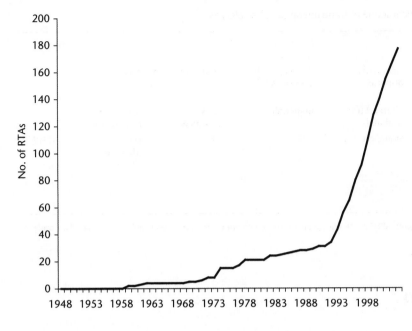

Fig. 5.1 Current RTAs by date of entry into force

Source:
www.wto.org/english/tratop_e/region_e/regfac_e.htm

China–Hong Kong), and sometimes these bilateral agreements link parties that are not geographically contiguous (for example, Korea and Chile). Because all these agreements are subject to the scrutiny of the WTO's Committee on Regional Trade Agreements, however, they tend also to be labelled 'regional'. How appropriate is such terminology is questionable. But it is not just the terminology that is problematic: the arguments of the large body of theoretical work on regional integration, which was developed with groupings involving multiple members from the same geographical region in mind, may not be applicable to arrangements that involve only two parties or those that involve states that are not geographical neighbours.

Table 5.1 demonstrates the complexity of the current configuration of 'regional' arrangements—essentially all strategies for trade liberalization that fall between unilateral action at the one extreme and negotiations at the global level in the WTO at the other. Bilateral agreements can occur either between neighbours or between countries that are far removed from one another. Regionalism, as conventionally understood, is a *minilateral* relationship, that is, one

that involves more than two countries, on a geographically concentrated basis, for example, the North American Free Trade Agreement (NAFTA) or the ASEAN Free Trade Area (AFTA) (Table 5.5, at the end of the chapter, lists the principal minilateral regional trade groupings). In recent years, however, two other forms of minilateral groupings have emerged among members that are geographically dispersed. *Transregional* groupings link individual countries located in different parts of the world. A good example is the Asia-Pacific Economic Cooperation (APEC) grouping, whose membership comprises twenty-one countries from the Americas, Asia, Oceania, and Europe (Russia). Many of the recently negotiated bilateral RTAs, for instance, USA–Jordan, Singapore–New Zealand, link countries from different geographical areas. *Interregional* arrangements link two established minilateral economic arrangements, as between the European Union and MERCOSUR (the Southern Common Market, comprising Argentina, Brazil, Paraguay, and Uruguay). By the end of 2002, more than twenty-five transregional and interregional agreements were operational.

Table 5.1 Example of the geographical scope of trade liberalization strategies

Unilateral	Bilateral		Minilateral			Global
	Geographically concentrated	Geographically dispersed	Geographically concentrated	Geographically dispersed		
	Bilateral within region	**Bilateral trans-regional**	**Regionalism**	**Trans regionalism**	**Inter regionalism**	
Trade liberalization in SE Asia, Australia, and NZ in 1980s and 1990s	Australia–New Zealand CER	Singapore–USA	NAFTA	APEC[a]	EU–Mercosur CER–AFTA	GATT/WTO

[a] Unlike the other RTAs discussed in this chapter, APEC is not a discriminatory arrangement (its members have pledged to reduce their trade barriers on imports from all sources).

Source: Adapted from Aggarwal (2001: 238).

Why regionalism?

Economists assert that an economy's welfare can be maximized, other than in very exceptional circumstances, if governments lower trade barriers on a nondiscriminatory basis (either through unilateral action or through negotiations at the global level that adhere to the WTO's principle of non-discrimination). Regional trade agreements, on the other hand, can reduce global welfare by distorting the allocation of resources, and may even lead to welfare losses for their members (see Box 5.2). Moreover, from the political scientist's perspective, it is usually more efficient to negotiate a single agreement with a large number of states than to undertake a series of negotiations with individual states or with small groupings (because it both economizes on the resources needed for negotiations and also increases the opportunities for trade-offs in reaching a package deal).

Why, then, has regionalism not only been attractive to governments throughout the post-war period but apparently has become increasingly so in the last two decades? Governments usually have multiple motives in entering an arrangement as complex as a regional partnership: it would be naïve to expect to find a single factor that explains governments' actions across all regional agreements. Moreover, governments often enter regional economic agreements primarily for political rather than economic reasons.

Political motivations for entering regional trade agreements

Economic cooperation and confidence building

Regionalism frequently involves the use of economic means for political ends: the improvement of inter-state relations and/or the enhancement of security within a region. In international relationships that have a history of conflict or where no tradition of partnership exists, cooperation on economic matters can be a core element in a process of confidence building.

The origins of post-war European economic integration provide an excellent example. The European Coal and Steel Community (ECSC), created by the 1951 Treaty of Paris, was the first of the institutions of what eventually was to evolve into the European Union. The ECSC, founded by France, West Germany, Italy, Belgium, the Netherlands, and Luxembourg, pooled the coal and steel resources of its members by providing a unified market for these commodities (perceived as critical to any military capacity); it also created a unified labour market in this sector. The underlying objective was to manage the rebuilding of Germany's economy post-war and to integrate it with those of its neighbours, thereby helping to restore

Box 5.2 The costs and benefits of preferential trade agreements: trade diversion and trade creation

Jacod Viner (1950) was the first author to present a systematic assessment of the economic costs and benefits of regional economic integration, and to demonstrate, contrary to the then conventional wisdom, that a selective removal of tariffs might not be welfare enhancing. He argued that increased trade between parties to a regional arrangement can occur through two mechanisms. *Trade creation* occurs when imports from a regional partner displace goods that have been produced domestically at higher cost, which can no longer compete once the tariffs on imports from the regional partner are removed. *Trade diversion* occurs when imports from a regional partner displace those that originated outside the regional arrangement, the displacement occurring because the extra-regional imports are no longer price competitive when the tariffs on trade within the region are removed. Consider, for instance, a hypothetical example of what might happen with the implementation of the North American Free Trade Agreement (Table 5.2 below). Let's assume that Indonesia was the lowest-cost source of imported cotton T-shirts for the United States. Before the implementation of NAFTA, when all countries faced the same level of tariffs on their exports to the US market, its T-shirts were preferred to the higher-cost production of Mexican firms. Assume that the tariff on T-shirts was 10 per cent, the cost of manufacturing and delivering an Indonesian T-shirt to the USA was $5 while that for a Mexican T-shirt was $5.40. Adding the 10 per cent tariff to the costs of manufacturing and delivery, the price paid by the importer before NAFTA would be $5.50 for an Indonesian shirt and $5.94 for a Mexican shirt.

Following the implementation of NAFTA, however, the tariff on imported T-shirts from Mexico is removed. For the importer, the Mexican T-shirt is now the least expensive ($5.40) because it is no longer subject to tariffs, while the Indonesian product will still face a 10 per cent tariff and still costs the importer $5.50. Assuming that the importer chooses the lowest-cost product, imports will be switched after the regional scheme goes into effect from the lowest-cost producer (Indonesia) to Mexico, a relatively expensive producer, which now benefits from zero tariffs in the US market.

Several consequences follow from this trade *diversion*. The consumer in the USA *may* gain because the cost to the importer of purchasing a T-shirt falls from $5.50 to $5.40 (although the producer/wholesaler/retailer may be able to capture some or all of this gain). The US government, however, loses the tariff revenue (50 cents for each imported T-shirt) that it previously derived from taxing Indonesian T-shirt imports (the new imports from Mexico not being subject to tax). For the US economy as whole, therefore, the potential gain to consumers is significantly exceeded by the loss of tariff revenue (which is of course a form of taxation income for the government). Considered again from the perspective of the US economy, real resources are wasted because more money is being spent ($5.40 compared with $5.00) for each imported T-shirt. And, unless exceptional circumstances prevail, the Indonesian economy will also suffer a welfare loss because of the decline in export revenue it experiences (and with the loss of the US market, it may also have to lower the price of its T-shirt exports to compete in other markets).

If trade diversion outweighs trade creation then the net effect of regional scheme on its members' welfare can be negative.

Table 5.2 The potential for trade diversion after the removal of tariffs on intra-regional trade ($)

	Cost of production	Tariff pre-NAFTA	Cost to importer pre-NAFTA	Tariff post-NAFTA	Cost to importer post-NAFTA
Indonesia	5.00	0.50 (10%)	5.50	0.50 (10%)	5.50
Mexico	5.40	0.54 (10%)	5.94	Zero	5.40

confidence amongst countries whose conflicts had embroiled the world in two major wars.

In a similar fashion, the Association of South-East Asian Nations, ASEAN, was founded in 1967 to promote economic cooperation in an attempt to build confidence and avoid conflict in a region that was the site of armed struggles in the Cold War era. Two of its founding members, Indonesia and Malaysia, had engaged in armed conflict in the period 1963–6 as the Indonesian government of President Sukarno attempted to destabilize the newly independent Malaysia. Over the years, ASEAN membership expanded and the organization successfully used cooperation on economic matters to overcome deep-seated inter-state rivalries and suspicions. In 1998, one of the visions of ASEAN's founders was realized when its membership was expanded to include all ten of the countries of South-East Asia (including Vietnam and Cambodia that had in the previous quarter of a century been at war with other ASEAN states and with one another).

In some instances, regional economic integration has been stimulated by a desire to enhance the security of regional partners against threats emanating from *outside* the membership of the regional arrangement. Such concerns played a role in ASEAN's foundation, the desire being to strengthen members against a perceived communist threat. And the Southern African Development Coordination Conference (SADCC) was founded in 1980 in an attempt to reduce members' dependence on South Africa during the apartheid era.

Regional economic cooperation and the 'new security agenda'

Offers by industrialized countries in recent years to extend regional economic cooperation have frequently been encouraged by concerns about 'non-traditional' security threats emanating from less developed partners. Such threats include environmental damage, illegal migration, organized crime, drug smuggling, and international terrorism. Regional cooperation may help address these issues directly, for example, NAFTA's provisions on the environment, or, proponents hope, indirectly by promoting economic development and thereby ameliorating the conditions that were perceived as fostering the security threats. Concerns about new security

threats played a part in European enthusiasm for new agreements with Mediterranean states, and in US interest in a free trade agreement with Mexico and its extension to other Western Hemisphere countries.

Regionalism as a bargaining tool

Many of the regional economic agreements that developing countries established in the 1950s through the 1970s were motivated by a desire to enhance their bargaining power with transnational corporations and with trading partners. They were often inspired by the work of the UN's Economic Commission for Latin America, and its principal theorist, Raul Prebisch, whose ideas were subsequently taken up by writers from the dependency school. Prebisch (1963, 1970) had argued that regional integration was essential to provide a sufficiently large market to enable the efficient operation of local industries to produce goods that had previously been imported. Moreover, a regional partnership would enhance bargaining power with external actors if the partners negotiated with one voice. One approach, as in the Andean Pact (founded in 1969 by Bolivia, Chile [which withdrew in 1976], Colombia, Ecuador, Peru) was to adopt a system of region-wide industrial licensing. The intention was to prevent TNCs from gaining concessions by playing off governments of the region against one another, and to use the carrot of access to a larger regional market to extract concessions from potential investors.

Less developed countries have also used regional partnerships as a way of gaining more aid from donor countries and organizations. Over the years, various governments and international organizations have encouraged regional economic integration among developing countries and have set aside some of their aid budgets to promote regional projects. The European Union has been a particularly enthusiastic supporter of regionalism in other parts of the world.

Moreover, a World Bank (2000: 20) study notes that by pooling their diplomatic resources in a regional arrangement, less developed countries are sometimes able to achieve greater prominence in international relations and to negotiate agreements that would not be available if they had acted individually, and to ensure election of their representatives to key positions in international organizations. The best example of successful pursuit of this strategy, the

Bank suggests, is CARICOM, the Caribbean Community and Common Market.

But it is not just developing countries that have perceived regional economic partnerships as a means for enhancing their bargaining power. The Japanese Ministry of Economy, Trade and Industry, for instance, in advocating participation in discriminatory regional arrangements, pointed to the possibility that they could increase Japan's leverage within the WTO (Ministry of Economy 2000). The foundation (in 1989) of APEC was linked to perceptions that it could help to pressure the European Union into trade concessions during GATT's Uruguay Round of trade negotiations (Ravenhill 2001). And some authors have suggested that the negotiation of the Treaty of Rome, which established the European Economic Community in 1957, was at least in part motivated by European countries' desires to increase their leverage against the United States in the upcoming GATT talks (Milward 1984, 1992).

Regionalism as a mechanism for locking-in reforms

Regional trade agreements can enhance the credibility of domestic economic reforms and thereby increase the attractiveness of economies to potential foreign investors (Rodrik 1989). Such considerations have become more important in an increasingly integrated global economy where countries are competing to stake their claims as preferred hosts for foreign direct investment (see Rugman, Chapter 10 this volume).

Commitments made within a regional forum can be more attractive to potential investors than those made in global institutions for several reasons. Countries' compliance with their commitments is likely to be more closely scrutinized within a regional grouping: the numbers of partners to be monitored is smaller than within the WTO with its close to 150 members, and any breaking of commitments is more likely to have a direct impact on regional partners and lead to swift retaliation. Some regional arrangements provide for regional institutions to monitor the implementation of agreements. Moreover, repeated interactions with a small number of partners within regional arrangements may make governments more concerned about their reputations (their credibility as collaborators) than they would be within more diffuse multilateral forums (Fernandez and Portes 1998).

Regional arrangements may be particularly effective in enhancing the credibility of commitments when less developed countries enter partnerships with an industrialized country as, for instance, in Mexico's participation in NAFTA (Haggard 1997). And the possibility that the policy coverage of the RTA may be more comprehensive than agreements at the global level—embracing, for instance, rules on competition policy and on the treatment of foreign investment—further enhances the potential of regional arrangements as a device for signalling to potential foreign investors the seriousness of a government's commitment to reform.

Regionalism to satisfy domestic political constituencies

Often the choice of trade policies faced by governments is not between liberalization at the global level and liberalization at the regional level, but between a regional agreement and unilateral liberalization. In contrast to a unilateral lowering of tariffs, which is usually politically difficult for governments because domestic groups believe that the government is giving something away (tariff protection) and not receiving anything in return from other countries, a regional trade agreement provides a means for a government to ensure that it receives concessions ('reciprocity') from its partners in return for those that it has offered. And, insofar as a regional agreement makes it easier politically for governments to undertake liberalization, and therefore enhances such activities, it may be beneficial not just to regional partners but to the wider international community.

Ease of negotiating and implementing agreements

The larger the number of states, the more likely it is that they will have a greater diversity of interests that will complicate negotiations. Moreover, the larger the number of members, the more difficult it is to monitor behaviour and to enforce sanctions in the event of non-compliance (Oye 1985; Keohane 1984). A regional agreement with a limited number of partners accordingly might be easier to negotiate and implement than one at the global level. This logic is particularly applicable to bilateral trade agreements.

On the other hand, numerous cases exist of large numbers of governments successfully concluding international agreements (within, for instance, the United Nations on issues that range from arms control to the environment to human rights (see, for example, Osherenko and Young 1993: 12). Kahler (1992) has argued persuasively that success in solving the numbers problem depends upon institutional design. Mechanisms for discussing issues and voting procedures can be adapted to counter the problems of numbers and diversity. A larger numbers of participants may bring potential for greater gains and more opportunities for trade-offs among the parties.

In short, the international relations literature is inconclusive on the relationship between the number of participants and the successful negotiation and implementation of agreements. But of greater importance to shaping state action are the perceptions that governments hold on this issue. And there is little doubt that many *believe* that regional agreements are easier to negotiate than those at the global level, given the numbers and diversity of WTO membership. The failure of the WTO ministerial meetings in Seattle in 1999 and in Cancun in 2003 reinforced these beliefs.

Economic motivations for regionalism

Here we can distinguish between two possibilities: (*a*) where governments, for economic reasons, prefer a regional economic agreement to unilateral liberalization or to a non-discriminatory multilateral agreement; and (*b*) where they prefer a regional agreement to the status quo.

Economic reasons for choosing regionalism over multilateralism

Regionalism enables continued protection of sectors that would not survive in global competition
Even though mainstream economic theory suggests that welfare gains will be maximized when trade liberalization occurs on a non-discriminatory basis, governments may nonetheless prefer a regional (discriminatory) trade agreement. This alternative is attractive, for instance, when they (and interest groups, such as manufacturers' or farmers' associations, which probably will be lobbying the government) believe that domestic producers will be successful in competition with regional partners and will benefit from the larger (protected) market that a regional scheme creates, but that they would not survive a competition with producers located outside the region. Added to this is the possibility (discussed in more detail later in this chapter) that governments will be able to completely exclude 'politically sensitive' non-competitive domestic sectors from the trade liberalization measures negotiated within a regional agreement whereas such exclusion would be more difficult at the global level.

A more benign variant of this argument is that a reform-minded government may seek to enter a regional agreement as a way to gradually expose inefficient domestic producers to international competition, with the expectation that competition from regional partners will generate reforms that will eventually enable the sector to be exposed to full international competition. In this scenario, regionalism is a stepping stone to broader liberalization.

Regionalism provides opportunities for 'deeper integration'
Regionalism may be more attractive than a multilateral treaty to pro-liberalization governments because it enables agreement on issues that would not be possible in the WTO where membership is more diverse. Since the early 1990s, a number of governments, such as those of the United States, Singapore, Chile, and Australia, which have been seeking to raise the tempo of trade liberalization, have turned to regional agreements in an attempt to promote 'deeper integration'. This concept refers to cooperation that goes beyond the traditional liberalization menu of removing tariff and non-tariff barriers. It may include, for instance, agreements on the environment, on the treatment of foreign direct investment, on domestic competition (anti-trust) policies, on intellectual property rights, and on labour standards. The North American Free Trade Agreement was one of the first free trade agreements to incorporate provisions on many of these matters. As trade liberalization within the WTO reduced the significance of border barriers so matters of 'deeper integration' have grown in importance as governments seek to establish a level playing field with their partners.

A regional approach may facilitate reaching agreement on these politically sensitive issues if the partner states share certain characteristics, for example, similar levels of economic development. Moreover, regional agreements, especially bilateral free trade areas, may also enable more powerful states to bring their weight to bear more effectively on weaker parties, for whom the price of gaining security of access to a larger market may be to accept undertakings on issues of 'deeper integration', such as their treatment of foreign investment, etc. (on this issue of unequal bargaining power in regional agreements see Helleiner 1996, and Perroni and Whalley 1994).

Economic reasons for preferring regionalism to unilateralism or the status quo

Larger markets and increased foreign investment
Governments may not have the option of choosing between a regional agreement and an agreement at the global level: the latter may simply not be available at the time. The choice that governments face is to stick with the status quo, to liberalize on a unilateral basis, or to seek a regional agreement. Besides the political advantages, noted above, that a regional agreement often has over unilateral action, economic advantages may also come into play. Coordinated liberalization on a regional basis broadens the geographical scope of liberalization and may also enable a widening of the product coverage of the agreement, thereby increasing the potential economic gains.

Compared with the status quo, a regional economic agreement can confer two principal economic benefits. First, it provides a larger 'home' market for domestic industries, possibly enabling them to produce more efficiently because of economies of scale. How significant an advantage is gained from regionalism will depend on the number of partner economies and their relative size: a firm in a large economy is unlikely to make significant gains in economies of scale if the regional partnership is with only a couple of much smaller economies.

Secondly, regionalism can increase the attractiveness of an economy to potential investors. Companies that previously supplied the separate national markets through exports from outside the region may now find that the unified regional market is of sufficient size to make local production (and hence foreign investment into the region) attractive. Gains from foreign direct investment may be particularly

> ### Box 5.3 Economies of scale
>
> In modern manufacturing, which often depends on the use of expensive machinery and on very large investments in research and development, large-scale production often enables firms to produce at a lower average cost per unit. These *economies of scale* can result not just from a more efficient use of machinery and of labour but also because specialist managers and workers can be employed, savings can be made in borrowing on financial markets (which generally charge higher rates of interest to smaller borrowers), raw materials can be purchased more cheaply when bought in bulk, and advertising costs are spread across a higher volume of output.
>
> A related concept is *economies of scope*. These occur when firms can spread various costs (including, for instance, research and development, accounting, marketing) across various products, which may, although they will not necessarily, be related (for instance, production of calculators and of LCD screens for laptop computers).

significant when a less developed country enters into a regional partnership with one or more industrialized economies. Companies may be able to take advantage of the relatively low-cost labour in the less developed country to supply the whole of the regional market from factories established there. The best example here is the dramatic increase that occurred in foreign direct investment into Mexico following the signature of NAFTA in 1994. Inflows of FDI to Mexico, which averaged $8 billion per year in the period 1990–5, rose to $14 billion in 1997 and to $24 billion in 2001 (UNCTAD 2002c: 304, Annex Table B.1). Some evidence also exists of similar effects elsewhere, for example, foreign direct investment inflows to ASEAN increased after it negotiated its free trade area (UNCTAD 2003: 47, Box II.5).

A related strategy is for governments to attempt to establish their economies as regional hubs. For a number of activities, companies will wish to establish only one office in a geographical area (it might, for instance, be a central office responsible for procurement, or for providing management services to all of the company's regional subsidiaries). One of the reasons why some governments appear to have chosen to negotiate multiple regional trade agreements is that this strategy enhances the prospects for attracting companies' 'regional' headquarters as the economy becomes a 'hub' for multiple regional 'spokes'. Singapore, an active proponent of regional trade agreements is a good example—it has a larger number of regional corporate headquarters than any other developing economy. Regional hubs may also be attractive to subsidiaries of multinational enterprises seeking to take advantage of the preferential access the RTAs provide to third country markets. For instance, US subsidiaries operating in Singapore enjoy duty-free access to the Japanese market for their production (subject to meeting the rules of origin in Singapore's economic partnership agreement with Japan), something not always available to them if they exported to Japan from their home base in the USA.

Key points

- Governments often enter regional trade agreements for political reasons.
- These include: enhancing security; improving their international bargaining positions; signalling to potential investors the seriousness of their commitment to reforms; to satisfy domestic constituencies' demands for 'reciprocity'; and because they perceive regional agreements are easier to negotiate than those within the WTO.
- Economic motivations for regionalism include access to a larger 'domestic' market; possibilities for attracting additional foreign direct investment; the possibility of engaging in 'deeper integration'; and the opportunity afforded to continue to protect politically sensitive, globally uncompetitive industries.

The rush to regionalism

The rush to regionalism in the 1990s is the second major wave of RTAs since the Second World War: the first occurred in the early 1960s, largely in response to the 1957 establishment of the European Economic Community (regionalism, however, has a much longer history, dating back several centuries: the previous peak in regional activity occurred in the interwar period when industrialized countries responded to the great depression by attempting to form closed trading blocs with less developed countries, in the case of European countries, with their colonies).

Many of the agreements negotiated in the 1960s linked less developed countries. In Africa, the growth of regionalism followed former European colonies gaining their independence in the late 1950s and early 1960s. As in Latin America, the other continent where regionalism took off in this period, the principal objectives of the regional agreements were to promote local industrialization to substitute for imports, and to enhance the bargaining power of participants vis-à-vis external actors (in Asia, few regional economic partnerships, with the exception of ASEAN,

emerged, not least because of Cold War conflicts that divided countries in this part of the world). In marked contrast with the most recent wave of regionalism, the agreements among less developed countries in the 1960s aimed to restrict imports from outside the region (in other words, they deliberately sought trade diversion—see Box 5.2—and to control foreign investors).

The landscape of interstate relations in Latin America and particularly in Africa soon became littered with the debris of failed regional arrangements. One reason was that few of the parties to regional arrangements were significant economic partners for one another. This was especially the case in Africa where the economies had been shaped in the colonial era to produce primary commodity exports for the European market. The share of intraregional trade (that is, trade with regional partners) in countries' overall trade was often less than 5 per cent. A consequence was that liberalization of intraregional trade in itself brought the participants few immediate benefits.

Moreover, liberalization of trade within a region often exacerbated existing inequalities among the partner states. Where companies had a choice of a single country location to serve the unified regional market, they usually preferred the city where infrastructure was most developed. Industries therefore tended to cluster around 'growth poles' and shunned the poorer-resourced towns and cities in the least developed parts of the region. The less developed countries in a regional partnership frequently found that they faced significant costs from trade diversion as imports from outside the region were replaced by relatively high-cost production from their partner states. They also lost tariff revenue, on which many less developed economies depend heavily as a source of government funding (both because of the removal of intra-regional tariffs and from the diversion of imports from outside the region to goods sourced from regional partners).

Some regional arrangements (including ASEAN and the Andean Pact) attempted to address the problems caused by this unbalanced growth by pursuing a policy of industrial licensing: the location of new industrial plants would be agreed by governments and allocated across different parts of the region to ensure that the less developed gained a share of the benefits from integration. But such an approach was politically unpopular with the governments of the more developed partners. They perceived the losses in investment forgone and the generally negative responses from foreign partners as exceeding any gains they made from collaboration with their less developed regional partners.

Arguments about the distribution of benefits from regionalism led to the collapse of many of the schemes established in the 1960s, and to a heightening of tensions between regional partners. Contrary to the idea that regionalism might improve inter-state security, disputes over the distribution of benefits from regional partnerships arguably contributed in some instances to the onset of armed conflicts between former regional partners, for example, the 'soccer war' between former Central American Common Market members Honduras and El Salvador in 1969, and hostilities between former East African Community members Uganda and Tanzania in 1979.

The new regionalism

The failure of many regional trade agreements among less developed countries in the 1970s (Figure 5.1 shows how few schemes from the 1960s and 1970s are still in force today) occurred at a time when there was a considerable degree of pessimism about the prospects for the European Community. There, integration had proceeded more slowly than many had anticipated, and progress had been punctuated by increasingly acrimonious disputes among the member governments. By the middle of the 1970s, when worldwide economic conditions were more turbulent than at any time since 1945 because of the Organization of Petroleum Exporting Countries-induced oil price rises and subsequent recession, regional integration no longer appeared to be a viable solution to the problems of interdependence that governments faced. To political leaders and academics alike, regional integration appeared increasingly obsolescent—the terminology the intellectual father of European integration studies, Ernst B. Haas (1975), applied at the time to theories of integration.

Two factors were to change the global context to make it far more favourable to regionalism in the 1990s. The first was the end of the Cold War. Regional economic agreements, like other aspects of international economic relations, are, in Aggarwal's (1985) terminology, 'nested' within the overall security context. A dramatic change in the security context opened up new possibilities for partnerships among countries that had previously been on opposite sides of the Cold War divide. In Europe, the disintegration of the former Soviet Union and the 1991 break-up of COMECON, the Council of Mutual Economic Assistance (founded in 1949 by the Soviet Union as an alternative to the assistance that the USA was providing Western Europe through the Marshall Plan, its membership expanded to include Czechoslovakia, East Germany, Poland, Hungary, Romania, Bulgaria, Mongolia, and Albania), opened the way for East European countries to enter into economic agreements with the European Union, and required new arrangements to be established amongst their former members if economic cooperation was to be sustained. Georgia, for instance, signed six free trade agreements with other former Soviet republics in the 1990s.

The concentration of new regional agreements in Europe in the 1990s underlines the importance of the East European fragmentation for the growth in the number of regional trade agreements. In Asia also, the end of the Cold War broke down the barriers that had previously prevented regional economic integration. In 1991, China joined the APEC grouping, which included its former Cold War foes Japan, the USA, and South Korea. In 2001, demonstrating the enormous improvement of relations that had occurred in East Asia over the previous decade, China began to negotiate a free trade agreement with ASEAN.

The second contextual factor was the growth in global interdependence, and the ascendancy of neo-liberal ideas in Western governments and in the international financial institutions. The growing integration of markets—for goods, services, and finance—placed increasing pressure on governments to pursue market-friendly policies. Potential foreign investors quickly voted with their feet when faced by governments that attempted to impose conditions on them: indeed, from the early 1980s onwards, the balance of bargaining power between investors and governments shifted dramatically so that investors were increasingly able to demand concessions from host governments on issues such as taxation, rather than accepting restrictions on their activities. Similarly, financial markets were quick to punish governments that were perceived to be inward-looking or inclined towards interventionist measures.

In this new context, the regional arrangements that developed were often designed to enhance states' participation in the global economy, to signal their openness to foreign investment, and to seek access to the markets of industrialized countries. Unlike the arrangements from the 1960s and 1970s, the new regionalism frequently involved partnerships between industrialized and less developed economies, that is, they were often North–South rather than South–South in orientation. The North American Free Trade Agreement is the obvious example; meanwhile, many less developed economies sought free trade agreements with the European Union, and by the early years of the new millennium, Japan had begun to negotiate free trade agreements with less developed economies in South-East Asia and Latin America.

It was not just less developed countries that responded to the increased market integration through seeking regional economic partnerships. The decision by European member states to deepen integration and to complete the implementation of a single internal market (brought into being by the Single European Act, signed in 1986), has been widely interpreted as an attempt to strengthen the capacity of European companies to compete in the new global market place (Sandholtz and Zysman 1989; Schirm 2002).

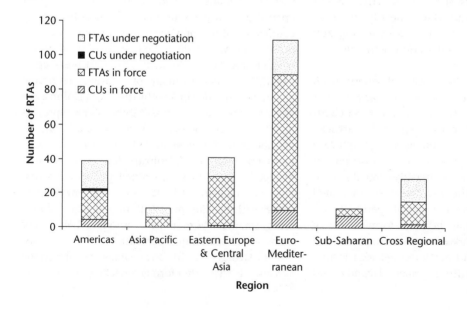

Fig. 5.2 Geographical distribution of RTAs, both in force and under negotiation

Source: WTO (2000*b*)

Table 5.3 Notified RTAs in goods by the date of entry into force and type of partners (as of January 2003)

	Developed-Developed	Developed-Developing	Developed-Transition	Developing-Developing	Developing-Transition	Transition-Transition	Total
1958–1964	2	0	0	1	0	0	3
1965–1969	0	0	0	0	1	0	1
1970–1974	5	3	0	2	0	0	10
1975–1979	0	5	0	1	0	0	6
1980–1984	2	1	0	1	0	0	4
1985–1989	1	1	0	2	0	0	4
1990–1994	3	3	12	5	0	6	29
1995–1999	3	7	10	4	12	28	64
2000–2002	0	11	4	5	4	6	30
TOTAL	16	31	26	21	17	40	151

Note: Developed countries include Canada, the United States, EU, EFTA, Japan, Australia, and New Zealand; transition countries include the former Soviet Union, Eastern and Central Europe, the Baltic States, and the Balkans; the remaining countries are classified as developing.

Source: WTO (2003c: Table 1B.9).

Table 5.3 illustrates a number of the factors contributing to the explosive growth in regionalism in the 1990s. Transition economies (the former Soviet bloc countries) were involved in more than one half of all RTAs signed in the 1990s (including forty RTAs that only involved other transition economies). Reflecting the desire of Southern countries to seek alliances with Northern partners, there was also a dramatic jump in the number of RTAs linking developed with developing countries in the 1990s. In contrast, only six of the more than 120 agreements initiated between 1990 and 2002 linked two or more developed economies.

A variety of other factors also contributed to the growth of regionalism in the 1990s.

Frustration with the difficulties of negotiating global agreements

The GATT began as a relatively small international institution dominated by Western industrial countries (see Winham, Chapter 4 in this volume). As more countries joined the GATT, so the difficulties of reaching agreement among an increasingly diverse group on an agenda that was becoming more complex were intensified. The consequence was that it took much longer to bring successive rounds of GATT talks to a conclusion.

When the Uruguay Round of GATT negotiations stalled over issues relating to trade in agricultural products, governments turned to regional agreements both as a substitute for a global agreement and as a means of increasing pressure on other countries to attempt to persuade them to make concessions in global talks. Similar considerations applied a decade later when the WTO prepared to launch a new round of global trade negotiations: membership of the WTO was approaching 150 economies and the agenda was yet more complex. The 'debacle in Seattle', the failure of the WTO's ministerial meeting in December 1999, convinced many governments (including that of Japan, see Ministry of Economy 2000), that negotiation of a new global agreement would not bring early results and that they should therefore look to RTAs if they wished to advance their trade agendas. The failure of the Cancun WTO ministerial meeting in September 2003 reinforced these beliefs.

Bandwagoning and balancing: 'contagion' effects

The fact that post-war regional integration has come in two waves points both to the likelihood that common responses have occurred across various parts of the globe to the same stimuli (especially, as noted above, to increased economic interdependence), and to the possibility that regionalism in one part of the world triggers regionalism elsewhere through 'demonstration', 'emulation', or 'contagion' effects.

The establishment of the European Common Market in 1957, with its apparently positive impacts both on inter-state relations and on the economies of its members, inspired a wave of imitations among less developed countries. Similarly, the completion of the single internal market in the EU in 1992 and the establishment of NAFTA in 1994 led governments elsewhere to take a keener interest in becoming participants in regional agreements. The Japanese government report cited above, for instance, presented a detailed review of academic studies of existing regional arrangements, concluding that they generally had a positive effect on the welfare of member states. For many governments, therefore, the new interest in regionalism was primarily a defensive response to developments elsewhere. And some governments that were already party to regional arrangements sought new ones in an attempt to reduce their dependence on existing regional partners. Mexico, for instance, began negotiations for free trade arrangements with the European Union and Japan as a means of reducing its heavy reliance on its NAFTA partners.

It was not just governments, however, that were prompted into action by regionalism elsewhere. The essence of preferential trade agreements is that they are discriminatory: non-members do not share the benefits they provide. Companies located in non-members therefore find that RTAs place them at a competitive disadvantage. They have an incentive to lobby their governments either to bandwagon by joining existing regional arrangements where such possibilities exist, or to negotiate a treaty that provides them with equivalent access to markets. For instance, following the implementation of NAFTA and the signature of the Mexico–EU Free Trade Agreement, Japanese manufacturers found themselves at a disadvantage in competing in the Mexican market. Whereas their American and European counterparts enjoyed duty-free access to Mexico, Japanese companies faced tariffs that averaged 16 per cent. The main business grouping, the Japan Federation of Economic Organizations, *Keidanren*, lobbied the government to sign a free trade agreement with Mexico that would give Japanese companies equivalent access to that enjoyed by their competitors (Ravenhill 2003).

The proliferation of preferential trade agreements across the globe, with the potential competitive disadvantages they bring for non-participants, increases the incentives for governments to either join existing agreements or to seek similar arrangements for their own exporters (Baldwin 1997; Oye 1992).

The change in the US attitude towards preferential agreements

The United States government was the strongest supporter of a non-discriminatory multilateral approach to trade in the negotiations that led to the creation of GATT at the end of the Second World War. Not only had it been a victim of the discriminatory colonial trading blocs that the European powers had created in the inter-war period, but it believed that their closing off international trade had made a significant contribution to the global recession of the 1930s. It was largely at US insistence that non-discrimination was enshrined as the cornerstone of the post-war global trade regime.

Washington was, however, willing to tolerate regional trading groupings that discriminated against its exports where it believed that these helped to achieve its political objectives through, for example, facilitating reconciliation between former enemies and strengthening the economies of the participants so that they would be less susceptible to the perceived communist threat. Security concerns trumped economic principles. The primary example was the European Economic Community (EEC). Washington had encouraged European recipients of Marshall Plan assistance (Box 5.4), to coordinate their plans (which led to the formation of the Organization for European Economic Cooperation, the forerunner to the OECD, the Organization for Economic Cooperation and Development). It put pressure on France to accommodate the rebuilding of Germany's industry and to devise a mechanism that would allay French concerns (which ultimately became the Schuman Plan for the European Coal and Steel Community). The US government supported the formation of the EEC in 1957 even though it was obvious that the new Community, like the ECSC, would not be fully compatible with GATT requirements for regional agreements, and would discriminate against US exports. At the same time it exerted pressure on the Europeans not to introduce any provisions that would increase discrimination against US economic interests. Its support for European integration was also accompanied by

---

Box 5.4 The Marshall Plan

Under the Marshall Plan, the US government provided $11.8 billion in grants and a further $1.5 billion in loans to assist in the rebuilding of European economies (and, in some instances, those of their colonies) in the years 1948–52. The United Kingdom received the largest volume of grants ($2.8 billion) followed by France ($2.5 billion), Italy ($1.4 billion), and West Germany ($1.2 billion). The Plan was an outgrowth of Washington's concerns about the perceived growth of Soviet influence in Europe. Funds were used for purposes such as purchasing new machinery for factories, providing technical assistance to enable Europeans to become familiar with new technologies, and the rebuilding of roads, railways, and ports. The bilateral assistance provided to Europe under the Marshall Plan far exceeded the funds available from the International Bank for Reconstruction and Development (World Bank). The Organization for European Economic Cooperation (which subsequently evolved into the Organization for Economic Cooperation and Development (OECD)) was created to manage the Marshall Plan aid.

American initiatives in the GATT for new rounds of global negotiations with the objective of reducing overall tariff levels and thus the discrimination its exporters would face in the European market (the 'Kennedy Round', 1963–7, was the response to the EEC's creation, and the 'Tokyo Round', 1973–9, the response to the first enlargement of the Community when it admitted Denmark, Ireland, and the United Kingdom in 1973).

Washington's attitude towards regional economic agreements among less developed countries was more ambivalent. Although it appreciated the possibility that regionalism might improve the security of the participants, its enthusiasm was tempered because of the anti-import and pro-interventionist frameworks that figured prominently in many of the regional schemes among less developing countries in the 1960s. Its support for regional economic integration among Latin American countries therefore was at best lukewarm. And, in other parts of the world, especially Asia, Washington opposed any movement towards a regional agreement from which it would be excluded.

The US attitude towards regional economic agreements changed in the early 1980s as it despaired of the slow progress in global trade liberalization and bristled at the growing trade distortions generated by the European Community's Common Agricultural Policy. United States Trade Representative William Brock announced in 1982 that Washington was willing to enter into regional trade agreements. Negotiation of a free trade agreement with Israel followed quickly. The USA also launched the Caribbean Basin Initiative, a programme of trade preferences for the island states of the region. Far more significant, however, was Washington's positive response to a Canadian proposal for negotiation of a free trade agreement. In one sense this was not a dramatic departure in American trade policy. Washington had offered such an agreement to Canada on several occasions over the previous century only to be rebuffed by a Canadian government concerned about maintaining its economic independence. Nonetheless, the signature of the Canada–US Free Trade Agreement in 1988 sent a dramatic signal to other members of the international community. This was reinforced in the following years when the first Bush administration indicated its willingness to construct a 'hub and spokes' framework that would link the USA in a series of free trade agreements with partners in Central and Latin America, Oceania, and East Asia.

The new approach to trade policy in the early 1990s was stated succinctly by Lawrence Summers, who became Under-Secretary of the Treasury for International Affairs in the first Clinton administration: that there should be a 'presumption in favor of all the lateral reductions in trade barriers, whether they be multi, uni, tri, plurilateral' (quoted in Frankel 1997: 5). In other words, the policy was one of 'anything goes' in trade policy as long as it contributed to trade liberalization, there no longer being a presumption that discriminatory regional agreements would be barriers to liberalization at the global level.

With the United States itself in the second half of the 1990s actively pursuing regionalism through NAFTA and advocating its extension into a Free Trade Area of the Americas, it would have been difficult for Washington to maintain its opposition to regionalism in other parts of the world. The change in attitude was particularly important in facilitating the development of preferential trade arrangements in East Asia. Whereas Washington had vigorously opposed a proposal from Malaysian Prime Minister Mahathir Mohamad in the early 1990s for the creation of an East Asian Economic Group, which would have excluded the countries of North America and Oceania that were members of the rival APEC grouping, by the late 1990s it acquiesced in the creation of an equivalent grouping (ASEAN Plus Three, the ten ASEAN members plus China, Japan, and South Korea), and in numerous East Asian moves to negotiate bilateral free trade arrangements.

Making existing preferential trade arrangements compatible with WTO requirements

Some of the new free trade areas came into being because industrialized countries perceived that they needed to make their trade agreements with less developed countries compatible with the WTO's regulations. Here the European Union has again been the most important actor.

The European Union had previously constructed a network of preferential trade arrangements with the countries of the southern Mediterranean and with the ACP grouping, which comprises over seventy countries in Africa, the Caribbean, and the Pacific, many of which had formerly been European colonies. These agreements had been negotiated in contexts entirely different from that prevailing in the second half of the 1990s. The arrangements with the ACP grouping were codified in the Lomé Conventions, the first of which had come into effect in 1975 at the height of the demands from less developed economies for the creation of a New International Economic Order. Reflecting a context in which industrialized countries were responsive to the demands from less developed economies for special treatment, the Conventions offered duty-free access to the European market for most ACP exports, without obliging the ACP countries to provide similar preferential treatment to European exports: in other words, they were non-reciprocal arrangements. (Treaties with southern Mediterranean countries, signed in 1975–7, offered similar duty-free access to the European market: the Mediterranean countries committed themselves to lower their tariffs on imports

from the European Community but the timetable for this process was not specified).

Besides the general trade provisions, the Lomé Conventions also included special arrangements for specific products, including bananas, beef, rum, and sugar, on which some countries' export earnings were heavily dependent, often enabling their sale in European markets at prices much higher than those prevailing elsewhere. In some instances, they rested on a segmentation of the European market, with, for instance, exports of ACP bananas being subject to different treatment in the United Kingdom and in France than they received in Germany and the Netherlands. The European Union, in fact, operated three different tariff regimes for bananas even though, as a common market, it had supposedly adopted a common external tariff. The new commitment to realizing a single internal market in the EU in 1992 made it impossible to maintain this arrangement for ACP bananas.

In an attempt to preserve the special position of ACP bananas, the European Union introduced an interventionist system of import licensing that discriminated against bananas coming from non-ACP countries (primarily Central and Latin America). Several of these producing countries challenged the new EU banana regime in the GATT; they were supported by the US government, which had been lobbied by the two giant US agribusiness firms, Dole and Chiquita, that handled most of the trade in Central and Latin American bananas. The outcome of the lengthy and convoluted dispute, which spanned the time period during which the WTO took over from the GATT, and which at one stage threatened to trigger a 'trade war' between the United States and the European Union, was that a WTO Dispute Settlement Panel found that the European provisions on bananas contravened several of its articles. The Europeans eventually backed down, committing themselves to introduce arrangements that were compatible with their WTO obligations.

The dispute illustrated how the WTO makes it possible for less developed countries to initiate a successful challenge against an aspect of the trade policies of an economic superpower, the EU. It also demonstrated the significance of the changed arrangements for dispute settlement with the transition from the GATT to the WTO: unlike the situation under the

GATT, when countries simply ignored dispute settlement judgements that they did not like, the EU had no viable alternative but to conform to the WTO's requirements. More important than the specifics of the banana dispute itself are the implications of the WTO's judgement for rules governing the relations between industrialized and less developed economies.

In finding that the EU's banana regime contravened several of its provisions, the WTO rejected European arguments that the trade arrangements with the ACP were legitimized by WTO rules on RTAs and on special treatment for less developed economies. The WTO found that the Lomé Convention did not conform to its rules for regional trade arrangements because the ACP countries were not required to remove their tariffs on European imports (under the requirements of Article XXIV, all parties to a regional economic agreement must liberalize 'substantially all trade' between them). Moreover, the Convention did not conform to the rules on preferences for less developed economies because it gave special treatment to one group (the ACP) but not to other economies at similar levels of development. These rulings left the EU with only one other avenue for seeking WTO legitimacy for the Convention: to apply under Article IX of the WTO for a special waiver from the most-favoured-nation rule. But the requirements for such a waiver are more stringent under the WTO than they were in the GATT, the waiver is only for a fixed term and would not prevent WTO members from subsequently challenging specific elements of the arrangements. In other words, a waiver would have provided little assurance to the ACP states that the provisions would not be disrupted in the future.

Faced with this dilemma, the EU decided that the only means through which it could provide long-term trade security for the ACP would be to abandon its previous approach and to negotiate arrangements that were compatible with WTO rules on regional trade agreements (Article XXIV). It proposed to do this through concluding a series of economic partnership agreements with groupings of ACP countries. A similar decision had been made earlier regarding the trade agreements with the countries of the southern Mediterranean: in its Barcelona Declaration of 1995, the EU stated its intention to negotiate WTO-compatible free trade agreements with these countries. These have subsequently been concluded with Tunisia (1995), Israel (1995), Morocco (1996), Jordan (1997), Egypt (1999), Algeria (2001), and Lebanon (2002).

Key points

- The regional trade agreements of the 1960s and 1970s aimed to promote regional industrialization behind tariff walls.
- They often broke down because of disagreements over the distribution of benefits and costs from regional cooperation.
- The new regionalism differs from this previous wave in seeking countries' increased integration into the world economy.
- Its origins lie in the end of the Cold War, the perceived success of RTAs elsewhere; frustrations with the pace of trade liberalization at the global level; a desire to make existing preferential trade relations compatible with WTO rules; and a change in US attitudes towards regionalism.

The political economy of regionalism

Private sector interests

Previous sections of this chapter have identified several reasons why governments and private sector actors might wish to pursue regional economic integration. It is straightforward, for instance, to suggest that when companies face high tariffs in markets where their competitors' products enter duty free because of the existence of free trade arrangements, they will lobby their governments to obtain similar arrangements. But other than for these defensive reasons, when might companies support the establishment of a regional free trade area rather than prefer either continued protectionism or non-discriminatory liberalization?

To address this question requires a starting point that is far removed from the assumptions of trade theory as developed in neoclassical economics (which assumes constant returns to scale and immobile factors of production, that is, unit costs of production are the same regardless of the size of the production run, and factors of production, for example capital, will not move across national boundaries). In particular, it rests on the possibility that companies will be able to produce more efficiently for a regional rather than a domestic market because they are able to capture economies of scale, on the increasing mobility of capital, and on observations regarding the geographical distribution of subsidiaries of transnational corporations.

The economies of scale argument assumes that regional integration is able to provide firms with the minimum market size required for them to capture scale economies whereas the domestic market alone is too small for this to happen. But why would firms not prefer multilateral liberalization so as to gain access to even larger global markets? The reason is that a regional agreement will provide an opportunity to retain tariff and other barriers against competitors from outside the region. The logic is that of strategic trade theory, one component of which asserts that it is possible for governments to provide an advantage to their domestic companies if they offer a protected domestic market that enables them to realize economies of scale (Krugman 1990; for an application of the argument to the regional level see Milner 1997*b*; and Chase 2003).

The other departure from conventional trade theory rests on an acknowledgement that contemporary manufacturing often involves conducting various stages of production in different geographical locations to take advantage of local characteristics such as relatively low-cost labour or a concentration of product- or industry-specific skills. From the 1980s onwards, United States and European firms, facing intense competition in their domestic market from imports from East Asia, established subsidiaries in relatively low-labour-cost neighbouring countries, from which they sourced components. The establishment of regional free trade areas facilitates this corporate strategy (and here it is appropriate to remember the North–South architecture of many of the new regional arrangements of the 1990s, for example, trade agreements between the European Union and Eastern European and Mediterranean countries, NAFTA, and the Caribbean Basin Initiative). Moreover, the rules of origin, in NAFTA for instance, that allow components sourced from US companies to be counted towards requirements that goods must meet if they are to be deemed to have been manufactured in Mexico, serve as a protectionist device that provides further advantage to US-based corporations (for further discussion see Cox 2000).

As Alan Rugman demonstrates in Chapter 10, even though multinational enterprises disperse their activities to capitalize on local characteristics, their production and sales are frequently concentrated within one geographical region. This geographical concentration of activities is likely to cause many MNEs to put their efforts into lobbying for regional trading agreements rather than for liberalization at the global level because their principal interest is in removing barriers to trade between those countries in which their manufacturing plants are located. This concentration on the regional level is encouraged by the better prospects there, compared with the global level of pursuing the 'deeper integration' that MNEs need for efficient integration of their production networks, for example, agreements on the treatment that foreign investment will receive, protection of intellectual property rights, and facilitation of the movement of skilled workers and management.

Economies of scale and regionalization of production may both incline companies towards lobbying for regional trade agreements but their impact on the attitudes of labour is likely to be more ambiguous. On the one hand, the possibility of gaining larger market share, longer production runs, and higher profits through the realization of economies of scale offers the prospect to labour of additional employment, higher wages, etc. On the other, the opportunity that the negotiation of a free trade area provides companies to regionalize their production will be likely to worry labour unions in relatively high-wage countries who will fear that labour-intensive stages of production will be moved to those parts of the region with lower labour costs. It was not surprising, therefore, that companies with regionalized production

Box 5.5 **Rules of origin**

Countries that enter into a free trade agreement inevitably are concerned that non-members should not exploit the benefits they provide to their partners. In particular, they fear that because free trade areas do not have a common external tariff, non-members will send goods into the free trade area through the country with the lowest tariff, and then use the free trade provisions of the grouping to access other members' markets. This *trade deflection* will lead to a loss of tariff revenue for the economies with higher tariffs and possibly to greater competition for their domestic producers.

Consider, for instance, the following hypothetical example. Assume that Mexico has a 5 per cent tariff on cameras whereas Canada and the United States both have a 12 per cent tariff. If they were able to take advantage of the introduction of free trade under NAFTA, Japanese camera manufacturers would export their cameras to Mexico and supply Canada and the United States from these exports. Both the Canadian and US governments would lose tariff revenue that they would otherwise collect on imports of Japanese cameras. And Japanese cameras (now subject to a lower tariff) would become more competitive than they otherwise would have been with cameras produced in Canada and the United States.

To prevent free trade areas from causing trade deflection of this type, their members typically adopt what are called rules of origin. These are intended to ensure that goods will only benefit from the provisions of the free trade agreement if they can be considered to have 'originated', that is, to have been produced, in the partner country. Goods that are merely passing through the partner or, for instance, have been re-stamped as 'Made in Mexico', will not qualify for duty-free access to other members' markets. Determining where a product has originated has become increasingly difficult in an integrated global economy with goods often being assembled from components manufactured in various countries.

Rules of origin typically take one or more of the following forms:

(*a*) A value-added criterion. This specifies that a particular percentage of the value of the export must have been generated within the partner country. For instance, to qualify as a local product for the purposes of NAFTA, 62.5 per cent of the value of an automobile must have been generated locally.

(*b*) A change of tariff heading criterion. The World Customs Organization has developed a 'Harmonized System Nomenclature' of tariff headings that classifies all products according to their degree of processing, ranging from raw materials through semi-processed products to finished manufactures. Under this criterion, a good is considered to have been produced domestically if a change in tariff heading results from the local processing/manufacture.

(*c*) A specific processing criterion. This stipulates that particular stages in the production of the export must have been undertaken locally. For instance, cloth may only be considered a local product if weaving has been undertaken locally.

(*d*) A specific components criterion. This establishes that particular parts of the finished good must have been manufactured locally for it to qualify for duty-free treatment. In NAFTA, colour television sets are considered to be local products only if their picture tubes have been manufactured locally. Usually, rules of origin allow for 'cumulation' so that components sourced from partner countries are counted as if they have been produced domestically (so that, for instance, a colour TV manufactured in Mexico which contains a picture tube manufactured in the USA would be classed as a local product for NAFTA rules of origin purposes).

As is evident from these examples, rules of origin are usually product-specific and can be very complex. Specification of the rules of origin often constitutes the bulk of the agreements that establish free trade areas. Those for NAFTA, for instance, run to close to 200 pages of small print. They require detailed, complex negotiations. The complexity of rules of origin is often viewed as a barrier to developing economies' participation in international trade, especially when they have to cope with multiple sets of rules that govern trade with different partners.

The negotiation of rules of origin, moreover, whose product-specific provisions often appear to be arbitrary, offers an opportunity for domestic interests to attempt to seek protection against the effects of regional trade liberalization. Setting a high value-added criterion may make it impossible for rival producers in partner countries to qualify for duty-free access to the domestic market. And the requirement that a specific component be produced locally may increase the discrimination against non-members and exclude them from the enlarged regional market. For instance, Schiff and Winters (2003: 80) cite the example of tomato ketchup. Under the 1988 Canada–US Free Trade Agreement (CUSFTA), ketchup produced from imported tomato paste qualified as a local product and received duty-free treatment. When the CUSFTA was converted into NAFTA, however, the new rules of origin stated that ketchup would be considered a local product only if it contained tomato paste manufactured within NAFTA. The result was *trade diversion* from Chile to Mexico: whereas Chile accounted for more than 80 per cent of US imports of tomato paste before NAFTA, after the introduction of the NAFTA rules of origin Chile's share dropped to 5 per cent whereas that of Mexico rose to 75 per cent.

networks lobbied in favour of NAFTA whereas labour unions (together with American firms that produced solely within the USA for the domestic market) expressed their concern that the agreement would generate, in the words of H. Ross Perot, a 'giant sucking sound' as US jobs were lost to Mexico (Chase 2003).

What drives regionalism forward?

As indicated in Box 5.1, governments that enter regional agreements that involve more than the creation of a free trade area inevitably have to agree to establish institutions that 'pool their sovereignty' on policies that have to be determined at the regional level, for instance, the determination of common external tariffs and other common foreign economic policies in customs unions. The deeper the integration, that is the broader the scope of policy issues on which members agree to cooperate, the greater will be the number of policy areas on which regional institutions will have to be given competence (unless members agree to a policy of mutual recognition whereby they accept policies/standards in other members as if they were their own).

Political scientists have long been fascinated by the question of whether, once a regional arrangement is established, it generates its own momentum towards not only closer economic but also closer political integration. The vast majority of regional economic agreements take the form of free trade areas, which, because they do not require setting a common external tariff, provide little stimulus for the establishment of a regional institution to coordinate policies. Most free trade areas do provide a process for the resolution of disputes between the parties over the interpretation and/or implementation of the free trade area's rules, but this is usually managed by secretariats within the governments of the member countries. For instance, although there is a NAFTA secretariat, which administers the dispute resolution procedures created by the agreement, this is a 'virtual' secretariat comprised of three sections located within the respective national governments. Very limited scope is available to such national agencies to act to promote deeper regional integration: indeed, the very lack of the creation of any alternative source of authority at the regional level is one of the attractions of free trade areas to many national governments. Even in those free trade areas where member governments have agreed to create a central secretariat, as in ASEAN, they often deliberately keep such institutions weak so that they do not develop as challengers to national governments.

With deeper integration, the scope for regional institutions to act autonomously may increase. The best example is the European Union, the only regional agreement that has fully implemented a common market and moved beyond this to form an economic union. It has by far the most complex of governance arrangements of any regional grouping. As Helen Wallace (2000: 44) suggests, 'much of what makes the EU so interesting . . . is the density of institutions and the evidence of institutional creativity. EU institutions provide both opportunities and constraints, and they serve to channel and to structure the behaviour of political actors from the participating countries.'

The principal political organs at the regional level are a supranational secretariat, the European Commission ('supranational' because it is autonomous from the governments of the member states and its officials have the responsibility of promoting the interests of the EU as a whole rather than those of specific members), an institution comprised of ministers from the national governments (the Council of Ministers), the European Parliament (directly elected since 1979 by voters in the member states), and the European Court of Justice (which is charged with interpreting the various EU treaties that member states have signed). The EU treaties now extend far beyond the liberalization of internal trade and the establishment of common foreign economic policies to include competition policies, environmental policies, common foreign and security policies, justice and home affairs, and regional development. The European Union and its member states now constitute a complex web of multilevel governance, with authority for making and implementing policies on various issues being split between institutions at the regional level, at the national level and, in some instances, at the subnational level (for further discussion see Bomberg and Stubb 2003; and Wallace and Wallace 2000).

Most of the theorizing in international relations on regionalism has concentrated on the European experience. The early experience of European integration inspired the development of *neo-functionalist* analysis (Haas 1958; Lindberg 1963). This approach suggested how a regional grouping could generate a momentum of its own that would lead to a deepening of cooperation. The logic was that cooperation in one area of economic activity would produce pressures for cooperation in other areas as the costs of pursuing uncoordinated policies became increasingly evident to member states, a process that the neo-functionalist theorists termed 'spillover'. Entrepreneurial leadership by regional institutions could intensify the pressures for further cooperation.

In the European Union, the European Commission has the power to take initiatives in the various areas where the members have agreed that the EU has competence; it thus has the capacity to shape agendas and to push for further cooperation at the European level. The European Court of Justice's responsibility for interpreting the treaties and for adjudicating disputes between member states affords it an opportunity that extends into the realm of policy making; over the last quarter of the twentieth century some of its judgements significantly extended the scope of European competence.

One element of neo-functional theorizing was to emphasize the significance of the unintended

consequences of previous actions and decisions. For instance, member states did not anticipate the important role that the Court of Justice would come to play in extending the scope of integration when they created a body that was intended to arbitrate disputes on the implementation of treaties. For scholars in the neo-functionalist tradition, the logic of spillover and the creative leadership provided by regional institutions can provide the integration process with a dynamic of its own (Sandholtz and Stone Sweet 1998 provide a recent example of theorizing from this perspective).

The neo-functionalist approach has consistently been challenged by scholars who assert that national states have primacy in the integration process. Stanley Hoffmann (1966) pioneered this challenge; the economic historian Alan Milward (1992) subsequently developed the theme that integration in Europe is best interpreted as a strategy pursued by national states to strengthen their own positions. Andrew Moravcsik (1998) presents the most theoretically sophisticated articulation of this 'liberal intergovernmental' argument, suggesting that the major steps forward in European integration were driven not by the European Commission or the Court of Justice but by member governments that were responding in a rational way to domestic economic interests. Key decisions on integration reflect bargains struck among member states; the most significant European institution therefore is not the supranational Commission but the intergovernmental Council of Ministers. For writers in this tradition, to the extent that member states delegate authority to community institutions, such moves are 'calculated, rational, and circumscribed' (Bomberg and Stubb 2003: 11).

In this hotly contested debate, as is often the case in international relations theorizing, authors writing from one perspective have been reluctant to acknowledge that the arguments of the competing school have any legitimacy. Because the EU embraces such a wide array of activities, and the competencies of its various actors and the balance of power between them have evolved over time, it is possible for both sides to this debate to find compelling examples that support their case. Rather than perceiving this issue as a dichotomy of government preferences versus the actions of supranational institutions, it would be more helpful to focus on the interaction between these two. Sandholtz (1993) has argued persuasively that state preferences themselves are not formed in a vacuum: membership in the EU itself has become an important influence on how governments define their interests.

To date, the failure of those other regional schemes that aspire to become common markets to realize their aspirations inevitably limits to the European context debates about the role that supranational institutions can play in driving integration forwards. Meanwhile, it is too early to tell whether the neo-functional logic of spillover will apply to some of the more significant free trade areas, most notably NAFTA, that were established in the 1990s.

Key points

- Corporations may prefer regionalism to global trade liberalization if it enables them to capture economies of scale while avoiding exposure to global competition.

- Regionalism may be particularly attractive to companies that seek 'deeper integration' to facilitate the operation of regional production networks.

- Unskilled labour in industrialized economies is likely to oppose regional integration if this includes less developed economies with significantly lower labour costs.

- Because most RTAs are free trade areas, they requiring little pooling of sovereignty and afford little scope for the emergence of sources of power at the regional level that rival national governments.

- In the EU, evidence from different sectors at different periods of time supports arguments from both the intergovernmental and the neo-functionalist perspectives.

The economic consequences of regional integration

The discussion of trade diversion in Box 5.2 reminds us that no assumption can be made that regional trade agreements will necessarily enhance the welfare of their participants. It is not straightforward to estimate the effect that RTAs have had on members' trade and their welfare more generally because the impact of many other variables has to be taken into consideration.

Regional agreements and members' trade

That the share of world trade conducted within RTAs has risen, as noted at the beginning of this chapter, reflects both an increase in the number of RTAs and an increase in the share of their total trade that members of RTAs conduct with one another. Table 5.4 shows for the major minilateral RTAs how the share of intra-regional trade in members' total trade evolved in the last quarter of the twentieth century.

The share of intraregional trade in the total trade of members of some regional agreements rose dramatically: most notable here were NAFTA, the Central American Common Market, CARICOM, and MERCOSUR. In contrast, ASEAN states were no more important as trading partners for one another in 2001 than they had been a quarter of a century before, despite implementing a free trade agreement in the interim. The record of many African RTAs was mixed: SADC was notably successful in increasing intra-regional trade, a reflection of the reintegration of the post-apartheid South Africa into the regional economy.

Simple statistics of this type, however, do not tell us whether the RTA itself has been a significant influence on trade among the member economies. Multiple factors other than the existence of a regional trade agreement can influence the volume of trade between any two countries. Among the most important of these are the size of the two economies, the levels of per capita income, the geographical distance

Table 5.4 Changes in the share of intra-regional trade in selected RTAs, 1970–2001

	1970	1980	1985	1990	1995	2000	2001
EU (1957)	59.5	60.8	59.2	65.9	62.4	62.1	61.2
NAFTA (1994)	36.0	33.6	43.9	41.4	46.2	55.7	54.8
CACM (1961)	26.0	24.4	14.4	15.4	21.7	13.7	15.0
Andean Group (1988)	1.8	3.8	3.2	4.2	12.2	8.8	11.2
CARICOM (1973)	4.2	5.3	6.3	8.1	12.1	14.6	13.4
MERCOSUR (1991)	9.4	11.6	5.5	8.9	20.3	20.7	20.8
ECOWAS (1975)	2.9	9.6	5.1	8.0	9.0	9.6	9.8
SADC (1992)	4.2	0.4	1.4	3.1	10.6	11.9	10.9
ASEAN/AFTA (1992)	22.4	17.4	18.6	19	24.6	23	22.4
GCC (1981)	4.6	3.0	4.9	8.0	6.8	5.0	5.1

Note: Figures in parentheses refer to year in which the RTA came into force.

Source: WTO (2003c: Table 1B.11).

between the two countries (and hence the transportation costs in trading), whether or not they share a common boundary, and whether or not their populations speak the same language. Such factors have to be built into any model that attempts to isolate the impact of the regional agreement itself on trade. Jeffrey Frankel (1997) has undertaken the most comprehensive modelling of this type. He finds that after allowing for the various factors identified above, regional trade agreements have had a (statistically significant) positive impact on the trade between their members. This positive effect is particularly pronounced for agreements among less developed economies, including ASEAN and MERCOSUR, but trade among EU member states was also 65 per cent above the level that would otherwise have been expected in the absence of a regional trade agreement. These results echo those in several other studies. The evidence points strongly to preferential trade agreements having caused changes in patterns of international trade.

These results in themselves, however, do not distinguish between trade creation and trade diversion effects, and thus tell us little about the welfare effects of the regional trade agreements. Again, isolating the causes of the increased trade is no easy task. The new preferences created for regional partners have to be viewed in the context of other changes in the participants' trade policies including, for instance, any reduction of their tariffs towards non-members of the regional agreement (as occurred in the 1980s and 1990s both through unilateral liberalization and through implementation of GATT/WTO agreements).

A major study by the World Bank (2000) finds that although the ratio of intra-regional trade to Gross Domestic Product (GDP) increased in all regional groupings reviewed, so too did the ratio of trade with extra-regional partners to GDP. In other words, not only did trade with regional partners grow in economic importance but so too did trade with countries outside the region. Consequently, the Bank concluded, while studies suggest that some trade diversion occurred in the EU, European Free Trade Association, and NAFTA, 'the picture is sufficiently mixed that it is not possible to conclude that trade diversion has been a major problem' (World Bank 2000: 48), a finding consistent with Frankel's (1997) comprehensive study (see also Krueger 1999).

That RTAs may distort members' trade patterns to only a limited extent is consistent with the lowering of MFN tariffs (and thus the preferential margins enjoyed by partner countries) that has occurred in the last two decades. In Canada, half of all MFN tariff lines are duty free; in the United States, the figure is 35 per cent. As noted in the previous chapter, the average tariff level in industrialized countries on imports of manufactured goods is less than 5 per cent.

A similar trend towards tariff reduction is also evident in most less developed countries, with an inevitable consequence for the preferential margins that RTAs create. In ASEAN, for instance, in roughly two-thirds of the tariff lines, MFN and preferential tariffs are identical. For many of the others, the preferential margin is so small in the most developed economies (Singapore and Malaysia) that few companies have found it worthwhile to meet the rules of origin requirements and file the necessary paperwork: less than 5 per cent of all intra-ASEAN trade takes advantage of preferential tariffs. Not only do many RTAs create few advantages for partners for many exports, they also seldom help in the most heavily protected areas: when 'sensitive' sectors are protected by high MFN tariffs, governments frequently also exempt them altogether from the regional agreement or minimize the liberalization provided.

Scale economies and competition effects

Regional trade agreements affect the welfare of their participants through impacts beyond those on trade itself. One argument made in support of RTAs is that they will lead to increased investment flows for participants. As noted earlier, inflows of foreign direct investment into Mexico increased substantially after the signature of NAFTA. Similarly, the establishment of the European Community and the subsequent deepening of European integration through the completion of the single internal market led to substantial increases in foreign direct investment in the EU, both intra-regionally, that is from one member state to another, and from external countries (Motta and Norman 1996).

The other area in which RTAs are often assumed to improve the welfare of participating countries is by increasing the size of the 'home' market. As noted earlier, this can be particularly important for firms dependent upon access to a market larger than that available within one country to achieve economies of scale. Moreover, regionalism may generate increased competition for domestic companies, thereby forcing them to become more efficient. Again, estimating these effects requires complex economic modelling

with often 'heroic' assumptions. Although the computer simulations reach dramatically different conclusions depending on the assumptions they use, the most frequent finding is that regional integration produces only a very limited positive aggregate effect on the economies of participants (on the Asia-Pacific region, for instance, see Scollay and Gilbert 2001). Critics suggest that these findings reflect the inability of the models to capture the 'dynamic' effects of regional integration, those that develop over time as companies benefit from scale economies and other efficiencies. Others, however, argue that the majority of benefits from regionalism come from increased competition rather than from realizing economies of scale, and that these competitive benefits can be achieved more effectively through non-discriminatory liberalization that exposes domestic companies to worldwide competition (Schiff and Winters 2003: 51–2).

In short, the verdict on the economic effects of regional trade arrangements is mixed and frequently inconclusive. Economic models suggest that there is little evidence that RTAs have generated significant trade diversion. They do appear to have been associated with increased inflows of foreign direct investment. Yet their overall effects on the economic welfare of participants, if positive, have been of limited magnitude. And in the most sophisticated of regional schemes, the European Union, any welfare benefits arising from improved competitiveness in manufacturing have been at least partially offset by the welfare losses caused by the EU's Common Agricultural Policy.

Key points

- Although considerable complexity is involved in attempting to isolate the economic effects of RTAs, evidence suggests that they have led to more trade among members than would otherwise be the case.

- RTAs do appear to have encouraged increased investment in member states.

- Economic simulations suggest that RTAs have had little aggregate effect on members' economic welfare.

- Little evidence exists that RTAs have produced significant trade diversion.

Regionalism and the WTO: stepping stone or stumbling block?

The advent of the new regionalism has been accompanied by a lively debate about its relationship to trade liberalization at the global level. Will regional trade agreements facilitate or obstruct global trade liberalization or, in Bhagwati's (1991) terminology, are regional agreements stepping stones or stumbling blocks?

Several arguments suggest how regional agreements might facilitate global negotiations:

1 Global negotiations involving regional groupings reduce the number of actors involved;

2 Reaching agreement on issues of deeper integration will be easier within regional groupings; these agreements can serve as models for global treaties;

3 Regional agreements can enhance the competitiveness of domestic industries, paving the way for full liberalization;

4 Regional agreements improve the financial position of export-oriented interests, thereby providing them with the means and incentive to lobby governments for broader liberalization.

The intuitively attractive argument that regional groupings simplify global negotiations by reducing the number of parties is counteracted by the difficulties that regional groupings often have in reaching a common position (witness the European Union on agricultural issues in global negotiations). Moreover, once a regional grouping has reached internal agreement on its own position, it may have little flexibility in bargaining with other actors. And there is no assurance that the common position adopted by a regional grouping will not be more restrictive than that held by a majority of its member states: in other words, the regional grouping can end up throwing its combined weight behind policies that might not have been supported by a majority of its members had they acted individually in the global negotiations. The recent proliferation of regional trade arrangements, many of which have overlapping memberships, suggests further complications should negotiations occur between 'regions' rather than between individual countries.

Until recently, little evidence existed to support arguments that agreement on contentious issues or on matters of 'deeper' integration could be reached more easily at the regional level. The European Union, for instance, has found it very difficult to liberalize the most politically sensitive areas of trade, especially in agriculture. In the OECD's words, 'regionalism has often failed to crack the hardest nuts' (2002: 20). And few regional agreements had moved beyond the basics of removing tariffs. Nonetheless, the recent wave of regionalism has provided greater encouragement for the argument that deeper integration on issues such as investment and the environment is more easily accomplished through regional negotiations (for further discussion see OECD 2002). Developments at the regional level on these issues, however, have yet to be translated into global agreements, so the idea of the regional positively influencing the global has yet to be substantiated.

The argument that regional agreements will enable industries to become internationally competitive and therefore that an RTA will ease the path towards non-discriminatory liberalization assumes that the level of competition at the regional level will be similar to that in the global market place to which firms will then be able to graduate. An alternative proposition is also intuitively plausible: that the regional market will be of sufficient size to enable firms to realize economies of scale, and that they will prefer to operate with the comfort provided by the external tariff of the regional grouping rather than be exposed to enhanced competition. Companies content with operating in the regional market may be financially strengthened through regional integration, and therefore may have an incentive to lobby against extending trade liberalization beyond the region.

Critics who see regional agreements as stumbling blocks in the path of global liberalization assert that:

1 They magnify the influence of power disparities in international trade relations, enabling larger economies to impose their will on smaller partners, gaining them advantages through rules of origin

that would not be achieved if liberalization occurred on a global basis, and thereby enhancing popular resentment in smaller, less developed economies against trade liberalization.

2 They lead to a diversion of scarce bureaucratic resources and political leadership away from global trade negotiations towards those at the regional level.

3 They give rise to what Bhagwati (1995) has termed a 'spaghetti bowl' effect of numerous, criss-crossing preferential arrangements with a multiplicity of tariff rates and different rules of origin. The complexity of regulations provides opportunities for special pleading by interest groups and generally increases the costs of engaging in international trade. With countries being members of several RTAs, each with its own set of rules, companies face difficult decisions on where to establish subsidiaries and where to source their inputs (OECD 2002: 18).

4 They provide exporters with the access to markets that they desire thereby removing their incentive to lobby the government for more complete domestic liberalization.

5 They enable governments to exempt sensitive political sectors from liberalization, thereby energizing protectionist forces and strengthening political resistance against liberalization at the global level.

The last two of these arguments rest on the possibility that regional arrangements will not be comprehensive in their product coverage because members are able to exploit the ambiguity of the WTO's rules on RTAs (Box 5.6 summarizes these rules). For the WTO to regard regional trade agreements as legitimate, average duties at the regional level must not be higher than those imposed by individual members before the agreement, and the arrangements must cover 'substantially all the trade' between the parties. The first of these obligations is ambiguous because it takes no account of rules of origin and non-tariff barriers; moreover, a substantial gap often exists between the tariff levels that countries have committed to in the WTO (so-called 'bound' rates) and the actual tariffs (usually lower) they have applied. In entering a regional agreement, countries, therefore, can keep the regional tariffs below their bound levels while actually imposing higher rates than they previously applied to non-members.

The ambiguities of the second obligation—the requirement that RTAs should cover substantially all trade—are of even greater import because they have enabled countries to exclude politically sensitive sectors from regional agreements. The European Union, for instance, did not include most of Mexico's and South Africa's agricultural exports in the free trade agreements it signed with these countries. Similarly, the Japanese government excluded the few agricultural products that Singapore exported to it from its free trade agreement with the island state.

The political significance is that free trade agreements that provide partial liberalization can provide exporters with what they want (access to foreign markets) while enabling governments to avoid tackling the problem of inefficient domestic industries. The result is a process of 'liberalization without political pain'. The continued protection that uncompetitive domestic industries enjoy by being exempted from regional liberalization may encourage them to lobby against any liberalization, whether at the regional or the global level. Meanwhile, the wider the network of preferential trade agreements, the less incentive will domestic exporters have for lobbying for liberalization at the global level. Take Mexico as the current extreme example. It has more than thirty preferential trade agreements with partners on all continents that collectively account for more than 60 per cent of global GDP and more than 97 per cent of its exports (the vast majority of course going to the United States). The signature of RTAs has substantially reduced the incentive for Mexican exporters to expend resources in lobbying for global liberalization.

The evidence

The sometimes contradictory arguments on the relationship between regional trade agreements and global trade liberalization rest on intuitively plausible hypotheses, but ones that are not easy to test. Moreover, the relatively brief period for which many of the new regional agreements have been operating makes it difficult to reach conclusions about their effects (and generalization is hazardous when the agreements themselves differ so markedly in their scope and content).

Box 5.6 **The World Trade Organization and preferential trade agreements**

Article XXIV of the GATT lays down the criteria that regional arrangements must meet to be regarded as legitimate by the WTO. Members' customs duties under the new agreement must not be higher or more restrictive than those previously imposed by the individual countries. The preferential agreement, according to Article XXIV.8, must also eliminate duties and other restrictions on 'substantially all the trade' between participants.

These provisions have generated enormous controversy over the years. In particular, members have failed to reach agreement on defining and applying the phrase 'substantially all the trade'. The WTO notes 'there exists neither an agreed definition of the percentage of trade to be covered by a WTO-consistent agreement nor common criteria against which the exclusion of a particular sector from the agreement could be assessed'. The European Union, a pioneer in negotiating preferential trade agreements, has argued that the Article XXIV.8 requirement has both a quantitative and a qualitative element, with at least 90 per cent of the trade between parties being covered and no major sector excluded. But other members have contested this interpretation, which raises its own problems of definition: How is the 90 per cent of trade to be measured (does it refer only to existing trade or to that which might take place should restrictions be removed)? And how does one define a 'major' sector? An agreed interpretation of Article XXIV.8 is one of the items on the agenda in the current Doha Round of multilateral negotiations.

The lack of agreement on Article XXIV.8 has stymied the work of the WTO's Committee on Regional Trade Agreements, created in February 1996 to examine preferential trade agreements and their implications for the multilateral trading system. Members have simply failed to determine whether or not any of the large number of

PTAs notified to the Committee since 1996 is fully compatible with the relevant rules. Lack of consensus has prevented the Committee from finalizing any of its reports. The WTO's record on this matter is similar to that of the GATT, which was able to agree on the compatibility with Article XXIV of only four of the more than fifty RTAs submitted to it for consideration. Political considerations have dominated decision making on this issue. Nowhere was this more evident than when a GATT Working Party considered whether the Treaty of Rome, which established the EEC in 1957, met the requirements for RTAs. Faced with a threat by the Europeans to quit GATT should their integration arrangements be found incompatible with the full requirements of Article XXIV (which they clearly were), the GATT Working Party failed to reach consensus in its deliberations. Ultimately, contracting parties' desire (as much for security as for economic reasons) for integration in Europe to proceed outweighed their concerns about the legality of the agreements. Subsequently, GATT and the WTO have simply failed to pass judgement on the vast majority of RTAs they have examined including CUSTA and NAFTA (one of the rare exceptions was GATT's approval in 1994 of the customs union between the Czech and Slovak Republics).

The rules relating to the establishment of preferential trading arrangements among less developed economies under the 'Enabling Clause' are even less restrictive than those under Article XXIV. They make no reference to coverage of trade, the complete elimination of duties or to a timetable for implementation. They require only that the regional agreement not constitute a barrier to most-favoured-nation trade reductions or cause 'undue difficulties' for other members. RTAs notified to the GATT/WTO under the Enabling Clause include AFTA and MERCOSUR.

Two pieces of evidence support those who believe that regional trading agreements have not been barriers to liberalization at the global level. The first is the successful conclusion of the Uruguay Round of GATT negotiations which, as documented in the previous chapter, produced major steps forward in liberalization at the global level (although most of the Uruguay Round's negotiations took place *before* many of the agreements that are part of the new wave of

regionalism came into being). The second is that members of many of the regional trade agreements, particularly those in Latin America, have lowered their barriers to non-member states more rapidly than did countries that were not members of regional agreements (Foroutan 1998). Although it is impossible to demonstrate a causal relationship here, the logic is straightforward: lowering barriers to non-members at the same time as entering a preferential trade

Table 5.5 Membership of Minilateral Regional Trading Agreements

AFTA	ASEAN Free Trade Area www.asean.or.id	Brunei Darussalam, Cambodia, Indonesia, Laos, Malaysia, Myanmar, Philippines, Singapore, Thailand, Vietnam
APEC	Asia-Pacific Economic Cooperation www.apecsec.org.sg	Australia, Brunei Darussalam, Canada, Chile, China, Hong Kong, Indonesia, Japan, Korea, Malaysia, Mexico, New Zealand, Papua New Guinea, Peru, Philippines, Russia, Singapore, Taiwan, Thailand, United States, Vietnam
BAFTA	Baltic Free-Trade Area	Estonia, Latvia, Lithuania
BANGKOK	Bangkok Agreement	Bangladesh, China, India, Republic of Korea, Laos, Sri Lanka
CAN	Andean Community www.comunidadandina.org	Bolivia, Colombia, Ecuador, Peru, Venezuela
CARICOM	Caribbean Community and Common Market www.caricom.org	Antigua & Barbuda, Bahamas, Barbados, Belize, Dominica, Grenada, Guyana, Haiti, Jamaica, Monserrat, Trinidad & Tobago, St Kitts & Nevis, St Lucia, St Vincent & the Grenadines, Surinam
CACM	Central American Common Market www.sice.oas.org/trade/cam ertoc.asp	Costa Rica, El Salvador, Guatemala, Honduras, Nicaragua
CEFTA	Central European Free Trade Agreement www.ijs.si/cefta/	Bulgaria, Czech Republic, Hungary, Poland, Romania, Slovak Republic, Slovenia
CEMAC	Economic and Monetary Community of Central Africa www.izf.net/izf/Institutions/ Integration/Default.htm	Cameroon, Central African Republic, Chad, Congo, Equatorial Guinea, Gabon
CER	Closer Economic Relations Trade Agreement www.dfat.gov.au/geo/ new_zealand/anz_cer/· anz_cer.html www.mft.govt.nz/foreign/ regions/australia/ tradeeconomic/ cerbackground.html	Australia, New Zealand
CIS	Commonwealth of Independent States www.cis.minsk.by	Azerbaijan, Armenia, Belarus, Georgia, Moldova, Kazakhstan, Russian Federation, Ukraine, Uzbekistan, Tajikistan, Kyrgyz Republic
COMESA	Common Market for Eastern and Southern Africa www.comesa.int	Angola, Burundi, Comoros, Democratic Republic of Congo, Djibouti, Egypt, Eritrea, Ethiopia, Kenya, Madagascar, Malawi, Mauritius, Namibia, Rwanda, Seychelles, Sudan, Swaziland, Uganda, Zambia, Zimbabwe
EAC	East African Cooperation www.eachq.org/	Kenya, Tanzania, Uganda
EAEC	Eurasian Economic Community	Belarus, Kazakhstan, Kyrgyz Republic, Russian Federation, Tajikistan
ECO	Economic Cooperation Organization www.ecosecretariat.org/	Afghanistan, Azerbaijan, Iran, Kazakhstan, Kyrgyz Republic, Pakistan, Tajikistan, Turkey, Turkmenistan, Uzbekistan
EEA	European Economic Area	EC, Iceland, Liechtenstein, Norway
EFTA	European Free Trade Association www.cefta.org	Iceland, Liechtenstein, Norway, Switzerland

EU	European Union europa.eu.int	Austria, Belgium, Denmark, Finland, France, Germany, Greece, Ireland, Italy, Luxembourg, Netherlands, Portugal, Spain, Sweden, United Kingdom
GCC	Gulf Cooperation Council **www.gcc-sg.org/**	Bahrain, Kuwait, Oman, Qatar, Saudi Arabia, United Arab Emirates
GSTP	General System of Trade Preferences among Developing Countries **www.g77.org/gstp/**	Algeria, Argentina, Bangladesh, Benin, Bolivia, Brazil, Cameroon, Chile, Colombia, Cuba, Democratic People's Republic of Korea, Ecuador, Egypt, Ghana, Guinea, Guyana, India, Indonesia, Islamic Republic of Iran, Iraq, Libya, Malaysia, Mexico, Morocco, Mozambique, Myanmar, Nicaragua, Nigeria, Pakistan, Peru, Philippines, Republic of Korea, Romania, Singapore, Sri Lanka, Sudan, Thailand, Trinidad and Tobago, Tunisia, United Republic of Tanzania, Venezuela, Vietnam, Yugoslavia, Zimbabwe
LAIA	Latin American Integration Association **www.aladi.org/**	Argentina, Bolivia, Brazil, Chile, Colombia, Cuba, Ecuador, Mexico, Paraguay, Peru, Uruguay, Venezuela
MERCOSUR	Southern Common Market **www.mercosur.org.uy/**	Argentina, Brazil, Paraguay, Uruguay
MSG	Melanesian Spearhead Group	Fiji, Papua, New Guinea, Solomon Islands, Vanuatu
NAFTA	North American Free Trade Agreement **www.nafta-sec-alena.org**	Canada, Mexico, United States
PTN	Protocol relating to Trade Negotiations among Developing Countries	Bangladesh, Brazil, Chile, Egypt, Israel, Mexico, Pakistan, Paraguay, Peru, Philippines, Republic of Korea, Romania, Tunisia, Turkey, Uruguay, Yugoslavia
SAPTA	South Asian Preferential Trade Arrangement **www.south-asia.com/ saarc/sapta.htm**	Bangladesh, Bhutan, India, Maldives, Nepal, Pakistan, Sri Lanka
SPARTECA	South Pacific Regional Trade and Economic Cooperation Agreement **www.forumsec.org.fj/docs/ SPARTECA/foreword.htm**	Australia, New Zealand, Cook Islands, Fiji, Kiribati, Marshall Islands, Micronesia, Nauru, Niue, Papua New Guinea, Solomon Islands, Tonga, Tuvalu, Vanuatu, Western Samoa
TRIPARTITE	Tripartite Agreement	Egypt, India, Yugoslavia
UEMOA/WAE MU	West African Economic and Monetary Union **www.uemoa.int/**	Benin, Burkina Faso, Côte d'Ivoire, Guinea Bissau, Mali, Niger, Senegal, Togo

arrangement reduces the risk of welfare loss through trade diversion. Critics of the new regionalism, however, point to evidence that after joining regional arrangements, Israel, Mexico, and MERCOSUR members when encountering economic difficulties all raised their tariffs against non-members.

Like so many other issues relating to the new regionalism, the link between RTAs and global liberalization remains inconclusive. Whether or not the current Doha Round of global trade negotiations is brought to a successful conclusion within a reasonable time frame will be a significant pointer to the validity of the contending arguments about the relationship between regionalism and the broader trade regime.

Key points

- A lively debate amongst writers on RTAs has produced several plausible arguments suggesting that regionalism can facilitate or hinder trade liberalization at the global level.

- The new regionalism is of such recent origin that the evidence on its effects remains inconclusive.

- The success of the Uruguay Round refuted the popular arguments in the late 1980s that the world economy was about to fragment into three rival trading blocs. But the results of the Doha Round will be a more significant indicator of the effects of the new regionalism on liberalization at the global level.

QUESTIONS

1 How does the 'new regionalism' differ from that of the 1960s and 1970s?

2 For what economic reasons might governments prefer trade liberalization at the regional rather than the global level?

3 What political benefits might membership of a regional agreement bring?

4 What are the likely sources of domestic political opposition to regionalism?

5 What is 'deeper' integration?

6 What were the sources of the failure of many of the regional trade agreements of the 1960s and 1970s?

7 Why did the United States government change its mind on the desirability of regional trade agreements?

8 How does trade creation differ from trade diversion?

9 Why are rules of origin regarded as a protectionist device?

10 What evidence is there that regional integration has had a positive impact on the economies of participating economies? And what has been its impact on non-members?

11 For what reasons might regionalism assist or impede trade liberalization at the global level?

FURTHER READING

General

Bhagwati, J., and Panagariya, A. (eds.) (1996), *The Economics of Preferential Trade Agreements* (Washington, DC: AEI Press). An accessible overview of arguments by economists against regionalism.

Fawcett, L., and Hurrell, A. (eds.) (1995), *Regionalism in World Politics: Regional Organization and International Order* (Oxford: Oxford University Press). An initial exploration of the new regionalism with overviews and case studies.

Frankel, J. A. (1997), *Regional Trading Blocs in the World Economic System* (Washington DC: Institute for International Economics). The most comprehensive examination of the effects of regional trade agreements.

Haas, E. B. (1975), *The Obsolescence of Regional Integration Theory* (Berkeley, Calif.: Institute of International Studies, University of California). A reconsideration of the relevance of early integration theory.

Mansfield, E. D., and Milner, H. V. (eds.) (1997), *The Political Economy of Regionalism* (New York, NY: Columbia University Press). A recent collection of articles from a political economy perspective on regionalism in general; it includes case studies of the principal geographical regions.

Moravcsik, A. (1998), *The Choice for Europe: Social Purpose and State Power from Messina to Maastricht* (Ithaca, NY: Cornell University Press). The most sophisticated statement of the liberal intergovernmental approach to regionalism.

World Bank (2000), *Trade Blocs* (New York, NY: Oxford University Press). A review of the evidence on the economic and political effects of regionalism and their relevance to less developed economies.

Africa

Bach, D. (ed.) (1999), *Regionalisation in Africa: Integration & Disintegration* (Bloomington: Indiana University Press). A collection that examines the relationship between regionalism, regionalization, and state disintegration in Africa.

The Americas

Cameron, M. A., and Tomlin, B. W. (2000), *The Making of NAFTA: How the Deal was Done* (Ithaca, NY: Cornell University Press). Analyses the negotiating process leading up to the signature of the NAFTA treaty.

Hufbauer, G. C., and Schott, J. J. (1993), *NAFTA: An Assessment* (Washington DC: Institute for International Economics). An early review of the terms of the NAFTA treaty.

Roett, R. (ed.) (1999), *Mercosur: Regional Integration, World Markets* (Boulder, Colo.: Lynne Rienner). A collection of articles on integration among MERCOSUR members and their relations with the global economy.

Asia-Pacific

Aggarwal, V. K., and Morrison, C. E. (eds.) (1998), *Asia-Pacific Crossroads: Regime Creation and the Future of APEC* (New York: St Martin's Press). A collection of articles on the foundation of APEC, the objectives of its founders, and its early impact.

Ravenhill, J. (2001), *APEC and the Construction of Asia-Pacific Regionalism* (Cambridge: Cambridge University Press). Applies the theoretical literature on regionalism to APEC's foundation and operating principles.

Europe

Bomberg, E. E., and Stubb, A. C. G. (2003), *The European Union: How Does It Work?* (Oxford: Oxford University Press). An up-to-date introductory text on the EU.

Milward, A. S. (1992), *The European Rescue of the Nation-State* (London: Routledge). A historical review of European integration from an intergovernmental perspective.

Wallace, H., and Wallace, W. (eds.) (2000), *Policy-Making in the European Union*, 4th edn. (Oxford: Oxford University Press). The most comprehensive and theoretically sophisticated overview of the various dimensions of EU integration.

WEB LINKS

Table 5.5 lists addresses for the websites maintained by most regional trade agreements.

www.wto.org/english/tratop_e/region_e/region_e.htm The WTO website's gateway to the Organization's material on regional trade agreements.

Part Three

Global finance

Global finance

6

The evolution of the international monetary and financial system

Eric Helleiner

READER'S GUIDE

The international monetary and financial system plays a central role in the global political economy. Since the late nineteenth century, the nature of this system has undergone several transformations in response to changing political and economic conditions at the domestic and international levels. The most dramatic change was the collapse of the integrated pre-1914 international monetary and financial regime during the inter-war years. The second transformation took place after the war when the Bretton Woods order was put in place. Since the early 1970s, another period of change has been under way as various features of the Bretton Woods order have unravelled: the gold exchange standard, the adjustable peg exchange-rate regime, the US dollar's global role, and the commitment to capital controls. These various changes have important political consequences for the key issue of who gets what, when, and how in the global political economy.

Introduction

It is often said that money makes the world go around. In an age of globalization, this saying appears more relevant than ever. International flows of money today dwarf the cross-border trade of goods. And the influence of these flows seems only enhanced by their unique speed and global reach.

If money is so influential, it is fitting that it should have a prominent place in the study of global political economy. Scholarly research on the political economy of international monetary and financial issues has indeed grown very rapidly in recent years. While perspectives vary enormously within this literature, scholars working in this field share the belief that the study of money and finance must adopt a wider lens than that adopted by most economists.

Economists are trained to view money and finance primarily as economic phenomena. From their standpoint, money serves the economic functions of acting as a medium of exchange, a unit of account, and a store of value. These functions are critical to large-scale economic life since they facilitate commerce, savings, and investment. Financial activity is seen by economists as primarily serving the economic functions of allocating credit within the economy. Given the key role of credit in modern economic life, the study of finance has a prominent place within the discipline of economics.

These descriptions of the economic role of money and finance are certainly accurate, but they are also limiting. Money and finance, after all, serve many political purposes as well (not to mention social and cultural ones). In all modern societies, control over the issuing and management of money and credit has been a key source of power, and the subject of intense political struggles. The organization and functioning of monetary and financial systems are, thus, rarely influenced by a narrow economic logic of maximizing efficiency. They also reflect various political rationales relating to pursuit of power, ideas, and interests (Kirshner 2003).

The interrelationship between politics and systems of money and finance is particularly apparent at the international level where no single political authority exists. What money should be used to facilitate international economic transactions and how should it be managed? What should be the nature of relationship be between national currencies? How should credit be created and allocated at the international level? The answers to these questions have profoundly important implications for politics not just within countries but also between them. It should not surprise us then that they provoke domestic and international political struggles, often of an intense kind.

This chapter highlights this point by providing an overview of the evolution of the international monetary and financial system since the late nineteenth century. The first section examines how changing political circumstances both internationally and domestically during the inter-war years undermined the stability of the globally integrated financial and monetary order of the pre-1914 era. The next section describes how a new international monetary and financial system— the Bretton Woods order—was created in 1944 for the post-war period with a number of distinct features. The following four sections analyse the causes and consequences of the unravelling of various features of that order since the early 1970s: the gold exchange standard, the adjustable peg exchange-rate regime, the US dollar's prominent global role, and the commitment to capital controls. In the next chapter, Louis Pauly addresses another feature of the contemporary international financial order: its vulnerability to crises.

The fate of a previous globally integrated financial and monetary order

Debates about contemporary economic globalization often note that this trend had an important precedent in the late nineteenth and early twentieth centuries. This is certainly true in the monetary and financial sector. Cross-border flows of money grew dramatically in this earlier period and even surpassed those in the current era in size according to some criteria. Some of these flows involved short-term capital movements that responded primarily to interest rate differentials between financial centres around the world. Others involved long-term capital exports from the leading European powers to locations around the world. The United Kingdom, in particular, exported enormous amounts of long-term capital after 1870, sums that were much larger as a percentage of its national income than any creditor country is exporting today (James 2001: 12).

These capital flows were facilitated by the emergence of an international monetary regime that was also highly integrated, indeed much more so than in the current period. By 1914, the currencies of most independent countries and colonized regions around the world were linked to the same standard of gold (see Box 6.1). The result was a fixed exchange-rate regime with almost global reach. Indeed, some European countries went even further to create regional 'monetary unions' in which the currencies of the member countries could circulate in each others' territory. Two such unions were created: the Latin Monetary Union (LMU) in 1865 (involving France, Switzerland, Belgium, and Italy) and the Scandinavian Monetary Union (SMU) in 1873 (involving Sweden and Denmark and then Norway too after 1875). A high-level international conference was even held in 1867 to consider the possibility of a worldwide 'monetary union' of this kind. As the scramble for colonies intensified after 1870, many imperial powers also often encouraged the circulation of their currencies in their newly acquired colonies during this period (Helleiner 2003: chapters 6, 8). These currency unions and imperial currency blocs were designed to make economic transactions within each union or bloc even easier to conduct.

The end of globalization

What can we learn from this era in our efforts to understand the political foundations of international money and finance? Perhaps the most interesting lesson is that this globally integrated financial and monetary order did not last. In the contemporary period, globalization is sometimes said to be irreversible. A study of the fate of this earlier globalization trend, however, reminds us to be more cautious. In particular, it highlights the importance of the political basis of international money and finance.

The first signs of disintegration came during the First World War when cross-border financial flows diminished dramatically and many countries abandoned the gold standard in favour of floating currencies. After the war ended, there was a concerted effort—led by the United Kingdom and the United States—to restore the pre-1914 international monetary and financial order, and this initiative was initially quite successful. Many countries did restore the gold standard during the 1920s and international capital flows—both short-term and long-term—also resumed on a very large scale by the late 1920s (Pauly 1997: chapter 3).

But this success was short-lived. In the early 1930s, a major international financial crisis triggered the collapse of both international lending and the international gold standard. This development signalled what Harold James (2001) has called 'the end of globalization'. The international monetary and financial system broke up into a series of relatively closed currency blocs. Within each bloc, currencies were usually fixed vis-à-vis each other and some international lending resumed. But between the blocs, currencies were often inconvertible and their value fluctuated considerably for much of the decade. International flows of capital between the blocs were also limited and often regulated tightly by new capital control regimes.

Hegemonic stability theory

What explains this dramatic change in the nature of the international monetary and financial regime? A prominent explanation within international political economy (IPE) scholarship has been that the transformation was related to a change in the distribution of power among states within the international monetary and financial arena (for example, Kindleberger 1973). According to this 'hegemonic stability theory', the pre-1914 international financial and monetary regime remained stable as long as it was sustained by British hegemonic leadership. Before the war, the United Kingdom's currency, sterling, was seen to be 'as good as gold' and it was used around the globe as a world currency. Britain was also the largest creditor to the world and London's financial markets had held a pre-eminent place in global finance. The United Kingdom's capital exports helped to finance global payments imbalances and they were usefully counter-cyclical; that is, foreign lending expanded when the UK entered a recession, thus compensating foreign countries for the loss of the UK export market. During international financial crises, the Bank of England is also said to have played a leadership role in stabilizing markets through lender-of-last-resort activities.

After the First World War, the United Kingdom lost its ability to perform its leadership role in stabilizing the global monetary and financial order. The country became a debtor to the world economy, while the United States replaced it as the lead creditor to the world economy. The US dollar also emerged as the strongest and most trustworthy world currency, and New York rivalled London's position as the key international financial centre. In these new circumstances, the United States might have taken on the kind of leadership role that the United Kingdom had played before the war. But it proved unwilling because of isolationist sentiments and domestic political conflicts between internationally oriented and more domestically focused economic interests. The resulting leadership vacuum is blamed for the instability and eventual breakdown of the gold standard and integrated financial order during the inter-war period.

Hegemonic stability theorists criticize several aspects of United States behaviour during the 1920s and early 1930s. Its capital exports during the 1920s were pro-cyclical; they expanded rapidly when the US economy was booming in the mid-to-late 1920s, but then came to a sudden stop in 1928 just as the growth of the US economy was slowing down. The collapse of US lending generated balance of payments crises for many foreign countries which had relied on US loans to cover their external payments deficits. The US then exacerbated these countries' difficulties by raising protectionist trade barriers against imports with the passage of the 1930 Smoot–Hawley Act. As confidence in international financial markets collapsed in the early 1930s, the USA also refused to take on the role of international-lender-of-last-resort or even to cancel war debts which were compounding the crisis.

Changing domestic political conditions

This interpretation of the evolution of the international monetary and financial system from the pre-1914 period into the inter-war period is not universally accepted (see for example, Eichengreen 1992; Simmons 1994; Calleo 1976). One line of criticism has been that it overstates the significance of UK leadership in sustaining the pre-1914 monetary and financial order. The distribution of financial and monetary power in that era is said to have been more plural than hegemonic, with stability being maintained by cooperation between leading central banks instead of unilateral UK leadership. Even more important, however, is the argument that the transformation of the international financial and monetary system was produced more by a change in the distribution of power *within* many states than between them.

According to this latter perspective, the stability of the pre-1914 international monetary and financial order was dependent on a very specific domestic political context. In that era, elite-dominated governments were strongly committed to the classical liberal idea that domestic monetary and fiscal policy should be geared to the external goal of maintaining the

Box 6.1 **The theory of the adjustment process under the international gold standard**

In theory, the international gold standard was a self-regulating international monetary order. External imbalances would be automatically corrected by domestic wage and price adjustments according to a process famously described by David Hume: the 'price-specie flow mechanism'. If a country experienced a balance of payments deficit, Hume noted that gold exports should depress domestic wages and prices in such a way that the country's international competitive position—and thus its trade position—would be improved. Hume's model assumed that most domestic money was gold coins, but the domestic monetary system of most countries on the gold standard during the late nineteenth and early twentieth centuries was dominated by fiduciary money in the form of bank notes and bank deposits. In this context, the monetary authority that issued notes and regulated the banking system had to simulate the automatic adjustments of the gold standard by following proper 'rules of the game'. In the event of a trade deficit, it was expected to tighten monetary conditions by curtailing the note issue and raising interest rates. The latter was designed not just to induce deflationary pressures (by increasing the cost of borrowing) but also to attract short-term capital flows to help finance the payments imbalance while the underlying macro-economic adjustment process was taking place. In practice, however, historians of the pre-1914 gold standard note that governments did not follow these 'rules of the game' as closely and consistently as the theory of the gold standard anticipated (Eichengreen 1985).

convertibility of the national currency into gold. When national currencies came under downward pressure in response to capital outflows or trade deficits, monetary and fiscal authorities usually responded by tightening monetary conditions and cutting spending. These moves were designed partly to induce deflationary pressures which improved the country's international competitive position, and thus its trade balance. Equally important, they were aimed at restoring the confidence of financial market actors and encouraging short-term capital inflows (see Box 6.1). Indeed, the very fact that governments were so committed to these policies and to the maintenance of their currency's peg to gold ensured that short-term capital movements were highly 'stabilizing' and 'equilibrating' in this period.

The strength of governments' commitments to these policies, however, rested on a particular domestic political order. Domestic deflationary pressures could be very painful for some domestic groups, particularly the poor whose wages were forced downwards (or who experienced unemployment if wages did not fall). The poor also often bore the brunt of the burden when government spending was cut. These policies were politically viable only because the poor had little voice in the political arena. In most countries, the electoral franchise remained narrow before 1914. In many countries, central banks were not even public bodies in this period. And in colonial or peripheral regions, monetary authorities were often controlled by foreign interests.

After the First World War, the domestic political order was transformed in many independent states. The electoral franchise was widened, the power of labour grew, and there was growing support for more interventionist economic policies. In this context, it was hardly surprising to find new demands for monetary and fiscal policies to respond to domestic needs rather than to the goal of maintaining external convertibility of the currency into gold and the confidence of foreign investors. Governments began to run fiscal deficits and central banks came under new public pressure to gear interest rates to address domestic unemployment.

It was these new domestic circumstances—rather than declining UK power—which many believe played the key role in undermining the stability of the integrated international and monetary system during the inter-war period. As governments ceased to play by the 'rules of the game', the 'self-regulating' character of the gold standard began to break down (see Box 6.1). Short-term international financial flows also became more volatile and speculative, as investors no longer had confidence in governments' commitments to maintain fixed rates and balanced budgets. Faced with these new domestic pressures, central banks also found it more difficult to cooperate in ways that promoted international monetary and financial stability.

In the context of the international financial crisis of 1931 and the Great Depression, many governments then chose simply to abandon the gold standard in order to escape its discipline. At the time, the collapse of international lending and export markets as well as speculative capital flight had left many countries with enormous balance of payments deficits. If they stayed on the gold standard, these deficits would be addressed by deflationary policies designed to press wages and prices downwards. A depreciation of the national currency provided a quicker, less painful manner of adjusting the country's wages and prices vis-à-vis those in foreign countries to boost exports and curtail imports.

A floating exchange rate also provided greater policy autonomy to pursue expansionary monetary policies that could address pressing domestic economic needs. While on the gold standard, a government that wanted to bolster economic growth by lowering interest rates would experience capital flight and a gold outflow, and it would be forced to reverse the policy in order to restore the stability of the currency. With a floating exchange rate, the government could simply let the exchange rate depreciate. The exchange rate would adjust to the changing level of domestic prices and wages instead of the other way around. This depreciation would also reinforce the expansionary intent of the initial policy since exports would be bolstered and imports discouraged. More generally, it is worth noting that a floating exchange rate was also attractive to many governments in the early 1930s because it would insulate the country from monetary instability abroad, particularly the deflationary pressures emanating from the USA at this time.

In addition to abandoning the gold standard, many governments during the 1930s turned to capital controls to reinforce their national policy autonomy. With this move, they insulated themselves from the disciplining power of speculative cross-border financial movements. If, for example, a government wanted to bolster domestic economic growth by lowering interest rates or engaging in deficit spending, it no longer had to worry about capital flight. For this reason, it was natural to find John Maynard Keynes, the leading advocate of such domestically oriented activist macro-economic management, emerge as one of the strongest supporters of capital controls in the early 1930s. As he put it in 1933, 'let finance be primarily national' (Keynes 1933: 758).

Key points

- In the late nineteenth and early twentieth centuries, a highly integrated global financial and monetary order existed. By the early 1930s, it had collapsed completely, and was replaced by a fragmented order organized around closed economic blocs and floating exchange rates.

- Some believe the reason for the breakdown of the pre-1914 order was the absence of a state acting as a hegemonic leader to perform such roles as the provision of stable international lending, the maintenance of an open market for foreign goods, and the stabilization of financial markets during crises.

- Others argue that the pre-1914 order was brought down more by a domestic political transformation across much of the world associated with expansion of the electoral franchise, the growing power of labour, and the new prominence of supporters of interventionist economic policies.

The Bretton Woods order

If an integrated international monetary and financial order was to be built again, it would need to be compatible with the new priority placed on domestic policy autonomy. An opportunity to create such an order finally arose in the early 1940s when US and UK policy makers began to plan the organization of the post-war international monetary and financial system.

Embedded liberalism

At the time, it was clear that the United States would emerge from the war as the dominant economic power and US policy makers were determined to play a leadership role in building and sustaining a more liberal and multilateral international economic order than that which had existed during the 1930s. The closed economic blocs and economic instability of the previous decade were thought to have contributed to the Great Depression and the Second World War. But US policy makers did not want to see a return to the classical liberal international economic order of the pre-1930s period. Instead, they hoped to find a way to reconcile liberal multilateralism with the new domestically oriented priorities to combat unemployment and promote social welfare that had emerged with the New Deal.

This objective to create what Ruggie (1982) has called an 'embedded liberal' international economic order was shared by Keynes who had emerged as the policy maker in charge of UK planning for the post-war world economy during the early 1940s. He worked together with his American counterpart, Harry Dexter White, to produce the blueprint for the post-war international monetary and financial order that was soon endorsed by forty-four countries at the 1944 Bretton Woods conference (Gardner 1980; Van Dormael 1978).

At first sight, the blueprint seemed to signal a return to a pre-1930s world. Signatories to the Bretton Woods agreements agreed to declare a par value of their currency in relation to the gold content of the US dollar in 1944. At the time, the US dollar was convertible into gold at a rate of $35 per ounce. By pegging their currencies in this way, countries appeared to be establishing an international gold standard—or to be more precise, a 'gold exchange' standard or 'gold-dollar' standard. And at one level, the objectives underlying the Bretton Woods agreements were indeed similar to those of the gold standard. The Bretton Woods architects sought to re-establish a world of international currency stability. Floating exchange rates were associated with beggar-thy-neighbour competitive devaluations, speculative financial flows, and the general breakdown of international economic integration.

A different kind of gold standard

But several other features of the Bretton Woods agreements made clear that this commitment did not signal a return to the kind of gold standard of the 1920s or pre-1914 period. First, countries were given the option of adjusting their countries' par value whenever their country was in 'fundamental

disequilibrium'. This was to be, in other words, a kind of 'adjustable peg' system in which countries could substitute exchange-rate devaluations for harsh domestic deflations when they experienced balance of payments deficits. Currency realignments of up to 10 per cent from the initial parity were to be approved automatically, while larger ones required the permission of the newly created International Monetary Fund (IMF). Even in the latter case, the priority given to domestic policy autonomy was made clear; the Articles of the Agreement of the IMF noted that the Fund 'shall not object to a proposed change because of the domestic social or political policies of the member proposing the change' (Article IV-5).

Second, although countries agreed to make their currencies convertible for current account transactions (that is, trade payments), they were given the right to control all capital movements. This provision was not intended to stop all private financial flows. Those that were 'equilibrating' and designed for productive investment were still welcomed. But the Bretton Woods architects inserted this provision because they worried about how speculative and disequilibrating flows could disrupt both stable exchange rates and national political autonomy. Regarding the latter, Keynes and White sought to protect governments from capital flight that was initiated for 'political reasons' or with the goal of evading domestic taxes or the 'burdens of social legislation' (quoted in Helleiner 1994: 34). Capital controls were also particularly important to enable governments to pursue macro-economic planning through an independent interest rate policy. As Keynes (1980: 149) put it, 'In my view the whole management of the domestic economy depends upon being free to have the appropriate rate of interest without reference to rates prevailing elsewhere in the world. Capital control is a corollary to this.'

The Bretton Woods architects further demonstrated their scepticism towards private international financial flows by establishing two public international financial institutions: the International Bank for Reconstruction and Development (IBRD) (known as the World Bank) and the IMF. At a broad level, these institutions—particularly the IMF—were given the task of promoting global monetary and financial cooperation. More specifically, they were to assume some aspects of international lending that had previously been left to private markets. The IBRD was designed to provide long-term loans for reconstruction and development after the war, a task that the private market was not trusted to perform. The IMF was to provide short-term loans to help countries finance their temporary balance of payments deficits, a function that was explicitly designed to reinforce those countries' policy autonomy and challenge the kind of external discipline that private speculative financial flows and the gold standard had imposed before the 1930s.

For the first decade and a half after the Second World War, the Bretton Woods system is sometimes said to have been in a 'virtual cold storage' (Skidelsky 2003: 125). It is certainly true that the IMF and IBRD played a very limited role during this period and that European countries did not make their currencies convertible until 1958 (the Bretton Woods agreements had allowed for a 'transition' period of no specified length during which countries could keep currencies inconvertible). At the same time, however, most governments outside the Soviet orbit were committed to the other principles outlined at Bretton Woods: the maintenance of an adjustable peg exchange-rate regime, the gold-dollar standard, and the control of capital movements. Moreover, although the IMF and World Bank were sidelined, other bodies—particularly the US government but also regional institutions such as the European Payments Union—acted in the ways that Keynes and White had hoped these institutions would. Public international lending was provided for temporary balance of payments support as well as for reconstruction and development. United States policy makers also promoted 'embedded liberal' ideals when they were engaged in monetary and financing advising

roles around the world (Helleiner 1994: chapter 3; 2003: chapter 9).

During the heyday of the Bretton Woods order from the late 1950s until 1971, the IMF and IBRD were once again assigned a more marginal role in the system than Keynes and White had hoped for. But governments remain committed to the other key features of the order. What then became of the Bretton Woods order? In some respects, it seems still alive. Currencies remain convertible, and the IMF and IBRD still exist (although their purpose has been radically altered, as is described in the next chapter). In the following sections, however, I explore the causes and consequences of the unravelling of the other features of the Bretton Woods regime since the early 1970s: the gold exchange standard, the adjustable peg exchange-rate system, the US dollar's prominent global role, and the commitment to capital controls.

Key points

- The Bretton Woods conference in 1944 created a new international monetary and financial order that was inspired by an 'embedded liberal' ideology and backed by US leadership.

- Governments joining this order committed themselves to: currency convertibility for current account payments, a gold-dollar standard, an adjustable peg exchange-rate regime, an acceptance of capital controls, and the creation of the IMF and World Bank.

- Many of the features of the Bretton Woods order were in place between 1945 and 1958, but this order reached its heyday between 1958 and 1971.

The crisis of the early 1970s

The breakdown of the gold exchange standard

The Bretton Woods system is usually said to have begun to collapse during the early 1970s when both the gold exchange standard and the adjustable peg

exchange-rate system broke down. The first sign of trouble came in August 1971 when the United States suddenly ended the convertibility of the US dollar into gold. Since other currencies had been tied to gold only via the US dollar, this move signalled the end of gold's role as a standard for other currencies as well.

This breakdown had in fact been predicted as far back as 1960 when Robert Triffin (1960) had highlighted why the dollar-gold standard was inherently unstable. In a system where the dollar was the central reserve currency, he argued international liquidity could be expanded only when the United States provided the world with more dollars by running a balance of payments deficit. But the more it did so, the more it risked undermining confidence in the dollar's convertibility into gold.

One potential solution to the 'Triffin dilemma' was to create a new international currency whose supply would not be tied to the balance of payments condition of any one particular country. Keynes had in fact proposed such a currency—which he called 'bancor'—during the negotiations leading up to the Bretton Woods conference. In 1965, the United States began to support the idea that the IMF could issue such a currency as a means to supplement the dollar's role as a reserve currency, and 'Special Drawing Rights' (SDR) were finally created for this purpose in 1969. The SDR was not a currency that individuals could use; instead, it could be used only by national monetary authorities as a reserve asset for settling inter-country payments imbalances (and subject to certain conditions). Despite its potential, IMF members have never been willing to issue significant quantities of SDR to enable this currency to play much of a role in the global monetary system.

During the 1960s, and especially after the mid-1960s, Triffin's predictions were increasingly borne out. United States currency abroad did grow considerably larger than the amount of gold held by the US government to back them up. In one sense, the situation was beneficial to the United States. The country was able to finance growing external deficits associated with the Vietnam War and its domestic Great Society programme (which produced rising imports) by simply printing dollars. Indeed, the United States was doing much more than providing the world with extra international liquidity by the late 1960s; it was actively exporting inflation by flooding the world with dollars. In another sense, however, the country was becoming increasingly vulnerable to a confidence crisis. If all holders of dollars suddenly decided to demand their convertibility into gold, the USA would not be able to meet the demand. Another cost to the USA was the fact that the dollar's fixed value in

gold was undermining the international competitiveness of US-based firms. If other countries had been willing to revalue their currencies, this competitiveness problem could have been addressed. But foreign governments resisted adjusting the value of their currencies in this way.

A crisis of confidence in the dollar's convertibility into gold was initially postponed when some key foreign allies—notably Germany and Japan—agreed not to convert their reserves into gold (sometimes as part of an explicit trade-off for US security protection; Zimmerman 2002). But other countries that were critical of US foreign policy in this period—France in particular—refused to adopt this practice, seeing it as a reinforcement of American hegemony (Kirshner 1995: 192–203). Private speculators also increasingly targeted the US dollar, especially after sterling was devalued in 1967. When speculative pressures against the dollar reached a peak in 1971, the United States was forced to a decision. It could either cut back the printing of dollars, or simply end the currency's convertibility into gold.

The US decision to take the latter course reflected its desire to free itself from the constraint on its policies that gold convertibility imposed (Gowa 1983). In the eyes of many observers, it also signalled an end to the kind of 'benevolent' hegemonic leadership that US policy makers had practised in the international monetary and financial realm since the 1940s. Some attributed this change in US policy to the fact that the United States was losing its hegemonic status in the international monetary and financial realm. From this perspective, the breakdown of the gold exchange standard provided further evidence to support the hegemonic stability theory that a stable integrated international monetary and financial order requires a hegemonic power. Others, however, suggested that US hegemonic power remained substantial in world money and finance, but what had changed was the US *interest* in leadership. Faced with new domestic and international priorities, US policy makers had chosen to exploit their position as the dominant power in this realm of the global economy to serve these ends. To support the thesis that the United States remained an important global monetary power, scholars pointed to the fact that the US dollar remained the unchallenged dominant world currency after 1971 (for example, Strange

1986; Calleo 1976)—a point to which we will return below.

The collapse of the adjustable peg exchange-rate regime

The second feature of the Bretton Woods monetary order that broke down in the early 1970s was the adjustable peg system. This development took place in 1973 when the world's major currencies began to float in value vis-à-vis each other. The new floating exchange-rate system was formalized in 1976 when the IMF's Articles of Agreement were amended to legalize floating exchange rates and to declare that each country now had responsibility to determine the par value of its currency.

The end of the adjustable peg system was triggered partly by the growing size of speculative international financial flows—a phenomenon explained in a later section—which complicated governments' efforts to defend their currency pegs. Equally important, however, was the fact that influential policy makers began to re-evaluate the merits of floating exchange rates. We have already seen how the Bretton Woods architects took a very negative view of the experience of floating exchange rates before the Second World War. Indeed, the drawbacks of floating exchange rates were deemed so obvious that there had been very few serious defences of them at the time. By the early 1970s, however, floating exchange rates had attracted a number of prominent advocates, particularly in the United States (Odell 1982).

These advocates argued that floating exchange rates could play a very useful role in facilitating smooth adjustments to external imbalances in a world where governments were no longer willing to accept the discipline of the gold standard. Under the Bretton Woods system, the idea of using exchange-rate changes for this purpose had, of course, already been endorsed; governments could adjust their currency's peg when the country was in 'fundamental disequilibrium'. But in practice, governments had been reluctant to made these changes because exchange-rate adjustments often generated political

controversy both at home and abroad. Governments usually made these adjustments only when large-scale speculative financial movements left them no option. The result had been a rather rigid and crisis-prone exchange-rate system in which countries often resorted instead to international economic controls, particularly on capital flows, to address imbalances. A floating exchange-rate system would allow that external imbalances to be addressed more smoothly and continuously, and without so much resort to controls.

It was also argued that floating exchange rates had unfairly earned a bad name during the 1930s. Advocates argued that floating exchange rates need not necessarily be associated with either competitive devaluations or with a retreat from international economic integration, as they had been in the 1930s. Their role in encouraging destabilizing speculative financial flows during the 1930s was also questioned. Financial movements in that decade, it was argued, had been volatile not because of floating exchange rates but because they were responding properly to the highly unstable underlying economic conditions of the time (for example, Friedman 1953).

Key points

- The breakdown of the Bretton Woods system is usually dated to the early 1970s when the gold exchange standard and the adjustable peg exchange-rate system collapsed.

- In 1971, the United States ended the gold convertibility of its currency, and, by extension, that of all other currencies. The US decision reflected its desire to free itself from the growing constraint on its policies that gold convertibility was imposing.

- The adjustable peg exchange-rate regime of Bretton Woods was replaced in 1973 by a system of floating exchange rates between the currencies of the leading economic powers. The changed was caused by heightened capital mobility and by a reconsideration of the merits of floating exchange rates among leading policy makers, particularly in the United States.

From floating exchange rates to monetary unions

Has the floating exchange-rate system performed in the ways that its advocates hoped? They were certainly correct that floating exchange rates have not discouraged the growth of international trade and investment to any significant degree. Indeed, by enabling governments to avoid using trade restrictions and capital controls, floating exchange rates may have helped accelerate international economic integration. Floating exchange rates have also undoubtedly often played an important role in facilitating adjustments to international economic imbalances. But critics have argued that their useful role in this respect should not be overstated.

Some have echoed the argument made in the 1930s that floating exchange rates have encouraged destabilizing speculative financial flows because of the uncertain international monetary environment they create. These flows, in turn, are said to generate further volatility and misalignments in currency values. One of the best-known advocates of this view is Susan Strange (1986) who suggests that floating exchange rates have encouraged a kind of 'casino capitalism' in which speculators have come increasingly to dominate foreign exchange markets. The consequences have been devastating from her standpoint: 'The great difference between an ordinary casino which you can go into or stay away from, and the global casino of high finance, is that in the latter all of us are involuntarily engaged in the day's play. A currency change can halve the value of a farmer's crop before he harvests it, or drive an exporter out of business . . . From school-leavers to pensioners, what goes on in the casino in the office blocks of the big financial centers is apt to have sudden, unpredictable and avoidable consequences for individual lives. The financial casino has everyone playing the game of Snakes and Ladders.'

It is certainly true that currency trading has grown very dramatically since the early 1970s; the size of daily foreign exchange trading increased from $US15 billion in 1973 to almost US$1,500 billion by 1998. The latter figure dwarfs the size of trading that would be necessary simply to service regular international trade and investment flows. The total value of exports of all countries *for the entire year* of 1997 was US$6.6 trillion (or $25 billion per day) (Gilpin 2000: 140; 2001: 261). As cross-border financial flows have grown dramatically, it is also accurate that exchange rates have sometimes been subject to considerable short-term volatility and longer-term misalignments. In these circumstances, a floating exchange rate has often been the source of, rather than the means of adjusting to, external economic imbalances.

International exchange-rate management: the Plaza to the Louvre

One of the more dramatic episodes of a long-term misalignment involved the appreciation of the US dollar in the early-to-mid 1980s. This currency movement was not responding to a US current account surplus; indeed, the country experienced a growing current account deficit at the time that stemmed from the country's rapid domestic economic expansion after 1982. Instead, the dollar's appreciation was caused by very large inflows of foreign capital, attracted by the country's high interest rates and its rapid economic expansion after 1982. The appreciation proved to be very disruptive; it exacerbated the US current account deficit and generated widespread protectionist sentiments within the USA by 1984–5.

This episode led the USA and other major industrial countries to consider briefly a move back towards more managed exchange rates. In September 1985, the Plaza Agreement was signed by the G5 (the United States, the United Kingdom, the Federal Republic of Germany, France, and Japan) which committed these countries to work together to encourage the US dollar to depreciate vis-à-vis the currencies of its major trading partners. After the dollar had fallen almost 50 per cent vis-à-vis the yen and deutschmark by February 1987, they then announced the Louvre Accord which established target ranges for the major currencies to be reached through closer macro-economic policy coordination (Funabashi 1988; Webb 1995; Henning 1987).

This enthusiasm for a more managed exchange-rate system between the world's major currencies proved to be short-lived. The three leading economic powers—the United States, Germany, and Japan—were not prepared to accept the kinds of serious constraints on their macro-economic policy autonomy that were required to make such a system effective. Many policy makers in Germany and Japan also argued that the US interest in macro-economic policy coordination seemed designed primarily to reduce its own external deficit by encouraging changes in macro-economic policy abroad rather than at home. This complaint had been heard once before during the late 1970s when the US policy makers last pressed Germany and Japan to coordinate macro-economic policies. In both instances, US policy makers sought to address their country's external payments deficit by pressing Germany and Japan to revalue their currencies and pursue more expansionary domestic economic policies. These moves would enable the United States to curtail its deficit without a domestic contraction by boosting US exports.

United States pressure in these two instances was applied not just through formal negotiations but also informally by 'talking down the dollar'. The latter encouraged financial traders to speculate against the dollar, leaving the German and Japanese governments with two options. They could defend the US currency through dollar purchases, thereby preserving the competitiveness of domestic industry vis-à-vis the important US market as well as the value of their dollar-denominated assets. In the end, however, these purchases would likely produce the other result that the USA wanted: an expanding domestic monetary supply in Japan and Germany caused by the increased purchase of dollars. Alternatively, if they accepted the dollar's depreciation, pressure for domestic expansionary policies would still come from another source—domestic industry and labour that was hurt by the country's loss of competitiveness vis-à-vis the United States. The effectiveness of this 'dollar weapon' rested on the US dollar's key currency status and the fact that the US market remained such an important one for Japanese and German businesses in this period. It was a strategy that met with some success for the USA in both instances, although it also left

the USA vulnerable to a crisis of confidence in the dollar at some key moments.

The creation of the euro

Although efforts to stabilize the relationship between the values of the world's major currencies have been limited since the early 1970s, some governments have moved to create stable monetary relations in smaller regional contexts. The most elaborate initiative of this kind has taken place in Europe. At the time of the breakdown of the Bretton Woods exchange-rate system, a number of the countries of the European Community (EC) attempted to stabilize exchange rates amongst themselves. These initial efforts were then followed up by the creation of the European Monetary System in 1979 which established a kind of 'mini-Bretton Woods' adjustable peg regime in which capital controls were still widely used and financial support was provided to protect each country's currency peg vis-à-vis other European currencies. Then, with the Maastricht Treaty in 1991, most members of European Union went one step further to commit to a full monetary union, which was created in 1999.

This long-standing resistance of many European governments to floating exchange rates within Europe has been driven partly by worries that exchange-rate volatility and misalignments would disrupt their efforts to build a closer economic community. Exchange-rate instability was deemed disruptive not only to private commerce but also to the complicated system of regional public payments within the European's Community Common Agricultural Policy. But why go so far as to abandon national currencies altogether by 1999?

One answer is that the adjustable peg system of the EMS became unsustainable after European governments committed themselves to abolish capital controls in 1988. The latter decision left European currency pegs vulnerable to increasingly powerful speculative financial flows, a fact demonstrated vividly in the 1992–3 European currency crisis. At this moment, European governments faced an important choice. If they sought to preserve financial liberalization and exchange-rate stability, they would have to give up their commitment to domestic monetary policy autonomy. Open macro-economic theory teaches

Box 6.2 **The 'impossible trinity' of open macro-economics**

Economists have pointed out that national governments face an inevitable trade-off between the three policy goals of exchange-rate stability, national monetary policy autonomy, and capital mobility. It is only ever possible for governments to realize two of these goals at the same time. In choosing an international monetary and financial regime, in other words, policy makers are faced with the choice of which goal to sacrifice within this 'impossible trinity'. If, for example, a national government wants to preserve capital mobility and a fixed exchange rate, it must abandon an independent monetary policy. The reason is straightforward. An independent expansionary monetary policy in an environment of capital mobility will trigger capital outflows—and downward pressure on the national currency—as domestic interest rates fall. In this context, it will be possible to maintain the fixed exchange rate only by pushing interest rates back up and thereby abandoning the initial monetary policy goal. If, however,

the government chooses to maintain the expansionary policy, it will need either to introduce capital controls or embrace a floating exchange rate, thereby sacrificing one of the other goals within the impossible trinity.

Historically, during the era of the gold standard, governments embraced fixed exchange rates and capital mobility, while abandoning national monetary policy autonomy. During the Bretton Woods order, national policy autonomy and fixed (although adjustable) exchange-rates were prioritized, while capital mobility was given up. Since the early 1970s, the leading powers have sacrificed a global regime of fixed exchange-rate regime in order to boost policy autonomy and capital mobility. Many governments within this system, however, have embraced fixed rates at the regional or bilateral level by using capital controls or by abandoning national policy autonomy.

---

us that it is not possible to achieve all three of these objectives simultaneously (see Box 6.2). If they agreed to abandon monetary policy autonomy within this 'impossible trinity', a logical next step was simply to create a monetary union which eliminated the possibility of future intra-regional exchange-rate crises altogether.

This choice was also made easier by the growing prominence of neo-liberal thought within European monetary policy-making circles (McNamara 1998). Neo-liberals were disillusioned with the kinds of activist national monetary policies that became popular in the age of 'embedded liberalism'. This sentiment emerged partly out of experiences of inflation and partly from the rational expectations revolution in the discipline of economics. The latter undermined a key idea that had sustained support for activist monetary policies: the Keynesian notion that there was a long-term trade-off between inflation and unemployment. By highlighting how experiences of inflation over time may encourage people to adjust their expectations, this new economic analysis suggested that activist monetary management could simply produce 'stagflation'; that is, a combination of high unemployment and high inflation. If people

began to anticipate higher and higher levels of inflation, this analysis argued that they would adjust their wage demands and pricing decisions accordingly, creating an upward inflationary spiral. To break these inflationary expectations, authorities would have to re-establish their credibility and reputation for producing stable money by a strong commitment to price stability. The perceived need for this kind of credibility and reputation has also been reinforced by the disciplining power of international capital markets (see for example, Andrews and Willett 1997).

The new influence of neo-liberal monetary thinking played an important role in generating support for European Monetary Union (EMU). By eliminating a key macro-economic rationale for wanting a national currency in the first place (that is, the commitment to activist national monetary management), it has made policy makers less resistant to the idea of giving these monetary structures up. Indeed, many policy makers saw currency union as a better way to achieve price stability than maintaining a national currency because the union appeared to allow them to 'import' the German central bank's anti-inflationary monetary policy. Like the German Bundesbank, the new European central bank was given a strict mandate to pursue price stability as its primary goal. Other neo-liberal policy makers also saw EMU as a way to prevent national policy makers from pursuing 'out-dated' Keynesian macroeconomic policies. This is not just because of the elimination of national monetary management but also because participants in EMU agreed under the 'Stability and Growth Pact' to limit the maximum size of their budget deficits and public debt. In addition, some neo-liberals have applauded the fact that EMU, by eliminating the possibility of national devaluations, might encourage greater price and wage flexibility within national economies as workers and firms are forced to confront the impact of external economic 'shocks' in a more direct fashion.

Because of this basis of support for EMU, many on the political left have been very wary of the project. They worry that it may produce domestic deregulation, cutbacks to the welfare state, and new constraints on states' abilities to address unemployment and other social and economic problems. The resultant costs, they suggest, will be borne disproportionately by vulnerable groups such as the poor and women (Gill 1998; B. Young 2002). Interestingly, however, there have also been many social democrats and unions across Europe—groups not usually friendly to neo-liberal thinking—who have been supportive of the drive to monetary union (Josselin 2001; Notermans 2001). Because it can protect a country from speculative currency attacks, some have seen EMU as creating a more stable macro-economic environment in which progressive supply-side reforms could be undertaken to promote equity, growth, and employment. In some countries, adopting the euro has also been seen as a way to lower domestic interest rates by reducing risk premiums that the markets were imposing, a result that has actually improved governments' budgetary positions and *prevented* cuts to the welfare state. Some social democrats and unions have also hoped that EMU might eventually help dilute the monetary influence of the neo-liberal Bundesbank across Europe and encourage coordinated EU-wide expansionary fiscal policies. In addition, some social democrats and unions have seen EMU as an opportunity to reinvigorate national corporatist social pacts in which cooperative wage bargaining, employment friendly taxation schemes, and other social protection measures can assume a key role in the process of adjusting to external economic shocks.

The EMU project also had a broader political meaning. In addition to challenging US power (see below), the creation of the euro has been seen as an important symbol of the process of fostering ever-closer European cooperation. Many analysts also argue that the decision to create the euro was linked to a broader political deal between Germany and other European countries at the time of the Maastricht Treaty. Many European countries—especially France—had become increasingly frustrated by the domination of the European monetary system by the German Bundesbank, and they pressed for EMU as a way to dilute its influence. Germany is then said to have accepted EMU when it came to be seen as a trade-off for European (and especially French) support for German reunification in 1989 (for example, see Kaltenthaler 1998).

Currency unions elsewhere?

The European experiment in creating a currency union has triggered talk of a similar move in some other regions. Is this likely to happen? Economists try to help address this question by analysing whether each region resembles an 'optimum currency area' (see Box 6.3). In practice, though, this kind of economic analysis has had little predictive power in the European context or elsewhere. One of the longest-standing monetary unions in the world is the CFA franc zone involving many ex-French colonies in west and central Africa, and its member countries do not come close to resembling an 'optimum currency area'. Like EMU, that monetary union was formed and has been sustained by certain political conditions. Particularly important in that case have been the power and political interests of France in the colonial and post-colonial context (Stasavage 2003).

The other region where interest in monetary union has been particularly significant is the Americas. Beginning in 1999, many policy makers in that region began to debate the idea of creating a currency union that would be based on the US dollar. Two countries—Ecuador and El Salvador—then went beyond talk to action and introduced the US dollar as their national currency in 2000 and 2001 respectively. The new interest in dollarization across Latin America is partly a product of the ascendancy of neo-liberal monetary

Box 6.3 **Monetary unions and the theory of optimum currency areas**

The theory of optimum currency areas was first developed by the Nobel prize-winning economist Robert Mundell (1961) to evaluate the pros and cons of forming a monetary union among a selected group of countries. While assuming the union will produce micro-economic benefits in the form of lower transaction costs for cross-border commerce, the theory focuses its analytical attention on the potential macro-economic costs associated with abandoning the exchange rate as a tool of macro-economic adjustment. If these costs are low, the region is said to approximate more closely an 'optimum currency area' that should be encouraged to create a monetary union.

To evaluate how significant these costs are in each regional context, the theory examines a number of criteria. If selected countries experience similar external shocks, for example, the theory notes that they are more likely to be good candidates for monetary union since they will each have less need for an independent exchange rate. Even if they experience asymmetric shocks, the macro-economic costs of abandoning national exchange rates may still be low if wages and price are very flexible within each country or if labour is highly mobile between countries or if there are mechanisms for transferring fiscal payments among the countries. Each of these conditions would enable adjustments to be made to external shocks in the absence of an exchange rate.

ideas there. As in Europe, many neo-liberals in the region see the abandonment of the national currency as a way to import price stability; in this case, from the US Federal Reserve. Advocates of dollarization have also argued that it will help to insulate countries from speculative financial flows and will attract stable long-term foreign investment.

The dollarization debate also emerges from a context where many Latin American countries have experienced a kind of informal, partial dollarization since the 1970s. Local residents have often turned to the US dollar as a store of value, a unit of account, and even a medium of exchange as a way to insulate themselves from domestic monetary and political uncertainty. The option has been made easier by the broader liberalization and deregulation of Latin American financial systems in this period. Since informal dollarization has already eroded national monetary sovereignty considerably, it has lessened resistance to the idea of formal dollarization.

Formal dollarization also has many opponents in Latin America. Critics highlight that countries that dollarize are giving up key tools—domestic monetary policy and the exchange rate—with which their governments can manage their domestic economies. The potential costs, they argue, have been well highlighted in Argentina's recent experience. Between 1991 and 2001, Argentina managed its national currency on a 'currency board' basis which tied the value of the currency tightly to the US dollar. When the

country began to experience growing current account deficits after the mid-1990s, the only way it could correct the problem—while retaining this monetary regime—was to undergo a costly deflation. This deflation produced high unemployment and dramatic cuts to government spending, and it contributed to the country's massive financial crisis of 2001–2.

Critics also point out that, while European countries are joining a monetary union in which they have some say, the adoption of the US dollar would leave Latin American countries as monetary dependencies. United States policy makers have begun to debate what kind of support they might provide to countries that adopt the US dollar and their answer to date has been very little. They have made it clear that dollarized countries would not be offered any role in the decision making of the US Federal Reserve, and that Fed officials have no intention of taking the concerns of dollarized countries into account when they set US monetary policy. United States policy makers are not even willing to consider providing lender-of-last-resort activities to institutions in dollarized countries. The only support they have seriously discussed is the sharing of the 'seigniorage' revenue that the United States would earn from the dollar's circulation in Latin American countries that formally dollarize (see Box 6.4).

All US currency held is an interest-free loan to the US government, and the portion held abroad is estimated to provide as much as $10 billion per year to the

---

Box 6.4 What is 'seigniorage'?

Seigniorage is usually defined as the difference between the nominal value of money and its cost of production. This difference is a kind of 'profit' for the issuer of money. In medieval Europe, this source of revenue was often a very important one for ruling authorities. They could earn it openly by adding a 'seigniorage' charge (above the normal mint charge that offset the cost of minting) when producing metallic coin. They also often earned more secretly by debasing their coin through a reduction of its weight or its 'fineness' (by increasing the proportion of non-precious alloy). If the surreptitious strategy was detected by the public, its effectiveness would be undermined as people would either not accept the coins or accept them only at a discount. In more modern times, metallic coins no longer dominate the monetary system, and governments now earn seigniorage also through the issuing of paper currency as well as indirectly through their regulation of the creation of bank deposit money. National monetary authorities earn seigniorage not just from the use of the money they issue by citizens within their borders. The international use of their currency will augment the seigniorage revenue they earn even further.

United States (Porter and Judson 1996: 883). Even this idea, however, was not able to pick up enough support to be endorsed by US Congress or the US financial officials when it was debated in 1999–2000. As Cohen (2002) puts it, US policy makers seem to prefer a policy of 'passive neutrality' on the question of dollarization in Latin America. In his view, the only scenario in which US policy makers might become much more supportive is if the euro began to pose a serious challenge to the dollar's international position.

Key points

- Floating exchange rates have performed an important role in facilitating balance of payments adjustments, but critics argue that they have also been subject to short-term volatility and longer-term misalignments.

- Efforts to stabilize the relationship between the values of the world's major currencies have been limited since the early 1970s, but initiatives to create more stable regional monetary relations have been more common, particularly in Europe where a monetary union was introduced in 1999.

- Some of the same factors that prompted the decision to create a European monetary union have triggered proposals for monetary unions elsewhere, most notably in the Americas. But a dollar-based monetary union in the Americas is not likely unless the United States becomes more supportive of the idea.

The dollar's declining global role?

Cohen's observation raises the question of the US dollar's future role as a world currency. When US policy makers ended the dollar's convertibility into gold in 1971, some predicted that the US currency's role as the dominant world currency would be challenged since the dollar was no longer 'as good as gold'. In fact, the dollar's central global role has endured. It has continued to be the currency of choice for denominating international trade across most of the world. It has also remained the most common currency held by many governments in foreign exchange reserves. In the private international financial markets that have grown dramatically in recent years (for reasons explained below), the US dollar has also been used more than any other currency as a store of value and for denominating transactions since the early 1970s (Cohen 1998: chapter 5). The US dollar has even been used to an increasing degree by market actors *within* many countries—not just in Latin America but elsewhere too—as a unit of account, a store of value, and even a medium of exchange over the past two decades (Cohen 1998).

In some respects, the US dollar's enduring central global position is a product of inertia. There are many 'network externalities' which reinforce the continued use of existing currencies, both within countries and at the international level, even when those currencies demonstrate considerable instability (Cohen 1998). Some foreign governments have also continued to hold their reserves in US dollars and denominated their international trade in dollars because of their broader political ties with the US (see, for example, Spiro 1999; Gilpin 1987). Perhaps most important in explaining the dollar's enduring global role, however, has been the fact that US financial markets, particularly its short-term markets, have remained among the most liquid, large and deep in the world. This has made the holding and use of US dollars particularly attractive to private actors and foreign governments. The two other leading economies—Japan and West Germany—have not cultivated liquid deregulated short-term money markets that rivalled those of the USA in which yen-denominated or deutschmark-denominated assets could be held.

Emerging challenges to the dollar's dominant position

Only very recently has the dollar's position as the dominant world currency begun to be challenged. One challenge has come from the creation of the euro in Europe. Some European policy makers have supported the euro's creation for this reason: they have seen it as a tool to challenge the dollar's pre-eminent global role and bolster Europe's power in the global political economy (Henning 1998: 563–5). In outlining the official rationale for monetary union in its 'One Market, One Money' report, the European Commission (1990: 194, 191), for example, praised how the euro would bring greater 'symmetry' to the global monetary order and force the United States to become 'more conscious of the limits of independent policy-making'.

What kind of a challenge will the euro pose to the US dollar? In 1990, the European Commission (1990: 182) predicted that the euro would be a particularly attractive international currency because it would be backed by a conservative central bank dedicated to price stability, and because it would be able to be held in unified European money markets that would be 'the largest in the world'. So far, however, the euro's challenge to the dollar has been less significant than this prediction. One reason has been that European financial markets remain highly decentralized and, in the words of Fred Bergsten (1997: 88), there is 'no central government borrower like the US Treasury to provide a fulcrum for the market'. Cohen (2003) also argues that the euro's international use is held back by uncertainties regarding the governance structure and thus broader political credibility of the whole initiative.

The European Commission (1990: 183) noted a second way in which the euro's creation might threaten the dollar. It observed that, with no more intra-EC foreign exchange intervention necessary, an estimated $230 billion of the total $400 billion of foreign exchange reserves of EC member states would no longer be needed, the majority of which was held in dollars. If these excess reserves were sold suddenly, Pauly (1992: 108) had predicted that the result would be 'destabilizing in the extreme' for the dollar. Again, however, European governments have so far shown little interest in provoking this kind of monetary confrontation with the United States.

More generally, it is also worth noting that the creation of a common European central bank might encourage Europe to present a more unified voice in international monetary politics. European Union countries could, for example, unify their voting stances in the IMF where they already hold a larger collective voting share than the United States. Indeed, Henning (1997) notes that some could even question—incorrectly in his view—whether this kind of a consolidated European quota will require a relocation of the Fund's headquarters away from Washington since its Articles of Agreement require that the Fund be located in the territory of its member with the largest quota.

The other challenge to the dollar's role comes from Japan where policy makers have recently become much more interested in promoting the international use of the yen, especially in the East Asian region (Grimes 2003). Despite Japan's emergence as the world's leading creditor in the 1980s, the yen remained used very little at the international level throughout that decade. Even the Japanese themselves relied heavily on the US dollar in their international transactions in both trade and finance. Indeed, the bulk of their assets held abroad remained in this foreign currency, a quite unprecedented and vulnerable situation for the world's largest creditor.

When this dependence played a central role in encouraging the Japanese bubble economy of the late 1980s, Japanese policy makers became more interested in promoting the yen's international use. As noted in the previous section, the US dollar fell dramatically in value between 1985 and 1987. To reduce the impact on Japan, the Bank of Japan was prompted to prevent its further fall by dropping Japanese interest rates and boosting Japanese growth through an expansionary monetary policy, policies which encouraged the domestic asset inflation. This experience generated a desire in Japan to reduce dependence on the dollar and encourage the yen to be used more, especially in the East Asian region where Japan's trade and investment was growing rapidly. This goal was reinforced by the East Asian financial crisis of 1997–8 which many Japanese policy makers felt was exacerbated by the region's over-reliance on US financial influence. To cultivate the yen's international role, the Japanese government has begun to pursue various initiatives such as fostering a more attractive short-term money market in Japan and encouraging the growth of yen-denominated lending from Japan. Internationalization of the yen, however, has been held back by the problems of the Japanese financial system, by the relatively closed nature of the Japanese economy, and by its economic stagnation in the 1990s at a time when China's economy continued to grow rapidly.

Consequences of dollar's declining role?

If the dollar's dominant global position is in fact challenged in the coming years, what will the consequences be? To begin with, the United States will lose some benefits that it has derived from the currency's status. In addition the international prestige that comes from issuing a dominant world currency, the US dollar's use abroad has produced extra 'seigniorage' revenue for the US government, as noted above (see Box 6.4). The pre-eminence of the dollar as a world currency has also enhanced the USA's ability to finance its external deficits. In addition, we have seen already how it has helped to persuade foreign governments to help correct these US deficits by adjusting their macro-economic policies. The USA may thus feel its policy autonomy more constrained as the dollar's global role diminishes, a constraint that may be felt particularly strongly if the USA continues to run very large current account deficits.

The erosion of the dollar's central global position will also have consequences for the world as a whole. In particular, it raises the question of whether the international monetary system will be more or less stable without a dominant monetary power. Drawing on the inter-war experience, some have predicted that increasing global monetary instability lies ahead. But others have suggested the opposite. David Calleo (1987: chapter 8) has long argued that a world monetary order based on more 'pluralistic' or 'balance of power' principles may be more likely to produce stability over time than one based on hegemony. A hegemonic power, in his view, is inevitably tempted to exploit its dominant position over time to serve its own interests rather than the interests of the stability of the system. Interestingly, European Commission president Jacques Delors advanced a similar argument in defending EMU in 1993; in his words, the creation of the euro would make the EU 'strong enough to force the United States and Japan to play by rules which would ensure much greater monetary stability around the world' (quoted in Henning 1998: 565).

Key points

- The US dollar continued to be a dominant global currency after it ceased to be convertible into gold in 1971. This was due in large part to the unique attractiveness of US financial markets.

- Recently, the US dollar's global role is beginning to be challenged by the euro and the yen, although these challenges should not be overstated.

- These challenges will impose new constraints on US policy making, but their wider systemic implications for global monetary stability are hard to predict.

The globalization of financial markets

The final feature of the Bretton Woods regime which has broken down since the early 1970s involves a trend that has already been mentioned a number of times: the globalization of private financial markets. Recall that the Bretton Woods architects endorsed an international financial order in which governments could control cross-border private financial flows and public international institutions would be assigned a key role in allocating short-term and long-term credit at the international level. Today, this world appears to be turned upside down. Enormous sums of private capital flow around the world quite freely on a twenty-four hour basis. And the size of these flows dwarfs the lending activities of the IMF and World Bank.

Explaining financial globalization

How did we get from there to here? The growth of global telecommunication networks has enabled money to be moved around the world much more easily than in the past. A number of market developments have also been significant. The dramatic expansion of international trade and multinational corporate activity from the 1960s onwards, for example, generated some of the growing demand for private international financial services. The 1973 oil price rise also provided a big boost to the globalization of finance when private banks took on the role of recycling the new wealth of oil-producing countries to countries in deficit. Private actors were also encouraged to diversify their assets internationally by the increasingly volatile currency environment after the breakdown of the Bretton Woods exchange-rate system in the early 1970s. The risks and costs of international financial activity were also lowered throughout this period by various market innovations such as the creation of currency futures, options, and swaps.

In addition to these technological and market developments, the globalization of finance has been a product of political choices and state decisions (Helleiner 1994). In particular, it has been encouraged by the fact that states increasingly liberalized the tight capital controls they employed in the early post-war years. The first step in a liberalizing direction took place when the British government encouraged the growth of the 'euro-market' in London during the 1960s. This was a financial market where the British government allowed international financial activity in foreign currencies—primarily US dollars in the early years—to be conducted on an unregulated basis. After the mid-1970s, the globalization of finance was encouraged further when many governments dismantled their capital control regimes which had been in place throughout the post-war period. The United States and United Kingdom led the way, abolishing their national capital controls in 1974 and 1979 respectively. They were soon followed by other advanced industrial countries. Indeed, by the 1990s, an almost fully liberal pattern of financial relations had emerged among advanced industrial states, giving market actors a degree of freedom in cross-border financial activity unparalleled since the 1920s.

Poorer countries have generally been less willing to abolish capital controls altogether. But an increasing number have done so and others have liberalized their existing controls in various ways in this period. Many small poorer states—particularly in the Caribbean—have also played a central role in fostering financial globalization by offering their territories as a regulation-free environment for international financial activity. Places such as the Grand Caymans Islands had emerged as very significant international banking centres in the world by the 1980s and 1990s (Palan 2003).

Why have states largely abandoned the restrictive Bretton Woods financial regime? Some scholars assign a prominent role to the growing influence of neo-liberal ideology among financial policy makers (for example, Helleiner 1994). As we have seen in the last section, neo-liberals were less sympathetic to the Bretton Woods idea that national policy autonomy needed to be protected. Where Keynes and White had endorsed the use of capital controls for this purpose, many neo-liberals have applauded the fact that international financial markets might impose an external discipline on governments that were pursuing policies that were not 'sound' from a neo-liberal standpoint. Neo-liberals have also criticized the role that capital controls might play in interfering with market freedoms and preventing the efficient allocation of capital internationally.

The liberalization of capital controls has also been seen by some policy makers as a kind of competitive strategy to attract mobile financial business and capital to their national territory (Cerny 1994). The British support for the euro-markets and their decision to abolish capital controls in 1979 were both designed to help rebuild London's status as a leading international financial centre in this way. The US support for financial liberalization (both at home *and abroad*) was also designed to bolster New York's international financial position as well as to attract foreign capital to the uniquely deep and liquid US financial markets in ways that could help finance US trade and budget deficits throughout this period. The smaller offshore financial centres have also seen the hosting of an international financial centre as a development strategy that could provide employment and some limited government revenue (from such things as licenses and fees). Once governments such as these had begun to liberalize and deregulate their financial systems, many other governments also felt competitive pressures to emulate their decisions in order to prevent mobile domestic capital and financial business from migrating abroad. As their country's firms became increasingly transnational and had access to foreign financial markets, policy makers also recognized that national capital controls could only be enforced in very rigid ways that would be costly to the national economy (Goodman and Pauly 1993).

Implications of financial globalization for national policy autonomy

What have been the implications of the globalization of finance? One set of implications is addressed in the next chapter: the vulnerability of global financial markets to financial crises. A second set of implications relates to the concerns of the Bretton Woods negotiators. As noted above, they worried that a liberal international financial order would undermine their efforts to create a stable exchange-rate system and to protect national policy autonomy. We have already seen how financial globalization has indeed complicated the task of maintaining fixed exchange rates. But what about its implications for national policy autonomy?

This question has generated much debate in the field of IPE. Some have argued that financial globalization has severely undermined national policy autonomy since it gives investors a powerful 'exit' option to exercise against governments that stray too far from their preferences. Like Keynes and White, proponents of this view argue that this discipline is felt particularly strongly by governments that pursue policies disliked by wealthy asset holders, such as large budget deficits, high taxation, expansionary macro-economic policies that risk inflation, or more generally policies that reflect left-of-centre political values (Kurzer 1993; Sinclair 1994; Harmes 1998; McKenzie and Lee 1991; Gill and Law 1989; Cerny 1994). These new constraints—what Thomas Friedman (2000) calls the 'Golden Straightjacket'—are said to help explain why governments across the world have shifted away from these kinds of policies since the 1970s.

Southern governments are seen to be especially vulnerable to the discipline of global financial markets. This is partly because their financial systems are so small relative to the enormous size of global financial flows. It is also because investors tend to be more skittish about the security of their assets in contexts where economic and political instability is higher and there is a higher prospect of default. The 1994 Mexican peso crisis and the 1997–8 East Asian financial crisis are cited to show how entire countries' economic prospects can be devastated overnight by a sudden loss of confidence in international financial markets. More generally, Southern countries have also suffered from the fact that their wealthy citizens have taken advantage of the new global markets to park their assets in safer Northern financial markets. During debt crises, the size of this 'flight capital' from many debtor countries has often equalled or surpassed that of the country's external debts. In other words, these countries were often creditors to the world economy at the very moment that their governments were managing a severe debt crisis; if this flight capital could be repatriated, these countries would have experienced no debt crisis and the associated loss of policy autonomy (Lissakers 1991).

Other scholars suggest that these arguments about the declining policy autonomy of national governments are overstated. We have seen already how macro-economic theory suggests that states can retain a high degree of monetary policy autonomy in an atmosphere of capital mobility if they are willing to allow the exchange rate to fluctuate (see Box 6.2). Indeed, according to this theory, monetary policy becomes even *more* effective in conditions of capital mobility. An expansionary monetary policy, for example, will trigger an outflow of capital which, in turn, will cause the exchange rate to depreciate, thus reinforcing the expansionary effect of the initial policy. Ton Notermans (2000), for example, has highlighted how European governments such as Sweden and Norway succeeded in pursuing expansionary monetary policies throughout the 1970s and 1980s by retaining a floating exchange. Indeed, from Notermans's perspective, these governments eventually abandoned expansionary macro-economic policies *not* because of the external constraint of financial globalization but because of a growing inability to contain inflation domestically as tripartite collective bargaining structures unravelled and domestic financial innovation undermined traditional monetary tools.

Michael Loriaux (1991) puts forward a similar analysis of the well-known experience of Mitterand's socialist government in France in the early 1980s. When this government abandoned its unilateral Keynesian expansion in 1983, many scholars pointed to the experience as a confirmation of the new constraints imposed by financial globalization. But Loriaux suggests that the constraint was a more domestic one. In the new atmosphere of floating exchange rates after 1973, he shows how the French government was increasingly unable to pursue expansionary policies because the inflationary consequences of a devaluation could not be easily contained. This inability to contain inflation stemmed from the existence of an 'overdraft economy' which resulted from the structure of the French domestic financial system. From this perspective, the French state lost control over its macro-economic policy *not* because of financial globalization but because its domestic financial system was ill-suited to the macro-economic imperatives of the new world of floating exchange rates. Ironically, as Loriaux points out, the financial deregulation and liberalization programme launched by the Mitterrand government after 1983 had the effect of *increasing* the ability of the state to control monetary policy rather than decreasing it. It enabled the state to regain control over monetary policy by eliminating the overdraft economy which had been fostered by the old financial system.

The importance of exchange-rate policy in providing a degree of macro-economic autonomy has also been highlighted in the case of capital flight from Latin American countries. Jonathan Crystal (1994) argues that much of the capital flight experienced by Latin American countries in the 1970s and 1980s could have been avoided through the use of different exchange-rate policies. He demonstrates how countries maintaining overvalued exchange rates have suffered much more serious capital flight than those that did not, and he shows how government decisions to maintain overvalued exchange rates reflected *domestic* political constraints rather than the influence of global financial markets.

Other authors suggest that the disciplining effect of global finance on governments with high levels of government spending, high taxation, or a more general left-of-centre political orientation has been exaggerated. Garrett (1995) has highlighted how many OECD governments have been able to use borrowing in international capital markets in the last two decades to finance *increased* government spending (see also Swank 2002). In the 1970s and again during much of the 1990s, countries in Latin America and East Asia also found that global financial markets offered funds that *enhanced* their fiscal autonomy in the short term. That these borrowing experiences often ended up in debt crises that undermined policy autonomy was a product of a number of factors often unrelated to financial globalization, such as unexpected sudden shocks to the world economy and particular patterns in the use of the borrowed funds. More generally, in a detailed study of the preferences of international financial market actors, Mosley (2003) found that these actors were concerned primarily with overall national inflation rates and aggregate levels of fiscal deficits; they did not worry about governments' overall level of spending, taxation, or their political orientation when considering investment decisions (although this result was less true when they considered investments in Southern countries).

Finally, those who think that the power of global financial markets over nation states has been overstated often point to the fact that states retain the ability to reimpose capital controls when their policy autonomy is threatened. The decision of the Malaysian government to adopt this strategy during the East Asian financial crisis provides one such example (Beeson 2000). Another prominent case has been Chile which has used controls on speculative capital inflows in order to manage its relationship with the global financial system more effectively (Soederberg 2002). These examples are cited to support the broader point that powerful global financial markets ultimately rest on political foundations that are established by nation states (Pauly 1997).

Distributive and environmental implications of financial globalization

International political economy scholars have also been interested in some other implications of financial globalization that attracted less attention at Bretton Woods. One of these has been its distributive impact within countries. Neo-Marxist scholars have argued that financial globalization has bolstered the power of an emerging internationally mobile capitalist class, while eroding that of labour. The emerging transnational capital class has gained 'structural power' through its new ability to exit—or simply threaten to exit—domestic political settings. This power has been used to reinforce neo-liberal ideology and a kind of 'internationalization of the state' which serves the interests of this new class (Gill and Law 1989).

Jeffrey Frieden (1991) has also highlighted new political divisions that have emerged within the business sector. While transnational corporations and owners of financial assets and services have gained from financial globalization, businesses that are more nationally based have often not. In a world of heightened capital mobility, he argues that these two groups are in fact increasingly at loggerheads over policy choices within the 'impossible trinity'. The former generally prefer exchange-rate stability because of

their involvement in international trade and finance, even if this involves a cost of abandoning monetary policy autonomy. Those in the non-tradable sector are inclined to defend monetary policy autonomy even if this involves accepting a floating exchange rate.

Some scholars have also analysed the gendered implications of financial globalization (Singh and Zammit 2000; van Staveren 2002). To the extent that global financial integration has been associated with the retrenchment of the welfare state, the costs have often been borne more by women than men. Cutbacks to government spending in areas such as health, education, public transportation, and other social services frequently have the effect of increasing the role played in these areas by the unpaid sector of the economy, a sector traditionally dominated by women. When countries experience international financial crises, other aspects of the burden of adjustment can also be strongly gendered. During the Asian financial crisis, incomes in the informal sectors—where women are heavily represented—fell particularly sharply and job cuts in the formal private sector often fell more heavily on women. Aslanbegui and Summerfield (2000: 87, 91) also note how 'across the region, migrant workers, the majority of whom were women, were expelled from host countries' and they quote the World Bank's observation that 'child labour, prostitution and domestic violence' increased during the crisis. Other analysts have also highlighted how even global financial markets themselves are overwhelmingly made up of male traders and they operate with a culture and discourse that is hyper-masculinized (McDowell 1997; De Goede 2000).

A final issue that received little attention at the time of the Bretton Woods conference concerns the environmental implications of global financial markets. Scholarship on this topic has been fairly limited within the field of IPE to date, but some interesting themes have been put forward by those who have addressed it. In particular, a number of analysts have suggested that speculative and volatile international financial flows reward instant economic results and short-term thinking in ways that greatly complicate the kind of long-term planning that is required for the promotion of environmental values. During the East Asian financial crisis, for example, governments scrapped environmental programmes and there was an intensification of deforestation, mining, and other economic activities that put pressure on natural ecosystems (Durbin and Welch 2002). Even two analysts working with the World Business Council on Sustainable Development acknowledge that 'it is clear that the globalization of investment flows is speeding the destruction of natural forests' (Schmidheiny and Zorraquin 1996: 10). International investors, they note, push firms to harvest an entire forest for a short-term windfall profit rather than managing the forest in a sustainable fashion over the long term. They conclude: 'sustainable development is concerned with the importance of the future. Financial markets discount the future routinely and heavily' (1996: 8). On the other hand, the short-termism of global financial markets should not be overstated because one powerful actor in global finance—the global insurance sector—does have a longer-term perspective that has led it to play a key role in lobbying for action on climate change in order to reduce the risk of future claims in this area (Paterson 2001).

Key points

- The globalization of financial markets has been driven not just by technological and market pressures but also by the decisions of states to liberalize capital controls that had been popular in the early post-war years.

- Global financial markets have eroded the policy autonomy of national governments, but the degree of this erosion is a hotly contested subject among IPE scholars.

- Financial globalization has also had important distributive consequences along class, sectoral, and gender lines. Its environmental implications may also be significant, but they require more detailed study.

Conclusion

The international monetary and financial system has undergone three important transformations since the late nineteenth century in response to changing economic and political conditions. During the inter-war years, the global integrated monetary and financial order of the pre-1914 period broke down. At the Bretton Woods conference of 1944, a new order was built on 'embedded liberal' principles. Since the early 1970s, the third change has been under way as a number of the features of the Bretton Woods system have broken down.

In some respects, the emerging international monetary and financial system is reminiscent of the pre-1914 world. The commitment to a liberal and integrated global financial order is similar, as is the interest in regional monetary unions (although these unions today are a more ambitious kind than the Latin Monetary Union and Scandinavian Monetary Union). Like their counterparts in that earlier era, many contemporary policy makers are also committed to the idea that the principal goal of monetary policy should be to maintain price stability. At the same time, however, the absence of a gold standard today and the commitment of many governments to floating exchange rates mark a sharp difference from the pre-1914 period. This contrast reflects the enduring commitment of many governments to the idea that first emerged during the inter-war period that exchange-rate adjustments can play a useful role in bolstering policy autonomy and facilitating balance of payments adjustments. The beginnings of a decline in the dollar's dominant position and the growing interest in large regional currency zones have also led some to draw parallels to the inter-war years.

Each of these transformations in the nature of the international monetary and financial system has had important consequences for the key question of who gets what, when, and how in the global political economy. Monetary and financial systems—both at the domestic and international levels—serve not just economic functions. They also have implications for various political projects relating to the pursuit of values such as power, ideas, and interests. For this reason, the study of money and finance cannot be left only to the economics profession which has traditionally dominated scholarship in this area. It needs also the attention of students of international political economy who have an interest in these wider political issues.

QUESTIONS

1   Does historical experience suggest that a hegemonic leader is necessary for a stable international monetary and financial system to exist?

2   What kind of a challenge are the euro and the yen likely to pose to the dollar's position as world currency in the coming years?

3   Has the floating exchange-rate system created a kind of 'casino capitalism' which is creating an increasingly unstable global political economy? Should the leading powers attempt to stabilize the relationship between the values of the major currencies?

4   Has the creation of the euro been a positive move for Europeans? Should other regions emulate the European example and are they likely to do so?

5   To what extent has financial globalization undermined the power and policy autonomy of national governments? Is financial globalization irreversible?

6   How important has financial globalization been in influencing class, sectoral, and gender relations within countries? What are its environmental consequences?

FURTHER READING

Block, F. (1977), *The Origins of International Economic Disorder* (Berkeley and Los Angeles: University of California Press). An important analysis of the creation and breakdown of the Bretton Woods monetary order.

Cohen, B. (1998), *The Geography of Money* (Ithaca, NY: Cornell University Press). An important analysis of the ways in which national currencies are being challenged in the current age by one of the pioneers of the field of the political economy of international money.

—— (2004), *The Future of Money* (Princeton: Princeton University Press). A kind of sequel to *The Geography of Money* which addresses key policy questions relating to the changing nature of money in the contemporary world.

Eichengreen, B. (1992), *Golden Fetters: The Gold Standard and the Great Depression: 1919–1939* (Oxford: Oxford University Press). A detailed analysis of international monetary and financial relations during the inter-war years.

Gallarotti, G. (1995), *The Anatomy of an International Monetary Regime* (New York: Oxford University Press). A comprehensive survey of the political economy of the international gold standard.

Germain, R. (1997), *The International Organization of Credit* (Cambridge: Cambridge University Press). A wide-ranging analysis of the evolution of the international financial system since the early modern age.

Henning, C. R. (1994), *Currencies and Politics in the United States, Germany and Japan* (Washington DC: Institute for International Economics). An insightful analysis of the politics of exchange-rate policy making in the three leading economic powers.

Kirshner, J. (1995), *Currency and Coercion: The Political Economy of International Monetary Power* (Princeton: Princeton University Press). A pioneering analysis of how monetary relations are used as an instrument of state power.

—— (ed.) (2002), *Monetary Orders* (Ithaca, NY: Cornell University Press). An edited collection that highlights effectively the political foundations of national and international monetary systems.

Strange, S. (1998), *Mad Money* (Ann Arbor: University of Michigan Press). An important critique of the contemporary international monetary and financial system from one of the leading IPE scholars in this field.

Walter, A. (1991), *World Power and World Money: The Role of Hegemony and International Monetary Order* (London: Harvester Wheatsheaf). An excellent survey of international monetary and financial history since the late nineteenth century with a special focus on the role of hegemony.

WEB LINKS

www.attac.org   The website of a leading international lobby group pressing for global financial reform.

www.bis.org   The website of the Bank for International Settlements. The Bank is the 'central bankers' bank' and it provides detailed analyses of international monetary and financial developments.

www.eurodad.org   The website of a leading non-governmental organization based in Europe that addresses international financial issues relating to poorer countries.

www.imf.org   The website of the International Monetary Fund.

www.stern.nyu.edu/globalmacro   A website run by Nouriel Roubini that provides a very large number of useful links for research on international monetary and financial issues.

7 The political economy of international financial crises

Louis W. Pauly

READER'S GUIDE

Since the early 1970s, the world economy has been embarked on an experiment involving, on the one hand, the opening and deepening of financial markets and, on the other, the dispersion of the political authority required to regulate global markets. The resulting governance dilemmas are nowhere clearer than in the circumstances surrounding financial crises capable of spilling across national borders. This chapter explores the political economy of crisis prevention and crisis management in the evolving world system. It pays particular attention to the challenges confronting emerging markets in recent years, and to the institutional responses of the leading states in the system.

Introduction

Financial crisis rocked the global economy from the late 1990s into the early years of the new century. It was not the first test of the post-1945 United States-led system, which had been built upon the idea of deepening international economic interdependence. Financial booms and busts have always characterized capitalism. They now spilled, however, more readily across national borders. After the collapse of the Bretton Woods exchange-rate system in the early 1970s, and the simultaneous liberalization of capital markets around the world, financial shocks capable of spreading great misery have intermittently recurred. But the panic that moved rapidly in 1997 and 1998 from East Asia to Russia and Latin America, and eventually to Wall Street, vividly threatened the system itself. Looming over economic policy-making circles around the world was the spectre of the terrible decade spanning the US stock market collapse in 1929 and the opening of the Second World War in 1939. As the crisis worsened, anyone who observed the faces of the world's leading finance ministers and central bank governors, anyone who listened carefully to their verbal attempts to calm international markets, anyone who monitored what they actually did as crisis managers would have been justified in wondering whether a new catastrophe lay just over the horizon.

After the Second World War, most countries were cautious about moving back to the kind of financial openness characteristic of the world economy in the pre-1914 period. Over time, this sense of caution dissipated and capital market liberalization came back in vogue. In the face of the crisis of the late 1990s, however, some countries responded to the crisis by reimposing capital controls, while others violated free market principles by effectively bailing out large private investors. Like Saul on the road to Damascus, one of the world's leading currency speculators offered a surprising diagnosis at the start of the system-shaking crisis. 'Financial markets are inherently unstable; left to their own devices, they are liable to break down. More important, many social values are not properly represented by market forces' (Soros 1997b; also see Soros 1997a and 1998). After the panic subsided, distinguished voices refused to let the memory fade. 'The crisis is over now, but countries such as Indonesia will feel its effects for years,' wrote the former chief economist of the World Bank (Stiglitz 2002: 89).

The preceding chapter set out the broad context for understanding the changing monetary dimension of our contemporary global economy. This chapter looks in depth at the political economy of recurring financial crises therein. For students of international relations and international economics, such moments in time are worth considerable attention. They open a unique window on the fragile political structures that continue to underpin globalizing markets. Those markets promise prosperity and peaceful interaction among the world's still distinctive societies, but they cannot in themselves ensure such outcomes. In this regard, the early chapters of the book drew attention to the importance of collaboration among the political authorities leading that system. International financial crises demonstrate both the continuing importance of such collaboration and the continuing difficulty of achieving it when it is most needed.

The complex politics of global finance

It is the *real* economy that really matters. The distinction economists and business journalists make between such an economy and the 'financial' economy reflects an important insight. The prices of stocks and bonds fluctuate continuously, so do the prices of all financial assets and liabilities. Every such price movement is meaningful to someone, somewhere. But financial gyrations only visibly matter to the lives of most people when they directly affect the fundamental mechanisms through which jobs are created or destroyed and goods and services are produced (the 'real' economy). In the democratic systems currently lying at the heart of an integrating global economy, financial market ups and downs can be constructive. When they facilitate innovation, production, and exchange, adjustments in the prices of financial assets are helpful to the real economy and serve to stabilize the underlying political order. Their specific political effects can be important, but they tend to be invisible to most. Economic benefits and costs are surely distributed and redistributed, but the process occurs in such a way that no particular group or groups with overwhelming political power become aggrieved enough to seek fundamental systemic change.

Turbulence in financial markets can also be destructive, however, and then its political effects tend to be very obvious and very negative. When panic feeds on itself and spreads the psychology of fear, the confidence of savers, investors, producers, and consumers is undercut. Crisis conditions can engender spiralling declines in real incomes and life prospects. When they impose costs deemed unbearable by the politically strong and mobilized, they can retard economic progress and destabilize political order. Early in the twenty-first century, Argentina tragically exemplified this negative syndrome (see Box 7.1).

The globalizing political economy gradually and intentionally built up in the wake of systemic turbulence in the mid-twentieth century rested on the assumption that it would eventually draw a widening circle of shared prosperity. Recurrent financial crises cast doubt on such an assumption. They raise a host of political challenges for national policy makers trying to secure the economic and social benefits promised by economic openness while minimizing associated social and political costs.

International economic interdependence formed a core element in the strategy of systemic stabilization and development designed and led by the United States and its key allies in the wake of the Second World War. The central idea, decidedly liberal, was not new, but its early architects deliberately tried to limit the extent to which the initial post-war strategy involved the banking industry. Who could forget the disappointed dreams of liberals earlier in the century? In 1912, the British intellectual, Norman Angell, had famously opined:

Commercial interdependence, which is the special mark of banking as it is the mark of no other profession or trade in quite the same degree . . . is surely doing a great deal to demonstrate that morality after all is not founded upon self-sacrifice, but enlightened self-interest . . . And such a clearer understanding is bound to improve, not merely the relationship of one group to another, but the relationship of all men to other men, to create a consciousness which must make for more efficient human co-operation, a better human society.

(Keegan 1998: 12)

Alas, Angell was to be proven wrong, both two years later, when the interdependence of bankers did nothing to prevent the coming of a catastrophic war, and even more decisively two decades later, when the self-interested actions of bankers and their national overseers helped plunge the world into an even deeper abyss.

The initial post-1945 political consensus reconceived the idea of what was desirable in commercial interdependence to exclude financial activity that was not trade related. In time, as we shall see, Angell's view once again became the common wisdom, albeit with a twist born of repeated financial crises and repeated reminders that the machinery of global capitalism required attentive political oversight. As John Ruggie put it, international market forces were embedded in domestic political economies that rendered market regulation and programmes aimed at guaranteeing minimum levels of social welfare legitimate (Ruggie 1982, 1998).

In the aftermath of the Second World War, in one form or another, the advanced industrial democracies leading the system built significant welfare states. In effect, national and local governments took responsibility for the security of their citizens, and they defined it more broadly than ever before to include not only physical safety but also minimum standards of living. The economic turmoil associated with financial crises had in earlier days been considered to be beyond the responsibility of governments to control. Now, however, economic stability, social security, and non-inflationary growth were considered to be not only legitimate but necessary policy objectives for which governments could and should be held to account.

Box 7.1 The policy challenges of financial openness: the case of Argentina

Blessed with abundant natural resources, diversified industries, and a well-educated labour force, Argentina might have become a regional beacon of prosperity during the twentieth century. Instead, political crises, bad luck, and economic policy mistakes plagued the country. After decade of troubles, hyperinflation struck in 1989. In April 1991, the government embarked upon a bold policy experiment to reverse the economy's course. The Convertibility Plan rigidly pegged the value of the peso to the US dollar and thereby constrained the ability of the central bank to print money. Simultaneously, the government announced a wide range of structural reforms to make the economy more flexible, competitive, and open. Initially, the plan achieved dramatic results. Inflation fell, international capital flowed in, and the economy grew by an average of 6 per cent through 1997. Late in 1998, however, a surprisingly severe recession began, and its effects were compounded by the unusual turbulence then being experienced in global financial markets. What happened next is still the subject of great controversy and debate, both inside Argentina and abroad.

As capital inflows dried up, some say the government did not react quickly enough with domestic policy adjustments. Others point to large loans from the IMF inadequately conditioned on such adjustments and to a currency devaluation by Brazil that undercut Argentina's export competitiveness. Still others blame the panic then gripping private foreign lenders and investors for reasons that had little to do with Argentina itself. In any event, in the middle of 2001 capital flew out of the country and the confidence of domestic as well as foreign investors

collapsed. Bank runs, the suspension of IMF loans, and severe political and social unrest ensued. In December 2001, the country partially defaulted on its international debts; the next month it abandoned its currency peg, and as the peso's value plummeted, the value of its debt, now largely denominated in US dollars, exploded. During 2002, the economy contracted by 20 per cent and unemployment rose to between 20 and 25 per cent of the workforce.

In retrospect, it became clear either that the currency regime should have been abandoned during more halcyon days in 1996 or 1997, or that its continuation should have been supported by tighter fiscal policies, a reduction in international borrowing, and lower labour costs. At the time, neither course of action had any domestic political traction, and international creditors, including the IMF, proved willing to ignore the logic that would later seem so obvious. Even so, according to a key IMF staffer, in 1998 'a crisis might have been avoided with good luck—for example, had the dollar depreciated against the euro, had Brazil not been forced to devalue, or had international capital markets not deteriorated—but Argentina's luck ran out' (Allen 2003: 131; also see Mussa 2002; and IMF 2003a).

In 2003, a new government and a chastened IMF worked to restore confidence, cut international debt and debt-servicing loads, and rekindle domestic production. Amidst encouraging signs and an upward bounce in the economy, painful negotiations commenced with external creditors. By then, however, most people in Argentina were much poorer than they had been a decade earlier.

Years of depression and war left another related legacy. Whereas the 1930s had been characterized by various measures that closed national economies off from one another, after 1945 the leading democratic welfare states increasingly sought to achieve core political objectives through freer but still managed economic interaction with one another. Fearing the kind of cross-border financial contagion experienced in the previous decade, however, they initially sought to limit that interaction mainly to trade. Gradually, international capital flows in the form of foreign direct investment became easier as well. National

financial markets, nevertheless, were kept distinctly separated. Nationally licensed banks and other financial intermediaries were typically considered to constitute the 'commanding heights' of economies governments were now trying to steer. They were closely regulated, and international capital movements not directly related to trade or permissible direct investment, remained limited.

As Eric Helleiner describes in the preceding chapter, these arrangements began to break down in the 1960s. The changing preferences of those same national governments lay behind a series of explicit and implicit policy choices that cumulatively pushed the system back toward one characterized by freer international capital movements. In democratic countries, the changing interests of key constituents shifted the ground upon which policy was made. Certainly, multinational corporations and large banks sought new sources of profit in more open markets, but a widening range of citizens also gradually became convinced of the virtues of portfolio diversification. Governments themselves, moreover, came increasingly to consider external markets as attractive places to sell official bonds and other securities. They believed as well that loosening the regulation of the non-domestic activities of financial institutions had the potential to generate jobs, prestige, and wealth. Benefits aside, leading governments also became convinced over time that the costs of attempting to maintain a relatively closed international financial system were increasing. Openness to capital flows through private markets in itself became broadly perceived as both necessary and sufficient for generating prosperity in the long run. Public-sector flows, whether in the form of overseas development assistance or facilities extended through multilateral organizations like the World Bank and International Monetary Fund, were intentionally kept limited.

We return to a consideration of these changing conditions permissive of large-scale international capital flows and of their consequences below. It is important to underline here, though, the fact that policies after 1945 intended to preserve the separation of national financial markets had by the opening of the 1970s clearly shifted in the direction of liberalization. By the 1980s, a similar shift was under way in much of the developing world. Even as such fundamental policy reorientations gathered steam, however, episodes of financial crisis continually reminded policy makers and market participants of certain historical lessons.

Stable, well-functioning national financial markets require stable, well-functioning regulatory authority underneath them. Market actors need clear operating rules. Property rights have to be established and adjudicated when conflicts arise. Predictable procedures have to be in place to handle inevitable bankruptcies. Someone has to provide the degree of insurance necessary to limit the chance that specific defaults on debt payments will cause the kind of cascading panic commonly witnessed in earlier times. Some agency has to be entrusted with the responsibility, and endowed with the capability, to act as lender-of-last-resort. Finally, and in light of the risk that such ultimate insurance facilities might tempt potential beneficiaries to act imprudently, a risk that economists call 'moral hazard', this last-resort lending function has to be linked with binding instruments for the prudential supervision of financial intermediaries.

After the experience of the 1930s, when financial contagion spread around the world, all advanced industrial states applied just such lessons in their national financial markets. Some gave the bulk of associated responsibilities to their central banks, while some split them between central banks and separate official agencies. Most initiated some kind of deposit insurance scheme to ameliorate the risk of domestic bank runs, but they all tried to leave as much scope as domestic circumstances would permit for self-discipline by market actors themselves. They nevertheless established back-up procedures to deal with emergencies. When no one else would lend sufficiently to financial institutions whose survival was deemed vital to national interests, some arm of the state had the ability and the mandate to intervene. Across the developing world, the challenge repeatedly confronted in recent decades, often unmet, has been to create similar facilities before they are actually needed.

National polities can certainly establish national regulators to govern national financial markets. When they fail to do so, it is appropriate to inquire into the reasons for internal weaknesses or for external political pressures exacerbating those weaknesses. But when those markets become ever more open, and ever more integrated internationally, how can adequate cross-national regulatory authority be maintained? All of the functions listed above still have to be fully met in a world potentially characterized by deeply integrated financial markets. What is missing, of course, is the international polity capable of creating policy instruments analogous to those that have been established at the national level. Therein lies the central political dilemma posed by the contemporary move toward financial openness. Moments of crisis focus an analytical spotlight on that very dilemma.

Key points

- Financial markets have always been prone to bouts of instability.
- During the twentieth century, leading states built up national regulatory and supervisory systems to limit the dangers of financial crises.

- Cross-national regulatory coordination became necessary after international capital movements accelerated in the 1970s, but remained politically difficult to ensure.

The nature and variety of international financial crises

Financial crises commence with sharp breaks in the prices of key financial instruments. The expectations of market participants suddenly change. Shocks course through markets, and participants seek to adjust their positions rapidly. Most commonly, the holders of financial claims rush to make them liquid and mobile. Driven by the fear of loss, they sell assets they expect to depreciate in value, and they buy assets they expect to rise in value. As in any market where demand rapidly shrinks and supply rapidly expands, the prices of unwanted assets plummet. When the panic subsides, it is often the case that those prices have overcorrected; the underlying value of the assets have become too inexpensive. Behind such radical breaks in financial markets that can seem abstract, actual institutions fail, wealth evaporates, and real human tragedies follow in train.

Contemporary crises

Over the post-1945 period, the consequences of crisis moments have varied in their severity and scope. The moments that particularly interest us here are those defined most often by plummeting prices in the value of a nation's banking assets at the core of its payments system (referred to as a banking crisis) and/or in the value of its currency relative to other currencies (referred to as a currency crisis). When foreign creditors are exposed to those kinds of shocks in a country's main financial markets, their reactions can generate crises that spill over national borders. Capital flight out of one market translates into capital flood in others. Excessive price declines in one asset

class translate into excessive price increases in another. Losses in the foreign portfolios of a nation's banks can translate into rising interest rates in the home markets of those banks. The failure of foreign subsidiaries can lead to the failure of parent institutions. The crisis-induced collapse of a particular nation's currency translates into the rapid appreciation of the currencies of trading partners. The pain of importers in one country is shared by exporters in another. Under conditions of deepening interdependence, in short, financial crises can be contagious.

The classic definition of a crisis revolves around the notion of a 'turning point'. Serious international financial crises mark crucial turning points not simply for the national or regional economies where they arise, but for the system as a whole. The most dangerous times for the system have occurred when banking crises and currency crises have coincided and threatened the real economies of leading states. More commonly, banking and currency crises have been limited to weaker economies in weaker states.

The human toll has been most visible and most tragic in these more limited cases, mainly in newly industrializing economies. Visible and invisible aftershocks of crisis moments, from bank failures to riots in the streets to undeniable declines in personal incomes and life prospects have repeated themselves. A financial crisis leads to rapid currency depreciation, sky-rocketing import prices, and the outright loss of bank deposits as institutional failures mount. Firms go bankrupt, societies become unhinged, and political responses follow.

From a systemic point of view, the most helpful political responses to financial crises aim at limiting real economic damage, preventing recurrences, and establishing better methods for managing crises when such prevention fails. The most damaging responses are those threatening the legitimacy of the post-1945 international consensus by pushing national economies back toward autarky. Believers in laissez-faire doctrines counsel policy passivity when financial crises occur; they assert that markets will correct themselves and that political intervention delays necessary economic adjustments. Real policy makers in real states have rarely been able to follow their advice. Students of political economy must understand why.

Indebtedness, uncertainty, and shocks

Capitalist economies rest on foundations of debt. Borrowing and lending fuel economic growth. In principle, the aggregate financial claims created by the interaction of consumers, producers, savers, and investors in an economy are eminently supportable as long as expected future incomes exceed expected future debt repayments. The same logic applies when once-separated economies become more integrated. At base, this involves the integration of markets for information.

Since we cannot know the future, expectations of future income flows are always uncertain. When the extent of such uncertainty can be estimated with any degree of precision, it becomes appropriate to speak of risks. Risks can be assessed, mitigated, and managed. Indeed, this is precisely what financial intermediaries do when they accept deposits from savers, pool the proceeds, and make loans to borrowers. Through such activities, financial claims are generated, priced, and exchanged. The different time horizons of savers and borrowers are 'mediated'. In the absence of the intermediary, the ability of a particular firm, or of a particular country, to invest would be limited to the amount that firm or that country could save out of its own resources at any given moment in time or out of the resources of others with whom it was itself in direct contact.

Specific financial claims (assets from the point of view of creditors, liabilities from the point of view of debtors) become insupportable all the time. Mistakes are made, misjudgements occur, market conditions change unexpectedly. In the wake of such 'shocks', the expectations of investors and financiers shift, and a rush to liquidate assets ensues. Currency values come under pressure. Debtors and creditors, especially creditors late through the exit door, share the pain through reductions in their wealth and restraints in their future economic prospects. When particular repayment difficulties cascade and insupportable claims multiply, the system as a whole feels the pain. Exchange rates cannot hold, financial asset prices tumble, and a generalized crisis can arise. Credit dries up, investors put their resources into low-risk/low-return instruments, and debtors default.

The history of capitalism is replete with such events, as well as with the efforts of national policy makers to ameliorate their consequences in the real economy. As Charles Kindleberger put it in the title of a famous book, manias, panics, and crashes seem to be inherent in any market-based system (Kindleberger 1978; see also Kindleberger and Laffargue 1982). Indeed, few close observers deny that modern financial markets are intrinsically fragile (Lamfalussy 2000). Contrary to George Soros, nevertheless, few participants are prepared to concede that they must necessarily be unstable or that better alternative mechanisms for broadly based resource redistribution in complex economic and social systems are feasible. The massive human failures associated with planned economies in the twentieth century are not easy to forget. The policy challenge taken seriously since the 1970s, therefore, has been to mitigate financial market fragility and render the interdependent market-based system as a whole more stable. The deeper political questions concerning the distributive justice of such a system, especially for those on its margins, would be taken seriously only much later.

Contemporary history highlights two crucial facts when financial markets cross legal and political borders: the probability of crisis increases as information flows become difficult, and the absence of a political entity capable of acting as the ultimate stabilizer becomes undeniable. As Barry Eichengreen puts it, 'Sharp changes in asset prices—sometimes so sharp as to threaten the stability of the financial system and the economy . . . are likely to be especially pervasive in developing countries, where the information and contracting environment is least advanced' (Eichengreen 2002: 4).

In this light, it becomes apparent why those analysts as well as policy makers who support the progressive engagement of developing countries in the post-1945 international system also tend to advocate explicit and more reliable forms of international cooperation. Deepening financial linkages bring with them unavoidable problems, the solutions to which require collective action. Information asymmetries combine with the political independence of participants to pose problems beyond the capacities of individual states to resolve. Only some kind of collaborative foundation for those markets can give participants confidence that those markets are working in the long run to the benefit of all. Early in the twenty-first century, such cooperative and collaborative structures remained fragile in themselves. Clearly, participants had an interest in working together to ensure systemic stability. But they were also motivated to compete with one another; an economist's information asymmetries and a political scientist's power asymmetries may be identical.

Incidence of international financial crises

As discussed in the previous chapter, economic historians commonly depict the period 1870 to 1914 as the first to witness the rapid expansion of cross-border financial markets. Although few countries were involved, by some measures the scale of international financial intermediation far exceeded anything that has since then developed. A golden age only for some,

the purchase and sale of financial claims to foreigners boomed. So too did defaults, especially around 1875 and then again when the world began marching toward what became known as the Great War. In an era when the values of the main currencies were meant to be firmly pegged to one another (recall the discussion in the previous chapter of the gold standard, which itself never worked perfectly), such defaults often translated into bank failures. After 1919, the incidence of banking crises escalated, but so too did currency crises when repegged exchange rates would not hold. The disastrous decade commencing in 1929 was characterized by the awful coincidence and global explosion of banking and currency crises (Kindleberger 1973). Figure 7.1 graphically summarizes the frequency of such crises since the emergence of industrial capitalism.

Currency crises continued to plague the system that eventually emerged from the ashes of the Second World War. Following the war, the United States and its victorious allies attempted to restore international trade, but they also deliberately restricted capital flows not related to exports and imports. Their simultaneous efforts to ensure internal financial stability did succeed in reducing the incidence of banking crises. But even after 1945 recurrent currency crises strained efforts to restore a stable exchange-rate system reminiscent of the pre-1914 gold standard era. Those efforts failed decisively in the early 1970s, when the link between the world's leading currency and the price of gold was decisively broken. After 1973, banking crises once again became a fact of international economic life; so too did their coincidence with currency crises. As Figure 7.2 shows, such twin crises were especially frequent in the

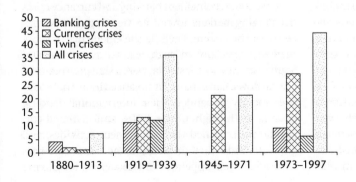

Fig. 7.1 Frequency of crises: industrial countries

Source: Data in Bordo and Eichengreen (2002).

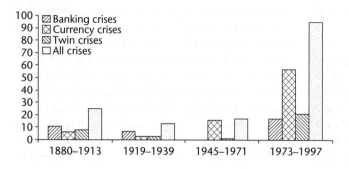

Fig. 7.2 Frequency of crises: emerging markets

Source: Data in Bordo and Eichengreen (2002).

markets of newly industrializing countries, which were now commonly referred to as 'emerging markets'.

From the standpoint of governments committed to helping their domestic markets 'emerge' and grow through international interaction, necessary financial resources may be gathered from four main sources: domestic savings, foreign governments, foreign investors, and foreign creditors. A rapidly increasing reliance in recent decades on the latter source surely had a great deal to do with political preferences. That reliance is, in any case, a fact. So too

are attendant banking and currency crises. Their repeated occurrence was presaged by the experience of industrial countries themselves.

Key points

- The most damaging financial crises occur when banking systems and currency markets simultaneously come under pressure.

- In recent years, such crises have occurred with most frequency in emerging-market nations.

The changing global context

From the 1940s through the 1970s, currency crises involving advanced industrial states repeatedly roiled the system and often forced adjustments in exchange-rate pegs. Banking crises did certainly occur in individual countries, but overall restrictions on international capital movements tended to keep the effects localized. In the aftermath of the abandonment of the pegged-rate system among the major currencies and the non-coincidental loosening of capital controls, however, the industrial countries confronted the first great banking crisis of the new era. In 1974, the failure of a German bank, Bankhaus I. D. Herstatt, to honour its foreign exchange contracts had knock-on effects globally, which ultimately even caused the Franklin National Bank of New York to fail as well (Spero 1980). Long memories recalled the collapse of the Credit-Anstalt Bank in Austria in 1931

and the contagion it spread through world markets (Schubert 1992). The post-1945 international economic system as a whole, however, did not revert to depression, and lessons were certainly learned in the years after the Bretton Woods exchange-rate system collapsed. We return to them below.

In the 1980s, coincident banking and currency crises in emerging markets now raised the most pressing concerns for the system. Fuelling the emergence of those markets, especially in such regions as Central and South America and East Asia, were rising international capital flows. Banks based in advanced industrial countries rapidly expanded their international lending operations throughout the 1970s, multinational corporations diversified their investment activities, and gradually individual investors in the richer countries expanded their appetites and capacities for buying

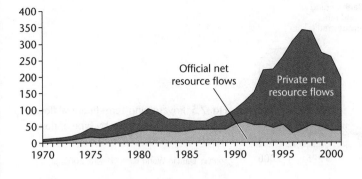

Fig. 7.3 Total long-term flows to developing countries (US$bn)

Source: Data in World Bank (1999*a*, 2002*a*).

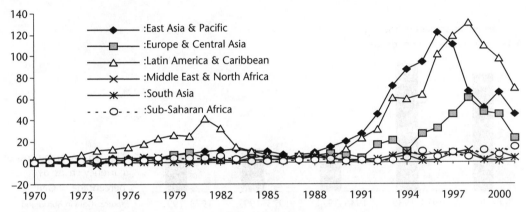

Fig. 7.4 Private long-term financial flows to developing countries: by region (US$bn)
Source: Data in World Bank (1999*a*, 2002*a*).

bonds and other financial instruments issued by governments and firms in developing countries. Some associated capital flows were trade related, some investment related, and some simply reflected the kind of financial speculation inherent in a capitalist system now becoming more global.

Movement toward financial openness in developing countries

From the 1970s onwards but most prominently in the late 1980s and early 1990s, industrial countries, and countries aspiring to that advanced status, moved collectively not only toward increased openness in their trade related current accounts but also in their investment related capital accounts. In essence, they rendered more interdependent an ever wider range of their still nationally regulated financial markets, and they opened themselves up to less regulated financial

markets now commonly labelled 'off-shore' (Palan 2003). Figures 7.3, 7.4, and 7.5, show the outcomes for developing countries as a group.

The explosion of international financial intermediation after the 1980s and the rising incidence of financial crises with cross-border effect were obviously related. For policy makers, the relevant questions were what they have always been. When real economic growth rates were sought in excess of those capable of being generated by domestic savings, how were the benefits and costs of financial openness to be distributed?

Opportunities and costs of openness

In principle, inward flows of privately owned capital make it possible for real economies to grow more rapidly. In practice, the extra costs associated with

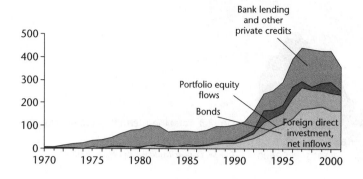

Fig. 7.5 Private long-term financial flows to developing countries: by type of flow (US$bn)

Source: Data in World Bank (1999a, 2002a).

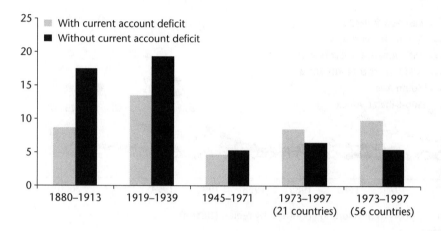

Fig. 7.6 Average cost of currency crises: as percentage of GNP

Source: Data in Bordo and Eichengreen (2002).

crisis-induced capital outflows, bank bailouts, and the lost confidence of investors occasionally threatens to undermine real economies, set back the process of industrialization, and disrupt underlying political and social orders. Figure 7.6 offers an indication of the historical costs of currency crises in terms of lost economic output.

Behind such statistical measures lies a human story repeated time after time in recent history. The costs of financial crises often include unemployment, increasing taxes, personal despair and hopelessness, family breakdown, and rising crime rates. In emerging markets, their public face can culminate in deepening poverty, *coups d'état*, and military dictatorship. Who would deny that it is best to avoid such outcomes? But their very possibility is inherent in the macro-policy choices both leading states and those aspiring to their level of prosperity made in the post-1945 period. With the final collapse in 1989 of the only alternative system once attractive to some, that

of state socialism and central planning, financial openness apparently marked the only feasible road to the future. To be sure, nevertheless, all but the most dependent states retained the ability to determine the speed with which they went down that road, and all but the weakest retained levers of power sufficient to influence the internal distribution of the benefits and costs thereby entailed.

National policy reform, international system consequences

In essence, by the 1980s it had become clear that states constituting the international economy had collectively moved away from one set of policy trade-offs and toward another. Immediately after the Second World War, they sought to reconcile their newfound desire for exchange-rate stability with their interest in maintaining independent monetary policies. Both as a matter of logic and of policy, they therefore had to tolerate limits on inward and outward capital flows (Mundell 1963). Four decades later, their priorities had changed. Now, capital mobility and monetary autonomy were privileged, and they were willing to tolerate floating exchange rates as well as a degree of volatility in their expanding financial markets.

In the 1970s, to be sure, some developing countries sought to limit the future role of privately owned international capital, and they demanded a 'new international economic order' (Krasner 1985). By the 1980s, most of them had also abandoned such a quest, a phenomenon referred to by one close observer as a 'silent revolution' (Boughton 2001). Few, however, joined the leading states in embracing a clearer trade-off between financial openness, monetary independence, and exchange-rate stability. In the latter regard, the painful earlier experience of leading states in attempting to hold onto exchange-rate pegs would be repeated. So too would be the experience of bank failures.

Over time, exchange rates measure the relative price levels across economies linked together by trade and investment. They can, however, also gyrate wildly in the face of speculative pressures or unanticipated economic or political shocks. As real economies become more open to trade and foreign investment, such volatility can be difficult to manage, both economically and politically. In the short run, exporters, importers, and investors may be able to hedge their foreign exposures, but this is costly and gets more problematic as time horizons expand. Standard, if still disputed, economic theory suggests that the way to ameliorate excessive currency volatility is to co-ordinate a range of national monetary and fiscal policies. Ever since the 1970s, leading states demonstrated only intermittent interest in doing so, despite rhetorical expressions to the contrary at successive high-profile meetings of the G7/8 and other collaborative bodies. They have instead left it to financial markets to attempt to impose whatever level of fiscal and monetary discipline was necessary to stabilize the system as a whole. In practice, the stronger the country—that is, the more it was capable of generating and retaining its own domestic savings and/or the more it was

capable of attracting foreign capital flows despite fiscal and monetary policies that might, in principle, be expected to have the opposite consequence—the lower such disciplinary effects turned out to be. In any event, through such macro-policy choices, leading states constructed a system that relied on the possibility of sharp reversals in capital flows to force on themselves and others that modicum of coordination required for economic interdependence to deepen. The possibility of financial crisis, in other words, was built into the system.

To be sure, as Helleiner noted in the previous chapter, some states sought to restore a degree of exchange-rate stability for themselves by limiting their own monetary independence within regional or bilateral arrangements. The member states of the Economic and Monetary Union in Europe took such a collective choice to its limit. But even they afterwards gave priority to financial openness and regional monetary autonomy over the stability of the exchange rate between the euro and other major currencies. By the 1980s, again, the system as a whole increasingly relied on open financial markets to encourage the cross-border adjustments entailed by international economic interaction. Such markets also became the source of most of the liquidity necessary for that interaction to occur.

In other words, having moved to an international economic system based on flexible exchange rates among the major currencies, leading states found that financial market liberalization represented a less politically costly alternative for the management of economic interdependence than any other. They did not forswear capital controls under any circumstances. But there gradually emerged a normative preference against anything other than temporary measures to limit international capital movements. Throughout the 1980s and early 1990s, despite prominent banking and currency crises in Mexico and other emerging markets, newly industrializing and many developing countries moved in the same direction. As official sources of development assistance dwindled relative to other capital flows, the implicit systemic promise was that emerging markets could attract the capital that they needed through ever more open private capital markets.

Nevertheless, even at the present time, capital flows continue to encounter friction at national borders.

It is costly to move money outside the national markets where it originates. There has yet to arise a truly global financial market characterized by perfect capital mobility. An evolving consensus on the liberalization of markets still heavily influenced by national governments certainly exists. But no international treaty on international capital flows analogous to that governing trade ever emerged to codify an underlying political understanding as to security, reciprocity, and safeguards. As the decade of the 1990s progressed, moreover, an assumption underneath the consensus, to the effect that private markets on their own would provide adequate financing for development if countries simply maintained sound macro-economic policies, became more difficult to sustain.

Enduring risks

Events surrounding the global financial crises of the late 1990s highlighted the reasons why states never codified their agreement to move toward financial openness after the Bretton Woods system broke down, and why policy makers in some developing countries came once again to doubt that a new system dominated by private firms and financiers based in rich countries would ultimately serve their interests. Any sense of obligation to move, say, toward complete financial openness certainly eroded as crisis conditions spread from country to country. Before the crises hit in the mid-1990s, some prominent voices were advocating an explicit amendment of the Articles of Agreement of the International Monetary Fund to extend the Fund's jurisdiction (and ethos of liberalization) from short-term balance-of-payments issues to long-term policies governing inward and outward capital movements. After Malaysia summarily reinstated capital controls in response to the financial crisis in 1997, and Chile experimented through the 1990s with sophisticated measures to restrain the inflow of short-term capital, debate on the proposition ceased. At the same time, a new chapter in a long-running policy debate on how best to deal with currency and banking crises opened. It is worth reviewing in some detail the chain of events set off by Thailand, for they vividly demonstrated the continuing tentativeness of the global trend toward financial openness itself (see Box 7.2).

Political sovereignty and economic interdependence

During periods of euphoria in financial markets, participants tend to forget historical lessons. When a fund manager is sitting on a portfolio earning 3 per cent per annum, it is difficult to watch colleagues earning 10 per cent. Watching too long may even cost that manager his or her job. But only the most ideological of participants in global markets choose entirely to ignore the past. The governments of leading states surely have not suffered from collective amnesia in the contemporary period.

The reluctance of those governments unambiguously to embrace the principle that capital had an inviolable legal right to cross borders, and their evident reluctance clearly to designate an international overseer for markets now ever more tightly linked together, is telling. The architects of the post-1973 order could not easily balance emergent market facts with political realities. They could not lodge ultimate political authority over international capital markets at the level where it logically belongs. No international agency has been authorized to regulate or supervise international capital flows, not the International Monetary Fund, not the World Bank, and not the Bank for International Settlements. None has been provided with the resources necessary to act as true lender-of-last-resort. States have instead opted to allow the financial institutions they themselves continue to license and supervise to expand their international operations on the understanding that national regulators would informally coordinate their supervisory policies and emergency practices to the extent necessary. At moments of confidence-withering crises, who would ultimately be responsible for bailing out financial institutions confronting the prospect of collapse? In the wake of actual financial crises in the decades following the breakdown of the Bretton Woods exchange-rate system, the answer became clearer and clearer. The basic operating principle remains 'home country control' (Kapstein 1994). Lender-of-last-resort facilities remain under the exclusive purview of individual states themselves. At most, pre-emptive or precautionary credit can be made available by states collectively, perhaps through treaty-based intergovernmental organizations like the International Monetary Fund, perhaps through

Box 7.2 The global financial panic of the late 1990s

In the mid-1990s, interest rates fell and stock markets boomed in North America and Western Europe. Banks and portfolio investors, including rapidly expanding mutual funds and so-called 'hedge' funds that pooled the capital of rich investors, increasingly looked abroad for higher returns. With those higher returns came higher risks.

At the same time, Japanese banks, confronting stagnant demand in a slumping home market, sought the higher earnings promised in neighbouring countries. Both public sector and private sector borrowers in emerging markets suddenly found new and ready sources of funds, and they borrowed heavily. Since interest rates were especially low on short-term debt, they loaded up, confident that they would easily be able to refinance their obligations when they came due.

In Thailand, much of this new debt was denominated in the local currency, which the Thai government valued at a pegged, not floating rate. By buying Thai securities or making loans denominated in Thai baht, investors and creditors, in essence, bet that the baht would hold its value at least until they had the chance to sell their investments or have their loans repaid. Early in 1997, however, Japanese banks, which then held about half of the country's foreign debt, began to lose confidence in the ability of Thailand to defend its exchange rate. They sought to reduce their exposures there as well as in a number of neighbouring countries, where they held large portfolios of short-term loans. Their pull-back prompted a regional liquidity crunch. Other creditors and investors, both domestic and foreign, fearing losses as local currencies came under pressure, headed toward the exits. A devaluation of the Thai baht became self-fulfilling, while other Asian nations whose industries competed to sell similar goods to the same foreign markets needed to defend their competitive edges by allowing their own currencies to depreciate.

Capital suddenly flew out of South Korea, Indonesia, and Malaysia, a phenomenon now exacerbated by the panicked reactions of thousands of mutual and hedge fund investors back in North America and Europe. Just as a bank hit by a run of depositors is forced hurriedly to raise cash by calling in loans, these funds had to meet demands for withdrawals by liquidating their assets. As their Thai assets declined in redeemable value, they withdrew what they could as quickly as possible from their Korean, Malaysian, Indonesian, and even Hong Kong and Singapore portfolios. The overall result was as predictable as it was painful. Liquidity dried up across the region, and the solvency of local institutions recently considered sound came into question.

The government of Malaysia tried to stem the panic by doing what foreign investors had come to consider unthinkable; it risked its future ability to re-enter global markets by intervening to impose capital controls to forbid the repatriation of what its prime minister labelled the immoral gains of speculators. Others took the more conventional route of calling in the IMF to provide emergency funding as a stop-gap measure until panic subsided. Borrowing from the Fund and other multilateral agencies came, as usual, with conditions attached, but in these instances the terms were particularly controversial. Whereas borrowing countries saw themselves struggling against a short-term problem, the Fund began insisting on more fundamental kinds of reform designed to make East Asian markets, including financial markets, more open to longer-term foreign investment, more transparent, and with a lesser role for government-sanctioned oligopolies. Talk of neo-imperialism by Western powers became commonplace as national incomes fell across the region, imports declined, and a cut-throat competition to maintain export industries ensued.

In the midst of the East Asian debacle, Russia's post-1991 experiment with frontier capitalism crashed into a wall of unsustainable foreign debt. In retrospect, it certainly seems that many foreign investors had unwisely discounted the possibility that Russia's new class of tycoons would take careful measures to spirit their own capital out of the country. By the summer of 1998, even a massive IMF loan could not bolster confidence in the value of the rouble. It also could not attract back private Russian capital invested in safe Western investments, nor could it sustain the confidence of the American and European investors in 'emerging market' funds that had recently and aggressively bought what turned out to be extremely risky securities backed by the Russian government. When the government defaulted in August and also devalued the rouble, seismic shocks were immediately felt at the core of the world's financial system. Stock markets plummeted around the world. Fearing that other emerging markets would follow Russia, panicked financiers pulled vast amounts of capital out of Mexico, Brazil, Argentina, and elsewhere.

In September, a particularly prominent hedge fund based in Greenwich, Connecticut, and bearing the now-ironic name, Long-Term Capital Management, found its heretofore extremely successful investment strategy wrecked by the crisis spreading from one emerging market to another. While the consensus view among American central bankers and financial market regulators would ordinarily have been to let such an entity bear the brunt of its mistakes, and even to fail, their view now was that such an outcome was too risky. Panic had gripped even Wall Street, and many top-tier commercial and investment banks were counter-parties in LTCM's transactions.

The legitimacy of the role of the US government and the Federal Reserve as lender-of-last-resort had not been seriously questioned since the experience of cascading bank failures during the 1930s. But direct intervention to save a speculative hedge fund was something else. In these unique circumstances, the solution was for official agencies coordinated by the New York Fed to encourage and support a consortium of large private banks that would ultimately bail LTCM out themselves. No one doubted that the full faith and credit of the US government would be available to stem the tide if required, but in the end the emergency operation succeeded and calm gradually returned to the markets of industrial countries. It would take longer for confidence to return to many emerging markets (for further details, see Blustein 2001).

less formal understandings, such as the recently negotiated series of bilateral swap arrangements in East Asia (Henning 2002). But no state has shown itself willing to delegate ultimate financial responsibility to any supranational institution.

Perhaps there was a moment in time, just after the Second World War, when one could sense a window opening on a world where states would actually delegate a coherent piece of their monetary, if not fiscal, sovereignty to a technical agency with a binding, enforceable mandate. By 1973, however, it was difficult to argue with the proposition that the final abandonment of the Bretton Woods exchange-rate system indicated that the coordination of national fiscal and monetary policies could only be voluntary and would likely only be episodic. How then could a reliable foundation for globalizing capitalism be constructed? If deeper financial interdependence remained a collective goal even as fiscal and monetary sovereignty remained sacrosanct, as it apparently did, then those same states confronted the logically alternative necessity of coordinating their more technical policies and instruments governing financial markets. From the Mexican debt crisis of 1981 through the Asian crisis of 1997, the actions of states individually and collectively indicated clearly that they understood this logic. That their progress was not smooth or always far-sighted should surprise no one familiar with the way most policies are actually constructed in democracies, the form of government shared in the states that built the world economy after 1973. The coordination of national policies is difficult in the best of times. The prospect of future systemic gains is, in truth, not often a successful motivator (see Aggarwal and Dupont, Chapter 2 in this volume). As an empirical proposition demonstrated time and again since 1973, the prospect of imminent national and systemic losses seems a much better motivator of necessary policy coordination (Aggarwal 1996).

Financial crises and the reactions of governmental authorities define the key dynamic. In short, the policy domain for serious collective action in the post-1973 era has necessarily taken in a broadening range of measures required for reducing but never entirely eliminating the chance that future cross-border financial crises will occur. At the same time, each new crisis, now including those in emerging markets, has led to the construction of new collaborative techniques for handling emergencies made inevitable by the persistent reluctance of state authorities to give up their political independence entirely. Outside of the idiosyncratic regional context of Europe, where the establishment of the euro zone suggests more ambitious political objectives, these efforts may be summarized under the rubrics of crisis prevention and crisis management.

Key points

- Financial crises generated policy innovations inside industrial states, and the pattern is repeating itself in many emerging-market nations.

- Sovereignty remains an important value in a globalizing economy.

- Collaborative efforts, often through international institutions, can assist developing countries as they open their financial markets.

Crisis prevention

No modern financial market exists for long without common standards understood by all participants. At the most basic level, financial information must be expressed in an understandable form. Accounting, auditing, and licensing rules form the bedrock. In all but the most limited local markets, or in all but the most libertarian utopias, such rules have not been spontaneously generated. Some actor must provide the collective goods of standard setting, adjudication, reform, and, ultimately, enforcement. Even illegal markets, if they are to persist, require someone to provide those minimal requirements. In legal markets, by definition, such collective goods are provided by the final maker of binding laws. To be sure, ultimate authorities can and do delegate the responsibility to define and promote technical standards in many of the world's financial markets. But all contemporary markets that are legal rest on standards and enforcement procedures associated with governmental authority in one form or another. Even central banks that we now conventionally label 'independent', like the European Central Bank, derive their authority from constitutional arrangements or interstate treaties.

Defining and defending public interests

Moments of financial crisis have tested this reasoning, even in recent times. International financial crises expose jurisdictional ambiguities and overlaps. But they are typically followed by new preventive measures, directly or indirectly supported by political authorities. They have not, however, yet been followed by the establishment of an unambiguous global standard setter or a global agency capable of final enforcement. The frontier of markets integrating themselves across political and legal boundaries therefore remains characterized in the final analysis by intergovernmental bodies charged with negotiating common cross-border understandings on appropriate standards and their enforcement (Bryant

2003). This is not to suggest that organizations created by private sector actors have been absent. For example, standard-setting bodies set up by accounting and other types of firms or private associations are increasingly common. In the United States, the United Kingdom, and elsewhere, governments have often been willing to let market participants attempt to reach agreement among themselves on best practices. When such attempts fail and markets are threatened with disruption, however, governments and central banks come out of the shadows.

Contemplating the ever-present possibility that a bank it regulated could fail and thereby compromise the financial system as a whole (called systemic risk), governments retained the ability either to dip into national treasuries to save it or to allow it to be liquidated in an orderly fashion. As banks expanded their international operations, regulators necessarily had to begin working with their foreign counterparts on common standards for prudential supervision and common approaches to the management of emergencies. Just as a common military defence among allies entails negotiating common understandings on burden sharing, so international bank regulation rests on the negotiation of such standards.

But regulated banks often bear the costs associated with prudential supervision. Over time, other kinds of financial intermediaries, like investment funds and trust companies, found ways to provide analogous services more cheaply. With the emergence of lightly regulated non-bank financial institutions in domestic and international markets in the 1960s and 1970s, the very same logic of international collaboration on standard setting and enforcement spread beyond the banking sector. The provision of insurance, stock underwriting and sales, and pooled investing services had by the 1990s clearly become global businesses. To some extent, most firms in these businesses remained supervised in some sense in their home markets, but the governmental agencies licensing and overseeing them often expressly tried to limit their own responsibility for bailing them out in an emergency. That is, their licensing authorities attempted to limit the risk those firms would make imprudent judgements and take excessive risks in the knowledge that they would not be allowed to fail. As in the banking sector though, setting standards, defining enforcement responsibilities, and preventing official liabilities became more complicated as functional and geographic barriers were permitted to erode throughout the post-1970s era. Drawing a clear dividing line between public interests and private risks, in other words, would rarely be a straightforward task any more.

Cross-national coordination on regulatory policies

Well into the 1980s, the main arenas within which financial regulators sought to coordinate their standard-setting and enforcement activities were easy to identify. Bilateral negotiations between national regulators and central banks were nothing new. After the Herstatt failure spread globally through foreign exchange markets, such interaction became multilateralized through a central bankers' club organized under the institutional auspices of the Bank for International Settlements (see Box 7.3 below). The Basel Committee on Banking Supervision technically reports to the governors of the world's leading central banks (the so-called G10, which actually now includes more than ten members), but it continues to be the key standard-setting forum for the largest financial institutions operating across national borders, institutions that still typically have a bank at the core of complicated conglomerate structures. The prevention of future international financial crises defines the core mandate of the Basel Committee. This has led it to experiment with protocols for minimum standards for back-up capital reserves to be held by banks, and to work with other national and regional bodies to bolster the transparency and effectiveness of prudential supervision beyond the banking sector narrowly defined. Over time, the work of the Basel Committee has come to be complemented and supplemented by other formal or informal intergovernmental bodies, as well as by the more prominent international work of various private-sector-led associations.

To the extent it can be labelled a coherent strategy, the efforts of leading states to prevent systemic financial collapse in recent decades have obviously been characterized by incremental institution building. They have favoured technical policy coordination to the extent necessary to ensure the deepening integration of stable, not risk-free, financial markets but not necessarily beyond that. Their success in systemic crisis prevention must be assessed against the counterfactual standard suggested in the famous Sherlock Holmes story that turns on the dog that did not bark.

In such a light, it would be hard to argue that the main architects of today's international capital markets have not made progress. In various national and regional crises, from the Herstatt crisis, to the Mexican and Latin American debt crises of the 1980s, and the Asian and Russian crises of the 1990s, systemic meltdown did not occur. Despite near misses, when expectations of disaster at the core of the system were perceived by policy makers to be on the verge of self-fulfilment, it seems unlikely that blind, dumb luck accounts completely for the persistence of the larger strategic idea of deepening international financial interdependence. A cynic might contend that stabilizing the core of the system—the New York-London-Frankfurt-Paris-Tokyo international payments, settlement, and investment nexus—is part of an implicit project that drains financial resources from the rest of the world. Such a view was certainly suggested by the pull-back of private capital from emerging markets after the Asian crisis. But the contemporary work programmes of the Basel Committee, the IMF, the World Bank, and other international organizations can more generously be interpreted as embodying the attempts of leading states to extend the project of global financial market construction safely beyond the core. Real resources were certainly being put into efforts to help establish reliable supervisory standards and instruments in a widening range of developing countries, often through expanding technical assistance by international organizations. Future market facts will ultimately tell the tale, for capital should in theory flow over the long term from capital-rich areas of the world, where returns should be relatively low, to capital-poor areas, where returns should be relatively high.

Broader policy context

Note, again, a fundamentally related policy arena where leading states have invested considerable rhetorical energy, and occasionally expended serious political capital, namely the arena of macro-economic policy. That sound fiscal and monetary policies in the states at the core of the world economy are required for international financial integration to proceed in a constructive manner is widely accepted, and for good reason. Steady, sustainable growth in real economies, low inflation, and spreading prosperity defines an objective much like motherhood. Everyone favours it, no one objects to it, and the principles supporting it are impeccable. The relevant political question, however, has remained the same ever since 1973. How can cooperative efforts to achieve fiscal and monetary stability be encouraged in the absence of some overarching agreement on an economic constraint, such as could theoretically be provided by a binding commitment to stable exchange rates? After 1973, leading states conceded that such a commitment could not be maintained; the most they could agree upon was a commitment to 'a stable system of exchange rates' facilitated by 'firm surveillance' by the International Monetary Fund (James 1995, 1996; Pauly 1997). (In the 1990s, the member states of the Economic and Monetary Union in Europe went further among themselves to construct a regional system of irrevocably fixed exchange rates and a common monetary policy, backed by explicit commitments to coordinate underlying fiscal policies and limit fiscal deficits through a 'Stability and Growth Pact'. In the early years of the twenty-first century, a number of members were having difficulties holding to the pact's original terms.)

Beyond technical measures designed to prevent crises in markets assumed to be more smoothly functioning over time, nothing could guarantee the sound macro-economic policy behaviour of the leading states. The system conducive to mutually beneficial financial interdependence tending in the direction of deeper and deeper cross-border integration continues to rest on the self-discipline and voluntary policy coordination of the leading states themselves. Properly functioning financial markets can, at most, send signals that might encourage such self-discipline; fiscal and current account deficits that can't easily be financed internally will have to be reduced, or financed externally at higher and higher real interest rates.

This was the essence of what came to be called the 'Washington Consensus' during the 1990s. Despite the scepticism elicited by each new financial crisis, it remains in place. By their actions if not always the rhetoric of their leaders, the governments of industrialized states and many emerging-market states apparently continue to see value in the reinforcement of such a market-based consensus through an ever-widening array of intergovernmental and private sector forums, where the standard setting, crisis prevention, and surveillance work embodied in the post-1973 IMF could be complemented (Cutler, Haufler, and Porter 1999). (See Box 7.3.)

Capital controls

The Washington Consensus notwithstanding, political economists remind us that one other policy instrument remains in the arsenal of states seeking to prevent financial crises from spilling over into their markets: the unilateral instrument of capital controls. In a world of globalizing finance, intentionally constructed by national authorities, circumstances can and do arise where the perceived costs of ideological consistency exceed the perceived benefits. In the post-1973 system, capital controls were, with good empirical evidence, depicted as increasingly ineffective. For industrial countries, they were indeed obsolescent, if never entirely obsolete (Goodman and Pauly 1993). They became more difficult to enforce, easier to evade, disruptive to long-term investment, and susceptible to political corruption. Nevertheless, individual states continue to experiment with more sophisticated measures, including managed currency floats and targeted foreign exchange market interventions, designed to attract desired capital flows (like loans and investments facilitating production and trade) and discourage unwanted flows (like speculative purchases of currencies in the expectation of quick gains).

Emerging markets tend to be governed by systems still incapable of the most subtle forms of

Box 7.3 Institutions for collaboration on international financial policies and practices

International Monetary Fund Designed at the Bretton Woods Conference, July 1944. (For details on its subsequent evolution, see this chapter and Helleiner, Chapter 6 in this volume.)

International Bank for Reconstruction and Development (World Bank) Also originally created at Bretton Woods. (See Wade, Chapter 11, and Thomas, Chapter 12 in this volume.)

Bank for International Settlements Established in 1930 to oversee Germany's war reparation payments. After the Second World War, this Basel, Switzerland based institution assisted European governments in their monetary and financial interactions. After the 1960s, its role in facilitating a multilateral payments system in Europe made it an obvious venue for intensifying dialogue among central bankers, now including the United States and other non-European countries, on a broad range of regulatory and supervisory issues. Today, the BIS sponsors and provides a meeting venue for several collaborative committees, including the Basel Committee of Banking Supervision, which is technically a committee of the world's leading central banks (commonly, if inaccurately, referred to as the G10), that seeks to develop and promote common understandings on such issues as minimum capital standards for banks operating internationally.

International Organization of Securities Commissions With a secretariat based in Montreal, Canada, IOSCO sponsors conferences and other linkages among the regulators of national stock and other securities markets. Designed to facilitate the sharing of information and best practices, it developed during the 1970s as buyers and sellers of securities increasingly moved their funds across national borders.

International Association of Insurance Supervisors Established in 1992 to encourage cooperation among regulators and supervisors of insurance companies. Since 1998, its secretariat has been housed in Basel, Switzerland, where it receives technical assistance from the BIS.

International Accounting Standards Board and **International Federation of Accountants** Private sector bodies organized by professional accounting associations to encourage international standardization of accounting principles and auditing practices. Activities intensified during the 1970s; came to prominence in the 1990s after a series of accounting scandals in the United States and other major markets.

United Nations Various UN commissions, agencies, and departments, such as the Department of Economic and Social Affairs in the New York-based secretariat, have mandates to review international financial developments and seek to promote understanding among member states on issues of equity and efficiency in the global economy. In the 1970s, the UN was a primary venue for debate on demands from developing countries for a 'New International Economic Order'. More recently, its focus has shifted to ensuring the availability of adequate financing for developing countries and to promoting internationally agreed Millennium Development Goals for poverty reduction and sustainable development (the 'Monterrey Consensus').

G7/G8 Dating back to informal meetings of European finance ministers after the collapse of the Bretton Woods exchange-rate arrangements, regular annual meetings of financial officials and heads of government now occur under this rubric. Originally five, then seven, including the United States, France, Britain, Germany, Japan, Canada, and Italy, now routinely includes Russia and representatives from the European Union. Meetings often involve the confidential sharing of information on financial and economic policies. Personal relationships thereby developed and reinforced are often seen to be useful when it comes to coordinating national policies rapidly in the face of international financial crises. There is no secretariat.

Organization for Economic Cooperation and Development Evolved out of post-Second World War efforts to coordinate policies on the use of Marshall Plan resources. Often now considered a think-tank for industrial countries contemplating various forms of economic policy coordination. Based in Paris, France.

Financial Action Task Force Initiated at the 1989 summit meeting of the G7 to examine measure to combat money laundering. A small secretariat based in the OECD, but not technically part of that organization, coordinates national efforts. Its mandate was expanded after 11 September 2001, and the Task Force now coordinates a range of work programmes designed to disrupt international networks involved in the financing of terrorism.

Joint Forum on Financial Conglomerates An effort spawned after 1996 by the Basel Committee of Bank Supervisors, IOSCO, and IAIS to promote common understandings on the regulation of private financial institutions increasingly bringing banking, securities underwriting, and insurance activities under one corporate roof.

Financial Stability Forum Following the international financial crises of the late 1990s, the G7 finance ministers and central bank governors sought to bring together national financial regulators from a wide range of countries hosting important international financial centres, together with international organizations involved in financial policy matters. The FSF began

meeting in April 1999; it has a small secretariat based at the BIS.

World Trade Organization Having grown out of the General Agreement on Tariffs and Trade, under which national trade policies have been liberalized on a multilateral basis ever since 1948, the WTO now has growing responsibilities for trade in various services, including a widening range of financial services.

Regional Development Banks With local mandates akin to the global development mandate of the World Bank, these multilateral organizations are now involved in providing technical advice for financial market deepening, regulation, and supervision in Africa, Latin America, East Asia, Eastern Europe, and Central Europe. (For more detailed descriptions, see Bryant 2003, Appendix; Solomon 1991; and Porter 2002.)

capital-influencing policies. In the late 1990s, even observers inclined to see all overt capital controls as apostasy and to predict long-term deleterious consequences from the undermining of future investor confidence, paid careful attention to tax policies adopted by Chile on short-term capital inflows designed to moderate speculative activity. Malaysia went even further by intervening (temporarily) in old-fashioned ways to impede outflows. Controversial as such policies were and remain, there is evidence that they can succeed in the short term in providing necessary breathing space for policy makers in national systems not yet capable of meeting the prudential, risk-management, and crisis-prevention standards of advanced industrial countries (Kaplan and Rodrik 2002; Haggard 2000; Lukauskas and Rivera-Batiz 2001). Still, it did not take long for internal pressures against the retention of such capital controls to build in Chile and Malaysia after crisis conditions eased, nor did external political pressures for re-engagement with globalizing markets let up. Given a systemic environment that continues to incline in the direction of expanding the scope for private-sector financing of central processes of economic adjustment, development, and growth, maintaining a realistic distinction between 'bad' speculation and 'good' investment becomes more difficult all the time. Like advanced

industrial states before them, emerging-market states especially in more halcyon times are clearly focusing less on designing better capital controls and more on finding better ways to manage financial crises when they occur. For that matter, all developing countries have a new appreciation for the importance of timing in the process of financial market deepening and opening; as the experiences of emerging markets demonstrated in the 1990s, excessively rapid liberalization programmes can end in disaster.

Key points

- Since the collapse of the Bretton Woods exchange-rate regime, governments have attempted to co-operate more intensively to prevent financial crises.

- Macro-economic policy choices condition the flow of capital across national borders.

- Policy coordination to reduce the chances that a localized financial crisis will spread has often involved talk about joint moves in fiscal and monetary policy making, but more substantive movement to render global markets more stable has occurred in the area of technical collaboration on regulatory and supervisory policies.

Crisis management

When the financial obligations of a business firm become unsustainable given available resources, the classic question is whether the underlying problem is one of illiquidity or insolvency. The distinction is rarely clear cut in practice, and one problem can easily slide into the other. In the typical case of illiquidity, creditors or investors in the firm might judge that a short-term loan or capital injection will get it past a payments crisis and enable it to find solid footing once again. In the case of insolvency, they would judge that it is no longer a going concern and that further lending would be worse than useless. One of two options might then be chosen. The firm could be taken over by its creditors and its balance sheet reorganized in an attempt to recreate some kind of viable business, or the firm's assets could be liquidated to retire as many of its liabilities as possible before finally closing its doors. In advanced capitalist systems, national bankruptcy laws exist to guide these procedures, and courts often are required to make the ultimate decisions. If Schumpeter was right and processes of creative destruction are the essence of modern capitalism, national governments use bankruptcy to clear their economic systems and enable those processes to repeat themselves. In the end, they no longer send failed entrepreneurs to debtors' prison but instead give them another chance.

Debt rescheduling and restructuring

Countries facing financial crises in an interdependent system are in a somewhat analogous position to a firm unable to meet its obligations. Aggregate debts become unsustainable, creditors demand repayment, and the resources available to settle accounts deteriorate in value. The national balance sheet requires adjustment. Crisis conditions may be generated by government overspending, by excessive imports, or by the building up of private-sector debt that cannot be financed domestically. Any of these situations might motivate the government to increase the rate of production of its monetary printing press. Inflation would normally be the consequence, and if

the fundamental problem is one of temporary illiquidity this might provide the necessary space for internal adjustments to occur. If much of a country's debt is owed to foreigners and is denominated in foreign currency, however, such a policy may quickly deepen the problem and easily turn it into one akin to the insolvency of a business firm. Inflation in the local currency by definition pushes up the value of foreign currency liabilities. Expecting further declines in the purchasing power of the local currency, domestic as well as foreign creditors and investors rush to preserve their capital, and even to get it out of the country. A deteriorating real exchange rate makes debt repayment more costly, imported goods required to facilitate revenue-generating production become more expensive, creditors and investors in future production lose confidence. The debtor government can default on its loans, or try to allow private firms under its purview to default with impunity, but then it risks cutting its economy off from future capital inflows that have no domestic substitute. The country becomes caught in the downward, vicious economic syndrome of deflation and depression. The situation in Argentina in 2001 provided a vivid example few emerging-market nations found attractive.

Obviously missing in such a scenario is a mechanism for the orderly bankruptcy of a national economy. Absent is a lender-of-last-resort, internationally agreed liquidation procedures, and a final court to replace managers and supervise the forced adjustment of the national balance sheet. This is, of course, no accident. In the conceptual extreme, the sovereignty of a state implies the absolute right both to resort to war and to default on debts. As a classic realist might argue, the ability in practice to claim such a right is in the final analysis a function of the raw power a state has in its possession to enforce its decision. In the real world, the sovereignty of particular states is compromised all the time (Krasner 1999). Unilateral defaults, payment moratoria, or standstills can be, and often are, declared by debtors. On the other hand, national assets can sometimes be unilaterally seized by aggrieved creditors. Gunboat diplomacy is nothing new, even if the technology has changed.

The architects of the post-1945 system contemplated the unruly form of international capitalism characteristic of the previous decade, and they deemed it a facilitator of war. At Bretton Woods, therefore, they took the first steps in designing mechanisms that would limit the extent to which sovereign participants in the system would resort to the ultimate policy instrument of debt default. Deepening theoretical debates among economists were never absent from their efforts then or during the following decades. But for practical policy makers in national capitals and the world's financial centres, the successors of the negotiators at Bretton Woods, crises and the real-time contemplation of counterfactuals more certainly determined actions. Time and again, from 1945 until the present moment, the main creditor states and the private financial institutions they licensed and regulated found themselves designing and redesigning substitutes for gunboat diplomacy, namely programmes that provided certain debtor states with the functional equivalent of last-resort lending facilities or of debt-restructuring services loosely analogous to those found in domestic bankruptcy courts. Ad hoc debt reschedulings and restructurings have been common since the 1980s. International banks as well as official agencies providing export credits informally organized themselves into negotiating groups (the so-called London Club and Paris Club, respectively) to manage such arrangements. Frequently, however, the threat of default has drawn attention from creditor governments themselves.

Whenever leading creditors have stepped into the breach created by their reluctance to accept unilateral defaults by debtor countries and by the simultaneous reluctance of sovereign debtors and creditors alike to design truly supranational organs of economic governance, they have in effect established precedents for the collaborative management of future crises. The practical economic consequences have analogues as well in domestic crisis situations. Bail-outs and debt restructuring perceived to be painless to creditors create the conditions for their imprudent behaviour in the future. Bail-outs perceived to be too painful for systemically significant debtors threaten to set back the continuing experiment in international economic interdependence and the cause of progressive development within the current system. So states have chosen collectively in practice to chart a middle path, where international institutions play a role in debt workouts, where technical devices, like collective action clauses in bond agreements, are used to encourage necessary concessions from creditors, but where the creation of supranational bankruptcy facilities is eschewed. That path remains an untidy one, unattractive to ideologues favouring the clarity existing in principle under crisis conditions at either of the imaginable extremes of untrammelled unilateralism or of irrevocably binding last-resort lending and bankruptcy procedures.

The rise of emerging markets and their special needs

In the early post-war decades, the main economic imbalances capable of derailing the system as a whole occurred in industrial countries. They typically manifested themselves as currency crises (often when governments sought to defend the par value of their currencies while running substantial trade deficits), so it was no coincidence that the International Monetary Fund was usually enlisted either to help resolve them or retroactively to bless new currency pegs or unorthodox financial arrangements. Ever since the 1980s, as noted above, the main crises capable of derailing the system have occurred in emerging markets, and more often than not, the IMF has again found itself at the centre of efforts to chart that middle path between financial anarchy and global governance. Many other institutions have also been involved one way or the other, but at moments of systemic crisis the main creditor states have shown a repeated inclination to work with and through the IMF and a small group of central banks.

The immediate objective of the IMF at such moments of crisis is to help break the psychology of fear and mistrust among its members and in the markets. Its ultimate mission, however, is to assist in stabilizing the financial underpinnings necessary for real national economies to become more deeply interdependent and more reliably prosperous through expanded trade. That the IMF was not dissolved after 1973 reflected much more than bureaucratic inertia.

Most importantly, the Fund's balance of payments financing facilities, which had grown over time in both size and flexibility, as well as its ability to attach policy conditions to the use of such facilities, proved to be extremely convenient to its major member states. This was demonstrated whenever an industrial state confronted financial problems capable of disrupting the international economic system or of seriously disturbing regional political stability. During the 1970s and 1980s, such situations arose mainly in the industrializing world, and especially in Latin America. After 1989, countries in transition from socialism became a focal point and, in the late 1990s, countries as diverse as Indonesia, Russia, and South Korea turned to the Fund for assistance.

In such cases, Fund officials demonstrated to their masters the usefulness of having an arbiter available, one that could at least provide surveillance over the key economic policies of members capable of generating external effects. Also proving itself useful was the Fund's legitimating role as a forum, wherein all member states were represented and had the right to voice opinions and vote on policies. Most importantly, however, the Fund proved handy when financing packages were required by members facing either routine or chronic balance of payments problems.

In retrospect, it is not surprising that the Fund evolved into the central crisis manager for emerging markets in a system that moved over time from one based on the interdependence of national exchange-rate policies and underlying macro-economic choices, toward one involving the deepening interaction of trade, investment, and financial policies. In this context, the leading states in the system confronted three basic choices every time one country or another found that it could not pay its bills to external customers or service its debts to external creditors:

1 They could do nothing, and risk the crisis spilling over to other countries and perhaps into their own domestic systems as well.

2 They could intervene directly by providing adequate financing from their own resources to the troubled country, and work directly with it to address the fundamental causes of the problem.

3 Or they could do the same indirectly, collectively, and more cheaply through the Fund and other collaborative institutions.

In practice, the third option often proved to be the least unattractive of the three, except for cases involving the weakest and most isolated developing countries. For countries whose periodic debt problems were widely perceived to be capable of seriously disrupting the system as a whole, the option of doing nothing, and of thereby letting markets attempt to force necessary adjustments, seldom seemed wise to actual policy makers charged with making such a decision. Similarly, the option of exposing their own taxpayers to the unmediated hazards of crisis resolution has typically proven itself to be almost as unattractive. The third option therefore nearly always found a sufficient number of advocates, in both creditor and debtor countries alike.

Institutional responses to emerging market crises

Against a changing global financial environment, the International Monetary Fund often eclipses other institutional competitors, an ability that many observers attribute to its close connections with the finance ministries of leading states and, in particular, of the United States. In the best-case scenarios, the Fund can use its own limited resources (in essence, the shareholders' equity or borrowings gathered over time from its member states); it can coordinate supplementary financing from other international institutions and from member state treasuries or central banks; it can potentially ameliorate moral hazard by imposing policy conditions that are politically tolerable to members in crisis; it can work with private banks, investment funds, and bondholders based in diverse national systems to coordinate the creditor side of debt restructurings; and it can provide a technical repository for lessons learned, lessons that might help reduce the likelihood of future crises. In the worst-case scenarios, such as when Russia defaulted in the mid-1990s and when Argentina did the same in 2001, moreover, the Fund can take on the politically important function of the scapegoat.

The IMF's crisis management role became more obvious as capital account liberalization became a clearer collective policy objective at the international level. It also became more complex as meeting that objective in developing countries implied dealing

with more fundamental issues of economic development, issues conventionally addressed by agencies like
the World Bank and regional development banks.
Leading states certainly pushed for more open financial markets, and the United States in particular came
to be associated with a vision for the system where
development and adjustment financing would only
be adequately supplied through private markets.
In the aftermath of the East Asian crisis of the late
1990s, the challenges thereby entailed for developing
countries clarified themselves. Economic development along capitalist lines required sophisticated
management, sound, confidence-inducing macro-
economic policy frameworks, and the rational order-
ing of processes through which real economies were
opened to external financial markets. States with shal-
low tax systems, weak legal systems, poor regulatory
structures, and fragile financial systems are likely also
to be desperate for capital inflows. Such states tend as
well to face domestic political constituencies supportive of fixed exchange-rate regimes. Throughout the
1990s, many such states found themselves pushed and
pulled to open their capital markets and make it easier
for external creditors to move into them. As some
discovered to their regret, however, this implied that
foreign banks, and increasingly foreign financial
investors with shorter time horizons, could also more
easily move out of those markets. They discovered too
that such movements could be triggered not only
by any objectively reasonable loss of confidence by
those investors in the integrity of domestic financial
institutions or in the value of the national currency.

They could be triggered by the expectation that other
investors might lose such confidence.

The psychology of what John Maynard Keynes
once famously described as the beauty contest at the
heart of capitalist financial markets, where one wisely
bets not on the contestant one deems most attractive
but rather on the contestant one think others will
consider the most attractive, is sometimes difficult to
manage even in the most advanced industrial states.
How much more difficult must it be expected to
remain in the industrializing world, and how utopian
it is to expect the least developed countries to construct the kind of managed exchange-rate floats and
crisis management tools that seem required to benefit
reliably from volatile global finance over the long
term (see Figure 7.7).

A new global architecture?

Key policy debates, not surprisingly, now revolve
around the theory and practice of crisis management
in emerging markets and around reducing the
exposure of the most needy countries to excessively
volatile capital flows (Tirole 2002; Eichengreen
2003; Bryant 2003; Tran Van Hoa 2002). After the
East Asian crisis, such debates filled library shelves
with myriad proposals for a new global financial
architecture.

Beyond the preventive measures discussed in
the previous section, proposals for crisis management are conventionally grouped into three main

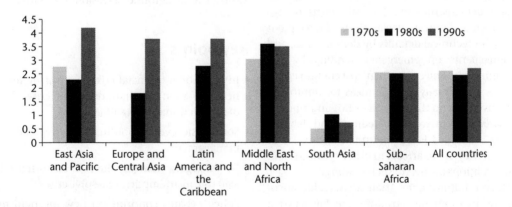

Fig. 7.7 Capital flow volatility: as percentage of GDP
Source: Data in World Bank (2001*a*).

categories: the unilateral, the multilateral, and the supranational (Eichengreen 2002: chapters 3, 4; Bryant 2003: chapters 8–10). In the first category, both conservative believers in the virtues of unfettered markets and the defenders of absolute sovereignty in developing countries join in a common cause. Crises, when they occur, are to be managed by unlucky or unwise external investors taking their lumps, and by debtor governments reverting to defaults and/or capital controls with attendant risks to their future access to external financing. In less extreme circumstances, private creditors and debtors would be left to their own devices to work out debt restructuring arrangements and to encourage reforms in national exchange-rate regimes.

At the other end of the spectrum, various proposals envisage the construction of global institutions that would come closer to serving as the functional equivalents of domestic emergency-lending, bankruptcy, and liquidation arrangements. Two successive deputy managing directors of the IMF made such proposals, one for the Fund to be legally empowered to play the role of lender-of-last-resort, and the next for the Fund to serve as a kind of ultimate bankruptcy court by overseeing a Sovereign Debt Restructuring Mechanism (Fischer 2000; Krueger 2002; Goodhart and Illing 2002).

In between these two extremes lie proposals to refine and improve the kinds of ad hoc measures used to resolve emerging market crises during the past twenty years. Typically, such measures have involved the establishment of committees to represent private or sovereign creditors, collective action clauses in negotiated debt instruments, domestic courts in creditor and debtor countries, declarations of repayment moratoria in technical defaults by debtor states, and tacit agreements on emergency lending by the finance ministries and central banks of creditor countries. They also usually include ideas for improving the effectiveness and the fairness of IMF intermediation between the interests of creditors and debtors, including continued Fund lending to debtor states even when they are in arrears to other creditors, and special conditions are tied to such lending.

In the years following the Asian crisis, zealots advocating the two extreme positions quickly receded from public view. The economic and political costs of their favourite proposals may be presumed to have become clear to those charged with actual decision-making responsibilities in both creditor and debtor countries alike. Until the next systemic threat arose, the most practical steps looked likely to evolve on the complicated middle terrain, where leading states and their most powerful constituents would continue pressing the cause of globalizing private finance, industrializing states would seek to harness associated opportunities and counter the unavoidable risks, and multilateral institutions like the IMF, led by creditor states but listening to debtors, would continue to search for stable political balances among their diverse memberships. The aspiration is well expressed as follows.

Markets cannot work without institutional supports. In particular, governments need to put in place the institutions that debtors and creditors require to smoothly resolve their differences. There needs to be a framework enabling them to do so without intolerable costs to the crisis country or unacceptable risks to the international financial system. But the mechanisms in question should not override market forces. Rather, it should enhance their efficiency. It should not make it harder for emerging markets to access external funding.

(Eichengreen 2002: 100)

Whether such an aspiration will be achievable for much of the developing world remains an open question. As in other international economic arenas, political economists at any given moment are left to assess the actual distribution of the costs and benefits of such a system. Again, the more practical minded among them attempt to make such an assessment against the background of feasible alternatives.

Key points

- International financial crises are usually more difficult to manage than domestic crises because of jurisdictional ambiguities.

- Some basic level of coordination is required in crisis management.

- For emerging markets, the IMF has often taken a lead role in attempting to resolve crises.

- Policy debates continue on new mechanisms for bankruptcy-like reorganizations of unsustainable debt in some developing nations.

Dilemmas of global governance

Globalizing financial markets remain at base a political experiment in an early stage. Once rejected as impracticable and excessively risky, since the 1970s the true architects of the international political economy—the United States, its key allies in the industrial world, and the most powerful domestic constituencies within them—have demonstrated little serious interest in advancing any alternative experiment. Ever more open financial markets might not ultimately succeed in generating a more stable, more prosperous, and fairer world order. But no other plan was on offer in the early twenty-first century. There was, however, a grudging recognition that private finance moving by its own lights would not be likely to provide adequate resources in the foreseeable future to the world's least developed countries. For this reason, proposals proliferated for significant increases in foreign aid budgets and for massive debt write-offs. Although some progress was recorded in this regard in the aftermath of the crisis years of the late 1990s, follow-through remained limited and tentative. Leaders and legislators in the world's major capitals clearly continued to hope that more open private financial markets would ultimately provide most of the external financial resources required by most countries aspiring to prosperity in a global economy.

Nevertheless, few with any historical memory believe that those markets could build a better world automatically. Few policy makers or close observers argued with any conviction that the global economic machinery being created by financial openness could manage itself. The critical issue then comes down to leadership in a system rendered more complicated, not only by the increased sophistication of that machinery but also by the contemporary dispersion of economic power.

A sense that reliable and just political leadership at the global level will turn out to be impracticable in the long run may lie deep in the consciousness of those attempting to build regional bulwarks as the experiment in economic and financial globalization continues (see Ravenhill, Chapter 5 in this volume). Still, the persistent reliance on multilateral institutions when practical policy makers confront collective problems, such as those associated with financial crisis prevention and especially crisis management, suggests that the post-1945 ideal of systemic collaboration remains alive. Students of political economy are left to contemplate the conditions under which increasingly interdependent states can govern themselves with an enlightened sense of their mutual interests.

QUESTIONS

1 What causes financial crises?

2 Why are certain crises contagious?

3 What special risks are associated with international finance, and how have regulators tried to keep pace with the risks inherent in international finance?

4 What alternatives to private financial markets exist for countries aspiring to development and economic prosperity?

5 What measures have been proposed for the prevention of financial crises?

6 How should international financial crises be more effectively managed?

7 What is the nature of the political limits on more effective crisis management?

8   What are the implications of current global crisis prevention and management systems for questions of distributive justice, both for the system as a whole and for specific countries?

FURTHER READING

Blustein, P. (2001), *The Chastening: Inside the Crisis that Rocked the Global System and Humbled the IMF* (New York: Public Affairs). An engaging, fast-paced account of the financial disturbances of the late 1990s. The author interviewed many of the major financiers, government officials, and political leaders involved; he weaves together a fascinating and disquieting tale.

Bryant, R. (2003), *Turbulent Waters: Cross-Border Finance and International Governance* (Washington DC: Brookings). A balanced exploration of the history and contemporary character of global finance by a leading economist attentive to the realities of national and international politics.

Edwards, S., and Frankel, J. A. (eds.) (2002), *Preventing Currency Crises in Emerging Markets* (Chicago: University of Chicago Press). An advanced compendium of economic papers on the multifaceted issues associated with pre-empting the problems most likely to create financial market instability.

Eichengreen, B. (2003), *Capital Flows and Crises* (Cambridge, Mass.: MIT Press). A prolific economist provides a highly readable account of the causes and consequences of international financial crises.

Goodhart, C., and Illing, G. (eds.) (2002), *Financial Crises, Contagion, and the Lender of Last Resort* (Oxford: Oxford University Press). An enlightening assessment of the strengths and weaknesses of institutions and practices at the global level aiming to govern interdependent financial markets.

Haggard, S. (ed.) (2000), *The Political Economy of the Asian Financial Crisis* (Washington DC: Institute for International Economics). A solid comparative examination of the political factors at work within the emerging markets most directly implicated in the financial turmoil of the 1990s.

James, H. (1996), *International Monetary Cooperation Since Bretton Woods* (Washington DC: International Monetary Fund). An accessible account of how the monetary dimension of the world economy evolved in the post-1945 era by an outstanding economic historian.

Kapstein, E. (1994), *Governing the Global Economy: International Finance and the State* (Cambridge, Mass.: Harvard University Press). A study by a political scientist who argues, in the wake of the international financial crises of the 1970s and 1980s, that clearer understandings emerged among advanced industrial countries on certain regulatory principles, especially the principle of home-country control.

Kindleberger, C. P. (1978), *Manias, Panics, and Crashes: A History of Financial Crises* (New York: Basic Books). A path-breaking orientation to the fragile financial underpinnings of modern capitalism.

Lukauskas, A. J., and Rivera-Batiz, F.L. (eds.) (2001), *The Political Economy of the East Asian Crisis and its Aftermath* (Cheltenham: Edward Elgar). A comprehensive survey by an interdisciplinary group of scholars.

Mussa, M. (2002), *Argentina and the Fund: From Triumph to Tragedy* (Washington DC: Institute for International Economics). A former chief economist of the IMF presents a troubling case study of chronic financial crisis and the responses of national and international institutions.

Pauly, L. W. (1997), *Who Elected the Bankers? Surveillance and Control in the World Economy* (Ithaca, NY: Cornell University Press). An examination of the emergence and institutionalization of international monetary and financial oversight in the wake of twentieth-century crises.

Stiglitz, J. E. (2002), *Globalization and its Discontents* (New York: W. W. Norton). A highly provocative critique of the reactions of governments and international organizations to the economic disasters befalling much of the developing world in recent years, by a well-known scholar and former chief economist of the World Bank.

Strange, S. (1998), *Mad Money: When Markets Outgrow Governments* (Ann Arbor: University of Michigan Press). The late, great international political economist provides a rousing introduction to the policy and technical innovations that dramatically increased the volume and volatility of global financial flows.

Tirole, J. (2002), *Financial Crises, Liquidity, and the International Monetary System* (Princeton: Princeton University Press). An insightful, theoretically challenging analysis of crucial differences between finance within a country and finance that crosses national borders, by a ranking European economist.

WEB LINKS

www.stern.nyu.edu/globalmacro/   Nouriel Roubini's Global Macroeconomic and Financial Policy Site at the Stern School of Business, New York University.

www.imf.org/   International Monetary Fund.

www.worldbank.org/   The World Bank Group.

www.un.org/esa/ffd/   United Nations, Department of Economic and Social Affairs, Financing for Development.

www.jubilee2000uk.org/   Jubilee Research.

www.g7.utoronto.ca/   G7/G8 Information Centre.

www.iif.com/   The Institute of International Finance, Inc.

Part Four

Globalization and its consequences

8 The logics of globalization

Anthony McGrew

READER'S GUIDE

In 1987, Robert Gilpin's *The Political Economy of International Relations* was published, a defining moment in the coming of age of international political economy as a distinctive field of academic enquiry. Less than two decades later, its 'replacement', *Global Political Economy*, was published, the new title reflecting, as Gilpin noted in the book's preface, fundamental changes which had taken place in the nature of the international economic order. Amongst the most critical of these developments he observes, is 'the globalization of the world economy' (Gilpin 2001: 3). The extent, historical significance, and consequences of this globalization, however, remain hotly contested in the academy and beyond. In this 'great globalization debate', which animates much of the study of contemporary political economy and international relations, the very concept of globalization is disputed as is its validity as a description or explanation of the dynamics of the current world economic order.

Commencing with a brief review of this debate, this chapter argues that globalization—understood simply as the widening, deepening, and speeding up of worldwide interconnectedness—aptly describes, even if by itself it does not explain, the emergence of a singular global political economy. But globalization is neither inevitable nor irresistible. Taking globalization seriously therefore necessarily involves a careful specification of its causes or logics, which is the principal task of this chapter. Unsurprisingly, since the very idea of globalization is deeply contested the question of its causes or logics tends to be neglected in the 'great debate'. In seeking to rectify this neglect the chapter will elucidate the principal accounts of globalization offering some critical judgements on which, if any, provide a convincing explanation of 'the globalization of the world economy'. By concentrating upon the causes of globalization the analysis brackets the matter of its presumed effects or consequences—for example on state sovereignty, patterns of inequality, or social democracy—which are the subject of other chapters. Nevertheless the discussion of causes has important implications for some of the crucial normative questions which concern the governance and future trajectory of globalization in the aftermath of 11 September 2001, the focus of the concluding section. In short, the chapter addresses three questions:

What is globalization?
What's driving it?
And so what? That is, why the analysis of its logics matters.

Introduction

In the aftermath of the cataclysmic attacks on the United States on 11 September 2001, there has been much talk of the end of globalization, deglobalization, or the onset of the post-global age. These momentous events, according to John Gray, herald a new epoch in world affairs: 'The era of globalisation is over' (Naím 2002). Measured in terms of flows within the circuits of the world economy, globalization, or to be more precise economic globalization, has undoubtedly stalled since the heady days of the turn of the century. Whether this truly marks the end of globalization as we have known it, or simply a hiatus in the global economic cycle, ultimately will be for future historians to judge.

Amongst those of a sceptical persuasion, the war on global terrorism presages a world of heightened nationalism, the reassertion of geopolitics and US military hegemony, the strong state, and the reimposition of borders, all but confirming the suspicion that globalization is so much 'globaloney'. This new climate of fear and insecurity, in other words, is debunking globalization as the great (popular) myth of the late twentieth century. By contrast, for many of a more globalist persuasion, the very events of 11 September and the climate of fear it has engendered are evidence of a pervasive 'clash of globalizations' rather than globalization's demise (Hoffmann 2002). Moreover, in contrast to Gray's pessimism, they assert that, despite 11 September, patterns of global inter-

dependence appear to have proved extremely resilient and enduring. What is at issue here, at least in part, are differing conceptual, theoretical, and historical interpretations of globalization.

Since it is such a 'slippery' and overused concept within the social sciences, and also has a colloquial life outside the academic world, it is hardly surprising that globalization should engender intense debate not to mention plain confusion. Because no singular or orthodox definition exists, it is crucial here to establish, from the outset, how the concept is understood within the global political economy literature. Accordingly, the first section will address several interrelated questions, namely:

What is globalization?
Is it happening?
And is it new?

Following this discussion the second section will identify and analyse the principal causes and the dominant theories of globalization. In so doing it will draw an important distinction between what Rosenberg (2000) refers to as 'theories of globalization' and 'globalization theory'. Finally, the third section will relate this discussion of theories of globalization to an understanding of the broader issues of the transformation and governance of the global political economy or, more crudely, why the analysis of causes matters.

Globalization today: another extraordinary episode?

Remarking upon a previous epoch of global economic transformation, John Maynard Keynes wrote of 'an extraordinary episode in the economic progress of man' in which 'the internationalization of . . . economic and social life . . . was nearly complete' (quoted in Grieco and Ikenberry 2002: 6). Many of his liberal contemporaries, such as Norman Angell, associated

(what later became known as) this *belle époque* (1870–1914) with the emergence of a new world order in which war was becoming increasingly unthinkable (McGrew 2002). The guns of August 1914 brutally suppressed such liberal idealism. This historic phase of liberal, or more accurately imperial, global economic integration nevertheless remains the classic benchmark against which many academic studies assess the current period (Hirst and Thompson 1999). Although there is fairly widespread and general agreement amongst students of global political economy that in the period since 1945, and in particular over the last two decades, there has been a remarkable intensification of transborder economic activity, this development lends itself to divergent interpretations (Gordon 1988; O'Brien 1992; Castells 1996; Dicken 2003; Held et al. 1999; Hirst and Thompson 1999; Gilpin 2001; Hoogvelt 2001—for further discussion, see Hay, Chapter 9 in this volume). Little agreement exists as to whether the trends disclose another 'extraordinary episode' in the evolution of the world economy or alternatively its growing segmentation or disintegration. Furthermore, since globalization encompasses more than simply the economic sphere, conclusions about its contemporary significance vary dramatically. At issue here, at least in part, are distinctive conceptions of globalization.

Within the political economy literature globalization is principally identified with a process of intensifying worldwide economic integration. Thus, for instance, Hirst and Thompson assert that 'We can only begin to assess the issue of globalization if we have some relatively clear and rigorous model of what a global economy would be like . . . ' (Hirst and Thompson 2003: 99). This presumption that globalization can be understood primarily as an economic process and can be assessed in relation to some idealized 'global economy' contrasts with the understanding of the concept in much of the wider social science literatures. Here globalization tends to be conceived as a multidimensional, rather than singular, process—evident across the cultural, political, ecological, military, and social domains—which is open-ended insofar as it discloses no historically determinate or fixed outcome (Held et al. 1999; Keohane and Nye 2003). Underlying these different conceptions are significant methodological disputes about how complex historical and social phenomena, such as globalization, are best studied (Rosenberg 1995). The lack of agreement suggests the need for some caution both in automatically privileging the economic in any systematic analysis of globalization but more especially in drawing general conclusions about globalization, as a social process, solely from an analysis of the economic sphere. Conflating global-

ization with economic globalization, in other words, is a categorical mistake. That said, few discussions of globalization can, or do, ignore its economic dimension.

Conceptually globalization is often elided with notions of liberalization, internationalization, universalization, Westernization, or modernization (Scholte 2000b). However, as Scholte argues, none of these terms captures its distinctive attributes or qualities. Within the global political economy literature economic globalization is generally specified in reasonably precise terms as 'the emergence and operation of a single, worldwide economy' (Grieco and Ikenberry 2002: 207). It is measured in respect of the growing intensity, extensity, and velocity of worldwide economic interactions and interconnectedness, from trade through production and finance, to migration. In this regard it is conceived as a *process*, rather than a fixed outcome or condition, insofar as it refers to a *historical tendency* towards heightened levels of worldwide economic interconnectedness. Indeed, there is a substantive conceptual difference between the notion of a *globalizing world economy*, in Gilpin's terms, and a fully or partially *globalized world economy* which implies a fixed state or condition of economic integration.

This distinction between 'becoming' and 'being', as will become apparent subsequently, is highlighted by Keohane and Nye, who differentiate between globalization—as a historical process—and globalism—the resulting condition at any particular historical moment (Keohane and Nye 2003). The implication is that since globalization is neither inevitable, determinate, nor irresistible it therefore, at particular historical moments, can result in thicker or thinner forms of globalism. Translated into the language of global political economy, globalization can be associated with thicker or thinner forms of worldwide economic integration.

Understood as a process, economic globalization also implies an evolving *transformation* or qualitative shift in the organization of the world economy. Quite simply, over time cumulative patterns and networks of transborder economic activity dissolve the separation of the world into discrete national economic units making the distinction between the domestic and world economy increasingly difficult to sustain both for academics and policy makers alike. In other words, globalization generates emergent or systemic properties such that the world economy increasingly begins to operate as a single system (Sayer 2000). This structural shift may be evident in, amongst other things, the formation of global markets, production networks, a global division of labour and business competition together with global systems of economic regulation and management that range from the World Trade Organization to the International Accounting Standards Board.

Underlying these shifts in the scale of economic organization are contemporary informatics technologies and infrastructures of communication and transportation. These have facilitated new forms and possibilities of virtual real-time worldwide economic organization and coordination. In the process, distance and time are being substantially reconfigured such that, for instance, economic and other shocks in one region of the world can rapidly diffuse around the globe with often serious local consequences (see, for example, Pauly, Chapter 7 in this volume). Although geography still matters it is nevertheless the case that globalization is associated with a process of *time-space compression*—literally a shrinking world—in which the sources of even very localized economic developments, from price rises to corporate restructuring, may be traced to economic conditions on another continent.

However, a single worldwide economy is not coextensive with a universal or planetary economy. More specifically, 'worldwide' is generally taken to refer to *interregional* or *intercontinental* patterns of economic exchange and enmeshment. Accordingly, globalization is conceived as embodying a *rescaling* of economic space manifested in the intensification of inter or supraregional and multicontinental networks and flows of economic activity (Brenner 1999). In effect, globalization denotes a relative *denationalization* of the world economy as significant aspects of economic life become organized increasingly on an interregional or multicontinental scale transcending bounded national economic space (Held et al. 1999; Keohane and Nye 2003). This rescaling, however, is not uniformly experienced across all regions or economies since globalization is also recognizably an uneven *process*. Differential patterns of enmeshment in, or alternatively marginalization from, the worldwide economy define its 'variable geometry' (Castells

---

Box 8.1 Globalization

Globalization is variously defined in the literature as:

1 'The intensification of worldwide social relations which link distant localities in such a way that local happenings are shaped by events occurring many miles away and vice versa' (Giddens 1990: 21).

2 'The integration of the world economy' (Gilpin 2001: 364).

3 'De-territorialization—or . . . the growth of supraterritorial relations between people' (Scholte 2000b: 46).

4 '[A] global economy . . . in which distinct national economies and, therefore, domestic strategies of national economic management are increasingly irrelevant' (Hirst and Thompson 1999).

5 '[T]he international integration of markets in goods, services, and capital' (Garrett 2000a).

2000). Such unevenness generates a distinctive geography of inclusion and exclusion such that the notion of a worldwide or global economy is less geographically inclusive than that of a planetary or universal economy. The implications of this distinction, as will become clear, are highly significant for any empirical assessment of economic globalization.

Having developed this general conception of economic globalization, its relevance and centrality to describing, understanding, and explaining the current global economic condition can be explored further. Several interrelated questions will be addressed:

- Is there substantive evidence of the globalization of economic activity?

- If so, is globalization now the principal dynamic of the contemporary world economy?

- And finally, even if it is, does it necessarily constitute a novel condition?

Within the existing literature there are, as noted previously, broadly two sets of responses to these questions: the globalist and the sceptical. In short, whereas globalists consider that world trends disclose unprecedented levels of economic globalization, such that there can be little question of the existence of a single worldwide economy, the sceptics are much less convinced. They conclude not only that globalization is highly exaggerated but also that contrary developments, from growing regionalism to intensifying geo-economic competition, are creating a more segmented and fragmented world economy. Of course, these two labels—globalists and sceptics—simplify the nature and sources of the underlying disagreement, not to mention concealing considerable theoretical heterogeneity within each camp and the common ground between them. Yet on the critical issue of whether globalization exists, they differ profoundly. The reasons for this will become clearer in subsequent pages. Here the discussion will concentrate upon trends in trade, finance, production, and labour as the principal constituents of the world economy.

Trade

It is the confluence of secular trends and patterns of world trade, capital flows, transnational production, and labour flows which, for globalists, affirms the validity of the globalization thesis. As Samir Amin concludes, though economic globalization is nothing new it has 'undeniably taken a qualitative step forward during the recent period' (1997: 31). For most of the post-war period world trade has grown much faster than world output. World exports, measured as a proportion of world output, were three times greater in 1998 than in 1950; the WTO estimates this ratio stood at around 29 per cent by 2001 (WTO 2001a). Despite 11 September and the subsequent downturn in the world economy, world trade in 2003 was over 25 per cent of world output, higher than for the entire preceding decade (WTO 2003a; Kearney 2003). Moreover trade now involves a larger number of countries than at any time in the recent past, except perhaps for the *belle époque*, while developing economies today account for a growing share of world export markets in both manufactures (almost a third) and the services sector (Held et al. 1999; WTO 2002).

Of course, world trade remains highly concentrated both geographically—OECD countries account for the bulk of world trade (some 70 per cent) and a number of East Asian countries for the bulk of developing

country trade—and sectorally—electronics account for 50 per cent of world exports (Held et al. 1999; WTO 2001a). This concentration is hardly surprising given that OECD countries account for the largest share of world economic output and are by far the largest economic units. Furthermore, the concentration of trade conceals major developments such as the emergence of a new global division of labour and the intensification of global competition through trade.

Patterns of trade have altered significantly over the last four decades. This reflects the changing location of manufacturing production as East Asia and other newly industrializing economies (NIEs) take on a new role as the world's factories. Falling costs of transportation, the communications revolution, liberalization, and the growth of transnational corporations have all contributed to a new global division of labour. Since 1990 developing economies have increased their share of world manufactures trade from 17 per cent to over 27 per cent (WTO 2001a: 3). At the same time, most developing economies have witnessed the decline of trade in raw materials and primary products whilst most OECD economies have experienced a significant rise in their trade in services.

These shifts represent a new pattern of specialization within the world economy which is also associated with the intensification of economic competition. In both the manufacturing, and to a lesser extent services, sectors the expansion of trade increases competitive pressures on domestic businesses. Lower-cost imports impose greater price competition whilst the dominance of intra-industry trade (trade in similar products or services) between OECD economies brings domestic business and foreign business in the same sector into direct competition. This has reinforced the search for competitive advantage through more efficient production methods or organization, including 'slicing up the value chain' or outsourcing production such that firms draw upon worldwide networks of suppliers that produce where greatest economies of scale or efficiency gains can be realized. One recent study suggests that intra-industry and inter-firm trade accounts for at least 30 per cent of the growth of world trade in the period 1970–90 (Hummels 2001). Through this new division of labour, productive, and competitive forces become further globalized whilst manufacturing systems in different regions and countries become more tightly integrated.

Insofar as dense trade flows occur between the major regions of the world economy—namely the Asia-Pacific, the North American Free Trade Agreement, and European Union cores—global markets in goods and services might be assumed to exist. The most obvious examples of such markets are those in key primary commodities, such as grain, which set benchmark world prices. But global markets are far from the textbook notion of perfectly integrated national markets. Despite the dramatic trade liberalization of the last forty years, significant non-tariff barriers to trade remain, whilst distance and history still continue to influence patterns of world trade. This is particularly evident in the significant growth of regionalism (see Ravenhill, Chapter 5 in this volume) over recent decades. Even so there is evidence of a tendency for price differentials for traded goods to narrow, as might be expected in a global market place (IMF 2002: 122). Moreover, studies suggest that distance is no longer as crucial a determinant of patterns of world trade as in the past (Coe et al. 2002). Neither too does regionalism appear to be producing a segmentation of the world economy into separate regional markets. Although patterns of regional trade present a complex picture, *intraregional* trade as a proportion of world merchandise trade, at an estimated 36 per cent, was lower in 2001 than throughout the 1990s (WTO 2001*a*: 6). As Table 5.4 (Ravenhill, Chapter 5 in this volume) indicates, the evidence does not demonstrate a secular trend towards the regional segmentation of the world economy. On the contrary it is rather inconclusive since in both the case of the European Union and Japan *inter*regional trade rose between 1990 and 2000, but remained constant for NAFTA, while simultaneously the growth of *intra*regional trade outpaced the growth of interregional trade in several regions during the same period.

Of course formally, under the rules of the WTO which today have acquired almost universal reach, regionalism is required to be compatible with the multilateral trade order (Ravenhill, Chapter 5 in this volume). This institutionalization of global rule making and adjudication in trade matters marks a seminal development in the political construction of a truly global trade system. Through its very existence and functioning, the WTO defines a global regulatory framework which effectively constitutes the normative and legal foundations of global markets and their operation. In this respect, global markets are not just spontaneous constructions but partly the product of the regulatory activities of multilateral bodies such as the WTO, not to mention the expanding role of transnational private merchant law (the new *lex mercatoria*) (Gill 1995; Cutler 2003). To this extent trade globalization is not simply about trends in world trade but also points to the critical importance of global and transnational trade authorities in *constituting* global markets.

Finance

Until comparatively recently international finance was considered principally an adjunct to trade, a necessary mechanism for enabling the international exchange of goods and services (Eichengreen 1996; Germain 1997). This direct association between finance and trade began to dissolve in the nineteenth century. By the twenty-first century it has become irrelevant or marginal at best. Daily turnover on foreign exchange markets more than doubled from $590 billion in 1989 to $1,210 billion in 2001 compared to daily world exports of approximately $25 billion (*BIS Quarterly Review* 2001; Grieco and Ikenberry 2002: 214). As a multiple of world trade, annual foreign exchange turnover in 1973 was around twice the value of world trade—but in 2001 was a staggering sixty times greater (Held and McGrew 2002: 48). This activity, facilitated by instantaneous global communications, is conducted around the clock between the world's major financial centres on each continent. A worldwide foreign exchange market exists that determines the value of traded currencies, influencing the level of key financial variables such as interest rates, and enabling the rapid movement of capital around the globe.

Following the significant liberalization of national financial markets in the last two decades, the level and geographical scope of global capital flows has also expanded enormously. By comparison with trade, which exhibited a compound growth rate of almost 10 per cent over the period 1964–2001, transborder financial flows grew at a compound rate of almost

19 per cent (Bryant 2003: 141). To put this in context Bryant calculates for the period 1964–2001 that if the growth of international bonds—a form of securitized international lending/borrowing measured here in terms of stocks not flows—had been at an equivalent level to the growth rate of all OECD economies, stocks of international bonds would be valued today at some $776 billion, only 11 per cent of the actual $7.2 trillion (Bryant 2003: 142). Similar patterns are evident for all other types of transborder capital flows, from international issues of shares—which expanded from $8 bn in the 1980s to a peak of $300 bn in 2000 and $100 bn in 2002—to cross-border trading in derivatives (new financial products)—which grew from $618.3 bn in 1986 to $23,873 bn in 2002—and transborder bank lending—which increased from $2,095 bn in 1983 to $11,483 bn in 2001 (BIS 2003; Held et al. 1999: chapter 4; Bryant 2003: 140)

As with trade, the bulk of capital flows (some 66 per cent) is accounted for by the major OECD economies. Whilst these interregional flows have intensified—64 per cent of transborder investments in stock markets is intercontinental—this is not replicated everywhere (IMF 2003b). Transborder financial flows are highly uneven such that whilst most emerging market economies have acquired access to world financial markets, many of the poorest economies remain subject to, rather than active participants in, their operation. Capital flows to developing states have fluctuated considerably over the last three decades, peaking in the mid-1990s prior to the East Asian crash and subsequently falling back, although they currently remain above the levels witnessed in the 1980s (IMF 2003b). The distribution of these flows is concentrated amongst the principal emerging market economies of Latin America, East Asia, and the European transition economies. Geography and history still exert some influence on capital flows. Of course, this is not to conclude that the dynamics and volatilities of transborder financial activities have no bearing upon those on the margins, for few economies can insulate themselves against the consequences of financial contagion in a real-time global financial system (Desai 2003).

Despite the unevenness of transborder capital flows the evidence suggests that since the 1980s there has been a significant integration of financial markets (Taylor 1996). Financial integration is a matter of degree, or a tendency, expressed in relative measurements of either greater or lesser intensity. It is normally assessed in relation to tendencies towards the convergence, deepening, and institutionalization of worldwide financial activity or performance. Obstfeld and Taylor's (1998, 2003) econometric studies, amongst others, identify a narrowing of interest-rate differentials between all the major OECD economies after 1960 (they returned to their pre-1914 levels), as might be expected from the existence and operation of global financial markets (Fujii and Chinn 2001; Goldberg, Lothian, and Kunev 2003; Obstfeld and Taylor 1998, 2003). Although short of complete convergence, international differentials remain comparable to those within most national economies (for a given financial asset) whilst they persist for much more limited periods than in the past (Goldberg, Lothian, and Kunev 2003; Fujii and Chinn 2001).

Moreover, although Feldstein and Horoika's classic study (1980) concludes that levels of national savings and investment appear to be highly correlated (see Hay, Chapter 9 of this volume), indicating significant barriers to financial integration, this correlation not only appears to have weakened during the 1990s—a period of intense transborder capital flows—but also Taylor suggests the original findings have to be interpreted with considerable caution (BIS *Quarterly Review* 2001: 32; Feldstein and Horoika 1980; Taylor 1996). This leads Bryant to conclude that 'the analogy of nearly autonomous national savings [and investment] reservoirs is no longer appropriate' (Bryant 2003: 152). While these studies indicate that global capital markets remain imperfect, the tendency, nevertheless, has been in the direction of greater, rather than lesser, financial integration.

Tendencies towards financial convergence have also been accompanied by processes of financial deepening. Finance pervades the operation and management of all modern economies representing for many, to borrow Hilferding's vocabulary, a new epoch of finance capitalism. To the extent that national financial systems are increasingly integrated (in real time) with global capital markets, the consequences of financial developments or volatility abroad is magnified and diffused rapidly at home. For instance, on 27 August 1998 the stock markets on every continent fell significantly in reaction to the spread of currency crises from Asia to Russia and Latin America (Desai 2003: 198). This synchrony in financial market movements across the globe is not uniform, since local conditions can make a difference, whilst it is more evident at times of crisis than normalcy. Nevertheless it denotes the heightened significance of global financial conditions for domestic financial stability and vice versa (Eichengreen 2002). This process of financial deepening arises out of the interaction between the greater 'financialization' of national economies and the scale of global financial activity. Evidence of this is to be found during the 1990s in, for instance, the increased foreign holdings of national public debt—in the euro zone an increase from 16 to 30 per cent and in the United States from 19 per cent to in excess of 35 per cent today—not to mention increased foreign holdings of shares, private financial assets, and the almost doubling of the ratio of foreign assets to national GDP for most OECD economies (Held et al. 1999; IMF 2002; Mosley 2003).

Associated with this financial deepening is a process of institutionalization as the organization and infrastructures of transborder finance become regularized and systematized through the activities of (public and private) global agencies and networks. This institutionalization is evident in the enormous expansion of multinational banking—for example, HSBC, 'the world's local bank'—as well as the surveillance and global standard-setting activities of the IMF, BIS, and the multiplicity of official and private transborder networks, from the Financial Action Task Force to the International Accounting Standards Board. It is through the operation of these institutions that the essential infrastructure of global financial markets is developed and extended, from the SWIFT global financial inter-Bank payments system to mechanisms for managing sovereign 'bankruptcy'. In the process the global or interregional integration of financial markets is reinforced.

Production

Although data on transborder capital flows include foreign direct investment (FDI), political economists analyse FDI separately because effectively it denotes the globalization of production. Outsourcing production around the world is now widespread in the most dynamic industrial sectors. Indeed, investment in overseas production has increased dramatically over the last three decades. Driving and dominating this process is the transnational corporation (TNC). By comparison with the recent past (say, 1990), transnational production rather than trade has become the principal means of servicing foreign markets. Transnational corporations account currently for more than 25 per cent of world production, 80 per cent of world industrial output, 33 per cent of world trade, and 10 per cent of world GDP (Gilpin 2001: 289; UNCTAD 2001, 2003). They have become important determinants of the location and organization of production and services in the world economy, especially within the most advanced and dynamic economic sectors, integrating and reordering business activity between and within the world's three principal economic regions and their associated hinterlands. These developments are characterized by, amongst other factors: an increased scale and scope; processes of transnational economic restructuring; and the consolidation of a new global division of labour.

Over the last three decades flows of FDI have not only become more geographically diffuse but also much more intense (Dunning 2000; UNCTAD 2001; for further discussion see Rugman, Chapter 10 in this volume). At the turn of the new century total world (inward) FDI reached a new peak of $1,271 billion, almost four times the level of 1995 and over six times that of a decade earlier (UNCTAD 2001: 3). Since then FDI flows have declined dramatically, with the slowdown in the world economy, to just over $651 billion in 2002 (UNCTAD 2003: 2). Even so, the scale of FDI remains over ten times that of 1982 and significant flows (more than $10 billion) reach more than fifty countries (including 24 developing economies) compared to seventeen (and seven LDCs) respectively in 1985 (UNCTAD 2001: 4). As UNCTAD notes the 'trend towards integration on ever larger geographical scales is relatively new. Supply chains have extended to new areas of the globe and integrated formerly distinct regional production activities' (UNCTAD 2002c: 13). This reflects a variety of factors including proximity to new markets and technological shifts in the capacity to organize and manage production at a distance (Dicken 2003). But it is not simply manufacturing production which is on the move but increasingly the provision of services, such as call centres, information processing, and legal and banking services (Held et al. 1999: chapter 5; UNCTAD 2001: 6).

Widely diffused as it is, nevertheless, both flows and stocks of FDI remain highly concentrated amongst and within the major OECD economies (see Rugman, Chapter 10 in this volume). Though some FDI reaches every continent it remains highly uneven in its dispersion. OECD economies account for some 70 per cent of FDI (inflows), 90 per cent of the world stock of (outward or exported) FDI, and 60 per cent of the world stock of (inward) FDI (UNCTAD 2003: 23). The trend denotes an increasing concentration of investment within and between the European Union, United States, and Japan as the largest economies and between these economies and the NIEs of Asia, (to a lesser extent) Latin America, and the East European transition economies. This concentration has been variously conceived as triadization or regionalization but such terms fail to capture the significant transregional flows of FDI and interregional networks of production (Dicken 2003; Dunning 2000). It is the very clustering of FDI around the three major economic regions combined with the intensity of interregional flows that reinforces the dynamic of global economic integration. As FDI has become more important (measured either in terms of the ratio of FDI to GDP, or FDI to domestic investment) for economic growth in both advanced, but most especially in developing economies, so it more readily and rapidly transmits any fluctuations in the business cycle within the world's major economies (UNCTAD 2003). This has been evident in each of the significant downturns in the world economy since the early 1970s.

In linking the dynamics of economies, FDI is also associated with processes of economic restructuring. Although the notion of 'footloose capital' is very much a cliché, the consequences of the mobility of capital are evident in structural changes across many OECD economies and the rise of NIEs in Asia and Latin America (Rowthorn and Wells 1987; Castells 1996; Dicken 2003; Kapstein 2000; Hoogvelt 2001). There is much debate both about the significance of the deindustrialization of OECD economies in recent decades and its causes (Piore and Sabel 1984; Krugman 1994; Wood 1994; Lawrence 1996b; Rodrik 1997; Burtless et al. 1998; Schwartz 2001). Although the impact of globalization, as opposed to technological change, on the decline of manufacturing employment in many OECD economies is disputed there is general agreement that capital mobility nevertheless plays a role in their continuous economic transformation. Deindustrialization in these economies is linked directly with the industrialization of many developing economies as production is shifted to lower-cost locations (Rowthorn and Wells 1987; Wood 1994; Lawrence 1996b; Rodrik 1997; Dicken 2003; Munck 2002). This is not to argue that the mobility of productive capital is unconstrained, since it is not. Proximity to local markets, institutional factors, and productivity calculations limit the potential for industrial capital to relocate abroad either rapidly or at all. Nevertheless, over time the cumulative impact of capital mobility, along with the expansion of trade, has contributed to structural changes in the world economy.

Amongst the most obvious of these structural changes is the evolution and consolidation of a new worldwide division of labour. A significant shift has occurred in the location of manufacturing production from OECD economies outwards to NIEs in East Asia, Latin America, and other parts of the developing world (Gilpin 2001: 140). To a much more limited degree, a similar trend is evident in some aspects of service provision, most notably in data processing and information provision (WTO 2001a). At the same time the raw material sector has declined, measured as a proportion of world FDI and trade, such that many developing economies have entered, or seek to enter, the manufacturing business. As a result of these shifts, the geography of world economic activity has been transformed in recent years with important consequences for the distribution of economic power and wealth, and ultimately for the politics of global economic relations (Gilpin 2001; Crafts and Venables 2003).

A second, and related structural change, has been the intensification of transnational and interregional competition for market share, technological advantage, and rapid product innovation. Such competition is no longer necessarily best conceived as occurring simply between self-contained national economic units, but rather increasingly between firms and businesses in different regions of the globe, insofar as the new geography of world economic activity links distant markets through the operations of giant multinational corporations (MNCs) and interregional production networks (Gilpin 2001: 180–2). Economic and corporate competition becomes globalized since it transcends regions, biting deeper into national economies and magnifying the consequences of local conditions and differences (Held et al. 1999: chapter 5). Domestic competition between supermarket chains for agricultural produce, for instance, turns farmers both at home and abroad into direct competitors. Given the existence of instantaneous communications it is not only the scope but also the rapidity with which global competition evolves which contributes significantly to its intensity (Harvey 1989; Castells 1996).

Labour

By comparison with capital, labour is relatively immobile. That said, labour flows are much more geographically extensive and, in terms of direction, reflect an almost mirror image of capital flows insofar as they have become primarily South *to* North (Held et al. 1999; Castles and Miller 2002; Chiswick and Hatton 2003). Outward flows of labour are a predominantly developing country phenomenon and, despite greater restrictions, they are, surprisingly, on a scale of the mass migrations of the early twentieth century (Chiswick and Hatton 2003: 74). Though complex in origin and destination, interregional, as opposed to regional, migration has expanded enormously over the period 1950–2000 (Chiswick and Hatton 2003). So, too, has skilled labour migration from South to North. These developments reflect tendencies towards the integration of distant labour markets (Silver 2003). Such tendencies might be expected to produce some convergence in wage rates (both North and South) most especially for the skilled, but overall a growing divergence between skilled and unskilled workers given the preponderance of the latter amongst migrants and in the South. There is some evidence to confirm such trends although the causal weight of migration—as opposed to other factors such as trade, technology, or capital mobility—is debated (Galbraith 2002; Firebaugh 2003; Lindert and Williamson 2003).

Economic globalization today: just how extraordinary?

For globalists, contemporary patterns of world trade, finance, production, and migration define a new epoch of economic globalization insofar as together they constitute the workings of a single, worldwide economy. Given the unevenness of economic globalization, however, the present epoch is better described as significantly, rather than fully, globalized—an epoch of thick as opposed to thin economic globalism. Though globalization is very much the dominant logic of the world economy, it is, as the references to regionalization and concentration suggest, by no means its sole logic. Those of a more sceptical persuasion pay greater attention to these subaltern logics as opposed to the alleged novelty of the present condition. In so doing they mount a rigorous intellectual challenge to the globalist case, although ultimately not a convincing or successful one.

Broadly, three arguments underlie the sceptical case. The first concerns the exaggerated nature of contemporary economic globalization; the second identifies limits to economic globalization; and the third emphasizes its irrelevance. Each will be briefly reviewed and discussed.

For Gilpin, 'although globalization had become the defining feature of the international economy at the beginning of the twenty-first century' the current world economy, by comparison with the *belle époque*, remains considerably less globalized and integrated (Gilpin 2001: 3). This is a view shared by many economic historians (for instance, O'Rourke and Williamson 2000). The implication is that, far from being unprecedented, economic globalization today is essentially a return to the developmental trajectory of the world economy inaugurated by the birth of the industrial age. Yet, for Gilpin amongst others, the world economy still has some way to go in order to achieve the levels of global capital, trade, and labour market integration of the pre-1914 era. The implication is that contemporary globalization is significantly exaggerated and thereby fundamentally misrepresented because globalists fail to locate it in its proper historical context (Hoogvelt 2001; see also Hay, Chapter 9 in this volume).

A concern with globalization as a historical process focuses upon its structural limits. Studies of the significant impacts of history, geography, borders, culture, and politics on worldwide economic integration suggest that the present phase of economic globalization, despite the globalists' claims, has not overcome the fundamental constraints of distance, national borders, and market segmentation (Feldstein and Horioka 1980; Gordon 1988; Boyer and Drache 1996; Burtless et al. 1998; Garrett 1998a; Weiss 1998; Riger and Liebfried 2003). Economic globalization is conceived as a highly contingent, rather than socially embedded, process so that any significant international economic or political crisis, such as the events of 11 September 2001, is more than likely to precipitate its rapid demise. The reimposition of many national controls on transborder movements of goods, capital, and people in the wake of the global war on terrorism prefigures the end of globalization, dependent as it is on a liberal world order of open borders.

Rather than globalization, the increased salience of these structural limits, combined with a more critical interrogation of actual international economic trends over the last three decades attests, suggest the sceptics, to the increasing segmentation rather than integration of the world economy (Berger and Dore 1996; Ruigrok and Tulder 1995; Boyer and Drache 1996; Hirst and Thompson 1999; Hay 2000; Rugman 2000). As argued in the Hay and Rugman chapters in this book (Chapters 9 and 10), the dominant patterns in the world economy over recent years have been increasing regionalization and concentration (or triadization) of economic activity. Whether by comparison with the belle époque, or by the theoretical standards of a perfectly integrated global economy, the current epoch is defined much more by the 'myth' of globalization than by its effective realization. The segmentation of

global markets along regional lines, and the dominance of OECD economies suggest the absence of significant global economic convergence that might be expected in a single, worldwide economy. Juxtaposed with recent developments, from the securitization of the world economy to the failure of the Cancun WTO trade round talks, the trends are indicative of a process of economic deglobalization rather than the emergence of a single, global economy.

These arguments amount to fundamental criticisms of the globalist case but they are by no means determinate or entirely convincing. Several points can be made in response to each of the three principal critiques.

Whether economic globalization is greater today than in the belle époque cannot be definitively determined, as many economic historians acknowledge (Obstfeld and Taylor 2003). As a point of comparison with the present it is perhaps more appropriate to identify the similarities and differences between the periods. Some of the most recent systematic studies suggest that levels of global economic integration are today comparable, if not more so on most measures, to the period of the belle époque (Geyer and Bright 1995; Bordo, Eichengreen, and Irwin 1999; Maddison 2001; Taylor 2002; Lindert and Williamson 2001; Obstfeld and Taylor 2003). As Bordo, Eichengreen, and Irwin conclude, 'the globalization of commodity and financial markets is historically unprecedented' (1999: 56). Table 8.1 demonstrates the world economy

---

Box 8.2 **Economic globalization after 9/11**

Trade

Value grew by 12.5% in 2000.

Value fell by 4% in 2001.

Value grew by 4% in 2002.

Trade value remains above level of 1980s and a much higher proportion of world GDP at around 29%.

Capital Flows

Growth of cross-border banking lending declined from $859.4 to $740.8 billion 2001–2, a fall of some 14%, but grew by 9% in the first half of 2003.

FDI inflows fell by 51% and outflows by 55% in 2002 compared to the historic peak of 2000, but remain above levels of the 1980s.

Inflows to LDCs fell by 23% 2002 but inward FDI stock was at a record 33% of GDP for LDCs compared to 19% for OECD and compared to 13% and 5% respectively for 1980.

International equity issues declined by two-thirds from $300 bn 2000 peak to $100 bn 2002.

Sources: BIS 2003; WTO (2002; 2003a); UNCTAD (2003).

Table 8.1 Epochal shifts in globalization since 1820

Epoch	Intercontinental commodity market integration		Migration and world labour markets		Integration of world capital markets
	Change in price gaps between continents	Why they changed	How migrant shares changed in receiving countries	Why they changed	What happened to integration (Feldstein–Horioka Slope Coefficient)
1820–1914	Price gaps cut by 81%	72% due to cheaper transport; 28% due to pre-1870 tariff cuts	Migrant shares rise	Passenger transport costs slashed, push and pull (immigration policies remain neutral)	60% progress from complete segmentation towards market integration
1914–50	Gaps double in width, return to 1870 level	New trade barriers only	Migrant shares fall	Restrictive immigration policies	Reversion to complete market segmentation
1950–2000, especially since 1970	Price gaps cut by 76%, now lower than in 1914	74% due to policies freeing trade, 26% due to cheaper transport	Migrant shares rise	Transport costs drop, push and pull again (no net change in immigration policies)	60% progress from complete segmentation toward market integration
Overall 1820–2000	Price gaps cut by 92%	18% due to trade policies; 82% due to cheaper transport	No clear change in US migrant shares but rises elsewhere	Policy restrictions, offsetting transport improvements	60% progress from complete segmentation toward market integration

Source: Lindert and Williamson (2003).

of the twenty-first century evidences very similar levels of integration whilst Dowrick and DeLong, two leading economic historians, conclude that 'It is hard to argue that there is any dimension . . . save mass migration in which we today are less "globalized" than our predecessors at the end of the first World War' (2003: 191).

That said, economic globalization today displays some profound *qualitative* differences from that of previous epochs. Most notable are: real-time world financial markets; the speed of economic exchange; the scale of gross economic flows of goods and short-term capital; the institutionalization of economic relations at an interregional level through global and regional organizations, MNCs, and transnational regulatory bodies; and finally the fact that globalization is much more unevenly experienced than in the *belle époque* (Geyer and Bright 1995; Deibert 1997; Held et al. 1999; Scholte 2000*b*).

The current phase of economic globalization undoubtedly displays many unique attributes—from the scale of short-term capital flows to transnational production—and a 'secular trend towards increased synchronization' of national business cycles. All of these trends produce novel political and economic dilemmas for governments (Eichengreen 1996; Rodrik 1997; Bordo and Helbling 2003: 431). As Garrett concludes, 'global market integration is qualitatively different and deeper today' (Garrett 2000*a*). Economic globalization today rivals that of the *belle époque* but it is organized and experienced in quite distinctive ways.

Most rigorous globalist accounts readily acknowledge there are limits to globalization. In rejecting the reductionist and teleological assumptions which inform many populist accounts of globalization as an inevitable and irresistible historical process, there is recognition of the significance of social, political, and institutional barriers which impede or even contest its advance. Economic globalization is conceived as a much more complex process than simply a juggernaut of world economic unification, in which distance and borders along with the weight of history and ties of culture are effectively annihilated in the construction of a single global economic space. It embodies processes of both global economic integration and segmentation, inclusion and exclusion, and convergence and divergence. National and local

economies, to varying degrees, are embedded in global economic systems whilst, to varying degrees, national and local factors mediate their impact. Distance, borders, and national differences still matter—but in different ways—under conditions of economic globalization. By comparison even the most advanced national economies are not as perfectly integrated, as is supposed by the economic textbooks, since subregional and sectoral differences do matter.

Moreover, since few economies are completely autarkic (autarky, the pursuit of national self-sufficiency as an economic strategy, appears defunct) national economic fortunes cannot be entirely decoupled from the dynamics of the world economy. This is evident in the manner and speed with which regional crises or slowdowns in world economic activity impact widely and rapidly across the globe (Bordo and Helbling 2003). In these respects the limits to globalization thesis is not incompatible with the notion of the world economy as imperfectly rather than perfectly integrated.

Not so, the sceptics proclaim, because the last three decades, they argue, have witnessed a significant regionalization of economic activity. Regionalization (see Chapters 5 and 10 in this volume) or the segmentation, rather than the globalization, of the world economy is now the principal trend (Hirst and Thompson 1999). Yet, on the contrary, interregional flows of trade, capital, and migrants have significantly increased over this period. As one leading economic historian has put it, since 1950, 'Interrelations between the different parts of the world economy have greatly intensified' (Maddison 2001: 125). This is not to argue that the regionalization and concentration of economic activity are not occurring but rather to conclude that they are not the dominant trends shaping the world economy nor are they necessarily incompatible with economic globalization since in several respects they can reinforce it (Schirm 2002). Regionalization can magnify the consequences of interregional economic integration (and vice versa). Moreover, the concentration of interregional flows within the OECD triad is principally evidence of the unevenness of economic globalization rather than regionalization *per se*.

That globalization has not measured up to the more stringent demands of neoclassical economic theory, which posits a perfectly integrated world market (of price and income convergence), is readily explicable to theorists of imperfect markets/competition and of institutional economics (Gilpin 2001). Except for the most ardent advocates of neo-liberal economics, few would argue that economic globalization can be assessed solely by measures of economic convergence because the most pronounced phase of global economic convergence, as economic historians note, was the inter-war period, paradoxically a period of unprecedented deglobalization when economies rapidly converged but towards economic collapse (Dowrick and DeLong 2003).

Economic globalization today, as in the past, is marked by patterns of both economic convergence and divergence or, in the language of classical Marxism, 'uneven (world) development'. This complexity is not captured by neoclassical or linear models of economic globalization which equate it solely with global economic convergence.

Of course, it might be contended that, since 11 September 2001, the limits to economic globalization have become even more apparent whilst the political conditions which have so far facilitated it are rapidly dissipating. For the first time in almost a decade the rate of growth of trade, capital flows, and foreign investment not only simultaneously turned negative (record falls of 4 per cent, 19 per cent to 67 per cent, and 41 per cent to 21 per cent for 2001 and 2002 respectively) but also endured for much longer than in previous global economic downturns (BIS 2003; WTO 2002; UNCTAD 2003). Corresponding falls in

the levels of trade, capital, and investment flows also set records (see Box 8.2). These falls have been experienced differentially across the world's regions and different economic sectors, with the OECD and least developed economies being subject to the most significant declines in transborder flows. Furthermore, this slowing of globalization has been accompanied by a dramatic change in the global political context evidenced in the shift from multilateralism to unilateralism, stability to growing insecurity, and soft power to hard power. For some this shift represents a permanent rejection of the liberal world order, which underwrote the second golden age of economic globalization, heralding a new period of deglobalization. For others it simply represents a slowing of the unprecedented intensity of economic globalization as it has been experienced over the last two decades.

At issue here are two related questions: whether the current slowdown of globalization is cyclical or structural and how far the altered global political environment is pushing in the latter direction. Much recent evidence suggests that economic globalization is far more socially embedded than the sceptics maintain since, despite record falls in transborder activities, these remain on almost all measures more intensive and extensive than a decade earlier (Kearney 2003). Nor is there any evidence to suggest that those domestic and transnational social forces upon which the advance of economic globalization is contingent have lost their ardour for it.

Given the scale of the global economic downturn, the prevailing political instability and global insecurity, a much greater contraction might have been expected. Overall the current condition is indicative of a cyclical downturn, since it began well before 11 September 2001, and as world growth prospects have improved so have the prospects for further economic globalization. Furthermore, as the worldwide economic and distributional impacts of slowing globalization have become increasingly apparent, those social forces which are its main beneficiaries have begun to reassert their domestic and transnational influence, especially in the wake of the failed WTO summit at Cancun, to advance the globalization project, even if in a slightly modified form. As Harold James explains in his analysis of the collapse of the previous era of globalization, the *belle époque*, 'the pendulum is so slow in swinging back from globality'

Box 8.3 **Sceptical argument**

1 Globalization is exaggerated and far from historically unprecedented.

2 The world economy was much more integrated and open during the *belle époque* of 1870–1914 when interest rates, commodity prices, and wages showed significant signs of convergence.

3 Regionalization and triadization, not globalization, are the dominant trends in the contemporary world economy.

4 Globalization is a myth which serves the interests of particular social and political forces.

today because of its global institutional embeddedness but also crucially because of the absence of any viable political alternative to an open world economy (James 2001: 224).

What then is to be made of economic globalization today? If not historically unprecedented, it is certainly more than comparable to that of the *belle époque* although today it is uniquely configured and constituted. As Garrett remarks, 'No matter how many different numbers are presented . . . the growth of international activity in the past thirty years remains staggering' (Garrett 2000*a*). Moreover, the combined and cumulative globalization of trade, finance, production, and to a lesser extent labour link together the economic prosperity and security of the world's major regions and through them the world's economic hinterlands. A worldwide economy is in the making constituted by, and through, the infrastructures and dynamics of economic globalization. This process of global economic integration, however, is highly uneven such that it is associated with both economic convergence and divergence, as different economies/subregions/sectors are differentially integrated into this globalizing world economic order. Globalization is the dominant, but not the sole, dynamic of the world economy whilst processes of regionalization (or segmentation) are in many respects compatible with, rather than necessarily contrary to, it.

Of course acknowledging that globalization is a key force in shaping the nature of the contemporary global political economy is quite separate from drawing any particular conclusions about its consequences for the state or the global economic condition. Such matters require separate investigation and theorization (see Hay, Chapter 9 in this volume). Having established the 'really existing condition' of globalization the focus in this chapter logically turns to the prior but cardinal question, namely, what forces are driving this further 'extraordinary episode' in the history of the world economy?

Key points

- Globalization is not a singular process but its economic dimension is critical.
- Economic globalization defines the principal trend in the contemporary global economy.
- It is associated with growing but uneven worldwide economic integration.
- Regionalization and segmentation are not entirely incompatible with economic globalization.
- To date globalizing tendencies have been moderated by the consequences of the war on terror but there is no evidence of a structural shift or epochal change in the direction of deglobalization.

The logics of globalization

Identifying the causes of economic globalization is a difficult and tricky intellectual task. Difficult because there are multiple dynamics at work, and tricky because the very notion of causation raises some thorny philosophical questions. Casting the latter aside for the moment, it is important to be clear about what is being explained here: in other words it is necessary to identify whether the focus is upon the *general* determinants of economic globalization or the determinants of the *current* phase of economic globalization. Explaining one is not quite the same as explaining the other (Robertson 2003). Given the story so far the focus will be primarily, but not

exclusively, upon the latter. The complexity of contemporary economic globalization is such that the search for a single, determinate logic is likely to prove unsuccessful since 'in explaining social change no single and sovereign mechanism can be specified' (Giddens 1984: 243).

In crude terms, the literature distinguishes between thick or thin conceptions of causation. In its thickest sense, causality implies determination in the last instance, insofar as causes are considered both necessary and/or sufficient to bring about, an event or given social phenomenon (Mellor 1995: 6). Thus technology, it is often argued, is the cause of globalization because it is sufficient to bring it about whilst it could not have occurred in its absence. Thinner conceptions of causation refer to dispositions, in the sense of the conditions, tendencies, or factors which make given events or social phenomena more rather than less likely or probable (McCullagh 1998: 173). So the liberalization of national economies, following the political revolution of neo-liberalism in the 1980s, can be viewed as a cause of economic globalization to the extent that it made it more rather than less probable, and thereby not simply a historical accident or arbitrary development. The thinnest conceptions of causation emphasize the contingency of events—that they could readily be otherwise—in that globalization is viewed almost as an accident of circumstances. However, since many complex social phenomena, such as economic globalization, involve a multiplicity of causes, few theorists of globalization adopt either a totally determinist or totally contingent explanatory account. Before examining these theories in some detail, it will be helpful to analyse the principal logics of globalization.

Principal logics

Explanations of economic globalization tend to focus on three interrelated factors or social forces, namely: technics (technological change and social organization); economics (markets and capitalism); and politics (ideas, interests, and institutions). Since they are so interrelated the principal methodological problem for analysts lies in unbundling the causal mechanisms involved (Garrett 2000a). Distinguishing them analytically is the first step. This will be followed in a subsequent section by an exploration of how some of the principal theories combine and configure these three causal logics in their explanatory accounts of contemporary economic globalization.

Technics is central to any account of globalization since it is a truism that without modern communications infrastructures in particular, a worldwide economy would not be possible. All writers refer to the transformation in communications and transport technologies and the way in which this has 'shrunk the globe'. 'Action at a distance' increasingly transcends national borders, not to mention continents, such that time and space are compressed. In this process the distinction between domestic economic activity and global economic activity becomes less easy to sustain as global markets evolve. Rather than the liberalization of national economies driving globalization, it can be argued that technological change drives liberalization, especially in the financial sector (Garrett 2000a). Modern communication technology not only provides the infrastructure of a real-time global economy but also facilitates new forms of transnational and global economic organization from production through to regulation.

This informatics revolution has underwritten not only the infrastructure of an evolving global economy but also, according to Dicken and others, a 'global shift' (Dicken 2003). This is expressed in the combined move towards service-based or post-industrial economies within the advanced core of the world economy and the associated rise of industrial economies in the developing world. To paraphrase Giddens, 'technology is inherently globalizing' insofar as contemporary economic globalization is conceived as a product of the second industrial revolution—the logic of the informatics age.

Crucial as technology is to any account of economic globalization so too is its specifically *economic* logic. This is discussed in two distinct sets of literature: that of orthodox economics which explains globalization in terms of market dynamics; and that of radical political economy which explains it in terms of the imperatives of capitalism. In the case of the former, globalization is considered a direct consequence of market competition whether, as in the case of trade, in terms of the operation of comparative or strategic advantage, or in relation to transnational production in terms of imperfect competition or the product cycle (Dunning 1993; Gilpin 2001).

The structure and functioning of markets is conceived as central to understanding the competitive dynamics which lead inevitably to the globalization of economic activity. Drawing upon both neoclassical and new economic theories, the principal concern is with identifying the specifically economic logic—understood in terms of the pursuit of profit, wealth, and market position—which explains the process of global economic integration and the location or distribution of economic activity. By contrast, radical political economy draws upon the Marxist tradition that locates economic globalization in the

---

Box 8.4 Economic theory and globalization

1 Neo-classical theory explains globalization in terms of comparative advantage, market forces, and economic convergence.

2 Free trade involves economies trading what they have—a comparative advantage or efficiency in producing—so in theory maximizing both the national and the global welfare.

3 Market forces and global competition ensure that similar goods and services are produced efficiently and at a minimum cost.

4 Market convergence ensures that prices and interest rates in a globalizing economy become increasing equalized or differences increasingly narrowed.

5 New trade theory, locational theory, and the theory of imperfect competition explain why perfectly competitive global markets do not exist and why market segmentation (differences and lack of complete convergence) occurs even in a globalizing world economy.

---

expansionary and universalizing logic of modern capitalism. This expansionary logic is a product of capitalism's structural contradictions—the tendency for overproduction combined with the relative impoverishment of workers—and its insatiable requirement for capital accumulation, that is, profit. Economic globalization is driven by the continual search amongst the corporate sector for new markets, cheaper labour, and new sources of profitability; a process facilitated and encouraged by governments and the agencies of global economic governance as they function to reproduce the very system on which their political legitimacy partly depends (Callinicos 2003). In short, the specifically economic logic of globalization arises from both the dynamics of markets and the dynamics of capitalism.

Politics—shorthand here for ideas, interests, and institutions—constitutes the third logic of economic globalization. Almost all accounts of contemporary globalization make reference to the rise and dominance of neo-liberal ideology throughout the OECD world, along with its associated policies of liberalization, deregulation, and privatization. If technology provides the physical infrastructure of economic globalization it is the significant movement towards 'market-driven politics' (Leys 2001)—greater emphasis on laissez-faire capitalism—which provides its normative infrastructure.

Irrespective of the party holding office, the dominant political trend over the last three decades in OECD states has been towards the liberalization of national economies and the easing of restrictions on capital mobility. This has enabled, some might argue driven, the creation of more integrated global markets and the globalization of production. Governments, or rather states, have been central to the process of economic globalization. They have been instrumental in establishing both the necessary national political conditions and policies, not to mention vital regional and global institutions, agreements, and policies, essential to its advancement. Promoted and advocated by a powerful configuration of domestic and transnational coalitions and lobbies, economic globalization is very much a political construction or project. It depends upon a particular configuration of social and political forces, both national and transnational, to sustain or accelerate its momentum against the background of an established but rising anti-globalization political backlash.

Central to the politics of the current globalization project is the hegemonic power and role of the United States, as the world's sole hyper-power. To the extent that a liberal world economic order, as Gilpin (2001) and others argue, is a by-product of US global dominance, then shifts in US strategic interests and domestic politics will have significant consequences for economic globalization. On the other hand, to the extent that the relative economic power of the United States has been eroded in recent years, the politics of globalization has become far more complex, not to say shaped, by the interplay between all the principal global economic players—states, international organizations, and transnational corporations—as well as the agencies of transnational civil society. In sum, contemporary economic globalization has an underlying political logic insofar as it is the product of political ideology, national or international public policy, the interests and interactions between states, global institutions, and global social forces.

In different measure and combination these three logics—technics, economics, and politics—inform the principal theories of globalization to be found in the existing literature. All theories, to differing degrees, draw upon these three logics in identifying the causal mechanisms of contemporary economic globalization. How they do so is explored in the following section.

Principal theories

As Rosenberg (2000) observes, there are many theories of globalization—its causes and dynamics—but little substantive globalization theory. This distinction is important in that it suggests that most existing theories of globalization are parasitic upon, if not entirely subservient to, the 'grand theories' of social science. To date, no discrete or singular globalization theory—which seeks to provide a coherent and systematic account of its causes, consequences, and developmental trajectory—can be said to exist. Nor is there any singular theory of globalization, only a proliferation of schools and analyses. Accordingly, the emphasis here will be upon the identification of distinctive types of theory and subsequently the elaboration and critical examination of their most significant formulations.

Few convincing accounts of economic globalization, given its complexity, locate its origins in a single causal logic. However, existing theories do make judgements both about the relative significance or configuration of different causal logics, in effect privileging some over others in their explanatory narratives. Along the continuum from thicker to thinner forms of causal explanation, accounts vary according to whether they give preference to the structural, the conjunctural, or to the contingent sources of economic globalization.

Broadly speaking, structural explanations are thick causal accounts because they tend towards the deter-

ministic: they highlight the imperatives or developmental logic of social and economic systems. Thus, structuralist accounts of economic globalization explain it in terms of the imperatives or drivers of technological advance and/or capital accumulation. Globalization is considered almost an *inevitable* consequence of either modern technologically advanced societies—recall Giddens' dictum that 'modernity is inherently globalizing'—or the expansionary imperatives of capitalism. Whilst structuralist accounts can answer the why and how questions of globalization— why it came about and how—they are less valuable in explaining its specific historical form (what kind?) or timing (why then?).

By contrast, conjunctural explanations are much better at explaining its timing and its form as well as its more historically specific causes. Conjunctural accounts, which are causally thinner than structural explanations, pay more attention to the confluence of particular historical circumstances, trends, and events which together combine to produce a given social phenomenon at a specific point in time and in a given form. As McCullagh (1998: 178) summarizes it, 'the cause of an event is a conjunction of things which together have a tendency to produce a certain kind of outcome'. Thus, contemporary economic globalization can be understood as a consequence of a multiplicity of tendencies (technological, economic, etc.) interacting with particular historical conditions and policies (the end of the Cold War) to produce its distinctive (neo-liberal) form. Rather than stressing the inevitability of globalization, conjunctural explanations stress its *conditionality*.

Finally, accounts which stress the contingency of economic globalization emphasize its causal indeterminacy—the lack of any convincing specifiable causal mechanism. Although such explanations may be less relevant to answering the 'why' question, they are particularly pertinent to addressing the 'how, when and what' type questions. As such these might be considered very thin, rather than thick, causal accounts of economic globalization because they stress its almost *incidental* or *arbitrary*, rather than inevitable or conditional, origins. Attention therefore tends to be focused much more upon the role of ideas—economic globalization as an idea or prevailing discourse—rather than seeking to identify specific causal patterns or mechanisms within the

Table 8.2 Economic globalization: types of theory

	Causal mechanism	Causal dynamics
Structural	Imperatives of domestic and international systems	Imperatives Inevitability Irresistible Determinate
Conjunctural	Emergent properties of confluence of separate logics and circumstances	Conditional Tendencies Dispositions Reversible
Constructivist	Ideas and discourses as constitutive	Contingent Unpredictable Incidental Indeterminate

empirical evidence of globalizing trends (Schirato and Webb 2003: 21). Accordingly, it can be argued that understanding the social or discursive construction of economic globalization is just as—some would say, more—important as identifying underlying causal patterns in the empirical data.

Structural theories of economic globalization can be distinguished by whether they privilege domestic or global structures. Those that emphasize the primacy of domestic structures locate the sources of economic globalization in the nature and dynamics of modern societies. Since the nineteenth century French philosopher Saint-Simon wrote of the universalizing logic of industrial societies, the primacy of technology as the motor of globalization has figured prominently in the political economy literature. This thesis is to be found, in more nuanced and less deterministic formulations in the work of Strange (1998), Garrett (2000*a*), Rosecrance (1999), and Ohmae (1990), amongst others.

Technology is privileged in such explanations not simply because it has shrunk the globe but also because it is often conceived as the principal dynamic of social change in advanced societies. Just as the technological revolution of industrialism transformed European agricultural societies, so today the information revolution is transforming the nature of production and social organization. In this 'virtualization' process, to borrow Rosecrance's (1999) label, borders no longer define the boundaries of national economic space whilst distance becomes a

less significant or costly barrier, although not entirely irrelevant, to the organization of production and economic activity. Moreover, this technological revolution enables firms and national economies, irrespective almost of geographic location, to exploit their comparative economic advantage and specialize further in the production and trading of those goods and services at which they are most efficient. Technological change, in other words, brings in its wake both economic change and political change in the form of globalized markets and the liberalization of economies. Since continual technological innovation is a structural (recursive) feature of modern (and modernizing) societies, then economic globalization, notwithstanding its cyclical fluctuations, is an inevitable feature of the contemporary global political economy.

That technology is a necessary requirement of economic globalization is not doubted, but for neo-Marxist theorists it is by no means a sufficient explanation. It is the capitalist form of the economy that is the crucial explanatory factor, not technology, which is subservient to the dynamics of capitalist accumulation and competition. Wood (2003: 14–15) summarizes this argument well: 'Capitalism . . . is driven by certain systemic imperatives, the imperatives of competition, profit-maximization and accumulation . . . globalization is their result rather than their cause.' The sources of globalization are therefore located in the requirement of capitalism constantly to acquire new markets and produce more efficiently in order to sustain levels of profitability and reproduce itself. Cultivating global markets and producing abroad to maximize profits and corporate efficiency are the consequence of the structural imperatives and contradictions of capitalist economies rather than technological innovation *per se*.

Moreover, these expansionary tendencies are shaped by intensifying economic competition and the resulting concentration of economic power in huge national and transnational corporations that can readily exploit new technologies and economies of scale to produce more efficiently and compete more effectively both at home and abroad. Liberalization and the rolling back of the state, reinforced by the disciplines of global institutions such as the WTO and IMF, are conceived ultimately as responses to these developments rather than the author of them. Such accounts do not deny the importance of political agency or the strategic action of states and other social forces, but rather assert that in the very last instance these are of only marginal causal significance in explaining economic globalization (though they are highly relevant to understanding the particular form it takes, for example, Empire in the nineteenth century versus Corporate globalization in the twentieth century).

In that the main engines of capitalist globalization are located in a small number of OECD economies, there is some disagreement as to whether the contemporary period is best described as a renewed phase of capitalist imperialism, a distinctly new form of globalized capitalism system or, alternatively, a historically novel global capitalist empire (Hardt and Negri 2000; Callinicos 2003; Gill 2003; Wood 2003). Irrespective of how it is characterized, the principal logic of contemporary economic globalization is located, in neo-Marxist theory, firmly with the imperatives of capitalist development.

Beyond these domestic level explanations, other structural theories give priority to international or global system level structures. Within all the major schools of theory in global political economy—realist, liberal, and neo-Marxist—frequent emphasis is placed upon the role of hegemony—or the dominance or pre-eminence of a single power or superpower—in creating and maintaining the conditions for an open world economy and so economic globalization. In effect, the hierarchical structure of power relations in the global political economy creates the necessary conditions for economic globalization. Despite their otherwise radically different theoretical positions, Gilpin, Ikenberry, and Wallerstein all assert that hegemony is an essential condition for the development and perpetuation of a globalizing world economy (Wallerstein 1983; Gilpin 1987; Ikenberry 2001). Without a hegemonic power capable of establishing a stable and managed world order, both through persuasion and coercion, economic globalization would be little more than an ideal. It is hegemony that makes an open world economy possible. That said it is also an essential precondition of economic globalization that the hegemonic power is a liberal-capitalist power and thus has a material interest in creating and sustaining a liberalized world economic order as opposed to a world empire. In this

respect hegemonic theory is entirely compatible with domestic level structural accounts which consider economic globalization a consequence of the imperatives of capitalist accumulation and market forces. However, to the extent that the hegemonic power becomes predatory or unilateralist the necessary conditions for economic globalization will be eroded.

By contrast the relative decline of the hegemon, as Keohane (1984) suggests, may have little impact to the extent that globalization is highly institutionalized. Under current conditions, the reassertion of US hegemony is likely to hamper, if not undermine, economic globalization if Washington pursues a unilateralist or predatory agenda, or alternatively reinvigorate it if it seeks to advance the further liberalization of the world economy. Of course, theory also points to the limits, contradictions, and ultimate erosion of hegemonic power suggesting that economic globalization has to be understood as a historical phenomenon (Gilpin 1981).

Whereas structural theories explain economic globalization as a path-dependent outcome of systemic—whether domestic or international—imperatives, by contrast *conjunctural* accounts are rooted in a much more historicized form of analysis. This is not to suggest that structural forces or tendencies are ignored—on the contrary they form the context of any historical analysis—but rather they are combined with a greater attention to the unique configuration of political, social, and global conditions which prefigured contemporary economic globalization. There is also a greater recognition of the role of strategic action by governments or other key agencies, and the interaction between social forces, political institutions, and ideas in advancing or constraining processes of global economic integration. Rather than an inevitability, economic globalization is understood as being 'rooted in history and shaped by particular political, social and cultural conditions . . . a conjunctural correlation of forces that are subject to reversal' (Petras and Veltmeyer 2001: 46). Amongst the most comprehensive studies in this context is Castells's three-volume study of the rise of 'global informational capitalism' (Castells 1996, 1997, 1998).

Castells sets out to explain the most recent phase of economic globalization, which he dates to the 1980s, rather than to produce a generalizable account of economic globalization *per se*. Castells identifies the principal sources of this new *belle époque* in the profound restructuring of the major capitalist economies, itself a response to the economic, and political crises of the 1970s (Castells 2000). This period was characterized by historic shifts in the technological, economic, and political spheres that, although insufficient in themselves to forge a new epoch of globalization, in conjunction provided the vital conditions which enabled it to flourish. Just as two atoms of hydrogen combine with one atom of oxygen to produce a new substance called water so, by analogy, the specific configuration and conjunction of developments in these three spheres—technics, economics, and politics—gave rise to the current epoch of globalization. In other words globalization emerged out of—in more technical language is an emergent property of—the particular confluence of historical developments in the technological, economic, and political domains (Sayer 2000: 12). What then were these significant developments?

According to Castells, they were respectively the information technology revolution, capitalist restructuring, and the political hegemony of the neoliberal project (Castells 2000: Prologue). Tracing these developments to the dissipation, in the 1970s, of the post-war system of managed capitalism, Castells identifies in the informatics revolution of the 1980s a new production paradigm that facilitated a process of global economic restructuring. As the major economies increasingly became service based (post-industrial) or in Castells's language 'informational', manufacturing industry began shifting abroad. This deindustrialization in the core economies was accompanied by industrialization in its hinterlands. However, as he argues, this 'Restructuring of business firms, and the new information technologies, while being at the source of globalizing trends, could not have evolved, by themselves, toward a networked global economy without policies of de-regulation, privatization, and the liberalization of trade and investment' (Castells 2000: 147).

Politics, but more specifically the advocacy and implementation of neo-liberal (market-enhancing) ideas, policies, and institutional (both national and global) reforms, played a significant role in this process to the extent that he argues, 'The decisive agents in setting up a new global economy were governments, and, in particular, the governments of the wealthiest countries, the G7, and their ancillary insti-

tutions' (Castells 2000: 137). The advance of this political project was also greatly assisted by the collapse of communism and thus any feasible political alternative to the capitalist model of development. For Castells, the emergence of a historically unique 'global informational capitalism' that has 'the institutional, organizational, and technological capacity to work as a unit in real time, or in chosen time, on a planetary scale' can be traced to the specific historical conjuncture of technological, economic, and political developments beginning in the 1980s (Castells 2000: 104).

Castells' analysis of globalization is amongst the most comprehensive and sophisticated. However, as with other conjunctural accounts (Scholte 2000b; Gill 2003), it is vulnerable to the criticism that in advocating an essentially multi-causal account, it simply avoids specifying a coherent or convincing causal mechanism. In simpler language, since almost *every* key factor is regarded as a cause of globalization by definition nothing in particular can be said to be its specific cause. To critics, conjunctural accounts do not so much explain—that is, identify a causal mechanism or mechanisms—so much as provide a rich description of economic globalization.

This judgement is a little harsh because it presumes a strongly scientific or positivistic model of causation identified with some determinate causal mechanism. By contrast, historical or interpretative models of causation accept such causal complexity (McCullagh 1998; Sayer 2000; Benton and Craib 2001). Nevertheless, for other critics a more fundamental problem is that conjunctural analyses fail to accept, although they imply, the essential indeterminacy or contingency of complex social phenomena, such as globalization, and thus cannot really claim adequately to explain it (Wendt 1998).

Economic globalization refers to both a process of growing material interconnectedness as well as the 'idea' or consciousnesses of that process. Obviously, the two are interrelated but in quite complex ways. *Social constructivist* analyses are far more interested in the idea of economic globalization and why it has become such a pervasive discourse or way of talking and theorizing about the world economy. Although they do not discount the relevance of globalization's material manifestations—in terms of flows of trade, investment—social constructivists are far more interested in its ideational or discursive construction. In this respect they argue, to paraphrase Wendt, that globalization is what states and others make of it, rather than a preordained or objective condition, and as such is a largely contingent or arbitrary phenomenon (Wendt 1992).

Rather than seeking to identify the causal mechanisms which generate globalization, constructivists seek to explore how widely shared ideas or discourses about economic globalization are constitutive of—that is, make real or give meaning to—the very process itself, for example, the popular discourse or idea of globalization as an inevitable or irresistible juggernaut of change. In simple terms there can be no economic globalization without the idea or discourse of economic globalization. This is not to argue that globalization is purely a product of the collective imagination. On the contrary it is simply to acknowledge that in naming or identifying the material trends in the world economy as a process of 'economic globalization', that process becomes socially or discursively constructed. This process of social construction, moreover, has an important bearing upon how globalization is explained and understood both in and beyond the academy. Accordingly, to make sense of globalization it is necessary to deconstruct or unpack the dominant ideas or discourses which inform how it is generally understood or conceived and the extent to which such ideas or discourses reflect or misconstrue contemporary world economic trends.

As Petras and Veltmeyer (2001: 11) observe, 'Globalization is both a description and a prescription, and as such, it serves as both an explanation . . . and an ideology that currently dominates thinking, policy making and political practice.' Those studies which have drawn upon the insights of this kind of social constructivist methodology generally tend to conclude that the genesis and diffusion of the 'idea of economic globalization' is more important to understanding and explaining the contemporary global economic condition than is a rigorous assessment of the actual evidence of global economic integration (Hay and Watson 1998; Rosamond 2001; Schmidt 2002). For the constructivists, the evidence is less important than the actual fact that to the extent that states, social forces, and international agencies perceive and understand the world principally within the discourse of globalization, they reproduce and perpetuate it to a large extent irrespective of what the actual historical trends disclose. There are also very good reasons why they do so, and in this context political interest and motivations—the power of political agency—becomes of critical importance. Irrespective of the objective existence of globalization, it is incontrovertible that the *idea* of economic globalization plays a crucial role in coordinating, communicating, and legitimating a range of diverse political projects, from the politics of the Third Way to the politics of the New Right (Schmidt 2002). Economic globalization, in such accounts, is therefore distinguished by its essential *contingency* more than its inevitability. It is as much, if not more of, an ideational, rather than an economic, construction. As such it is not determined by collective ideas but rather constituted by, and through, them with significant consequences for the politics of globalization (see Hay, Chapter 9 in this volume).

Making sense of the logics of economic globalization

How are these different accounts of the causes of economic globalization to be assessed? Do these distinctive types of theory offer competing or

---

Box 8.5 **Causal and constitutive theory**

1 Causal theories refer to explanations which identify specific or general causal mechanisms which can be said to be both necessary and/or sufficient to produce the social effects or social phenomenon which is the object of analysis.

2 Constitutive theories refer to explanations which demonstrate how ideas, values, and beliefs or discourses about the world actually construct 'reality' and thus constitute, in part, the very social phenomenon under investigation.

3 An intense debate exists as to whether causal and constitutive theories are different or similar kinds of explanations and, thus, whether in effect reasons can be considered, in the strictest sense, to be causes.

Table 8.3 Economic globalization summary: types of theories and forms of explanation

	Principal methodological focus	Causal mechanisms	Focus	Indicative account of globalization
Structural	Focus on organizing principles of domestic and international systems Holistic analysis Emphasis on dynamics or 'laws' of the social totality	Tends towards (economic, technological or political) determinism Emphasis upon inevitability, irresistible forces Path-dependent outcomes	Why and How questions	Ohmae/Rosecrance—technics primary causal logic Woods—imperatives of capitalism Gilpin/Wallerstein—political imperatives of hegemony-globalization as Americanization
Conjunctural	Unique configuration of social forces and historical circumstances Political decisions and agency	Emphasis on tendencies and conditional factors Confluence of events and circumstances Emergent properties	How When and What form	Castells—global informational capitalism product of conjuncture of technics, economics and political developments in 1980s
Constructivist	Role of ideas crucial in shaping how agents view and act on the world Discourse of globalization—globe talk—constructs the way the world is perceived Discourse of economic globalization constitutes it rather than simply mirrors it	Constitutive rather than causal explanation—globalization is made real through discourse Emphasis upon motivations, interests, ideas and political agency	When and What form	Schmidt—how the discourse of globalization came to play the crucial role in coordinating, communicating, and legitimating European government economic strategies in the 1990s

complementary explanations? Is a 'grand theory' of economic globalization attainable? Such questions flow naturally from an examination of the theoretical pluralism which is the hallmark of global political economy. If there is no singular or universal theory of globalization this is partly, but not exclusively, a consequence of the fact that there is no universally accepted set of criteria—or epistemology—by which the validity of theories of global political economy can be judged. This does not mean that rational judgements cannot be made as to which theories present a more or less convincing account of globalization but simply that such judgements cannot in any sense establish its 'truth'—or true causes. Quite simply the problem is that, as within the social sciences more generally, an appeal to the evidence or the 'facts' of globalization largely proves inconclusive since the 'facts' are often compatible with competing theories, that is, theories are underdetermined. Thus, for instance, the evidence discussed in the first part of the chapter supports theories which identify both technology and politics as the principal cause of globalization. Accordingly, rather than seeking the unattainable grail of objective truth a more productive approach may be to explore how these three distinctive types of theory might be combined and so contribute to a more comprehensive understanding and explanation of the logics of economic globalization.

In a very interesting article Eric Helleiner (1997) seeks to realize precisely that goal. Drawing upon the scholarship of Fernand Braudel, a renowned social historian, Helleiner concludes that to understand and explain economic globalization as a historical and social process it is necessary to adopt and combine different temporal perspectives. These distinct temporal perspectives reflect the different pace of historical time: from the *longue durée* of centuries over which change can appear to have a glacial momentum shaped as it is by deeper social structures and recurrent patterns of socio-economic organization, through the 'episodic', 'epochal', or conjunctural in which the pattern of socio-economic change over several decades seems to prefigure the emergence of a new era or social formation, to *l'histoire événementielle* or contemporary existence in which social agents—from individuals to governments—are daily engaged in reacting to, or in, seeking to shape, events and circumstances as they perceive and interpret them. As Helleiner (1997: 95) suggests, these 'three temporal perspectives are useful not just in describing economic globalization, but also in understanding and explaining it'.

A direct correspondence may be observed between these temporal perspectives and the three types of theory elaborated in the preceding section: the *longue durée* is associated with structural theory; the episodic with conjunctural theory; and the existential/contingent with constructivist theory.

As Gilpin (2001: 364) observes, 'globalization has been taking place for centuries'. Understood as a process of secular historical development, economic globalization might therefore be best explained through the medium of structural theories which locate its causes in the dynamics of enduring systems or recurrent patterns of socio-economic organization. Thus economic globalization can be understood as an intrinsic feature of the modern age: of modern societies and the modern international state system or, to use a grand term, modernity. Conceived from a temporal vantage point of the *longue durée*, economic globalization appears as a chronic or persistent—although by no means linear—historical trend which, as Helleiner (1997: 95) comments, 'also makes it seem an almost irreversible one'. To understand and explain economic globalization therefore, requires some account of the deeply embedded structures of the global political economy—capitalism, industrialism, hegemony, etc.—which are its underlying drivers. At one level such accounts are essential, since although they cannot explain its specific historical features or rhythms, they do offer insights into why economic globalization has been a recurring feature of the global political economy for many centuries.

By contrast, particular historical episodes or epochs of intensifying economic globalization, like that of today, are better explained by conjunctural theories. Such theories principally seek to account for the cyclical and historical rhythms of economic globalization: how and why it accelerates or contracts at different historical moments and the specific configuration it takes—from empire to global markets. In so doing such accounts emphasize discontinuity, rather than continuity (as in structural accounts) with the past. Thus the entire debate about whether contemporary globalization is unprecedented by comparison with the *belle époque* is indicative of an episodic temporal perspective. Understood from such a perspective the origins of contemporary economic globalization are to be located in a particular conjunction of factors and forces within a specific historical context. This provides a different frame of reference to the structural, because it suggests that economic globalization is 'also a clearly reversible process' since the conjuncture of forces which hold it together at any one moment may (or will) eventually dissipate (Helleiner 1997: 95). Conjunctural accounts thereby complement structural theories because they provide an explanation of globalization's episodic and discontinuous evolutionary pattern, offering specific insights into what drives it forward (or backward) at particular moments in history.

Finally, from an existential or immediate temporal perspective, Helleiner notes that economic globalization 'often appears as a political weapon used and promoted by certain groups' as 'a project in which the local is increasingly "globalized" . . . in an active and deliberate way' (Helleiner 1997: 96).

Explanations that emphasize motivations, strategic actions, and the political struggles over globalization offer significant insights into its immediate origins. Such accounts complement both structural and conjunctural theories because they can explain how and why economic globalization comes to be constructed through the multiplicity of actions of, and interactions between, individual and collective (political and economic) subjects or agents, from consumers to corporations and protestors to politicians. From this existential perspective economic globalization appears entirely contingent or arbitrary. This requires an explanation of the motives, interests, ideas, and institutions that are constitutive of such action. In providing this, constructivist theories of economic globalization—which emphasize its essential contingency—function to correct those marked tendencies in structural and conjunctural accounts which downplay the significance of political agency—ideas, motivations, and choices. In so doing the former very much complements the latter.

For much the same reasoning that economic globalization is considered causally complex, necessitating a multi-causal analysis, so too, following Helleiner (1997: 102), must it also be conceived as a 'layered' historical process, that is, 'taking place at several different historical speeds'. Accordingly, understanding and explaining the current phase of economic globalization requires a causal analysis which is not only sensitive to its multiple logics—technics, economics, and politics—but also to its multiple speeds—the *longue durée*, episodic, and existential. No single theory, or account, of economic globalization meets, or is ever likely to, such demanding requirements (Rosenberg 2000). This should not induce academic despondency, since as argued, by drawing upon intellectually compatible structural, conjunctural, and constructivist theories a more systematic and layered analysis of economic globalization is entirely feasible,

even if this falls short of the explanatory properties of an ideal globalization theory.

Key points

- Economic globalization is conceived as having three logics: technics, economics, and politics.

- There are three main types of theory associated with economic globalization: structural, conjunctural, and constructivist.

- These can be distinguished in terms of their causal mechanisms: imperatives, conditional, and contingent.

- Understanding globalization as a historical process involves examining it in terms of three speeds of social change: the *longue durée*, the episodic, and the existential moment.

- The three theories of globalization correspond with each of these three speeds so explaining economic globalization from a different temporal perspective.

- The three theories of economic globalization are, therefore, in principal complementary producing a layered explanation from its structured to its contingent origins.

A world transformed? The prospects for economic globalization

Accepting the existing condition of economic globalization does not presuppose any particular line of argument about its future development or its consequences or ramifications for the global political economy. Nevertheless, it is possible to offer some general remarks, rooted in the previous discussion, in response to the provocative 'so what?' question, that is, why does the study of causes matter?

Drawing upon the analytical and temporal distinctions in the preceding analysis it is possible to sketch out three broad arguments about the politics and

governance of economic globalization and thus its future trajectory. These are necessarily truncated and oversimplified rehearsals of the more substantive debates discussed in other chapters (see in particular Hay, Chapter 9 in this volume). It is in identifying the consequences of economic globalization for politics and governance that dramatic differences of interpretation between the structural, conjunctural, and constructivist theories become evident. As noted, the *longue durée* perspective is associated with structural theories of economic globalization which in turn tend to accept its inevitability, if not inexorability. Governance and politics—whether at a global, national, or local level—are thereby conceived as highly constrained by the limits and opportunities for active intervention imposed by the operation of global markets, capitalist imperatives, and US hegemony. Operating within these parameters, the role of politics and governance is principally functional: to stabilize the global political economy and provide it with some legitimacy, most especially in times of crisis. Beyond these parameters they have a marginal impact, especially in 'taming' or resisting globalization, such that they tend to be regarded as largely epiphenomenal—that is having a symbolic but not a practical function. Of course only in its most hyperglobalist or deterministic formulations is the room for politics so narrowly defined (Greider 1997). In sum: globalization conceived as the result of technological, capitalist, or hegemonic imperatives induces a sensitivity to the limits to politics consonant with the reproduction of the global political economy in its current capitalist form: the future trajectory of economic globalization is unlikely to be fundamentally altered by the ebb and flow of current political developments.

By contrast, episodic or cyclical perspectives, and their associated conjunctural analyses, give particular weight to politics and governance in coordinating and managing the global political economy. In key respects the politics of the major states and the institutions of global economic governance are conceived as playing a critical role in forging and managing economic globalization. As Castells (2000: 147) argues, economic globalization and the globalized economy to which it gave rise 'was politically constituted'. Politics, in other words, provides the ideological, institutional, and motivational resin which sutured together the conjuncture of circumstances and the correlation of social forces that facilitated and fuelled the current epoch of economic globalization. However, once unleashed, the dynamics of economic globalization cannot be readily undone such that the politics and governance of the global political economy is transformed into a contest between the very powerful technological, economic, and social forces driving globalization forward and those much weaker (but arguably more numerous) social forces

contesting its logic. As Castells (2000: 147) concludes any 'decoupling from the global economy implies a staggering cost: the devastation of the economy in the short-term, and the closing of access to sources of growth'. Under these conditions politics is a critical, although not necessarily the determining, factor in shaping the future trajectory of economic globalization. In particular, political choices are constrained. In other words the future trajectory of globalization, notwithstanding major war or economic collapse, will be shaped through the interaction between its political and its economic logics: that is, in the vortex of politics and markets. In this respect a *political economy* reading of globalization is thereby all but essential.

Finally, a temporal perspective which focuses upon current events encourages an emphasis upon the contingency of economic globalization and thus its essential political malleability. Insofar as globalization is what politicians and social forces make of it, then its future trajectory will be principally a consequence of their perceptions and political decisions. To the extent that substantive political agendas, interests, priorities, and policies are modified in response to the hegemonically defined threat of global terrorism then the globalization project may be increasingly displaced by the new war on global terror. The politics and governance of globalization will be transformed from a major focus of public and academic attention to a largely incidental matter. For many this may be a comforting thought—the real end to globalization—but for others it will simply represent the substitution of one hegemonic social construction of the global political economy by yet another which is distinguished only by its entirely more alarming and incoherent logic (Mann 2003).

The future trajectory of economic globalization is wholly speculative. That it is so is both a source of intellectual despair and huge relief. Despair since it reaffirms the explanatory weakness of existing theories. Relief because it confirms the future remains to be made, even if not within conditions of human choosing, to paraphrase Marx. As such, the politics and governance of globalization undoubtedly will play a significant role in the making of the twenty-first-century global political economy, hopefully for the better, but quite possibly for the worse.

QUESTIONS

1   What are the principal causes of globalization?

2   Is economic globalization a product of technology or of capitalism, or both?

3   'Technics made globalization.' Discuss.

4   In what sense, if any, do constructivist theories provide a convincing account of the origins of economic globalization?

5   Which is more convincing: the globalist or sceptical analysis of economic globalization?

6   Outline the globalist case and critically evaluate it with reference to the historical evidence.

7   Why does it matter if the world economy was more economically integrated in the *belle époque*?

8   How does Braudel's analysis help us to understand the logics of economic globalization?

9   Critically assess the argument that economic globalization is simply a political project.

10   'Economic globalization is much more limited than many realize' (Gilpin 2001). Critically assess this proposition with reference to contemporary global economic trends.

FURTHER READING

Amin, S. (1997), *Capitalism in the Age of Globalization* (London: Zed Press). A useful overview of contemporary Marxist thinking about globalization, its driving forces and consequences for states.

Castells, M. (2000), *The Rise of the Network Society* (Oxford: Blackwells). This is now a contemporary classic account of the political economy of globalization which is comprehensive in its analysis of the new global informational capitalism.

Dicken, P. (2003), *Global Shift: Transforming the World Economy,* 4th edn. (London: Sage). This is an excellent introduction and comprehensive account of the new global division of labour and the globalization of production in the world economy.

Garrett, G. (2000), 'The Causes of Globalization', *Comparative Political Studies*, 33/6: 945–91. A really interesting and thorough exploration of the causal dynamics of globalization written from a rather orthodox political economy position but nevertheless critical of much of the contemporary sceptical analysis.

Giddens, A. (1990), *The Consequences of Modernity* (Cambridge: Polity Press). A classic statement of the rootedness of globalization in the long-term historical processes of modernization or modernity. It is less a political economy than a historical sociological account of globalization which takes it seriously as a transformative force.

Gilpin, R. (2001), *Global Political Economy* (Princeton: Princeton University Press). A more sceptical view of economic globalization which, although taking it seriously, conceives it as an expression of Americanization or American hegemony.

Held, D., McGrew, A., Goldblatt, D., and Perraton, J. (1999), *Global Transformations: Politics, Economics and Culture* (Cambridge: Polity Press). A comprehensive exploration of the nature and dynamics of globalization as a historical process which is transforming the nature of world order and the landscape of the global political economy.

Hirst, P., and Thompson, G. (1999), *Globalization in Question* (Cambridge: Polity Press). An excellent and sober critique of the hyperglobalist arguments which is thoroughly sceptical about the globalization thesis, viewing it as a return to the *belle époque* and heavily shaped by states.

Robertson, R. (2003), *The Three Waves of Globalization: A History of Developing Global Consciousness* (London: Zed Press). A very good account of globalization as a long-term historical process driven by a combination of economic and political factors.

Rosenberg, J. (2000), *The Follies of Globalization Theory* (London: Verso). A very erudite and rigorous critique of the globalization literature which, although sceptical about its wilder claims, considers globalization can only be understood from a historical materialist perspective.

Scholte, J. A. (2000), *Globalization: A Critical Introduction* (London: Macmillan). An excellent introduction to the globalization debate from its causes to its consequences for the global political economy from within a critical political economy perspective.

Wood, E. M. (2003), *Empire of Capital* (London: Verso). A novel reworking of the classical Marxist account of imperialism which takes globalization seriously as a new phase of capitalist development accompanied by a unique form of empire.

WEB LINKS

www.isn.ethz.ch/linkslib/   Good links to security and global economy nexus.

www.wto.org   Official WTO site with useful material of its policies and data on world trade.

www.theglobalsite.ac.uk   Good site for the globalization debate and related links.

www.wtowatch.org   Unofficial site operated by NGOs critical of WTO and economic globalization.

www.polity.co.uk/global   Good site for the globalization debate and many good links.

www.stern.nyu.edu/globalmacro   Excellent site for whole range of material on global economy and economic globalization.

www.csf.colorado.edu/ipe/   Good site for general material on IPE.

www.nber.org   Excellent studies of economic globalization in NBER Working Paper series.

9 Globalization's impact on states

Colin Hay

READER'S GUIDE

There is no topic more controversial in the field of global political economy than the impact of globalization on the accountability, autonomy, capacity, and sovereignty of the nation state. Arguably, the democratic character of governance in contemporary societies is at stake in such debates. This chapter reviews the extensive controversy which surrounds such questions, focusing attention on the principal mechanisms in and through which globalization is seen to impact upon the nation state and the empirical evidence which might either substantiate or question the existence of such mechanisms. It provides a detailed assessment of the case for and against the globalization thesis, examining the extent to which global economic integration might be seen to restrict the parameters of domestic political autonomy. It concludes by considering the complex and sometimes paradoxical relationship between globalization, democracy, and the nation state.

Introduction

It is over thirty years since Charles Kindleberger boldly proclaimed that 'the nation-state is just about through as an economic unit' (1969: 207). Since then we have witnessed a remarkable profusion of apocalyptic predictions of the demise of the nation state. In such accounts, globalization is invariably cast in the role of prosecutor, judge, jury, and executioner. Yet despite such doom-laden prognoses, government expenditure continues to account for a significant and, in many cases, rising share of Gross Domestic Product, whilst the nation state remains the principal focus of political identification and the principal locus of political debate and contestation in an interdependent world. Given this seeming paradox it is perhaps not surprising that the question of the impact of globalization on the development of the state has become a subject of considerable interest and intense controversy. Opinions range widely.

Though perhaps less influential than once it was, the view that globalization is in the process of, or has already, precipitated a terminal crisis of the nation state is still widespread. Others see such apocalyptic claims as wild and unfounded extrapolations from anecdotal evidence. Proponents of such a view, they suggest, confuse a crisis of the *form* of the nation state for a crisis of the nation state *per se*. Yet others see globalization as a process driven by states that has, in many cases, served to strengthen and certainly to increase the significance of state intervention for economic performance. Still others question the role of globalization in such dynamics, suggesting either that globalization—though real—has little to do with the developmental trajectory of the nation state or that the claim that we have witnessed a systematic process of globalization is itself mythical. Finally, there are those who suggest that the very *idea* of globalization as a harsh and non-negotiable economic constraint has itself exerted a powerful influence in confining the political ambitions of elected officials to those consistent with the pervasive neo-liberal orthodoxy. It is this, rather than globalization *per se*, they suggest, that has given rise to the impression of a waning of the nation state's autonomy, capacity, and sovereignty.

Much more than academic pride is at stake in such debates. For whether or not we see globalization as restricting the parameters of political choice domestically, and whether or not we see the nation state as having a present or, indeed, a future will have a very significant bearing on the space for political autonomy we perceive there to be. This, in turn, has significant consequences for the extent to which we might legitimately hold elected officials accountable for their conduct in office. Given the significance of the issues we are dealing with, it is important to proceed with a certain degree of caution.

We should perhaps be wary of accepting uncritically, as many have, that globalization leaves states (and the governments which give effect to state power) with no alternative other than to capitulate to the demands and desires of mobile investors. For to do so is effectively to deny the possibility of the democratic governance of economic processes in contemporary societies, certainly at the national level. In other words, there is a certain danger that in accepting over hastily an influential conception of the inevitable demise of the nation state's capacity and autonomy we provide a convenient alibi for politicians keen to justify otherwise unpalatable social and economic reforms by appeal to the harsh economic realities of a global age. Maybe our politicians deserve such an alibi; maybe the constraints of the global economy are so exacting and all-pervasive to warrant the appeal to such a 'logic of no alternative'; maybe these are valid and defensible conclusions. The crucial point for now is that we cannot allow ourselves to accept at face value such claims without a detailed consideration—both theoretical and empirical—of the arguments for *and against* such a view.

Though space does not permit a fully comprehensive exploration of the relevant issues, it is my aim in what follows to survey the existing literature in this area and, in so doing, to provide a basis for such an assessment. It is important to emphasize at the outset, however, that there is no agreed or emerging consensus on globalization's impact upon the state. Commentators are divided and they are likely to remain divided. As we shall see this is, at least in part, due to the rather slippery nature of the term globalization itself, which has come to mean a range of rather different things to a range of different analysts.

The chapter proceeds in four sections. In the first of these, I seek to establish a few necessary preliminaries, distinguishing in particular between the politics of globalization and the globalization of politics. In the second, I identify the principal mechanisms in and through which globalization is seen to impact upon the nation state before turning, in the third, to the empirical evidence which might either substantiate or question the existence of such mechanisms. In the final section, and by way of a conclusion, I consider the complex and sometimes paradoxical relationship between globalization, democracy, and the nation state, looking both at the impact of globalization on states and the state's impact on globalization.

The globalization of politics and the politics of globalization

It is crucial at the outset that we distinguish between the globalization of politics and the politics of globalization. This is particularly important given the tendency, especially prevalent amongst international/global political economists, to talk about globalization as if it were a transparent, self-sustaining, and purely economic dynamic (on the dangers of such 'economism' see also Teivainen 2002). It is a key contention of this chapter that globalization is not a tendency that is furthered or, indeed, countered in the *absence of political actors*. As such, it has a politics that must be a central ingredient of any adequate account of its development.

By the *globalization of politics*, I refer to the displacement of political capacities and responsibilities from the national and/or regional levels to the genuinely global level, through the development of institutions of global governance (such as the IMF and the World Bank).

By the *politics of globalization*, I refer to the politics of the process of globalization itself, to the political drivers of globalization and to the consequences of such a process for political conflict, practice, and the distribution of political responsibility.

Whether, and to what extent, we observe a globalization of politics is a matter of empirical judgement. It is likely to relate, amongst other things, to our evaluation of the extent and significance of genuinely global institutions of governance, the relative significance of regional institutions, and the degree to which the emergence of global institutions might be seen to give rise to a politics independent of and irreducible to that between discrete nation states or regions. Yet whatever specific judgement we reach— and opinion again varies considerably (compare, for instance, Archibugi 2003; Buzan, Held, and McGrew 1998; Krasner 1999)—we must acknowledge that if globalization exists at all, and even if it is confined exclusively to the economic and cultural spheres, it has a politics. Whilst we may well deny the globalization of politics, then, unless we deny globalization itself we cannot deny the *politics* of globalization. It is with the latter that this chapter is principally concerned.

More specifically, we will focus on three analytically separable, but nonetheless interconnected, dimensions of the politics of globalization:

1 The implications and consequences of globalization (whether economic, political, or cultural) for the capacity and autonomy of the nation state.

2 The interpretation of the opportunities and constraints associated with globalization and the consequent appeal, in political contexts, to the language of globalization (often, as we shall see, to justify social and economic reforms).

3 The role of political actors, particularly state actors, in the political 'authoring' of globalization and the processes which either sustain or impede its development.

The first of these might be seen as the *structural* dimension, relating as it does to the constraints and

---

Box 9.1   The politics of globalization: key controversies

- The extent to which globalization might be seen to diminish the autonomy and 'perforate' the sovereignty of the nation state (on 'perforated sovereignty' see Duchacek 1990; Jessop 2002).

- The extent to which globalization might be seen to establish powerful tendencies towards global political convergence and homogenization.

- The extent to which it is right to identify a globalization of political problems—the proliferation of issues that require a response in the form of concerted global action.

- The extent to which we can point to a parallel globalization of political solutions and the corresponding emergence of more or less dedicated institutions, mechanisms, and processes of *global governance*.

- The extent to which we can identify the global diffusion of 'best practice' policy solutions (or potential solutions) and/or policy models in the form of the transfer of ideas about 'good' practice between nations (whether by choice or imposition).

- The extent to which globalization might be seen to promote the development of a global polity or *cosmopolis* capable of transcending the state (see, for instance, Archibugi 2003; Zolo 1997).

---

opportunities of the external environment for domestic political actors. The second relates to the *ideational* dimension and, more specifically, to the ways in which political actors understand the constraints and opportunities that the external environment presents to them. The third relates to the *intentional*, *strategic*, or *agential* dimension—to the role of political actors in the creation and recreation of the very external environment in which they find themselves. Together they suggest an approach to the question of the impact of globalization on the state and the state's impact on globalization in which political actors are always present, in which the ideas they hold about their environment shape their political conduct, and in which they are never unburdened of the constraints (and opportunities) of the environment they have created (for a further elaboration, see Hay 2002*b*: 253–60).

Such a perspective is applied, in the pages that follow, to a series of more substantive issues and controversies. These might together be taken to comprise an agenda for a consideration of the politics of globalization (see Box 9.1).

Each set of issues, as we shall see, reveals a separate and distinct politics of globalization. By drawing attention to the multifaceted politics of globalization in this way, my aim is to contribute to the attempt to restore political (and one might hope democratic) scrutiny and accountability to processes more conventionally seen as economic and inexorable—and, consequently, as not subject to political deliberation (see, more generally, Hay 2002*a*).

Key points

- The impact of globalization on the autonomy, capacity, and sovereignty of the nation state is much disputed.

- It is important to distinguish between the politics of globalization (the political drivers of the process of globalization) and the globalization of politics (the displacement of political responsibilities and capacities from the level of the nation state through the emergence of institutions and processes of global governance). Globalization has a politics whether or not politics has become globalized.

- It is equally important to distinguish between and to acknowledge the structural, ideational, and strategic dimensions of the process of globalization. The first of these relates to the constraints and opportunities presented by globalization; the second to the way in which those structural factors are understood; the third to the role of political actors in 'authoring' the process of globalization itself.

Globalization and the crisis of the nation state

If we are to assess the impact (if any) of globalization on the viability of the nation state, we must first identify the principal mechanisms in and through which globalization is held, in conventional accounts, to limit the capacity, autonomy, and sovereignty of the nation state. Before doing so, however, it is perhaps important to emphasize that most strong variants of the globalization thesis—which present the nation state as a casualty of globalization—tend to do so without pointing directly or explicitly to the mechanism or mechanisms involved (see, for instance, Ohmae 1990, 1995; Reich 1992). At best, it seems, they treat the existence of such mechanisms as self-evident. What we tend to see, instead, is what Andreas Busch (2000: 34) refers to as 'casual empiricism'—the anecdotal appeal to, and extrapolation from, single pieces of evidence which appear to confirm the general tenor of the argument being advanced.

At times, however, casual empiricism gives way to 'casual theoreticism'. Here, tangential reference is made to the increased bargaining power and/or mobility of capital in an era of globalization. In so doing, 'hyperglobalists' appeal, whether they are aware of it or not, to mechanisms derived from neoclassical open economy macro-economic models (for reviews of the relevant literature, see Obstfeld and Rogoff 1996; Rødseth 2000; Ugur 2001). This is an important point and gives a first clue as to the character of the hyperglobalization thesis. For it serves to indicate that, for such authors, it is *economic* globalization that is the principal factor limiting the capacity and autonomy of the state in the contemporary context. In short, economic globalization gives mobile international investors the upper hand over domestic political authorities.

Without going into any technical detail it is useful to examine further such open economic macro-economics models. In particular, it is important that we:

1 establish the assumptions on which such models are predicated;

2 assess the plausibility of such assumptions; and

3 consider the sensitivity of the conclusions derived from such assumptions (for the viability or otherwise

of the nation state) to modifications in the initial premises *from* which they are derived.

The hyperglobalization thesis

Arguably the key factor determining the inevitability of state retrenchment for hyperglobalists is the heightened mobility of capital. The logic to which they appeal is, in fact, very similar to that elaborated by Adam Smith in 1776.

The . . . proprietor of stock is properly a citizen of the world, and is not necessarily attached to any particular country. He would be apt to abandon the country in which he is exposed to a vexatious inquisition, in order to be assessed a burdensome tax, and would remove his stock to some country where he could either carry on his business or enjoy his fortune at his ease. A tax that tended to drive away stock from a particular country, would so far tend to dry up every source of revenue, both to the sovereign and to the society. Not only the profits of stock, but the rent of land and the wages of labour, would necessarily be more or less diminished by its removal.

(Smith 1776/1976: 848–9; cited in Swank 2002: 245)

Updated and restated in more familiar terms, the argument goes something like this. In closed national economies, such as those which (supposedly) characterized the early post-war period, capital is essentially immobile and national in character; it has no 'exit' option. In such an environment governments can impose punitive taxation regimes upon unwilling and relatively impotent national capitals with little cost to the domestic economy (save for the tendency for capitalists to hoard rather than to reinvest their profits). With open economy conditions, such as are conventionally held to characterize the contemporary era, this is no longer the case. Capital may now exit from national economic environments at minimal cost (indeed, in most neoclassical inspired models, at zero cost).

Accordingly, by playing off the regulatory regimes of different economies against one another, capital can ensure for itself the highest rate of return on its investment. *Ceteris paribus*, capital will exit high-taxation regimes for low-taxation regimes, comprehensive welfare states for residual states, highly regulated labour markets for flexible labour markets, and economies characterized by strict environmental regulations and high union density for those characterized by lax environmental standards and low union density. The clear prediction would be that capital will seek out the high growth regimes of, for instance, newly industrialized countries (like the Philippines or Malaysia) unencumbered by a powerful environmental lobby, burdensome welfare traditions, rigid labour market institutions, and correspondingly higher rates of taxation.

The process pits national economy against national economy in an increasingly intense competitive struggle. States must effectively clamber over one another in an ever more frenzied attempt to produce a more favourable investment environment for mobile ('footloose') foreign direct investors than their competitors. Yet this is not a one-shot game—and an early influx of foreign direct investment only increases the dependence of the state upon its continued 'locational competitiveness'. If investment is to be retained in such an environment, states must constantly strive to improve the investment opportunities they can offer relative to their competitors. Any failure to do so can only precipitate a haemorrhaging of invested funds, labour shedding, and, in turn, economic crisis. A neo-Darwinian survival of the fittest effectively guarantees that states must internalize the preferences of capital, offering ever more attractive investment incentives, ever more flexible labour markets, and ever less restrictive environmental regulations, if

they are not to be emptied of investment, economic activity, and employment. Big government, if not perhaps the state itself, is rendered increasingly anachronistic—a guarantor not of the interests of citizens or even consumers, but a sure means to disinvestment and economic crisis.

Little wonder, then, that the hyperglobalization thesis tends to predict 'social dumping', 'competitive deregulation', and a 'race to the bottom' in terms of social and environmental standards, a process lubricated by the 'deregulatory arbitrage' of footloose and fancy-free transnational corporations.

The policy implications of such an account are painfully clear. As globalization serves to establish competitive selection mechanisms within the international economy, there is little choice but to cast all regulatory impediments to the efficient operation of the market on the bonfire of welfare institutions, regulatory controls, and labour market rigidities.

Plausible, familiar, and compelling though such a logic may well appear, it serves us well to isolate the assumptions on which it is predicated. For, as we shall see, it is these, rather than any inexorable process of globalization, which ultimately summon the crisis of the nation state. They are principally fivefold, and each can be challenged on both theoretical and empirical grounds (see Box 9.2).

Each of these premises is at best dubious, at worst demonstrably false. Such assumptions, it should perhaps be noted, are not justified in neoclassical economics in terms of their accuracy, but because they are convenient and make possible abstract

---

Box 9.2 Core assumptions of the 'hyperglobalization' thesis

1 That capital invests where it can secure the greatest net return on that investment and is possessed of perfect information of the means by which to do so;

2 That markets for goods and services are fully integrated globally and that, consequently, national economies must prove themselves internationally competitive if economic growth is to be sustained;

3 That capital enjoys perfect mobility and the cost of 'exit' (disinvestment) is zero;

4 That capital will invariably secure the greatest return on its investment by minimizing its labour costs in flexible labour markets and by relocating its productive activities in economies with the lowest rates of corporate taxation; and, consequently,

5 That the welfare state (and the taxation receipts out of which it is funded) represent nothing other than lost capital to mobile asset holders and have no positive externalities for the competitiveness and productivity of the national economy.

quasi-mathematical modelling. That defence, whatever one thinks of it, is simply not available to proponents of the hyperglobalization thesis whose borrowings from neoclassical economics rarely extend past the assumptions to the algebra.

Consider each assumption in turn. Whilst it may seem entirely appropriate to attribute to capital the sole motive of seeking the greatest return on its investment, the political and economic history of capital provides little or no support for the notion that capital is blessed either with complete information or even with a relatively clear and consistent conception of what its own best interest is. Moreover, as the political economy of the advanced capitalist democracies demonstrates well, capital has a history of resisting social and economic reforms which it has later come both to rely upon and actively to defend (see, for instance, Swenson 2000).

The second assumption is, again, a convenient fiction, used in neoclassical macro-economics to make possible the modelling of an open economy. Few if any economists would defend the claim that markets for goods or services are fully integrated or clear instantly. Indeed, the degree of integration of such markets is an empirical question and, as such, an issue to which we return in the next section.

If the first two assumptions are problematic, then the third is demonstrably false, at least with respect to certain types of capital. For whilst portfolio capital may indeed exhibit almost perfect mobility in a digital economy, the same is simply not the case for capital invested in infrastructure, machinery, and personnel. Consider inward foreign direct investment. Once attracted to a particular locality, foreign direct investors acquire a range of non-recuperable or 'sunk' costs—such as their investment in physical infrastructure, plant, and machinery. Consequently, their exit options become seriously depleted. Whilst it is entirely 'rational' for foreign direct investors to proclaim loudly their mobility, exit is perhaps most effective as a threat.

What this in turn suggests is that predictions of the haemorrhaging of invested capital from generous welfare states are almost certainly misplaced. A combination of exit threats and concerns arising from the hyperglobalization thesis about the *likelihood* of exit may well have had an independent effect on the trajectory of fiscal and labour market reform. But there

would seem no a priori reason to hold generous welfare state and high corporate taxation burdens incompatible with the attraction and retention of foreign direct investment. As we shall see in greater detail in the next section, this is precisely what we find from the empirical record. Not only have the most generous welfare states consistently proved the most attractive locations for inward foreign direct investors (Locke and Kochan 1985; Swank 2002), but volumes of foreign direct investment (expressed as a share of GDP) are in fact found to be positively correlated with levels of corporate taxation, union density, labour costs, and the degree of regulation of the labour market (Cooke and Noble 1998; Dunning 1988; Traxler and Woitech 2000; Wilensky 2002: 654–5). As Duane Swank notes, 'contrary to the claims of the international capital mobility thesis . . . the general fiscal capacity of democratic governments to fund a variety of levels and mixes of social protection and services may be relatively resilient in the face of internationalisation of markets' (2002: 276). Here it is perhaps instructive to note that despite a marked tendency for direct corporate taxation to fall in recent years in line with the predictions of such neoclassically inspired models, the overall burden of taxation on firms has in fact remained remarkably constant, rising marginally since the mid-1980s (Kiser and Laing 2001; Steinmo 2003).

No less problematic are assumptions four and five—that capital can only compete in a more intensely competitive environment on the basis of productivity gains secured through tax reductions and cost shedding (through rationalization, downsizing, and the flexibilization of labour) and that the welfare state is, for business, merely a drain on profits. Such assumptions reflect a narrowly Anglo-US conception of competitiveness—and, as we shall see presently, are difficult to reconcile with the empirical evidence. Though ever more influential, the hyperglobalization thesis extrapolates wildly and inappropriately from labour-intensive sectors of the international economy in which competitiveness is conventionally enhanced in this way to the global economy more generally. It fails to appreciate that foreign direct investors in capital-intensive sectors of the international economy are attracted to locations like the Northern European economies neither for the flexibility of their labour markets nor for the cheapness of the wage and non-wage labour costs that they impose, but for the access they provide to a highly skilled, reliable, and innovative labour force. High wages and high non-wage labour costs (in the form of payroll taxes) would seem to be a price many multi-national corporations regard as worth paying for a dynamic and highly skilled workforce.

At this point it might be objected that the above paragraphs relate principally to foreign direct investors and hence to productive/invested capital as opposed to investment/portfolio capital. This is a valid point. Indeed, although the hyperglobalization thesis has rather more to say about the former, it has much to say about the latter too.

Its assumptions about finance capital and financial markets are similar to those about productive/invested capital and markets in goods and services. Yet the small differences are significant. Referring again to Box 9.2, the first assumption applies equally to invested and investment capital and is equally problematic. Yet whether it is accurate or not arguably matters rather less in the case of portfolio capital. For such investors do not need to act rationally or with perfect information in order to inflict considerable damage on the currencies against which they may be tempted to speculate and the stocks and shares they may be tempted to dump—as the influential literature on 'irrational exuberance' and 'herding instincts' in financial markets makes very clear (see, for instance, Schiller 2001). Assumption two also applies equally to financial markets and to those in goods and services. All are assumed global and perfectly integrated. This may seem like a more plausible assumption to make of financial markets but, as we shall see in the next section, as an empirical claim it is not easily reconciled with the available evidence. Assumption three, though problematic for productive/invested capital as already discussed, again seems more plausible for portfolio investors. Stocks and shares can certainly be traded, and assets swapped from one denomination to another, in the flickering of a cursor. Yet whether this *potential* is reflected in the actual behaviour of financial markets is, again, an empirical question and the subject of some debate. This, too, is discussed further in the next section. Assumptions four and five are not directly relevant to finance capital, but they can be adapted to financial actors. Hyperglobalists tend to assume that portfolio investors have a clear interest in, and preference for, strong and stable currencies

backed both by implacable independent central banks with hawkish anti-inflationary credentials and governments wedded in theory and in practice to fiscal moderation and prudence. Any departure from this new financial orthodoxy, it is assumed, will precipitate a flurry of speculation against the currency and a haemorrhaging of investment from assets denominated in that currency. Governments provoke the wrath of the financial markets at their peril. This, again, is an intuitively plausible proposition that would seem to be borne out by a series of high-profile speculative flurries against 'rogue' governments. It is, however, an empirical claim and, as we shall see later, one that a growing body of scholarship reveals to be considerably at odds with the empirical evidence.

As the above paragraphs perhaps serve to indicate, the theoretical case against the hyperglobalization thesis is strongest with respect to the assumptions made about productive/invested capital. Its assumptions about investment/portfolio capital, if perhaps overly simplistic, are, on the face of it, more plausible. Yet they give rise to a series of substantive claims and predictions which have prompted an important empirical challenge to the thesis. This provides the principal focus for the next section. Before turning to such issues, however, it is important that we first consider the implications of the hyperglobalization thesis for the question of convergence, prior to examining an alternative and rather more political account of the origins of the contemporary crisis of the nation state.

Convergence, dual convergence, or divergence?

Through attempts to enhance labour market flexibility, welfare retrenchment, and the intensification of tax competition between states, the hyperglobalization thesis predicts a simple convergence amongst previously distinct 'models' or 'varieties' of capitalism—on an Anglo-US or liberal ideal type. This can be represented schematically (see Figure 9.1).

Globalization is the driving force, unleashing as it does an intense competitive struggle between contending models of capitalism. It exposes all economies (here, A–E) to common pressures which, in turn, produce common outcomes. Since liberal models of capitalism best approximate the preferences of mobile capital for open markets, low-taxation regimes, and

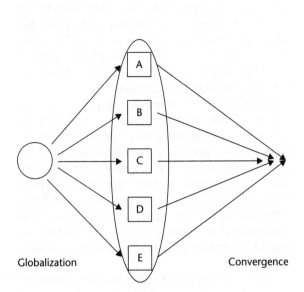

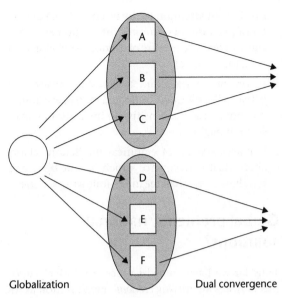

Fig. 9.1 The hyperglobalization thesis.
Globalization (perfect capital mobility and perfect competition under open economy conditions) generates common pressure (inputs); states and/or political-economic regimes have no independent mediating role (no insitutional effects); hence convergence on best practice assuming complete information, rational action, and Darwinian competition—in short, *common inputs produce common outputs.*

light regulation, they rapidly establish themselves as the model to be emulated. Convergence on this Anglo-US ideal type is held to be rapid, lubricated by exit from more highly regulated regimes.

Influential though this simple convergence thesis is, it is not as unquestioned as once it was. An alternative and increasingly influential account points to a rather more complex process of 'dual' or 'co-convergence', again driven by globalization (see above).

In this contending account more attention is paid to the role of institutional factors in mediating the state's response to globalization. Models of capitalism are differentiated by virtue of the rather different institutions they embody. In the now conventional classification, *liberal market economies* (such as the USA and the UK) and *coordinated market economies* (such as Germany, Sweden, and the Netherlands) are contrasted (Hall and Soskice 2001).

The competitive pressures unleashed by globalization may make similar demands of these institutions (such as balanced budgets, flexible labour markets, and

Fig. 9.2 The dual convergence thesis.
Globalization produces a variety of common pressures to which competing models of capitalism are differentially exposed; this exposure tends to promote a dual process of convergence accentuating the difference between liberal market economies and coordinated market economies—in short, *globalization generates common pressures; these are refracted institutionally to produce a dual convergence.*

the control of inflation), but these can be delivered in different ways in different institutional domains. Consequently, the 'varieties of capitalism' approach, as it has come to be known, predicts not a simple or singular process of convergence on the liberal (or Anglo-US) model, but a complex or dual convergence in which capitalist polities cluster ever more closely around the liberal and coordinated ideal types (Hall and Soskice 2001; see also Garrett 1998*b*, 2000*b*; Iversen, Pontusson, and Soskice 2000; Kitschelt et al. 1999).

In its sensitivity to institutional variations amongst different models of capitalism and in its recognition that common external pressures need not translate into common outcomes, the 'varieties of capitalism' approach represents a considerable advance on the hyperglobalization thesis. Yet in a number of significant respects it, too, is problematic (see also Blyth 2003; Goodin 2003; Hay 2004; Watson 2003).

1 It may, unwittingly, borrow too much from the hyperglobalization thesis in presenting globalization as the principal agent of convergence (paying

insufficient attention to the often regional character of processes of economic integration and/or to the differential exposure of economies to globalization, for instance).

2 In drawing a rigid and rather static distinction between liberal and coordinated market economies it is not perhaps as sensitive to institutional diversity as it might be.

3 It makes a series of empirical predictions/claims about dual convergence which are, at best, contestable—as we shall see in the following section.

Global problems, national solutions?

Thus far we have tended to focus exclusively upon mechanisms identifying *economic* globalization as the key determinant of the contemporary crisis of the nation state. Yet arguably altogether more plausible is a rather more political mechanism. Strictly speaking this does not so much point to the diminished capacity and sovereignty of the state in an era of globalization, as to the globalization of the problems with which the nation state is confronted—and its inability to deal with such problems. Indeed, it points to the more general lack of the political capacity to deal with genuinely global problems and risks that result from the continued ascendancy of the nation state as a political unit.

The classic example here is the problem of high-consequence global environmental risks (Beck 1992; Giddens 1990). This is well expressed in the so-called 'tragedy of the commons' first identified by Garrett Hardin (1968). Hardin provides an intuitively plausible and all too compelling model of the seemingly intractable problem of environmental degradation in contemporary societies. The systematic exploitation and pollution of the environment, it is argued, is set to continue since individual corporations and states, despite a clear collective interest, choose not to impose upon themselves the costs of unilateral environmental action. Their logic is entirely rational, though potentially catastrophic in its cumulative consequences. Such actors know that environmental regulation is costly and, particularly in an open international economy, a burden on competitiveness. Accordingly, in the absence of an international agency capable of enforcing the compliance of all states and all corporations, the anticipation of free riding is sufficient to ensure that corporations and states do not burden themselves with additional costs and taxes. The long-term effects for the environment are all too obvious, preventing as it does, a global solution to a genuinely global problem.

The extent to which the narrowly perceived self-interest of states and governments can subvert the development of effective mechanisms and institutions of global governance is well evidenced by the Bush administration's withdrawal from the 1997 Kyoto Protocol (committing signatories to staged reductions in greenhouse gas emissions); and, for its critics, by the fact that such a protocol, even if fully implemented, would only serve to reduce slightly the pace of an ongoing process of environmental degradation.

This is a most important example, and a number of broader implications might be drawn from it (see Box 9.3).

Key points

- Many of the strongest versions of the globalization thesis fail to specify the mechanism by which globalization might be seen to limit the capacity, autonomy, and sovereignty of the nation state.

- Nonetheless, a variety of such mechanisms have been posited. These are principally economic in character and often rely upon stylized assumptions about the behaviour of capital drawn from open economy neoclassical economics. These assumptions can be questioned theoretically and empirically.

- The hyperglobalization thesis predicts a simple convergence between 'models of capitalism' under conditions of (economic) globalization; the more recent 'varieties of capitalism' perspective predicts a more complex process of dual convergence. There are theoretical problems with both sets of predictions.

- The nation state has always suffered from a limited capacity to deal with genuinely global problems; such problems are proliferating. The 'tragedy of the commons' provides a compelling model of the consequences of this lack of capacity, pointing to the need for effective and democratic institutions of global governance.

Box 9.3 The implications of the 'tragedy of the commons'

1 The 'tragedy of the commons' is, effectively, a modern-day morality tale. It is indicative of a more general disparity between the need for and supply of effective institutions and mechanisms of global governance. For whilst it is easy to point to genuinely global problems requiring for their resolution coordinated global responses, it is far more difficult to find examples of the latter.

2 As this perhaps suggests, the 'tragedy of the commons' is not really a story of the crisis of the nation state at all. For it is the continued capacity of many (if perhaps not all) states to behave unilaterally and to veto international agreements that preclude the appropriate globally coordinated collective response. In other words, political globalization (effective and authoritative institutions of global governance) is impeded by the retention of the nation state's sovereignty. This is less a crisis of the nation state, then, than a crisis produced by the resilience of the nation state.

3 Whilst the proliferation of genuinely global political problems does point to the incapacity of a system of sovereign states to deal with the challenges it now faces, it does not indicate any particular incapacity of states to deal with the problems and issues they have always dealt with. This is, then, less of a story of a loss of capacity than of the proliferation of issues with which the nation state has never had the capacity to deal effctively.

4 Finally, and rather perversely, the disparity between the need for and supply of global solutions to global problems is merely exacerbated by economic globalization. For this has served to drive states, at pain of economic crisis, to elevate considerations of competitiveness over all other concerns, including environmental protection. There is a clear and obvious danger that the narrow pursuit of short-term economic advantage will come at the long-term price of a looming environmental, economic, and political catastrophe.

Globalization and state retrenchment: the evidence assessed

As suggested in the previous section, the hyperglobalization thesis tends to present a theoretical, indeed largely hypothetical, argument for the contemporary crisis of the nation state. If its assumptions are accepted then the predicted crisis of the nation state is little more than a logical inference. Yet, as we have seen, there may be good theoretical grounds for challenging some of these assumptions and with them the claimed inevitability of the state's loss of capacity, autonomy, sovereignty, and legitimacy. In the end, however, these are empirical questions—and it is to the empirical evidence itself that we must turn if we are to assess the validity of the hyperglobalization thesis and to assess the impact, if any, of globalization on states. It is to this task that we now turn. We begin first by considering the dependent variable.

The dependent variable: state retrenchment

It is perhaps appropriate to begin with the simplest data which most directly address the contemporary condition of the state. If the state were to experience a potentially terminal crisis we might expect to see clear evidence of systematic state retrenchment. Moreover, we would expect this to be most pronounced in highly open economies whose public spending had traditionally accounted for a high proportion of gross domestic product. Table 9.1 presents data on government expenditure expressed as a proportion of Gross Domestic Product for a number of developed countries from the 1960s, conventionally the point of departure for political economies of globalization.

Table 9.1 Government expenditure as a share of GDP

	AUL	AUS	BEL	CAN	DEN	FIN	FRA	GER	IRE
1960	22.1	32.1	34.6	28.9	24.6	26.6	34.6	32.0	28.0
1965	25.6	37.9	36.5	29.1	29.6	30.8	38.4	36.3	33.1
1970	25.5	39.2	42.1	35.7	40.2	30.5	38.9	37.6	39.6
1975	32.4	46.2	51.3	40.7	47.5	38.4	43.5	47.1	46.5
1980	34.1	48.5	58.7	41.5	56.2	39.4	46.2	46.9	50.8
1985	38.5	51.7	62.3	47.1	59.3	45.0	52.2	47.5	54.8
1990	37.7	49.4	55.3	47.8	58.6	46.8	49.9	45.7	41.4
1996	35.9	51.6	52.9	44.7	63.6[d]	1.0[d]	55.0	49.1	42.0
2000	32.9	46.9	46.8	41.9[a]	51.1	43.7	47.5	44.5	35.0[b]
Net growth[e] (%)	49	46	35	45	108	64	37	39	25
Growth to peak (%)	74	61	80	65	158	129	59	53	96
Decline from peak (%)	15	9	25	12	20	28	14	9	36

	ITA	JAP	NTL	NOR	NZL	SWE	SWZ	UK	USA
1960	30.1	18.3	33.7	32.0	26.9	31.1	17.2	32.6	27.2
1965	34.3	18.6	38.7	34.2	—	36.0	19.7	36.4	27.2
1970	34.2	19.3	45.5	41.0	—	43.7	21.3	39.3	31.6
1975	43.2	27.3	55.9	46.6	—	49	28.7	46.9	34.6
1980	45.6	32.7	62.5	49.4	38.1	65.7	29.7	44.6	33.6
1985	50.8	32.7	59.7	45.6	—	64.3	31.0	46.2	36.4
1990	53.6	32.3	57.5	54.9	41.3	60.8	30.9	42.3	36.6
1996	52.7	35.9	49.2	49.2	34.0	59.1	39.4	43.0	32.4
2000	44.1	31.9	41.7	39.4	36.4	52.2	33.4[b]	37.7	32.7[c]
Net growth[e] (%)	47	74	24	23	35	68	94	16	20
Growth to peak (%)	69	96	85	72	[54]	111	129	44	35
Decline from peak (%)	18	11	10	28	[12]	21	15	20	11

Key: AUL = Australia; AUS = Austria; BEL = Belgium; CAN = Canada; DEN = Denmark; FIN = Finland; GER = Germany; IRE = Ireland; ITA = Italy; JAP = Japan; NTL = Netherlands; NOR = Norway; NZL = New Zealand; SWE = Sweden; SWZ = Switzerland; UK = United Kingdom; USA = United States

[a] 1998
[b] 1999
[c] 1997
[d] 1994
[e] Net growth here refers to the percentage increase in the share of GDP devoted to government expenditure.

Source: Calculated from OECD, Economic Outlook, various years.

The evidence itself is fairly unequivocal. These, for the most part extremely open and developed economies, show little sign of systematic retrenchment in the so-called era of globalization. There is certainly some evidence in the last decade or so of a decline in the proportion of GDP devoted to public spending. Though invariably greatest where unemployment has fallen most, this is consistent with the predictions of the hyperglobalization thesis to some extent. Yet what is perhaps more important is that in each and every case the size of the state (as expressed as a share of GDP) has increased considerably over the period, peaking in most cases in the early to mid-1990s.

Of course, state expenditure is not the only means of gauging quantitatively the role of the state. Figure 9.3 presents time-series data on the proportion of the

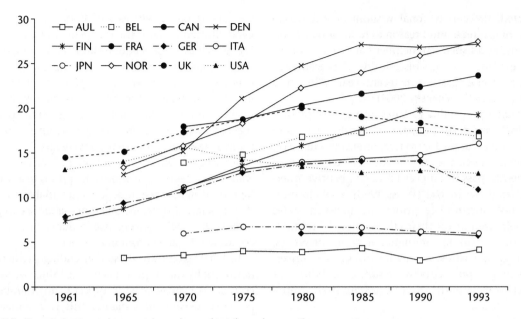

Fig. 9.3 Government employment (as a share of total employment)

Sources: Calculated from OECD, *Labour Force Statistics*, various years; OECD Health Data, ECO-SANTE, 1995; Huber, Ragin, and Stephens 1997.

total workforce employed directly by the state since the 1960s.

Again the evidence is unequivocal. This period, the much-vaunted era of globalization, has witnessed the development of the largest states the world has ever seen and there is little evidence of this trend being reversed.

It would certainly seem that globalization is compatible with a far higher level of state expenditure than the hyperglobalization thesis would seem to imply. This presents something of a paradox: a widely accepted conception of state crisis and retrenchment which seems to stand in some tension to the available empirical evidence. There are at least four potential solutions to this conundrum, each with rather different implications:

1. That the conventional wisdom on the subject is indeed correct, that 'big government' represents an ultimately unsustainable drain on competitiveness in an era of globalization, but that the institutional form of the state has become so entrenched and embedded as to make its reform and retrenchment an incremental process down which we are now only slowly embarking. (Though perhaps the most plausible

defence of the 'crisis of the nation state' thesis, this argument is rarely made in the existing literature. It might, however, draw inspiration from the work of historical institutionalists who have consistently pointed to the inertial nature of complex institutions like the state; see, especially, Pierson 1994, 1996).

2. That the conventional wisdom, though somewhat overstated, is basically correct, since the aggregate empirical evidence in fact masks the actual degree of retrenchment. Once we control for demographic and other 'welfare inflationary' pressures (such as higher levels of unemployment and the near exponential growth in health care costs since the 1960s), observed state expenditure is in fact substantially below what we would anticipate, were consistent level of generosity and coverage to have been maintained (Barr 1998; Esping-Andersen 1996*a*, 1996*b*; Rhodes 1996, 1997). We have not witnessed, nor should we expect to witness, a terminal crisis of the nation state, but we have already experienced a significant process of state retrenchment driven by globalization.

3. That whilst the aggregate evidence may indeed mask the real degree of retrenchment that has

occurred, the conventional wisdom is still wrong since there is no a priori reason to hold globalization responsible for such retrenchment and/or no consistent evidence of an historically unprecedented process of globalization in recent years (Hirst and Thompson 1999; Wilensky 2002).

4. That, in expecting globalization to precipitate a terminal crisis of the state, the conventional wisdom is simply inaccurate. Far from representing a drain on competitiveness, the state is the very condition of competitiveness in an ever more competitive international/global market (Weiss 1998). Globalization does not discriminate principally between states on their size but on their effectiveness in promoting and sustaining international competitiveness. Consequently, whilst we might expect to see convergence on best practice between states, we should not expect to see a withering of the state itself (Cerny 1995, 1997).

As this already serves to indicate, there are a number of ways of rehabilitating an albeit somewhat respecified variant of the globalization thesis in the light of the above evidence. We probably can reject the notion that globalization has precipitated a terminal crisis of the nation state. Yet the evidence considered thus far is by no means incompatible with the claim that globalization circumscribes the parameters of domestic political choice and is the principal determinant of the state's developmental trajectory. If we are to assess that claim then we need to turn our attentions from the dependent variable (the extent of state retrenchment) to the independent variable (the process of globalization itself). Before doing so, however, it is important that we first consider one remaining aspect of the dependent variable—the question of convergence.

The dependent variable: convergence or dual convergence

Having originally placed their emphasis upon the crisis and transcendence of the nation state as a political unit responsible for regulating an economic jurisdiction (Ohmae 1990, 1995), proponents of the hyperglobalization thesis now more frequently cast institutional and policy convergence as the dependent variable (Gray 1998; Parker 1998; Teeple 1995). Globalization remains the independent variable and is depicted as a stable equilibrium and as an entirely non-negotiable external economic imperative which exposes all economies within the global system to near identical pressures and challenges. In a highly competitive environment in which only the fittest survive, successful adaptation will rapidly be emulated, resulting in a powerful tendency to convergence.

As we have seen, the institutional sensitivity of the 'varieties of capitalism' approach appeals to a similar logic (and an identical independent variable), in predicting a rather different outcome—a more complex process of dual convergence around liberal and coordinated market economic models.

To what extent are these contending predictions borne out by the empirical evidence? Since we might consider convergence with respect to any number of potential dependent variables this is a somewhat contentious issue that we cannot hope to do full justice to here. Space prevents an exhaustive survey. Nonetheless, we would once again expect the convergence or co-convergence theses to be most relevant to the most developed and most open economies in the world system. Moreover, given that welfare expenditure is most frequently described in the globalization literature as the kind of unnecessary indulgence which can no longer be afforded in an era of heightened competition amongst nations, we might expect to find the strongest evidence of convergence or co-convergence amongst European welfare states.

Yet the evidence simply does not bear out that expectation (see also Hay 2003). Limits of space allow us only to consider social transfer payments (expressed as a percentage of GDP). These are, in essence, a measure of basic welfare expenditure. For ease of comparison they are here standardized at 100 for 1960. Precisely because these are standardized measures, they are bound to show an initial divergence. Yet, the convergence thesis would lead us to expect that initial divergence to be checked considerably by the 1980s and 1990s. It would predict, in short, an oval shaped distribution. And the co-convergence thesis would predict the emergence of two clusters—one grouped around Germany, the other grouped around the United Kingdom.

Neither prediction is borne out by the evidence (see Figure 9.4). Instead, consistent paths are mapped out

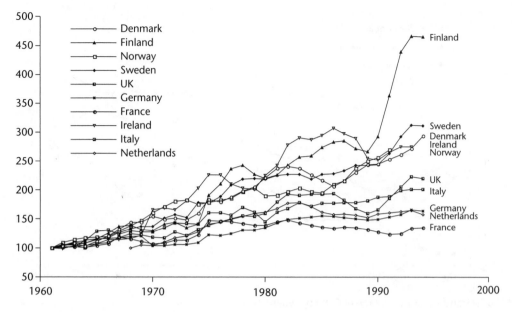

Fig. 9.4 Social transfers of EU member states as percentage of GDP (1960 = 100)

Source: Calculated from *Eurostat Yearbook,* various year.

from the 1960s which social models continue to follow for the most part to the present day. The wide initial variance in growth rates is sustained over time. This is not a story of systematic welfare retrenchment, nor is it a story of the diminishing distinctiveness of regime types—which seem, if anything, to be reinforced over time. Indeed, it is the Nordic welfare states that have grown the most. Under globalization, it would seem, the most generous welfare states have thrived.

Second, we might consider the raw unstandardized data itself—that is, social transfers expressed as a share of GDP. To aid the analysis, European welfare regimes are here grouped in terms of the conventional threefold classification. The *Nordic* regime type refers to Sweden, Denmark, Finland, and Norway; the *conservative* regime type refers to Germany, the Netherlands, Italy, and France; and the *liberal* regime type to the United Kingdom and Ireland.

What the raw data reveals is that it is only relatively recently that the distinctiveness of the Nordic social democratic regime type has emerged. This is the most generous in terms of welfare provision and, one might expect, the most exposed by virtue of globalization as a consequence. Again, it seems, the evidence is in

some tension with the predictions of the existing literature (see Figure 9.5). For, far from being associated with welfare retrenchment the period of (supposedly) most intensive globalization (the 1980s to the present day) has been associated with the emergence and consolidation—not the retrenchment—of the most generous welfare states the world has ever known.

Finally, we might also note that the standard deviation (a measure of dispersion about the mean) for social transfers rises over time, indicating divergence not convergence.

Of course, we cannot infer from such evidence that globalization is not an agent of convergence or co-convergence, merely that the evidence considered here is not consistent with such a claim. It is also important to note that even were this a valid inference to draw, it would be wrong to conclude from this that globalization has no impact on the nation state. For if globalization serves, as some have suggested, to increase the sensitivity of economic performance to the *quality* of public policy (see, for instance, Weiss 1998), then there is no particular reason to expect either a crisis of the state or convergence. Moreover, if, as is widely assumed, globalization generates common pressures for neo-liberalization and this has

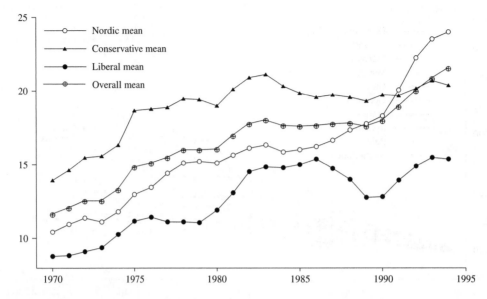

Fig. 9.5 Social transfers (as percentage of GDP) by regime type

Source: Calculated from *Eurostat Yearbook,* various year.

been more enthusiastically embraced in regimes already characterized by their liberalism, we might expect to see at least an initial period of divergence.

But what evidence is there of an historically unprecedented phase of globalization capable of generating such pressures? We turn now to the independent variable.

The independent variable: globalization

As already noted, proponents of the hyperglobalization thesis have rarely felt the need to defend the intuitively plausible claim that we live in a fully integrated global economy. Casual and anecdotal appeals to supporting evidence largely exhaust the empirical content of this literature. Yet in recent years a more rigorous and systematically evidential assessment of patterns of economic integration has emerged. Its authors invariably draw a rather different set of conclusions. Thus, on the basis of an exhaustive (if not uncontroversial) assessment of the empirical evidence sceptics such as Paul Hirst and Grahame Thompson conclude that globalization is, in fact, a rather inaccurate description of existing patterns of international economic integration and cannot

credibly explain the development of the state in recent years (1999; for an important critical response to their work see Held et al. 1999).

The principal claims of this literature are summarized in Box 9.4 and discussed in more detail in the proceeding pages.

The comparative history of global economic integration

It is conventional, as already noted, to date the current era of globalization from the 1960s. And it is certainly the case that if we plot economic data from the early 1960s to the present day we see clear evidence of an almost exponential increase in trade and capital flows (expressed as shares of global GDP). Yet, it would be wrong to infer from this the development of an unprecedented integration of the global economy, without first considering the history of economic integration.

If we do that, then what becomes very clear is the sensitivity of the conclusions drawn by proponents of the globalization thesis to their preferred start date. If we extend the time frame, choosing as a starting point the late nineteenth or early twentieth century, a rather different picture emerges. Consider first economic openness with respect to trade (the value of imports plus exports expressed as a share of GDP).

Box 9.4 The empirical case against the globalization thesis

1 Although the period since the 1960s has seen the growing openness of national economies (such that imports plus exports are equivalent to a growing proportion of Gross Domestic Product), there is still some considerable way to go before pre-First World War figures are likely to be exceeded (Bairoch 1996; Hirst and Thompson 1999).

2 There continues to be a positive and, indeed, strengthening relationship between public spending (as a share of Gross Domestic Product) and economic openness (Cameron 1978; Katzenstein 1985; Garrett 1998b; Rodrik 1996, 1997).

3 There is no inverse relationship, as might be expected, between the volume of inward foreign direct investment and levels of corporate taxation, environmental and labour market regulations, generosity of welfare benefits or state expenditure as a share of Gross Domestic Product (Cooke and Noble 1998; Dunning 1988; Traxler and Woitech 2000; Wilensky 2002).

4 Trade and international flows of capital (such as foreign direct investment) tend to be extremely concentrated within the core 'triad' (of Europe, North America, and Pacific Asia) providing evidence of regionalization and 'triadization' but hardly of globalization (Frankel 1997; Hirst and Thompson 1999; Petrella 1996; Rugman, Chapter 10 in this volume).

5 The pace of economic integration is higher *within* regions (such as Europe, North America, or Pacific Asia) than it is *between* regions, suggesting that regionalization rather than globalization is the overriding dynamic in the process of international economic integration (Frankel 1997; Hay 2004; Kleinknecht and ter Wengel 1998; Ravenhill, Chapter 5 in this volume).

6 Financial integration has failed to produce the anticipated convergence in interest rates which one would expect from a fully integrated global capital market (Hirst and Thompson 1999; Zevin 1992);

7 Financial integration has failed to produce the anticipated divergence between rates of domestic savings and rates of domestic investment which one would expect in a fully integrated global capital market—the so-called 'Feldstein–Horioka puzzle' (Feldstein and Horioka 1980; see also Epstein 1996: 212–5; Watson 2001).

8 Though the liberalization of financial markets has certainly increased the speed, severity, and significance of investors' reactions to government policy, capital market participants appear far less discriminating or well-informed in their political risk assessment than is conventionally assumed (Mosley 2003; Swank 2002). Consequently, policy makers may retain rather more autonomy than is widely accepted.

As Hirst and Thompson note, 'apart from the dramatic differences in the openness to trade of different economies demonstrated by these figures . . . the startling feature is that trade to GDP ratios were consistently higher in 1913 than they were in 1973 . . . Even in 1995 . . . the US was the only country that was considerably more open than it was in 1913' (1999: 27). True, the composition of trade in, say, 1913 is likely to be remarkably different from that in 1973 or 1995, reflective in the case of the United Kingdom, the Netherlands, and Germany by a strongly colonial dimension. Nonetheless, in inviting a closer examination of the character and not just the quantity of trade and in pointing, in purely quantitative terms, to the by no means unprecedented level of international trade today, Hirst and Thompson provide a powerful challenge to the conventional literature.

The data with respect to capital flows reveal a similar pattern. Between 1870 and 1914 international capital flows between the G7 economies averaged some 4 per cent of GDP, peaking at around 6 per cent in 1914. Between 1914 and 1970 they declined to 1.5 per cent of GDP. Since 1970 they have charted a consistent upward trajectory, rising to 3 per cent of GDP by the early 1990s. Yet they still have a long way to go to reach the figures of the pre-First World War period (Hirst and Thompson 1999: 28, Figure 2.4; Bairoch 1996: 184; Lewis 1981; Turner 1981). In quantitative, if not perhaps in qualitative terms, the current period is not unprecedented or, indeed, unsurpassed.

In sum, then, whilst from the mid-1970s there has been an increasing trend towards financial and trade integration, economic openness was greater in the pre-First World War years than in the 1990s.

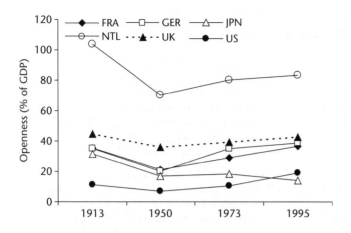

Fig. 9.6 Ratio of merchandise trade to GDP at current prices

Sources: Calculated from Maddison (1987: table A-23); OECD, National Accounts, 1997; Hirst and Thompson (1999: 27, table 2.3).

'Stateness' and openness

Arguably more significant, and certainly less contested, are recent attempts to reproduce and update David Cameron's (1978) path-breaking study of the covariance of economic openness and public expenditure. Such findings are particularly damaging to the globalization orthodoxy which predicts a strong inverse correlation between 'stateness' and openness—high levels of state expenditure (expressed as a proportion of GDP) *should* suppress the globalization of the domestic economy.

What Cameron demonstrated in a now famous paper published in the *American Political Science Review* in 1978 was a strong positive correlation between trade openness and social protection, funded through taxation. In other words, international economic integration seemed to go hand in hand with comprehensive social provision. Moreover, openness was also positively correlated with social democratic tenure, union power, and the degree of regulation of the labour market.

More damaging still to the orthodox globalization thesis has been more recent research in this vein by, amongst others, Peter Katzenstein (1985), Geoffrey Garrett (1998b), and Dani Rodrik (1996, 1997). What these authors demonstrate is that the strength of the correlation between openness and government expenditure in OECD countries has only grown in subsequent decades. For proponents of the hyperglobalization thesis this takes some explaining. Yet for Dani Rodrik (1997: 53) it is easily explained:

What should we make of this? I will argue that the puzzle is solved by considering the importance of social insurance and

the role of government in providing cover against external risk. Societies that expose themselves to greater amounts of external risk demand (and receive) a larger government role as shelter from the vicissitudes of global markets. In the context of the advanced industrial economies specifically, this translates into more generous social programmes. Hence the conclusion that the social welfare state is the flip side of the open economy!

Rodrik's is, of course, not the only possible explanation. Equally plausible is that high levels of state expenditure are a result of success in international markets—a consequence rather than a condition of the globalization of the domestic economy. Yet whichever way round it is, economic openness would seem far more compatible with state expenditure than is conventionally assumed.

The determinants of inward foreign direct investment

As we saw in an earlier section, orthodox accounts of globalization tend to make a series of clear and more or less plausible assumptions about the preferences and interests of mobile investors. Such assumptions, as was shown, are directly responsible for the influential thesis that states enhance their locational competitiveness to foreign direct investors by offering targeted investment incentives, eliminating labour market rigidities, reducing the burden of corporate taxation, and ensuring that environmental regulations are not overly restrictive. Alter the assumptions and a rather different set of inferences (and consequent policy implications) follow.

Recent scholarship, which examines the *revealed* preferences of foreign direct investors as exhibited in actual investment decisions (rather than making a priori assumptions about such preferences), challenges the globalization orthodoxy in important respects. Particularly notable here is the work of W. N. Cooke and D. S. Noble on the geographical distribution of foreign direct investment from the United States (1998). This work contains a number of significant findings, each troubling to proponents of the hyperglobalization thesis.

1. It is direct market access and/or proximity to market that is the single greatest determinant of investment location. Inward direct investors value, above all else, geographical proximity to a substantial and affluent market. Consequently, the greatest single predictor of the volume of inward investment is total income within a 1,000-kilometre radius of the investment site.

2. Once access and proximity to market are controlled for, educational attainment/skill level is the most critical factor in determining the attractiveness of an industrial relations regime. Yet the effect is complex and not as anticipated. As Cooke and Noble note, 'with respect to investments in low-skill-low-wage countries, the evidence indicates that US multinational corporations have sought to match lower work force education with the limited labour skill requirements of operations that get located in low-skill-low-wage countries . . . [A]cross low-wage-low-skill countries US multinationals invest more in locations with the lowest levels of education' (1998: 596). This much is consistent with the hyperglobalization thesis. Yet, 'in contrast, it appears that, in matching the high labour skills requirements of operations located in high-skill-high-wage countries, US multinationals invest more in countries with both higher average education levels and higher hourly compensation costs' (1998: 596). This reveals a globally segmented market for inward investment, in which it is only developing countries that are compelled to compete in terms of labour costs. Investors, it would seem, are perfectly prepared to pay the price of the highly trained and appropriately skilled workforce that (some) developed economies are capable of providing.

3. Moreover, and in seeming confirmation of this, it is not just the quantity (duration or level of attainment) of education that is important. Though it is difficult to gauge empirically, the evidence strongly supports the thesis that it is the *quality* and not the *cost* of skilled labour that is the key determinant of investment behaviour. Again, it would seem, cost (direct or indirect) is no impediment to investment if the perceived return provides adequate compensation for that cost. Thus, skill and productivity differences between economies make a significant and additional difference in attracting inward investment. Comparing the United Kingdom and Germany, Cooke and Noble explain, 'both have comparable average years of education . . . but substantially different average hourly compensation costs . . . Germany's unmeasured skill base has garnered about $2.3 billion more in US FDI per industry than has the UK's unmeasured skill base . . . high-skill-high-wage countries that further enhance skill levels can attract significant additional US foreign direct investment' (1998: 602).

4. The conclusion is clear, 'countries need not encourage . . . wage restraint, since high hourly compensation costs do not reduce . . . foreign direct investment, provided these costs are matched by higher skills and productivity' (1998: 602).

This, and other evidence like it (see, for instance Dunning 1988; Traxler and Woitech 2000; Swank 2002; Wilensky 2002) seriously challenges both the assumptions on which the hyperglobalization thesis is predicated and the predictions it makes about exit from highly regulated labour market regimes with generous welfare states funded out of taxation receipts.

Globalization or 'triadization'

In the highly contentious political economy of globalization, perhaps no issue is more controversial than the geographical character of the process of international economic integration that we have witnessed since the 1960s. It is, in particular, the challenge posed to the conventional wisdom by the recent work of arch globalization sceptics, Paul Hirst and Grahame Thompson, that has provided the central focus of attention and controversy (1996, 1999; see also Allen and Thompson 1997; Petrella 1996: 77–81; and, for a flavour of the critical responses, Held and McGrew 2002: 38–57; Perraton et al. 1997).

Hirst and Thompson, along with a growing crescendo of 'sceptics', have questioned the extent to which the term globalization accurately characterizes both the pattern of economic integration within the international political economy today or the trajectory of relations of economic integration and interdependence since the 1960s. Rather than a process of globalization, they suggest, a process of 'triadization' is and has been under way (1996: 2, 63–7). By triadization they refer to the selective and uneven process of deepening economic integration between the 'triad' economies; and by the 'triad' economies they refer to North America, South-East Asia, and Europe. In short, some economies are more global than others and this must ultimately lead us to challenge the appropriateness of the appellation 'globalization'. For a significant and rising proportion of international economic activity is conducted within and between the triad economies. This is true of trade, foreign direct investment, and finance. For Hirst and Thompson, then, the developmental path of the international economy is far more accurately characterized by pointing to the effects of two separate processes:

1 A more general process of intraregional economic integration or 'regionalization' (discussed in more detail presently); and

2 A more specific process of interregional economic integration drawing the triad economies into an ever denser web of complex interdependencies.

The appeal, and indeed much of the novelty, of Hirst and Thompson's work when first published was its reliance on a substantial body of empirical evidence. Until their contribution the innumerable empirical assertions made in the literature on globalization were largely unsubstantiated or defended only in a loose and anecdotal sense. Indeed, Hirst and Thompson's iconoclastic claim was that such assertions simply could not be defended evidentially. In so doing they pointed to the far from global character of flows of trade, investment, and finance. Space does not permit a detailed exploration of this evidence (though see Rugman, Chapter 10 in this volume). Suffice it to note that, between 1991 and 1996, over 60 per cent of all flows of foreign direct investment were conducted within and between the triad economies and, in 1995, over 75 per cent of the accumulated stock of foreign direct investment was located within the same triad bloc (1999: 71; see also Brewer and Young 1998: 58–60). Between 1980 and

1991 the figures were almost identical (1996: 68). The triadic concentration in the accumulated stock of outward foreign direct investment is even more pronounced (see Figure 9.7).

Moreover, in 1996, despite accounting for only 14.5 per cent of the world's population these economies accounted for some two-thirds of global exports (1999: 73), a figure marginally lower than that for 1992 (70 per cent), but significantly greater than for either 1990 (64 per cent), 1980 (55 per cent), or 1970 (61 per cent) (1996: 69; Petrella 1996: 79). Finally, as Riccardo Petrella notes, 'during the 1980s, the triad accounted for around four-fifths of all international capital flows . . . [whilst] the developing countries' share fell from 25 per cent in the 1970s to 19 per cent' (1996: 77).

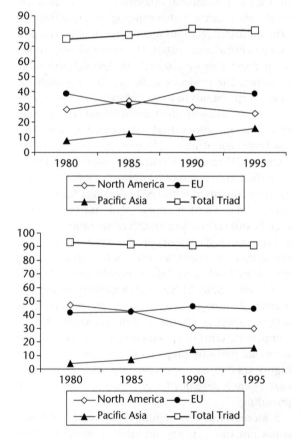

Fig. 9.7 Inward FDI stock (share of total)

Source: Calculated from Brewer and Young (1998: table 2.7 and 2.8).

How much damage this does to the globalization thesis depends, to a large extent, on what one takes that thesis to be. Indeed, arguably the debate is largely semantic (see also Scholte 2000*b*: 14–20). Sceptics like Hirst and Thompson and Petrella adopt a rather more exacting definition of globalization, it seems, than many of the hyperglobalization theorists. If, to count as evidence of globalization, processes either have to be genuinely global in scope or operative in unleashing such dynamics, then globalization characterizes poorly the condition and trajectory of the international economy. If, on the other hand, globalization means little more than economic openness (as witnessed by greater volumes of trade, investment, and financial flows as a share of global GDP) then globalization is certainly under way but it is unlikely to have the effects so frequently attributed to it. This is the challenge the sceptics present—one, it would seem, that is largely borne out by the empirical evidence.

Globalization or regionalization

Hirst and Thompson's emphasis, particularly in the first edition of *Globalization in Question*, is on the process of 'triadization' and hence upon a series of interregional processes of economic integration linking North America, South-East Asia, and Europe (1996). Yet, as indicated above, this rests on the prior identification of a more general tendency towards regionalization (within, and indeed beyond, the triad economies). In fact, in the second edition of *Globalization in Question*, the significance of triadization is somewhat downplayed as, on the basis of a re-examination and updating of the available evidence, regionalization now emerges as the pervasive tendency within the international economy (1999: especially 99–103). Here, again, Hirst and Thompson's work provides a powerful statement of a developing consensus amongst sceptical voices.

Yet it is the work of Jeffrey Frankel that is perhaps the most comprehensive on the question of regionalization (see especially 1997, 1998). On the basis of a detailed examination of the empirical record he demonstrates that, with respect to trade, any tendency to globalization or even *inter*regional economic integration has been swamped by the rapid growth in *intra*regional integration. Intraregional trade accounts for an ever-growing share of global economic activity, suggesting once again that globalization is in fact an increasingly inaccurate characterization of both the process of economic integration and the resulting pattern of economic interdependencies (see Ravenhill, Chapter 5 in this volume, Table 5.3).

Such findings have been replicated for foreign direct investment flows to and from Europe (Hay 2004; Kleinknecht and ter Wengel 1998). Whilst this provides strong evidence of regionalization it does not exhaust the case against the globalization thesis. Arguably rather more discriminating empirically is data on the regional concentration of trade. As Frankel explains, 'to obtain a useable measure of regional concentration, we need to adjust the intraregional trade share by a measure of each group's importance in world trade' (1997: 25–6). This is achieved by dividing each regional grouping's trade share by that region's share of total world trade. The resulting index of intraregional concentration, again, reveals a pervasive regionalization tendency. For, in a globalizing world we would expect the value of such intraregional concentration ratios to fall consistently over time. As Figure 9.8 makes very clear, with the sole exception of East Asia, the effect is one of trendless fluctuation or further regionalization rather than globalization.

Finally, so-called gravity models (a form of regression analysis in econometrics) have been used to examine the sensitivity of trade and, indeed, foreign direct investment to distance for a number of European countries (Hay 2003, 2004). A gravity model predicts that trade (and/or foreign direct investment) will decay exponentially with distance. In an era of globalization, in which transportation costs have been diminished and barriers to trade eliminated, we would expect to see the decreasing sensitivity of trade (and investment) to distance. Accordingly, the gravity model should become ever less effective in predicting patterns of trade (and investment). Yet, unremarkably perhaps given the evidence discussed above, far from showing a consistent pattern of globalization since the 1960s, the gravity model becomes an ever better fit to the data. This demonstrates, once again, a pervasive regionalization tendency in which trade and investment become more not less sensitive to geographical distance. European economies, it would seem, have experienced a consistent and ongoing process of deglobalization since the 1960s as the process of European

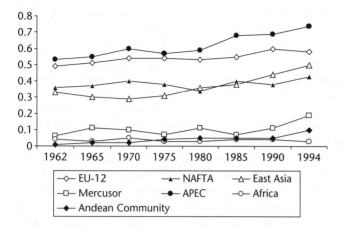

Fig. 9.8 Intraregional trade as a proportion of total trade

Source: Calculated from Frankel (1997: 22–4).

economic integration has accelerated. Similar tendencies would appear to be under way in many, if perhaps not all, regions within the international economy. As this suggests, globalization is a tendency that has, in the majority of cases, been swamped in recent decades by a regionalizing counter-tendency.

Capital market integration and interest-rate convergence

Thus far we have examined evidence principally relating to trade and foreign direct investment and it is important that we now turn our attention to the degree of integration (or globalization) of financial markets. It is often assumed that even if the case against the globalization thesis is credible with respect to trade and foreign direct investment (for the reasons discussed above), the thesis is rather more robust with respect to financial markets and, moreover, that the effects of financial market integration on the autonomy of the nation state are most pronounced (see, for instance, Cerny 1995, 1997). Yet, as we shall see, recent evidence casts some doubt on this claim too.

The first surprising piece of empirical evidence for proponents of the globalization thesis is the observed failure of interest rates to converge. In a fully integrated capital market a common international rate of interest on short-term and long-term loans would emerge almost instantaneously, for fairly obvious reasons. All things being equal, borrowers will seek out the lowest rate of interest available to them, just as savers will seek the highest rate of return (and hence interest) on their savings.

Yet, as numerous commentators have noted, and despite some controversy about which precise index to use and what specific inferences to draw from such evidence, interest-rate differentials persist and show little sign of being eroded (Bayoumi and Rose 1993; Frankel 1991; Kasman and Pigott 1988; Osler 1991; and for a review, Simmons 1999: 57–61). Moreover, as Robert Zevin has argued, 'every available descriptor of financial markets in the late nineteenth and early twentieth century suggests that they were more fully integrated than they were before or have been since' (1992: 51–2).

This is an important observation which again draws our attention to the less than totally unprecedented character of the contemporary phase of economic integration. This is relatively easily accounted for. Quite simply, capital market integration occurred (to the extent that it did occur) far earlier than most have assumed. This is why there is no clear contemporary evidence of (further) interest-rate convergence. As Hirst and Thompson suggest, 'the coming of the electronic telegraph system after 1870 in effect established more or less instantaneous information communications between all the major international financial and business centres' (1999: 37–8). The shift in the 1870s from ships to telegraph was far more significant than that from telegraph to telematics in the 1970s.

Savings and investment correlations: the 'Feldstein–Horioka' paradox

Interest-rate convergence is not the only index of financial globalization. In a perfectly integrated capital market we would expect to see a clear divergence of domestic savings and investment rates. In a system of closed and bounded national economies these should correlate absolutely (or very closely). In a genuinely open economy (a perfectly integrated capital market), we would expect the correlation to break down as investors become genuinely global, sourcing their investments from around the world. Indeed, we would expect the correlation to fall to zero (Feldstein and Horioka 1980; see also Bayoumi 1997: 17–19). Consequently, a persistent correlation between domestic savings and investment levels provides strong evidence of a lack of integration of capital markets.

What do we observe? The evidence is again relatively unambiguous. As a large number of commentators have noted, national savings–investment correlations show no consistent pattern of decline in the 1980s and 1990s (Bayoumi 1990; Epstein 1996; Feldstein and Bacchetta 1991; Feldstein and Horioka 1980; Tesar 1991). As Hirst and Thompson suggest, this 'testifies to the continued robust relative autonomy of financial systems' (1999: 38). Indeed, the 'savings retention coefficient' (the proportion of incremental savings invested domestically) remains at 67 per cent for the period 1991–5 (Obstfeld 1993).

This, again, is an important finding and one that continues to trouble international macro-economists, for whom it remains something of a paradox even after over two decades. The 'Feldstein–Horioka puzzle', as it has come to be known, has given rise to an extensive literature and considerable controversy (for reviews of which see Bayoumi 1997: 30–53; Obstfeld and Rogoff 1996: 161–4; Rødseth 2000: 163–4). Unremarkably, a series of challenges have been mounted to the notion that it provides clear evidence of the lack of integration of capital markets. Yet, as we shall see, none of these caveats is ultimately devastating.

1. As a number of commentators have noted, aggregate indices of national investment do not discriminate between public and private investment (see, for instance, Bayoumi 1990). Savings–investment correlations might, then, mask a decrease in the savings–investment correlation for private investors. This is certainly accurate, yet the effect is likely to be relatively small; the essential paradox remains.

2. If, as Hirst and Thompson conjecture, there were 'no significant difference between the return on financial investment' from one economy to the next, 'then we might not expect a large redistribution of capital relative to savings' (1999: 40). Consequently, domestic savings–investment relations might prove persistent. Under such conditions we would be wrong to infer low levels of capital market integration. Yet, though plausible, the empirical evidence does not bear this out. For although there was, indeed, some convergence in returns on investment in the 1970s between the developed economies, this has given way to subsequent divergence (1999: 41). Again, the paradox remains.

3. In growing desperation, perhaps, international macro-economists have increasingly turned to hypothetical solutions to the paradox. If, they suggest, the global economy had experienced a productivity shock we would expect profitability to increase. This would result, in turn, in an increased propensity for both savings and investment. Under such conditions, the anticipated correlation between savings and investment would be spurious, at least in terms of the degree of capital market integration—as it would be generated in the absence of domestic investment being sourced from domestic savings (Ghosh 1995; Rødseth 2000: 164). This hypothetical solution to the paradox is both plausible and ingenious but it is significantly compromised by the fact that such productivity shocks are both relatively rare and, generally, short-term in nature. The persistent and seemingly long-term character of domestic savings–investment correlations (first observed in 1980) would suggest that a productivity shock is simply not responsible for the Feldstein–Horioka paradox.

4. Finally, and rather more plausibly, it has been suggested that economists have tended to draw the wrong (or, at least, an exaggerated) inference from the persistence of domestic savings–investment correlations. For, whilst in a perfectly integrated text-book capital market we might expect such correlations to tend to zero, in a real-world capital market, even a highly integrated one, we would expect some correlation to persist (Watson 2001). Real markets are not perfectly integrated, nor are they likely to become so.

Whether this provides the elusive 'solution' to the 'Feldstein–Horioka puzzle' or merely demonstrates further the dubious nature of the premises which continue to inform influential understandings of globalization (as reflected in unrealistic expectations about the degree of capital mobility we should expect to see) is a moot point.

The expressed and exhibited preferences of financial market actors

A persistent theme of this chapter has been the disparity between the a priori theoretical assumptions made in the conventional literature about the preferences of economic actors (principally investors) and the *actual* preferences of such actors (as revealed in their conduct). We have seen how the behaviour of foreign direct investors is rather different in 'reality' from that attributed to them in much of the existing literature. The same is equally true of financial investors, however more intuitively plausible the conventional assumptions may seem for such actors.

Here the recent work of Layna Mosley (2003) is especially notable. Mosley's work is unique in the existing literature in its attempt to gauge empirically both the *expressed preferences* of market participants through an extensive series of interviews with fund managers and the *revealed preferences* of market participants through a detailed statistical analysis of their investment decisions. Her conclusions are extremely important and do some considerable damage to the conventional wisdom.

Though the liberalization of financial markets has certainly increased the speed, severity, and significance of investors' reactions to government policy, capital market participants appear far less discriminating or well informed in their political risk assessment than is conventionally assumed. For advanced capitalist democracies, the range of government policies considered by market participants in making investment decisions is, in fact, extremely limited. As Mosley explains:

Governments are pressured strongly to satisfy financial market preferences in terms of overall inflation and government budget deficit levels but retain domestic policymaking latitude in other areas. The means by which governments achieve macropolicy outcomes, and the nature of government policies in other areas, do not concern financial market participants . . . [G]overnments retain a significant amount of policy autonomy and political accountability. If, for domestic reasons, they prefer to retain traditional social democratic policies, for instance, they are quite able to do so (2003: 305).

This is a most important finding, all the more so given the methodological rigour of the study from which it derives. It would seem to support Duane Swank's own important findings. On the basis of a detailed statistical analysis, he demonstrates the existence of a complex interaction effect between welfare state expenditure, on the one hand, and international capital mobility, on the other. When budgets are in balance, capital market liberalization produces a positive effect on welfare effort; when budgets are moderately in deficit there is no effect; and when budget deficits exceed 10 per cent of GDP the effect becomes negative. As Swank concludes, contrary to the prevailing consensus, 'rises in international capital openness, or exposure to international capital markets, do not exert significant downward pressure on the welfare state at moderate levels of budget imbalance [and] when budget deficits don't exist, some expansion of social protection is possible even in the context of international capital mobility' (2002: 94).

It would seem that the constraints imposed by financial market integration upon domestic political autonomy, certainly in the advanced capitalist economies, have been grossly exaggerated. Yet the picture is not an undifferentiated one. For developing countries, as Mosley again demonstrates in considerable detail, financial market participants are rather more exacting in the demands they make of government policy and correspondingly more severe in the constraints they impose.

Key points

- There is little evidence of systematic state retrenchment at the hands of globalization.

- There is little evidence of systematic convergence or dual convergence between models or varieties of capitalism under conditions of globalization.

- The impact of globalization of the nation state suggested in the hyperglobalization thesis has been challenged empirically by a number of authors. They have pointed to the less than unprecedented degree of integration of the global economy today, the positive correlation between openness and public spending, the factors which attract foreign direct investors, the regional and triadic character of international trade and investment, the far from fully integrated character of financial markets, and the investment behaviour of financial market actors.

Conclusions

What are we to make of this? The overall picture that emerges is rather more complex than that with which we began. Whilst the economic processes usually labelled globalization have led to a greater degree of economic integration than at any point in the post-war period, current levels of economic interdependence are neither unprecedented historically nor perhaps as genuinely 'global' as is invariably assumed.

The impact of such processes on the capacity, autonomy, and sovereignty of the state is also complex. For whilst there is certainly some evidence of state retrenchment in recent years, especially once one controls for the higher demands placed upon welfare states by demographic change and higher rates of unemployment, there would seem to be no clear evidence that globalization is the driver of this retrenchment. Indeed, the evidence reviewed in the previous section would strongly suggest that the constraints imposed upon domestic political autonomy by heightened levels of economic integration (with respect to trade, foreign direct investment, or finance) have been grossly exaggerated. Yet this does not mean that globalization has had no impact on the nation state—merely that we need to be extremely cautious in attributing state retrenchment today to globalization.

Rather more plausible, and sadly overlooked in much of the existing literature, is the impact of *ideas* about globalization. If it is conceded that policy makers increasingly view the world they face through a series of assumptions about globalization, then their conduct in office is likely to be shaped significantly by those assumptions. Arguably, then, the idea of globalization may be more influential in shaping the developmental trajectory of the nation state today than the reality of globalization (see Box 9.5).

This raises an important point about democratic legitimacy and accountability today. For it is all very well to argue that state autonomy remains essentially intact in an era of globalization. But if such autonomy is perceived to have been eroded by all credible candidates for political office, then such autonomy is purely hypothetical. Whilst globalization may not have narrowed the field of democratic choice itself, the idea of globalization may well have done so—as parties across the political spectrum converge on a set of prudent economic and social policies designed to appease footloose multinational investors. Arguably this has much to do with the widespread contemporary disaffection with liberal democratic regimes (see, for instance, Pharr and Putnam 2000). Democracy is no less a casualty in such a scenario. This makes the public scrutiny of influential assumptions and ideas about globalization a most urgent political priority. It establishes once again the phenomenal importance of the ongoing controversy which surrounds the question of globalization's impact on the state.

One final point might also be noted. Whilst there is in fact little evidence for the thesis that the nation state's capacity and autonomy has been significantly eroded by virtue of globalization, it is nonetheless the case that globalization poses a series of problems for the nation state which it has never had the capacity to deal with. We have seen, and are likely to continue to see, a proliferation of interlinked and genuinely global political, economic, and, above all, environmental problems requiring, for their resolution, effective institutions of global governance. This final point is perhaps the most troubling of all. It is certainly tempting to dismiss globalization

Box 9.5 The role of ideas about globalization: tax competition between states

Consider tax competition between states. The hyperglobalization thesis suggests that in a globalized context characterized by the heightened mobility of capital, vicious competition between states will serve to drive down the level of corporate taxation. Accordingly, any failure on the part of a state to render its corporate taxation levels competitive in comparative terms, through tax cuts, will result in a punitive depreciation in net revenue as capital exercises its mobility to exit. If governments believe the thesis to be true, or find it to their advantage to present it as true, they will act in a manner consistent with its predictions, thereby contributing to an aggregate depreciation in corporate taxation—whether they are right to do so or not.

To elaborate, were we to envisage a (hypothetical) scenario in which the hyperglobalization thesis were accurate, the free mobility of capital would indeed serve to establish tax competition between fiscal authorities seeking to retain existing investment levels whilst enticing mobile foreign direct investors to relocate. The price of any attempt to buck the trend is immediate capital flight with consequent effects on budget revenue. In such a scenario any rational administration aware (or assuming itself

to be aware) of the mobility of capital will cut corporate taxes with the effect that no exit will be observed (Scenario 1). Any administration foolish enough to discount or test the mobility of capital by retaining high levels of corporate taxation will be rudely awakened from its state of blissful ignorance or stubborn scepticism by a rapid exodus of capital (Scenario 2). In a world of perfect capital mobility, then, the learning curve is likely to prove very steep indeed.

Yet, were we to assume instead that we inhabit a world in which the mobility of capital is much exaggerated and in which capital has a clear vested interest in threatening exit, the scenario unfolds rather differently. Here, fiscal authorities lulled into accepting the hyperglobalization thesis by the (ultimately hollow) exit threats of capital will cut rates of corporate tax, (falsely) attributing the lack of capital flight to their competitive taxation regime (Scenario 3). Yet, were they to resist this logic by calling capital's bluff they might retain substantial taxation receipts without fear of capital flight (Scenario 4). The crucial point, however, is that whilst politicians believe the hyperglobalization thesis—and act upon it—we cannot

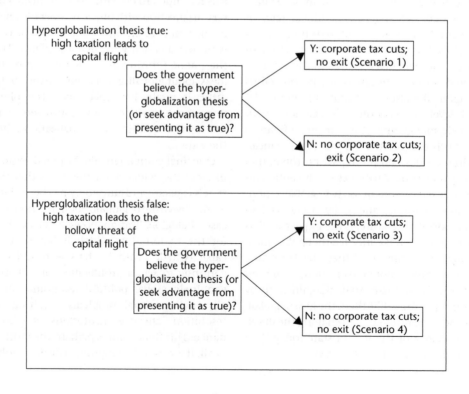

differentiate between Scenario 1 (in which the thesis is true) and Scenario 3 (in which it is false). Though in the former Scenario, globalization is a genuine constraint on political autonomy and in the latter it is merely a social construction, the outcomes are the same. As this demonstrates, in the end at least in this scenario it is ideas about globalization . . . rather than globalization *per se* which affects political and economic outcomes. [This makes the role of international institutions in the dissemination of ideas about globalization especially significant].

Source: Adapted from Hay (2002*b*: 202–4).

as a myth or as a process with minimal impact upon the historical capacities of the state. Yet the problem of the lack of the political capacity to deal with urgent global problems in an effective and democratic way remains. The challenges we face are essentially twofold:

1 To find ways of designing effective and democratic institutions of global governance capable of commanding political support and legitimacy; and

2 To find ways of passing responsibility and indeed sovereignty from a system of nation states that still provides the focus of political identification and citizenship to such institutions.

At the point at which we prove ourselves capable of responding to both of these challenges, we might legitimately begin to speak of a transcendence (if not perhaps a crisis) of the nation state. But that point is still a very, very long way off.

QUESTIONS

1 Is there, or has there been, a crisis of the nation state?

2 What is meant by the globalization of politics and has it occurred?

3 What mechanisms can be pointed to suggesting a clear link between globalization and state retrenchment?

4 What are the key assumptions of the hyperglobalization thesis? Are they plausible?

5 Is globalization an agent of convergence, dual convergence, divergence, or continued diversity?

6 How does the model of the 'tragedy of the commons' illuminate the problem of global governance?

7 Assess the evidence on whether state retrenchment has taken place.

8 What impact has globalization had on the development of the nation state?

9 Are the constraints on the autonomy and capacity of the nation state arising from globalization largely real or imagined?

FURTHER READING

Cerny, P. G. (1997), 'Paradoxes of the Competition State: The Dynamics of Political Globalization', *Government and Opposition*, 32/2: 251–74. The clearest exposition of the highly influential 'competition state' thesis.

Garrett, G. (2000), 'Shrinking States? Globalization and National Autonomy', in N. Woods (eds.), *The Political Economy of Globalization* (Basingstoke: Palgrave). A clear and comprehensive survey of the existing literature and supporting evidence by an influential commentator.

Hirst, P., and Thompson, G. (1999), *Globalization in Question*, 2nd edn. (Cambridge: Polity). The definitive statement of the case against the globalization orthodoxy.

Jessop, B. (2002), *The Future of the Capitalist State* (Cambridge: Polity). The product of almost two decades of scholarship, this is perhaps the most important single work on the condition of the state today. Though dense and at times difficult, it rewards close reading.

Mosley, L. (2003), *Global Capital and National Governments* (Cambridge: Cambridge University Press). An exceptionally important recent addition to the existing literature and a comprehensive reappraisal of the conventional wisdom about the domestic political constraints issuing from financial markets.

Ohmae, K. (1996), *The End of the Nation State* (New York: Free Press). Though widely discredited, still the core exponent and defender of the hyperglobalization thesis.

Weiss, L. (1998), *The Myth of the Powerless State: Governing the Economy in a Global Era* (Cambridge: Polity). A clear and accessible defence of the continued centrality and importance of the nation state in an era of globalization.

10 Globalization and regional international production

Alan M. Rugman

READER'S GUIDE

Foreign Direct Investment (FDI) has grown enormously in the past twenty-five years; it increased particularly rapidly in the 1990s. Many authors see FDI as the principal motor of globalization. Why do firms undertake FDI rather than supply foreign markets through exports from their home base or through licensing a local firm to manufacture their product? This has been the central question in the large theoretical literature on the multinational enterprise. The consensus is that an 'eclectic' approach best explains FDI. This approach identifies three factors—firm-specific advantages; the capacity of a company to 'internalize' its advantages; and location-specific advantages—as critical in decisions to undertake FDI.

The majority of international production is conducted by a relatively small set of multinational enterprises (MNEs) from the 'core triad' of the European Union, the United States, and Japan. Indeed, as few as 500 MNEs account for 90 per cent of the world's stock of FDI and also for 40 per cent of the world's trade. These firm-level data reinforce the aggregate trade and FDI data reported in Rugman (2000), showing that there has been increased *intraregional* activity over the last twenty years. In other words, there is little or no evidence of globalization of manufacturing production, only of regionalization. These data on the regional production of MNEs have major implications for both corporate strategy and government policy. These are explored in the concluding section of this chapter.

Introduction

Foreign Direct Investment is the engine of international business. In contrast to portfolio investment, which is the purchase of financial securities in other firms for the purpose of realizing financial gains when these marketable assets are sold, FDI is defined as the investment of equity funds across national boundaries. Every time a company builds a factory or marketing office; purchases a distributor, plant, or competitor; or acquires control of a natural resource, it is engaging in FDI. Unlike trade, FDI represents the physical expansion of operations across national borders. The MNE is a company that has established an international presence by engaging in FDI.

According to UNCTAD's *World Investment Report*, the world stock of FDI has more than tripled over the last eleven years. In 2002, world FDI outward stock

Table 10.1 World inward stocks of FDI, 1990 and 2002 (in US$bn and percentages)

Region	1990	% total	2002	% total
Developed countries	1,400	71.6	4,595	64.5
North America	508	26.0	1,573	22.1
Western Europe	781	40.0	2,780	39.0
Other developed countries	94	4.8	242	3.4
Developing countries	551	28.2	2,340	32.9
China	25	1.3	448	6.3
Hong Kong	201	10.3	433	6.1
Least developed countries	8	0.4	46	0.6
World	1,954	100.0	7,123	100.0

Note: Numbers may not add to 100% due to rounding.
Source: Adapted from UNCTAD (2003).

Box 10.1 **FDI into China**

In the 1990s, the expectation that China would join the World Trade Organization (which it did in 2001), led many companies to establish themselves in one of the fastest growing markets in the world and to take advantage of the country's low production costs. Indeed, between 1990 and 2001, the inward stock of FDI in the country increased nearly sixteen-fold. China now holds 6 per cent of the world's stock of FDI, compared to 1.3 per cent in 1990. A large percentage of foreign investment into China (in 2002, approximately 36 per cent) originates in Hong Kong, much of which is believed to be capital that was originally sent from China itself to avoid various government restrictions. Hong Kong and China together account for more than one-third of the total inward stock of FDI held by developing countries.

The 'round-tripping' of capital between China and Hong Kong illustrates some of the difficulties involved in measuring FDI. Developing countries often do not have the bureaucratic capacity to collect FDI statistics systematically (consequently, UNCTAD's *World Investment Report*, generally regarded as the most authoritative

comprehensive source of data on FDI, sometimes relies on data from the MNE's home country). Different countries adopt different conventions as to what constitutes control of a company from the point of view of the management of its assets. For example, some may regard foreign ownership of 10 per cent in an enterprise as constituting 'control', while others may consider that a figure of 50 per cent or more is required to establish 'control'. Some governments use data from applications they receive from MNEs for approval for investments to measure their 'expected' value: others rely on the value of investments actually made. Further difficulties arise in attempting to estimate the market value of stocks of FDI.

Data on 'flows' of investment across national boundaries typically ignore another important source of FDI: the reinvestment of profits in host countries by the established subsidiaries of MNEs. Because data on 'stocks' of FDI reflect more accurately the contribution of MNEs to host country economies, this chapter reports the figures for stocks rather than for flows (both are available in the *World Investment Report*).

was estimated at $6,866 billion. For the same year, inward stocks of FDI were estimated at $7,122 billion. Developed countries accounted for the largest portion of this, 64.5 per cent. In other words, the vast majority of FDI occurs between industrialized countries (although their share in all FDI has declined since 1990, when they accounted for 73.9 per cent of all inward stocks of FDI). In contrast, the share of inward stocks of FDI in developing countries increased from 28.2 per cent to 32.9 per cent between 1990 and 2002 (see Table 10.1). A significant factor in the growing share of developing countries in overall FDI flows has been the huge increase in foreign investment in China (see Box 10.1).

Analysis of the multinational enterprise

The reasons why firms engage in FDI include:

1 to diversify against the risks and uncertainties of their domestic business cycle;

2 to tap the growing world market for goods and services;

3 in response to increased foreign competition in their home market;

4 to decrease costs by setting operations closer to foreign customers or take advantage of the lower costs of production;

5 to overcome trade barriers imposed by governments; and

6 to take advantage of technological expertise in a foreign country (for further discussion, see Rugman and Hodgetts 2003: chapter 2).

Because more than one factor frequently motivates a firm's decision to undertake FDI, the literature on the MNE now accepts that an 'eclectic' approach is required to understand the reasons behind the investments made by MNEs. This eclectic approach to the theory of FDI was originally developed by John Dunning (1981). It provides a consolidation of the literature on FDI that draws on industrial organization theories, location theory, and market imperfections approaches (see Box 10.2). The eclectic theory specifies a set of three conditions that must be met if a firm is to engage in FDI.

Firm-specific advantages (FSA)

The firm must possess net ownership advantages vis-à-vis firms of other nationalities in serving particular (and, in practice, mainly foreign) markets. These firm-specific (or ownership) advantages largely take the form of the possession of intangible assets, which are, at least for a period of time, exclusive or specific to the firm possessing them.

Internalization advantages

A firm possessing an advantage can either use the advantage itself (internalize it) or can sell or lease the advantage to other firms. This choice is usually

---

Box 10.2 **Dunning's eclectic theory of international production**

Ownership-specific (firm-specific) advantages

  Firm-specific knowledge advantages

  Management, marketing, financial skills

  Vertical integration

    Control of resources

    Control of markets

  Risk diversification

Internalization (by MNEs)

  To enforce property rights and overcome other transaction costs

  To reduce buyer uncertainty

  To overcome government regulations

Location-specific (country-specific) advantages

  National production functions

  Government controls and regulations

  Political risk; cultural values

explained in the context of transactions costs and internalization theory (Rugman 1981). There are costs involved in use of markets and in internal coordination and control. The FDI decision depends on which option presents the best net return (revenue minus cost), when the risks associated with each alternative are taken into account. According to internalization theory, both natural and unnatural market imperfections induce internalization by MNEs. The firm must consider not only government-imposed regulations, but also natural barriers and other transaction costs such as the creation of buyer uncertainty.

Assuming that a firm possesses unique ownership advantages, if it is to engage in FDI it must be more beneficial for it to internalize its FSA, for example, to secure property rights over its firm-specific advantages in knowledge, rather than to sell or lease them to foreign firms. This internalization is done through an extension of its own activities rather than by externalizing them through contacts at arm's-length prices (which, in any case, may not exist) with independent firms. The management of the firm must judge that

alternatives to internalization such as licensing, management contracts, franchises, technical service agreements, turnkey projects, and subcontracts are either not a feasible or the most profitable method of appropriating its firm-specific advantages.

Country-specific (location-specific) advantages (CSAs)

Assuming that the conditions stated in the two preceding sections are satisfied, if FDI is to take place it must be profitable for the enterprise to locate abroad, that is, to utilize these firm-specific advantages in conjunction with at least some factor inputs (including natural resources) outside its home country. Otherwise foreign markets would be served entirely by exports and home markets by domestic production. Therefore, the location-specific advantages of the MNE are important elements in its choice of modality for servicing foreign markets.

Relevance of the Dunning Model

The net ownership, or firm-specific, advantages are required to offset the costs incurred by the MNE of operating at a distance from its home base. In the literature on the MNE, these costs are referred to, following Williamson (1975), as *transaction costs*. Transactions costs arise from the difficulties of communicating over large distances and of controlling many subsidiaries. Both factors come into play once production decisions are made across national boundaries. In contrast, these costs of operating internationally are not incurred by a local firm. The MNE must possess advantages that offset the disadvantages (additional costs) incurred in operating transnationally. If assets corresponding to those conferring the advantages to the MNE were available to local host-country firms, the MNE would not be able to compensate for the transaction costs of operating at a distance.

The use of the advantage in the host country is required if FDI is to take place. The cost of moving resources used in the host country must exceed the costs of controlling a subsidiary at a distance plus the

costs of trade. Otherwise, the resource would be exported or moved to the home country, production would take place in the home country, and the foreign country market would be served by exports.

Sources of firm-specific advantages

The range of advantages that can lead to FDI is large but can be summarized as follows:

1. Proprietary technology due to research and development activities.

2. Managerial, marketing, or other skills specific to the organizational function of the firm.

3. Product differentiation, trademarks, or brand names.

4. Large size, reflecting scale economies.

5. Large capital requirements for plants of the minimum efficient size.

Sources of internalization advantages

The conditions that favour internalization include:

1 The high costs of making and enforcing contracts.

2 Buyer uncertainty about the value of the technology being sold.

3 A need to control the use or resale of the product.

4 Advantages to using price discrimination or cross-subsidization.

Sources of country-specific advantages

The location-specific advantages of the host country can include:

1 Natural resources.

2 Efficient and skilled relatively low-cost labour force.

3 Trade barriers restricting imports.

Box 10.3 Porter's diamond of competitive advantage

Whereas conventional economic theory suggests that countries must be content to work with the natural factor endowments that they possess, Porter (1990) suggested that firms can help to improve a country's international competitiveness by utilizing new advanced factor endowments such as skilled labour, an advanced knowledge and scientific base, and a competitive environment for domestic firms. The four key factors that affect national competitive advantage are presented in the diamond figure below. The individual points on the diamond and their interaction determine the four factors that Porter argues lead to national competitive advantage. First is factor conditions, the availability of natural resources and the quality and quantity of the labour force. Second is demand conditions, the size and quality of a country's demand, as measured by its Gross Domestic Product. Third is the amount of home market rivalry and the managerial skills in a country. Fourth are the related and supporting industries, mainly in the service sector infrastructure. An additional two factors affect international competitiveness: chance and government. This single diamond model applies well to a large regional market in the 'triad', such as the United States, European Union, and Japan, but it is not as useful for managers of firms in small, open, trading economies such as Australia, Canada, Norway, Korea, etc. These countries have firms whose managers follow a 'double diamond' approach. They look at the diamond in their home country but also simultaneously at the diamond of their largest trading partner. These models are discussed in Rugman and Hodgetts 2003: chapter 15.

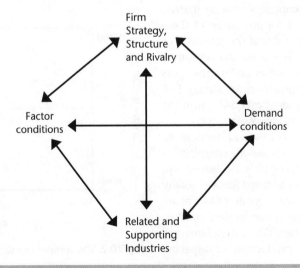

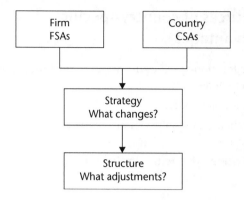

Fig. 10.1 The basic components of international business

The first and second of these CSAs can result in FDI that leads to exports as well as to production for the local market. The third CSA will be associated with production for the local market only.

Tariff and non-tariff barriers to trade, the country's competitive environment, and government regula-

tions also influence CSAs. Building on these CSAs, the firm makes decisions about the efficient international configuration and coordination between segments of its value chain (operations, marketing, R&D, and logistics). The skill in making such organizational decisions represents a strong, managerial firm-specific asset in itself.

In a perfect market situation, free trade would be the most efficient means of servicing markets abroad; however, given the many barriers to trade presently affecting the market, MNEs are a necessary alternative. The ability of MNEs to create internal markets enables them to bypass the barriers to trade that governments often erect.

Managers and most MNEs use strategies that build on the interactions of country-specific advantages and firm-specific advantages (see Figure 10.1). They do this to position themselves in a unique strategic space. In Porter's (1990) terminology, the CSAs form the basis of the global platform from which the multinational firm derives a home-base 'diamond' advantage of global competitiveness (see Box 10.3).

The FSA/CSA matrix

To help formulate the strategic options available to the MNE, it is useful to identify the relative strengths and weaknesses of the country-specific advantages they can access and the firm-specific advantages they possess. Figure 10.2, the competitive strategy matrix, provides a useful framework for discussion of these issues. It should be emphasized that the 'strength' or 'weakness' of FSAs and CSAs is a relative notion. It depends upon the relevant market and on the CSAs and FSAs of potential competitors. A strong FSA implies that, when faced by identical CSAs, a firm has a potential competitive advantage over its rivals.

Quadrants 1, 2, and 3 correspond broadly to the three generic strategies for achieving competitiveness, suggested by Porter (1980): cost leadership, differentiation, and focus. Quadrant 3 firms generally can follow any of these strategies. Quadrant 1 firms are generally resource based and/or mature firms producing a commodity-type product. Given their late stage in the product life cycle, production firm-specific

advantages flowing from the possession of intangible skills are less important than the country-specific advantages of location and energy costs, which are the main sources of the firm's competitive advantage.

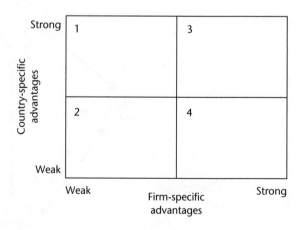

Fig. 10.2 The competitive strategy matrix

Thus these firms are following low-cost and price competition strategies. Firms in quadrant 4 include those with strong firm-specific advantages in marketing, brand names, and customization. These firms follow basically a differentiation strategy. In quadrant 4, firm-specific advantages dominate, so for firms in this quadrant, the home-country CSAs are not essential for strategic success in world markets. Quadrant 2 comprises inefficient, floundering firms with no consistent strategy, nor any intrinsic CSAs or FSAs. These firms are either preparing to exit production or to restructure. Quadrant 2 can also represent domestically based small and medium-sized firms with little global exposure.

In terms of business strategy, quadrants 3 and 2 are unambiguous in their implications. A quadrant 3 firm can benefit from strategies of both low cost and differentiation. By developing dynamic organizational capabilities and maintaining an effective strategy, the firm can maintain its overall position in quadrant 3. In contrast, firms in quadrant 2 have no alternative but to restructure or to eventually leave the market.

Quadrants 4 and 1 are credible positions for different types of firms to occupy. For instance, a quadrant 4 firm that has strong firm-specific advantages in marketing (for example, brand name recognition) can operate regionally or globally without reliance on its home-market CSA, or the CSAs of the host nation. For such a firm, quadrant 4 does not signal a CSA weakness; rather, country-specific advantages are simply not relevant. In contrast, quadrant 1 has mature multinational companies or product lines determined more by country-specific advantages than by firm-specific advantages. By improving potential FSAs in marketing or through product innovation and increasing value added through vertical integration, the quadrant 1 firm can move to quadrant 3, where its profitability should be enhanced.

The CSAs are best defined as those available in the *home* country of the MNE. They can be redefined to represent the home *region* rather than an individual country, for example, the European Union rather than Germany, and Asia rather than Korea. The CSAs can also be used analytically to refer to *host*-nation advantages, but this is not undertaken in the discussion in this chapter. To make the matrix work it is useful to use it sequentially for separate analytical discussions of home and host-nation CSAs.

The second part of the chapter examines how MNEs in the manufacturing sector have chosen to capitalize on the firm-specific and country-specific advantages available to them.

Key points

- FDI has grown very rapidly in recent years. Most FDI takes place among industrialized economies although the share of less developed countries (LDCs) in total FDI stocks is rising.

- An 'eclectic' explanation, which focuses on the interaction of firm-specific advantages, internalization, and country-specific advantages, best explains the decision by MNEs to engage in FDI.

- The combination and relative strength of firm-specific and country-specific advantages determine the competitiveness of firms and the range of feasible strategies a firm can pursue.

Globalization, regionalization, and the MNE

The asymmetrical dominance of the largest 500 MNEs in accounting for nearly all of the world's international production has often been confused with globalization. Indeed, a basic definition of economic globalization is the worldwide spread of goods and services by MNEs, leading to commonality of production and consumption (the same goods being produced by the same MNEs in all parts of the world). However, writers on globalization often make three mistakes:

1 They often confuse international sales with globalization. In fact, most of the sales of the world's 500 largest MNEs are *within* their home regions.

2 They often argue that globalization is driven by US MNEs. In fact, there are as many European as US MNEs and there are also many large Asian

---

Box 10.4 **The Regional Nature of Global Multinational Activity Survey**

The data on the Regional Nature of Global Multinational Activity (RNGMA) were collected from official documents of the world's 500 largest companies (according to the *Fortune* Global 500 in 2002). Wherever possible the Annual Report, and in the case of US companies and those with large operations in the United States 10-K SEC (Securities and Exchange Commission) filings, were used to obtain data on regional sales.

It is important to note that although the aggregate GDPs of Europe and North America are roughly equal, that of the Asia-Pacific region is substantially smaller than these two so one would expect, other things being equal, that the Asia-Pacific would be a relatively less important market for MNEs.

Of the largest 500 firms in the world, information was only available for 380 companies. These 380 companies comprise *The Regional Nature of Global Multinational Activity (RNGMA)*. These companies represent 76 per cent of the *Fortune* Global 500 MNEs and 79.2 per cent of their revenues. Of the RNGMA's 380 companies, 200 are service companies and 180 are manufacturing companies. The RNGMA simplifies the *Fortune* Global 500 industry classifications codes into sixteen broad categories. Of these, nine are manufacturing categories and seven are service categories. For more details on the survey, see Rugman (2005).

Appendix 10.1 lists the world's 180 largest manufacturing MNEs.

MNEs. Of the fifty largest MNEs in manufacturing, twenty-five have their home region in North America, fifteen in Europe, and ten in the Asia-Pacific. In other words, there is a 'triad' of MNEs from North America, Europe, and Asia. No single region of the triad is dominant.

3 There is no evidence of commonality, that is, in the manufacturing sector there is no spread of production on a uniform, global basis. Rather, each set of triad-based MNEs develops and expands international production mainly within their home region of the triad. Extremely few MNEs operate globally; nearly all are regionally based (Rugman 2000).

In this section, we analyse recent data on the activities of the world's 206 largest *manufacturing* MNEs (see Box 10.4). The other large firms in the list of the top 500 MNEs are in service sectors, such as retail and finance. There are data reported here on geographic sales for 180 manufacturing MNEs (for the remaining twenty-six no suitable data are available). These data show that the production of manufacturing MNEs is mainly *intra*regional, within their home regions of the 'broad triad' of the European Union, the North American Free Trade Agreement, and Asia. The average share of intraregional sales in the worldwide sales of manufacturing MNEs is about 62 per cent. We find that the world's largest MNEs are not global but

regionally based in terms of breadth and depth of market coverage. These firm-level data reinforce the analysis of aggregate trade and FDI data in Rugman (2000), showing that an increase of *intra*regional activity has occurred over the last twenty years.

In other words, there is little or no evidence of globalization, only regionalization. 'Globalization' reflects a special, and rather unusual, outcome of international business. In contrast, the regional/triad-based form of geographical market coverage appears to be a more typical reflection of international production patterns. These data have major implications for both corporate strategy and government policy, which are explored later in this chapter.

We also include a set of case studies of major MNEs in each of our major classifications of regional-based production activity. These classifications are:

1 Home-regional: these MNEs have over 50 per cent of their sales in their home region.

2 Bi-regional: these MNEs have at least 20 per cent of sales in two regions of the triad, including its own, and more than 50 per cent of total sales are made outside the home region.

3 Host-regional: these are a special case of bi-regional MNEs, but with more than 50 per cent of their sales in one region other than their home.

4 Global: these MNEs have at least 20 per cent of their sales in each of the three broad regions of the triad of North America, Europe, and Asia, but less than 50 per cent in any one region.

As truly 'global' MNEs we discuss three of the total of eight cases that fall in this category in our survey. These are IBM, Flextronics, and Canon. As home-region based bi-regional MNEs we discuss two of the twenty-four cases. These are Toyota and Lafarge. We also discuss one of the three bi-regional 'host' region cases, Honda. Finally, we discuss three of the 131 home-region cases. These are General Motors, VW, and NEC.

Evidence on regionalization

This study focuses on the 180 manufacturing firms included in the RNGMA survey (for discussion of services see Rugman and Girod 2003, and Rugman 2005). As Table 10.2 shows, all of the firms in some sectors are included in the survey, for example, in aerospace and defence, and in 'other natural resource manufacturing'. The latter sector includes all MNEs in forest and paper products, metals, mining, and crude oil production. However, in energy, petroleum, and refining, data on only thirty-one of the forty-three in the top 500 are included. Three of these firms have 100 per cent of their sales in their home region and are likely to be entirely domestic (Allegheny Electric, Valero Energy, and Sunoco all sell only in their home US market).

Table 10.3 reports the average *intra*regional sales of the firms in each of the nine manufacturing sectors, rearranged in decreasing order of sales intensity. The largest percentage of home intraregional sales are

Table 10.2 The top 500 MNEs, by industry, 2001

Industry category	No of Firms in the Fortune 500	No. of Firms in the RNGMA	% of total
Manufacturing	**206**	**180**	**87.4**
1 Aerospace and Defense	11	11	100.0
2 Chemicals and Pharmaceuticals	19	18	94.7
3 Computer, Office & Electronics	39	36	92.3
4 Construction, Building Materials and Glass	12	11	91.7
5 Energy, Petroleum & Refining	43	31	72.1
6 Food, Drug & Tobacco	18	14	77.8
7 Motor Vehicle and Parts	31	29	93.5
8 Other Manufacturing	13	13	100.0
9 Natural Resource Manufacturing	20	17	85.0
Services	**294**	**200**	**68.0**
1 Banks	62	40	64.5
2 Entertainment, Printing & Publishing	9	9	100.0
3 Merchandisers	77	63	81.8
4 Other Financial Services	58	27	46.6
5 Other Services	25	21	84.0
6 Telecommunications & Utilities	43	27	62.8
7 Transportation Services	20	13	65.0
TOTAL	500	**380**	**76.0**

Table 10.3 A comparison between the service and manufacturing sectors, 2001

Industry category	Weighted average intraregional sales
Manufacturing	
1 Natural Resource Manufacturing	77.6
2 Construction, Building Materials and Glass	73.5
3 Aerospace and Defense	66.3
4 Energy, Petroleum & Refining	66.0
5 Motor Vehicle and Parts	60.6
6 Other Manufacturing	57.8
7 Chemicals and Pharmaceuticals	56.5
8 Computer, Office & Electronics	56.2
9 Food, Drug & Tobacco	55.0
Services	
1 Merchandisers	87.9
2 Telecommunications & Utilities	87.6
3 Transportation Services	83.7
4 Banks	78.3
5 Other Services	75.8
6 Entertainment, Printing & Publishing	73.1
7 Other Financial Services	71.9

in the more 'location-bound' sectors, such as natural resource manufacturing, construction aerospace, and energy. All of these sectors show 66 per cent intra-regional sales or higher. In contrast, in the sectors where value added in production is made at the customer end, the intraregional sales are lower, for example, in food, drugs and tobacco at 55 per cent, in computers and electronics at 56 per cent, and in chemicals and pharmaceuticals at 57 per cent. Motor vehicles are in between, at 61 per cent. The service sectors are generally even more home-region based than are the manufacturing MNEs examined here (Rugman 2003). Indeed, average share of intra-regional sales in total sales of the world's 180 largest manufacturing companies is 61.8 per cent compared to 81.9 per cent for the 200 service companies.

Table 10.4 shows how the manufacturing MNEs appear under our four classifications. We have identified nine global MNEs; twenty-four bi-regionals; another three host-region bi-regionals; and 131 home-region MNEs. There are insufficient data on

geographical sales to classify thirteen of the MNEs in manufacturing in the survey.

Table 10.5 shows that seven of the nine global MNEs are in computer and electrical equipment. The high value to weight ratio of components and final products in this sector mean relatively low transport costs for these MNEs. In contrast, most of the other manufacturing MNEs are more 'location bound', for example, the twenty-nine automobile and auto parts MNEs; the seventeen chemical and pharmaceutical MNEs, etc.

The following set of tables list the MNEs in each of the four geographic sales classifications. In Table 10.5, the nine global MNEs are reported. From North America are: IBM, Intel, and Coca-Cola. From Europe are Philips, Nokia, and Dior. From Asia are Sony, Canon, and Flextronics. These nine MNEs have an average of 38.3 per cent of their sales in their home region (global firms are defined as having at least 20 per cent of their sales in each other region of the triad but less than 50 per cent in their home region).

Table 10.6 lists the twenty-four bi-regional MNEs with at least 20 per cent of sales in two regions of the triad and at least 50 per cent sales outside their home region. There are sixteen European, five North American, and three Asian. The average home-region intra-regional sales are 41.7 per cent.

Table 10.7 reports the three 'host'-region-based manufacturing MNEs. These are DaimlerChrysler, which is now headquartered in Europe but has 60.1 per cent of its sales in North America; Japan's Honda, with 53.9 per cent sales in North America; and, another European MNE, AstraZeneca, with 52.8 per cent of its sales in North America. These three MNEs average 29.2 per cent home-region sales.

Table 10.8 reports only the largest twenty-five of the 131 home-region MNEs in manufacturing. These 131 MNEs have an average of 61.8 per cent of sales in their home region of the triad. There are seventy-two from North America, twenty-five from Europe, thirty-three from Asia, and one non-triad MNE.

Table 10.9 reports a set of eight 'near miss' global MNEs. Three or four of these companies barely miss the requirements of a global MNE. These include 3M, Anglo American, Eastman Kodak, and potentially Shell. For most of these companies, however, there was insufficient information on geographic sales to classify them as global. These later companies

Table 10.4 The regional nature of global manufacturing MNEs, by industry and type, 2001

Industry category	Global	Bi-regional	Host-region oriented	Home-region oriented	Insufficient information
1 Aerospace & Defence	—	2	—	8	1
2 Chem. & Pharm.	—	4	1	11	2
3 Computer, Office & Elec.	7	4	—	22	3
4 Const., Building Mat. & Glass	—	2	—	9	—
5 Energy, Petroleum & Ref.	—	1	—	27	3
6 Food, Drug & Tobacco	1	2	—	9	2
7 Motor Vehicle and Parts	—	4	2	23	—
8 Other Natural Resource Mnfg.	—	1	—	15	1
9 Other Mnfg.	1	4	—	7	1
TOTAL	9	24	3	131	13
			% of total		
1 Aerospace & Defence	—	8.3	—	6.1	7.7
2 Chem. & Pharm.	—	16.7	33.3	8.4	15.4
3 Computer, Office & Elec.	77.8	16.7	—	16.8	23.1
4 Const., Building Mat. & Glass	—	8.3	—	6.9	—
5 Energy, Petroleum & Ref.	—	4.2	—	20.6	23.1
6 Food, Drug & Tobacco	11.1	8.3	—	6.9	15.4
7 Motor Vehicle & Parts	—	16.7	66.7	17.6	—
8 Other Natural Resource Mnfg.	—	4.2	—	11.5	7.7
9 Other Mnfg.	11.1	16.7	—	5.3	7.7
TOTAL	100.0	100.0	100.0	100.0	100.0

include Exxon Mobile, Nestlé, Compaq Computer, Shell, and Aventis. We cannot classify these last companies as they do not provide objective data showing at least 20 per cent of their total sales in each region of the triad. Nor do they show less than 50 per cent of their sales in their home region of the triad.

In the next section we turn to a more detailed discussion of several actual MNEs in each of the four major categories in the Regional Nature of Global Multinational Activity survey.

Case studies

Home-region

General Motors
The world's largest manufacturer of automobiles is General Motors (GM). In 2002, the company's

revenues totalled $187 billion; GM accounted for nearly 15 per cent of the world's market for trucks and automobiles. General Motors produces and manufactures vehicles in all three triad markets. Nonetheless, 57 per cent of its sales originate in the United States, its home national market. Including Canada in North America, this number rises to 73.4 per cent of total sales. On the production aspect, North America accounts for 74 per cent of production capacity. An international company yes, but by no means a global company.

The company is also most successful in the North American market, where it holds 28 per cent of the market compared to 8.7 per cent of the European market and 4.2 per cent of the Asian market. In the United States, GM has a competitive advantage in that it is already well situated in the market and has a loyal consumer base. In other countries, however, it faces

Table 10.5 Global manufacturing MNEs, 2001

Rank	500 rank	Company	Industry	Region	Revenues in bn US$	F/T Sales	% intra-regional	NA % of total	EUR % of total	AP % of total
1	19	Intl. Business Machines	Computer, Office & Elec.	NA	85.9	64.8	43.5	43.5	28.0	20.0
2	37	Sony	Computer, Office & Elec.	AP	60.6	67.2	32.8	29.8	20.2	32.8
3	143	Royal Philips Electronics	Computer, Office Office & Elec.	EUR	29.0	na	43.0	28.7	43.0	21.5
4	147	Nokia	Computer, Office & Elec.	EUR	27.9	98.5	49.0	25.0	49.0	26.0
5	162	Intel	Computer, Office & Elec.	NA	26.5	64.6	35.4	35.4	24.5	40.2
6	190	Canon	Computer, Office & Elec.	AP	23.9	71.5	28.5	33.8	20.8	28.5
7	239	Coca-Cola	Food, Drug & Tobacco	NA	20.1	na	38.4	38.4	22.4	24.9
8	388	Flextronics International	Computer, Office & Elec.	AP	13.1	na	22.4	46.3	30.9	22.4
9	446	Dior (Christian)	Other Mnfg.	EUR	11.3	83.4	36.0	26.0	36.0	32.0
Weighted average					**33.1**		**38.3**			
TOTAL					**298.3**					

competition from foreign automakers that know their home regions very well. In Europe, Volkswagen, BMW, and DaimlerChrysler build performance cars. In Asia, competitors build smaller, more fuel efficient cars that cater to local preferences. That is, each region has a particular competitive environment in which the major world players compete for market share. Local competitors are more adept at meeting the demands of their regional markets because they possess know-how on consumer preferences, government regulations, and market trends. While foreign companies might hire local personnel, purchase local car manufacturers, and do extensive market research, companies headquartered in that region are often more capable of responding to the changing circumstances of their primary market.

General Motors' primary market is North America, in particular the United States. It derives most of its revenue and most of its profits from its home-region operations. GM's strategy must balance the benefit of investing in foreign regions with the benefits of investing in its home-region market. Foreign markets, though potentially profitable, do not offer GM

sufficient incentive to switch the focus of its strategy. This is because the United States is the largest market for automobiles in the world and GM depends heavily on it to continue to be the largest world player.

NEC

In 1899, the first Japanese joint venture with foreign capital was established when Western Electric Company of the United States became a partner in the creation of Nippon Electric Company (NEC). Initially a telephone and switching systems manufacturer, the company had moved into radio, microwave communication, transistors, and computers by the late 1950s.

The company's first international excursion was an export contract with Korea in 1951 to supply radio equipment. In 1958, Taiwan Telecommunication Company became NEC's first post-war FDI venture. By the early 1970s the company had additional operations in the United States, Mexico, Brazil, China, and Australia. Despite over fifty years of international expansion, Japan still accounts for about 83 per cent of the company's revenues. North America accounts

Table 10.6 Bi-regional manufacturing MNEs, 2001

Rank	500 rank	Company	Industry	Region	Revenues in bn US$	F/T Sales	% intra-regional	NA % of total	EUR % of total	AP % of total
1	4	BP	Energy, Petroleum & Ref.	EUR	174.2	80.4	36.3	48.1	36.3	na
2	10	Toyota Motor	Motor Vehicle & Parts	AP	120.8	50.8	49.2	36.6	7.7	49.2
3	58	Nissan Motor	Motor Vehicle & Parts	AP	49.6	50.3	49.7	34.6	11.0	49.7
4	68	Unilever	Food, Drug & Tobacco	EUR	46.1	na	38.7	46.6	38.7	15.4
5	138	Motorola	Computer, Office & Elec.	NA	30.0	56.0	44.0	44.0	14.0	26.0
6	140	GlaxoSmithKline	Chem. & Pharm.	EUR	29.5	50.8	28.6	49.2	28.6	na
7	153	EADS	Aerospace & Defence	EUR	27.6	na	44.9	33.7	44.9	10.2
8	158	Bayer	Chem. & Pharm.	EUR	27.1	na	40.3	32.7	40.3	16.1
9	210	L.M. Ericsson	Computer, Office & Elec.	EUR	22.4	97.0	46.0	13.2	46.0	25.9
10	228	Alstom	Other Mnfg.	EUR	20.7	88.0	45.1	28.0	45.1	16.1
11	230	Aventis	Chem. & Pharm.	EUR	20.5	87.2	32.1	38.8	32.1	6.4
12	262	Diageo	Food, Drug & Tobacco	EUR	18.6	na	31.8	49.9	31.8	7.7
13	268	Sun Microsystems	Computer, Office & Elec.	NA	18.3	52.6	47.4	47.4	30.2	17.2
14	285	Bridgestone	Motor Vehicle & Parts	AP	17.6	61.2	38.8	43.0	10.1	38.8
15	288	Roche Group	Chem. & Pharm.	EUR	17.3	98.2	36.8	38.6	36.8	11.7
16	316	3M	Other Mnfg.	NA	16.1	53.1	46.9	46.9	24.6	18.9
17	317	Skanska	Const., Building Mat. & Glass	EUR	15.9	83.0	40.0	41.0	40.0	na
18	342	Michelin	Motor Vehicle & Parts	EUR	14.6	na	47.0	40.0	47.0	na
19	383	Eastman Kodak	Other Mnfg.	NA	13.2	na	48.5	48.5	24.7	17.2
20	386	Electrolux	Computer, Office & Elec.	EUR	13.1	na	47.0	39.0	47.0	9.0
21	390	BAE Systems	Aerospace & Defence	EUR	13.0	82.7	38.1	32.3	38.1	2.7
22	408	Alcan	Other Natural Resource Mnfg.	NA	12.6	95.4	41.1	41.1	39.6	13.9
23	415	L'Oréal	Other Mnfg.	EUR	12.3	na	48.5	32.4	48.5	na
24	416	Lafarge	Const., Building Mat. & Glass	EUR	12.3	na	40.0	32.0	40.0	8.0
Weighted average					**31.8**		**41.7**			
TOTAL					763.5					

for an additional 5 per cent while the remaining 12 per cent are sales in other parts of the world. An even higher percentage of its long-lived assets—those which hold value after one year—90 per cent, is in its home market of Japan. Clearly, NEC remains very Japanese.

In the early 2000s, the company began to experience heavy losses in North America as a result of the

Table 10.7 Host-region based manufacturing MNEs, 2001

Rank	500 rank	Company	Industry	Region	Revenues in bn US$	F/T Sales	% intra-regional	NA % of total	EUR total	AP % of total
1	7	DaimlerChrysler	Motor Vehicle & Parts	EUR	136.9	na	29.9	60.1	29.9	na
2	41	Honda Motor	Motor Vehicle & Parts	AP	58.9	73.1	26.9	53.9	8.1	26.9
3	301	AstraZeneca	Chem. & Pharm.	EUR	16.5	na	32.0	52.8	32.0	5.2
Weighted average					**70.8**		**29.2**			
TOTAL					**212.3**					

Table 10.8 The top 25 home-region based manufacturing companies, 2001

Rank	500 rank	Company	Industry	Region	Revenues in bn US$	F/T Sales	% intra-regional	NA % of total	EUR % of total	AP % of total
1	3	General Motors	Motor Vehicle & Parts	NA	177.3	25.5	81.1	81.1	14.6	na
2	5	Ford Motor	Motor Vehicle & Parts	NA	162.4	33.3	66.7	66.7	21.9	na
3	15	Total Fina Elf	Energy, Petroleum & Ref.	EUR	94.3	na	55.6	8.4	55.6	na
4	21	Volkswagen	Motor Vehicle & Parts	EUR	79.3	72.3	68.2	20.1	68.2	5.3
5	22	Siemens	Computer, Office & Elec.	EUR	77.4	78.0	52.0	30.0	52.0	13.0
6	24	Philip Morris	Food, Drug & Tobacco	NA	72.9	42.1	57.9	57.9	25.8	na
7	32	Hitachi	Computer, Office & Elec.	AP	63.9	31.0	80.0	11.0	7.0	80.0
8	36	American Electric Power	Energy, Petroleum & Ref.	NA	61.3	12.3	87.7	87.7	11.8	na
9	39	Duke Energy	Energy, Petroleum & Ref.	NA	59.5	13.1	96.5	96.5	na	na
10	42	Boeing	Aerospace & Defence	NA	58.2	33.3	66.7	66.7	14.5	16.3
11	43	El Paso	Energy, Petroleum & Ref.	NA	57.5	2.8	97.2	97.2	na	na
12	45	Matsushita Electric Ind.	Computer, Office & Elec.	AP	55.0	35.1	64.9	12.4	6.9	64.9
13	49	Fiat	Motor Vehicle & Parts	EUR	51.9	65.6	73.3	13.0	73.3	na
14	53	RWE	Energy, Petroleum & Ref.	EUR	50.7	37.9	75.0	19.5	75.0	5.1
15	62	Merck	Chem. & Pharm.	NA	47.7	16.4	83.6	83.6	na	na
16	67	Reliant Energy	Energy, Petroleum & Ref.	NA	46.2	8.6	91.4	91.4	na	na
17	71	ENI	Energy, Petroleum & Ref.	EUR	44.6	44.3	80.4	12.1	80.4	3.1
18	77	Toshiba	Computer, Office & Elec.	AP	43.1	37.0	75.3	13.9	8.7	75.3
19	78	Dynegy	Energy, Petroleum & Ref.	NA	42.2	23.7	90.7	90.7	na	na
20	84	NEC	Computer, Office & Elec.	AP	40.8	20.4	79.6	7.0	na	79.6
21	87	Aquila	Energy, Petroleum & Ref.	NA	40.4	18.4	91.0	91.0	na	na
22	88	Fujitsu	Computer, Office & Elec.	AP	40.0	28.2	71.8	11.4	12.2	71.8
23	92	Pemex	Energy, Petroleum & Ref.	NA	39.4	34.4	91.7	91.7	3.7	na
24	93	Procter & Gamble	Other Mnfg.	NA	39.2	48.2	55.0	55.0	27.0	10.0
25	99	Suez	Energy, Petroleum & Ref.	EUR	37.9	50.0	74.0	11.0	74.0	5.0

Table 10.9 The 'near miss' global manufacturing MNEs, 2001

500 rank	Company	Industry	Region	Revenues in bn US$	F/T Sales	% intra-regional	NA % of total	EUR % of total	AP % of total
2	Exxon Mobile	Energy, Petroleum & Ref.	NA	191.6	69.6	37.5	37.5	8.9	10.4
8	Royal Dutch/ Shell Group	Energy, Petroleum & Ref.	EUR	135.2	na	46.1	15.6	46.1	na
55	Nestlé	Food, Drug & Tobacco	EUR	50.2	na	31.6	31.4	31.6	na
117	Compaq Computer	Computer, Office & Elec.	NA	33.6	62.0	38.0	38.0	36.0	na
230	Aventis	Chem. & Pharm.	EUR	20.5	87.2	32.1	38.8	32.1	6.4
316	3M	Other Mnfg.	NA	16.1	53.1	46.9	46.9	24.6	18.9
341	Anglo American	Other Natural Resource Manufacturing	EUR	14.8	86.7	46.1	18.9	46.1	17.8
383	Eastman Kodak	Other Mnfg.	NA	13.2	na	48.5	48.5	24.7	17.2

US recession. Heavy competition, as well as the worldwide effect of the US slowdown, forced the company into $417 million in losses in 2002. The heaviest losses were in North America ($237 million), but the company also lost significantly in its home market ($126 million). The remaining $52 million in losses were in other markets.

Unlike IBM, NEC has not succeeded in diversifying sales to the other two regions of the triad. To become more global it needs to focus on the large US market. If NEC is to become global it must change its management capabilities. Other Japanese companies have been able to become bi-regional with the United States, but the centralized hierarchical structure of a typical Japanese company, like NEC, has proved to be incompatible with success in the US market.

NEC is following other manufacturers on the road to China. In 2002, NEC announced plans to raise Chinese manufacture and assembly of PCs destined for the Japanese from 10 per cent to 70 per cent. The company already outsourced parts to these cheaper regions, but up to that point had continued to retain most assembly operations in Japan. For NEC, China is not only one of the cheapest countries in which to produce, but it is also conveniently located within its home region of Asia-Pacific. Success in China will reinforce NEC's concentration on its home region.

Volkswagen
In March 1998, Germany's Volkswagen revamped its strategy in the US market by introducing the New Beetle. The car's appeal is the 1960s and 1970s nostalgia of the VW Beetle. In 2002, Volkswagen delivered over 420,000 vehicles to the United States market and accounted for approximately 10.1 per cent of the passenger car import market. Including imports and domestic production, Volkswagen holds about 6.6 per cent of the US passenger car market.

Although the Volkswagen comeback into the US market has been a success, the North American market is still a minor part of the company's operations. In 2002, only 19.9 per cent of total revenues originated in North America. It is the European market that Volkswagen depends on for the vast majority of its revenue. Like GM, which concentrates on the US market, VW's primary market is at home—in this case, in Europe. Its cars reflect the European taste for performance, safety, and durability. Germany accounted for 27.5 per cent of total sales. Including other European countries, the (home) intraregional sales of VW rose to 69.3 per cent. Volkswagen is a highly regional company, and while it has enjoyed significant success in other regions, the company's main strategic market continues to be its home region.

Over the last few years, Volkswagen has increasingly relied on foreign markets for its revenue and production. Between 1993 and 2002, production outside Germany rose from 53.3 per cent of all units to 64.5 per cent. However, many of these factories are located in Eastern Europe. Similarly, unit sales in foreign markets increased from 69.1 per cent to 81.8 per cent, but a large portion of these units are actually sold in the

European regional market. Units delivered to Europe accounted for 63.2 per cent of total deliveries in 2002.

Volkswagen has a larger share of the overall car market in its home region. The company holds 30 per cent of its domestic market and 17.9 per cent of the European market (including Germany). This is well above its market share in the other two triad regions (see Table 10.8). Although the company has had some success in developing countries, with 25.1 per cent of the Mexican market and 20.2 per cent of the South American market, its revenues from these regions account for a very small fraction of total revenues because of the small size of these economies and their automobile markets.

Bi-regional

Toyota

In 2002, two regional markets accounted for well over 80 per cent of Toyota's revenues: Asia (with Japan alone providing 45 per cent of total revenues) and North America, which supplied 38.8 per cent of total revenues. Europe only accounts for 8.8 per cent of revenues. In terms of units sold, the result is similar: Asia and Oceania account for 46.2 per cent of unit sales (Japan accounts for 38.3 per cent); North America for 30.8 per cent; and Europe for 15 per cent. This distribution of revenue and units sold makes Toyota a bi-regional company. Market share shows a slightly different picture. Toyota holds approximately 40 per cent of the Japanese market but only 10 per cent of the North American market. Moreover, production is not as dispersed as sales around the world; 75.9 per cent of all Toyota cars are still produced in Japan. Only 14.9 per cent are produced in North America. Other regions account for less than 10 per cent of the company's global production.

Over the last ten years, Toyota's intraregional percentage of sales has decreased from 57.1 per cent to 46.2 per cent. One major reason for this is the declining significance of the Japanese market itself (in part a reflection of the recent stagnation of the Japanese economy), where sales decreased from 48.4 per cent of total revenues in 1993 to 38.3 per cent in 2002. In contrast, North America, European, and non-triad sales have steadily increased in importance. In 1993, Toyota derived 25.4 per cent of its sales from North America. This rose to 30.8 per cent in 2002; EU

restrictions on imports of Japanese cars were one reason why Toyota historically had been unable to be successful in the European market. European sales accounted for a mere 9.9 per cent of total sales in 1993, but by 2002, by which time Toyota had begun assembly within the European Union, Toyota almost doubled the number of units sold so that, in this year, the region accounted for 15 per cent of total sales. This increase in Europe is not just a reflection of local production but also of Toyota's learning to cater to the European market.

Many Asian economies were in a slump in the 1990s, and Europe has been a money pit. This is why the North American market is very important for all Japanese manufacturers. Japanese carmakers began to manufacture in the United States, the largest North American national market, in the 1980s to protect themselves from imports restrictions. North America is Toyota's second largest regional market in terms of revenues. It is also highly profitable. In 2002, one-fourth of Toyota's profits originated in this region.

Toyota manufactures locally over two-thirds of the cars it sells in the United States. The company's Canadian plant also serves this regional market, and a Mexican plant in Tijuana is expected to increase local production when it opens in 2005.

Local responsiveness is important. Toyota introduced its luxury models to accommodate the ageing and wealthier North American baby boomers in the 1990s. Today, the company is introducing cars to target the young American customer, the demographic echo of the baby boomers. Because 60 per cent of US car buyers remain loyal to the brand of their first car, it is imperative for Toyota and its competitors to service this young market.

American consumers, for their part, have been responsive to the company's reputation for quality and in particular for the lower ticket price at which Toyota's cars are sold. In fact, during economic downturns in which consumers seek more value for their money, Toyota performs better than its rivals in the United States. The company's cars are not only less expensive, but they also consume less gasoline than American cars. The resale value is also higher for Toyota cars. One major advantage for Toyota is that it has some of the best manufacturing facilities in the world, and it combines this with excellent relationships with its suppliers. The company is so efficient that, despite the lower price of its cars, it makes an average profit of $1,000 on each car sold compared to $330 for GM.

Toyota's European operations are money losers, but the company continues to try to access this market and increase its market share from its 3.8 per cent level in 2002. To boost its image for performance in the region, the company recently began to compete in Formula One races. To protect itself from currency risk, Toyota will now produce a higher percentage of its cars within the region. That also means more local procurement of components. To this end, Porsche was asked to produce engines for its European models. Porsche already produces transmissions for the company. The company expects to increase its European market share to 5 per cent by 2005.

Always a pioneer, Toyota is one of the most efficient companies at outsourcing production to suppliers with whom it enjoys an amicable long-term relationship. If the auto industry is to become more like the electronics industry (as many believe must occur), vehicle brand owners, such as Toyota, GM, VW, will be the equivalent of original equipment manufacturers (OEMs) in the electronics industry, such as Nokia, IBM, and Microsoft, and will concentrate on designing, engineering, and marketing vehicles to be sold under their brand while others take care of the petty details of manufacturing. Toyota is well ahead of other triad automakers on the way to outsourcing manufacturing.

Lafarge

One of the world's largest cement firms is French MNE, Lafarge. It has a presence in seventy-five countries and while it operates from its European base, it is expanding in North America and Asia. In 2001, Lafarge derived 40 per cent of its sales from Western Europe, 32 per cent from North America, and 8 per cent from Asia-Pacific. The remaining 20 per cent of revenues originate in Central and Eastern Europe, Africa, the Indian Ocean, the Mediterranean Basin, and Latin America.

This is an extraordinary market presence for Lafarge, across the triad, in an industry that is essentially location bound. Cement is very costly to transport, so virtually all production is local and close to large urban areas. Only marine transportation is at all viable (for example, across the Great Lakes, where Canadian firms export to the United States). However, even then most cement plants are not near

ports as they need to be near limestone deposits. Since transport is so costly, firms that wish to operate internationally in this industry engage in foreign direct investment, buying up local cement firms, and thereby becoming MNEs.

Building on its world leadership in cement and concrete, Lafarge is also a top ranking construction company in aggregates, roofing, and gypsum. The group had sales of $14.6 billion euros in 2002, and employs 77,000 people across the world. It offers more than 5,000 services and products, ranging from ultra-high performance concrete, ready-mix concrete, improved roofing material, plasterboard insulation systems, etc.

Lafarge was created in 1833. In 2001 it acquired Blue Circle industries, a UK cement and building company, bringing its total production capacity of cement from 107 million tons to 150 million tons, or 10 per cent of world capacity. The merger reinforced Lafarge's position as top dog in Europe, and Blue Circle's operations in Asia catapulted the company into that region. In North America, however, Lafarge was forced to sell part of Blue Circle's concrete business to satisfy regulators.

In sum, because the only economies of scale that a cement firm can attain are in its logistic systems, in production technology, and in management, the world's concrete industry is dominated by triad-based MNEs, in which European firms and a North American (US-Mexican) firm are competing in both the rich markets of the European Union and North America and also developing markets.

Host-region bi-regional

Honda

Toyota may be the largest Japanese automaker in the world, but in the United States, it is Honda that rules the road. In 2002, the Honda Accord was the best-selling passenger car in the United States. Not surprisingly, given the size of the US market, the company generates over half its revenues (55.6 per cent) in North America. Its home market of Japan accounts for only 23.3 per cent of sales. European sales account for 11.2 per cent of sales while sales to other markets account for the remaining 9.9 per cent. Most of the company's long-lived assets are also in its host region of North America, 53 per cent.

This unusual dependence on the North American market is the result of its rival Toyota's dominance of the Japanese market. The relative spread of revenues across the triad is not only influenced by the ability of a company to penetrate a foreign market, but also by how much of the domestic market it can attain. A small car manufacturer might have better opportunities for growth, despite the costs and difficulties of operating overseas, in another region of the triad than in its own home region.

Honda's future success is expected to rely on the company's three strategic directions: to create value; 'glocalization', a term the company coined to mean localized global operations; and a commitment to the future. To increase value, the company relies on continued innovation. Honda's modular production methods are giving it an edge against the competition. Around the world, the company is known for its smaller, less expensive, more efficient, and environmentally friendly cars.

Glocalization is the company's commitment to a global supply chain that is responsive to local customers. 'Made by Global Honda' has already been chosen as the expression that will represent this global supply network that will link facilities in different regions. Honda divides its business into five regional operations: its domestic market of Japan; North America; Latin America; Europe, the Middle East, and Africa; and Asia and Oceania. The Japanese market is expected to be served through imports from China, Thailand, Malaysia, and Indonesia. To maintain its local responsiveness, the company has research and development (R&D) facilities in each of the triad markets.

Global firms

International Business Machines (IBM)

In 1911, the C-T-R (Computer-Tabulating-Recording) company was founded by the acquisition of four equipment manufacturers. The new company acquired the expertise of its predecessors, including recording equipment and punch card tabulating technology. C-T-R opened an office in Canada in 1917 under the name of International Business Machines Company. It was only in 1924 that C-T-R officially changed the name of all its operations to International Business Machines Company, better

known as IBM. In the early 1980s, IBM struck it big by pioneering the personal computer (PC), which sold for as little as $1,565. Today, IBM is one of the largest manufacturers of PCs, laptops, and other customer-end computer products, as well as servers, networking solutions, and hardware.

Always an innovator, the company has also led the way in globalization. IBM is one of only ten truly global companies in the *Fortune* Global 500. It has revenues of $85.9 billion, operations in over 160 countries, and research laboratories in eight locations in six countries.

When C-T-R was founded in 1911, it inherited the international operations of its predecessors. IBM was born as a multinational enterprise. For instance, IBM Canada was founded to consolidate the Canadian operations of three companies that had been acquired by C-T-R.

In 1917 the company entered the Latin American market by opening an office in Brazil. By the early 1930s, IBM had secured contracts with Argentinean, Mexican, Ecuadorean, Chilean, Cuban, Uruguayan, and Peruvian governments and large corporations. In 1929, the Compañía Internacional de Maquinas Comerciales S.A. was organized in Mexico.

In Asia, the company opened its first office in Bombay, India in 1920. It entered the Philippines in 1925 and shortly afterwards IBM equipment was installed in Osaka, Japan, for the Nippon Mutual Life Insurance Company. Entry into the Chinese market was accomplished in 1934, with the installation of IBM machines at the Peking Union Medical College.

IBM's entry into the European market started when the International Time Recording Company, an IBM forerunner, opened a branch in France in 1914. By 1919 a consolidated IBM was introduced to the European market. Foreign production began in 1924 with the completion of factories in Germany and France. The same year, a company was organized in France to carry on IBM's business in that market.

IBM was able to compete internationally because it functioned in a developing industry that relies on breakthrough technology. Local competitors, at the time, were scarce and customers were typically either large corporations or governments.

Although there is a global diversity to IBM's revenue generation stream, its home region, the

Americas, is the most important of all its regional operations. For the year 2001, IBM derived 43.5 per cent of all its revenue from the Americas (35.2 per cent in the United States alone) compared to 28 per cent in Europe, the Middle East, and Africa and 20 per cent in Asia. The remaining 8.5 per cent of its revenue derives from IBM's uncategorized global operations. If we look at the company's long-lived assets, 62.9 per cent are in the United States alone. This is because a large part of the core operations are still in the United States. For instance, the largest research centres remain US based. Also, as the company has expanded production overseas, it has not done so by acquiring foreign assets but by entering into outsourcing contracts. More than two-thirds of the company's Intel-based products, for instance, are manufactured in worldwide factories by contract manufacturers, including Sanmina-SCI and Solectron.

Flextronics

Since the recent emergence of 'electronic-manufacturing service providers' (EMS), corporate rivals such as Sony and Philips, or Ericsson, Alcatel, and Motorola, have chosen to share the same factories to build competing products. Today, companies largely unknown to the public, such as Flextronics, Solectron, Sanmina-SCI, Celestica, and Jabil, among others, produce such well-known products as IBM PCs, the Microsoft Xbox video console, Web TV set-top boxes for Philips and Sony, and portable phones for Ericsson, Alcatel, and Motorola. In 2002, EMS industry revenues were estimated at $134 billion. The two largest EMS companies, Flextronics and Solectron, account for 9.7 per cent and 9.2 per cent of this market respectively.

That the electronics industry is pioneering contract manufacturing is no accident. The industry's products are easily transported by air, allowing parts to travel the world before the finished product is completed. This allows an EMS to identify the specific advantages of each region and to develop a worldwide production network that coordinates procurement, inventory management, vendor management, packaging, and services that minimizes both time-to-market and production costs.

Today's electronic manufacturers have come a long way from the cheap labour-based contractors that used to dominate the industry. Robotic automation is now a significant part of the production process and is mostly handled by specialists. It is their manufacturing expertise that makes for lower costs, but EMS provide many more advantages to OEMs (Box 10.5). They decrease the risk of manufacturing because OEMs no longer need to make large investments in a new factory to introduce a new product that might or might not prove to be successful in the market place. Electronic-manufacturing service providers can also purchase inputs at lower prices because of scale economies: they are not only making cell phones for Alcatel, but also those for Motorola and Ericsson, thereby strengthening their purchasing power. By outsourcing manufacturing, OEMs can concentrate their activities in those parts of the value chain where they enjoy firm-specific advantages.

Contract manufacturing accounts for less than one-fourth of electronic manufacturing; however, there are reasons to believe that EMS companies will dominate the industry in the future. This process will redefine the role of OEMs in the electronics industry to that of design and marketing.

Although most end customers who purchase its products have never heard of Flextronics, the MNE is ranked at number 388 on the *Fortune* Global 500 list, and is the largest EMS. With headquarters in Singapore, Flextronics specializes in handheld electronics devices, IT infrastructure, communications infrastructure, computer and office automation, and consumer electronics. The company's operations allow its customers, large multinationals such as Xerox, Casio, and Ericsson, to take over at the end of the manufacturing supply chain, if they take over at all. For instance, Ericsson might meet with Flextronics and agree to outsource its production of mobile phones. Flextronics engineers then collaborate with Ericsson in the design of a prototype. A compromise is reached between market-based design based on Ericsson's know-how and technology, and production-friendly design based on Flextronics know-how of the production process. Flextronics then takes over supplies logistics, manufacturing, distribution, and after-sales support. Ericsson's post-production role is minimized to marketing its brand-named product through its traditional channels. In only twelve years since its incorporation in 1990, Flextronics sales have grown to $13.1 billion while its operations now span twenty-eight countries across the world.

Box 10.5 OEM (Original equipment manufacturer)

The term OEM often causes confusion because it has two usages that are contradictory. In its original usage, OEM referred to companies that manufactured equipment to the specifications provided by other companies who then sold the product under their own brand name. For instance, Korean companies used to manufacture the vast majority of the world's production of microwave ovens. Korean companies such as LG (formerly known as Lucky Goldstar) would manufacture ovens that were sold under the brand name of well-known Western firms, for example, GE. In this usage of the term, LG was the OEM.

More recently, the term OEM has been applied to the companies that outsource manufacturing and which acquire products for sale under their brand names. In this usage, continuing with the example above, it would be GE that would be the OEM. In this chapter, the term OEM is used in this second sense. For example, Motorola is an OEM that purchases products for marketing under its brand name from electronic-manufacturing service providers such as Flextronics.

Flextronics expansion was accomplished through friendly takeovers of plants from its customers. For example, in 2001, Flextronics purchased half of Xerox's office equipment making operations for $220 million. The deal came with a five-year outsourcing contract for Flextronics to manufacture Xerox products. A similar deal was accomplished in 2000 when Casio sold a Japanese factory, and in 2001 when Ericsson transferred plants in Brazil, Malaysia, Sweden, the United States, and the United Kingdom to Flextronics. Most of these deal/contracts include employment protection for the plant employees. Once Flextronics takes over a factory, it redesigns it to its manufacturing standards and begins production of branded products for different, and sometimes competing, companies.

In 2001, only 24.4 per cent of Flextronics revenues and 26 per cent of its production originated in its home-region market of Asia. European sales were the highest, accounting for 45.5 per cent of total revenues. North American sales accounted for an additional 30.1 per cent of sales. At a national-market level, Malaysia is the company's largest market; 18 per cent of all revenues originate here. Another 16 per cent of its sales originate in Mexico while Hungary and Sweden account for 12 per cent and 11 per cent respectively. No other country accounts for more than 10 per cent of Flextronics' revenues, which is a bit of puzzle. How can an MNE with contracts with large triad-based MNEs derive most of its sales in non-triad national markets? One obvious answer is that revenues are being reported at point of sales to subsidiaries of foreign

MNEs who then distribute the products in triad markets. There is nothing strange about this as Flextronics' involvement in the process is finished once the product is delivered to one of its sales offices, and it reports its sales as that. Complications arise, though, because we are unable to make assumptions as to the final markets that Flextronics depends on through its clients.

Flextronics is also a global company in terms of production. Its home region of Asia accounts for 42 per cent of the company's production while North America, mainly Mexico, accounts for 32 per cent. Europe, where most of Flextronics plants are located in Eastern countries, accounts for the remaining 26 per cent of production.

Canon

Few companies can claim to be truly global multinationals, but with revenues, production, and employees distributed across the world, the Canon Group of Japan comes as close as any company to fitting that title. With $23.9 million revenues and over 90,000 employees, Canon develops, manufactures, and markets cameras, business machines, and optical products around the world. The company had its beginnings in 1933, when Precision Optical Instruments Laboratory was established to conduct research into cameras in Roppongi, Minato-ku, and Tokyo.

Canon's international expansion started in 1955 with the opening of a New York branch. By 1962, sole distributors had been established in Europe and Latin America, but by 1963, the sole distributor system was abolished to make way for company-owned subsidiaries under the direct control of the Japanese headquarters. By 1979, overseas sales had reached ¥100 billion.

By 2001, the company was generating 71.5 per cent of its revenues outside of Japan, or $17.1 billion. The Americas accounted for 33.8 per cent of total revenues, Asia accounted for 28.5 per cent, and Western Europe for 20.8 per cent. The remaining 16.9 per cent of revenues were generated in other areas, including Eastern Europe.

The company's strategic international expansion goes beyond marketing to include production, research, and development. Taiwan became the site of Canon's first foreign production facility in 1970. Two years later the company opened a manufacturing plant in Germany. By 2001, Canon had production facilities in all parts of the triad—Western Europe, the Asia-Pacific region, and North America. Asia, including Japan, however, is still home to the vast majority of Canon's production facilities, which account for close to half its total employees. Since its founding, Canon's R&D has been centralized in Japan, but in 1990, R&D centres were opened in the United States, Australia, France, Thailand, and the People's Republic of China. Each R&D facility specializes in a specific

product line and is coordinated by a centralized R&D lab in Japan. Approximately 8 per cent of Canon's revenues are spent in R&D. Together with its R&D this has made Canon one of the best world innovators. The company is the largest holder of patents after IBM.

The relative importance of each of the triad regions has led the company to organize itself regionally. In the Americas, Canon USA oversees the entire region's operations. The subsidiary employs 10,908 people and has its own marketing, R&D, and production facilities. In Europe, the company has two complementary regional headquarters. These two companies oversee marketing in Western and Eastern Europe and have 12,875 employees. European operations also include two manufacturing plants in Germany and France and R&D centres in the United Kingdom and France. The third region is Asia and Oceania, excluding Japan. In terms of employees, this is the largest region outside of Japan with 25,028 people.

Over the last few years, Canon has been reorganizing its production facilities to take advantage of its global scope, selecting suppliers and production facilities across the world to minimize costs and decrease production time.

Conclusions

The previous case studies have described companies in all our categories of geographic sales. While comparisons across industries can be made relatively easily, based on the nature of the inputs, government regulations, production processes, and transportation costs in each industry, differences of firm strategy within the same industry are more difficult to explain. In the automobile industry, for instance, GM and Volkswagen are examples of home-region oriented companies while Toyota is an example of a bi-regional company and Honda of a host-region oriented company.

There are many factors that contribute to the international strategy of a company. Some of these are firm specific. For instance, Toyota and Honda have outstanding production facilities that translate into a competitive advantage in the two major regions of

the triad in which they operate. In addition, they efficiently produce smaller, cleaner cars. General Motors is an icon of American manufacturing and enjoys the loyalty of many US consumers. General Motors builds larger cars that appeal to a large segment of its home-region consumers. Germany's Volkswagen has the reputation for performance and durability demanded by European consumers.

A set of country-specific factors also affects the international business strategy of MNEs. For instance, Toyota is the largest Japanese automaker and, like GM, enjoys consumer loyalty in its home region. Honda, on the other hand, is a smaller player in the Japanese market. It needs international expansion into the United States to grow. The United States is the largest market for automobiles and the most profitable market for Japanese companies. Other country-specific factors include the size of the host economy, its economic and political stability, the strength of the competition, and the preferences of its consumers.

Yet another set of factors that affect the international business strategies of MNEs are government regulations. Both Honda and Toyota switched to FDI to replace exporting and thereby established manufacturing plants in the United States in response to US government regulations designed to protect its national manufacturers. Ironically, it might well be that this decision to transfer production facilities to the United States can now be credited with the success of these companies in this host market. Tariffs and non-tariff barriers to trade (for instance, the barriers that the European Union erected against car imports) might affect a firm's decision to open manufacturing plants in its home region or to relocate to a host region.

Trade-related regulations are just one way in which governments might affect the decision to open international subsidiaries. Labour laws, environmental laws, tax regimes, and approval processes for food and drugs are all country-specific factors affecting the international expansion of firms. In short, there are a number of interrelated firm, country, and governmental factors that influence the regional business strategy of a particular MNE.

The implications for strategy and government policy are many. In terms of their proposed strategies, firms must reconsider the globalization myth. Most firms have been unable to successfully transplant their operations to other regions of the triad. Firms should first look to their home region and craft regional strategies. For the vast majority of international firms, which rely on their home region for 80 per cent of their sales, this means working to strengthen or retain their competitive position in their own home regions. For bi-regional and global companies, a strategy of regionally responsive units for each of the regions in which they operate should be implemented. Because of the significance of home regions in the total sales of most MNEs, governments seeking to attract FDI should attempt to strengthen regional integration programmes both within existing regional trade blocks and by encouraging the accession of new members into the regional groupings.

Key points

- The vast majority of the world's largest MNEs in manufacturing operate not globally but regionally measured by the geographical distribution of their total sales.

- Seven of the nine MNEs in the survey that are categorized as 'global' in their operations are in computer and electrical equipment. The high value to weight ratio of components and final products in this sector means that they incur relatively low transport costs.

- Companies with the highest percentage of home intra-regional sales are in the more 'location-bound' sectors, such as natural resource manufacturing, construction aerospace, and energy.

- In some manufacturing sectors, notably automobiles, different combinations of firm-specific and country-specific advantages have caused MNEs to adopt quite different strategies—with some characterized as home-regional and others as host-regional and bi-regional in the geographical distribution of their sales.

CASE REFERENCES

IBM

IBM (2001), *Annual Report*.

Canon

Canon (2002), *Canon Fact Book*.
—— (2002), *The Canon Story*.

Flextronics

Anon. (2000), 'Have Factory, Will Travel', *The Economist*, 10 Feb.

—— (2001), 'Gadget wars', *The Economist*, 8 May.

—— (2001), 'Let the Bad Times Roll', *The Economist*, 5 Apr.

—— (2003), 'IBM Outsourcing to Solectron, Sanmina-SCI', *Internet News*, 7 Jan.

Sprague, J. (2002), 'Invasion of the Factory Snatchers', *Fortune*, 15 Aug.

Flextronics (2002), *Annual Report*.

General Motors

Anon. (2002), 'A Duo of Dunces', *The Economist*, 7 Mar.

General Motors (2002), *Annual Report*.

Honda

Honda (2002), *Annual Report*.

Boorstin, J. (2002), 'Going Cheap: Japan's Hottest Carmakers', *Fortune*, 15 May.

Taylor, A. (2002), 'Honda Goes Its Own Way', *Fortune*, 8 July.

Lafarge

Anon. (1999), 'Bagged Cement', *The Economist*, 17 July.

—— (2000), 'The Cemex Way', *The Economist*, 14 June.

NEC

Anon. (2001), 'NEC confirms job cuts', *BBC.co.uk*, 27 July.

—— (2001), 'NEC Weighs Anti-dumping Complaint', *BBC.co.uk*, 24 Oct.

—— (2001), 'Xerox Sells Half its Plants for $220 Million', *BBC.co.uk*, 2 Oct.

—— (2002), 'NEC to Switch Plant to China', *BBC.co.uk*, 27 Feb.

NEC (2002), *Annual Report*.

Toyota

Anon. (2002), 'Toyota Targets European Expansion', *BBC.co.uk*, 6 Mar.

—— (2002), 'Twenty Years Down the Road', *The Economist*, 12 Sept.

Toyota (2002), *Annual Report*.

Volkswagen

Tierney, C., and Muller, J. (2001), 'Another Trip Down Memory Lane', *Business Week*, 23 July.

—— Zammert, A., Muller, J., and Kerwin, K. (2001), 'Volkswagen', *Business Week*, 23 July.

QUESTIONS

1 What explains the rapid growth in foreign direct investment in recent years?

2 What is Dunning's eclectic approach to explaining foreign direct investment?

3 How do firm-specific advantages differ from country-specific advantages?

4 What are the principal sources of firm-specific advantages?

5 What are the principal sources of country-specific advantages?

6 What are the principal characteristics of firms that are 'global' in the distribution of their sales?

7 In what ways does the Regional Nature of Global Multinational Activity Survey cast doubt on arguments that the world is experiencing globalization?

FURTHER READING

Buckley, P. J., and Casson, M. (1976), *The Future of the Multinational Enterprise* (London: Macmillan). The classic original statement of the theory of internalization.

Dunning, J. H. (1981), *International Production and the Multinational Enterprise* (London: Allen & Unwin). An incisive and cogent explanation of the 'eclectic' theory of the multinational enterprise.

Rugman, A. (1981), *Inside the Multinationals: The Economics of Internal Markets* (New York: Columbia University Press). An extension of internalization theory to North American multinationals, their research and development and their strategies.

—— (2000), *The End of Globalization* (London: Random House; New York: Amacom-McGraw Hill). A book using aggregate country-level data to provide the first evidence on the prevalence of intra-regional trade and investment.

—— (2005), *The Regional Multinationals* (Cambridge: Cambridge University Press). Presents firm-level data on intra-regional sales and analyses the nature of global versus regional strategy for multinationals.

—— and Hodgetts, R. (2003), *International Business* (London: Prentice Hall). A leading textbook in the business school field of international business, explaining both firm and country-level factors affecting the strategies of multinational enterprises.

Williamson, O. (1975), *Markets and Hierarchies* (New York: Free Press). The classic explanation of transaction cost economics, relevant for the theory of multinational enterprises.

WEB LINKS

http://r0.unctad.org/wir/ World Investment Report.

www.templeton.ox.ac.uk/pdf/Briefings/13-TB.pdf Templeton Global Performance Index.

Appendix 10.1 The largest 180 manufacturing multinational enterprises

Rank	500 Rank	Company	Region	F/T Sales	% intra regional	% extra regional	NA % of total	EUR % of total	AP % of total	
1	2	Exxon Mobile	NA	69.6	37.5	62.5	37.5	8.9	10.4	I
2	3	General Motors	NA	25.5	81.1	18.9	81.1	14.6	na	D
3	4	BP	EUR	80.4	36.3	63.7	48.1	36.3	na	B
4	5	Ford Motor	NA	33.3	66.7	33.3	66.7	21.9	na	D
5	7	DaimlerChrysler	EUR	na	29.9	70.1	60.1	29.9	na	S
6	8	Royal Dutch/Shell Group	EUR	na	46.1	53.9	15.6	46.1	na	I
7	10	Toyato Motor	AP	50.8	49.2	50.8	36.6	7.7	49.2	B
8	14	Chevrontexaco	NA	56.5	43.5	56.5	43.5	na	na	I
9	15	Total Fina Elf	EUR	na	55.6	44.4	8.4	55.6	na	D
10	19	Intl. Business Machines	NA	64.8	43.5	56.5	43.5	28.0	20.0	G
11	21	Volkswagen	EUR	72.3	68.2	31.8	20.1	68.2	5.3	D
12	22	Siemens	EUR	78.0	68.2	31.8	20.1	68.2	5.3	D
13	24	Philip Morris	NA	42.1	57.9	42.1	57.9	25.8	na	D
14	32	Hitachi	AP	31.0	80.0	20.0	11.0	7.0	80.0	D
15	36	American Electric Power	NA	12.3	87.7	12.3	87.7	11.8	na	D
16	37	Sony	AP	67.2	32.8	67.2	29.8	20.2	32.8	G
17	39	Duke Energy	NA	13.1	96.5	3.5	96.5	na	na	D
18	41	Honda Motor	AP	35.1	64.9	35.1	12.4	6.9	64.9	S
19	42	Boeing	NA	33.3	66.7	33.3	66.7	14.5	16.3	D
20	43	El Paso	NA	2.8	97.2	2.8	97.2	na	na	D
21	45	Matsushita Electric Industrial	AP	35.1	64.9	35.1	12.4	6.9	64.9	D
22	49	Fiat	EUR	65.6	73.3	26.7	13.0	73.3	na	D
23	53	RWE	EUR	37.9	75.0	25.0	19.5	75.0	5.1	D
24	55	Nestlé	EUR	na	31.6	68.4	31.4	31.6	na	I
25	58	Nissan Motor	AP	50.3	49.7	50.3	34.6	11.0	49.7	B
26	62	Merck	NA	16.4	83.6	16.4	83.6	na	na	D
27	67	Reliant Energy	NA	8.6	91.4	8.6	91.4	na	na	D
28	68	Unilever	EUR	na	38.7	61.3	46.6	38.7	15.4	B
29	70	Hewlett packard (q)	NA	58.4	41.6	58.4	18.8	na	na	I
30	71	ENI	EUR	44.3	80.4	19.6	12.1	80.4	3.1	D
31	77	Toshiba	AP	37.0	75.3	24.7	13.9	8.7	75.3	D
32	78	Dynegy	NA	23.7	90.7	9.3	90.7	na	na	D
33	84	NEC	AP	20.4	79.6	20.4	7.0	na	79.6	D
34	87	Aquila	NA	18.4	91.0	9.0	91.0	na	na	D
35	88	Fujitsu	AP	28.2	71.8	28.2	11.4	12.2	71.8	D
36	92	Pemex (q)	NA	34.4	91.7	8.3	91.7	3.7	na	D
37	93	Procter & Gamble	NA	48.2	55.0	45.0	55.0	27.0	10.0	D
38	99	Suez	EUR	50.0	74.0	26.0	11.0	74.0	5.0	D

Rank	500 Rank	Company	Region	F/T Sales	% intra regional	% extra regional	NA % of total	EUR % of total	AP % of total	
39	103	Tyco International	NA	na	65.4	34.6	65.4	21.2	12.4	D
40	110	Marathon Oil	NA	3.6	96.4	3.6	97.6	na	na	D
41	112	BMW	EUR	73.4	57.3	42.7	31.7	57.3	na	D
42	116	Thyssen Krupp	EUR	63.8	61.1	38.9	21.9	61.1	na	D
43	117	Compaq Computer (q)	NA	62.0	38.0	62.0	38.0	36.0	na	I
44	121	Johnson & Johnson	NA	32.7	67.3	32.7	67.3	20.9	na	D
45	122	Conoco	NA	42.4	57.6	42.4	57.6	na	na	D
46	125	Renault	EUR	60.8	89.1	10.9	na	89.1	na	D
47	127	Pfizer	NA	38.2	61.8	38.2	61.8	na	6.5	D
48	129	Mirant	NA	16.0	95.2	4.8	95.2	1.8	na	D
49	131	Dell Computer	NA	na	71.7	28.3	71.7	20.1	8.2	D
50	133	Hyundai Motor	AP	20.9	81.6	18.4	18.1	0.3	81.6	D
51	138	Motorola	NA	56.0	44.0	56.0	44.0	14.0	26.0	B
52	140	GlaxoSmithKline	EUR	50.8	28.6	71.4	49.2	28.6	na	B
53	141	Mitsubishi Electric	AP	26.3	83.1	16.9	8.9	6.0	83.1	D
54	142	BASF	EUR	77.8	55.3	44.7	23.6	55.3	14.4	D
55	143	Royal Philips Electronics	EUR	na	43.0	57.0	28.7	43.0	21.5	G
56	147	Nokia	EUR	98.5	49.0	51.0	25.0	49.0	26.0	G
57	149	United Technologies	NA	53.0	47.0	53.0	47.0	17.0	12.0	I
58	152	Dow Chemical	NA	57.9	42.1	57.9	42.1	32.0	na	I
59	153	EADS	EUR	na	44.9	55.1	33.7	44.9	10.2	B
60	155	Saint-Gobain	EUR	67.9	63.9	36.1	22.3	63.9	na	D
61	156	ConAgra	NA	14.7	85.3	14.7	85.3	na	na	D
62	158	Bayer	EUR	na	40.3	59.7	32.7	40.3	16.1	B
63	159	PepsiCo	NA	32.4	67.6	32.4	67.6	na	na	D
64	162	Intel	NA	64.6	35.4	64.6	35.4	24.5	40.2	G
65	163	International Paper	NA	22.0	78.0	22.0	78.0	10.0	7.0	D
66	164	Statoil	EUR	24.6	86.8	13.2	10.0	86.8	na	D
67	166	Delphi	NA	na	77.7	22.3	77.7	18.4	na	D
68	171	Mitsubishi Motors	AP	40.9	62.8	37.2	22.1	12.1	62.8	D
69	172	DuPont de Numerous (E.I.)	NA	51.2	55.1	44.9	55.1	26.0	14.8	D
70	173	Georgia-Pacific	NA	13.2	86.8	13.2	86.8	na	na	D
71	180	Lucent Technologies	NA	35.3	64.7	35.3	64.7	na	na	D
72	182	Lockheed Martin	NA	17.0	83.0	17.0	83.0	na	na	D
73	185	Petrobrás (q)	Other	12.0	88.0	12.0	na	na	na	D
74	188	Philips Petroleum	NA	9.1	90.9	9.1	90.9	na	na	D
75	190	Canon	AP	71.5	28.5	71.5	33.8	20.8	28.5	G
76	194	ABB	EUR	na	53.9	46.1	25.1	53.9	11.3	D
77	195	Honeywell Intl.	NA	26.3	73.7	26.3	73.7	18.0	na	D
78	197	Nippon Mitsubishi Oil	AP	19.2	87.9	12.1	1.9	10.2	87.9	D
79	204	Mitsubishi Heavy Industries	AP	7.9	93.2	6.8	4.7	1.9	93.2	D
80	205	Alcoa	NA	34.0	73.0	27.0	73.0	20.0	7.0	D
81	210	L.M. Ericsson	EUR	97.0	46.0	54.0	13.2	46.0	25.9	B
82	213	Cisco Systems	NA	na	59.7	40.3	59.7	24.8	15.5	D
83	218	Bristol-Myers Squibb	NA	32.3	67.7	32.3	67.7	18.6	7.0	D

Rank	500 Rank	Company	Region	F/T Sales	% intra regional	% extra regional	NA % of total	EUR % of total	AP % of total	
84	228	Alstom	EUR	88.1	45.1	54.9	28.0	45.1	16.1	B
85	229	Nippon Steel	AP	17.8	82.2	17.8	na	na	82.2	D
86	230	Aventis (q)	EUR	87.2	32.1	67.9	38.8	32.1	6.4	B
87	232	Caterpillar (q)	NA	na	53.9	46.1	53.9	26.9	10.6	D
88	239	Coca-Cola	NA	na	38.4	61.6	38.4	22.4	24.9	G
89	240	Archer Daniels Midland	NA	34.6	65.4	64.6	65.4	na	na	D
90	250	Pharmacia	NA	43.5	56.5	43.5	56.5	na	6.7	D
91	251	Fuji Photo Film	AP	51.6	48.4	51.6	na	na	48.4	I
92	252	Denso	AP	32.4	73.1	26.9	20.0	6.8	73.1	D
93	257	Novartis	EUR	na	32.0	68.0	43.0	32.0	na	I
94	261	Solectron	NA	50.8	49.2	50.8	49.2	18.2	na	I
95	262	Diageo	EUR	na	31.8	68.2	49.9	31.8	7.7	B
96	263	Nortel Networks	NA	94.6	54.4	45.6	54.4	na	na	D
97	264	Johnson Controls	NA	na	62.9	37.1	62.9	25.6	na	D
98	266	Bouygues	EUR	53.0	62.0	38.0	2.0	62.0	13.0	D
99	267	Volvo	EUR	na	51.6	48.4	30.2	51.6	6.0	D
100	268	Sun Microsystems	NA	52.6	47.4	52.6	47.4	30.2	17.2	B
101	271	British American Tobacco (q)	EUR	na	31.3	68.7	na	31.3	9.9	I
102	278	Visteon	NA	29.0	71.0	29.0	71.0	15.6	na	D
103	281	BHP Billiton	AP	67.9	66.1	33.9	12.6	13.0	66.1	D
104	282	Sara Lee	NA	42.9	57.1	42.9	57.1	na	na	D
105	285	Bridgestone	AP	61.2	38.8	61.2	43.0	10.1	38.8	B
106	288	Roche Group	EUR	98.2	36.8	63.2	38.6	36.8	11.7	B
107	291	Norsk Hydro	EUR	91.8	77.0	23.0	11.8	77.0	4.2	D
108	293	Sanyo Electric	AP	49.0	72.7	27.3	17.0	8.7	72.7	D
109	295	Raytheon	NA	16.4	83.6	16.4	83.6	na	na	D
110	296	Mazda Motor	AP	34.3	65.7	34.3	24.4	7.0	65.7	D
111	300	Xerox	NA	41.0	59.0	41.0	59.0	29.6	na	D
112	301	AstraZeneca	EUR	na	32.0	68.0	52.8	32.0	5.2	S
113	302	Kajima	AP	9.9	92.2	7.8	6.9	1.0	92.2	D
114	306	TRW	NA	40.7	59.3	40.7	59.3	na	na	D
115	307	Japan Tobacco	AP	9.5	90.5	9.5	na	5.8	90.5	D
116	308	Vinci	EUR	38.0	89.0	11.0	5.0	89.0	na	D
117	309	Abbott Laboratories	NA	37.1	65.8	34.2	65.8	na	4.6	D
118	316	3M (q)	NA	53.1	46.9	53.1	46.9	24.6	18.9	B
119	317	Skanska	EUR	83.0	40.0	60.0	41.0	40.0	na	B
120	322	Coca-Cola Enterprises	NA	na	76.8	23.2	76.8	23.2	na	D
121	326	Emerson Electric	NA	40.0	60.0	40.0	60.0	19.9	9.1	D
122	327	Onex	NA	77.0	65.0	35.0	65.0	22.0	na	D
123	336	Valero Energy	NA	na	100.0	—	100.0	—	—	D
124	341	Anglo American	EUR	86.7	46.1	53.9	18.9	46.1	17.8	I
125	342	Michelin	EUR	na	47.0	53.0	40.0	47.0	na	B
126	343	Man Group	EUR	72.6	68.7	31.3	15.6	68.7	12.7	D
127	344	Wayerhauser	NA	18.9	86.4	13.6	86.4	2.9	4.8	D
128	345	Kimberly-Clark	NA	na	55.0	45.0	55.0	15.0	na	D

Rank	500 Rank	Company	Region	F/T Sales	% intra regional	% extra regional	NA % of total	EUR % of total	AP % of total	
129	346	Sharp	AP	32.5	80.0	20.0	18.7	9.5	80.0	D
130	350	Mitsubishi Chemical	AP	13.1	86.9	13.1	na	na	86.9	D
131	352	Goodyear Tire & Rubber (q)	NA	45.9	64.1	45.9	54.1	na	na	D
132	354	Wyeth	NA	36.1	63.9	36.1	63.9	na	na	D
133	355	Occidental Petroleum	NA	13.2	87.7	12.3	87.7	na	na	D
134	360	Bombardier	NA	92.2	60.7	39.3	60.7	30.9	4.5	D
135	365	RAG	EUR	29.2	83.8	16.2	na	83.8	na	D
136	369	Lear	NA	51.4	58.2	41.8	58.2	31.6	na	D
137	373	Northrop Grumman	NA	9.6	90.4	9.6	90.4	na	na	D
138	376	Amerada Hess	NA	26.8	73.2	26.8	73.2	23.7	na	D

11 Globalization, poverty, and inequality

Robert Hunter Wade

READER'S GUIDE

The liberal argument says that world poverty and income inequality have fallen over the past two decades or so for the first time in more than a century and a half. The falls have been driven in large part by the rising density of economic integration across national borders. This 'globalization' has made for a more market-driven, more efficient use of world resources, which has raised developing country growth rates, not only of average income but also the bottom deciles' income.

The dynamics of globalization thus yield 'mutual benefit', thanks to which the interests of rich countries and poor countries, dominant classes and subordinate classes, are now aligned in favour of free markets and greater equity, contrary to the standard 'conflicting interests' assumption of the Left. The divide between North and South, between rich world and poor world, between geographical core and geographical periphery, is not a structural feature of the world economy, but merely a lag in the catch up of the poor world to the prosperity of the rich world. The World Trade Organization (WTO), the World Bank, the International Monetary Fund (IMF) and other multilateral economic organizations are rightly mandated to deregulate markets and harmonize national regulations so as to give economic actors a global 'level playing' field undistorted by state restrictions.

But how much confidence can we have in the claim that world poverty and inequality have been falling, thanks to globalization? This chapter summarizes some doubts about the reality of falls in world poverty and income inequality and about why economic globalization may not have had the impact on poverty and inequality that liberal arguments suggest. It concludes by asking whether we should be concerned about rising inequality, and how we might analyse the political economy of statistics.

Introduction

'Evidence suggests the 1980s and 1990s were decades of declining global inequality and reductions in the proportion of the world's population in extreme poverty' (Martin Wolf, *Financial Times*, 8 May 2002).

'World inequalities did rise over a period of a century from the middle of the nineteenth century up to the early 1960s [*sic*]. But since that time this trend has been halted' (Anthony Giddens, director of the London School of Economics, 2002).

'Over the past 20 years the number of people living on less than $1 a day has fallen by 200 million, after rising steadily for 200 years' (James Wolfensohn, president of the World Bank, 2002*a*).

'[G]lobalization has dramatically increased inequality between and within nations' (Jay Mazur, US union leader, 2000).

Economic globalization has been one of the central vectors of change in the world economy since the 1970s. The world trade to world production ratio has risen higher than ever before and is continuing to rise, foreign investment to total investment likewise, and national economic growth rates in the West have become increasingly correlated. Public policy in the West has swung away from the social protections put in place after the Depression and the Second World War. It has come to emphasize deregulation, open capital accounts, privatization, cuts in some welfare state services, flexible labour markets, restrictions on labour unions (though it does not emphasize cuts in agricultural subsidies or lifting of restrictions on cross-border movement of labour). Not only Reagan, Thatcher, and their successors in the United States and the United Kingdom, but also left-of-centre parties and governments in Europe, Japan, and Australasia have been talking the same language. And through their predominance in multilateral economic organizations (MEOs) like the IMF, the World Bank, and the WTO they have sought to 'internationalize' the new priorities to developing countries—to make them the universal norm. To a remarkable degree, anything that constrains the preferences of international capitalists has been delegitimized in the name of the imperative of global 'competitiveness' and 'efficiency'.

In economics, institutional economics, Keynesian economics, development economics—previously flourishing approaches—have been pushed to the margins by neo-liberal economics presented as the universal science of human behaviour. Neo-liberal economics rests upon the epistemological assumption that, in the words of former Treasury Secretary Larry Summers, 'the laws of economics, it's often forgotten, are like the laws of engineering. There's only one set of laws and they work everywhere.' The laws reflect the assumption that 'Markets are an expression of the deepest truths about human nature and . . . as a result, they will ultimately be correct', in the words of *Time* magazine's paraphrase of the core belief of Federal Reserve Chairman Alan Greenspan (J. C. Ramo, 15 February 1999). Neo-liberal free markets are seen as the 'natural' form of capitalism, analogous to Rousseau's Noble Savage. As the Noble Savage is corrupted by society, so natural capitalism is corrupted by politics and government intervention, as in developmental states and the Western European social market economies (Wade 2003*a*).

The world system has therefore been developing both a strong normative consensus and a set of international political structures, notably the MEOs, that regulate interactions within and across national borders. These international structures are being operated as a condominium among a small number of prosperous states, made up almost entirely of the early-industrialized Atlantic states, with a common interest not in conquering other states so as to extract tribute but in establishing rules and norms that reinforce their own pre-eminence, economic, political, cultural, and military.

Of course, these states do not justify them in these terms, but in terms of the best interests of the world. They claim that the neo-liberal agenda, as described above, will do most to promote the catch-up of developing countries to the prosperity of the now prosperous democracies. One large part of the evidence used to support this claim comes from trends in world income inequality and poverty.

The liberal argument says that world income inequality and the number of people living in extreme poverty have both fallen over the past two decades or so, for the first time in more than a century and a half. This gratifying result is due in large part to the rising density of economic integration between countries, which has generated rising efficiency of resource use worldwide as countries and regions specialize in line with their comparative advantage. Hence the globalizing direction of change in the world system serves the great majority of the world's people well. The core solution for lagging regions, Africa above all, is freer domestic and international trade and investment, leading to deeper integration into the world economy.

Evidence from the current long wave of globalization thus confirms neo-liberal economic theory—more open economies are more prosperous, economies that liberalize more experience a faster rate of progress, and people who resist further economic liberalization must be acting out of vested interests. The world economy is an open system in the sense that country mobility up the wealth/income hierarchy is unlimited by the structure; and the hierarchy itself is in the process of being flattened, the North–South, core–periphery, rich country–poor country divide is being eroded away. The same evidence also validates the rationale of the WTO, the World Bank, the IMF, and other MEOs as the world's agents for creating a global 'level playing' field undistorted by state-imposed restrictions on markets. This line of argument is championed by the more powerful of the centres of 'thinking for the world' that influence international policy making, including the intergovernmental organizations like the World Bank, the IMF, and the WTO, also the USA and UK Treasuries, and opinion-shaping media like the *Financial Times* and *The Economist*.

The standard Left assumption, in contrast, is that the rich and powerful countries and classes have little interest in greater equity. Consistent with this view, the 'anti-globalization' argument (better described as 'anti-neo-liberal') asserts that world poverty and inequality have been rising, not falling, due to forces unleashed by globalization (for example, union leader Jay Mazur's quote above). The line of solution is some degree of tightening of public policy limits on the operation of market forces; though within the broad 'anti-globalization' camp there is a much wider range of views about solutions than exists in the liberal camp.

Each side tends to conduct the debate as if its case was overwhelming, and only an intellectually deficient or dishonest person could see merit in other's case. For example, Martin Wolf (8 February 2000) of the *Financial Times* claims that the 'anti-globalization' argument is nothing less than 'the big lie'. If translated into public policy it would only cause more poverty and inequality, while pretending to do the opposite. On the other hand, reports from the grass roots even in middle-income countries like Mexico—one of neo-liberalism's star pupils over the past twenty years—suggest that the promised benefits are not arriving. According to one such report in the *Washington Post*,

The three main options for high school graduates—attending college, getting a job in Mexico or crossing the border illegally to work in the United States—have become tougher in the past few years . . . The result is that the generation being counted on to drive Mexico's future finds itself stuck. A historically high number of Mexicans—more than 20 million people, a fifth of the population, are 15 to 24 years old. These young people have been promised much: They are reaching working age a decade after implementation of a free trade agreement with the United States that was supposed to bring new jobs, higher wages and a better life than their parents had. They are also coming of age as Mexico moves beyond its authoritarian past. But millions are finding more obstacles than opportunities in the new democratic era. (Jordan, 4 October 2003: A15).

This chapter summarizes some doubts about the reality of falls in world poverty and income inequality and about the role of globalization. The bottom line is that there is a non-trivial probability that the liberal argument is wrong.

Key points

- Public policy in Western industrialized countries in the last quarter of a century has emphasized deregulation, privatization, restrictions on labour unions, and cuts in state services and welfare. The international financial institutions and the WTO have sought to ensure developing countries also adopt these policies.

- In economics, neo-liberal approaches are dominant and presented as a universal science of human behaviour.

- Liberal approaches argue that both poverty and inequality have fallen in the last two decades. Globalization has had a beneficial impact on all. Deeper integration into the global economy is the solution for less developed countries.

- The anti-neo-liberal argument suggests in contrast that world poverty and inequality have been rising.
- Evidence suggests that the neo-liberal argument on poverty and inequality may be wrong.

Regional variation

First, an overview of world income distribution and growth. Figure 11.1 shows the distribution of world population by the average country income (with the two giants, China and India, divided into rural and urban sectors). Here incomes are measured at purchasing power parity exchange rates rather than current market exchange rates (Box 11.1). The questions concern the shape of the distribution and the trends over time.

World Gross Domestic Product (GDP) has grown about two percentage points faster than world population over the past two decades; and the (population-weighted) GDP of developing countries as a group has grown a little faster than that of the high-income

countries. This is good news, environmental concerns aside. But regional variance is large. Sub-Saharan Africa's economic performance has been dire over the past two decades; its average real income today is below the level of twenty years ago. Latin America's economic performance has been poor; its average income is about the same as twenty years ago. South Asia's has been better than average since the 1990s. China's has been excellent through the 1980s and 1990s, as also the rest of (non-Japan) East and South-East Asia's, apart from the crisis of 1997–8.

This collage can be shown as a ratio of regional Gross National Product (GNP) per capita to the GNP per capita of the 'core' regions. Table 11.1 shows the

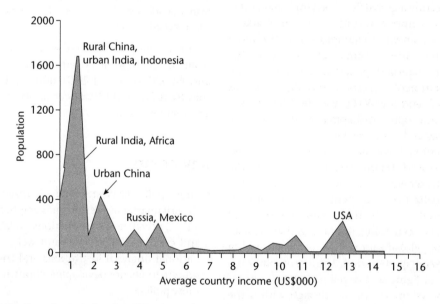

Fig. 11.1 Distribution of population (in million according to average per capita country income where they live, in 000$PPP per year)

Source: Milanovic 2002*b*.

trends from 1960 to 1999. Here incomes are converted into US$ at current exchange rates in order to measure *international* purchasing power. Over the three decades, the per capita incomes of Sub-Saharan Africa, Latin America, and West Asia and North Africa have fallen as a fraction of the core's; South Asia's remained more or less constant; East Asia's (minus China) rose sharply; China's rose sharply but from a very low base. But the most striking feature is not the trends but the sheer size of the gaps, testimony to the failure of 'catch-up'; even success-story East Asia today has an average per capita income only about 13 per cent of the core's. It is a safe bet that most development experts, asked in 1960 to predict these ratios for 2000, would have guessed much higher. To put the gaps in tangible terms, consider an 'economic hardship' index as the number of hours of work needed for an adult male entry-level employee of McDonald's to earn the equivalent of one Big Mac. In the 'core' zone of Western Europe, North America, and Japan the figure is in the range of 0.25 to 0.6 hours; in the

'semi-periphery' of South Korea and Malaysia, 1.5 hours; China, 2.2 hours; India, nearly 3 hours.

The variance can also be shown in terms of the distribution of world income by regions and income percentiles. Figure 11.2 shows the regional distribution of people at each income percentile for two years, 1990 and 1999. Here incomes are expressed in purchasing power parity dollars (PPP$) in order to measure, notionally at least, *domestic* purchasing power.

One sees the African collapse in the increased share of the African population in the bottom quintile, even within the short period of 1990 to 1999; also the falling back of the eastern and central European populations from the second to the third from top quintile; and the rising share of the East Asian population in the second from top quintile.

Figure 11.3 shows, in the top half, the world's population plotted against the log of PPP$ income, taking account of both between-country and within-country income distribution; and the breakdown by region. The bottom half shows the world's income plotted against income level, from which one sees the relative amount of income accruing to people at

---

Box 11.1 Purchasing power parity

Purchasing power parity (PPP) is a method of adjusting relative incomes in different countries to take account of the fact that market exchange rates do not accurately reflect purchasing power. It rests on the 'law of one price': the idea that competitive markets will equalize the price of an identical good in different countries when prices are expressed in the same currency and transportation and transactions costs are excluded. If exchange rates reflected local purchasing power then a dollar would buy the same amount of goods in all countries.

The Economist publishes a simple exercise at calculating purchasing power parities each year in its 'Big Mac' index, which compares the price of a McDonald's hamburger around the world in local currencies and translated into dollars at current exchange rates (**www.economist.com/markets/Bigmac/Index.cfm**). More sophisticated calculations of PPP use local prices of a 'basket' of goods and services. As discussed below, one of the problems with PPP calculations is that at different levels of per capita income, people consume very different mixtures of goods and services.

Table 11.1 GNP per capita for region as percentage of core's GNP per capita

Region	1960	1980	1999
Sub-Saharan Africa	5	4	2
Latin America	20	18	12
West Asia and North Africa	9	9	7
South Asia	2	1	2
East Asia (w/o China and Japan)	6	8	13
China	1	1	3
South	5	4	5
North America	124	100	101
Western Europe	111	104	98
Southern Europe	52	60	60
Australia and NZ	95	75	73
Japan	79	134	145
North (=core)	**100**	**100**	**100**

Note: Based on World Bank data. GNP at current exchange rates.

Source: Arrighi, Silver, and Brewer (2003).

A. 1990

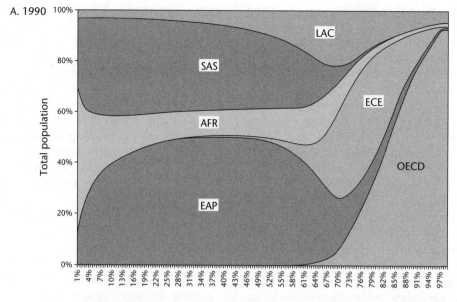

B. 1999

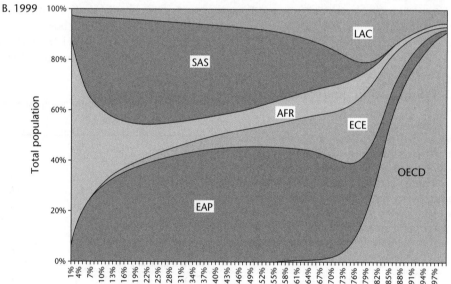

Fig. 11.2 World income distribution, by region and by percentile of income distribution, 1990, 1999

Note: LAC = Latin America and Caribbean; SAS = South Asia; AFR = Africa; ECE = East and Central Europe; EAP = East Asia and Pacific; OECD = Organization for Economic Cooperation and Development. Based on World Institute for Development Economics Research (WIDER) data. PPP$.

Source: Dikhanov and Ward (2003).

different income levels and in different regions. Residents of South Asia and East Asia predominate at income levels below the median, and residents of the OECD countries predominate at the top.

Finally, Figure 11.4 shows the movement in the bimodal shape of the overall PPP$ income-to-population distribution between 1970 and 1999. The 1999 distribution has shifted forward compared to

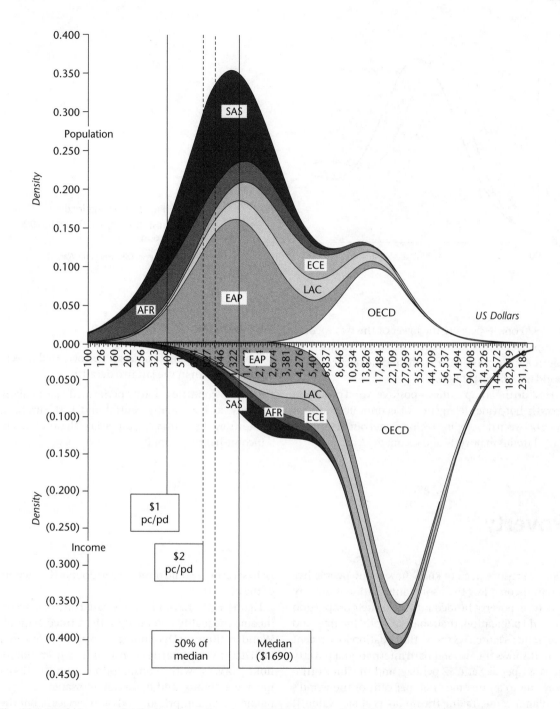

Fig. 11.3 World income distribution, by region: top half, distribution of world population against income; bottom half, distribution of world income against income, 1999

Source: Dikhanov and Ward (2003).

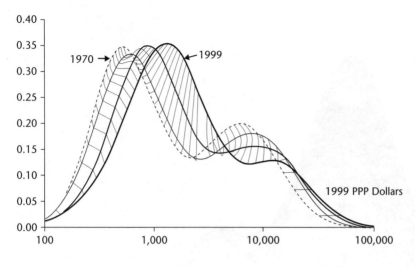

Fig. 11.4 World income distribution, 1970, 1980, 1990, 1999

Source: Dikhanov and Ward (2003).

the 1970 one, especially the lower of the two income humps, reflecting the arrival of large numbers of South and East Asians into the middle deciles of the world income distribution.

How do the complexities—positive world per capita growth but wide divergence of economic performance between developing regions—net out in terms of global trends in poverty and inequality?

Key points

- Substantial regional variation has occurred in economic growth in the last two decades.
- African countries have performed particularly poorly, as have many central and East European countries. In contrast, East Asia's share of world income has risen rapidly.

Poverty

On poverty, we need to know how many people live on an income less than some international poverty line (the 'poverty headcount'); also their proportion of world population; their share of world income; and the trends. Figure 11.3 shows the situation for a recent year. It shows the two standard international poverty lines, $1 per day and $2 per day; and the line corresponding to an income of 50 per cent of the world's median income. Taking the numbers at face value, it is striking that even the higher $2 per day absolute poverty line is below a 'minimum' *relative* poverty line of half of the median. It is striking, too, how small a share of world income goes to those on less than $1 per day, and how small a share of the income of the

richest earners would be needed to double the income of the poorest.

Figures 11.2, 11.3, and 11.4 are based on a data set on income inequality compiled by the United Nation's World Institute for Development Economics Research (WIDER) (which marries consumption from household surveys with consumption from national income accounts, and makes an allowance for non-public sector non-priced goods and services). But the standard poverty numbers—the ones normally used in discussions about the state of the world—come from the World Bank's own data set. This is the source of the claims that, in the words of President James Wolfensohn, 'Over the past 20 years the number of people living on less than $1 a day has fallen by 200 million, after rising steadily for 200 years' (World Bank 2002*d*: Foreword). And 'the proportion of people worldwide living in absolute poverty has dropped steadily in recent decades, from 29% in 1990 to a record low of 23% in 1998' (Wolfensohn 2001). The opening sentence of the Bank's 'World Development Indicators 2001' says, 'Of the world's 6 billion people 1.2 billion live on less than $1 a day', the same number in 1987 and 1998 (World Bank 2001*b*: 3); see also World Bank (2002*b*).

I now show that the Bank's figures contain a large margin of error, and the errors *probably* flatter the result in one direction. For discussions about the Bank's poverty numbers I am particularly indebted to Sanjay Reddy (Reddy and Pogge 2003; see also Ravallion 2002; and Reddy and Pogge 2002). In this chapter, I do not consider the additional problems that arise when estimating the impact of economic growth on poverty (see Deaton 2003).

To get the world extreme poverty headcount the Bank first defines an international poverty line for a given base year by using purchasing power parity conversion factors (PPPs) to convert the purchasing power of an average of the official national poverty lines of a set of low-income countries into the US dollar amount needed to have the same notional purchasing power in the United States in the same year. (In its first global poverty estimation this procedure yielded a conveniently understandable US$1 per day for the base year of 1985. The Bank also calculates a poverty headcount with $2/day, which suffers from the same limitations as the $1/day line.) Then the Bank uses PPP conversion factors to estimate the amount of local currency, country by country, needed to have the same purchasing power in the same year as in the US base case. (So by this method Rs.10 may have the same purchasing power in India in 1985 as US$1 in the United States in the same year.) This gives an international poverty line equivalent to US$1 per day, expressed in domestic currency (Rs.10 per day in the Indian example). From household surveys the Bank then estimates the number of people in the country living on less than this international poverty line, for that year. It sums the country totals to get the world total. Finally, the Bank uses national consumer price indices to keep real purchasing power constant across time, and adjusts the international poverty line for each country upwards with inflation.

Large margin of error

Consider the reasons to expect a large margin of error, regardless of direction.

First, the poverty headcount is very sensitive to the precise level of the international poverty lines. Recent research on China suggests that a 10 per cent increase in the line brings a roughly 20 per cent increase in the poverty headcount.

Second, the poverty headcount is very sensitive to the reliability of household surveys of income and expenditure. The available surveys are of widely varying quality, and many do not follow a standard template. The point is not that household surveys are less reliable than other possible sources (for example, national income accounts); but simply that they do contain large amounts of error.

Third, by far the two most important countries for the overall trend, China and India, have PPP-adjusted income figures that contain an even bigger component of guesswork than for most other significant countries. The main sources of PPP income figures (the Penn World Tables and the International Comparison Project) are based on two large-scale international price benchmarking exercises for calculating purchasing power parity exchange rates, one in 1985 in sixty countries, the second in 1993 in 110 countries. The government of China declined to participate in both. The purchasing power parity exchange rate for China is based on guestimates from small, ad hoc price surveys in a few cities, adjusted by rules of thumb to take account of the huge price differences between urban and rural areas and between eastern and western regions. The government of India declined to participate in the 1993 exercise. The price comparisons for India are extrapolations from 1985 qualified by small, ad hoc price surveys in later years. The lack of reliable price comparisons for China and India—hence the lack of reliable evidence on the purchasing power of even average incomes, let alone incomes of the poor—compromises any statement about levels and trends in world poverty (Reddy and Pogge 2003).

Fourth, the often-cited comparison between 1980 and 1998—1.4 billion in extreme poverty in 1980, 1.2 billion in 1998—is not valid because the Bank introduced a new methodology in the late 1990s which makes the figures non-comparable. The Bank has

Table 11.2 1993 poverty rate, using old and new World Bank methodology

	Old poverty rate (%)	New poverty rate (%)
Sub-Saharan Africa	39.1	49.7
Latin America	23.5	15.3
Middle East/North Africa	4.1	1.9

Note: The poverty rate is the proportion of the population living on less than $1 a day.

Source: Deaton (2001).

recalculated the poverty numbers with the new method only back to 1987, and we do not know what the 1980 figure would be if calculated in the same way.

We do know, however, that the new method caused a huge change in the poverty count even for the same country in the same year using the same survey data (published in World Bank 2001c). Table 11.2 shows the method-induced changes by regions for 1993. Angus Deaton comments that 'Changes of this size risk swamping real changes', 'and it seems impossible to make statements about changes in world poverty when the ground underneath one's feet is changing in this way' (Deaton 2001: 128).

Downward bias

Further sources of error bias the results downwards, making the number of people in poverty seem lower than it really is. The bias probably increases over time, making the trend look rosier than it is. There are at least three reasons.

First, the Bank's international poverty line underestimates the income or expenditure needed for an individual (or household) to avoid periods of food-clothing-shelter consumption too low to maintain health and well-being. (And it avoids altogether the problem that basic needs include unpriced public goods like clean water and access to basic health care.) The Bank's line refers to an 'average consumption' bundle, not to a basket of goods and services that makes sense for measuring poverty (though '$1 per day' does have intuitive appeal to a Western audience being asked to support aid). Suppose it costs Rs.30 to

buy an equivalent bundle of food in India (defined in terms of calories and micro-nutrients) as can be bought in the USA with $1; and that it costs Rs.3 to buy an equivalent bundle of services (haircuts, massages) as $1 in the United States (Pogge and Reddy 2003). Current methods of calculating purchasing power parity, based on an *average* consumption bundle of food, services and other things, may yield a PPP exchange rate of, say, $PPP1 = Rs.10, meaning that Rs.10 in India buys the equivalent average consumption bundle (food, services, etc.) as $1 in the United States. But this is misleading because the poor person, spending most income on food, can buy with Rs.10 only a third of the food purchasable with $1 in the United States. To take the international poverty line for India as Rs.10 therefore biases the number of poor downwards.

We have no way of knowing what proportion of food-clothing-shelter needs the Bank's international poverty line captures. But we can be fairly sure that if the Bank used a basic needs poverty line rather than its present artificial one the number of absolute poor would rise, because the national poverty lines equivalent to a global basic needs poverty line would probably rise, perhaps by 25 to 40 per cent (Reddy and Pogge's estimate, the range reflecting calculations based on PPP conversion factors for 1985 and 1993, and for 'all-food' and 'bread-and-cereals' indices).

A 30 to 40 per cent increase in a basic-needs-based international poverty line would, for the reason mentioned earlier, increase the world total of people in extreme poverty by a large fraction, probably at least 30 to 40 per cent. A recent study for Latin America shows that national extreme poverty rates, using poverty lines derived from calorific and demographic characteristics, may be more than *twice* as high as those based on the World Bank's $1/day line. For example, the World Bank estimates Brazil's extreme poverty rate (using its international poverty line) at 5 per cent; the Economic Commission for Latin America, using a calories-and-demography poverty line, estimates the rate at 14 per cent (similarly, Bolivia's extreme poverty rate according to the World Bank line was 11 per cent, according to the ECLA line, 23 per cent; Chile, 4 per cent, 8 per cent; Colombia, 11 per cent, 24 per cent; Mexico, 18 per cent, 21 per cent) (ECLA 2001: 51).

In short, we can be reasonably confident that switching from the Bank's rather arbitrarily derived international poverty line to one reflecting the purchasing power necessary to achieve elementary human capabilities would substantially raise the number of people in extreme poverty in any year.

The second point is that the Bank's new international poverty line of $1.08/day *lowers* the equivalent national poverty lines in most countries compared to the earlier $PPP1 line. It lowers them in 77 per cent of the ninety-four countries for which data are available, containing 82 per cent of their population. It lowers the old international poverty line for China by 14 per cent, for India, by 9 per cent, for the whole sample by an average of 13 per cent (Reddy and Pogge 2003). As noted, even a small downwards shift in the poverty line pushes a large number of people out of poverty.

Third, future 'updating' of the international poverty line will continue artificially to lower the true numbers, because worldwide average consumption patterns (on which the international poverty line is based) are shifting toward services whose prices relative to food and shelter are lower in poor than in rich countries, giving the false impression that the cost of the basic consumption goods required by the poor is falling. This effect is amplified by the widespread removal of price controls on 'necessities' and the lowering of tariffs on luxuries.

All these problems have to be resolved in one way or another in any estimate of world poverty, whoever makes it. But the fact that the World Bank is effectively the monopoly provider introduces a further complication. The number of poor people is politically sensitive. The Bank's many critics (from the political right as well as the left) like to use the poverty numbers as one of many pointers to the conclusion that it has accomplished 'precious little', in the words of US Treasury Secretary O'Neill.

A comparison of two recent Bank publications suggests how the Bank's statements about poverty are affected by its tactics and the ideological predispositions of those in the ideas-controlling positions. *The World Development Report 2000/2001: Attacking Poverty* says that the number of people living on less than $1 a day *increased* by 20 million from 1.18 billion in 1987 to 1.20 billion in 1998. When it was being written in the late 1990s the key ideas-controlling positions in the Bank were held by Joe Stiglitz and Ravi Kanbur (respectively, chief economist and director of the *World Development Report 2000/2001*), not noted

champions of neo-liberal economics (see Wade 2002, which uses Stiglitz's firing and Kanbur's resignation to illuminate the US role in the Bank's generation of knowledge). At that time, the Bank was trying to mobilize support for making the Comprehensive Development Framework the new template for all its work, for which purpose *lack* of progress in development helped. Then came the majority report of the Meltzer Commission (2000), for the US Congress, which said the Bank was failing at its central task of poverty reduction and therefore should be sharply cut back—as shown by the fact that the number of people in absolute poverty remained constant at 1.2 billion between 1987 and 1998 (Meltzer 2001 later described the fall in the proportion of the world's population in poverty from 28 per cent in 1987 to 24 per cent in 1998 as a 'modest' decline, the better to hammer the Bank). Now the Bank needed to emphasize progress. The next major Bank publication, *Globalization, Growth, and Poverty: Building an Inclusive World Economy*, claimed that the number of people living in poverty *decreased* by 200 million in the eighteen years from 1980 to 1998 (World Bank 2002*b*; Deaton 2002). By this time Stiglitz and Kanbur were gone and David Dollar, a prominent Bank economist, was ascendant. He was chief author of *Globalization, Growth and Poverty*.

Conclusions about poverty

We can be fairly sure that the Bank's poverty headcount has a large margin of error in *all* years, in the sense that it may be significantly different from the headcount that would result from the use of PPP conversion factors based more closely on the real costs of living of the poor (defined in terms of income needed to buy enough calories, micro-nutrients and other necessities in order not to be poor). By the same token we should question the Bank's confidence that the 1980s to 1990s trend is downwards.

We do not know for sure how the late 1990s revisions to the method and the PPP numbers alter the poverty headcount in any one year and how they alter the trend over the 1980s and 1990s. But for the reasons given it is quite likely that the Bank's numbers substantially underestimate the true numbers of the world's population living in extreme poverty, and make the trend look better than it is.

On the other hand, it is quite plausible that the *proportion* of the world's population living in extreme poverty has fallen over the past twenty years or so. For one thing, household surveys are more likely to miss the rich than the poor, so that their results may overstate the *proportion* of the population in poverty. For another, for all the problems with Chinese and Indian income figures, we know enough about trends in other variables—including life expectancy, heights, and other non-income measures—to be confident that their poverty headcounts have indeed fallen dramatically over the past twenty years. Moreover, the magnitude of world population increase over the past twenty years is so large that the Bank's poverty numbers would have to be *huge* underestimates for the world poverty rate not to have fallen. Any more

precise statement about the *absolute* number of the world's people living in extreme poverty and the change over time currently rests on quicksand.

Key points

- World Bank data probably significantly underestimates the number of people living in poverty.
- Conversion of incomes in purchasing power parity terms provides a more accurate estimation the cost of living and of the incidence of poverty. Conversion in market exchange rate terms is better as a proxy for international purchasing power and for influence in the world polity.

Inequality

The world poverty headcount could move in one direction while world income distribution moves in the other. The liberal argument says that they have both moved together: the world poverty headcount has fallen over the past twenty years, and world income inequality has also fallen. But in the past several years world income distribution has become a hot topic of debate in international economics and in sociology (much hotter than trends in world poverty). Disagreement about the overall inequality trend should not be surprising given the collage of economic performance by region; different ways of measuring emphasize different parts of the collage.

The only valid short answer to the question, 'what is the trend of world income distribution?', is, 'it depends'. It depends on which combination out of many plausible combination of measures and samples we choose (in addition to the studies referenced elsewhere I draw on Firebaugh 1999; Jones 1997; Pritchett 1997; Quah 1997; UNDP 1999; Kanbur 2002; Korzeniewicz and Moran 1997; Korzeniewicz and Moran 2000). Whereas we *could* get better data on the poor to the extent that the poverty headcount would command general agreement, there is no single best combination of measures of world income inequality.

The choices include: (*a*) alternative measures of income (GDP per capita converted to US dollars using

market exchange rates or GDP per capita adjusted for differences in purchasing power across countries); (*b*) alternative weightings of countries (each country weighted as one unit or by population); (*c*) alternative measures of distribution (including the Gini or some other average coefficient; see Box 11.2), or ratios of the income of the richer deciles of world population to that of poorer deciles, or average income of a set of developing countries to that of a set of developed countries; (*d*) alternatives sources of data on incomes (national income accounts or household surveys); (*e*) alternative samples of countries and time periods.

Here are six propositions.

Proposition 1: International purchasing power and market exchange rates

With incomes converted into a common numeraire (the US dollar) by market exchange rates—giving a measure of the relative international purchasing power of residents of different countries, world income distribution has become rapidly more unequal.

No one disputes this. The dispute is about what the figures mean. Most economists say that

Box 11.2 **The Gini coefficient**

Income inequality is usually measured through surveys of household income. Households are then ranked from lowest to highest on the basis of income and divided into equal population groups, typically fifths (quintiles), or tenths (deciles). The share of income received by each population group is then compared with the share the population group would receive if all households received an equal share of the income.

The Gini coefficient is a number between zero and one that measures the degree of inequality in the distribution of income in a given society. The coefficient would be zero for a society in which each member received exactly the same income; it would be 1.0 for a country in

which one member received all the income and the rest nothing.

In practice, coefficient values range from around 0.25 for historically egalitarian countries such as Bulgaria, Finland, Hungary, Japan, and Sweden to around 0.6 for countries with highly skewed distributions of income including Brazil, Central African Republic, Chile, Guatemala, Nicaragua, and Sierra Leone. In the United States, the growth of inequality in the last three decades is reflected in an increase in the Gini coefficient from 0.35 in the 1970s to 0.40 in the 1990s.

For further information on measuring inequality see the World Income Inequality Database page at **www.undp. org/poverty/initiatives/wider/wiid_measure.htm**

---

exchange-rate-based income measures are irrelevant, and hence would dismiss the data in Table 11.1 as meaningless. Gross Domestic Product incomes should always be adjusted by PPP exchange rates to take account of differences in purchasing power, they say. This makes a big difference to the size of the gap between rich and poor. As noted earlier, the PPP adjustment is made by computing the relative prices for a general bundle of goods and services in different countries. The PPP adjustment generally raises the relative income of poor countries, making world income distribution more equal than with market exchange rates.

Market exchange-rate-based income comparisons do suffer from all the ways in which official exchange rates do not reflect the 'real' economy: from distortions in the official rates, exclusion of goods and services that are not traded, and sudden changes in the official exchange rate that may be driven more by capital movements than by trade movements. Nevertheless, we should reject the argument that incomes converted via PPP exchange rates should always be used in preference to incomes converted at market exchange rates.

The practical reasons concern the weaknesses of the PPP numbers. As noted, the PPP numbers for China and India have a large margin of error; for example, plausibly constructed PPP numbers for China differ by a factor of two. The same for countries of the former Soviet Union before the 1990s. So if incomes

converted via market exchange rates do not give an accurate measure of relative purchasing power, neither do the PPP numbers for countries that carry heavy weight in world trends. Our confidence in the trends in PPP income distribution should be correspondingly limited.

Practical problems aside, it is true that PPP adjustment is in principle preferable when one is interested in relative domestic purchasing power or, more generally, material well-being. However, we may be interested in income not only as a measure of material well-being. We may *also* be interested in relative income as a proxy for the relative purchasing power of residents of different countries over goods and services produced in *other* countries, and hence as a proxy for influence, power, and privilege. If we are interested in any of the questions about the economic and geo-political impact of one country (or region) on the rest of the world—including the capacity of developing countries to repay their debts, to import capital goods, and to participate in international organizations—we should use market exchange rates.

The reason why many poor small countries are hardly represented in multilateral negotiations that concern them directly is that they cannot afford the cost of hotels, offices, and salaries in places like Washington DC, and Geneva, which must be paid not in PPP dollars but in hard currency bought with their own currency at market exchange rates. And the reason they cannot afford to pay the foreign exchange costs of living up to many of their international commitments—hiring foreign experts to help them exercise control over their banking sectors so that they can implement their part of the anti-money-laundering regime, for example—likewise reflects their low market exchange-rate incomes.

Moreover, these same impacts shape internal state capacity. For example, we should use market exchange rates in order to pick up the key point that the long run deterioration in the exchange rates of most developing countries is putting developing countries under increasing internal 'stress'. When a rising amount of real domestic resources has to go into acquiring a given quantity of imports—say, of capital goods—other domestic uses of those resources are squeezed, including measures to reduce poverty, to finance civil services and schools and the like. This backwash effect is occluded in PPP calculations.

Hence we need to pay attention to what is happening to market exchange-rate world income distribution. It is widening fast, unambiguously.

The next four propositions refer to inequality of PPP-adjusted incomes, as an approximation to domestic purchasing power.

Proposition 2: Income polarization

With decile measurements of inequality (richest over poorest decile) rather than the Gini or other measure of inequality over the worldwide distribution of income, PPP-income distribution has become more unequal over the past three decades. World income polarization has widened. The broad result is hardly surprising: the top 10 per cent is comprised almost entirely of people living in the core countries of North America, Western Europe, and Japan, where incomes have grown over the past twenty to thirty years, while a large chunk of the bottom 10 per cent is comprised of African countries where incomes have stagnated or fallen. According to one study, the trend of richest to poorest decile goes like this: 1970–92, 1980–109, 1990–104, 1999–104 (Dikhanov and Ward 2003). Another study finds a sharp jump in the ratio between 1988 and 1993 of the order of 25 per cent (Milanovic 2002a). The polarizing trend would be more dramatic if we took the top 1 per cent's income over the bottom 10 per cent's.

Proposition 3: Between-country inequality, countries weighted equally

With per capita GDPs, equal country weights (China = Uganda), and a coefficient like the Gini covering the whole distribution, between-country world income inequality has increased since at least 1980.

Of course, we would not weight countries equally if we were interested simply in relative well-being. But we would weight them equally—treat each country as a unit of observation, analogous to a laboratory test observation—if we were interested in growth theory and the growth impacts of public policies, resource endowments, and the like. We might, for example, arrange (unweighted) countries by the openness of their trade regime and see whether the more open countries have better economic performance.

The same broad inequality-widening trend is obtained using a somewhat different measure of inequality—the dispersion of per capita GDPs across the world's (equally weighted) countries. Dispersion increased over the long period, 1950 to 1998, and especially fast over the 1990s. Moreover, the dispersion of per capita GDP growth rates has also risen over time, suggesting wider variation in performance among countries at each income level. A study by the Economic Commission for Latin America using these dispersion measures concludes that there is 'no doubt as to the existence of a definite trend towards distributive inequality worldwide, both across and within countries' (ECLA 2002: 85). (The dispersion of per capita GDP/PPP is measured as the average logarithmic deviation, the dispersion of growth rates as the standard deviation.)

Proposition 4: Between-country inequality, countries weighted by population

With the same measures as Proposition 3 but countries weighted by population, inequality has been constant or falling since around 1980.

This is the result that Martin Wolf, *The Economist*, and many others celebrate. What they do not emphasize is that the result comes from fast average growth in China. Exclude China and even this measure of inequality shows widening inequality since 1980. We can conclude that even using the one combination of measures most favourable to the liberal case, falling between-country income inequality is a function of China; *it is not generalized.*

In any case this measure—the average income of each country weighted by population—is interesting only as an approximation to what we are really interested in, which is income distribution among all the world's people or households regardless of which country they reside in. We would not be interested in measuring income inequality within the United States by calculating the average income for each state weighted by population if we had data for all US households.

Proposition 5: Between- and within-country inequality

Several serious studies, using different samples and time periods and different measures of inequality, all measuring both between- and within-country distributions, find that world income inequality has increased over a period within the past two to three decades.

Studies which attempt to measure income distribution among all the world's people show widely varying results, depending on things like the precise measure of inequality, the sample of countries, the time period, and the sources of income data. But several studies, which use various measures and methodologies, point to widening inequality (Dowrick and Akmal 2002; Milanovic 2002*a*; Dikhanov and Ward 2003).

Proposition 6: Manufacturing pay dispersion

Pay inequality within countries was stable or declining from the early 1960s to around 1980–2, then sharply increased from 1980–2 to the present. 1980–2 is a turning point towards greater inequality in manufacturing pay worldwide.

More doubts are cast on the falling inequality hypothesis by trends in manufacturing pay inequality within countries, that come out of research by James K. Galbraith and associates (University of Texas Inequality Project, **http://utip.gov.utexas.edu**; also Galbraith 2002). Pay data has the great advantage over income data that pay is a much less ambiguous variable, it has been collected systematically by the United Nations Industrial Development Organization (UNIDO) since the early 1960s, and gives many more observation points for each country than any data set on incomes. The disadvantage of pay data, of course, is that it treats only a small part of the economy of many developing countries, and provides only a proxy for incomes and expenditure. It is of limited use if our interest is only in relative well-being (though of more use if our interest is in the effects of trade, manufacturing innovation, etc.). But not as limited as may seem at first sight; because what is happening to pay rates in formal-sector manufacturing reflects larger trends, including income differences between countries and income differences within countries (since the pay of unskilled, entry-port jobs in manufacturing is closely related to the opportunity cost of time in the 'informal' or agricultural sectors).

Case studies

China and India

With 38 per cent of world population China and India shape world trends in poverty and inequality. They have grown very fast over the past decade (India) or two (China), if the figures are taken at face value. China's average purchasing power parity income rose from 0.3 of the world average in 1990 to 0.45 in 1998, or 15 percentage points in only eight years.

We can be sure that world poverty and inequality are less than they would be had China and India grown more slowly. About any stronger conclusion we have to be cautious. First, recall that China and India's purchasing power parity numbers are even more unreliable than those for the average developing country, because of their non-participation in the international price comparisons on which the PPP calculations rest. Second, China's growth is probably substantially overstated. Many analysts have recently been revising China's growth statistics downwards. Whereas government figures show annual real GDP growth of 7 to 8 per cent in 1998 and 1999 one authority on Chinese statistics estimates that the economy may not have grown at all. He puts the real figure at between −2 and +2 per cent (J. Kynge, *Financial Times*, 27 February 2002; Rawski 2002). As another example from Rawski's analysis, Chinese government figures show total real GDP growth of 25 per cent between 1997 and 2000, whereas energy consumption figures show a drop of 13 per cent (not all of which is likely to be due to replacement of inefficient coal-fired furnaces). Rawski estimates the growth rate since 2000 has been about half the official rate (see also A. Waldron, *Financial Times*, 4 July 2002).

Over the 1990s, China's annual growth rate is more likely to have been around 6 to 7 per cent than the 8 to 10 per cent that the official statistics show. This one change (assuming constant internal distribution) lowers the probability that world interpersonal distribution has become more equal.

We have to be cautious about going from China's fast growth to falls in world income inequality not only because China's growth rates and income level are probably overstated but also because the rise in inequality within China and India partly offsets the reduction in world income inequality that comes from relatively fast growth—though careful calculations of the relative strength of the two contrary effects have not yet been made. Evidence for rising inequality in India over the past two decades is set out in Jha (2000). Deaton (2002) agrees that inequality in India has been increasing 'in recent years', and that consumption by the poor did not rise as fast as average consumption. China's surging inequality is now greater than before the communists won the civil war in 1949, and inequality between regions is probably higher than in any other sizeable country. The ratio of the average income of the richest to poorest province (Guangdong to Guizhou) rose from around 3.2 in 1991 (current yuan) to 4.8 in 1993, and remained at 4.8 in 1998–2001. The corresponding figure for India in the late 1990s was 4.2, the United States, 1.9.

The United States and other Anglo political economies

Canada excepted, all the countries of English settlement, led by the United States, have experienced big increases in income inequality over the past twenty to thirty years. In the United States, the top 1 per cent of families enjoyed a growth of after-tax income of almost 160 per cent between 1979 and 1997, while families in the middle of the distribution had a 10 per cent increase (P. Krugman, *New York Times*, 20 October 2002). Within the top 1 per cent most of the gains have been concentrated in the top 0.1 per cent. This is not a matter of reward to education. Inequality has expanded hugely among the college educated. Whatever the causes, the fact is that the United States is now back to the same level of inequality of income as in the decades before 1929, the era of the 'robber barons' and the Great Gatsby.

Country mobility

How much do countries move in the income hierarchy? One study uses 'real' GNP per capita data (GNP deflated in local currency to a common base year, then converted to dollars at the exchange rate for that base year) from 1960 to 1999, and finds a robustly tri-modal distribution of world population against the log of GNP per capita (Babones 2002). The three income zones might be taken as empirical correlates of the conceptual zones of core, semi-periphery, and periphery. Of the 100 countries in the sample, seventy-two remained in the same income zone over the whole period, sampled at five-yearly intervals (for example, Australia remained in zone 1, Brazil in zone 2, Bolivia in zone 3). The remaining twenty-eight countries moved at least once from one zone to another (for example, Argentina from 1 to 2). No country moved more than one zone. (South Korea, Hong Kong, and Singapore were in the middle, not low zone in 1960.) There are about as many cases of upwards movement as downwards. Compared to the rate of potential mobility (each country moving one zone at each measurement date) the rate of actual mobility was 3.1 per cent.

The absolute income gap

Our measures of inequality refer to relative incomes, not absolute incomes. Inequality between developing countries as a group and developed countries as a group remains constant if the ratio of developing country income to developed country income remains at 5 per cent. But this of course implies a big rise in the absolute size of the gap. The absolute gap between a country with average income of $1,000 growing at 6 per cent and a country with average income $30,000 growing at 1 per cent continues to widen until after the fortieth year!

China and India are reducing the absolute gap with the faltering middle-income states like Mexico, Brazil, Russia, and Argentina, but not with the countries of North America, Western Europe, and Japan. Dikhanov and Ward's figures show that, overall, the absolute gap between the average income of the top decile of world population and the bottom decile increased from $PPP 18,690 in 1970 to $PPP 28,902 in 1999 (Dikhanov and Ward 2003). We can be sure that absolute gaps between people and countries are increasing fast and will continue to increase for several generations.

Conclusions about inequality trends

The only set of measurements where the evidence clearly supports the neo-liberal argument of falling inequality is the one using population-weighted countries' per capita PPP-adjusted incomes, plus a measure of average inequality, and taking China's income statistics at face value. On the other hand, polarization (using decile ratios) has increased. And several studies that measure inequality over the whole distribution and use either household survey data or measures of combined inequality between countries and within countries (as distinct from only inequality between countries' average income) show widening inequality since around 1980. The conclusion is that world inequality, measured in plausible ways, is probably rising, despite China's fast growth. The conclusion is reinforced by evidence from the dispersion in pay rates within worldwide manufacturing, which has become steadily wider since the early 1980s having remained roughly constant from 1960 to the early 1980s.

Key points

- The impact that globalization has had on inequality depends on the measure used.
- A fall in inequality between countries is due entirely to rapid economic growth in China.
- Inequality within China and India has increased substantially in recent years.
- Large increases in inequality have occurred in all English-speaking industrialized economies with the exception of Canada.

Globalization

Let us consider the other end of the argument—that the allegedly positive trends in poverty and inequality have been driven by rising integration of poorer countries into the world economy, as seen in rising trade/GDP, foreign direct investment/GDP, and the like. Clearly, the proposition is not well supported at the world level if we agree that globalization has been rising while poverty and income inequality have not been falling. Indeed, it is striking that the pronounced convergence of economic policy towards 'openness' worldwide over the past twenty years has gone with divergence of economic performance. But it might still be possible to argue that globalization explains differences between countries: that more open economies and/or ones that open faster have a better record than less open ones and/or ones than open more slowly.

This is what World Bank studies claim. One of the best known, *Globalization, Growth and Poverty* (World Bank 2002*b*), distinguishes 'newly globalizing' countries, also called 'more globalized' countries, from 'non-globalizing' countries or 'less globalized' countries.

It measures globalizing by *changes* in the ratio of trade to GDP between 1977 and 1997. Ranking developing countries by the amount of change, it calls the top third the globalizing or more globalized countries, the remaining two-thirds, the non-globalizing or less globalized countries. It finds that the former have had faster economic growth, no increase in inequality, and faster reduction of poverty than the latter. 'Thus globalization clearly can be a force for poverty reduction', it concludes.

Not so fast. First, using 'change in the trade/GDP ratio' as the measure of globalization skews the results (Rodrik 1999, 2001). The globalizers include China and India, as well as countries like Nepal, Cote d'Ivoire, Rwanda, Haiti, and Argentina. It is quite possible that 'more globalized' countries are *less* open than many 'less globalized' countries, both in terms of trade/GDP and in terms of the magnitude of tariffs and non-tariff barriers. Because, for instance, a country with high trade/GDP and very free trade policy would still be categorized as 'non-globalized' if its *increase* in trade/GDP over 1977–97 was small enough to put it in the bottom two-thirds of the sample. It turns out that many of the globalizing countries initially had very *low* trade/GDP in 1977 and still had relatively low trade/GDP at the *end* of the period in 1997 (reflecting more than just the fact that larger economies tend to have lower ratios of trade/GDP). To call relatively closed economies 'globalizers' and to call countries with much higher ratios of trade/GDP and much freer trade regimes 'non-globalizers' is an audacious use of language.

But it yields the right result. Excluding countries with high but not rising levels of trade to GDP from the category of more globalized eliminates many poor countries dependent on a few natural resource commodity exports, which have had poor economic performance. The structure of their economy and the low skill endowment of the population make them very dependent on trade. If they were included as globalized their poor economic performance would question the proposition that the more globalized countries do better. On the other hand, including China and India as 'globalizers' over the 1977–97 period—despite relatively low trade/GDP and relatively protective trade regimes—guarantees that the globalizers, weighted by population, show better performance than the non-globalizers.

The second big problem is causality. The argument assumes that fast trade growth is the major cause of good economic performance. It does not examine the reverse causation, that fast economic growth leads to fast trade growth. Nor does it consider that other variables correlated with trade growth may be more important causes of economic performance: quality of government, for example. One re-examination of the Bank's study using indicators such as press freedom, democratic accountability, corruption, and civil rights finds that the globalizer countries do indeed have higher quality of government indicators than the non-globalizer countries, on average (Besley 2002).

Third, the argument fudges almost to vanishing point the distinction between trade quantities and trade policy, and implies, quite wrongly, that rising trade quantities—and the developmental benefits thereof—are the consequence of trade liberalization.

Certainly, many countries—including China and India—have benefited from their more intensive engagement in international trade and investment over the past one or two decades. But this is not to say that their improved performance is largely due to their more intensive external integration. They began to open their own markets *after* building up industrial capacity and fast growth behind high barriers. And throughout their period of so-called 'openness' they have maintained protection and other market restrictions that would earn them a bad report card from the World Bank and IMF were they not growing so quickly. China began its fast growth with a high degree of equality of assets and income, brought about in distinctly 'non-globalized' conditions and unlikely to have been achieved in an open economy and democratic polity (Rodrik 1999).

Their experience—and that of Japan, South Korea, and Taiwan earlier—shows that countries do not have to adopt liberal trade policies in order to reap large benefits from trade (Wade 2003a). They all experienced relatively fast growth behind protective barriers; a significant part of their growth came from replacing imports of consumption goods with domestic production; and more and more of their rapidly expanding imports consisted of capital goods and intermediate goods. As they became richer they tended to liberalize their trade—providing the basis for the misunderstanding that trade liberalization drove their growth. For all the Bank study's qualifications (such as 'We label the top third "more globalized" without in any sense implying that they adopted pro-trade policies. The rise in trade may have been due to other policies or even to pure chance'), it concludes that trade liberalization has been the driving force of the increase in developing countries' trade. 'The result of this trade liberalization in the developing world has been a large increase in both imports and exports,' it says. On this shaky basis the Bank rests its case that developing countries must push hard towards near-free trade as a core ingredient of their development strategy, the better to enhance competition and create efficient, rent-free markets. Even when the Bank or other development agencies articulate the softer principle—trade liberalization is the necessary direction of change but countries may do it at different speeds—all the attention remains focused on the liberalization part, none on how to make protective regimes more effective (other than just by liberalizing them).

In short, the Bank's argument about the benign effects of globalization on growth, poverty, and income distribution does not survive scrutiny at either end of the causal chain. A recent cross-country study of the relationship between openness and income distribution strikes another blow. Milanovic (2002a) finds that among the subset of countries with low and middle levels of average income (below roughly $5,000 per capita in PPP terms, that of Chile and the Czech Republic), higher levels of trade openness are associated with *more* inequality, while among higher-income countries more openness goes with less inequality.

Key points

- Arguments that reductions in poverty and inequality are associated with integration of poorer economies into the global economy rely on a measure (changes in the ratio of trade to GDP) that skews the results and makes unwarranted assumptions about the direction of the causality in the relationship between trade and growth.

What accounts for the failure of the liberal argument?

If the number of people in absolute poverty is probably not falling and probably higher than the World Bank says, and if income inequality by several plausible measures is not falling and probably rising, why? Is it because developing countries have failed to industrialize, which is what the development economics and modernization theory of the 1950s to the 1970s would point to?

No. If we take manufacturing's share of GDP or of employment we find a remarkable convergence—manufacturing now constitutes a *larger* share of both production and employment in developing countries than in developed countries (Arrighi, Silver, and Brewer 2003). But each additional increment of manufacturing in developing countries is yielding less income over time. This is not what one would expect if manufacturing in developing countries was embedded in a dynamic capitalism. The failure of the industrialization prediction may help to explain why

industrialization has been relegated to the margins of today's development agenda. The World Bank scarcely refers to it. In the Bank's eyes, development is about poverty alleviation, market access, good governance, and environmental protection, not about capitalist industrialization.

What other factors might explain the shift in the distribution of world population towards the extremes of the world income distribution and the shift in income distribution towards the top end? The subject warrants an extended treatment; here I make only a few points about the way that well-functioning capitalist markets generate 'uneven' development (see further Wade 2004).

Spatial clustering of high value-added activities
In the simple version of neo-liberal theory, capital and technology move from high-income, high-cost zones to low-income, low-cost zones, and low-cost

labour moves in the opposite direction. The result is convergence of factor incomes, eventually. If this were the dominant trend in today's world—as dominant as in economic models—we should see falling poverty and inequality.

To understand the 'fact' of non-convergence—or failure of catch-up—we have to understand a general property of modern economic growth. Some kinds of economic activities and production methods have more positive effects on growth and productivity than others (Box 11.3). They are activities rich in increasing returns (to scale, to agglomeration), in contrast to activities with decreasing returns. To oversimplify, increasing return activities are those characterized by falling marginal costs as output rises, diminishing returns, by rising marginal costs with output; they tend to have large unpriced 'spillover' benefits that can be captured by other firms in the locality (which therefore enjoy lower costs than otherwise); and they tend to yield higher value-added than diminishing return activities. This is the non-neoclassical realm of analysts such as Marshall, Young, Schumpeter, Kaldor, Myrdal, Hirschman, Streeten, Seers, Akyuz, Arthur, Krugman, and Jane Jacobs; and also Marx, whose defining features of capitalism included 'the centralization of capital' and 'the entanglement of all peoples in the net of the world-market'.

Countries and regions with higher proportions of increasing return activities enjoy higher levels of real incomes, in a virtuous circle; countries and regions with higher proportions of diminishing return activities have lower incomes, in a vicious circle. The central national-level development problem is to shift the resources of a national economy, at the margin, away from diminishing return activities and towards increasing return activities; away from the activities that Malthus wrote about and towards those that Schumpeter wrote about. As a first approximation, this means to shift resources out of agriculture and primary commodities and into manufacturing and related services (or into higher-level processing of primary commodities).

To understand the paradox of substantial catch-up of developing countries as a group to developed country levels of manufacturing/GDP without a corresponding catch-up of income, one has to start with the manufacturing value chain. The value chain is the sequence of operations that go to make final products, including R&D, design, procurement, manufacturing, assembly, distribution, advertising, sales. Thanks in part to the communications advances associated with globalization, manufacturing value chains have become spatially disarticulated, and value-added has 'migrated' to the two ends of the value chain—to R&D, design, distribution, and advertising. Activities within the value chain that are more subject to diminishing returns have been shifting to low wage zones while those more subject to increasing returns tend to stay at home.

In other words, the increasing returns/high value-added activities in manufacturing and in services continue to cluster in the high-cost, high-wage zone of the world economy, even when markets are working well (and not as a result of 'market imperfections'). German skilled workers cost more than fifteen times to employ as Chinese skilled workers; yet Germany remains a powerful centre of manufacturing. Japanese skilled workers cost even more; yet Japan too remains a powerful centre of manufacturing, despite being only 700 kilometres from Shanghai across the East China Sea.

Why then are locations 'sticky' for the increasing return/high value-added activities? First, costs per unit of output may not be lower in the lower-wage zone, because lower wages may be more than offset by lower productivity. In any case, the cost of employing people has fallen to a small proportion of total costs in automated assembly operations, often 10 per cent or less. As the technology content of many engineering products—such as vehicle parts and aircraft—becomes increasingly sophisticated, this raises the premium on the company keeping highly skilled workers to develop and manufacture these products; and one way to keep them is to pay them highly. The fact that wages are a small part of total costs means that higher wage payments do not have much effect on the net incentive to move to the low-wage zone of the world economy.

Second, the 'capability' of a firm relative to its rivals (the maximum quality level it can achieve, and its cost of production) depends not only on the sum of the skills of its workforce, but also on the *collective* or firm-level knowledge and social organization of its employees. In the case of increasing return/higher value-added activities, much of this knowledge and social organization is *tacit*, transferred mainly through face-to-face relationships—not transferred easily between people in different places in the form of machinery or (technical and organizational) blueprints. The value of tacit knowledge typically increases as a share of total value even as the ratio of tacit to codified knowledge falls with computerization. If a firm or plant were to move its increasing return activities to a lower-wage zone and some of its employees were not mobile, the costs to the firm's capacity, including the loss of tacit knowledge, may outweigh the advantages of relocation.

Third, tacit knowledge transfer is bigger the shorter the physical and cultural distance; and some other forms of transactions costs fall in the same way. This is a powerful driver of spatial clustering in increasing return activities. Firms in a network of spatially concentrated input–output linkages can derive (unpriced) spillover benefits from the presence of the other firms and supporting infrastructure. They all get access to nests of producers' goods and services, ranges of skills, people practised at adapting and innovating, and tacit knowledge—in short, to the external economies of human capital that are a major source of increasing returns to location in the high-wage zone. These spillover benefits compound the tendency for any one firm not to move to a low-wage zone, or to transplant only its *low* value-added assembly activities by outsourcing or establishing subsidiaries while holding at home the core activities that depend on varied inputs, tacit knowledge, social contacts, and closeness to consumers.

Further, as skill shortages develop in the core and the supply of skilled people rises in the low-wage zone, firms nowadays can remain rooted in the core because skilled people are increasingly crossing borders to find them.

Firm immobility is reinforced by the fact that for many products and services, quality and value-added go up not continuously but in steps (ball-bearings below a quality threshold are useless). Getting to higher steps may require big investments, critical masses, targeted assistance from public entities, long-term supply contracts with multinational corporations seeking local suppliers. 'Normal' market processes—now fortified by WTO agreements that make many forms of industrial policy illegal (Wade 2003*b*)—can therefore prevent firms and countries in the low-wage zone from transforming themselves into attractive sites for higher-quality work.

The empirical significance of these effects is suggested by the fact that about two-thirds of manufacturing output in the OECD is sold by one firm to another firm within the OECD. In addition, parent companies based in the OECD, especially in some of the biggest manufacturing sectors (including electronics and vehicles), have formed increasingly concentrated vertical production networks in which they put a rising proportion of routine manufacturing operations in lower-tier suppliers in the low-wage zone, often locally owned companies, while keeping control of the high value-added activities of proprietary technology, branding, and marketing. They then use their market power and intense competition among the lower-tier suppliers to extract more value-added from them. The lower-tier suppliers are first to suffer in a recession.

Box 11.3 **Spillovers**

Spillovers occur when knowledge, for example, of technology, is accessible by individuals and companies other than those who have invested in its original production. For instance, individuals who leave a company to establish their own business often take with them knowledge that their previous employer had paid to create. Some aspects of knowledge, therefore, frequently have the character of a public good.

Such spillovers are often concentrated geographically (ease of communication facilitates transfer of knowledge,

especially of the tacit variety), and are themselves a significant factor in the geographical concentration of particular industrial sectors, for example, Silicon Valley.

The significance of spillovers of knowledge is emphasized by the literatures on 'new' economic growth (Romer 1986; Grossman and Helpman 1991), and on the significance of technological innovation in economic growth (Dosi, Pavitt, and Soete 1990).

This is not the end of the sticky location story. At the next round, the greater wealth and variety of economic activities in the high-wage zone—not to mention institutions that manage conflict and encourage risk taking, such as legally guaranteed civil rights, social insurance, a legal system that supports limited liability, and socially more homogeneous populations—mean that the high-wage zone can more readily absorb the Schumpeterian shocks from innovation and bankruptcies, as activity shifts from products and processes with more intense competition to those with less competition closer to the innovation end. There is less resistance to the 'creative destruction' of market processes, despite the fact that organizing people to resist tends to be easier than in the low-wage zone. Enron may go bankrupt but there are plenty more companies to take on its business and employ its employees.

Diminishing returns in the manufacturing rungs of the value chain

Over the 1980s and 1990s many firms in the North moved the more labour-intensive parts of their value chains to low-wage locations, and many analysts expected that the plants and firms in developing countries which undertook this work would be able to rise up the chain, undertaking progressively higher value-added work. (In apparel, this would mean moving from stitching of imported cut pieces, to cutting and stitching, to 'full package' production including designs.) They expected too that this upwards mobility would be developmentally nutritious; and that the trade flows associated with the expansion of North–South production networks would be as good for development as the arms-length trade assumed in the standard economic models.

The evidence suggests that plants and firms in the low-wage zone have indeed moved up the chain—but the resulting increase in competition between low-wage producers in the higher stages of manufacturing has caused a fall in returns at the higher stages (Schrank 2002). One study of 'a decade's worth of hard data' found 'an almost uniform wage meltdown in the apparel industry in the Third World' (A. Tonelson, *Washington Post*, 2 June 2002). The trends in apparel also apply in other assembly-intensive industries, including consumer electronics.

China is often held up as the prime example of an economy that has benefited massively from the expansion of production tied to Northern value chains. But in fact exports from foreign-funded enterprises have yielded much less value-added for the national economy than the roughly equal value of exports from national firms, because the import content of the foreign-funded enterprises remains much higher (UNCTAD 2002b: chapter 5).

Here is a micro-economic explanation of the macro trend to worldwide convergence of manufacturing but non-convergence of incomes. Each increment of manufacturing in developing countries is yielding less value-added in the South and more in the North.

In short, the several mechanisms described here—particularly the combination of spatial clustering of high value-added activities in the prosperous zone and the fall in returns to the more advanced stages of manufacturing as more Southern producers enter them—help to explain a stably divided world in which high wages remain high in one zone while low wages elsewhere remain low even as the industrialization gap has closed. The important point is that well-functioning free markets in a highly economically globalized world produce, 'spontaneously', an equilibrium division of activities between the high-wage zone and the low-wage zone that is hardly desirable for the low-wage zone.

To spell out the causality further, one might hypothesize that rising levels of (especially manufacturing) trade to GDP raise the income share of the rich in low-income developing countries, who have education and control over critical trade-related services, while shrinking the share of the bulk of the population with minimal or no education. The consumption preferences of the rich lock the low-income countries into dependence on sophisticated imports from the high-income countries, restricting the replacement of imports by national production that is a key to expanding prosperity rooted in diversifying production from the national economy rather than in narrow export specialization for foreign markets.

Oligopolistic industrial organization in the high-income zone reinforces the inequalities by supporting mark-up pricing, which generates falling terms of trade for the low-wage zone.

Falling terms of trade facing developing countries are a major proximate cause of the persistence of the North–South divide. The prices of exports from developing countries, not only of primary commodities but also of manufacturing goods, have fallen sharply over the past two decades in relation to the prices of exports from developed countries, depressing the share of world income going to the low-income zone. The harnessing of China's vast reservoirs of labour has particularly depressed the terms of trade for developing country manufactures. The sharp fall in the developing countries' manufacturing terms of trade soon after 1984 is largely due to China's dramatic entry into manufacturing exports. At a stretch one could say that China's biggest export is deflation.

East Asia

Even about East Asia's ability to continue to defy economic gravity we should not get too optimistic. Only a miniscule portion of world R&D work is done in (non-Japan) East Asia. Virtually all of it continues to be done in the triad countries of North America, Western Europe, and Japan. Even Singapore, which looks to be an Asian centre of R&D, does not do 'real' R&D; its R&D labs mostly concentrate on adapting products developed in North America and Europe for the regional market and listening in on what competitors are doing (Amsden, Tschang, and Goto 2001). The much heralded 'globalization of R&D' is really about movement within the high-income zone.

China still relies heavily on foreign investment and imported components for its higher-tech manufactured output; and incoming foreign investment is still mainly seeking low-cost labour, tax breaks, and implied promises of protection, as distinct from rapidly rising skills. Even its IT engineering complex around Shanghai depends heavily on Taiwanese and other foreign know-how. Japanese alarm bells have been ringing at graphs showing Japan's personal computer exports to the United States falling as

China's rise; but the figures conceal the fact that the computers are assembled in China using high value-added technology from Japan and elsewhere. Some of the technology is spilling into the heads of the millions of Chinese employees, almost certainly more than is occurring in other developing countries (China has 200 'technicians' per million people, using the UNESCO definition, compared to 108 in India, 30 in Thailand, 318 in South Korea, 301 in Singapore; UNCTAD 2002*b*: 167). Nevertheless, if China is prevented by WTO rules from deploying the sorts of industrial policies used earlier in the capitalist economies of East Asia—so as to generate productive 'rent seeking' in activities important for the economy's future growth—it may remain for a prolonged period as an assembly platform for low value-added exports.

These qualifications, added to doubts about the accuracy of China's growth statistics, should caution us about a scenario of declining world income inequality based on China's continued fast growth and transformation.

In short, the benign effects of free markets in spreading benefits around the world, as celebrated in the liberal argument, are probably offset by other tendencies, yielding divergence between a high value-added, high-wage, highly versatile zone and a low value-added, low-wage, narrowly specialized zone—even as ratios of manufacturing to GDP, total trade/GDP, and manufacturing exports/total exports rise in the latter, and even as income inequality in the former rises towards the latter's.

Key points

- The failure of globalization to reduce levels of poverty and inequality is not due to a lack of industrialization in developing economies. Rather it is due to:

  - The clustering of higher value-added activities in the high-wage zone of the world economy;

  - Increasing competition and decreasing returns in manufacturing in less developed economies.

Conclusions

Should we worry about rising inequality?

The neo-liberal argument says that inequality provides incentives for effort and risk-taking, and thereby raises efficiency. We should not worry provided that it does not somehow make the poor worse off than otherwise.

The counter-argument is that this productive incentive effect applies only at moderate levels of inequality. At higher levels, such as in the United States over the past twenty years, inequality erodes social norms of citizenship and creates incentives to divert effort into unproductive activities calculated to redistribute income into the hands of top managers and shareholders.

Higher-income inequality within nations goes with: (1) higher poverty (using World Bank data and the number of people below the Bank's international poverty line; Besley and Burgess 2002); (2) slower economic growth; (3) higher unemployment; and (4) higher violent crime (Lee and Bankston 1999; Hsieh and Pugh 1993; Fajnzylber, Lederman, and Loayza 1998). Higher violence is only the tip of a distribution of social relationships skewed towards the aggressive end of the spectrum, with low average levels of trust and social capital. In short, inequality at the national level should certainly be a target of public policy.

The liberal argument is even less concerned about widening inequality between countries than it is about inequality within countries, because we cannot do anything directly to lessen international inequality. But on the face of it, the more globalized the world becomes, the more that the reasons why we should be concerned about within-country inequalities also apply between countries. If globalization actually increases inequality within and between countries, as is consistent with a lot of evidence, increases in world inequality above moderate levels may cut world aggregate demand and thereby world economic growth, producing a vicious circle of rising world inequality and lower world growth.

And rising inequality between countries impacts directly on national political economy in the poorer states, as rich people who earlier compared themselves to others in their neighbourhood or nation now compare themselves to others in the United States or Western Europe, and feel deprived and perhaps angry.

Inequality above moderate levels may, for example, predispose the elites to become more corrupt as they compare themselves to elites in rich countries and squeeze their own populations in order to sustain a comparable living standard, enfeebling whatever norms of citizenship have emerged. It may encourage the educated people of poor countries to migrate to the rich countries, and encourage unskilled people to seek illegal entry. It may generate conflict between states, and—because the market exchange-rate income gap is so big—make it cheap for rich states to intervene to support one side or the other in civil strife. Rising inequality in market exchange-rate terms—helped by a high US dollar, a low (long-run) oil price, and the new intellectual property agreement of the WTO—allows the United States to finance the military sinews of its emerging empire more cheaply (Wade 2003c). Moreover, these effects may be presumed to operate in response to widening absolute income gaps even if relative income gaps are narrowing (and therefore inequality falling by our normal measures).

The effects of inequality within and between countries depend on prevailing norms. Where power hierarchy and income inequality are thought to be the natural condition of man the negative effects can be expected to be lighter than where prevailing norms sanction equality and where the sense of relative deprivation is likely to be stronger. The significance for the future is that norms of equality and democracy are being energetically promoted by the prosperous democracies in the rest of the world, at the same time as the lived experience in much of the rest of the world belongs to another planet.

The political economy of statistics

Concerns about global warming gave rise to a coordinated worldwide project to get better climatological data; and the same response is needed to get better data on poverty and inequality. The World Bank is one of the key actors. It has moved from major to minor source of foreign finance for most developing countries outside Africa. But it remains an important world organization because it wields a disproportionate influence in setting the development agenda, in offering an imprimatur of 'sound finance' that crowds in other resources, and in providing finance—allocated by partly non-commercial criteria—at times when other finance is not available. Its statistics and development research are crucial to its legitimacy (Kapur 2002). Other regional development banks and aid agencies have largely given up on statistics and research, ceding the ground to the World Bank. Alternative views come only from a few 'urban guerrillas' in pockets of academia and the UN system (for a good example of a heterodox book from a corner of the UN system, see UNDP 2003*b*: the WTO lobbied to prevent its publication).

Think of two models of a statistical organization that is part of a larger organization working in politically sensitive areas. The 'exogenous' model says that the statistics are produced by professionals exercising their best judgement in the face of difficulties that have no optimal solutions, who are managerially insulated from the overall tactical goals of the organization. The 'endogenous' model says that the statistics are produced by staff who act as agents of the senior managers (the principals), the senior managers expect them to help advance the tactical goals of the organization just like other staff, and the statistics staff therefore have to massage the data beyond the limits of professional integrity (or else quit).

Certainly the simple endogenous model does not fit the Bank; but nor does the other. The Bank is committed to an Official View of how countries should seek poverty reduction, rooted in market opening, privatization, deregulation, with some democratic governance, civil society, and environmental protection thrown in; it is exposed to arm twisting by the G7 member states and international non-governmental organizations; it must secure their support and defend itself against criticism. It seeks to advance its broad market-opening agenda not through coercion but mainly by establishing a sense that the agenda is right and fitting. Without this it would lose the support of the G7 states, Wall Street, and fractions of developing country elites. The units of the Bank that produce the statistics are partly insulated from the resulting pressures, especially by their membership in 'epistemic communities' of professionals inside and outside the Bank; but not wholly insulated. To say otherwise is to deny that the Bank is subject to the Chinese proverb, 'Officials make the figures, and the figures make the officials'; or to Goodhart's Law, which states that an indicator's measurement will be distorted if it is used as a target. Charles Goodhart was thinking of monetary policy, but the point also applies to variables used to make overall evaluations of the performance of multilateral economic organizations.

But little is known about the balance in the Bank between autonomy and compliance, or the mechanisms of compliance, or the latitude of the statisticians to adjust the country numbers provided by colleagues elsewhere in the organization which they believe to have been fiddled.

Some of the Bank's statistics are also provided by independent sources, which provide a check. Others, including the poverty numbers, are produced only by the Bank, and these are more subject to Goodhart's Law. The Bank should appoint an independent auditor to verify its main development statistics or cede the work to an independent agency, perhaps under UN auspices (but if done by, say, UNCTAD, the opposite bias might be introduced). And it would help if the Bank's figures on poverty and inequality made clearer than they do the possible biases and the likely margins of error.

If the trends in poverty and inequality really are in the wrong direction we need to know more about why, at the level of the whole, the increasing returns of the Matthew effect— 'To him who hath shall be given'—continues to dominate decreasing returns. And we need to know more about whether the structure of the world economy is open enough to permit the upward mobility of large demographic masses, or whether there is something in the functioning of world capitalism in the current framework that precludes a shrinking of the gap between bottom and top and pushes some demographic masses down the income scale as others rise. The answer should inform discussion of international public policies.

QUESTIONS

1   What arguments do liberal writers use to make the case that globalization reduces poverty and inequality?

2   What evidence is there to support the liberal position on the relationship between globalization and poverty/inequality?

3   What are the advantages of using purchasing power parity measures for comparing incomes across countries?

4   What are the main difficulties in measuring the number of people living in poverty?

5   What are the advantages and disadvantages of the various ways of examining the extent of inequality within and between countries?

6   How much change has there been in the global distribution of income in the last 40 years?

7   What are the principal reasons why the liberal argument on the relationship between globalization and poverty/inequality might be incorrect?

8   Why might there be problems with the statistics that the World Bank and other international agencies use on poverty and inequality?

9   Why should one be concerned about rising levels of inequality in the global economy?

FURTHER READING

Deaton, A. (2001), 'Counting the World's Poor: Problems and Possible Solutions', *World Bank Research Observer*, 16/2: 125–47. A non-technical account of some of the issues involved in estimating the number of people living in extreme poverty.

Galbraith, J. K. (2002), 'A Perfect Crime: Inequality in the Age of Globalization', *Daedalus*, 131/1: 11–25. A non-technical discussion of inequality trends, including a new source of data.

Pritchett, L. (1997), 'Divergence Big Time', *Journal of Economic Perspectives*, 11/3: 3–18. A powerful statement of the argument that inequality has been rising.

Reddy, S. G., and Pogge, T. W. (2003), 'How *Not* to Count the Poor', **www.socialanalysis.org** 26 March, available at **www.columbia.edu/~sr793/count.pdf.** A detailed examination of the methodological examination of the World Bank's poverty statistics.

Rodrik, D. (1999), *The New Global Economy and Developing Countries: Making Openness Work* (Baltimore: Johns Hopkins University Press for the Overseas Development Council). A powerful argument for development strategy that is not mainly just a liberalization strategy.

Wolf, M. (2000), 'The Big Lie of Global Inequality', *Financial Times*, 8 Feb. A good summary of the case that global inequality is falling.

WEB LINKS

http://utip.gov.utexas.edu   University of Texas Inequality Project.

www.unido.org/   United Nations Industrial Development Organization.

www.columbia.edu/~sr793/   Monitoring Global Poverty.

www.worldbank.org/poverty/   World Bank PovertyNet.

www.bris.ac.uk/poverty/   Townsend Centre for International Poverty Research.

12 Globalization and development in the South

Caroline Thomas

READER'S GUIDE

After half a century of development initiatives, the countries and peoples of the South continue to experience unequal development. Opinion is divided as to precise contribution of domestic and/or external/structural factors to this situation. This is clear in assessments of the impact of globalization on the South. Despite—or some would argue because of—two decades of intense global economic integration, 2 billion people live in countries experiencing falling incomes and rising poverty. Frustration is widespread at the uneven distribution of the economic benefits of globalization between and within regions and states. The very poor economic outlook for much of the South is a serious cause for concern, as is the lack of voice for Southern governments and peoples in global development policy. In response, there have been some modifications in global development policy, especially the much publicized Poverty Reduction with Growth strategy, which emphasizes country ownership and growth with poverty reduction. Hope for further significant improvement is vested in the potential of the Monterrey Compact, which specifies the roles and responsibilities of rich and poor governments and other stakeholders in improving the situation in the South. Whether this will evolve from rhetoric into policy remains to be seen, and even if it does, questions remain as to its adequacy or appropriateness.

Introduction

The aim of this chapter is to explore the development impact of globalization on the South. Before we can begin, we must clarify terms. Each of our key terms of reference has been hotly debated.

The meaning of 'development' is heavily contested and the subject of an extensive debate in the literature (for example, Rahnema and Bawtree 1997). Here, we take development to mean more than simply economic growth, as it was understood in early post-war decades (Rostow 1960). We understand development as structural transformation: the economic growth of national economies, coupled with a material improvement in the lives of their citizens evidenced in poverty reduction and increased equity. In other words, national economic growth must be accompanied by human development—measured by the United Nations Development Programme (UNDP) as an aggregate of income, life expectancy, and literacy—for development to be occurring. The former without the latter does not equal development.

'Globalization' has been interpreted in many ways by scholars, policy analysts, politicians, and global citizens (Held and McGrew 2000). For our purposes, the definition offered by Hans Kohler (2002: 1), Managing Director of the International Monetary Fund (IMF), is accepted: 'the process through which an increasingly free flow of ideas, people, goods, services and capital leads to the integration of economies and societies'. Thus our concern is with the development impact of global economic integration, focusing in particular on the last twenty-five years when privatization, deregulation, and liberalization has proceeded rapidly.

By 'South' we mean the majority of the world's countries, which do not have the opportunity to play a significant role in global rule making and policy formulation, and/or where the overwhelming majority of the world's poor citizens reside. Many other terms have been used to refer to this grouping, but 'South' has been selected here because it leaves open the issue of membership and therefore is more dynamic than some of the alternatives. It sits more comfortably than some alternatives (for instance, Third World) with the political reality of the post-1989 world.

Over the last two decades, global economic integration has become synonymous with global development policy. In other words, privatization of public enterprises, deregulation, and the liberalization of trade, investment, and finance has been promoted as global development policy for the South. But to what extent is global economic integration supporting development in the South? On the basis of available evidence, what do we expect the future might hold in terms of development outcomes if we continue on our current path? What, if anything, needs changing to get a better result in development terms? And what are the prospects for the international community reaching agreement on such changes?

In order to address these questions, this chapter is divided into four sections. The first is concerned with the current development challenge, and the response of the international community. The second and third sections explore how we got here. A brief overview of development history from the Second World War to the end of the 1970s is followed by more detailed evaluative study of the period since the early 1980s when global economic integration has proceeded rapidly. The fourth section explores what might be done to achieve better development outcomes, and assesses whether the Monterrey Consensus really represents a compact for development. An important theme occurs repeatedly throughout fifty years of the North–South development debate, and remains unresolved: the extent to which international and/or domestic structures and policies pose a barrier to development, and what must be done.

Getting our terms straight

The literature on North–South relations and development uses a multiplicity of terms, such as Third World, South, or G77, to refer to the poorer countries, or specific subgroups, in the international system. Many of these terms are indicative rather than fixed, reflecting the difficulty of categorizing a very heterogeneous set of countries with diverse histories and changing trajectories. Some relate to ways in which countries define themselves; others, to how they have been classified by commentators and/or international agencies. Some of the most common of these terms are presented in Box 12.1. It would be useful to familiarize yourself with these straight away, as they will crop up frequently.

The development challenge in the South

Let's assess where we are. The development experience of the South over the last half-century has not been uniform across space or time. *Differentiation* has been the key defining word. While broadly speaking, we can identify the 1950s, 1960s, and 1970s as periods of growth for the South, the quality and location of that growth differed greatly, with some regions, countries, and social groups faring better than others at various times. The picture was mixed. What is special about the 1980s and 1990s, however—the period in post-war history when global economic integration has proceeded most rapidly—is that these mixed results have intensified, with deepening economic differentiation between regions, within regions, and within countries (see Wade, Chapter 11 in this volume). *Polarization is arguably more apt than differentiation* to describe the impact of globalization on the South over the last two decades. The message is clear: the potential for global economic integration to support development in the South cannot be assumed, and therefore must come under scrutiny.

The top priority in terms of the global development challenge is those countries where poverty is widespread, deeply entrenched, and even getting worse. Also important, however, are those countries which have made economic progress, such as China, India, Mexico, and Brazil, but where the gaps within the country are widening as certain regions or groups of the populace fail to enjoy the benefits of growth; indeed the improvement of some groups may even be at the direct expense of others.

A New Partnership for Development?

How is the development challenge to be tackled? This depends on how the causes of the problem are understood, and how responsibility for action is constructed within the international system. Hitherto, a culture of blame has permeated North–South relations, with a failure to acknowledge shared responsibilities. The North has laid the blame for lack of development on domestic factors in Southern countries, whilst failing to acknowledge that structural aspects of the global economic order such as changes in the terms of trade systematically discriminate against Southern countries (see Box 12.2). Southern countries have drawn attention to systematic factors and Northern policy choices and double standards which have undermined the South, whilst ignoring their own domestic policy failings, corruption, and so forth.

However, we may be witnessing a change: at least at a rhetorical level, we can identify an embryonic development compact based on *collective responsibility*. The development challenge has been articulated in terms of the United Nation's Millennium Development Goals (MDGs) (see Box 12.3). Governments of rich and poor states have accepted—at least in theory—their *collective responsibility* for human development in a world where the benefits of globalization are spread unevenly and where the gap between rhetoric and performance in development policy is stark.

Box 12.1 Definitions

Third World. A term (*tiers monde*) coined by the French demographer, Alfred Sauvy, used during the Cold War to distinguish the non-industrialized countries, including China, from the industrialized countries of Western Europe, North America, Japan, and Australasia (First World) and the planned economies of the USSR and Eastern Europe (Second World). Despite obvious negative connotations, the term 'Third World' came to refer to a self-defining group of mostly post-colonial states with relatively low per capita incomes. Despite obvious and growing diversity in economic achievement amongst this grouping, a common, unifying experience persists: lack of voice in global affairs and vulnerability to external forces beyond their control, such as commodity price fluctuations, transnational corporate policies, and IMF/ World Bank/WTO decisions.

NAM. The central defining characteristic of the Non-Aligned Movement is a commitment to political independence, and this reflects its inception during the era of anti-colonial struggle and the Cold War. Its origin is in the Asia-Africa Conference held in Bandung, Indonesia, in 1955, which brought together twenty-nine mostly former colonies under the leadership of Prime Ministers Nehru of India, Nasser of Egypt, and Soekarno of Indonesia. The aim was to discuss common problems and develop common positions on international affairs which reflected the interests and priorities of developing countries. At the first Conference of Non-Aligned Heads of States in Belgrade in 1961, twenty-five countries were represented, drawn not on regional grounds as in Bandung, but rather on commitment to shared principles: support for national liberation, and an independent or non-aligned foreign policy. The latter was considered especially important in the context of the ideological bipolar division of the world between the two superpowers, the United States and the Union of Soviet Socialist Republics. Today membership stands at 115. Its remit has expanded beyond the early political interests to embrace policy advocacy on global economic and other issues. This shift has been intensified post-Cold War (**www.nam.gov.za/background/history.htm**).

G20/G20 Plus. A powerful new bloc of developing countries which came into its own at the Cancun trade talks in September 2003, where it was united by clearly articulated economic interests on which it negotiated forcefully with the European Union and the United States. The alliance includes the world's most populous countries and most of its fastest growing economies, for example India, China, Brazil, Malaysia, Indonesia, South Africa, and Nigeria.

G77. The Group of Seventy-Seven was established by seventy-seven developing countries in June 1964 at the end of the first meeting of the United Nations Conference on Trade and Development (UNCTAD) in Geneva. It is the largest grouping of Southern countries in the United Nations system. The membership currently stands at 131 states, but the grouping retains its original name. The G77 defines its aims as threefold: to articulate and promote the collective economic interests of its members; to enhance its joint negotiating capacity on major economic issues in the UN system; and to promote economic and technical cooperation among developing countries (**www.g77.org/**).

LDCs. Previously less developed countries, synonymous with Third World or the South, but more commonly used now to refer to the least developed countries (which are also called LLDCs) as defined by the United Nations.

LIC. Low-income country.

MIC. Middle-income country.

NIE. Newly industrializing economy—an economy which seems to be on a sound path towards joining the ranks of rich, industrialized states or, indeed now ranks as an industrial economy. In the early 1960s, commentators applied the label to the Latin American states of Brazil, Mexico, and Argentina. Later, it was applied most frequently to the East Asian states of Taiwan, Hong Kong, South Korea, and Singapore. Others, such as Thailand and Malaysia, more recently have had the label applied to them.

The South/the Global South. With the passing of the Cold War and the accompanying transition of the former centrally planned economies into the global market, the terminology of First, Second, and Third World seemed to have less relevance. The expectation was that the Second World would join the ranks of the First, and the new line-up would be advanced Northern economies and the rest—the South. However, in practice the former Second World states have more in common with the Third World countries, being characterized by lack of voice in global affairs and widespread poverty. European Union enlargement may alter this for some.

The new globalizers. The term used currently by the World Bank to refer to those countries which it believes have best taken advantage of the opportunities offered by global economic integration, such as China, India, Mexico, and Malaysia, by breaking into global manufacturing markets and making some progress towards poverty reduction.

Box 12.2 **Terms of trade**

The price of exports of a given state relative to the price of its imports.

The Prebisch–Singer thesis forecast a consistent, long-run tendency for the prices of primary products to decline in relation to manufactured products (Raffer and Singer 2001: 16).

This has been borne out. The impact on Southern countries which export primary products has been *declining*

terms of trade: the price of their primary product exports has grown more slowly than the cost of manufactured imports. In practice, this means that Southern countries have had to run in order to stand still: for example, over time, they have needed to export more quantities of tea or coffee in order to generate the foreign exchange necessary for one imported tractor or computer. See Figure 12.1.

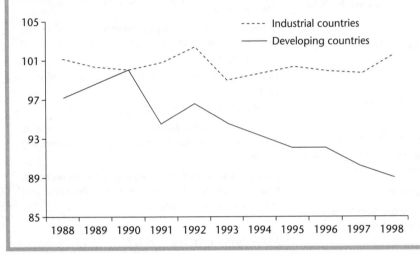

Fig. 12.1 Terms of trade for industrialized and developing countries
Source: Oxfam 2002*b*: 39.

In March 2002, the responsibilities and roles of rich and poor alike were restated in the UN's global level summit in Monterrey, the International Conference on Financing for Development. There, the rich and poor countries struck a global deal. The Monterrey Consensus (see Box 12.4) acknowledged the existence of two fundamental aspects to the development challenge—the domestic and the external/structural—and this represents a potentially important step forward.

However, a note of caution is in order: the history of North–South relations is littered with unfulfilled promises. For example, the OECD countries committed as long ago as 1969 to an Official Development Assistance (ODA) target of 0.7 per cent Gross National Product. Yet thirty-five years on, only a handful of countries have reached this target.

The task is to make the compact work. With the UNDP (2003*a*) estimating that on current performance, Sub-Saharan Africa (SSA) will not halve extreme poverty until 2147—that is, 150 years away—the responsibility is huge. However, even if both North and South keep to their side of the bargain, the question remains as to whether this is appropriate for meeting today's challenge. Moreover, with projected global population of 8 billion by 2025, an even more difficult question is whether it is appropriate for meeting tomorrow's challenge.

The question of voice

A key element in making the compact work lies in translating the commitment to enhancing the voice of the South in global governance into practice. As will be shown below, the South has felt aggrieved at its long-standing lack of effective voice in drawing up the rules and institutions which govern the global economy, and at its lack of opportunity to influence

Box 12.3 The millennium development goals and targets for 2015

1 Eradicate extreme poverty and hunger

Halve the proportion of people living on less than a dollar a day and those who suffer from hunger.

2 Achieve universal primary education

Ensure that all boys and girls complete primary school.

3 Promote gender equality and empower women

Eliminate gender disparities in primary and secondary education preferably by 2005, and at all levels by 2015.

4 Reduce child mortality

Reduce by two-thirds the mortality rate among children under 5.

5 Improve maternal health

Reduce by three-quarters the ratio of women dying in childbirth.

6 Combat HIV/AIDS, malaria, and other diseases

Halt and begin to reverse the spread of HIV/AIDS and the incidence of malaria and other major diseases.

7 Ensure environmental sustainability

Integrate the principles of sustainable development into country policies and programmes and reverse the loss of environmental resources.

Reduce by half the proportion of people without access to safe drinking water.

By 2020 achieve significant improvement in the lives of at least 100 million slum dwellers.

8 Develop a global partnership for development

Develop further an open trading and financial system that includes a commitment to good governance, development, and poverty reduction—nationally and internationally.

Address the least developed countries' special needs, and the special needs of landlocked and small island developing states.

Deal comprehensively with developing countries' debt problems.

Develop decent and productive work for youth.

In cooperation with pharmaceutical companies, provide access to affordable essential drugs in developing countries.

In cooperation with the private sector, make available the benefits of new technologies—especially information and communications technologies.

Source: **www.undp.org**

Box 12.4 The Monterrey Consensus: a compact for development

- **Poor states**: pledged to strengthen the rule of law, reduce corruption, and improve the environment for private sector growth.

- **Rich states**: pledged more generous financial assistance, better access to their markets for goods from poor countries, and lasting debt relief.

In addition, the compact included a commitment to enhancing the voice of the South in global governance.

policy evolution within that framework. It is important to note that formal representation at a table does not necessarily translate into influence. Progress on this issue is vital.

Key points

- The South refers to the states of the world which do not have a significant voice in global rule making and/or where the majority of the world's poor live.

- Too many states and people are being excluded from the economic benefits of globalization.

- The international community of states has signed up to the Millennium Development Goals and Targets for achievement by 2015.

- The Monterrey Consensus represents a potentially significant partnership for development between North and South.

- The issue of voice for the South remains a major challenge.

Development history: 1945 to 1980

Hopes on independence

On gaining political independence fifty years ago, nationalist leaders in the South wanted to pursue economic independence and the development imperative was strong. They identified industrialization as the path to growth, wealth, and economic independence. They believed that their countries' poor economic status resulted from the imperial policy of using them as the source of raw materials, and depriving them of the opportunity to produce manufactured goods for local consumption or trade.

Some Southern states such as India and China had a rich history of manufacturing. Indeed, in the mid to late eighteenth century, the largest manufacturing areas in the world lay in the Yangtze Delta in mid-China, and Bengal in India, and it is likely that the average standard of living in Europe at that time was slightly lower than in those regions (Davis 2002: 34). India and China had a bitter memory of the military and economic policies of the imperial powers which had been geared towards the destruction of their commercial and manufacturing bases.

Some of the Latin American states (independent since the nineteenth century), had a more recent experience of industrialization. Although still dependent on primary exports at the end of the Second World War, they had been developing their industrial bases since the 1930s. This had been largely in response to the economic insecurity they felt during the Depression, when their dependence on the industrialized states for markets for their primary products and as sources of manufactured goods had cost them dear. The unreliability of export commodity prices in the 1920s and 1930s had hurt them badly, and resulted in a shortage of foreign exchange for imported manufactures. This had made local manufacture rather than import for the domestic market essential (Rapley 1996: 12). The Latin American governments believed that

this kind of *import substitution* which involved both *large public and private enterprises* would *protect them against the unreliable international market*. The newly independent African and Asian countries wanted to follow this example, in the hope of 'catching up' with the industrialized countries of the North and breaking out of the condition of economic dependence.

Were 'breaking out' and 'catching up' realistic goals and, if so, how might they be achieved? Two schools of thought emerged on this and continue to inform analysis. The first is the structuralist approach, which identified underlying structures in the international economy which worked against the South. Southern countries due to their colonial history were tied into structures of production and trade which militated against their advancement. Many, for example, were dependent on the production of one or two primary commodities for sale in the market of their former colonizer. Hence they were extremely vulnerable to factors outside their control. Structuralists believed that it was possible to reform these patterns to the advantage of the South. The second approach, modernization theory, identified domestic constraints as the obstacle to development, and did not engage with the issue of international economic structures. They too believed development was possible, if the internal context was reformed (see Box 12.5). The writings of several of the key authors associated with the two approaches, plus pertinent critiques, have been drawn together in a useful collection by Seligson and Passe-Smith (1993).

Development context and experience

From the perspective of the South, the international system of states in 1945 looked very different to that of today. Not only were the African states still colonies, but major Southern countries such as India

Box 12.5 Obstacles to development: domestic or structural?

Structuralist theory

- Developed from 1950 on the basis of analyses of North–South trade and promoted vigorously by the UN's Economic Commission for Latin America in the 1950s.

- Identified the obstacles to Southern development in *structural* differences between production and trade in the North and the South rooted in colonial history.

- Southern economies were dominated by the primary sector—production of raw materials, agricultural products, etc. In Northern economies the industrial sector was more important.

- The South relied on the export of primary products to pay for manufactured imports from the North. But the price of those manufactured imports rose faster than the price of primary exports.

- Outcome: the South would have to run in order to stand still because of *deteriorating terms of trade*.

- Result: the South could not catch up, and moreover, the gap between South and North would get bigger.

- Conclusion: this could be avoided by reforming the system so that the South would benefit.

- Development required a concentration on industrial rather than primary sector and a breaking of dependence on the North by increasing intra-South trade.

- Action: the state was to be the catalyst for this change and should support import-substitution-industrialization (this could be facilitated by regional cooperation—see Ravenhill, Chapter 5 in this volume).

- Key authors: Amin (1976); Baran (1976); Frank (1971); Wallerstein (1975).

Modernization theory

- Developed in the United States in the 1950s and 1960s in the context of ideological competition between the two superpowers, the USA and the USSR.

- Based on behaviouralism: the belief that scientific study could determine the ingredients of successful development in the North, and these could be applied in the South to deliver similar results.

- Identified a linear path to development, from a traditional, agrarian society to a modern, industrial, mass consumption one.

- Economic growth would go through set stages, one of which was economic 'take off' indicative of self-sustaining development.

- Identified obstacles to development as domestic, for example, administrative inefficiency, weak legal system, and insufficient mobilization of domestic resources.

- Structures created by imperialism were irrelevant to future development of the South.

- Action: development required Southern countries to embrace liberal Western values of economics, politics, and society.

- Domestic efforts to mobilize resources would be helped by some private foreign investment.

- Export-led growth was the path to development.

- Key authors: Inkeles and Smith (1974); Rostow (1960).

---

and Indonesia were yet to gain their independence. Post-1945, when colonies achieved independent statehood, they found themselves born into a global economic order in which they were expected to grow through export-led trade, and without any aid or special treatment. Moreover, they had had no effective voice in shaping that order. Southern countries felt the global economic order inherently discriminated against them. The history of North–South relations thereafter is the story of their struggle to gain a greater voice and a better deal in the global economic order (Thomas 1987; Adams 1993).

As discussed in Chapter 1 in this volume, the essential character and management of the post-war international economy was discussed at Bretton Woods in 1944, by invitation of the United States.

At the time of Bretton Woods, there was little anticipation that rapid decolonization would occur. Therefore, apart from the Latin Americans, 'development' seemed to be an issue for individual colonial powers (see Box 12.6).

Chapter 1 in this volume showed how the Bretton Woods system created two multilateral organizations (the IMF and the World Bank, or International Bank

---

Box 12.6 Representation but no effective voice: the South's experience at Bretton Woods

It goes without saying that the influence of the under-developed countries on these (Bretton Woods) negotiations and on the nature of the institutions that emerged was nil or negligible. Of the forty-three countries invited to attend the Bretton Woods Conference, 27 were from the underdeveloped regions of Africa, Asia, and Latin America, with the overwhelming majority (19) being Latin American countries. Indeed there were only three African countries present (Egypt, Ethiopia, and Liberia) and five countries from Asia (India, Iran, Iraq, the Philippines, and China). The bulk of Africa was still under European colonial rule, as was a large part of Asia. Given the complexity of the issues involved, the late stage at which they were brought into the picture, and the minimal bargaining power that they could in any event exert, it is not surprising that the influence of these countries on the conference and its outcome was minimal (Adams 1993: 22).

---

for Reconstruction and Development—IBRD) and one standing conference (the General Agreement on Tariffs and Trade). While liberal in orientation, this system represented a compromise. The North believed that the economic protectionism of the 1930s had fuelled international instability. Therefore the recipe for peace and prosperity henceforth would be economic liberalism. However, Northern leaders were aware of the political imperative in their own states for meeting social issues such as full employment, and thus *they wanted a clear role for governments in the operation of the market* (Ruggie 1982).

In the immediate post-war period, the IMF and the World Bank, unsurprisingly, were preoccupied with the needs of Northern countries. Southern countries soon felt that the Bretton Woods system operated against their interests. The South was dissatisfied with its lack of voice in the IMF and World Bank, and potential violations of sovereignty (Thomas 1987; Woods 2001). Those institutions operated a system of weighted voting. Moreover, the United States was (and remains) the only state with unilateral veto power (Thomas 2000). The problem of lack of representation was made all the more acute because while theoretically part of the United Nations family, the IMF and World Bank, unlike other arms of the UN, were not (and never have been) accountable to the UN General Assembly, where the principle of one state one vote operated. Instead they answer to their major shareholders (Raffer and Singer 2001).

Southern countries had many concerns over policies, all stemming from the fact that their special needs had not been considered in the establishment of the Bretton Woods structure. Indeed it was only after

the numerical balance in the United Nations shifted dramatically in the late 1950s with the decolonization of Africa that Southern concerns began to be taken on board. The IBRD, for example, during its early years, concentrated on market-rate finance for reconstruction, rather than concessional (that is, low interest-rate) finance for development (which was not forthcoming until 1960) (Spero 1977). The Southern experience of the GATT was similar. The General Agreement on Tariffs and Trade promoted trade as the engine of growth, but the South felt that equal treatment rules and reciprocal tariff-cutting arrangements under GATT were unfair, and made things worse not better for them. They needed to protect their infant industries, and they needed preferential access to the markets of the North. Also, they needed stable commodity prices, but the GATT was not geared towards this (Raffer and Singer 2001). GATT did not even recognize a distinction between developed and developing countries until 1964 (Tussie 1987). Moreover GATT had relatively few Southern members until the Uruguay Round negotiations in the mid-1980s (Winham 2000). Also, the IMF was simply not interested in the South in its early years. It was not until 1963 that it responded to calls from the South for special resources, with the creation of the Compensatory Finance Facility (Williams 1994: 60).

As regards aid (other than to Northern countries through the Marshall Plan), it was only in the context of the Cold War that this took off. In the mid-1950s, the US government assumed that aid would spur growth and development in the South and thereby bring these countries into the Western camp. By this time the United States priority of rebuilding the

European and Japanese economies was well on its way to being achieved.

As more Southern states (especially those of Africa) gained independence, the early political solidarity of the South expressed through the non-aligned movement (NAM) was transferred to the economic arena. The South was able to start collective organization both in General Assembly and in the Economic and Social Council (ECOSOC). These forums operated on the basis of one state one vote, and therefore provided a more congenial environment in which to work collectively to put pressure on the North for a better economic deal. The NAM provided further impetus for the collective articulation of demands. With the growing competition between the superpowers for allies in the South from the mid-1950s onwards, opportunities opened up not only to receive aid (often a double-edged sword in the circumstances) but to bargain for changes.

A noteworthy achievement for the South came in 1964 with the establishment of the United Nations Conference on Trade and Development (UNCTAD), a standing conference on trade and development outside of the Western-founded GATT. This was followed by the formation of the G77, through which the South would pursue collective representation in the United Nations (Spero 1977; Adams 1993). The Southern victory had a hollow ring, however. The Western powers did not object to the establishment of UNCTAD, secure in the knowledge that funding and economic policies would be determined through the IMF and the World Bank where weighted voting operated in their favour. Yet UNCTAD's intangible achievements, in terms of its role as a pressure group for the developing world, and as a focus for critiques of mainstream development thinking, were significant in its first decade (see Box 12.7).

The decade of the 1970s was to be the high point of Southern achievement in terms of participating in decisions and effecting outcomes on the global economic stage (Williams 1994: 60–2). The negotiating environment changed dramatically for the South in the early 1970s (Adams 1993; South Commission 1990). Several factors contributed to this change: the Bretton Woods system of fixed exchange rates was abandoned in 1971; the OPEC countries acting as a cartel quadrupled the price of oil in 1973; commodity prices were strong during the first half of the 1970s. Even though oil-importing Southern countries were hurting economically, politically the South remained united, enjoying

---

Box 12.7 Development achievement in the South, 1945–80

Throughout this period, development in the South was led by the state rather than the market. There were many variations in national policy. Some states (for example, in Latin America, South Asia, and SSA) pursued import substitution, while others (for example, in East Asia) used selective protection in key industries as preparation for export-led growth. A few (for example, Tanzania, Burma) attempted self-sufficiency. Some (for example, in East Asia) emphasized growth with equity (Watkins 1998: 18). Others (for example, in Latin America) ignored issues of equity and human capital. *The common thread was the important role of the state as the motor of development. This was in accord with the conventional wisdom of development economics of the period.*

The 1950s and 1960s have been described as an *'optimistic'* period of growth for the South (Singer and Roy 1993). However, despite this, the South was still being left further behind the North. The South's share of world trade fell during the 1950s from one-third to one-fifth, and expansion of their export earnings decelerated over the decade. Nevertheless, the proportion of the South's people living in absolute poverty fell.

In the 1970s, growth continued in the South, but Singer and Roy identify this as 'illusory', based on the accumulation of debt. Nevertheless, the proportion of people living in absolute poverty continued to fall. When overall averages for per capita growth rates are unpacked, great variation in achievement is apparent, with many states experiencing negative or very low growth rates (for example, SSA), some moderate (Latin America), and some high (East Asia).

But growth alone is an inadequate measure of development. Again, variations are apparent. In the oil states of the Gulf, for example, the high rates of growth experienced after 1973 did not translate into similar achievements in various aspects of human development. Also, the gross inequity which characterized many Latin American states meant that they needed to grow more than the East Asian states to make an impact on poverty reduction.

the new found empowerment. The North felt insecure; not yet understanding that oil was a special case, it was concerned that the cartel action could be repeated for other commodities, giving yet more bargaining power to the South (Spero 1977). It was also troubled at this time by inflation and unemployment.

In 1974, the South called for a New International Economic Order (NIEO) at the UN General Assembly, and followed this a year later with a Charter on the Rights and Duties of States (Thomas 1985: 122–51). At core these represented a political demand for sovereignty to be taken seriously. There were a number of economic demands, several geared toward reducing the vulnerability of the South to external factors (for example, index linking the price of raw materials to the price of manufactured goods) and exercising sovereignty (for example, control over foreign investment and domestic natural resources). Despite the shock of oil price rises, the Northern states were in no mood to make concessions (Rothstein 1979; Hansen 1979; Bhagwati and Ruggie 1984; Zartman 1987).

At the IMF, the South fought for increased financial flows, and this was realized through a number of mechanisms such as the two-year Oil Facility in 1974 to help countries hurting due to the oil price rise, and the Trust Fund in 1976 to support the poorest countries with concessional loans (Williams 1994: 61).

This period of heightened diplomatic activity by the South in the United Nations and the IMF coincided with a change of commitment in the World Bank from highly visible infrastructural projects to poverty-focused aid. The presidency of Robert McNamara (1968–81) is best remembered for an emphasis on redistribution with growth, illustrated by the emergence of integrated rural development projects which tackled multiple causes of poverty in parallel—health, education, rural finance, as well as infrastructure (Mosley and Eeckhout 2000: 133–4). McNamara first highlighted the issue of growth with equity at the joint meetings of the IMF and World Bank in 1973. A year later, the Bank supported the publication of *Redistribution with Growth* (Chenery et al. 1974), and in 1978 it published its first *World Development Report*, on the prospects for enhanced growth and poverty alleviation. However, the changed focus of the Bank did not mean that the institution or its president supported the claims of the South for an NIEO. Indeed, by 1979, McNamara

was calling at the Manila UNCTAD conference for structural adjustment (see below).

Oil price rises were a double-edged sword for the non-oil-exporting South, and their economic difficulties mounted. In addition to the oil shock, volatile commodity prices in the second half of the 1970s and declining terms of trade further weakened their position. Keen to maintain rates of growth comparable to the 1960s, many Southern governments borrowed recycled petrodollars at low but floating rates of interest from private banks. (SSA states were unable to borrow much from private banks, but got into similar trouble by borrowing from official creditors.) When the United States responded to a second oil price hike in 1979 by raising interest rates, Southern countries found themselves in severe trouble. Interest payments on debts rose, and they needed to borrow more to deal with deficits and debt repayment.

At the end of the 1970s, the Soviet bloc was still intact, and the G77/non-aligned group, while weak, still functioned—albeit under increasing strain due to growing divisions between oil-exporting and importing developing countries apparent at the 1979 UNCTAD Manila Conference. While the calls for an NIEO had receded, there still existed the idea and the reality that there was more than one model of development on offer—but not for much longer. Governance in the international system would shift from the relatively open, discursive multilateral UN system of the 1970s, to governance through the narrowly defined IMF and World Bank under the direction of the G7 in the 1980s.

Key points

- Post-1945, Southern states pursued several paths to development, but all identified the state as the motor of development, and industrialization as the means to catch up with the economic achievement of the North.

- Structuralist theory and modernization theory emerged as the two main approaches to explain the development problem.

- The South felt the liberal Bretton Woods Economic Order did not address their special needs.

- The South campaigned for changes through the UN system.

- Empowered by the OPEC cartel action, they called for an NIEO in 1974.
- Oil price rises hurt Southern countries, and they tried to maintain earlier growth rates via borrowing.

- The political response of the North to the second oil price rises in the late 1970s sealed the fate of the South. Interest rate rises on floating rate debt, coupled with falling commodity prices, meant the debt crisis was born.

Development policy since 1980: from state led to market led

The beginning of the 1980s marked a very significant shift in development policy from state led to market led. The overwhelming need of many states in the South for immediate and longer-term external finance was so great that it had no effective bargaining power vis-à-vis the First World. This weakness coincided with the ascendancy of a neo-liberal agenda (see below) within the domestic politics of the United States and the United Kingdom. The post-war liberal principle of a state-guided market gave way to neo-liberalism; the scene was set for the expansion of market fundamentalism across the South.

The G7 accorded the World Bank a higher and more exclusive profile in global development policy, and the IMF an entirely new one, as the major Western powers decided to use these institutions to manage Third World debt. They worked on the assumption that needy countries suffered from short-term cash flow problems which could be remedied by policy reforms. Thus loans were made conditional on policy changes: the role of the state was to be reduced and redefined, and the market was to operate unhindered.

By the early 1990s, with the demise of the eastern bloc, the IMF and World Bank were portrayed globally as *the exclusive holders of legitimate knowledge about development*; and they held a monopoly on policy advice. This meant that the role of external/structural factors in the development challenge was downplayed. Crucially, these institutions disbursed most of the multilateral aid, and they provided a green light for other lenders. The amount and significance of ODA declined substantially in the 1990s, and Southern countries competed to attract growing volumes of private capital in line with neo-liberal policies (see below). There seemed to be no possibility of resourcing alternative pathways for development.

Over the period 1986 to 1994, the Uruguay Round GATT trade negotiations were under way, and these too reflected and reinforced the ascendancy of the neo-liberal agenda and the lack of political leverage or bargaining power of the South (UNDP et al. 2003).

During the 1990s, the G7 increasingly used its summits to frame development policy politically. Under its direction, since the mid-1990s, the World Bank has pushed forward the harmonization of donor policies and coherence between the policies of the IMF, the World Bank, and the WTO in support of free trade. This has further strengthened the already overwhelming influence of the North on development policy for the South, as bilateral donors line up behind international financial institution (IFI) policies. Against this formidable line-up, the political space for Southern voice and leverage is virtually non-existent.

Neo-liberal development policy for the South

Neo-liberal development policies are referred to as the 'Washington Consensus' (WC). These policies are based on the assumption that global economic integration through free trade is the most effective route to promote growth, and the benefits of growth will trickle down throughout society. Broadly, they involve three stages (Green 1995: 4). The first stage is to control inflation by *stabilization*, and *to get rid of government spending deficits*. The money supply is reduced by *cutting public spending* and *raising interest rates*. The second stage is *structural adjustment*—this involves letting the market operate unhindered by state controls; *privatizing* public enterprises; *liberalizing* trade, investment, and finance. The third stage is *export-led growth*—which involves encouraging foreign investors to bring in capital and technology unhindered by government regulation (see Box 12.8).

The WC was applied as a universal blueprint for development throughout the Third World and former Second World. The debt crises in Latin America and Africa in the 1980s gave the IMF and the World Bank the opportunity to institutionalize structural adjustment programmes as a debt management strategy in those regions. Post-1989, the treatment was consolidated in the economies in transition, several of which were already borrowing from the IFIs. In the late 1990s, in the context of financial crisis, it was the turn of the East Asian states.

The IMF and World Bank diagnosed the problems of all these regions and their constituent countries in the same way, and made loans conditional on a standard package of policy advice. But their problems were not the same, and uniform solutions were not appropriate. The Latin Americans, for example, had very high inflation, low savings rates, and large balance of payments problems (Green 1995), whereas the East Asians enjoyed low inflation, high savings, and balanced budgets (Bullard, Bello, and Malhotra 1998). The debts of African states were to public creditors—bilateral and multilateral, while the Latin American states were more indebted to private banks.

From the late 1980s onwards, anxieties grew regarding the model's ability to deliver the promised economic growth, and also its social and environmental impact (Cornia, Jolly, and Stewart/UNICEF 1987; South Commission 1990; Walton and Seddon 1994). Moreover, Southern debt continued to mount. Also the conditions attached to loans raised concerns that the model was being externally imposed on needy, vulnerable client states in violation of national sovereignty.

In the early to mid-1990s the IMF and World Bank responded to these criticisms by attempting to make their prescriptions for growth more palatable on the ground. They offered some support for limited, targeted poverty-reduction actions such as micro-credit, social safety nets, and social funds (Vivian 1995; Subbarao et al. 1997). 1996 saw a change in approach to debt. Up till then, the debt problem had been seen as one of *illiquidity*, and emphasis had been on debt collection, debt rescheduling, and aid/structural adjustment. In 1996, the Heavily Indebted Poor Countries' initiative (HIPC) was based on the recognition that the least developed (LDCs) were *insolvent*. It was designed to reduce the debt stock of the LDCs and to bring those countries to a position of debt sustainability. It would remove the debt overhang which was seen as a disincentive to private investment, and a barrier to the government expenditures needed to improve physical and human infrastructures.

But while the IMF and World Bank made a few modifications to their prescriptions for the South, the conclusion of the GATT Uruguay Round in 1994 reflected the economic interest and political influence of the

---

Box 12.8 From state-led to market-led development

- In the context of mounting Southern debt, the IMF and the World Bank were given a prominent new role by the United States in making global development policy and monitoring its implementation.

- Loans to the South were dependent on the adoption of stringent policy conditions.

- They universalized a neo-liberal approach to development: state-led development was replaced by market-led development.

- Export-led growth was the route to enable Southern countries to generate the foreign exchange necessary to repay their debts and to promote development through a trickle-down process.

- They identified the causes of poverty and underdevelopment as *internal* to states, rather than external/structural or a combination of both.

- The state was redefined as an enabler for the private sector; it was to facilitate deregulation, privatization, and liberalization, and regulate activities of the private sector.

- Good governance was the key, including tackling corruption, holding free elections, and developing and enforcing property rights and contracts.

- Other possible paths to development were closed off, as IMF/World Bank loans were the necessary green light for finance from other public and private sources.

United States and the Europeans for whom trade in services, intellectual property, and investment issues were becoming increasingly important (Winham 2000: 169; UNDP 2003a: 11). The special needs of the South in these issues were ignored. For example, in the Trade-Related Investment Measures (TRIMS) (UNDP et al. 2003: 11). Also, in much of the South (especially, but not only, the heavily indebted) agriculture rather than services was the most pressing issue, yet this was of less interest to the North and was left unresolved.

The basic WC model remained, promoted by a wider group of actors. From the mid-1990s policy coordination for development went wider and deeper than before. It involved the IMF, World Bank, and also the new World Trade Organization (WTO) in new areas and enmeshed them with new partners, particularly private partners and civil society groups. Most noticeable during this period was the privatization of global governance, in which corporate and private interests hid beneath the apparel of public governance. Examples in the field of development policy are wide-ranging. One is corporate sponsorship of UN conferences, influencing their agendas and outcomes—such as UNCED (the United Nations Conference on Environment and Development), which gave a green light for self-regulation by transnational corporations. Another example is the overt corporate role in shaping policy at the WTO, seen in striking fashion in the formulation of Trade-Related Intellectual Property Rights (TRIPs) (Drahos 2002).

The results were very disappointing. By the late 1990s, it was no longer politically tenable for the IMF and World Bank to argue that the WC model had not been applied long enough or fully enough for the expected growth and trickle-down to occur. Evidence was mounting that inequalities had increased between and within states while the model had been applied, and there was no sign of this trend reversing.

1. *Economic growth.* Lower than expected, and often of an insufficient quality. In SSA, for example, it remained under 2.5 per cent annually during the 1980s and the 1990s (and on a per capita basis was frequently negative) (UNCTAD 2002b). East Asia, which had enjoyed strong rates, suffered reversals in the late 1990s (see Box 12.9).

2. *Indebtedness.* Remained a serious problem, particularly for the most heavily indebted countries where the situation actually got worse, with the nominal stock of debt exploding relative to exports.

The HIPC did not achieve the desired results; it amounted to 'too little, too late' (see Table 12.1).

The total debt stock of the net-debtor developing countries almost doubled in the 1990s, from US$1.3 trillion to 2.2 trillion, while their debt service payments to export ratio increased from 19.6 per cent in 1991 to 22.3 per cent in 1999. The HIPC country share of this stock was $65 billion in 2002.

3. *Trade liberalization.* The share of world trade enjoyed by Southern countries has increased, and the composition of Southern exports has changed, with the share of manufactured goods growing relative to primary commodities (see Figure 12.2).

But the East Asian newly industrializing economies (NIEs) mainly account for this growth, with their 75 per cent share of Southern manufactured exports (compared with less than 2 per cent for South Asia and SSA combined) (Oxfam 2002b: 10) and their increasing role in the high-tech export market. The LDCs which rely on the export of primary commodities have suffered a continuous, significant decline in market prices (real terms) of their products (see Table 12.2 and Figure 12.3).

Box 12.9 **Economic growth and human development**

Economic growth is necessary but insufficient for human development. And the quality of growth, not just its quantity, is crucial for human well-being. Growth can be jobless, rather than job creating; ruthless, rather than poverty reducing; voiceless, rather than participatory; rootless, rather than culturally enshrined; and futureless, rather than environmentally friendly. Growth that is jobless, ruthless, voiceless, rootless, and future-less is not conducive to human development.

Source: UNDP 2003a: 23.

Table 12.1 External debt as a percentage of GDP (period average)

Category	1980–4	1985–9	1990–4	1995–2000
HIPC	38	70	120	103
Other IDA countries	21	33	38	33
Other lower-middle-income countries	22	30	27	26

Source: Gautam (for World Bank's OED) 2003: 5.

The commodity-exporting countries have become far more open to trade, yet they are earning less. Why is this so? UNCTAD (2002*b*) identifies the reasons as their continued concentration on production of primary commodities that have been characterized by stagnant markets and declining prices, and their failure to shift production into technology-intensive products. This experience lends support to the structuralist position outlined earlier. A secular decline in the terms of trade of primary commodity producers has occurred, costing SSA for example 50 cents for every US dollar received in aid since the late 1970s (Oxfam 2002*b*: 10; see Figure 12.1 in Box 12.2, above). The Southern countries which have been able to develop the export of manufactures have fared much better (but even the World Bank's 'new globalizers' have competed with one another on the basis of wage levels). This helps explain increasing polarization within the South between the NIEs and the states of SSA.

The South's share of world trade would be higher were it not for the double standards practised by the North. It has been estimated that if Africa, East Asia, South Asia, and Latin America were each to increase their share of world exports by 1 per cent, then 128 million people could be lifted out of poverty (Oxfam 2002*b*: 5). In the case of Africa, this 1 per cent increase would generate US $70 billion—which as Oxfam notes (2002*b*: 8) is 5 times the amount received through aid and debt relief. Moreover, a 5 per cent increase in the share of world trade for Southern countries would deliver US$350 billion—seven times the amount they receive in aid (see Figure 12.4).

But the North stands in the way of this expansion of Southern trade. The North demands that the South open its borders to trade, while protecting its own domestic markets from Southern imports, for example by escalating tariffs on processed goods (as opposed to raw materials). The very products in

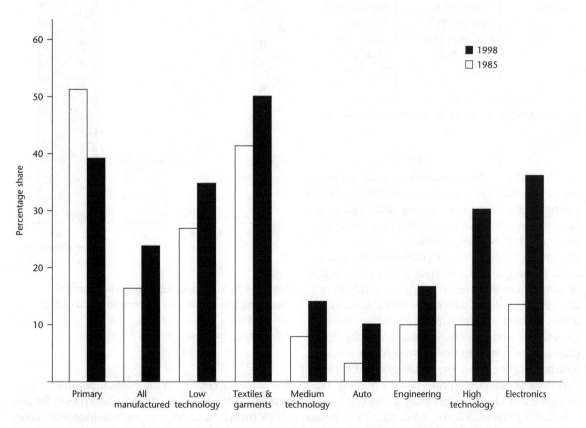

Fig. 12.2 Share of developing countries in world exports: selected product groups (1985 and 1998)
Source: Oxfam 2002*b*: 152.

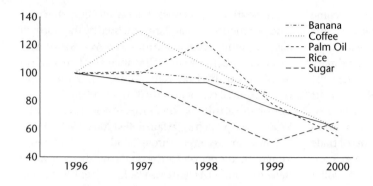

Fig. 12.3 Decline in real prices 1996–2000 (index 1996 = 100) for developing countries' top five commodities (excluding tobacco)

Source: Oxfam 2002*b*: 151.

Table 12.2 Commodity price decreases, real terms, 1980–2000

Decrease 0–25%	Decrease 25–50%	Decrease over 50%
Banana[a] −4.4	Aluminium −27.2	Cocoa −71.2
Fertiliser −23.1	Coconut oil −44.3	Coffee −64.5
Iron ore[a] −19.5	Copper −30.9	Lead −58.3
Phosphate	Cotton −47.6	Palm oil −55.8
rock −21.6	Fishmeal −31.9	Rice −60.9
Tea −7.5	Groundnut oil −30.9	Rubber −59.6
	Maize −41.6	Sugar −76.6
	Soybean −39.0	Tin −73.0
	Wheat −45.2	

Source: Adapted from Oxfam 2002*b*: 151, based on IMF (various years).

[a]1980–99.

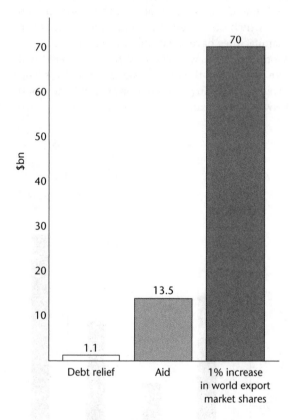

Fig. 12.4 SSA: Aid and debt relief versus foreign exchange gains from a 1% increase in world market shares ($bn)

Source: Oxfam 2002*b*: 50.

which Southern countries can most easily develop a manufacturing base and gain a competitive edge, for example, labour-intensive clothing and textiles, meet Northern protectionist barriers *four times higher* than those faced by Northern producers (Watkins 2002). Also, the North subsidizes its own domestic production, resulting in global dumping and the destruction of Southern production. This is seen starkly in relation to agriculture, where Northern subsidies to domestic farmers have topped $1 billion per day. Livelihoods have been devastated in the South, for example, the cotton growers of West Africa, and local food markets destroyed. The UNDP (2003*a*: 155) notes that the European Union cash subsidy to every dairy cow exceeds total per capita EU aid to SSA.

4. *Social problems.* Global deprivation has spread geographically. The effect of shock therapy on the former Soviet Union was to throw 60 million people

below the poverty line in the 1990s. In South-East Asia, severe reversals following the financial crises of the late 1990s (which in some cases, such as Indonesia, compounded political disintegration) threw millions back below the poverty line virtually overnight. In SSA, poverty deepened in the 1980s and 1990s as structural adjustment took its social toll. Public infrastructures such as health, education, and transport eroded, as governments were forced to cut public spending, and the World Bank advocated the use of user fees (Save the Children 2001; GUFPC 2003; Thomas and Weber 2004). Privatization, for example of water, failed to expand services to the poorest, as transnational corporations practised 'cherry picking'. Market-based entitlement deprived the poor of access to essential services. In SSA this has happened while the region and its people have faced their greatest health emergency—the HIV/AIDS pandemic (Poku 2001). Aggressive US trade policy has prevented poor states from taking advantage of the limited opportunities open to them in the WTO's TRIPs to access cheap drugs (Thomas 2002).

Trade liberalization can contribute to social problems and polarization. International trade theory assumes that increased openness to trade will result in more equal income distribution within poor countries. But recent research by Milanovic (2002*a*) found that in countries with a low per capita income level, such as in Sub-Saharan Africa, it is the rich who benefit from trade openness, while in countries where average income has risen, such as Chile or the Czech Republic, openness seems to be related to the rise in the relative income of the poor and middle class relative to the rich.

5. *Official Development Assistance.* The quantity and quality of flows were disappointing. Even though Southern states implemented structural adjustment, sufficient new money failed to flow in as expected. In real per capita terms, ODA to the LDCs fell 46 per cent in the 1990s (UNCTAD 2002*b*: 215). Over the 1990s, ODA declined from 0.33 per cent of donor country Gross National Product (GNP), to 0.22 per cent—despite the OECD countries' 1969 commitment mentioned earlier to an ODA target of 0.7 per cent of GNP! The hopes for a 'peace dividend' after the demise of the Eastern bloc came to nothing; indeed, former Second World states competed with Third World states for the declining pot of aid. The tying of aid to the purchase of goods and services and technical cooperation from donor countries eroded its value; for example, in 1997, technical cooperation amounted to 40 per cent of bilateral ODA.

6. *Private capital flows.* Private flows to the South, which had dropped sharply after the debt crisis broke in 1982, increased dramatically. By 1996 they accounted for 85 per cent of resource flows. But only about a dozen countries benefited. Moreover, the quality of the flows posed problems for recipients: short-term portfolio investment grew fastest, and its volatile nature had the potential to undermine rather than support development efforts in recipient countries. The East Asian states discovered this to their cost.

7. *Foreign Direct Investment.* Although the South's overall share of global FDI was on the increase during the 1990s—and rose from 18 per cent in the late 1990s to 28 per cent in 2001 (UNCTAD 2002*c*: 5)—the quantity and quality were disappointing for much of the South. The quantity of Southern FDI in 2000 (\$240 billion) seems impressive when compared with the amount of ODA (\$56 billion) (Oxfam 2002*b*: 35). But this must be seen against the pattern of distribution: it was highly concentrated in about ten states, with China dominating, and the majority of Southern countries received very little. Indeed in 2001, five developing countries accounted for 62 per cent of Southern FDI, while forty-nine LDCs attracted just 2 per cent of the Southern FDI, or 0.5 per cent of global FDI. Moreover, FDI still contributes a relatively small share of gross capital formation in most Southern countries (with some notable exceptions such as Malaysia and Singapore).

Assessments of the efficacy of this FDI are mixed. While UNCTAD (2002*c*) is generally positive, suggesting that FDI can bring benefits providing the host governments have the correct policy mix in place to encourage spillovers, some other assessments are more cautious. The International Labour Organization (ILO), for example, has voiced significant concerns regarding the conditions for 43 million workers in rapidly expanding Export Processing Zones (EPZs). EPZs, in order to attract FDI, are designed as tax free havens without standard national social or environmental regulation (ILO 2002; Oxfam 2002*b*: 181).

Key points

- A significant shift in development policies from state-led to market-led approaches emerged at the beginning of the 1980s, coinciding with the rise of neo-liberalism.

- The World Bank and the IMF were assigned new roles in managing Third World debt, using conditionality attached to their lending to promote the neo-liberal policy agenda (the 'Washington consensus') in LDCs.

- Despite an extended experience of structural adjustment, the economic performance of most developing countries has been disappointing.
- Industrialized countries' continuing protection of their markets hampered LDCs' development efforts, as did the relatively small amounts of foreign aid provided.

Post-Washington consensus

These poor achievements fuelled criticism of the WC, with NGOs and civil society movements being particularly effective in their attacks. The Jubilee 2000 campaign against Third World debt became extremely important, impacting on the G7 governments. The effects of financial crises in Mexico, East Asia, and Russia intensified the critique, as it was clearly not only the poorest states where the WC didn't seem to be working. Protests took place at WTO meetings and G7 summits. Criticism of the WC model mounted even within the IMF and World Bank themselves, with some notable individuals such the World Bank's Joseph Stiglitz (2002) calling for change. Clearly, the pace of global economic integration would be threatened, unless the benefits of the process were more evenly shared. Concerns about the possible link between poverty and conflict were voiced forcefully by the leaders of the IMF and World Bank (Thomas 2000: 3), and these were to be reinforced by the events of 11 September 2001. The Post-Washington Consensus (PWC) was born.

Whereas the WC aimed for growth, the PWC stresses that growth alone is not enough, it must be made 'pro-poor'; and that poverty reduction is crucial for development. Under the WC the IMF and World Bank decided on the universal development blueprint; under the PWC, national governments must *own* development strategies, and civil society must *participate* in their formulation. Blueprints must not be imposed by external actors. Conditions should relate to *processes* rather than to *policies*.

The PWC discourse took off in 1999, with the ideas officially launched in World Bank's President Wolfensohn's Comprehensive Development Framework. The donor/creditor relationship looked set to change, as the language of *partnership* between

donors and recipients permeated development discourse. National Poverty Reduction Strategy Papers (PRSPs) were identified by the IMF and the World Bank as the litmus test of a country's suitability for debt relief under the HIPC and for new funds from multilateral and bilateral lenders. The *Enhanced* HIPC was launched, which moved away from the original HIPC's emphasis on debt sustainability, to a new emphasis on deeper, faster, broader relief linked directly to poverty reduction. Once a country qualified for debt relief under the Enhanced HIPC, *access* to relief would depend on acceptance by the IMF and World Bank Boards of the national PRSP.

The idea of the PRSP has been adopted rapidly by the official aid community, and it is now the centrepiece for policy dialogue in *all* countries seeking concessional funds. In April 2002, James Wolfensohn's first recommendation, in setting out a post- Monterrey action plan to the DAC was the use of PRSPs as 'anchors for securing fresh donor support' (Wolfensohn 2002*b*).

The language of the PWC is different from the WC, but in practice has much changed? Previous efforts to change institutional direction—such as the McNamara era of 'Growth with Equity'—do not inspire confidence in the capacity to change the institutional culture in the World Bank, see, for instance Ayres (1983). It is still early days for the PWC. However, critics have raised some legitimate concerns. Two related issues will be discussed here in respect of the PRSP, the central vehicle for the new approach: continuity in the policy focus with the WC, and the issue of ownership/sovereignty.

PRSPs: the issue of ownership

PRSPs were to be country-driven and owned, rather than imposed by outside actors such as the World Bank. But the PRSP actually *enables* the IMF and World Bank to assume even more extensive powers over developing countries than under the WC, as they are able to validate an *entire national development strategy*, including its social and political aspects. This is so even though they are only lending or underwriting a very small part of that strategy (Abugre 2000). Moreover, with the entire spectrum of donors aligning behind a single development strategy, as part of their coherence and harmonization strategy, there is little room for flexibility or diversity amongst borrowers. Thus sovereignty can be further undermined.

PRSPs: the issue of policy

While the PRSPs encourage governments to focus more attention on some poverty issues such as health and education, an important potential failing is *the continued absence of a real discussion of the link between macroeconomic policy and poverty creation, or inequality, or possible alternatives to the WC orthodoxy*. The primacy of *export-led growth as the route to development is not held up for scrutiny, but rather assumed as common sense*. Also, the Poverty and Social Impact Analysis (PSIA) to map potential effects of policies on the poor does not seem to be occurring effectively when policies are considered.

Given the emphasis on country ownership, how can we explain the limited nature of the debate? One reason is necessity. The poorest countries, starved of investment resources and crippled with debt burden, are desperate for immediate debt reduction so as to free up resources for the import of essential items without which they cannot function. Therefore they are under intense pressure to develop PRSPs quickly, because without these they cannot receive debt reduction under the Enhanced HIPC or new loans. They are drawing up these plans, however, in full knowledge that if their plans do not fit with the world-view of the World Bank and Fund, they are unlikely to get approval, and this knowledge is bound to affect the shape of the plans. In some cases, the World Bank or IMF have actually been involved in the drawing up of the national paper. It is well known that in the case of Nicaragua, the draft PRSP was available in English in Washington before it was even available in Managua! A second reason may be the intellectual hegemony of the Bank: 'Through its global and national-level studies, and its extensive network of official, journalist and academic contacts, the Bank has a strong influence on policy debates' (Wilks and Lefrancois 2002: 8). The IFIs even provide a 1,000 page PRSP Sourcebook. Other reasons include the lack of bureaucratic capacity in many HIPCs, and the lack of well-organized domestic NGOs to participate in the process.

Despite the intention that PRSP loan conditions are related to processes, this doesn't seem to be supported by country experience. This is not entirely surprising. Since the World Bank and Fund understand poverty reduction to occur within the context of a trade-led growth-oriented strategy, the parameters of the national strategy are assumed. An inquiry conducted by a network of leading Southern NGOs of experience in Latin America, Africa, and Asia suggested that: 'In every case examined the most important element of the PRSPs or interim PRSPs devised are the mandatory policy matrices. These orientations detail the now standardized Bank-Fund assortment of policy "reform" including liberalisation, privatisation, fiscal and administrative reform, assets management' (Jubilee South et al. 2002). Many loan conditions are the same as twenty years ago.

The same inquiry revealed that important issues are ignored, such as 'Policy and political measures indispensable in many cases to effective poverty and inequality reduction . . . land and agrarian reform, progressive taxation, support for domestic markets and protection, food sovereignty, the protection of the environment and labour vis-à-vis investors, assurances of social rights and entitlements, and other forms of governmental protection vis-à-vis the free market' (Jubilee South et al. 2002: paragraph 5).

Development: roads to failure and success in the South

An early evaluation suggests that the PWC strategy is not sufficiently different from the WC as to make a crucial difference to outcomes in terms of growth and poverty reduction. In particular, the continued emphasis on the need for domestic policy reform, and growth via trade liberalization, coupled with the continued neglect of structural issues, is unbalanced.

This was all too evident in the WTO's Doha Conference in November 2001. It was decided through undemocratic means (for example, the exclusive Green Room process—see Box 12.10) that instead of using its 'Development Round' to redress profound imbalances in its rules and the structure of trade, rather it would expand its power and remit. Despite the opposition of many developing countries and social movements, the WTO would negotiate agreements on four new areas—the 'Singapore' issues, placed on the agenda at a WTO Ministerial meeting in Singapore in 1996: investment, competition, transparency in government procurement, and trade facilitation (Khor 2001). More than 100 NGOs from North and South joined together to declare the Doha Declaration—touted by supporters as a 'development agenda'—'Everything but development' (Joint Statement 2001).

Box 12.10 **The Green Room process**

GATT negotiations developed a pattern known as the Green Room process. Representatives from a limited number of states sat at a table, exchanged drafts, and negotiated. An 'inner circle' of consensus was developed, and this was then sold to other members, so the circle of consensus expanded (Drahos 2002: 167).

The pattern continued with the WTO, where its supporters argue that the entire membership cannot negotiate on issues as this would take far too long. The process has come under attack from the developing countries and the global NGO community who argue that democracy should not be sacrificed on the altar of efficiency. They say that while in theory the WTO is based on one state one vote, this type of consensus formation is undemocratic and operates against the spirit of international cooperation.

Participation in Green Room meetings is by invitation only, and there are no published selection criteria for membership. The director-general (or occasionally the chairman) invites a small number of states—maybe twenty-five—to discuss compromise texts on specific issues, and there is no written record of the discussions. The agenda is set, and the consensus built, among the few, on the behalf of the entire membership. The consensus is then presented to the majority as a take-it-or-leave-it package. The implications are far reaching, as the WTO creates legally binding and enforceable agreements for member governments worldwide.

(Adapted from NGO Coalition 2002, and Khor 1999.)

Box 12.11 **Trade liberalization: precedes or follows high rates of growth in India and China?**

'China and India implemented their main trade reforms about a decade after the onset of higher growth. Moreover, their trade restrictions remain among the highest in the world. The increase in China's growth started in the late 1970s. Trade liberalization did not start in earnest until much later, in the second half of the 1980s and especially in the 1990s—once the trend growth rate had already increased substantially. India's growth rate increased substantially in the early 1980s, while serious trade reform did not start until 1991–93.' (UNDP 2002: 31)

These UNDP findings are extremely important, for they suggest that the unadulterated free trade mantra which still dominates IMF/World Bank/WTO policy on how to promote global economic integration (and therefore development) may well be misplaced. The study is not suggesting that states should never liberalize trade. Rather, it is suggesting that *the sequencing and intensity of trade liberalization policies may well be crucial for growth, and for human development*. In other words, states need to be mindful in their application of trade liberalization, and not see it as an end in itself which will necessarily bring the desired results.

Moreover, the trade liberalization agenda is pushed further in the South, whilst the North continues to undermine Southern efforts by protection, subsidies, and dumping. When in May 2002 United States President Bush introduced a six-year, $51.7 billion farm law, designed to boost crop and dairy subsidies for US farmers by 67 per cent, this sounded a death knell for many Southern farmers who will be unable to compete on the world market against these heavily subsidized US exports. The European Union is guilty of the same crime, and its 2003 reform of the Common Agricultural Policy has done nothing significant to rectify the problem.

We can conclude that the development strategy and policies advocated for the South by the IMF, World Bank, and WTO are unlikely to deliver the UN-sanctioned outcomes, the MDGs.

In contrast, evidence from the history of development of the East Asian NIEs, plus more recent evidence from India and China, suggests that growth with poverty reduction is achievable by a different route— one which assigns *an important place to the role of the state in development, and within this basic approach, encourages appropriate diversity rather than a policy straitjacket*.

Despite World Bank assessments claiming these countries' achievements as evidence of the market's ability to deliver, many analysts within those countries and even in UN organizations argue the contrary (as do some former high-ranking members of the World Bank who have departed from office) (Bello 1997). As Box 12.11 shows, trade liberalization *followed* rather than *preceded* high growth in India and China.

Opinion remains divided. It is argued forcefully by various Southern governments and an international network of NGOs from South and North that progress in the East Asian NIEs, as well as more recently in India and China, has been state—rather than market—led, with a high degree of government intervention in a form of state-assisted capitalism. State planning was crucial, with governments deciding which 'infant industries' to protect with tariffs, and then encouraging exports when selected industries were strong enough to compete internationally. Governments negotiated favourable local content laws and technology transfer.

In the area of finance, they argue that the evidence suggests that states (and of course their people) which went against WC/PWC prescriptions regarding liberalization have weathered the storm of global financial volatility better than those which did not (Bello, Bullard, and Malhotra 2000). Malaysia defied IMF prescriptions and imposed capital controls, and recovered from the crisis of the late 1990s more quickly than others which did not. The lesson was not lost on countries such as Hong Kong and Taiwan. China and India also have capital controls. Chile is often cited as a successful example of WC policies in Latin America, but this isn't strictly true as it too uses capital controls.

Such views on the central role of governments in development are still not shared by the IMF, or by mainstream economists, and dominant figures in the World Bank hierarchy would also have reservations. However, many are willing to accept that the state in success stories has played a positive role in non-sector-specific intervention, for example, education and technical training, maintaining low rates of inflation, government deficits, etc. Regarding capital controls (of which there are many different types), they may concede that these are likely to be successful at best only as a temporary, short-term measure in today's globalized financial market, offering countries a breathing space (Hood 2001).

Despite this ongoing debate, one message is clear: the WC/PWC has not delivered growth with equity; in other words, it has not delivered development. However, development is occurring through other routes. Knowledge of these successes must inform future development paths.

Key points

- Poor performance under structural adjustment programmes led to criticism of the international financial institutions; this was intensified following the financial crises of the late 1990s.

- The international financial institutions and the governments of industrialized economies responded to these criticisms by adopting a new approach that emphasized poverty eradication (the 'post-Washington consensus').

- Although the Poverty Reduction Strategy Papers that are at the heart of the post-Washington consensus approach were intended to be devised by developing countries, the international financial institutions still dictate their terms.

- Debate continues over the appropriate role for the state in development, and the lessons to be learned from the success of the East Asian newly industrializing economies.

Development prerequisites

In this section, the task is to outline some indicative examples of the prerequisites of development in the South, based on the experience of the last two decades. As recognized in the Monterrey Consensus 2002, discussed in the first section, these include both domestic and external/structural elements. In contrast to that Consensus, however, the evidence from the development successes and failures discussed in the third section suggests *that the appropriateness of market-led policies should be considered mindfully, rather than simply assumed.*

Voice for South

There must be a greater voice for Southern states and peoples within the global governance of development (see Box 12.12). Civil society groups have been campaigning on this issue since the mid to late 1990s. The impact of their efforts was clear in the Monterrey Consensus, which referred to the need of the IMF and World Bank to 'continue to enhance the participation of all developing countries . . . in their decision-making' (UN 2002: point 63). To date, this has been confined to capacity building; for example, supporting the efforts of the two African Executive Directors at the IMF, rather than increasing African representation on the Executive Boards of the IMF and World Bank. This must go much further, ideally to ensure that all member states can fairly represent themselves, and to remove veto power from a single country (Thomas 2004). With regard to the WTO, many Southern countries can afford at best only token representation at Geneva, while Northern delegations are extensive and reflect considerable technical expertise. Again, efforts to enhance the competency of Southern delegations are inadequate and divert attention from the bigger issue of representation. Thus, profound imbalance must be redressed.

Voice for the South is not simply a matter of *national representation* within the international arena; importantly it embraces voice for people at the *grass roots* within the South. While the PRSPs in theory include civil society in the making of national development plans, in practice this has not developed very far. If the making of PRSPs develops in the spirit which was intended, then the process would represent a potentially very important step towards genuinely expanding grass-roots participation in the formulation and therefore ownership of development policy in the South (Cheru 2001).

Equity: the neglected element of domestic reform

The IFIs and donor states continue to define domestic reform in the South primarily in terms of reducing corruption, strengthening the rule of law, and fostering an enabling environment for the private sector. These are very important. Yet one of the most important domestic underpinnings for development is *government commitment to growth with equity*.

Differences in income distribution are crucial in explaining interregional differences in poverty reduction (Watkins 1998: 38). In highly unequal societies, such as Brazil, the benefits of growth are distributed highly unequally. This means that unequal countries have to grow much more than more equal countries to bring benefits to the poor. This is supported by recent research of Milanovic on the impact of trade liberalization on poverty reduction, cited above.

Where governments have been committed to growth with equity, as in East Asia, progress has been very encouraging indeed—especially when compared with areas where this has not been so, such as Latin America and SSA. East Asian governments have not been large spenders per capita on health and education, but the quality and target of their spending has ensured that *most people have access to basic services*.

Debt write-off

The forty-two HIPCs (see Appendix 12.1 for map and list) owe 350 billion dollars. Civil society groups have been campaigning since 1996 under the Jubilee 2000 umbrella for debt write-off for these states. So far the response of the North has been inadequate. While the HIPC represents an improvement on what came before in terms of dealing with the debt of the poorest, the fact that it is geared towards *sustainable debt* rather than *speedy total debt cancellation* is a major failing. Only 10 per cent has been written off. No matter

---

Box 12.12 **Making the rules: 'global' in name only**

'. . . the main problem, from the perspective of poor countries . . . is simply that the rules drawn up, and decisions handed down, at the WTO, the IMF and other international tribunals, are drawn up and handed down almost entirely by the rich countries. They have the negotiators, the expertise, the financial leverage, and in some cases (such as the IMF and World Bank) the weighted vote to win virtually every dispute. Even when rich countries clearly violate an agreement, their poor-country counterparts may lack the resources (meaning, often, simply the lawyers) to lodge a successful protest' (Finnegan 2003: 16).

how hard the HIPC countries try, the continuous fall in commodity prices, and the continued deterioration in terms of trade, makes sustainable debt repayment a fanciful idea, and outside their control.

More—and more effective—aid

The sharp declines in aid of the 1990s must be reversed, and aid flows must become more predictable to have maximum effect. Less developed countries cannot mobilize adequate resources domestically to stimulate self-sustained growth. The World Bank has estimated that reaching the MDGs by 2015 will depend on a number of factors. In addition to domestic policy reform in the South recommended by the World Bank, *an additional $40–60 billion per year in assistance will be needed until 2015* (World Bank 2002c). This figure has been criticized as a gross underestimate by Oxfam International, which suggests an extra $100 billion is more realistic (Oxfam 2002a).

How can these extra resources for development be generated? The donor community has historically been long on promises and short on delivery regarding ODA. At Monterrey, they promised to increase annual ODA by $16 billion by 2006—far short of the projected needs. Donor countries must be encouraged to live up to their commitments, and in this respect NGOs have suggested a legally binding treaty to make donors comply with internationally agreed ODA targets. While this may seem politically unrealistic, history shows us that dramatic changes in attitude often occur unexpectedly.

In addition, new ways to fund additional resources can be explored (CAFOD et al. 2003). Several ideas have been put forward. A Tobin Tax—a tax on foreign exchange transactions—could contribute to new development funds (Raffer and Singer 2001; Jetin and de Brunhof 2000). First mooted in the 1970s, it has gained more political momentum in the wake of the global financial crises that have accompanied capital liberalization. The primary aim of the tax would be to reduce the instability which has wreaked havoc with the international financial system and destroyed livelihoods in the South. A secondary benefit of the tax is that it could generate extra resources for development. Another way to raise money for development would be through stronger international cooperation on taxation. For example, it has been

suggested that tax havens result in losses to Western governments of $50 billion per annum—money which could be directed to development (Wabl 2002). A third possibility is the idea of development bonds, launched by United Kingdom Chancellor Gordon Brown (CAFOD et al. 2003). While sceptics will raise concerns about political acceptability, workability, etc. of such measures, supporters will point to the step-by-step building of a new consensus which they see as gradually eroding the legitimacy of neo-liberalism.

When funds are forthcoming from the North, it is imperative that they are not tied to purchases of goods or services of Northern donors, and that they are put to the most effective use possible at point of delivery. UNCTAD (2002a: 222) suggests that there should be selective targeting of areas where the money could make a real difference in poverty alleviation, and highlights agriculture as an obvious target.

Trade for development

The WTO and its supporters must work to make trade supportive of the development concerns of the South, or the institution will never gain legitimacy in the eyes of the majority of its members, and the global trading order will continue to be perceived as structurally tilted against the South.

The WTO's Doha Agenda (WTO 2003c), despite being billed as a development agenda, has not been perceived as such by the South. The Doha Development Round has failed to open the markets of the rich countries to Southern exports; it has not delivered on access to affordable generic medicine; and it has not dealt with Northern farm subsidies and dumping. A multilateral trade system serious about development would have to put Special and Differential Treatment for the South at the heart of its agenda. This has been an issue for the past half-century and it will not go away.

As mentioned above, greater efforts must be made to give the South a bigger role in the decision making of the WTO. This will ensure that the attention of that institution will become more focused on the needs of the Southern countries for special and different treatment within the global trading order. It would also put more pressure on the developed countries to play by the rules which they have drawn up, and put the onus on them to get rid of their protectionism, stop dumping and put an end to domestic subsidies. It would ensure that key issues such commodity price stabilization are addressed (UNCTAD 2002*a*).

The failure to reach agreement in Cancun in September 2003 reflected the South's level of frustration with the North, and consequent unwillingness to go along with new issues while their existing trade problems were sidelined by the North. Importantly, it represented a coming of age of the South within the WTO, as a powerful new bloc of the economically stronger Southern countries—the G20—made its presence felt. Time will tell whether this bloc will work effectively to represent the diverse interests of the entire South, or whether the particular interests of the LDCs will be lost along the way.

Other prerequisites

The list of development prerequisites is long. Aspects not discussed here due to space constraints include,

for example, technology transfer, accountability for the North via a commitment to development index (UNDP 2003*a*: 161), greater South–South cooperation, and the regulation of capital in the interests of development. These can be followed up via the bibliography and further reading.

Key points

The experience of the last two decades suggests the following prerequisites for development:

- an enhanced role for the South in key global institutions;
- commitment to growth with equity, and to poverty eradication;
- the writing-off of the debts of the HIPC;
- additional and more effective aid;
- reform of the trade regime to remove impediments to developing countries' exports.

Conclusion

Over the last two decades, market-led globalization has been substituted for nationally driven development policies in the South. The result has been unsatisfactory: the deepening impoverishment of entire world regions, states, and the majority of humanity, amidst greater but ever concentrated wealth and opportunity. In these circumstances there is a legitimate worry that the current course of globalization may not be appropriate to meet the development challenge that lies ahead. In continuing to advocate this path for the South, the IMF, World Bank, and the WTO and the G7 from whom they take their cue, are promoting policies at odds with the achievement of the MDGs accepted by the UN General Assembly.

It will take far more than a tweaking of the prevailing order to promote growth with equity in the South. Reform within developing countries is a necessary but insufficient condition to achieve these goals; it must extend outside the borders of developing countries to

encompass global economic and financial structures, and the process of governance itself. Only when both parts of the equation, the domestic and the structural/external, are addressed, will there be a chance for the language of the PWC to be translated into sustainable results for the majority of humankind.

But even that may be insufficient. Since 1945, the development challenge has been understood largely in terms of modernization theory or structuralist theory. Both of these approaches allow for gains for the South within the existing global economic order. But to date these gains have not been extensive enough, nor have they reached enough people. Time will tell whether another approach is necessary to promote development for all humanity, one which prioritizes the needs of all human beings rather than capital or a narrow band of humanity. If this is necessary, then it will require a rejection of the current global economic and political order, rather than accommodation of the South within it.

QUESTIONS

1 Why are there so many different terms to refer to the poorer states in the international system?

2 Why did the poorer states find the United Nations a more congenial environment than the International Monetary Fund and the World Bank in the early post-war decades?

3 Explain modernization theory and structuralist theory.

4 Why did the developing countries call for a New International Economic Order in 1973 and what did they hope to achieve?

5 What was the 'Washington Consensus'?

6 How far does the World Bank's recent emphasis on national Poverty Reduction Strategy Papers represent a change of policy on development matters?

7 What are the Millennium Development Goals and to what extent are they owned by North and South?

8 What is the significance of the Monterrey Consensus?

9 Why has trade liberalization not delivered expected results for the least developed countries?

10 How could financial resources for development be increased?

11 What do you think are the most important prerequisites for development in the South, and why?

FURTHER READING

General

Chossudovsky, M. (1997), *The Globalisation of Poverty: Impacts of IMF and World Bank Reforms* (London: Zed and Penang: Third World Network). The author draws on examples from the Third World and Eastern Europe to provide a lucid and cogent critique of IFI policies.

Hoogevelt, A. (1997), *Globalisation and the Postcolonial World: The New Political Economy of Development* (Basingstoke: Macmillan). A historically and theoretically well-informed comparison of the impacts of globalization and the responses to it in Sub-Saharan Africa, the Middle East, East Asia, and Latin America.

Trade

Barratt Brown, M. (1993), *Fair Trade* (London: Zed Books).

World Bank Institute (2003), *Development Outreach*, July, whole edition on Trade for Development, **www1.worldbank.org/devoutreach/**. Interesting collection of accessible articles from different viewpoints.

Investment

Picciotto, S., and Mayne, R. (eds.) (1999), *Regulating International Business: Beyond Liberalization* (Basingstoke: Macmillan).

Madeley, J. (1999), *Big Business, Poor Peoples: The Impact of Transnational Corporations on the World's Poor* (London: Zed).

Aid

Randel, J., German, T. and Ewing, D. (eds.) (2000), *The Reality of Aid 2000: An Independent Review of Poverty Reduction and Development Assistance* (London: Earthscan).

Health

Kim, J., Millen, J., Irwin, A. and Gershman, J. (eds.) (2000), *Dying for Growth: Global Inequality and the Health of the Poor* (Monroe, Me.: Common Courage Press). An excellent reader on effects of WC on health.

Farmer, P. (2003), *Pathologies of Power: Health, Human Rights and the War on the Poor* (Berkeley and Los Angeles: University of California Press).

Development

Preston, P. (1996), *Development Theory: An Introduction* (Oxford: Blackwell). A good general reader.

Sachs, G. (1993), *The Development Dictionary* (London: Zed Books). Thought-provoking definitions which challenge mainstream analyses.

Development and security

Duffield, M. (2001), *Global Governance and the New Wars* (London: Zed). An original and fascinating book that examines the current framing by donors of the link between security and development.

WEB LINKS

Southern NGOs/Independent Research Institutes

www.twnside.org.sg   Third World Network (based in Malaysia).

www.focusweb.org   Focus on the Global South (based in Thailand).

www.choike.org   Choike: a portal on Southern civil societies (based in Uruguay).

www.seatini.org   SEATINI: Southern and Eastern African Trade Information and Negotiations Institute (based in Zimbabwe).

Southern Intergovernmental Organizations

www.g77.org   G77.

www.nam.gov.za/   NAM.

www.southcentre.org   South Centre.

Northern NGOs

www.eurodad.org   European Network on Debt and Development.

www.brettonwoods.org   Bretton Woods Project: scrutinizes and attempts to influence the World Bank and International Monetary Fund (IMF).

International Organizations

www.imf.org   IMF.

www.worldbank.org   IBRD.

www.wto.org/english/tratop_e/dda_e.htm   Doha Development Agenda.

www.unctad.org   UNCTAD.

Appendix 12.1 HIPC Countries

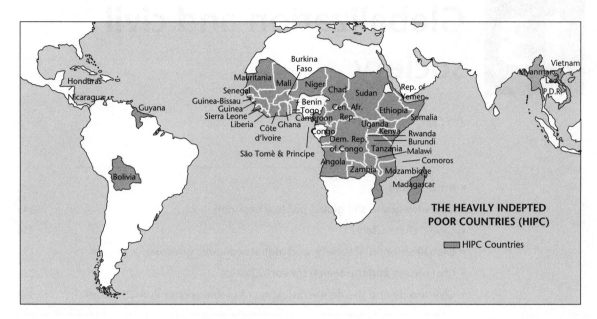

THE HEAVILY INDEPTED
POOR COUNTRIES (HIPC)

HIPC Countries

Source: **www.worldbank.org/hipc/about/map/map.html**

13 Globalization and civil society

Marc Williams

READER'S GUIDE

In the last decade, political scientists and political economists have given increasing attention to the role of civil society actors in the global political economy. This recent awareness of the activities of civil society activism does not, of course, mean that such actors were previously absent from the workings of the global political economy. Nevertheless, it appears that as a consequence of globalization and the reduction in East–West tensions that civil society actors have been playing increasingly important roles in the governance of the global political economy. This chapter attempts to assess the significance of civil society in the contemporary global political economy. It does so in three stages. The first stage consists of an identification of civil society and civil society actors. This section outlines the usefulness of the concept 'civil society' and explores the diversity of civil society actors. Underlying the new focus on civil society activism is a recognition that globalization has ushered in profound quantitative and qualitative changes and that these developments have transformed the structures and processes of global governance in important ways. The second section of the chapter explores how and why civil society actors have been brought to the forefront of contemporary debate. The third section focuses on the impacts of civil society on the global political economy, looking in particular at different forms of engagement by civil society actors in the world economy and assesses the significance of these activities.

Introduction

In April 2000, Joseph Stiglitz, a Nobel Prize-winning economist, and former chief economist and senior vice-president of the World Bank wrote,

Next week's meeting of the International Monetary Fund will bring to Washington D.C., many of the same demonstrators who trashed the World Trade Organization in Seattle last fall. They'll say the IMF is arrogant. They'll say the IMF doesn't really listen to the developing countries it is supposed to help. They'll say the IMF is secretive and insulated from democratic accountability. They'll say the IMF's economic 'remedies' often make things worse—turning slowdowns into recessions and recessions into depressions. (Stiglitz 2000)

Stiglitz conceded that the demonstrators did have a point, an opinion in sharp contrast with the views of most mainstream commentators.

The actions of anti-globalization protesters present a highly visible face of civil society activism in the world economy. Nevertheless, although receiving extensive media coverage, such actions represent a fragment of the various ways in which civic associations have engaged with the contemporary global economy. Violent anti-globalization protests capture attention but fail to indicate the myriad ways in which civil society impacts on global economic activity.

The relative importance of civil society for developments in the world economy is a new topic for students of global political economy (GPE). Until recently the study of international political economy (IPE) with its focus on the state and the market gave almost no attention to transnational actors other than to large international firms. But two tensions created by the shifting context of globalization have clearly illustrated the array of non-state and non-corporate actors that play a role in the global political economy.

Within the global political economy globalization has generated conflict among state and non-state actors, and prompted a search for regulatory frameworks to lessen the impact of globalizing processes. This process of internationalizing national economies creates a search for new forms of transnational governance and regulation. Central to this process has been the rise of social movements, non-governmental organizations (NGOs), transnational networks, and other actors linking civil society across national boundaries. Civil society actors have presented challenges to the existing practices of the global economy and in particular argue for the development of alternative forms of governance.

The expansion of global finance and the extension of trade rules create another set of tensions. As economic activity becomes increasingly liberalized it ignites a conflict between supporters of further economic liberalization and domestic interest groups intent on protecting national and sectional interests from further economic liberalization. For example, the strengthening of the international trade regime has provided the political space in which social movement activists have sought to challenge the liberal ideology of free trade (see Winham, Chapter 4 in this volume).

The increased visibility of civil society actors and the attention to civil society by policy makers and analysts is not sufficient in itself to indicate the importance of civil society in the determination of outcomes in the global political economy. Questions concerning the importance of civil society actors for an understanding of change in the global political economy are linked to debates concerning the meaning of civil society and the impact of globalization on patterns of political authority. Therefore, before surveying different forms of engagement by civil society actors in the world economy this chapter examines the concept of civil society and assesses the extent to which globalizing processes have changed the political conditions under which various actors participate in the global political economy.

Civil society and the global political economy

Civil society is an old concept but has recently been revived in discussions of international relations and international political economy. However, recent attention by political scientists to civil society exhibits considerable disagreement among them concerning the concept and its applicability to political economy. This observation prompts a number of questions. What is meant by civil society? Is there a global civil society? Why have analysts begun to employ the term in the past decade?

What is civil society?

The idea of civil society has variously been traced back to the Roman historian and political thinker Cicero

(Thomas 1998) and the English political theorist John Locke (Kaldor 2003). In common with many concepts used by political scientists there is no agreed definition of the term. Contemporary confusion over the meaning of civil society is perhaps, traceable to the chequered history of the concept (see Box 13.1). Varying uses of the term in contemporary discourse, to some extent, reflect the fact that it has no settled historical meaning but has changed its meaning over time. The search for a single, dominant meaning of the term is therefore a fruitless and pointless exercise. This statement is not meant to suggest that we should not discuss the intellectual heritage of the terms we use but rather to make the point that most important political concepts have complex histories, and their meanings are frequently disputed. Instead of

---

Box 13.1 Civil society: evolution of a concept

The concept of civil society has been utilized by many political thinkers but is particularly associated with the writings of Cicero, Locke, Hegel, and Gramsci, and it is through attention to the meanings these writers attached to the term that we can see both the varied ways in which it has been used and the common features attendant on its usage. The modern usage of the term civil society has its origins in the writings of the Roman philosopher Cicero. He distinguished between a state of affairs in which law prevailed and one in which it did not. In the former case a civilized political community could develop whereas in the latter it was not possible to develop the bonds of 'civic partnership' (Thomas 1998: 50). The early modern political theorists rejuvenated the concept of civil society in their search for the most appropriate political forms of republican administration and justice. The English philosopher John Locke used the term to signify a society in which relations were governed by a social contract. Thus, in Locke's formulation, political society is coterminous with civil society insofar as the rule of law has been established. Thus the rule of law provides the foundation for civil association. With the German philosopher Hegel, the concept was altered in a significant way. For both Cicero and Locke no separation was made between

the state and civil society. Indeed, it could be said that civil society represented a particular (preferable) type of state. It was one in which a person could best attain the good life. In his formulation Hegel sharply delineated the state from civil society. According to Hegel, there were three key social institutions—the family, civil society, and the state. Civil society exists as an intermediate realm between the family and the state. For Hegel, the state was the highest form of social institution and the institution most conducive to the realization of freedom. In his thought civil society played a crucial role in the development of the state. With the creation of the state civil society did not disappear but remained essential to the transformation in political relations through, for example, the development of legal systems to protect the rights of individuals. In the early part of the twentieth century, the Italian Marxist Antonio Gramsci developed his idea of civil society to distinguish between the sphere of coercion and domination represented by the state and the sphere of civil society in which hegemony is maintained through consensual rather than coercive mechanisms. As this brief survey shows, the concept has evolved from being initially associated with the state or one form of state to its current formulation where civil society is juxtaposed to the state.

searching for a single meaning it is best to accept that such terms carry a variety of meanings. It is in this sense that this chapter explores the concept of civil society and the related concept of global civil society. Essentially therefore we have to note two features of the concept. First, the changing historical usages of the term, and second, any fundamental, core meanings associated with its use over time.

Current usage of the term civil society builds on and is indeed indebted to its historical heritage. In contemporary usage the term exhibits four core features. The first common feature of definitions of civil society is the reference to civil society as the free association of a group of individuals in pursuit of a common aim. In this sense, the term is indebted to Cicero and Locke with their emphasis on the rule of law. In other words, a society founded on law indicates one in which consent rather than coercion is the norm. Membership in civil society is therefore voluntary and is not based on coercion. It can be argued, for example, that membership in some forms of state (especially in authoritarian and totalitarian states) may be maintained through the coercive apparatus of statehood. In contradistinction civil society implies voluntary association.

This emphasis on the importance of voluntary relations takes us to the second feature of contemporary usages of civil society, namely, the emphasis on civil society as a sphere distinct from the state. In this respect contemporary usage follows the distinction made by Hegel. The private character of civic associations is not, however, always easy to sustain in the real world. The boundaries between official or state activity and non-official or civil society activity may not always be easy to demarcate and maintain; for example, some NGOs have a close association with states and the literature on NGOs refers to 'government-organized non-governmental organizations' and 'quasi-non-governmental organizations' (Gordenker and Weiss 1996: 20–1). Nevertheless, the non-state character of civil society is an important feature of contemporary uses of the term. Civil society in this sense refers to a voluntary political space that is not part of the formal state apparatus, and is frequently portrayed as being 'below the state' (Wapner 1996: 158).

A third area of agreement in current usage concerns the identification of civil society as a sphere distinct

from the market. Civil society is frequently distinguished from the commercial or profit-oriented realm. The term most frequently used to describe civil society is the non-profit (or not-for-profit) sector. Once again this distinction can become difficult to sustain. For example, are business lobby groups part of civil society? Organizations representative of business interests are not in themselves profit-making entities and yet they represent firms that are driven by the profit motive.

Despite the difficulties attendant on drawing firm lines between state and non-state, market and non-market activities, these features are standard in most definitions of civil society. From the above, it should be apparent that civil society is not a single entity but rather a political space inhabited by a variety of civic associations. Thus we can define civil society as that voluntary sphere in which individuals come together from outside the state and the market in order to promote common interests. It is 'the process through which individuals negotiate, argue, struggle against or agree with each other and with the centres of political and economic authority' (Kaldor 2003: 585).

Apart from this consensus on the four main attributes of civil society there is one further issue that frequently arises in contemporary discussions of civil society. The term civil society and its historical associations with the law give rise to an expectation that civil society represents a space of civility and a channel for democracy. But, to what extent is civil society civil or civilized? On the one hand, much contemporary thinking emphasizes the link between civil society and democracy. That is, emphasis is given to the importance of civil society in the construction of democratic politics. We can observe an emphasis on this positive role of civil society as a contributor to democracy both in the attention given to the development of civil society by Western governments and international organizations through democratization schemes, and in the role played by civil society in the 1980s in Eastern Europe and Latin America in opposition to oppressive regimes. These developments, notwithstanding, it is important to note that certain groups in civil society may be far from civil. Civil society, after all, includes fascist and racist groups with no commitment to a democratic agenda. And one would be hard pressed to find evidence of the democratic credentials of terrorist groups such as al-Qaeda, or criminal organizations operating across national boundaries.

Civil society organizations

The definition of civil society as a political space implies the existence of civil society actors. And, indeed, much of the analytical focus in political economy is on the role and activities of civil society actors. It therefore becomes important to identify the range of actors engaged in civil society. The absence of a single definition of civil society is reflected in the array of terms used for civil society actors, and the absence of definitional clarity concerning the groups selected for scrutiny. There is, nevertheless, agreement that a variety of actors engage in civil activity within states and across national borders. Given the diversity of terms used to describe actors in civil society this chapter will use two generic terms for convenience—civil society actors and civic associations.

Within the vast array of actors engaged in civil society, two organizational forms are given most prominence in the literature—NGOs and social movements. An NGO can be defined as an organization with a formal structure formed by private individuals for the purpose of engaging in non-profit-making activities. Non-governmental organizations vary from small, national organizations to large, international or transnational organizations. From the perspective of the global political economy both national and international NGOs may attempt to exert influence over policy making. NGOs are important organizational nodes in social movements.

The term social movement refers to a collection of individuals and groups united on the basis of shared interests and identities in the collective pursuit of common political goals. The formation and development of a social movement depends on the existence of groups or people who mobilize resources in pursuit of a certain cause and who determine the way in which these resources are pooled and directed towards social change. Social movements are developed in an attempt to effect social change. Social movements are not homogeneous, and any particular social movement is comprised of diverse

organizations at local, national, and transnational levels. Nevertheless, despite the variety in, for example, size, resources, ideology, activities, and organizational forms a certain commonality of values and commitment to a set of goals enables us to conceive of the existence of a social movement.

This diversity among NGOs and social movements is reflected in a variety of ways. Civil society actors can be differentiated according to their area of expertise, focus or interest, size and resources, geography and level of organization, aims, tactics, and strategies.

Expertise

In terms of membership and policy focus, civic associations extend into most if not all areas of social life. Examples of civic associations include, among others, academic and research institutes, business lobby groups, community-based organizations, charitable foundations, consumer groups, development groups, environmental groups, human rights organizations, religious organizations, social reformist organizations, trade unions, and women's groups. Social movements with a focus on the world economy include the environmental movement, human rights movement, labour movement, and the women's movement.

Focus, size, and resources

Civic associations vary enormously in size and resources, from grass-roots organizations working in villages in the developing world to sophisticated NGOs or trade unions with large memberships and financial and human resources adequate to their needs. Furthermore, civic associations may pool their resources and increase their size through engaging in network activity (Keck and Sikkink 1998). Once again, no single organizational form exists with some networks operating according to hierarchical principles—for example, the Roman Catholic Church—and others based on non-hierarchical principles—for example, the Peoples' Global Action (PGA) a network of anti-globalization groups. As far as funding and resources are concerned, enormous disparities exist for both national and international civil society groups. The issue of resources must of course be seen not in absolute terms but in relation to the goals and objectives of the civil society actor. While some groups are well funded and have access to resources adequate for their tasks, other groups are poorly funded and resourced.

While it is not possible to make any generalizations on this point, the resource issue is particularly symptomatic of another difference among civil society actors, namely the geographic differentiation between Southern and Northern civic associations. On the whole civic associations from the Western, industrialized world are better provisioned than their counterparts from the developing world. This disparity of financial resources and human capital is often referred to in terms of the necessity to build the capacity of Southern civic associations. The resource issue is critical to success in achieving outcomes since it is difficult to participate effectively in global politics in the absence of adequate resources.

Level of engagement

Civil society is composed of actors at the grass roots, national, regional, and international levels. Civic associations may operate at more than one level and may also over time alter the level at which they operate. When analysing the global political economy it is important to examine the activities of groups at the domestic level as well as at the international level. Civil society actors in the contemporary global political economy should not be viewed solely as transnational civic associations since the ability of a national civic association to affect the foreign economic policies of its national government can also be of importance in determining outcomes.

Engagement with governments and attitudes towards liberal capitalism

Some groups are interested in becoming a part of the policy dialogue in order to influence developments through a direct engagement in the political process while other groups reject such forms of engagement. In examining the activities of civil society groups, we can distinguish between conformist, reformist, and radical attitudes and behaviour (Scholte, O'Brien, and Williams 1999). This division reflects different attitudes to the prevailing global economic structure and the current dominant norms of liberal capitalism. Conformist civil society organizations are generally supportive of the status quo and focus their efforts at

bolstering it and initiating change that maintains the underlying principles and norms of the existing economic order. Business associations, philanthropic foundations, and research institutes tend to fall into this category. Reformist civic associations are based on an acceptance of the fundamental premises of liberal capitalism but recognition that the present system is flawed and requires reform in order to be sustainable in the long term. Examples of organizations in this category include academic bodies, consumer advocates, human rights groups, and labour unions. Radical groups are opposed, in principle, to liberal capitalism and seek a transformation of the system. In this category are anarchist groups, some environmentalist groups, and religious fundamentalists. Conformists and reformists are more likely to seek (and achieve) inclusion in decision making, and also to engage in effective lobbying.

Tactics

Some groups direct their activities to governmental agencies and firms while others engage instead with the public. These various forms of engagement arise from varying capacities to access decision makers and from the attitude of the civic association to dialogue with policy makers. Ottaway (2001: 273) distinguishes between inclusion in decision making, lobbying activities, and confrontation. Some groups may use more than one approach depending on the issue and their access to governmental officials. One recurrent theme in much of the literature on civil society is the importance of the media and the use of modern technologies in generating publicity and mobilizing opinion. But even with these tactics caution has to be exercised since not all civil society actors use these methods. Indeed, some civil society organizations do not possess the capacity to use the Internet or to engage the media in a sophisticated manner.

Key points

- Civil society is that sphere of social life that exists outside the state and the market.
- There are a variety of actors in civil society.
- Civil society organizations differ in form, size, resources, tactics, and objectives.

Global civil society?

The existence of cross-national linkages between national civic associations, and the direction of attention by civil society actors to the international activities of states, firms, and international organizations, have led some analysts to conclude that it is no longer sufficient to speak solely of civil society in national terms. A number of different terms have been used to describe the transborder activities of civic associations. Some writers use the term international civil society (Otto 1996) and others mention transnational civil society (Edwards 2001: 2). However, the term most frequently used in this context is global civil society (Lipschutz 1992; Macdonald 1994). Since the term global civil society has become the most widely used one, this chapter will follow conventional usage. It is, nevertheless, important to note that this term remains controversial. Some writers evince scepticism concerning the applicability of the term global civil society for two principal reasons (Edwards 2001; Germain and Kenny 1998; Thomas 1998). On the one hand it is argued that the concept of civil society is only applicable at the domestic level because an internationalized state does not exist. Civil society does not and cannot exist at the global level in the absence of a global state. From this perspective, civil society requires the existence of a state to bring it into being. On the other hand, some contend that although transnational interactions have increased the depth of interactions at the global level 'there are few global citizens to constitute a global civil society in the deepest meaning of that term' (Edwards 2001: 2).

Other political scientists, although accepting that civil society is defined by its relationship to the state, nevertheless maintain that 'Civil society can become globalized to the extent that society increasingly represents itself globally, across nation-state boundaries, through the formation of global institutions' (Shaw 1994: 650). The term global civil society implies the existence of meaningful interactions across state borders by civil society actors. Moreover, it signifies that this activity has an element of globalism. Within the International Relations literature terms such as world, global, and transnational are frequently used interchangeably to signify relations that are in some sense beyond conventional interstate or international relations. Given this imprecision it is fruitless to search for any meaningful difference between the terms transnational civil society and global civil society since such distinctions reflect the preferences of scholars rather than any agreement on specific criteria that distinguishes 'transnational' from 'global'. What these terms have in common is the sense that the relations they describe are in significant ways quantitatively and qualitatively different from interstate relations.

Thus the term global civil society signifies the existence of a sphere of activity that cannot be confined within a framework in which political relations are dominated by the presence of states. For Lipschutz, global civil society as a space for political interaction is one 'focused on the self-conscious constructions of networks of knowledge and action, by decentred local actors' (1992: 390). In what senses, if any, is there a voluntary sphere in which individuals come together from outside the state and the market in order to promote common interests that also in important ways transcends the boundaries of states? And, which civic associations inhabit this sphere?

There are a number of ways in which it can be claimed that a global civil society exists. One way of accounting for the existence of a global civil society is to note the intensity and extensity of interconnections between civic associations transcending domestic politics. In other words, if civil society at the domestic level is based on frequent and extensive interactions among civic associations, then global civil society is based on a dense network of regular and wide-ranging interactions among groups and organizations operating across national borders. In other words, the patterns and forms of interaction are global. Recent academic work has explored the activities of transnational advocacy networks (Keck and Sikkink 1998), global social movements (O'Brien et al. 2000; Williams 2003), and NGOs (Clark, Friedman, and Hochstetler 1998) in the construction of global civil society. The international activities of non-governmental organizations, the development of social movement activity transcending national boundaries, and the growth of advocacy networks suggest the emergence of civil society beyond the state. Although most NGOs work solely at the domestic level, NGOs are also key organizations in constituting a global civil society. Non-governmental organizations work at a number of different levels in order to influence the structures of global governance. They 'create and activate global networks, participate in multilateral arenas, facilitate interstate cooperation, act within states and enhance public participation' (O'Brien et al. 2000: 16). An *advocacy network* brings together a number of NGOs and grassroots organizations mobilizing to influence policy makers. A *global social movement* is one that operates across national boundaries as well as within the domestic sphere.

A second way in which a global civil society can be posited concerns the existence of issues that are intrinsically transnational or global in character (Turner 1998: 32). There are a plethora of issues from the AIDS/HIV pandemic to global warming and human rights protection that cannot be envisaged as the preserve of a single nation. Insofar as various civil society groups and organizations concern themselves with these issues then a global civil society exists. For example, the development of international law, especially international human rights law is increasingly founded on the notion of common and collective interests across national frontiers. And within this process, transnational civil society actors have been prominent. The political campaign that resulted in the creation of the International Criminal Court provides an excellent example of such activism (see Pace and Panganiban 2002).

Civil society is global in a third sense when civic associations have shared transnational or global goals. Undoubtedly many international campaigns by NGOs represent interests shaped by national considerations. However, it is also possible to find evidence of common interest across national borders. For some such solidarity gives birth to the concept of the transnational or global citizen (Otto 1996: 128; Solomon 2002: 74). But even if such notions of cosmopolitan citizenship appear far-fetched the campaigns of, particularly, human rights advocates and supporters of development assistance indicate a transworld solidarity that is not reducible to national sentiments. Furthermore, groups that link individuals on the basis of ethnicity, gender, and sexual preference, for example, are premissed on a different ethic from that behind national identity. Global civil society thus exists in a normative and ideational sense. Some groups and organizations clearly identify with a global or transnational ethos and transcend the territorial loyalties inscribed in the state system.

The three features discussed above—a transnational network of interconnections and global interactions; shared issues; and common goals—suggest the existence of a global civil society. A global civil society reflects a combination of global issues and transnational actors. Because the agenda of contemporary politics does not and, indeed, cannot stop at the boundaries of the nation state, the growth of policy interdependencies among countries has created connections not only at the official level but also among social actors. In other words, increasing interconnectedness includes economic, political, cultural, and social dimensions. Therefore, citizen attention and organizational energies are focused outside the state as well as within its boundaries. In short, global civil society refers to the transnational organization of civil society actors.

The first part of this chapter has provided evidence of the existence of civil society and civil society actors in the global political economy. The next stage suggests why global civil society has developed and how it affects the global political economy.

The emergence of global civil society

The organization of citizen activity across national boundaries is not new. For example, the creation of the International Red Cross and the anti-slavery movement are two instances of transnational citizen mobilization in the nineteenth century. But the creation of a global civil society is a recent development in world politics. The growth of a space for transnational voluntary association and the concomitant rise in transborder civic activism is the result of a number of factors. The emergence of global civil society is in part the result of changes in domestic politics and the response of individuals and groups to these changes. It is also a result of structural change in the global political economy and the activities of political actors seeking to shape their own destinies in light of these developments. Attention has to be given to changes at both the domestic and international levels since neither perspective individually fully accounts for this complex phenomenon.

A focus at the domestic level highlights the role of agency, and sees civic associations as the main actors. It emphasizes self-organization, autonomy, and transnational 'interconnectedness'. Such a perspective gives greater weight to 'bottom-up' or 'grassroots' processes in explaining how global civil society functions. On the other hand, a focus on developments at the global level provides for greater emphasis on the structural transformations created by the globalization of economics and the internationalization of politics.

Domestic politics and the emergence of global civil society

In looking at the domestic level three factors are generally conceived as the main driving forces behind the emergence of a global civil society—the revival of the concept of domestic civil society, the changing nature of the state, and new ideas about what constitutes good governance.

The revival of the concept of civil society in national societies was an important development in the emergence of a global civil society. The concept of civil society resurfaced in Eastern Europe and Latin America during the 1980s. Kaldor (1999) argues that a deliberate engagement with the concept of civil society led to the emergence of new social networks in direct opposition to the state. The activities of Eastern European dissidents and Latin American human rights groups challenged the primacy of the state. These developments although taking place simultaneously were largely separate in their challenges to authoritarian regimes. Nevertheless, they shifted civil society from an analytical construct to the activist realm. Moreover, as the concept moved to the activist sphere it also transcended national boundaries. For example, the association between peace and human rights generated by the civic discontent of 1980s Cold War totalitarian societies was crucial to this revived civil society in Eastern Europe. Peace and human rights are intrinsically global issues, and as social movements and citizen groups organized around these issues the civil society associations

developed a transnational character. Moreover, with the end of the Cold War many transitional societies have accorded an important role to civil society organizations in the process of economic and political reconstruction.

A second factor located at the domestic level is linked with the changing nature of the state. It has been argued that the decline in welfare provisions, as the Keynesian state was replaced with the neo-liberal state (see Hay, Chapter 9 in this volume), best explains the emergence of transnational civil society associations. In these circumstances 'change from below' has been the result of a growing awareness by citizens of the necessity of using non-state associations in order to achieve political goals (Lipschutz 1992: 419). Lipschutz (1992: 391) further contends that a new form of collective identity emerges in which new social movements construct 'imagined communities' to facilitate the creation of many heterogeneous transnational political networks within global civil society to challenge the nation-state system.

Lipschutz's arguments were constructed to explain developments in the advanced industrialized countries but a related development took place in the developing world where as a result of structural adjustment policies the state became increasingly incapable of providing welfare services. Into this vacuum stepped the non-profit sector. Increased delivery of basic needs such as education and health by NGOs also resulted in an expanded advocacy role in response to perceived alienation. The so-called post-Washington consensus that replaced neo-liberal policies in the late 1990s accorded an important role to civil society organizations in the construction of development policies and the provision of development services (Edwards 2001: 2).

In both the developed and developing world, the rise of global civil society has been coterminous with the rise of neo-liberalism. In the developed world, the neo-liberal agenda resulted in the erosion of welfare rights, which populations had previously considered sacrosanct, while in the developing world neo-liberal policies rolled back state protection and exposed many people to degrees of economic vulnerability they had never envisaged as possible. Whether civic associations were created as advocacy organizations or in a service capacity, an expansion in the number of civil society actors occurred in the 1980s and 1990s.

These largely national organizations were brought into contact through the similarities of experience and the development of analyses that linked national performance to global changes.

A third factor (linked to the previous two) relates to change in what can be termed the ideational sphere. The discourse of good governance (Clark 2001: 20) has helped to shape citizens' perceptions of the limitations of official agencies. Scepticism concerning the adequacy of official services has sparked a rise in citizen mobilization. The growth of domestic civic associational activity rarely remains focused solely on the national sphere given the increased interdependence between national societies. A good case in point is the Asian financial crisis.

Global structural change and the emergence of global civil society

Here we highlight three main developments to account for the growth in global civil society—global economic integration; advances in communications technology; and the renewed impetus given to international politics by the end of the Cold War. Together these created a new global space which placed constraints upon state sovereignty from above. These structural changes at the global level have created a 'space' for autonomous political participation, and a 'need' for governance on a global level to match unchecked economic globalization. In this sense globalization caused civil society to 'go global'.

There are many facets of global economic integration that have spurred the rise in transborder citizen activism. Globalization involves economic, political, and cultural change, and civil society groups have mobilized in relation to all three sectors. Increased economic integration has sparked fear of the loss of economic sovereignty. This is exemplified in the reaction to the creation of the North American Free Trade Agreement (NAFTA). The negotiations leading to NAFTA presented an opportunity for citizen action and protest. The organized campaign by civil society against the proposed OECD Multilateral Agreement on Investment (MAI) is another example of civic action in response to perceived erosion of sovereignty. But transnational social movement activity in response to economic globalization has also been spurred by other concerns. The volatility of financial markets, for example, and the financial crises affecting Mexico, parts of Asia, Russia, and Argentina in the past decade (see Pauley, Chapter 7 in this volume) have all sparked the mobilization of citizen groups on a transnational basis. Furthermore, the fruits and rewards of globalization have not been distributed equally, with the result that social justice issues have spurred transnational activity by civil society organizations. For example, the deterioration of conditions in the developing world drew increasing attention to the Third World debt problem, and gave rise to a major initiative by transnational civil society actors. The Jubilee 2000 coalition brought together development, religious, and human rights activists in response to the Third World debt crisis. And, the increased prominence of global economic institutions has stimulated a diverse array of transnational civil society organizations to engage directly with these global economic institutions. This is a direct result of the enhanced role given to the International Monetary Fund (IMF) and World Bank in the 1980s and the strengthening of the rule-making authority of organizations such as the World Trade Organization (WTO) in the 1990s.

Moreover, cultural globalization is resisted by a number of groups who resent the erosion of what they see as important national or religious values. This example highlights the contradictory nature of the relationship between globalization and civil society. Civil society actors use the most sophisticated of modern technologies to argue against the spread of ideas and technology.

Innovations in communications and information technology facilitate the organizational energies of civil society organizations. One result of technological change has been the decline in the cost of collecting and disseminating information. The cost of communications has been significantly reduced with widespread access to the Internet, fax, and email and, furthermore, relatively inexpensive air travel makes it easier for social movement activists to travel to conferences, workshops, and other meetings. The declining cost of communications also signals a reduction in state control over sources of information. Access to and ability to disseminate information at relatively low costs provides an alternative source to official viewpoints. New technologies such as the Internet make it increasingly difficult for states to block access to alternative sources of information. Another result of technological change has been the speed with which information is transmitted. Instead of taking days (or weeks or months) for a letter to arrive, information can now be transmitted instantaneously. This enables groups to organize across boundaries and mobilize resources. This rapidity and ease of information increases the available resources at the disposal of civil society. It facilitates the educational, campaigning, and lobbying activities of civic associations. The speed of action, reaction, and mobilization is increased through real time accounts of events. For example, the Zapatistas utilized the Internet to stimulate political mobilization against the status quo and disseminate alternatives to the prevailing institutions and structures of governance (Cleaver 1998; Reinke 2002).

For some analysts, the recent emergence of global civil society is linked with the decline of sovereignty, brought about by structural changes in the international system. Some analysts emphasize the importance of the end of the Cold War in this development (Marden 1997: 48; Keane 2001: 23). And others suggest the development of 'multilayered governance',

that is, regulation is moving away from a focus on the state and is increasingly located at local, national, regional, and global levels (Scholte 2000*a*: 185). Thus the decline of sovereignty suggests that the emergence of global civil society is linked to the development of global collective identities (Williams 2003).

Key points

- Global civil society refers to the transnational political sphere in which civic associations negotiate, discuss and lobby on transnational issues.
- Global civil society arose because of:
  the revival of the concept of civil society at the national level;
  the changing nature of the state;
  the development of the doctrine of good governance;
  changes in the global economy;
  innovations in communications and information technology;
  changing world order.

Globalization, civil society, and global economic governance

We have noted the existence of civil society and the emergence of global civil society but we cannot assume that civil society actors play important roles in the structures of global governance without first examining the impact of globalization on national and international policy making. Before looking in detail at the ways in which civil society actors engage in the global political economy it is necessary to enquire into the changing structures of global governance. In what ways and to what extent has globalization changed the relative positions of state and non-state actors in the world economy?

Globalization is variously defined and understood but can be perceived as comprising material and normative dimensions. It can be defined as describing sets of processes—technological, financial, economic, social, environmental, and cultural—that are increasing

global interconnectedness and interdependence. Globalization thus alters the context of economic and political problems and generates new concerns about the development and implementation of economic and political agreements. If governance is understood as the sum of the many ways that individuals and institutions, public and private, manage their common affairs (Commission on Global Governance 1995), it follows that globalization has important repercussions for national and international governance. While the state and the firm remain important actors within governance structures, civic associations have increasingly become visible players. And their activities are best understood in terms of their interactions with states and corporate actors.

The state remains a significant actor in the construction and maintenance of global governance arrangements but its role is changing. On the one hand, even if territorial space is 'shrinking' the state retains formal control of territorial space and is the legitimate source of domestic authority. In other words, states are positioned in the global political economy in ways that have crucial consequences for the organization of economic and political activity. They continue to perform an organizational role for 'internal affairs' within national, regional, and global structures. And they retain the legal right to negotiate and ratify multilateral treaties. Moreover, there is ample evidence of the significance of the state's role as architects and drivers of globalization (Kymlicka 2000; Weiss 1997).

On the other hand, globalization has had an impact on the state and therefore its ability to negotiate and implement international agreements. For many governments globalization means a forced transformation in the way they define their existence as a state and the authority and power that they wield. States have become increasingly permeable to influences and transactions outside their borders and as such their sovereignty and ability to control these transnational events are declining, with a resulting inability to offset the negative and unwanted impacts of globalization. For example, the emergence of intensified global competitive pressures has enforced a financial discipline on governments that to a large degree have taken economic development out of their control (Held et al. 1999: 13). Most states today actively seek foreign investment and compete with each other to provide conditions conducive to the operation of transnational corporations. The emergence of neo-liberal ideology and the competition state thus signifies a changing world order in which some corporations have more (economic) power than the states whose borders they operate across, and are in a position to use their investment power to dictate the rules they are willing to follow.

Under conditions of globalization, corporate actors are playing increasingly important roles in opening up national economies to the forces of the market. As key agents of globalization they are also important in trying to influence the emerging patterns of governance. They do so through three mechanisms—market power, pressure group politics, and private authority. Transnational corporations exert market power through their control over assets held to be valuable by states and individuals. They engage in pressure group politics within domestic political systems and at the international level. Firms attempt to exert influence over decisions made by states and international organizations. Corporations have been instrumental in trying to control the agenda through the increased mobilization of national and international networks and umbrella organizations to articulate a business perspective on globalization. Private authority refers to the situation in which firms exercise legitimate decision-making power over a particular issue area. Cutler, Haufler, and Porter (1999) have identified six mechanisms through which private authority is exercised: industry norms; coordination service firms (for example, bond ratings); production alliances; cartels; business associations; and private regimes. Of course, a diversity of corporate interests and strategies reflecting national, industry, and sectoral differences, rather than a monolithic or single corporate interest, is visible in the global economy.

How have civil society actors engaged with the changing forms of the state and the shifting nature of corporate power? How have these changes spurred civic associations to engage with the global political economy? Developments in two areas—regulation and liberalization—provide a context within which to understand the impact of globalization on civil society and global governance. Regulation in this context refers to both material and ideational change.

Economic globalization has had a fundamental impact on patterns of regulation, with movement from a system in which national laws were primary to one in which some regulatory activities have been shifted to subnational, regional, and international levels. This phenomenon of devolution, regionalization, and internationalization of regulatory activities presents increased political spaces and opportunities for civic associations to support, protest, or resist. The recognition that self-interest must sometimes be advanced collectively, coupled with the emergence of new problems associated with globalization, has led to the emergence of new forms of global governance. There has been growing state participation in regional and international organizations and increasingly states have delegated greater power to these bodies (see Ravenhill, Chapter 5 and Winham, Chapter 4 in this volume). This is evident, for example, in the enhanced competence of the World Trade

Organization compared with its predecessor, the General Agreement on Tariffs and Trade. Moreover, the debates over the content of regulation and contestation over the site of regulatory activity have spurred civil society actors to engage with states and firms. Examples of these activities will be developed below. Another important facet of changing patterns of regulation has been a trend towards privatization. And the increasing power of corporate actors in this movement away from public provision towards privatized governance has spurred local and transnational forms of resistance from social movement activists.

Financial and trade liberalization and their attendant impact on states and corporations have opened up avenues for greater citizen participation in the global economy. The opening up of national economies to world markets, deregulation, and the removal of many protectionist policies has meant that competition between firms is now increasingly global. Moreover, the removal of most capital controls has led to an unprecedented increase in the expansion and integration of financial markets around the world. The world financial market has become increasingly autonomous, separated from the real economy, and has contributed to financial instability and financial crises (see Pauly, Chapter 7 in this volume). A series of financial crises in the last decade in Mexico, Russia, East Asia, and Argentina led among other things to increasing civil society criticism of the polices of national governments, international financial institutions, and transnational corporations. The activities of civic groups in advocacy roles in this ideational struggle was also matched by the active engagement of civic associations in material provisioning to counter the devastating impacts of these crises on the most marginal sectors of their respective societies.

An extensive literature on NGOs, social movements, and other types of civic associations documents important and constructive roles for civil society actors in global economic governance. One important role is that of advocacy. Civic associations provide an important voice for groups unrepresented by state or corporate interests, and therefore contribute to the greater democratization of governance structures. For example, NGOs have articulated dissent and protest most notably against the neo-liberal

policies of organizations such as the International Monetary Fund, the World Bank, and the World Trade Organization. By giving voice to the marginalized, civil society actors are contributing to global democracy. A second role is that of material provision and refers to those activities in which NGOs (in particular) act as service providers. Increasingly civic associations have provided welfare, development relief, and humanitarian assistance. In instances where the state either cannot or chooses not to provide assistance, civic associations have been critical in supporting the material needs of people.

Civic associations are also increasingly providing a legitimating function in the global economy. The authority of civic groups is crucial to the acceptance of many practices in the global political economy. The campaign against child labour is an example of such legitimizing practices at work. Non-governmental organizations also provide important links between the local and global thereby contributing to the effectiveness of various institutions. As political actors, they use bargaining power to influence national and international decision making, and to facilitate international cooperation. They have been at the forefront of attempts to mobilize citizen action against policies they perceive to be harmful. Developmental, environmental, and human rights NGOs, for example, have helped the process of institutional development through, for example, agenda-setting activities. Finally, civic associations conduct research and disseminate their findings to the public and policy makers. Environmental groups, development organizations, human rights groups, trade unions, and women's groups have all played important roles in disseminating information.

There is widespread agreement that civic associations are playing increasingly important advocacy roles within the global political economy. The extent to which they have developed into salient actors in the negotiation and implementation of global environmental governance remains open to question. It can be argued that in their engagement with state and market actors, civic associations have contributed in limited ways to both negotiation and implementation of governance arrangements. Regarding the negotiation of governing arrangements, civic associations have become directly involved through participation in official delegations and through discussions with official negotiators. For example, at the Cancun ministerial meeting of the WTO in September 2003 the European Union delegation included members of the European Parliament and representatives from civil society organizations as observers, and negotiators from developing countries relied heavily on research and analysis conducted by NGOs in formulating their bargaining positions. Non-governmental organization engagement with corporate social responsibility provides an illustration of the role of civic associations in the implementation of governance arrangements.

A number of NGOs have entered into a variety of constructive strategic engagements with transnational corporations. Strategic engagement in this context refers to a collaborative partnership between a firm and an NGO in which the NGO shapes the market behaviour of the firm. The relationship between the Environmental Defence Fund and McDonald's in the past decade has included deliberations of company policy on issues such as recycling and the use of antibiotics in food animal production.

In the absence of civic associations, many issues would have remained unknown to governments and populations. Civil society, often through links with the media, has educated the public about specific dangers. This has especially been the case with environmental issues.

Key points

- Globalization has transformed global economic governance.
- States remain important actors.
- Corporations exercise influence through market power, pressure group activity, and private authority.
- Civil society actors play key roles in governance structures—advocacy, material provision, mobilization, legitimation, and coordination.

Civil society and the search for social justice

The two tensions identified earlier—the search for regulatory frameworks and the expansion of economic activity—present a useful framework for a discussion of the diverse patterns of engagement between civic associations and the global political economy. Civic associations have confronted the state and market and have increasingly become engaged in the search for social justice. As previously indicated, the activities of diverse civil society organizations span a wide range of issues. Advocacy efforts by civic associations target states, intergovernmental organizations, and transnational corporations. As suggested previously, no single strategy or approach exists among the various civic associations and an array of objectives and tactics is apparent in the engagement between civil society and other institutions in the world economy. In the context of an evolving and dynamic global economy three issues have emerged as important sites of struggle—inequality, security, and democracy.

Globalization is a highly uneven process that creates winners and losers. Recent evidence supports the claim that globalization is associated with rising inequality (between rich states and poor states) rather than increasing equality (see Wade, Chapter 11 in this volume). While the causes of inequality remain disputed, some attention has to be focused on processes of trade and financial liberalization. This is partly because trade liberalization remains a selective process. For example, while industrialized countries continue to provide substantial subsidies to their agricultural sectors, they exert pressure on developing countries to open their domestic economies as a condition of economic support (see Thomas, Chapter 12 in this volume). And, the flow of capital has been uneven with foreign direct investment in the developing world concentrated in a relatively small number of countries. Moreover, rapid advances in telecommunications and information technology, and the increasing digital divide, threaten to further marginalize developing countries and deny them the opportunities of globalization. By determining the location and distribution of wealth and productive power in the world economy, globalization defines and reshapes global patterns of hierarchy and inequality. Civil society organizations, especially those concerned with development, human rights, and labour conditions, have addressed the problems created by inequality.

Processes of globalization have profound consequences for human security. The search for security is no longer confined solely to freedom from military threat. In a world characterized by economic, environmental, societal, and cultural problems states, firms, and civil society all confront increasing insecurities. Civil society actors have worked to enhance the security of vulnerable groups and vulnerable populations. From labour issues (campaigns on labour standards) to indigenous issues (campaigns on biodiversity); from women's issues (campaigns on gender equity) to health (campaigns on essential medicines) civic associations have emerged as agents for change, promoting, contesting, and resisting liberalization and regulatory processes.

Equally, the changing global economic order poses fundamental questions regarding the exercise of democratic governance. In particular, citizens have become increasingly concerned with the nature of economic governance, especially the democratic accountability of firms and intergovernmental institutions. Coleman and Porter (2000) suggest six criteria that can be used in judging the democratic credentials of an institution or regime—transparency; openness to direct participation; quality of discourse; representation; effectiveness; and fairness.

How, in specific terms, have civic associations responded to the impact of globalization on equality, security, and democracy? Given the diversity of civil society actors and the range of issues it is difficult to arrive at definitive and generalizable conclusions. An analysis of three key structures in the global political economy—trade, finance, and production—provides some preliminary answers.

Civil society and international trade

Civil society actors attempt to influence trade policy and practice through lobbying and advocacy activities at national, regional, and international levels. Trade-related civic associations direct their attention to states, corporations, and intergovernmental organiza-

tions. Some organizations are primarily based at the national level with an interest in the impact of trade on local communities. Such organizations tend to direct their focus towards national governments. Other organizations have a focus outside the nation state and devise strategies targeted towards national governments, international organizations, and transnational corporations. No single civil society approach to trade issues exists. Support for or opposition to further trade liberalization arises from ideological preference and special interest. Some civil society actors have been promoters of liberalization in general, others have supported particular liberalization initiatives, and others have attempted to counter liberalization measures.

There are three types of trade-related NGOs (Scholte, O'Brien, and Williams 1999). *Conformists* are sympathetic to the goal of trade liberalization and the expansion of the regulatory activities of the WTO. However, some conformist groups are critical of certain aspects of the organization of the trade agenda. Among the more active conformist groups are organizations representing business interests such as the Business Council for Sustainable Development, and the International Chamber of Commerce, farmers associations such as the American Farm Bureau, and economic research institutes such as the Institute for International Economics.

Reformists support liberal trade rules, but on either social justice or democracy principles campaign for changes to WTO rules and procedures. In terms of policies, reformers have mounted specific 'issue' campaigns and, in relation to procedural change, they have campaigned for the transformation of the WTO from what they term a secretive and unrepresentative organization into one reflecting general democratic principles. Reformist groups include trade unions such as the International Confederation of Free Trade Unions, environmental groups such as the World Wide Fund for Nature, and development organizations such as Oxfam. Both conformists and reformists adopt engagement strategies.

The third main approach to the WTO is taken by those civil society organizations that adopt a *radical* stance. Members of radical groups criticize the WTO and campaign to limit its powers or to replace the organization. The Peoples' Global Action (PGA) is the best known of the various radical coalitions active on trade issues.

The relationship between trade and growth, and the benefits and costs of further trade liberalization, lie at the centre of civil society engagement with the world trading system. Civil society actors have been involved in the exploration and contestation of the benefits of trade liberalization. One of the major issues for civil society actors has been the social impact of trade, and these concerns have been heightened by the expansion of the trade agenda. Development and human rights activists have been prominent in attempts to counter the uneven impacts of trade liberalization.

The Agreement on Trade-Related Aspects of Intellectual Property Rights (TRIPS) provides an example of competing civil society perspectives and activism. The agreement was actively promoted by a coalition of American transnational companies that campaigned at national and international levels (Sell 2000). Its inclusion in the WTO was actively opposed by reformist and radical groups, and the operation of TRIPS continues to spark major debate. A critical issue confronting the TRIPS Agreement was how it prevented developing countries from gaining inexpensive access to essential medicines. A furore arose over the inability of patients in the developing world suffering from HIV/AIDS to gain access to cheaper pharmaceutical products. A campaign against TRIPS and especially its seemingly restrictive application to medicines was launched by civil society actors (see, for example, Orbinski 2002; Panagariya 2002).

Some civil society organizations have played a different role in the politics of trade through the promotion of fair trade as an alternative to the existing trading system. A leading American fair trade association defines fair trade as 'an equitable and fair partnership between marketers in North America and producers in Asia, Africa, Latin America, and other parts of the world. A fair trade partnership works to provide low-income artisans and farmers with a living wage for their work.' It lists the following criteria as essential to fair trade (see **www.fairtradefederation. com/memcrit.html**):

- 'Paying a fair wage in the local context.
- Offering employees opportunities for advancement.
- Providing equal employment opportunities for all people, particularly the most disadvantaged.

- Engaging in environmentally sustainable practices.
- Being open to public accountability.
- Building long-term trade relationships.
- Providing healthy and safe working conditions within the local context.
- Providing financial and technical assistance to producers whenever possible.'

Supporters of fair trade look to a future in which 'For consumers concerned with fairness in the Third World, their shopping baskets can become a powerful statement of their commitment to the poor' (Coote 1992: 178). But such sentiments have been the subject of scathing criticism from radical commentators. Robins, for instance, asserts that 'maybe it's true that the best the world's poor can hope for is better pimps for their products' (quoted in Johnston 2002: 38), while Josée Johnston (2002) suggests that fair trade is not a radical option but rather another element in consumer culture.

Civil society and global finance

The main actors in the global financial structure are banks, states, and transnational corporations. Financial innovation and liberalization have presented problems for national monetary authorities and attempts to manage international capital markets. In what ways, if any, have civil society actors affected developments in the global financial system? Civil society actors have engaged with financial issues in a number of ways and in various forums. Among the key issues addressed by civil society have been financial crises, the lending policies of the IMF, and the relationship between capital markets and national governments. Two important campaigns by civil society organizations provide an insight into the engagement by civil society with the global financial structure.

In relation to attempts to reduce global inequalities and promote social justice, the struggle to provide debt relief for heavily indebted poor countries is arguably the most significant campaign undertaken by civil society actors. The indebtedness of developing countries emerged as a key political issue in the 1980s. Debt servicing and repayment obligations spiraled following the debt crisis in the early 1980s

---

Box 13.2 **The 1980s debt crisis**

The 1980s debt crisis emerged in August 1982 when Mexico announced that it could no longer service its debt. This announcement sent shock waves through the banking community and lending was stopped to Mexico and a number of other states (many in South America) that had borrowed heavily. No consensus exists on the causes of the debt crisis but the following factors were influential: imprudent lending by banks; the second oil shock in 1979; an increase in interest rates; recession in the world economy; and capital flight from indebted countries.

The debt crisis affected both oil-exporting developing countries and oil-importing developing countries.

Oil-exporters such as Mexico, Venezuela, and Nigeria were affected because they had borrowed heavily to fund their industrialization schemes, and falling oil prices affected their ability to repay loans.

The consequences of the debt crisis were severe and impoverishment affected development. The response of the international financial institutions was to impose structural adjustment reforms that proved controversial and heightened tension between civil society groups and global institutions.

(see Box 13.2). The massive debt burden of developing countries undermines their technological and organizational capacities, and the long-term diversion of funds from social investment increases poverty and conflict.

Initiatives for debt relief have been developed in the context of multilateral negotiations at G7 (G8) summits, the Paris Club, and the IMF and World Bank. The international debt regime was created by states and financial institutions and it reflects the preferences of the major creditor counties. The target of civil society action was therefore the governments of industrialized countries, which effectively exercise control over decisions concerning debt reduction and cancellation. Organized civic action to attempt to break the cycle of debt has been occurring for decades. Civic associations challenged the power of creditor states and an economic order that tolerate the debt burdens of poor countries. At the forefront of the campaign for debt reduction is a global coalition, the Jubilee Movement (see Box 13.3). The Jubilee Movement mobilizes thousands of people, via direct action and awareness-raising campaigns, to demand the establishment of a new international economic order through cancellation of poor countries' debt and the construction of new sets of relationships between North and South.

The critique offered by anti-debt campaigners provides a critical assessment of the existing global economic order and is based on a vision of a poverty-free world order. The anti-debt social movement argued

that the prevailing economic order was oppressive and unjust. The mobilization of civic associations provided a direct challenge to the foundational principles of the liberal economic order.

A debt crisis can be conceived as two separate but interrelated crises, one financial and the other socioeconomic. The financial crisis essentially affects governments and large investors while the socio-economic crisis impacts on a country's population. By the time Jubilee 2000 was launched, the financial crisis had been solved but the socio-economic crisis remained. The importance of Jubilee Research (as it is now called) lies in its ability to keep debt as a high-profile issue on the global financial agenda. The British Prime Minister Tony Blair gave recognition to the significance of the movement in 1998 when he said, 'I pay tribute to the Jubilee 2000 campaign and its dignified breaking-the-chain demonstration in Birmingham. The most persuasive case for debt relief is that it is only when countries can escape the burden of debt that they are able to benefit economically' (quoted in Hajnal 2002: 220).

The success of the anti-debt movement is difficult to measure. It is possible to claim, for example, that the Cologne Debt Initiative that increased debt forgiveness was the result of campaign pressure (Michael 2001) but it is also possible to indicate the continued existence of the Jubilee Movement as proof of its lack of success. To a large extent the politics of debt relief indicates the strength and weakness of civil society in the global political economy. The key decision makers

Box 13.3 Jubilee 2000 and the Jubilee Movement

The Jubilee Movement is the successor to Jubilee 2000. Established in 1996 in the United Kingdom by Bill Peters and Martin Dent, Jubilee 2000 was a global civil society coalition campaigning for debt relief. The movement takes its name from the biblical idea of debt forgiveness in 'Jubilee' years (Leviticus ch. 25 and Deuteronomy ch. 15). The idea of debt forgiveness based on Jubilee principles emerged in the early 1990s and later developed the organizational form of Jubilee 2000. The campaign focused on debt relief by 2000 (hence its name). Initially a Christian-based movement, after the official launch of Jubilee 2000 the coalition widened to include non-faith-based organizations. Jubilee 2000 utilized an array of strategies including research and analysis, mass mobilization, lobbying, and media campaigns. The key goal of Jubilee 2000 is brilliantly captured in the organization's slogan, 'Drop the Debt'. At the end of 2000, Jubilee 2000 ceased to exist but the transnational advocacy network it had spawned continues. By the end of 2000 there were member organizations in sixty-nine countries.

remain states and successful change is only possible through the actions of states. Civil society cannot, by itself, provide the solution to the debt burdens of developing countries. But civil society has obviously played a legitimating role in this process. It maintained the profile of debt and mobilized sufficient numbers of people (including many high-profile ones) with the result that debt relief became and remains a priority for political leaders. The anti-debt coalition was successful in arguing that debt reduction is an issue of justice and not solely one of economic efficiency. And, the partial fulfilment of Jubilee 2000's demands for the cancellation of poor countries' debts indicates the opportunity for social movements to affect international economic decision making.

Another issue relevant to international finance concerns rules on the flow of investment. One important recent campaign by civil society actors concerned protest against a proposed code for the treatment of foreign investment. Negotiations for a Multilateral Agreement on Investment (MAI) were launched at the May 1995 Ministerial Meeting of the Organisation for Economic Cooperation and Development (OECD). The aim was the conclusion of an agreement to liberalize investment regimes and provide protection for transnational investors. This agreement would initially have applied to the OECD member states but it was hoped that it would progressively be adopted by other non-OECD states that would undoubtedly have come under pressure to do so. Although the negotiations on the MAI were conducted between governments, consultations were entered into with civil society groups. The campaign against the MAI was triggered in October 1997 when a network of twenty-five NGOs withdrew from the consultative process with the OECD. The campaign against the MAI is often hailed as a triumph for civil society (Goodman 2002). Can this judgement be supported and what does the role of the anti-MAI coalition tell us about civil society and the global economy?

Between October 1997 when the NGOs launched their campaign and the effective end of the negotiations in October 1998 when the French government withdrew from the negotiating process, the MAI emerged from obscurity to a highly visible and contentious political issue. It was this movement from a secret and specialized bargaining environment to a public sphere that signalled the beginning of the end for the MAI. Anti-MAI campaigners were successful in creating a global coalition to protest against the proposed treaty. The main issue for the campaigners concerned the loss of national control over the policies of transnational firms. A successful conclusion to the MAI negotiations always hinged on a compromise among the twenty-nine OECD states concerning which sectors would be exempt from the general obligations of the treaty. By making the terms of the treaty public, anti-MAI campaigners ensured that groups seeking exemption from the stipulations of the treaty would lobby their governments. The political pressure on governments intensified as domestic lobby groups sought protection from 'globalization from above' (see Goodman and Ranald 2000).

Critical to the success of the campaign was the use of the Internet (Smith and Smythe 1999), which was used by a wide variety of civic associations and government agencies. The campaigners effectively questioned the legitimacy of the OECD process. Giving credence to this challenge to the OECD was the broad nature of the coalition both in terms of geographic spread (for example, across the North–South divide), and also in terms of diverse constituencies represented (for example, cultural groups, environmental groups, public advocacy organizations, religious groups, and trade unions).

As ever, it is difficult to generalize from a single case—but three main lessons can be drawn from the anti-MAI campaign. First, civic associations successfully exploited the 'legitimacy deficit' of the OECD. The role of civil society in legitimizing change in the global political economy is increasingly of importance to state and market actors. Secondly, the campaign worked because it successfully garnered the energies of cross-national groups on an issue with cross-cutting cleavages. National governments faced pressure from diverse constituencies. The final lesson concerns the importance of the Internet as a tool for transnational mobilization, in this case to mobilize a network of resistance.

Civil society and global production

The key actors in the global production structure remain corporations and states. Civil society organizations are not directly engaged in productive activities but elements within civil society have developed specific campaigns directed at transnational corporations.

Labour standards have become an issue of central importance in the discourse on globalization. Although this issue is predominantly analysed from the perspective of the international trading system, it is at base one concerning the conditions under which products are made. Child labour, women's labour, and trade union rights have featured prominently in the political debates around labour standards. Civic associations at the national level and transnational coalitions have challenged the employment practices of transnational corporations. At the centre of the labour standards debate is the relationship between capital and labour. And once again, the diversity of civic action is apparent on this issue. For example, the

proposal that core labour standards be included in the WTO was opposed by some Southern NGOs because they perceived this proposal as a device to protect the jobs of Northern workers (O'Brien et al. 2000: 85–6).

Civil society interest in the conditions of workers in developing countries is not confined to attempts to change national or international regulation but is also directed at specific corporations. Two strategies are frequently employed to highlight the practices of corporations. Non-governmental organizations use the media to highlight abuses, and they also organize national and international boycotts of a firm's products. The Nike campaign (see Box 13.4) provides an illustration of one such campaign.

In pursuit of transformations in the practices of companies, NGOs have engaged directly with firms in attempts to change their practices and priorities. Some civic associations have adopted confrontational strategies and others have sought dialogue with firms (see Evans, Goodman, and Landsbury 2001). Other campaigns have been against the marketing practices of transnational corporations. Before the rhetoric of globalization became commonplace, the food giant Nestlé was the subject of an intense campaign because of its promotion of infant formula in the developing world (see Box 13.5).

Another issue has concerned the goods produced by companies. The most significant international campaign was that against landmines. Non-governmental organizations acted as catalysts in politicizing the issue, played an educational role for society, garnered support from key individuals and policy makers, and framed the issue as a humanitarian crisis (Price 1998). An absolute ban on anti-personnel mines was agreed to in 1997 and an international treaty to ban landmines entered into force in March 1999. The importance of civil society in this process is not only documented in the literature (see, for example Price 1998; Warkentin and Mingst 2000) but was recognized by the Nobel Foundation with the award of the 1997 Nobel Peace Prize to the International Campaign to Ban Landmines, a transnational coalition formed by six NGOs—Handicap International (France), Human Rights Watch (US), Medico International (Germany), Mines Advisory Group (UK), Physicians for Human Rights (US), and Vietnam Veterans of America (US).

Box 13.4 **The Nike campaign**

The campaign process

In 1992 *Harper's* magazine published an article by Jeff Ballinger entitled 'Nike, the New Free-Trade Heel: Nike's Profits Jump on the Backs of Asian Workers'. This marked the beginning of a campaign against Nike. The campaigners accused Nike of using sweatshop labour in factories in Asia in which its shoes were manufactured.

Campaign obstacles included Nike's positive corporate image; the difficulty of interesting Americans in Indonesian affairs; Nike's contracts with major college and university athletic teams; Nike's adoption of a Code of Conduct asserting that the company carefully monitored wages and working conditions; and the public perception that it was unfair to target Nike when other footwear companies were allegedly engaged in similar action.

The debate over NAFTA with its emphasis on trade and labour rights gave the campaign a boost but it was not until 1996 and the transformation of the campaign into a broad-based movement that intense pressure was exerted on Nike.

1997—student activist groups and sportswriters included in the coalition.

1997–8—Nike experienced unprecedented declines in sales and earnings. In May 1997, the company's shares fell 13 per cent and in the fiscal year 1998, it experienced a 49 per cent fall in earnings.

The actors

Faith-based investment community, for example, Interfaith Center on Corporate Responsibility (ICCR).

Global Exchange.

Campaign for Labor Rights.

Press for Change.

Justice! Do it Nike.

Student/campus groups.

Politicians, for example, seventy-five members of the US Congress signed on to a resolution criticizing Nike in October 1997 (Shaw 2001: 96).

The outcome

Success

February 2001: Global Alliance for Workers and Communities conducted a factory assessment programme, paid for by Nike, and 'found evidence of inadequate wages, forced and illegal overtime, denial of sick leave, menstrual leave and annual leave and unacceptable levels of sexual harassment and verbal abuse' (Connor 2001: 92). This forced Nike to 'admit that serious labor abuses do exist in its suppliers' factories in Indonesia'.

'Anti-Nike activists have crystallized opposition to socially irresponsible economic globalization around an easily understood core idea: a living wage for all workers' (Shaw 2001: 94).

12 May 1998: Phil Knight, CEO of Nike, addressed the National Press Club, pledging to significantly reform Nike's overseas labour practices by raising the minimum age for new workers to eighteen years, to improve worker health and safety conditions, and to allow labour and human rights groups to monitor working conditions in its factories, but failed to commit to raising workers' wages (Shaw 2001: 93).

Reason behind this reform: Knight's acknowledgement that 'Nike's product has become synonymous with slave wages, forced overtime, and arbitrary abuse'.

Key points

- Civil society groups have formed transnational coalitions to campaign for changes to the practices of states, corporations, and international institutions.

- Civil society organizations have utilized communications technology as an important part of their campaign strategy.

- Civil society actors have played crucial leadership roles in some campaigns.

- The record of success is mixed.

- The attitudes of civil society actors are diverse; different positions can be found on issues relating to trade, finance, and production.

Box 13.5 The Nestlé campaign

Issue background

The campaign received its initial impetus from medical authorities in the late 1960s, who drew attention to the trends in less developed countries of increased bottle feeding, a decline in breastfeeding, and a dramatic increase in the number of malnourished and sick babies. At the same time, the marketing of infant formula products was based on unethical practices such as women employed on a commission basis, dressed in nurses' uniforms frequenting maternity wards; promotion through the healthcare system.

The campaign process

1977—Boycott of Nestlé products launched; Infant Formula Action Coalition (INFACT) established in Minneapolis, and targeted Nestlé as the world's largest seller of infant formula products.

Push for a code of conduct negotiated in the World Health Organization (WHO). A code was successfully drafted in 1980. WHO was unable to implement the code but Nestlé took important steps to achieve implementation of the Code.

The actors

Broad coalition of faith-based groups, development groups, and women's groups.

The outcome

The boycott and the campaign against violations of the WHO Code continues.

Successes

• The boycott campaign was an important force in the creation and implementation of the World Health Organization's international code of marketing for breastmilk substitutes;

• a major step in the development of a framework for evaluating corporate accountability, and the understanding of the intersection between human rights and commercial interests;

• by formally recognizing boycott groups such as INFACT, the WHO gave consumer activist groups official NGO status and thus enhanced legitimacy, and set a precedent for the equal treatment of consumer interests and commercial interests in the development of international health policy;

• the creation of a global monitoring organization, the International Baby Food Action Network (IBFAN) became the model for pesticide monitoring in developing nations.

By 1981, the manufacturers had eliminated many of the worst promotional practices.

Failures

• Significant expansion of formula companies in developing countries;

• increased promotion of formula products through the health care system;

• violations of the WHO code still take place (Sklair 2002).

Civil society and the democratization of global economic institutions

Reformist and radical civic groups have been at the forefront of a campaign advocating reform of the three major global economic institutions (GEIs). The civil society critics have targeted the policies of the institutions and also their democratic credentials. Here we will focus on the campaign for the democratization of the IMF, World Bank, and the WTO through an examination of the claims of the critics, and an assessment of the political significance of the movement for change. While radical critics such as anti-globalization protestors reject the cosmopolitan underpinnings of these organizations and campaign for their abolition, the reformist critics believe that these organizations can be transformed so that they become more representative, accountable, and transparent. It is the reformist argument that will be examined below.

The civil society critique: representation, accountability, and transparency

At the centre of the civil society critique of the GEIs is a rejection of the intergovernmental character of the institutions. From this perspective, the restriction of decision making to governments cannot satisfactorily capture the range of stakeholders likely to be affected by the activities of the GEIs. In an era of globalization, a focus on intergovernmental relations is too limiting since the degree of autonomy and independence implied in the traditional concept of sovereignty is absent. State control has effectively been diminished by shifting patterns of regulation. It is precisely the increasing authority of regional and global institutions that is the problem. As states cede regulatory activities to regional and global organizations, these bodies cannot be conceived solely as the instruments of their member states. They themselves constitute centres of authority. That is, through their expanded mandates, governments and their citizens are increasingly subject to new forms of regulation over which there is little direct control. The critics allege that under globalization the three GEIs have increased their power and influence and hence are not subject to direct state control. Therefore, these organizations should be transformed so that non-state actors can play important roles. In other words, the GEIs should include the wide range of stakeholders affected by policy decisions. Global economic institutions, it is argued, should be accountable not solely to their member states but to diverse communities around the world directly affected by their activities. Finally, some civil society groups are sceptical of the extent to which governmental delegates are representative of the inhabitants of their states.

The critics claim that the GEIs are not accountable because their decision-making structures are undemocratic. Critics of the World Bank and IMF contend that the weighted voting systems of these organizations undermine their democratic credentials. Decisions made on the basis of weighted voting gives major industrialized countries (especially the United States) control over the agenda. And, although the WTO's formal provision of consensus decision-making rules suggests a more democratic organization, the major trading nations (the so-called QUAD countries) use informal mechanisms to maintain influence over key decisions. In other words, intergovernmental negotiations, it is claimed, effectively disbar civil society groups from providing a valuable watchdog function for the wider public.

The critics allege that transparency is lacking in two respects. They argue that decisions are frequently made in secret and that the visible part of proceedings is a mere masquerade with little relation to the real exercise of power that takes place outside the public gaze. Secondly, it is argued that access to the information on which decisions are based should be more readily available. Although all three organizations have in different ways become more open in providing access to documents, critics from civil society nevertheless contend that this openness is severely limited and hampers the monitoring functions of civic associations. Organizations lacking in transparency, and with a restricted membership it is argued cannot effectively be accountable to their constituents. In short, GEIs as structures of global governance are not representative, accountable, or transparent since their operations are shrouded in secrecy and decisions are removed from effective scrutiny by national legislatures.

In addition to the negative case made above, three broad claims have been made for the increased participation of civil society groups in the IMF, World Bank, and WTO. The first is based on an assumption common to pluralist theories of democracy in which it is claimed that the more voices heard, the better the policy output. Opening up these organizations to civic actors will provide decision makers with more ideas and views and improve the results of policy deliberations. Furthermore, proceedings that are not transparent perpetuate a secretive image of the organizations and diminish public confidence and support for their work.

Second, civic actors claim that they possess specialized knowledge and can therefore make a constructive contribution to global economic governance.

Increased participation of civic associations will ensure that a full range of potential consequences are addressed because they can provide information and technical expertise, not necessarily available in intergovernmental deliberations.

The third claim concerns the necessity for broad public support for development assistance and further trade liberalization. Enhanced participation by NGOs in the World Bank and WTO will increase public support for these organizations since governments rely on public support for increasing aid budgets and implementing trade liberalization. Broad-based support fostered by public participation ensures that policies are likely to be implemented. Moreover, wider public participation counters the role of vested interests and therefore ensures that policies are taken in the public interest. Furthermore, civic associations contend that greater representation is necessary to ensure a wider range of interests are taken into account in the decision-making process.

Responsiveness of the GEIs

In what ways are civil society criticisms of the democratic credentials of the IMF, World Bank, and WTO politically significant? In other words, to what extent have civic associations affected the decision making of key GEI members and elicited responses from these organizations? The response from the GEIs has not been consistent and reflects the differential ability of civil society actors to exert pressure on individual GEIs. While state interests and interstate conflicts remain the key determinants of decisions in the IMF, World Bank, and WTO, nevertheless, the campaign against the democratic credentials of the three organizations has elicited a degree of change in all three institutions.

The member governments of the GEIs have not accepted the claim that these institutions are not representative. It can be argued that the IMF, World Bank, and WTO are representative in the sense that they are universal organizations and they boast wide membership both in terms of geographic coverage and in the diversity of the economic and political characteristics of its member states. Not only are most of the world's states members of the GEIs but, in terms of the activities covered by these organizations,

no significant states are denied membership. The issue of representation has, nevertheless, been addressed by all three organizations through the establishment of linkages with civil society organizations. The World Bank has the longest and most established linkage with civil society organizations. In 1982 the World Bank established the NGO–World Bank Committee in response to criticisms of its lending policies, and it has developed a number of other formal mechanisms since the 1990s. The latest development was the creation of the World Bank–Civil Society Joint Facilitation Committee in 2001 (JFC). The JFC is a transitional body (eighteen months' duration) with the aim of producing a 'framework for World Bank–civil society engagement'. The WTO's response to the issue of representation was to mandate the secretariat to initiate consultations and dialogue with civil society organizations. This involves direct contacts between the director-general and NGOs, and symposia for NGOs to discuss trade, development, and environment issues. Moreover, it encourages NGOs to attend its Ministerial Meetings.

As far as accountability is concerned, the key states in the GEIs assert that the decision-making rules of the three organizations are fair. In response to the critique of the weighted voting system, they argue that the simple one person, one vote model of domestic systems is inapplicable to the World Bank and the IMF. These are financial organizations and a weighted voting system is necessary to protect the interests of the major shareholders who provide the money that is lent to other members. In the absence of contributions from the leading industrialized states, a pool of finance for borrowing states would not exist. And given that decisions in the WTO are based on consensus, it can be argued that such an approach is ultra-democratic since every member country has a voice. Moreover, agreements negotiated within the WTO often have to be ratified by national parliaments.

Democratic decision making, however, should not be confused with the exercise of influence. Countries do have differential bargaining power and that is reflected in the decisions of these organizations but this does not undermine their democratic credentials.

The World Bank and the IMF have responded to the issue of accountability through the creation of independent audit and evaluation mechanisms. In 1993 the World Bank established its Inspection Panel. The task of the Inspection Panel is to hear complaints brought by civic associations representing citizens harmed by World Bank policies. In 2000 the International Finance Corporation (IFC) and the Multilateral Investment Guarantee Agency (MIGA), two organizations in the World Bank Group, created the Compliance Adviser/Ombudsman Office to hear complaints. And the IMF established an Independent Evaluation Office in July 2001.

The issue on which the greatest progress has been made in response to the civil society critique is that of transparency. The WTO initiated a process to make its documents more readily available to the public. A policy of derestricting documents was taken in 1996 and this was further liberalized in 2001. Furthermore, the WTO maintains a website that provides instant electronic access to most of its documents. Under its Information Disclosure Policy the World Bank provides access to its policy and project documents on its website. It has also established Public Information Centres in more than sixty-five countries. Similarly, from the mid-1990s the IMF began to provide greater access to its documents, making available material relating to its loan arrangements, a process that was accelerated after criticisms of the Fund's response to the Asian financial crisis of 1997–8. And like the WTO and the World Bank it maintains an accessible website.

Key points

- Civil society actors contend that global economic institutions are unrepresentative, unaccountable, and non-transparent.

- Global economic institutions have responded to these criticisms and have initiated policies to increase their interactions with civil society organizations.

QUESTIONS

1 What is meant by 'civil society'?

2 What is the difference between a non-governmental organization and a social movement?

3 In what sense, if any, is there a global civil society?

4 Account for the emergence of global civil society.

5 How does globalization affect traditional economic governance?

6 How have civil society actors transformed global economic governance?

7 How, and in what ways, have civic associations influenced the international trading regime?

8 What evidence is there to suggest that the anti-debt movement has influenced the international debt regime?

9 What role did civil society play in the defeat of the MAI?

10 How convincing is the civil society critique of the democratic credentials of global economic institutions?

11 Why have global economic institutions responded to criticism from civic associations?

FURTHER READING

Arts, B., Noortmann, M., and Reinalda, B. (eds.) (2001), *Non-State Actors in International Relations* (Aldershot: Ashgate). A collection of essays with a good mix of theoretical articles and empirical case studies.

Cameron, M. A., Lawson, R. J., and Tomlin, B. W. (eds.) (1998), *To Walk without Fear: The Global Movement to Ban Landmines* (Toronto: Oxford University Press). A collection of essays by participants and observers on a successful campaign.

Clark, J. (1991), *Democratizing Development: The Role of Voluntary Agencies* (London: Earthscan). The classic study of the NGOs as development actors.

Cohen, J. L., and Arato, A. (1992), *Civil Society and Political Theory* (Cambridge, Mass.: MIT Press). An introduction to historical uses of the term civil society.

Cohen, R., and Rai, S. (eds.) (2000), *Global Social Movements: Towards a Cosmopolitan Politics* (London: Athlone Press). A collection of essays on the practice and promise of social movements.

Florini, A. M. (ed.) (2000), *The Third Force: The Rise of Transnational Civil Society* (Washington DC: Carnegie Endowment for International Peace). Contains some good case studies.

Fox, J. A., and Brown, D. (eds.) (1998), *The Struggle for Accountability: The World Bank, NGOs and Grassroots Movements* (Cambridge, Mass.: MIT Press). A well-documented study of engagement between the World Bank and its environmental critics.

—— —— (eds.) (1998), *Accountability within Transnational Coalitions: The Struggle for Accountability* (Cambridge, Mass.: MIT Press). An early academic study of accountability in civic associations.

Glasius, M., Kaldor, M. and Anheier, H. (eds.) (2002), *Global Civil Society 2002* (Oxford: Oxford University Press). The successor to the important 2001 Yearbook this continues the comprehensive coverage of the first volume.

Keane, J. (2003), *Global Civil Society* (Cambridge: Cambridge University Press). An accessible introduction to the concept of global civil society.

Nelson, P. (1995), *The World Bank and NGOs: The Limits of Apolitical Development* (London: Macmillan). One of the early studies of the World Bank's engagement with NGOs.

O'Brien, R., et al. (2000), *Contesting Global Governance: Multilateral Economic Institutions and Global Social Movements* (Cambridge: Cambridge University Press). The most empirically detailed and theoretically sophisticated of recent books on global social movements.

Smith, J., Chatfield, C., and Pagnucco, R. (eds.) (1997), *Transnational Social Movements and Global Politics: Solidarity beyond the State* (Syracuse, NY: Syracuse University Press). A social movements approach to transnational activity.

WEB LINKS

www.debtlinks.org   A gateway to organizations researching and campaigning for the cancellation of Third World debt.

www.globalpolicy.org/ngos   A gateway to recent articles on NGO activity with sections on business; social and economic justice; and international and regional institutions.

www.icbl.org   International Campaign to Ban Landmines.

www.ictsd.org   The International Centre for Trade and Sustainable Development has provided an excellent website on trade issues.

www.iccbw.org International Chamber of Commerce.

www.imf.org/external/np/exr/cs/eng/index.asp The International Monetary Fund's Civil Society Newsletter.

www.jubilee2000uk.org The UK site of Jubilee Research, a successor to Jubilee 2000.

www.oxfam.org Oxfam International.

www.nadir.org/nadir/initiativ/agp/en Peoples' Global Action.

www.citizen.org/trade/ Public Citizens' Global Trade Watch provides a gateway to resources on trade politics.

web.worldbank.org/WBSITE/EXTERNAL/TOPICS/CSO/0 The World Bank's gateway to material on civil society.

www.wto.org/english/forums_e/ngo_e/ngo_e.htm The World Trade Organization's gateway to information for NGOs.

14

Globalization and the environment

Peter Dauvergne

READER'S GUIDE

Globalization is transforming the health of the planet. There is nothing particularly controversial about this statement. Yet sharp disagreements arise over the nature of this transformation. Is globalization a force of progress and environmental solutions? Or is it a *cause* of our current global environmental crisis? This chapter explores these questions by examining the debates around some of the most contentious issues at the core of economic globalization and the environment: economic growth, production, and consumption; trade; and transnational investment. It begins with a glance at the general arguments about how globalization affects the global environment. Then, to set the stage for an analysis of more specific arguments about the global political economy of the environment, it sketches the history of global environmentalism—in particular the emergence of global environmental institutions (including regimes) with the norm of sustainable development. The last section builds on these arguments to assess the effectiveness of North–South environmental financing and global environmental regimes.

Introduction: globalization and environmental change

Globalization is altering the global environment. Few scholars of global environmental politics would challenge this statement (see Box 14.1). The nature of the change, however, is hotly debated. Some argue it is a source of progress and ingenuity and cooperation, of a future world with much better environmental conditions for all. Others argue it is accelerating the process of the capitalist exploitation of nature and humanity, spinning the globe faster and faster toward an ecological meltdown.

Globalization and a healthy planet

The optimists see globalization as a process that fosters economic growth and raises per capita incomes, both essential to generate the funds and political will for global environmental management. Optimists see other environmental benefits from globalization as well. It is promoting global integration and cooperation as well as common environmental norms and standards, which are enhancing the capacity of a system of sovereign states to manage problems like ozone depletion and climate change. It is pushing states to liberalize trade and foreign investment, promote specialization, and eliminate subsidies, which in the past have contributed to market failures and sub-optimal economic and environmental outcomes. It is enhancing the capacity of developing states for environmental management through the transfer of technologies, knowledge, and development assistance. And it is contributing to a host of domestic reforms to policies—such as better environmental laws, stronger institutions, and more secure property rights.

Optimists such as environmental writers Julian Simon, Gregg Easterbrook, and Bjørn Lomborg see a past full of progress and a future full of hope and socio-ecological triumph. There is every reason to believe that economic growth and technological progress will continue forever. 'The standard of living', Simon (1996: 12) argues, 'has risen along with the size of the world's population since the beginning of recorded time. There is no convincing economic reason why these trends toward a better life should not continue indefinitely.' Simon's lifetime of work has stirred a hornet's nest of environmental critics. Writers like Easterbrook, however, see him as

---

Box 14.1 Globalization

This chapter assumes globalization is an ongoing and accelerating process that is restructuring and increasing the connections among economies, institutions, and civil societies. This dynamic and multidimensional process is integrating trade, production, and finance as well as strengthening global norms and global social forces. A constellation of forces drives globalization, including new and faster technologies (like computers) as well as the increasing dominance of capitalism and Western ideologies. In the simplest terms, it is leading to a 'world as a single place', where changes in distant lands affect people around the globe more quickly, and with greater frequency and intensity (Scholte 1997: 14). It is, in the words of Thomas Friedman (2002), 'the integration of everything with everything else . . . the integration of markets, finance, and technology in a way that shrinks the world from a size medium to a size small. Globalization enables each of us, wherever we live, to reach around the world farther, faster, deeper, and cheaper than ever before and at the same time allows the world to reach into each of us farther, faster, deeper, and cheaper than ever before.' This does not assume the process of globalization is even or equal within or across countries. The rich in Europe and America are unquestionably benefiting far more than the poor of Africa, Asia, and Latin America. The process is also not inevitable. States and societies can resist and reverse globalization.

profound and brave. 'There was a time', Easterbook (1995: xxi) argues, 'when to cry alarm regarding environmental affairs was the daring position. Now it's the safe position: People get upset when you say things may turn out fine.' Writers like Lomborg add, too, that there is little statistical evidence of a global environmental crisis—that this common misperception is more a result of media hype and non-governmental organization (NGO) fund-raising antics than real problems. 'Mankind's lot', Lomborg (2001: 4) asserts, 'has actually improved in terms of practically every measurable indicator . . . We are not running out of energy or natural resources . . . Acid rain does not kill the forests, and the air and water around us are becoming less and less polluted.'

Simon, Easterbrook, and Lomborg are at the extreme end of the optimists. Most supporters of globalization—those in governments like the United States and the United Kingdom and in global institutions like the World Bank and World Trade Organization—emphasize the need for a practical view that looks toward future generations. These supporters argue that some degree of change and loss is inevitable, but the consistent trend under globalization is toward a future that looks like Britain, France, and the United States, not one that looks like Ethiopia, Cambodia, and Guyana. History demonstrates the great strides of humanity. Just a hundred years back cities like London and New York were filthy and unhealthy. Today, health conditions in virtually every city in the North are vastly superior. One of the greatest feats has been the increase in food production. In the middle of the last century close to half of the people in the South were starving. By 1970 it was less than one-third; today it is less than one-fifth (WFS 1996: 1; Lomborg 2001: 61).

Just over two hundred years ago Thomas Malthus (1798) predicted that exponential population growth would, following the laws of basic maths, inevitably surpass arithmetic food production: mass starvation would thus ensue. Since then many scholars, now commonly called Malthusians or neo-Malthusians, have continued to tout the same logic. Yet, optimists stress, Malthus was flat-out wrong, primarily because he discounted the ability of human ingenuity to increase agricultural yields. The Green Revolution of the 1960s saw scientists and farmers work together to produce fast-growth, pest-resistant, high-yield crops

able to grow just about anywhere (with irrigation, fertilizers, and pesticides). There is, as a result, plenty of food today. And it is far cheaper—global food prices have fallen two-thirds in real terms since 1957. People starve at present because of inefficient distribution and incompetent governments, not because of insufficient global food supplies. For optimists, perhaps the most revealing statistic of all is global life expectancy: in 1900 it was a mere thirty years; in 1950 it was forty-six years; today it is over sixty-six years (Lomborg 2001: 50–51, 61; World Bank 2002d). Granted, such progress has demanded inevitable change, including some global environmental changes. But, optimists stress, science and human ingenuity have time and again shown the capacity to respond with even more progress.

The view that globalization is a basically positive ecological force dominates global economic and environmental negotiations and institutional decision making. The debate here ranges over how to best channel globalization so as to minimize environmental damage and maximize socio-economic progress (which, in the long run, must occur for effective global environmental management). Some argue for few, if any, restraints. Others see a need to guide globalization with national environmental agencies and strong global norms and institutions. There are, however, many scholars and activists who challenge the core assumptions behind these views—that is, they see globalization as a core cause of the current ecological crisis.

Globalization and ecological collapse

Environmental critics of globalization worry it is luring humanity toward a global fate not unlike Easter Island of 300 years ago, where ecological decay drove a once thriving people to violence and cannibalism in just a few centuries (Rees 2002: 249). Particularly worrying, so-called progress and scientific reason has created, in the words of Paul Ehrlich's (1968) infamous book title, 'a population bomb', an explosion from less than 300 million people at the time of Christ to over 6 billion today (see Figure 14.1). Globalization, critics contend, is compounding the ecological impact of the 260,000 people added to the planet

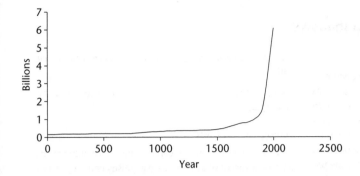

Fig. 14.1 World population AD 1–2000
Source: Facing the Future: People and Planet:
www.popinfo.org/index.htm

every day. It reinforces the neo-classical economic assumption that indefinite economic growth is both possible and necessary. It assumes, too, that it is possible and logical for the South to follow the development path of the North and continue to industrialize and intensify agricultural production. The globe can barely sustain the current population. How, critics ask, can it sustain another 3 billion in 2050? How can Africa sustain an additional 1 billion people in 2050, more than double its current population? (See Population Reference Bureau 2002: 4.)

The net effect of globalization, moreover, is to enlarge the *ecological footprint* of *each* person on the planet, by promoting ever more economic growth as well as cultivating an almost religious faith in the value of consumption—in the value of electronic toys, cars, and fast food (Robbins 2002)—all of which requires more and more natural resources, energy, and infrastructure to produce. The growing integration and disparities among economies are also increasing the extent and number of *ecological shadows*, which tend to shift the ecological damage of more powerful economies to weaker economies (see Box 14.2).

Critics contend, too, that globalization is encouraging ever more economic growth and production with no real concern about unequal or unsustainable patterns of consumption. It exacerbates the ecological inequality within and between countries and marginalizes women, indigenous peoples, and the poor. The global political economy is constructing, for critics like William Rees and Laura Westra (2003), a world of 'eco-apartheid' and 'eco-violence'. Globalization tears, too, at the fabric of local communities, destroying historic patterns of trust, cooperation, and knowledge so essential to ecological and social balance.

In short, it destroys the living environments of much of the world's people.

There can be, in the view of critics, no environmental justice or biological balance in a globalized world where the super-rich like Bill Gates and J. K. Rowling live alongside (metaphorically, that is, in their mansions) the 1.2 billion who live on less than US$1 per day and the 2.8 billion who live on less than US$2 per day. Over a billion people do not have access to clean water (UNFPA 2001: 5). Nearly 800 million people in the South suffer from chronic malnutrition (World Bank 2002d: 40). Unhealthy environments aggravate illnesses, contributing, for example, to the deaths of more than 4.7 million children under the age of 5 in 2000 (WHO 2002). The future under current patterns of globalization, critics argue, is one of greater horrors still: of pandemics like AIDS, which UNAIDS (2002) predicts will kill 68 million people between 2000 and 2020. Over 80 per cent of these victims will come from Sub-Saharan Africa, where already average life expectancy has fallen to just 47 years. What is needed, critics like Colin Hines (2000) argue, is not globalization, but localization.

The latest biological trends, critics note further, confirm the beginnings of a global Easter Island. Humans are now the dominant predator in every ecosystem (even in the seemingly limitless Pacific and Atlantic Oceans), and unless strict restraints are put in place humans will exhaust the globe's natural resources, fill its sinks, and overstep the earth's capacity to support life. Half the world's forests and wetlands are already gone. Every day another thirty to 100 species go extinct. One of the more worrying findings in recent years, say critics, is the ten-year survey by Ransom Myers and Boris Worm (2003), which

Box 14.2 **Ecological footprints and shadows**

Ecological footprints

Bill Rees and Mathis Wackernagel created this concept to measure the sustainability of human lifestyles. It translates human consumption of renewable natural resources into hectares of average biologically productive land. A person's footprint is the total area in global hectares (one hectare of average biological productivity) required to sustain his or her lifestyle: food and water, clothes, shelter, transportation, and consumer goods and services. The concept allows an analyst to compare the average ecological impact of people from Africa to Australia to China to the United Kingdom to the United States. The average global ecological footprint in 1999 was 2.3 global hectares per person. There were, however, great differences across the globe. In Africa it was 1.36 global hectares (with lows in Mozambique of 0.47 and Burundi of 0.48) and in China it was 1.54. In contrast, the average footprint of someone in the United Kingdom was 5.35 and in the United States it was 9.7.

This measure also allows an analyst to compare the world ecological footprint with the total biological productive capacity of the earth. The total productive capacity of the earth in 1999 was roughly 11.4 billion hectares. From 1961 to 1999 the world ecological footprint grew by 80 per cent, reaching 13.7 billion hectares in 1999—20 per cent above the earth's biological capacity. Humanity, the WWF laments, is now 'running an ecological deficit with the Earth'.

Sources: Wackernagel and Rees (1996); WWF (2002): 2–4, 22–8.

Ecological shadows

This concept is designed to capture the extent of the environmental impact of a nation state in jurisdictions beyond its sovereign control. Ecological shadows arise as economies, through both intentional and unintentional patterns of consumption, trade, investment, and financing, transfer the environmental harm of its citizens outside its territory. This concept is particularly useful for analysing the environmental impact of more powerful economies on weaker (dependent) economies. The United States, for example, casts a large ecological shadow over South America. Such shadows can extend down a chain of weaker economies. Japan, for example, casts an ecological shadow over Thailand, which in turn casts a shadow over neighbours like Cambodia and Laos. Ecological shadows do not arise from straightforward North–South exploitation. Often, elites in weak economies in the South profit personally from these ecological shadows, commonly acting as the agents of the ecological destruction, for example, as miners, fishers, and loggers.

Sources: MacNeill, Winsemius, and Yakushiji (1991); Dauvergne (1997).

---

found a 90 per cent decline in the ocean's large predatory fish—such as tuna, swordfish, marlin, cod, and flounder—over the last fifty years. The waters of Ernest Hemingway's *Old Man and the Sea* will soon be empty of the majestic marlin, a startling testimony, critics warn, not to the environmental consequences of the exploits of men like Hemingway's old man Santiago, but to the greed of industrial fishing boats plying the oceans to feed global markets.

Supporters and critics of a globalizing world, then, hold starkly different pictures of the current and future state of the global environment. The trends and statistics to support the statement 'globalization is good for the environment' seem convincing. Yet so do the trends and statistics that 'globalization is bad for the environment'. The truth seems to lie some-where in the middle: globalization is producing *both* constructive and destructive ecological processes. The goal is to somehow harness globalization to ensure sustainability. What has the global community done so far to harness globalization and manage global environmental affairs? The next section turns to examine the history of environmentalism with an eye on this question.

Key points

- Some perceive the *net* ecological impact of globalization as positive, as a force of progress and better lives. It fosters economic growth and cooperative institutions, both necessary in the long run to manage the global environment.

- Others see the *net* impact as negative, as a force sinking the globe into a bog of ecological decay. It is accelerating the destructive process of too many people consuming too many natural resources without any concern for equality or justice.

- Both the pro- and anti-globalization camps present persuasive data and arguments. Globalization involves multiple and complex sets of overlapping processes. Inevitably, there will be manifold and at times cross-cutting effects on the global environment.

History of global environmentalism

Collective human efforts to control nature began in earnest 8,000 to 15,000 years ago as nomadic hunters-and-gatherers in various locales began to shift to settled agriculture. Great civilizations sprang up, inventing such wonders as the plough (animal drawn), the wheel, writing, and numbers. Often, nature was subsumed in the quest for human progress, and many civilizations cut down regional forests, degraded land, and polluted local waters. Environmental decay even toppled a few great civilizations, such as Mesopotamia (a land between the Tigris and Euphrates Rivers, part of contemporary Iraq), where a poorly designed irrigation system gradually poisoned the agricultural land with salt. For most of the history of civilization, however, the scale of human activity has been too small to alter the global environment—that is, to induce climate change, deplete the ozone layer, empty the oceans, or destroy global biodiversity stocks.

This began to change with the dawn of the industrial revolution some 300 years ago. Production and energy use (including the burning of coal) began to rise rapidly. The global population of 600 million or so began to multiply. There were a billion people by the early 1800s; 2 billion by the end of the 1920s. The wealthy began to extract more natural resources, faster, from increasingly remote parts of the globe (often through colonial administrations). Such activities strained local and regional environments. The evidence was stark. Smog in cities like London and New York killed thousands in the nineteenth and twentieth centuries. Once seemingly boundless species, like the plains bison of North America, were brought to near extinction. Some, like the passenger pigeon, a bird that once migrated through eastern North America in millions, went extinct (in 1914).

Governments reacted to these environmental disasters with new national and regional policies. At first these were aimed primarily at either conservation of wildlife or more effective resource management. Canada and the United States, for example, signed the Migratory Birds Treaty in 1918. Colonial powers reacted as well, putting in place policies (like sustained yield management) to try and ensure more efficient and rational resource extraction. After the Second World War, ordinary citizens began to become increasingly worried about the biological impacts of industrialization and agricultural production. Anxiety mounted after Rachel Carson's (1962) best-seller, *Silent Spring*, shocked popular consciousness with images of pesticide-laden food chains and dying ecosystems.

Worries about the health of the 'global environment' began to emerge around this time as well. The picture of the earth from space, beautiful and fragile and borderless, became a compelling global ecological image. These concerns fed into the sense of mutual economic vulnerability of post-war economies (including those in the North and South). Ehrlich's 1968 best-seller, *The Population Bomb*, added a new and perturbing image: the earth left barren by an exploding population. 'In the 1970s', he boldly predicted, 'the world will undergo famines—hundreds of millions of people are going to starve to death' (1968: xi).

Concern over the health of the global environment continued to rise in the late 1960s and early 1970s. Experts met in 1968 at the United Nations Biosphere Conference to discuss global environmental problems. The first Earth Day was held in the United States in April 1970. Twenty million rallied, one of the largest organized demonstrations in the history of the United States. That same year the US government founded the Environmental Protection Agency (EPA). Canada created a Department of the Environment the following year. The outcome of this growing societal and political concern was the United Nations Conference on the Human Environment, held in Stockholm, Sweden, in June 1972.

The Stockholm Conference and the 1970s

The Stockholm Conference, organized by Canada's Maurice Strong, was the first global United Nations conference for state officials on the environment. There were 1,200 delegates from over a hundred countries. Swedish Prime Minister Olaf Palme and Indian Prime Minister Indira Gandhi were the only heads of state to attend. Russia and the communist bloc countries boycotted the conference to protest against the exclusion of East Germany.

The North was initially interested in addressing industrial pollution, nature conservation, and population growth. The South was more worried about development, and did not want the anxieties of rich conservationists to deny poorer countries the benefits of economic growth and industrialization (an ongoing source of conflict). There were tensions, too, over who would pay and who was responsible for solving global environmental problems. Many Southern delegates saw global capitalism as a core reason for poverty, and there was general anger that global economic institutions were pushing developing countries to export raw materials on declining terms of trade. The phrase 'the pollution of poverty' was coined at Stockholm, to express the idea that poverty was the greatest global environmental threat. Many delegates from the South called for global economic reforms to help solve the pollution of poverty.

In the end, conference delegates tried to reconcile the desire (need) for economic development in the South with the need to protect the global environment for all. Most governments came to recognize a mutual interdependence and vulnerability of North and South. The official conference documents, however, *did not* emphasize the Southern calls for global economic reforms. The conference produced a Declaration on the Human Environment (with twenty-six principles), an Action Plan for the Human Environment (with 109 recommendations), and a Resolution on Institutional and Financial Arrangements. These were non-binding on signatory states—and most scholars agree that Stockholm produced few practical commitments to address global environmental change.

The Stockholm Conference did, however, signal a growing concern among national governments over the global environment. It also led to a General Assembly decision to create the United Nations Environment Programme (UNEP), officially launched in 1973, with Maurice Strong as the first executive director. The United Nations Environment Programme was designed as a relatively weak global institution. It was headquartered in Nairobi, Kenya, rather than in New York, Geneva, or Vienna. And it was established as a coordinating programme with a small budget rather than as a specialized agency. This was in the interest of all sides. The North did not want to finance a large institution. The South did not want a global institution with the power to interfere with development goals. And other United Nation agencies did not want to relinquish significant 'turf' (Elliot 1998: 11–13).

After Stockholm, OPEC's restrictions on oil supplies in 1973–4 rocked the global economy. Oil prices quadrupled, inflation soared, and economic growth became sluggish worldwide. This economic turbulence deflated some of the potential for more aggressive global environmental initiatives after Stockholm. The South, in particular, became even more worried about the effects on debt levels and prospects for industrial development. Still, the debate over how to handle global environmental change continued, sparked by groundbreaking books like the Club of Rome's (1972) *Limits to Growth* and E. F. Schumacher's (1973) *Small is Beautiful*. The global community also signed noteworthy global environmental treaties just after Stockholm. These include the Convention on the Prevention of Marine Pollution by Dumping of Wastes and other Matter (the London Convention, 1972, entered into force in 1975), the Convention on International Trade in Endangered Species of Wild Flora and Fauna (CITES, 1973, entered into force in 1975), and the Convention for the Prevention of Pollution by Ships (MARPOL, 1973, entered into force in 1975).

Environment slid more into the background of global affairs in the second half of the 1970s and first half of the 1980s. There was nevertheless a great deal of environmental activity. Scientists continued to research global environmental change. Non-governmental organizations continued to campaign and pressure governments and firms. Individual states, including in the South, continued to establish environmental agencies. States continued as well to sign and ratify global environmental agreements, such as the 1980 Convention on the Conservation of Antarctic Marine Living Resources (entered into force in 1982). The global community, too, continued to debate and make some headway on how best to manage the need for development (especially in the South) with the need for a healthy global environment. Problems like the depletion of the ozone layer, and disasters like the nuclear accident at Three Mile Island in 1979, the Union Carbide chemical leak in Bhopal in 1984, and the Chernobyl nuclear meltdown in 1986, added a sense of urgency. Slowly, environmental issues began again to move back up the global agenda. The debate by the mid-1980s began increasingly to focus on the concept of *sustainable development*. The publication in 1987 of the World Commission on Environment and Development report, *Our Common Future*, synthesized and consolidated the global debates over environment and development, defining sustainable development as 'development that meets the needs of the present without compromising the ability of future generations to meet their own needs' (WCED 1987: 43).

The Brundtland Commission

The World Commission on Environment and Development, commonly known as the Brundtland Commission, was chaired by the former prime minister of Norway, Gro Harlem Brundtland. There were twenty-three members serving in an expert rather than official state capacity—thirteen were from the South, including India, China, and Brazil. Among G7 countries only France and the United Kingdom did not have representatives. The Commission's report *Our Common Future*, commonly known as the Brundtland Report, is widely seen as a watershed in the evolution of environmental debates within the global community of state representatives. The content of the Brundtland Report is an ingenious

compromise. It does not foresee any necessary limits to growth, and industrialization and natural resource production are, under correct management, acceptable, indeed inevitable for some countries. The report calls for a transfer of environmental technologies and economic assistance to support sustainable development in the South. It calls, too, for more effective controls on population growth, as well as better education and food security in the South. It portrays poverty as a core cause of unsustainable development. The source of much of the poverty in the South, it argues, is the position of developing economies within the global structure. The best way forward, then, is to stimulate—not slow—economic growth: not the unchecked growth of the 1960s and 1970s, however, but growth from sustainable development.

States continued to negotiate and sign global environmental treaties leading up to and after the publication of the Brundtland Report. These include the 1985 Vienna Convention for the Protection of the Ozone Layer, the 1987 Montreal Protocol on Substances that Deplete the Ozone Layer, and the 1989 Basel Convention on the Control of Transboundary Movements of Hazardous Waste and their Disposal. By the late 1980s global environmental issues had again crept back to the top of the global agenda, culminating in a 1989 United Nations General Assembly resolution to hold the first summit of world leaders on the global environment: what became the 1992 United Nations Conference on Environment and Development (UNCED), held in Rio de Janeiro, Brazil.

The Rio (Earth) Summit

The UNCED Conference is popularly known as the Rio or Earth Summit. Again, as with the Stockholm Conference twenty years earlier, Maurice Strong was the secretary-general and the main organizer (Strong 2000). The Rio Summit was the largest United Nations conference to date, with most countries and 117 heads of state participating. There were thousands of non-governmental representatives at the official conference as well as at a parallel NGO forum. The recommendations in the Brundtland Report and the notion of sustainable development formed the core of the debate at Rio. Most countries endorsed the

Brundtland definition of sustainable development. Many developing countries, however, wanted specific assurances of transfers of environmental technologies and economic assistance from the North to support the additional costs of green growth. Many Northern states, on the other hand, were reluctant to assume further financial commitments (Rogers 1993: 238–9).

The Rio Summit put environment and development on the agendas of global leaders. It reinforced, too, the Brundtland Commission assumption that more growth was compatible with a better global environment. Two official Rio Summit documents of particular note are the Rio Declaration on Environment and Development, and Agenda 21. The Rio Declaration is a set of twenty-seven principles on the rights and responsibilities of states for environment and development. These principles include far more of the South's concerns about the right to development than the Stockholm Declaration on the Human Environment. Agenda 21 is a 300-page action programme to promote sustainable development (UN 1992).

The Rio Summit also produced the Non-legally Binding Authoritative Statement of Principles for a Global Consensus on the Management, Conservation and Sustainable Development of all Types of Forests. The original intent was to sign a legally binding forest treaty, but after irreconcilable differences arose among negotiators over the terms of an agreement the conference settled for a non-binding statement of principles (Brack, Calder, and Dolun 2001: 2). Rio also opened two conventions for signature: the United Nations Framework Convention on Climate Change and the Convention on Biological Diversity. Negotiations began, too, on a treaty on desertification. Finally, the conference established the United Nations Commission on Sustainable Development to monitor and evaluate the progress on meeting the Rio objectives.

The Rio Summit was a historic global conference hailed by many states as a great success. Critics from all sides, however, lamented the inadequate amount of 'promised' funds—especially from the North—to implement Agenda 21. More radical environmentalists, too, attacked the Brundtland definition of sustainable development—in particular its support for more economic growth and industrialization. Among activists, there was in addition a general concern that the negotiators ignored the root cause of global environmental change: the inequalities, unsustainable industrial production and growth, and overconsumption that arise from corporate globalization and free trade. That, in fact, industry captured the agenda at Rio (Chatterjee and Finger 1994), and the outcomes were little more than an incompetent doctor (the state system) slapping a Band-Aid onto a cancerous tumour (capitalism). Other critics also felt the Rio Summit entrenched a top-down set of solutions, without nearly enough focus on the needs of local communities or the plight of women and indigenous peoples (Shiva 1993; Lohmann 1993).

The decade after Rio saw global environmental issues again slip down the list of state priorities. States turned to the threats of terrorism, chemical and biological warfare, and global financial crises. The global community nevertheless kept signing and ratifying environmental treaties. The Convention on Biological Diversity, for example, was opened for signature in 1992 (entered into force in 1993). The United Nations Convention on the Law of the Sea, though first opened for signature in 1982, entered into force in 1994. The United Nations Convention to Combat Desertification in Those Countries Experiencing Serious Drought and/or Desertification, Particularly in Africa was opened for signature in 1994 (entered into force in 1996). The Kyoto Protocol to the United Nations Framework Convention on Climate Change was opened for signature in 1998 (not in force as of July 2004). The Stockholm Convention on Persistent Organic Pollutants (POPs) was opened for signature in 2001 (in force as of May 2004) (see Table 14.1).

The global community also continued to discuss and review the progress of Agenda 21 and the implementation of sustainable development, including a 1997 special session of the United Nations General Assembly, known as the Earth Summit +5. The global community prepared as well for the World Summit on Sustainable Development, eventually held in Johannesburg, South Africa, in 2002.

Johannesburg and beyond

The World Summit on Sustainable Development is popularly called Rio +10 or the Johannesburg Summit. The purpose was to evaluate the progress of

Table 14.1 Examples of international environmental agreements

Name of the agreement	Opened for signature	Entered into force	Website
International Convention for the Regulation of Whaling	1946	1948	www.iwcoffice.org
Convention on Wetlands of International Importance Especially as Waterfowl Habitat (Ramsar)	1971	1975	www.ramsar.org
Convention on the Prevention of Marine Pollution by Dumping Wastes and Other Matter (London Convention)	1972	1975	www.imo.org
Convention on the International Trade in Endangered Species of Wild Flora and Fauna (CITES)	1973	1975	www.cites.org
Convention on the Conservation of Antarctic Marine Living Resources	1980	1982, as part of the Antarctic Treaty System	www.ccamlr.org
Montreal Protocol on Substances that Deplete the Ozone Layer	1987	1989	www.unep.org/ozone
Basel Convention on the Control of Transboundary Movements of Hazardous Wastes and their Disposal	1989	1992	www.basel.int
Convention on Biological Diversity	1992	1993	www.biodiv.org
United Nations Convention on the Law of the Sea (LOS)	1982	1994	www.un.org/Depts/los
United Nations Convention to Combat Desertification in Those Countries Experiencing Serious Drought and/or Desertification, Particularly in Africa	1994	1996	www.unccd.int
Kyoto Protocol to the United Nations Framework Convention on Climate Change	1998	Not in force as of July 2004	www.unfccc.int
Stockholm Convention on Persistent Organic Pollutants (POPs)	2001	2004	www.chem.unep.ch/pops

Source: Compiled by the author.

sustainable development since the Rio Summit in 1992. It was also designed to establish specific targets to improve implementation of the Rio goals as well as develop a strategy to implement the United Nation's Millennium Development Goals (Mehta 2003: 122). The Johannesburg Summit—with over 180 nations, over 10,000 delegates, at least 8,000 civil society representatives, and 4,000 members of the press, as well as countless ordinary citizens—was even larger than the Rio Summit. Revealingly, however, there were only about 100 heads of state, fewer than at Rio.

The official documents of Johannesburg were similar to Rio and Stockholm in their broad calls for global sustainability. The two most important were the Johannesburg Declaration on Sustainable Development, a list of challenges and general commitments, and the Johannesburg Plan of Implementation to meet these. These are non-binding, but nevertheless represent significant political compromises. One of the most contentious issues, as was the case too at Rio, was financing. But Johannesburg also added two equally tough topics: the impact of globalization on sustainable development as well as specific timetables/targets to meet goals (Mehta 2003: 122). The Johannesburg Declaration on Sustainable Development (2002) reflects the debates over globalization. Point 12 declares: 'The deep fault line that divides human society between the rich and the poor and the ever-increasing gap between the developed and developing worlds pose a major threat to global prosperity, security and stability.' Point 14 states: 'Globalization has added a new dimension to [global environmental problems]. The rapid integration of markets, the increasing mobility of capital and significant upsurge in investment flows around the world have opened new challenges and opportunities for the pursuit of sustainable development. But the benefits and costs of globalization are unevenly distributed, with developing countries facing special difficulties in meeting this challenge.'

Was the Johannesburg Summit a success? The answer naturally depends on the definition of success. No doubt, like Stockholm and Rio, it helped to focus the attention of world leaders on global environmental change. The preparation and outcomes also cemented sustainable development as the core organizing concept for global and national environmental institutions. Some see the outcomes as constructive and as more realistic than the outcomes of Rio. Others, though, see the conference as a symbol of the global failure to sincerely tackle global environmental problems. They see the targets and timetables as weak, and the Johannesburg Declaration as little more than a restatement of the past, doing little to promote global sustainability (Burg 2003: 116–18). These critics also see the official statements on globalization as little more than bland and evasive whitewash. The Johannesburg Summit added yet another layer to global environmentalism, but as with Stockholm and Rio it seems highly unlikely it will stem the tide of ecological decay. Paul Wapner (2003: 7), in his assessment of the Johannesburg Summit outcomes, sums this up nicely: 'The strains on the earth's sources, sinks and sites have intensified dramatically since Rio and show no sign of decreasing in the near future.' In short, critics worry that environmentalism piloted by the principle of sustainable development is too weak to manage global environmental change. It does not, in particular, have the depth or content to restrain the ecological impacts of the globalization of production, consumption, trade, and corporations—the focus of the next section of the chapter.

Key points

- Environmental change began to accelerate some 300 years ago, after the Industrial Revolution intensified production and colonizers reached into distant lands.

- By the late 1960s governments began to recognize the need to cooperate to address global environmental problems. The result was the 1972 United Nations Conference on the Human Environment.

- A global compromise gradually emerged in the 1970s and 1980s around the concept of sustainable development, as defined by the Brundtland Commission in 1987.

- The Rio Summit in 1992 set an ambitious agenda for global sustainable development. Progress, however, was slow and uneven over the next decade. Ten years later the Johannesburg Summit endeavoured to facilitate implementation of the Rio goals.

- The net result has left thick layers of global environmentalism (treaties, norms, and institutions) with the Brundtland Commission's concept of sustainable development at the core. Supporters see this as evidence of the global community's capacity to handle global environmental change. Critics see it as camouflage for 'business as usual'.

Economic growth, trade, and corporations

What is the ecological impact of economic growth, trade, and corporations under globalization? Some see the net impact as positive for the health of the planet. It pulls destitute people—who are prone to degrade surrounding environments to survive—out of poverty. And it raises national per capita incomes, which generate the funds, technologies, and political will to implement sustainable development. In the short run, such growth produces more food and better medical care, which in turn lengthens life expectancy and allows the global population to rise. This undeniably creates global ecological pressures. But, advocates of economic growth contend, this is a temporary problem. The global population will stabilize at 9 or 10 billion, probably in fifty years or so, in part because globalization is raising the standards of living and education levels of women in the South.

Others see economic growth and corporate globalization as core causes of the global environmental crisis. These forces are distributing environmental effects unequally, where the rich get richer and the poor remain confined in ever-worse environments. It is also driving up per capita consumption in the South (without improving well-being) and over-consumption in the North. Already the number of humans is well beyond the earth's carrying capacity. The global population may well stabilize in fifty years' time. But that is still another 3 to 4 billion people to feed, clothe, and shelter. How many earths, these critics wonder, are we planning to live on?

Which side is correct? To begin, the next section outlines the environmental arguments for more economic growth, more free trade, and more foreign investment.

Trading for growth and a better environment

A world free of poverty, say economists at institutions like the World Bank, is critical for the long-term health of the planet. The struggle of the poor to survive is a core cause of problems like deforestation, desertification, and unsanitary water. The poor forage for wood to cook and heat homes. They exhaust nearby natural resources, such as fresh water, seafood, and wildlife. They cultivate unsuitable land to grow food and earn income. And they despoil local waterways with garbage and sewage. Stating these facts, advocates of economic growth argue, is not an attempt to assign blame. Rather, the point is far simpler: poor people have little choice if they wish to survive.

The poor and uneducated, too, tend to have more children than the rich, which creates a spiral of poverty and ecological collapse as ever more people forage for food, water, and shelter on increasingly fragile lands. This spiral occurs for many reasons besides just weak economic growth. Other factors include insecure property rights, the failure of family planning, inadequate government services and regulations, trade distortions, and insufficient investment and development assistance. The spiral downward accelerates during times of slow growth—that is, during an economic recession or depression—since firms are less willing to invest in cleaner technologies, and states are less willing and less able to enforce environmental laws. A quick glance at environmental management in Asia during the 1997–9 financial crisis confirms this (Dauvergne 1999).

Admittedly, advocates note, economic growth can worsen environmental conditions in the short run. Air and water quality, for example, can deteriorate in the early stages of industrial production. Yet in the long run, once a society harnesses sufficient per capita wealth, environmental standards will invariably rise. Advocates of economic growth commonly illustrate this with the Environmental Kuznets Curve (see Figure 14.2). This Curve demonstrates that pollution (such as smog and lead) will rise along with economic growth during the early stages of industrial development. This occurs because governments focus on increasing industrial growth and national income rather than on pollution controls. Yet this is a temporary phenomenon. Once per capita income reaches high levels (in the past often between US$5,000 and US$8,000), pollution begins to fall (Grossman and Krueger 1995). This partly occurs because citizens demand better living environments, and partly because firms and governments now have the financial and institutional capacity to respond effectively. It partly arises, too, because strong economies naturally tend to move away from heavy industry and toward service and information industries.

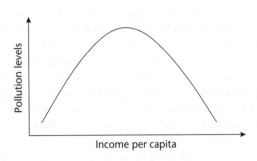

Fig. 14.2 Environmental Kuznets Curve

The Environmental Kuznets Curve usually draws on data for industrial pollution rather than natural resources. A recent study, however, found a correlation between lower deforestation and higher national income in Asia, Latin America, and Africa (Bhattarai and Hammig 2001).

Japan's environmental history fits the Environmental Kuznets Curve well. After the Second World War industrial production and economic growth in Japan soared, and by the 1960s Japan was suffering from acute pollution, 'not unlike many of the heavily polluted areas of India, China, and Southeast Asia today' (Schreurs 2002: 36). Citizen protests over the health consequences of pollution escalated in the 1960s and 1970s. In response, the Japanese government passed strict environmental regulations and Japanese business developed new environmental technologies (McKean 1981; Broadbent 1998). The result was a dramatic improvement in the domestic environment.

Environmental advocates of economic growth do not generally propose that states with low per capita incomes should blindly pursue economic growth. For most, the Environmental Kuznets Curve suggests two critical lessons. First, that in the long run economic growth will improve environmental institutions and governance. Second, that, following the logic of the Environmental Kuznets Curve, it is feasible to use measures such as ecological markets, technological advances, sound policies, and global institutions to help countries with low per capita incomes to 'tunnel' through the middle of the Curve, attaining high per capita incomes with less environmental damage.

The globalization of free trade—following the principles of absolute and comparative advantage—will also help these weak economies tunnel through the Environmental Kuznets Curve. Free trade fosters efficient worldwide production as well as the transfer of environmental technologies and higher environmental standards from the North to the South (Neumayer 2001; WTO 1999b). This means humanity is able to produce more goods with fewer resources, which stimulates global economic growth and raises national per capita incomes. The extra income from efficient production is necessary, too, for sustainable development. More income means that more can be spent to preserve the environment as well as enforce environmental regulations. World Trade Organization director-general, Mike Moore, succinctly explains the logic: 'Every WTO Member Government supports open trade because it leads to higher living standards for working families which in turn leads to a cleaner environment' (WTO 1999b).

Trade liberalization, too, produces significant environmental rewards. Trade barriers distort price signals of natural resources. Prices therefore do not reflect real scarcities or pollution costs, which in turn creates waste and overconsumption. Liberalization also fosters cleaner production processes, as firms that produce goods behind trade barriers face less competition and have fewer incentives to upgrade facilities or use resources efficiently. States with more liberal trade policies are also, advocates argue, more likely to meet global environmental standards. 'Liberalized trade', the World Bank (1992: 67) explains, 'fosters greater efficiency and higher productivity and may actually reduce pollution by encouraging the growth of less-polluting industries and the adoption and diffusion of cleaner technologies.' Trade liberalization can further pressure producers with low environmental standards to raise these standards to gain access to markets with higher standards. This 'trading up' of environmental standards, David Vogel (1995) argues, occurred for example when California's strict auto emission standards pushed up standards across the United States as well as in Japan and Germany. Germany's willingness to support tougher European Union standards in part reflected its experience in the US market.

Restricting trade for environmental reasons, advocates of open trade argue, is on occasion necessary— such as to protect endangered species or control the dumping of hazardous waste and dangerous chemicals. Yet far more often restricting trade on environmental grounds is illogical and counter-productive. Sound policies and incentives within an open trading structure lead to much better long-term environmental management. Green markets—where prices throughout a trade chain internalize environmental and social costs, and where consumers voluntarily pay higher prices for these products—are another effective means to promote sustainable development.

The globalization of corporations, argue supporters, will further promote sustainable development. Transnational corporations (TNCs) transfer critical technologies, expertise, and funds into the South. Without this investment, economies stagnate and slip backwards and sustain environmental degradation—a quick glance at North Korea or Sub-Saharan Africa confirms this. Transnational corporations that invest in the South also tend to employ higher environmental standards than local laws require—what Roniel Garcia-Johnson (2000) calls 'exporting environmentalism'. This occurs for a host of reasons: partly because of more sophisticated technologies and management techniques; partly because of pressure from states, NGOs, shareholders, and consumers; partly because of internal codes of conduct and risk-management strategies; and partly because the resulting efficiencies can provide a competitive advantage.

There is as well a trend among all firms since the 1980s to voluntarily 'green' operations (Schmidheiny 1992). For example, Responsible Care—an environmental and safety code for the chemical industry—was established in 1985. The Global Environmental Management Initiative (GEMI) was created by the International Chamber of Commerce in 1990 to implement the Chamber's business charter for sustainable development (Sklair 2001: 204). There was a flood of voluntary industry codes after the 1992 Rio Summit. The ISO 14001 certifiable standards for environmental management have been widely adopted by business since the mid-1990s (see Box 14.3). Industry founded the World Business Council of Sustainable Development in 1995 to address 'the challenges and opportunities of sustainable development based on three fundamental and inseparable pillars: the generation of economic wealth, environmental improvement and social responsibility' (Holme and Watts 2000: 5). The Johannesburg Summit saw the business community stress the need for voluntary corporate leadership to promote sustainable development. Corporations are now embracing the principle of Corporate Social Responsibility. Chairman and Chief Executive Officer of AT&T, C. Michael Armstrong, explains the logic of the greening of AT&T: 'AT&T understands the need for a global alliance of business, society and the environment. In the 21st century, the world won't tolerate businesses that don't take that partnership seriously, but it will eventually reward companies that do' (quoted in Holme and Watts 2000: 1).

Box 14.3 ISO 14000 and ISO 14001

The International Organization for Standardization (ISO), headquartered in Geneva, advances voluntary international standards for particular products and for environmental management. The ISO develops these standards relying on consensus and voluntary participation among ISO member countries. ISO 14000 is a series of voluntary environmental standards, including for environmental auditing, performance, labelling, and most importantly, the ISO 14001 Environmental Management System (EMS) Standard. The ISO 14001 standard allows for certification from an external authority. It requires a community or organization to implement practices and procedures that together comprise a system of environmental management. It also requires a policy to prevent pollution and continually improve environmental performance.

Source: ISO website, at **www.iso14000.com**

Most states and global institutions accept the need for more economic growth, more open trade and more foreign investment. There are critics, however, many of whom see the relentless pursuit of growth, trade, and investment under globalization as a primary cause of the global environmental crisis.

Trading away the earth for unequal consumption

Critics contend that the Environmental Kuznets Curve is misleading. They see the link between growth and lower long-term pollution as simplistic. It is possible, critics argue, for economies to get stuck along the curve, never reaching a point where pollution declines (Arrow et al. 1998; Tisdell 2001: 187). The Curve does not account for the integrity of the ecosystem as a whole and it ignores irreplaceable losses (such as biodiversity and species loss). It discounts, too, the potential for cumulative ecological change to erupt into a sudden and uncontainable crisis. It does not address the possibility that, as the amount of one toxic substance declines, the amount of another may rise. The Curve, moreover, only works for a limited range of pollutants and resources. It fails, for example, for CO_2 emissions (the leading cause of global warming), which have been steadily rising alongside growth. Finally, a decline of a particular pollutant in one country may occur because industrial production shifts offshore. Japan's domestic environment was able to improve, for example, partly because dirty industries shifted into South-East and North-East Asia (Hall 2002).

Environmental critics of economic growth argue further that production patterns and unequal consumption—not poverty—are the driving forces of global environmental decay. The earth is already beyond its carrying capacity. The push for constant economic growth under globalization, critics contend, means that industrialization, intensive agriculture, and unsustainable natural resource extraction will continue to rise. Globalization also 'distances' production from consumption, so end users do not 'see' the ecological effects of individual purchases or disposal (Princen 1997; Clapp 2002). Products like computers often become obsolete in a few years, partly because of the design. This, along with advertising, is contributing to ever higher levels of consumption in both the North and South. Total consumption, for example, doubled in real terms from 1973 to 1998. There has been a fourfold rise in energy consumption since 1950. These rises, moreover, have not solved the gross inequalities between consumption in the South and North. Africa's per capita consumption has been declining over the past two decades. Meanwhile the North, with about 15 per cent of the global population, accounts for about three-quarters of global consumption expenditure (UNDP 1998: 46, 50). The United States alone, with a mere 5 per cent of the global population, consumes 30 per cent of the world's resources (Myers 1997: 34). Much of this consumption, critics argue, is wasteful and excessive—creating a world where obesity is the latest crisis of the North and malnutrition is the everlasting crisis of the South.

Global free trade, critics contend, merely adds to the earth's unsustainable ecological burden (Daly 1993, 1996, 2002). The prices of traded goods generally do not reflect the full environmental and social costs of production—the value, for example, of an old-growth tree as a source of biodiversity—leaving consumer prices far too low and consumption far too high for global sustainability (Arden-Clarke 1992). Environmental critics further argue that trade and trade agreements put downward pressure on environmental standards. This occurs because governments, in a bid to become more competitive in global markets, sometimes lower or fail to strengthen environmental management. Some see this as creating a 'race to the bottom'; others see it as leaving countries 'stuck at the bottom' (Esty 1994; Porter 1999). For many, the only solution to the ecological drawbacks of trade is to impose strict controls over trade.

Production under free trade may well become more 'efficient', critics add, but the steady increase in the production of goods overrides any environmental gains—creating, for example, a world full of billions of fuel-efficient cars rather than millions of fuel-inefficient cars. Global free trade, moreover, is in fact far from 'free'. Nor is it equal or fair as highly mobile capital exploits the so-called comparative advantages of weak economies. The ideology of free trade in reality translates into patterns of exchange that exploit the labour and environments of the South and protect the interests of the North (such as farmers). The South ends up exporting unsustainable quantities of natural resources and absorbing ecological damage so the North can prosper. Production-for-export from the South tends to rely on either unsustainable quantities of natural resources or on dirty and unsafe factories (and, of course, cheap labour). Logging and mining sites and textile and electronic factories in Latin America, Africa, and the Asia-Pacific highlight the ecological damage of such production (Marchak 1995; Gedicks 2001; Karliner 1997). Global trade, critics conclude, in effect allows the North to live beyond its carrying capacity, doing so by using up the carrying capacity of the South.

Critics see corporate globalization as a fundamental cause of the escalating global ecological crisis. Transnational corporations are viewed as engines of environmental exploitation, plundering the globe's limited resources for quick profits. In particular, critics see *pollution havens* and *double standards* as real or potential threats to sustainability. A pollution haven refers to governments using lower environmental standards to induce firms to invest, thus creating a haven for polluters. It does not, as David

Wheeler (2002: 1) points out, 'necessarily refer to a region that is seriously polluted'. What really matters is 'the willingness of the host government to "play the environment card" to promote growth'. A double standard refers to cases where a firm applies one set of standards at home and another set overseas (generally lower standards in countries with weaker laws). Double standards are common, and most economists would agree, a normal outcome of the process of development. The case of the American TNC, Union Carbide, in Bhopal, India, the site of the worst industrial accident in history, is perhaps the best-known case of double standards (the US headquarters was responsible for the plant's design) (MacKenzie 2002). But there are countless others, too (Karliner 1997; Frey 1998; Ofreneo 1993). The American firms General Electric, Ford, General Motors, and Westinghouse all, for example, operate plants in Northern Mexico, thus avoiding California's much tougher regulations on toxic emissions. Critics blame these TNCs for polluting local rivers, soils, and water supplies near these plants (Bryant and Bailey 1997: 109).

There is, then, little debate about the existence of double standards. The existence of pollution havens, however, is hotly debated. Critics of TNCs commonly assert that corporate globalization is producing pollution havens around the globe. The process of globalization spreads these because corporations are increasingly willing to relocate for the smallest differences in costs. Governments, meanwhile, are more prone to use lax regulations to entice investors. Most economists, however, argue that the reason for double standards *is not* a result of host governments intentionally and explicitly playing the environment card. There are, they claim, in fact few, if any, permanent pollution havens anywhere in the world (Wheeler 2002). There are many reasons. For some industries it is impractical or too risky to relocate for market or infrastructural reasons. The main reason, however, is that costs like labour and technology are far higher than environmental costs (Ferrantino 1997: 52). It therefore does not make financial sense for a firm to relocate on environmental grounds alone.

A second and much larger strand of environmental literature, which is critical of corporations, focuses less on the differential environmental practices of firms and more on practices 'on the ground'. These critics have filled libraries documenting the destructive and illegal practices of loggers, miners, oil companies, chemical companies, and so on (Dauvergne 2001; Gedicks 2001; Clapp 2001). Besides academics, research institutes like the World Resources Institute and countless numbers of NGOs also research and publish such findings. This research leads popular writers like Joshua Karliner (1997) to call the world a 'Corporate Planet' and David Korten (1995) to conclude that 'Corporations Rule the World'.

Key points

Advocates argue that the wealth from the globalization of trade and TNCs creates:

- Poverty alleviation, better education, population controls, and a stronger capacity of states and global institutions to implement sustainable development.

- Technological innovation and less harmful forms of production (for example, a shift from industry and agriculture to service and knowledge).

- Corporate investment that 'exports environmentalism' by transferring funds, new technologies, and higher standards to the South.

- Opportunities to use creative policies and incentives to tunnel through the Environmental Kuznets Curve.

Critics see unequal and destructive economic growth, trade, and investment that:

- Burden the South with unequal environmental costs and low environmental standards.

- Allow corporations to plunder the globe's fragile ecosystems.

- Generate consumer prices that ignore environmental and social costs of production.

- Drive overconsumption in the North and unbalanced consumption in the South, putting total global consumption well beyond the earth's carrying capacity.

A sustainable future? Financing and regimes

There is, then, a great divide between environmentalists who support and those who oppose globalization. Most agree, however, that it will no doubt require new consumption patterns, innovative markets, technological advances, corporate ethics, and cooperation to ensure a sustainable global economy. There are indeed reforms ongoing in all of these areas. Yet the global community has put much of its energy into funding sustainable development and into forming and strengthening global environmental agreements. Is sustainable development an effective core principle? Is funding sufficient? Can international agreements and sustainable development ensure globalization is a positive environmental force? Many in the global community—states and state negotiators in particular—believe in sustainable development and environmental agreements. Others, however, see them as, at best, harmless, and at worst, themselves causes of global environmental harm as the effort to reach a compromise lowers expectations, creates long delays, and ultimately contributes to ineffective policies. The next section addresses these issues with particular attention to global environmental financing and the political economy of three international regimes: ozone depletion, climate change, and forestry.

Financing sustainable development: the GEF

Few deny that the South requires assistance to implement sustainable development. How else can the South find the funds and personnel to address issues like climate change or global biodiversity? Yet critics lament the failure of environmental assistance. Some see total assistance as far too low—far below the repeated global promise of total overseas development assistance of 0.7 per cent of gross national income. The OECD average is just 0.22 per cent, while the United States is the lowest of the major donors, supplying a mere 0.11 per cent in 2001. Assistance for sustainable development is even lower. At the Rio Summit, for example, the North was only willing to commit to US$125 billion of the US$625 billion estimated as needed to implement Agenda 21 (UNEP 2002: 17).

Other critics see development assistance as a cause of global ecological stress. These critics see the conditions attached to this 'aid' as a tool of donors and corporate allies to exploit labour and natural resources in the South. Multilateral donors like the World Bank and bilateral donors like Japan (the world's largest bilateral donor over the 1990s), for example, use loans to require governments to eliminate trade barriers and support foreign investors. Heavy foreign debts, these critics contend, further aggravate ecological pressures as states export natural resources to earn the foreign exchange to service and repay the debt (Rich 1994).

The Global Environment Facility (GEF) is one of the few financial sources to specifically fund global environmental initiatives in the South. The GEF was first set up as a pilot facility in 1991 just before the Rio Summit. It formally became a permanent body in 1994. The GEF has three implementing agencies—the World Bank, the United Nations Development Programme (UNDP), and the UNEP—although the World Bank is the most influential. The Global Environment Facility is formally housed in the World Bank, though functionally independent. The UNDP handles technical assistance and the UNEP coordinates between the GEF and global environmental agreements. There are fourteen donor states, eighteen recipient states, and five NGOs on the GEF Council. GEF finances global environmental policies and programmes in developing countries, including ozone depletion, biodiversity, climate change, and persistent organic pollutants (Streck 2001). The GEF currently supports over 1,000 projects in over 140 countries. The total amount of GEF grants by 2003 was US$4 billion. The GEF has also managed to leverage US$12 billion in co-financing from other sources.

The GEF disburses grants and technical funds to cover the additional costs for developing countries of a project targeting a global environmental objective (such as to mitigate climate change or protect biodiversity). Some see GEF as a critical step forward to help the South absorb the financial costs of global sustainability. Others, like Bruce Rich of the NGO Environmental Defense, have lashed out at GEF, especially during the pilot phase: 'The formulation of the Global Environment Facility', he argues (1994: 176–7), 'was a model of the Bank's preferred way of doing business: Top-down, secretive, with a basic contempt for public participation, access to information, involvement of democratically elected legislatures, and informed discussion of alternatives.' These critics see GEF as little more than a financial Band-Aid that stresses top-down technological fixes rather than long-term solutions (Young 2003). These critics worry, too, that the World Bank is tying GEF grants to other World Bank loans that finance projects that damage the environment. Korinna Horta of Environmental Defense states: 'The World Bank mocks the principles and policies of the GEF by hypocritically funding and mitigating environmental destruction. The GEF "greenwashes" business as usual for the Bank' (Halifax Initiative 2002; also see Horta, Round, and Young 2002).

No doubt, funding for global sustainability is far from adequate. The global community has in some ways made more progress developing and strengthening environmental regimes.

Political economy of regimes

The global community has put great faith in international environmental agreements to guide globalization, promote cooperation, rein in free riders, and avoid the natural drift of a system of sovereign states toward a 'tragedy of the commons' (see Box 14.4). There has been a steady increase over the last three decades in the number of international and regional environmental negotiations, and today there are several hundred agreements (see Table 14.1 above, for examples).

An international environmental regime encompasses more than just international legal agreements. Steven Krasner's (1983: 2) definition of international regime is the classic one: 'sets of implicit or explicit principles, norms, rules and decision-making procedures around which actors' expectations converge in a given area of international relations' (see Aggarwal

and Dupont, Chapter 2 in this volume). Yet most international environmental regimes revolve around an international agreement. Such regimes tend to evolve in four phases. They begin with the recognition of a problem, including the scientific debates about the causes and severity, and the emergence of an agenda. The science here is often speculative, especially if, as with climate change, it involves looking hundreds of years into the future. Working through the science can create decades of delay during this phase as various 'experts' make claims and counterclaims. Dramatic events, like an oil spill or a chemical leak or a 'hole' in the ozone layer, can catalyse action toward the next stage—the negotiation of the rules and decision-making procedures. Here, coalitions of states or a powerful state like the USA can play a critical role either in the emergence or veto of an agreement. States may also shift gears during this phase—for example, signing an agreement then withdrawing later (for example, refusing to ratify). As with the emergence of an agenda, scientists or experts with collective policy preferences can play a key role in defining the content of an agreement (Haas 1992). So can networks of activists who work across traditional sovereign borders (Keck and Sikkink 1998). Once an agreement enters into force, parties to the agreement need to implement policies that meet their obligations. This phase can further strengthen or weaken a regime, as many states, even those legitimately striving to meet obligations, may be unable (or unwilling) to do so for technical or political reasons. Finally, regimes continue to evolve even after implementation begins, strengthening and weakening as norms shift (or sometimes as negotiators amend the formal rules).

There is a growing literature on evaluating the effectiveness of international environmental regimes (Victor, Raustiala, and Skolnikoff 1998; Young 1999, 2002; Vogler 2000, 2003). Some global environmental regimes are weak, with little influence over the behaviour of states and firms or, if there is influence, with little impact on global ecological conditions. An array of factors shape regime effectiveness. These include the scope and nature of the international rules as well as the strength of the national policies designed to meet international obligations.

National agencies are generally responsible for monitoring and enforcing international environmental

---

Box 14.4 **Tragedy of the commons**

Garrett Hardin (1968), in a now notorious article in *Science*, drew a vivid analogy of access and historical collapse of the English commons with access and future collapse of modern-day commons (like the high seas or the atmosphere or an unregulated forest). Look, he says, at a grazing pasture 'open to all'. It is in the rational self-interest of a farmer to breed and graze as many animals as possible. The addition of one more animal will enhance the wealth of the owner far more than it will degrade the pasture for the owner's herd. Without controls, however, the logic of personal gain will inevitably overfill and destroy the pasture. The process is the same for all commons with rising populations and unrestricted access. 'Ruin is the destination toward which all men rush', he argues 'each pursuing his own best interest in a society that believes in the freedom of the commons. Freedom in a commons brings ruin to all.' The only solution, he concludes, is 'mutual coercion, mutually agreed upon by the majority of the people affected'.

---

laws. To encourage compliance, however, parties generally submit implementation data to secretariats as well as attend regular meetings to review implementation. Some agreements also link financing to compliance (especially important in the South). The secretariats, however, often lack the staff and funds to verify data (as well as push laggards to submit). The combined total in 1999 of professional staff of the Framework Convention on Climate Change, the Convention on Biological Diversity, the Montreal Protocol, CITES, and the Convention to Combat Desertification was a mere 100 people. The combined total budget was just US$43.5 million (Porter, Brown, and Chasek 2000: 150). Both figures are tiny in comparison with the international financial institutions (see Winham, Chapter 4 in this volume). Non-governmental organizations also play a key role here, publicizing violations and conducting independent studies of national implementation. The NGO Environmental Defense, for example, has been 'critical' in ensuring US regulations in fact implement the Montreal Protocol (Porter, Brown, and Chasek 2000: 149).

Implementation can pose great technical and political problems for governments in the South. Often, these governments do not have the finances, personnel, or technologies to monitor and enforce environmental legislation. Systemic corruption may further hinder enforcement. The cost of compliance, too, is frequently greater in the South than in the North, as the South has less infrastructure and experience in meeting environmental obligations, although, as mentioned earlier, funds like the ones from the GEF can help to offset the higher costs of compliance in the South. Countries in the North, however, also struggle with implementing international environmental agreements. Scientific uncertainty may create long bureaucratic delays in implementation. Lobby groups and bureaucracies may work to weaken national legislation designed to meet international obligations. In democratic federations like Canada the federal government may sign and ratify an agreement, but then face stiff opposition from some of the provinces, as happened after the federal government ratified the Kyoto Protocol in 2002.

For all of these reasons, then, it is a formidable challenge for state negotiators and implementers to develop and uphold an effective international environmental regime. Perhaps the most common example of a 'successful' regime is the one to reduce the production and consumption of chlorofluorocarbons (CFCs), the main cause of the depletion of the ozone layer.

Ozone depletion regime

Production and consumption of CFCs, first invented in 1928, rose quickly from the 1950s to the 1970s. The main use was in aerosols, refrigerators, insulation, and solvents. In 1974 Mario Molina and F. Sherwood Rowland, who went on to win the 1985 Nobel Prize in Chemistry, published an article hypothesizing that CFCs were drifting into the atmosphere, breaking apart, releasing chlorine, then reacting to deplete the ozone layer. Ozone is a molecule of three oxygen atoms able to absorb harmful ultraviolet light. The ozone layer refers to the region of high concentrations of ozone in the stratosphere. (The stratosphere is 15–50 kilometres above the earth's surface. Below is the troposphere where weather occurs.) The ozone layer protects us from the harmful effects of ultraviolet radiation from the sun, which can contribute to skin cancer and cataracts, decrease our immunity to diseases, and make plants less productive.

In the decade after Molina and Rowland's seminal article, global negotiators slowly worked toward a collective consensus on the causes and consequences of ozone depletion. This effort gained momentum in 1985 after British scientists found a 'hole' (in fact a severe thinning) in the ozone layer over Antarctica. This hole, which persisted for three months, was the size of North America. The same year the global community signed the Vienna Convention for the Protection of the Ozone Layer, a framework convention without legally binding targets. The 1987 Montreal Protocol on Substances that Deplete the Ozone Layer was adopted two years later, setting mandatory targets to reduce the production of ozone-depleting CFCs and Halons (Halons are another significant ozone-depleting substance found, for example, in fire extinguishers).

Significantly, in 1990 the South agreed to phase out consumption of CFCs and Halons by 2010. The Parties to the Montreal Protocol created the Montreal Protocol Fund to assist developing countries with implementation. This is unusual, as most international agreements do not contain a funding mechanism, and instead rely on traditional development assistance and, more recently, the GEF. So far, the Montreal Protocol Fund has supplied more than US$1

billion to phase out the consumption of ozone-depleting substances in the South. Partly as a result, many developing countries were already 'on track' by the mid-1990s to phase out CFCs and Halons ahead of schedule (Greene 1997: 329), and the South was able to reduce CFC consumption by about 15 per cent from 1986 to 2001 (UNEP 2003: 5).

Conferences of the Parties in London in 1990, Copenhagen in 1992, Montreal in 1997, and Beijing in 1999 amended and strengthened the Montreal Protocol. These conferences also added other ozone-depleting substances and accelerated the phase-out schedules. Over this time, the Vienna Convention and the Montreal Protocol became truly global agreements, and today both have over 180 Parties. The result has been a dramatic fall in global CFC production (see Figure 14.3).

The damage to the ozone layer, it is important to emphasize, is still a serious problem. Today the thickness of ozone over Antarctica, for example, is generally 40 to 55 per cent of its pre-1980 level (UNEP 2000a: 5). The stratospheric concentration of CFCs also continues to increase because the long life of CFCs means 'old' emissions are still rising into the stratosphere. Nevertheless, the UNEP (2000b: chapter 2) now predicts that the ozone layer will repair itself and return to pre-1980 levels by 2050, preventing 1.5 million cases of melanoma cancer and 130 million cases of eye cataracts (UNEP 2003: 4). This is indeed an exceptional turn-around. 'The ozone layer regime is remarkable', Marvin Soroos (1997: 169) argues, 'not only for the series of agreements limiting and phasing out the production and use of ozone-depleting substances but also for the broad acceptance of them and

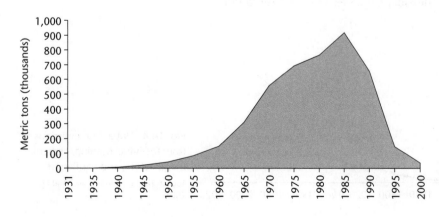

Fig. 14.3 Global CFC production

Source: Alternative Fluorocarbons Environmental Acceptability Study, available at **http://www.afeas.org**

the apparent high rate of compliance with the controls.' Most other scholars would agree. Edward Parson (2003: vii) calls it a 'striking success', noting: 'With near-universal participation of nations and energetic support from industry, the ozone regime has reduced worldwide use of ozone-depleting chemicals by 95 per cent, and use is still falling.'

Yet in many ways this was an exceptional case, one that may well tell us little about our ability to handle future global environmental crises like climate change. The consequences of less ozone were easy for the general public to understand, with skin cancer a particular worry in the North. Even more important, the causes and solutions were relatively straightforward. In the mid-1980s, twenty-one firms in sixteen countries were responsible for CFC production, with the North accounting for about 88 per cent of production. Especially notable, by 1986 the chemical company DuPont, the largest producer of CFCs (accounting for one-quarter of global production), had decided to seek substitutes for CFCs (Grundmann 2001; Parson 2003). Two years later Dupont announced it would phase out production of CFCs. The shift to CFC substitutes did not harm its profits; indeed, in many ways it gave DuPont a competitive edge as other producers soon followed suit.

Climate change regime

Most other global environmental problems involve far greater complexities and uncertainties, and will require far greater sacrifices to solve. Climate change is perhaps the most complex of all. Human activities are altering the relative volumes of greenhouse gases—such as carbon dioxide, methane, and nitrogen oxides—in the earth's atmosphere. Figure 14.4, for example, shows the rapid increase in global emissions of carbon dioxide over the last century. The planet is warming as the 'new' atmosphere traps more heat, a process akin to rolling up a car window on a hot day. The Intergovernmental Panel on Climate Change (IPCC 2001) calculates that the mean global surface temperature has already risen by 0.3–0.6 degrees Celsius over the last 100 years. This may seem minor, but it was the largest rise of any century in the last millennium. The problem appears to be getting worse. The 1990s was the warmest decade and 1998 was the warmest year since records began. This century could be worse still. Various studies predict a rise of between 1.4 and 5.8 degrees Celsius by 2100—the fastest rate of change since the last ice age. The IPCC (2001) estimates that seas could rise by as much as 88 centimetres by the end of the century, displacing millions in low-lying coastal areas in countries like Bangladesh and submerging low-lying countries like the Marshall Islands and the Maldives.

Climate change especially alarms environmental critics of economic globalization as the primary greenhouse gases arise from core economic activities, such as automobiles, power plants, oil refineries, factories, agriculture, and deforestation. At the same time many of the consequences, such as melting polar ice, rising seas, severe storms, new diseases, and drought, are beyond the lifetimes of politicians and business leaders. No doubt, to lower greenhouse gas emissions will require significant changes to global economic production and consumption patterns. It will require, too, governmental, corporate, and personal sacrifices. Replacing CFCs, these critics note, is simply not a comparable sacrifice (Paterson 1996; Newell 2000).

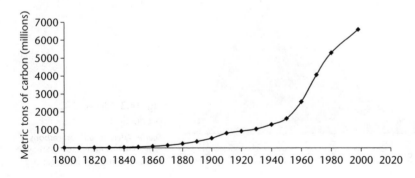

Fig. 14.4 Global CO_2 emissions from fossil-fuel burning, cement manufacture, and gas flaring

Source: Marland, Boden, and Andres 2001.

The South sees the North as largely responsible for climate change, as developed countries account for three-quarters of cumulative emissions of carbon dioxide from 1950 to 1992. The North, on the other hand, often notes the need for global efforts, as carbon dioxide emissions from the South are likely to equal those from the North by 2035. Nevertheless, specific views on climate change do not split cleanly along North–South lines. The European Union, Japan, and Canada, for example, have supported global efforts to combat climate change while the United States and Australia have remained sceptical, at times even questioning the science of global warming. Meanwhile, the states in the Organization of Petroleum Exporting Countries (OPEC) oppose efforts to reduce the global dependence on oil while, predictably, the thirty countries in the Alliance of Small Island States support every possible effort to halt the rise of sea levels.

The 1997 Kyoto Protocol to the 1992 Climate Change Convention is the core agreement in the climate change regime. It requires developed countries to reduce emissions of six greenhouse gases, on average, by 5 per cent below 1990 levels between 2008 and 2012 (calculated as an average over these years). If achieved, emissions levels in 2010 would be about 20 per cent lower than without the Protocol. Not all governments have the same 'target'. The European Union agreed to reduce emissions by 8 per cent below 1990 levels, the United States by 7 per cent, and Japan and Canada by 6 per cent. The Russian Federation agreed to stabilize emissions at 1990 levels. Australia managed to negotiate an increase of 8 per cent above 1990 levels. Developing countries are exempt from legally binding commitments in the Kyoto Protocol, although some, like India and China, set voluntary reduction targets.

The Kyoto Protocol will enter into force ninety days after at least fifty-five Parties, accounting for 55 per cent of the 1990 carbon dioxide emissions of the developed countries, ratify it. So far, as of April 2004, over 100 states have ratified, including the European Union, Japan, and Canada—in total accounting for 44.2 per cent of 1990 emissions. The United States, however, which accounts for 36.1 per cent of 1990 carbon dioxide emissions of developed countries, withdrew support in 2001. Later, the United States vowed to reduce greenhouse gases 'by 18 per cent over the next decade through voluntary, incentive-based, and existing mandatory measures' (Switzer 2004: 293). The Kyoto Protocol may still enter into force even without the United States. It now lies in the hands of Russia, which accounts for 17.4 per cent of 1990 levels. Regardless, however, most analysts agree that even with full compliance the Kyoto Protocol will not lower greenhouse gas emissions to levels that will 'solve' climate change. More radical groups like Greenpeace argue for a global emission reduction more in the range of 80 per cent.

Forests regime

Most environmental regimes, as with ozone and climate change, contain a core international agreement. But some, like the international forests regime, are emerging without a core global treaty. The international forests regime includes the norms and principles arising from numerous global meetings since the Rio Summit to discuss the benefits and drawbacks of negotiating a global treaty for forest management. It consists, too, of the forest-related clauses of international conventions like the ones on biodiversity, desertification, climate change, and wetlands. It also includes the sustainable forest principles of institutions like the International Tropical Timber Organization (ITTO), and the standards of organizations like the Forest Stewardship Council (FSC) (see Box 14.5). At the core of the regime is the concept of sustainable forest management. Humphreys (1999: 251) writes, 'The forests regime has coalesced around the core concept of sustainable forest management (SFM) and the norm that forests should be conserved and used in a sustainable manner.' Other global principles include the value of conservation, ecosystem integrity, protected areas, indigenous knowledge and values, and participation of civil society (Humphreys 1999, 2003).

Yet global norms and principles are only a small part of the basket of rules—both formal and informal—that shape forest management. National and local leaders often ignore the concept of sustainable forest management as well as the non-binding principles of institutions like the ITTO and FSC. The international forests regime is particularly weak and ineffective in Asia, Africa, and South America, most

Box 14.5 **ITTO and FSC**

International Tropical Timber Organization

The 1983 International Tropical Timber Agreement (in force from 1985) created the International Tropical Timber Organization (ITTO), headquartered in Yokohama, Japan. A successor agreement was negotiated in 1994 (in force since 1997). The ITTO's mandate is to facilitate consultation and cooperation among member countries that produce and consume tropical timber. There are fifty-nine members (as of 2004), representing 90 per cent of world trade in tropical timber. The organization is committed to assisting members with meeting the so-called Year 2000 Objective, which calls for members to only trade tropical timber products that originate from sustainably managed forests by the year 2000. (This is still being pursued despite the passing of the target year.) The Bali Partnership Fund is designed to assist producers with implementing sustainable forest management.

Source: ITTO website, at **www.itto.or.jp/**

Forest Stewardship Council

The non-profit Forest Stewardship Council was founded in 1993 to promote more effective forest management. Its members include environmental organizations, forest industries, indigenous and community groups, and forest certification bodies. The FSC accredits and monitors organizations that certify that forest products come from 'a well-managed forest'—that is, a forest that meets the FSC's Principles and Criteria of Forest Stewardship. The FSC visits certified forests to ensure compliance. It further supports the development of regional, national, and local standards that implement these principles and criteria. The FSC logo on a wood product is ultimately designed to provide a 'credible guarantee' to the consumer 'that the product comes from a well-managed forest'.

Source: FSC website, at **www.fscoax.org/**

notably where timber profits prop up corrupt politicians, bureaucrats, and military officers. This explains in part why tropical deforestation has persisted largely unimpeded over the last few decades despite a global outcry and repeated government promises to do better (Dauvergne 2001).

International regimes, then, can solve global environmental problems. The history of the depletion of the ozone layer confirms this. Yet the regimes for climate change and deforestation, for different reasons, are still largely ineffective. Supporters of regimes argue this in part reflects the complexity of the causes and consequences of these problems, as well as the need for economic sacrifices to solve them. For them, this suggests a need to work even harder to strengthen these regimes. For critics of regimes, however, the failure to slow climate change and deforestation suggests the innate limitations of regimes as a mechanism to constrain and guide economic globalization. The energy expended on seemingly endless international negotiations on climate change and deforestation, some critics argue, would be better spent elsewhere, perhaps in labs developing new technologies or in communities developing new ethics. A few of these critics even see the focus on the development of

agreements like an international forests convention as a strategic move by powerful actors to delay real action and ensure 'business as usual' continues for as long as possible (Dauvergne forthcoming).

Key points

- All sides agree that the South needs financial and technical support to pursue global sustainability.

- Some see current efforts—for example the GEF—as a critical lifeline for weak economies. Others see such financing as too small to matter. Still others see global development assistance as a cause of the global environmental crisis as states export natural resources to service and repay foreign debt.

- Environmental regimes are the primary global mechanism for coordinating environmental management across states. It is exceedingly difficult, however, to create and maintain an effective environmental regime.

- Most agree the ozone regime has been effective, largely because the causes, consequences, and solutions of ozone depletion are straightforward.

- The climate and deforestation regimes are much weaker than the ozone regime. Advocates of regimes see this as temporary, a result of the sheer complexity and difficulty of the science, politics, and economics of climate change and deforestation. Critics, on the other hand, see weak regimes for problems like climate change and deforestation as inevitable within the current global political economy; for some, these are not a part of the solution, but part of the reasons for failure.

- Most advocates and critics of regimes agree, however, that solutions to climate change and deforestation will require far more than financing and regimes. Solving them will require a level of innovation, cooperation, and sacrifice never seen before in the history of global environmental politics.

Conclusion

What, then, is the nature of global environmental change in an era of globalization? Is globalization a force for environmental progress or crisis? Are global environmental regimes and the norm of sustainable development effectively channelling globalization to ensure a sustainable future? The record is mixed. For some problems, like ozone depletion, global cooperation has indeed been effective. But for problems like tropical deforestation, the global community appears to be making no headway at all. Perhaps the greatest environmental problem of all is climate change. Here, it also appears that global efforts are failing. Can sustainable development and regimes alone 'solve' deforestation and climate change? The answer seems clear. No. These may indeed help. But such great problems will require new national policies, new corporate ethics, more North–South financial transfers, innovative markets, technological advances, and new forms of cooperation. It will be a bumpy path forward: one that will, because of the nature of the global political economy and global environmental change, no doubt, most unjustly, impose the greatest hardships on the world's poorest and least powerful peoples. That much seems certain.

The chapter did not strive to convince the reader to believe in a particular set of arguments. Already far too many globalization and anti-globalization 'environmental ideologues' preach or chant at, rather than talk to, each other. The goal was instead to deepen the understanding of the range of reasonable and logical arguments about the environmental impacts of the ongoing changes to the global political economy. The hope is that one day those who choose to act on their beliefs—from joining the World Bank's environment team to protesting at an anti-globalization rally—will do so with the humility of knowing the complexities and uncertainties of the relationship between globalization and the environment.

QUESTIONS

1 What, in the broadest terms, is the relationship between globalization and global environmental change?

2 What is the globalization of environmentalism? Is the overall trend positive or negative?

3 Is the Environmental Kuznets Curve a useful policy tool?

4 Which is more common: 'pollution havens' or 'exporting environmentalism'?

5 What are the effects of inequality and consumption on global environmental conditions?

6   What are the effects of trade and corporations on global environmental conditions?

7   What are the effects of financing and regimes on global environmental conditions?

8   Is there a global environmental crisis? If yes, why? If no, why?

9   Can we solve global environmental problems within the current political and economic structures? If yes, how? If no, why?

FURTHER READING

Clapp, J., and Dauvergne, P. (forthcoming), *Paths to a Green World: The Political Economy of the Global Environment* (Cambridge, Mass.: MIT Press). Maps out an original typology to classify the dominant worldviews regarding the impact of the global political economy on the global environment.

Conca, K., and Dabelko, G. D. (eds.) (forthcoming), *Green Planet Blues: Environmental Politics from Stockholm to Johannesburg*, 3rd edn. (Boulder, Colo.: Westview Press). Surveys and extracts core concepts and arguments from seminal articles in global environmental politics.

Dauvergne, P. (ed.) (forthcoming), *Handbook of Global Environmental Politics* (Cheltenham: Edward Elgar). Collection of original and cutting-edge articles by many of the world's premier scholars of global environmental politics.

Dryzek, J. (1997), *The Politics of the Earth: Environmental Discourses* (Oxford: Oxford University Press). Analysis of the history of environmental discourses. Collection of accompanying readings is available in: J. Dryzek and D. Schlosberg (eds.) (1998), *Debating the Earth: The Environmental Politics Reader* (Oxford: Oxford University Press).

Global Environmental Politics (**www.mitpress.mit.edu/GEP**). Scholarly journal that contains the latest innovative and original research on environment and the global political economy (first issue Feb. 2001).

Haas, P. M. (ed.) (2003), *Environment in the New Global Economy* (Cheltenham: Edward Elgar). A collection of sixty seminal articles on environment, globalization, and the global political economy (previously published, dating from 1944 to 2001).

Lipschutz, R. D. (2004), *Global Environmental Politics: Power, Perspectives, and Practice* (Washington DC: CQ Press). A text on the politics of the global environment that among other issues examines green thought, capitalism, power, and international environmental policies.

Paterson, M. (2000), *Understanding Global Environmental Politics: Domination, Accumulation, Resistance* (London: Macmillan and St Martin's). Draws on the literature in international relations to provide a critical account of the environmental impacts of the global political economy.

Pojman, L. P. (ed.) (2001), *Environmental Ethics: Readings in Theory and Application*, 3rd edn. (Belmont, Calif.: Wadsworth/Thomson Learning). Balanced collection of many of the most influential articles in environmental philosophy and politics, including deep ecology, generational obligations, population, hunger, economics, and sustainability.

Porter, G., Brown, J. W., and Chasek, P. (2000), *Global Environmental Politics*, 3rd edn. (Boulder, Colo.: Westview Press). Introduces the academic study of global environmental politics with a focus on international agreements.

Princen, T., Maniates, M. F., and Conca, K. (eds.) (2002), *Confronting Consumption* (Cambridge, Mass.: MIT Press). Breaks new ground in the understanding of consumption as a core problem for the global political economy.

Young, O. R. (2002), *The Institutional Dimensions of Environmental Change: Fit, Interplay, and Scale* (Cambridge, Mass.: MIT Press). Leading scholar of environmental regimes analyses the role of institutions in causing and constraining environmental change.

WEB LINKS

www.unep.org   United Nations Environment Programme and **www.undp.org**   United Nations Development Programme. Provide entries into environment and development data and projects of the United Nations.

www.gefweb.org   Global Environment Facility. Outlines projects and programmes to finance protection of the global environment in developing countries.

www.wri.org   World Resources Institute. Source of scientific environmental research and non-governmental policy proposals. Includes agriculture, biodiversity, forests, climate change, marine ecosystems, water, and health.

www.iisd.org   International Institute for Sustainable Development. Monitors the proceedings of global environmental negotiations and conferences.

www.worldwatch.org   WorldWatch Institute. Source of data on the global environmental 'crisis'. Challenges some of the data (and interpretations) of the United Nations, World Bank, and governments.

References

Abugre, C. (2000), 'Who Governs Low Income Countries? An Interview with Charles Abugre on the PRS Initiative', *News and Notices for IMF and World Bank Watchers*, 2/3, Autumn, **www.attac.org/fra/toil/doc/gci301.htm**

Adams, N. (1993), *Worlds Apart: The North–South Divide and the International System* (London: Zed).

Aggarwal, V. K. (1985), *Liberal Protectionism: The International Politics of Organized Textile Trade* (Berkeley and Los Angeles: University of California Press).

—— (1994), 'Comparing Regional Cooperation Efforts in Asia-Pacific and North America', in A. Mack and J. Ravenhill (eds.), *Pacific Cooperation: Building Economic and Security Regimes in the Asia-Pacific Region* (Sydney: Allen Unwin).

—— (1996), *Debt Games: Strategic Interaction in International Debt Rescheduling* (Cambridge: Cambridge University Press).

—— (2001), 'Economics: International Trade', in P. J. Simmons and C. de Jonge Oudraat (eds.), *Managing Global Issues: Lessons Learned* (Washington DC: Carnegie Endowment for International Peace).

—— and Dupont, C. (1999), 'Goods, Games and Institutions', *International Political Science Review*, 20/4: 393–409.

Allen, J., and Thompson, G. F. (1997), 'Think Global, and Then Think Again: Economic Globalization in Context', *Area*, 29/3: 213–27.

Allen, M. (2003), 'Some Lessons from the Argentine Crisis: A Fund Staff View', in J. J. Teunissen and A. Akkerman (eds.), *The Crisis That Was Not Prevented: Lessons for Argentina, the IMF, and Globalisation* (The Hague: FONDAD).

Alt, J., and Gilligan, M. (1994), 'The Political Economy of Trading States', *Journal of Political Philosophy*, 2/2: 165–92.

Amin, S. (1976), *Unequal Development* (New York: Monthly Review Press).

—— (1997), *Capitalism in the Age of Globalization* (London: Zed Press).

Amsden, A. H. (1989), *Asia's Next Giant: South Korea and Late Industrialization* (New York: Oxford University Press).

—— Tschang, T., and Goto, A. (2001), 'A New Classification of R&D Characteristics for International Comparison (with a Singapore Case Study)' (Tokyo: Asian Development Bank Institute).

Andrews, D., and Willett, T. (1997), 'Financial Interdependence and the State', *International Organization*, 51/3: 479–511.

Archibugi, D. (ed.) (2003), *Debating Cosmopolitics* (London: Verso).

Arden-Clarke, C. (1992), 'South–North Terms of Trade: Environmental Protection and Sustainable Development', *International Environmental Affairs*, 4/2: 122–39.

Arrighi, G., Silver, B. J., and Brewer, B. D. (2003), 'Industrial Convergence, Globalization, and the Persistence of the North–South Divide', *Studies in Comparative International Development*, 38/1: 3–31.

Arrow, K., Bolin, B., Costanza, R., Dasgupta, P., Folk, C., Holling, C. S., Jansson, B., Levin, S., Mäler, K., Perrings, C., and Pimentel, D. (1998), 'Economic Growth, Carrying Capacity and the Environment', *Science*, 268 (28 Apr. 1995), in J. Dryzek and D. Schlosberg (eds.), *Debating the Earth: The Environmental Politics Reader* (Oxford: Oxford University Press).

Arup, C. (2000), *The New World Trade Organization Agreements: Globalizing Law through Services and Intellectual Property* (Cambridge: Cambridge University Press).

Aslanbeigui, N., and Summerfield, G. (2000), 'The Asian Crisis, Gender and the International Financial Architecture', *Feminist Economics*, 6/3: 81–103.

Ault, A., and Sandberg, E. (2002) 'Our Policies, their Consequences: Zambian Women's Lives under "Structural Adjustment" ', in I. Grewal and C. Kaplan (eds.), *An Introduction to Women's Studies: Gender in a Transnational World* (Boston: McGraw-Hill).

Axelrod, R., and Keohane, R. O. (1986), 'Achieving Cooperation under Anarchy: Strategies and Institutions', *World Politics*, 38/1: 226–54.

Ayres, R. L. (1983), *Banking on the Poor: The World Bank and World Poverty* (Cambridge, Mass.: MIT Press).

Babones, S. (2002), 'The Structure of the World-Economy, 1960–1999' (Chicago: 97th annual meeting of the American Sociological Association).

Bachrach, P., and Baratz, M. S. (1970), *Power and Poverty: Theory and Practice* (New York: Oxford University Press).

Bailey, M., Goldstein, J., and Weingast, B. (1997), 'The Institutional Roots of American Trade Policy', *World Politics*, 49/3: 309–38.

Bairoch, P. (1996), 'Globalization Myths and Realities: One Century of External Trade and Foreign Investment', in R. Boyer and D. Drache (eds.), *States against Market: The Limits of Globalization* (London: Routledge).

Baldwin, R. E. (1997), 'The Causes of Regionalism', *World Economy*, 20/7: 865–88.

Baran, P. A. (1976), *The Political Economy of Growth* (Harmondsworth: Penguin).

Barr, N. (1998), *The Economics of the Welfare State*, 3rd edn. (Oxford: Oxford University Press).

Barry, N. (1982), 'The Tradition of Spontaneous Order', *Literature of Liberty*, V/2: 7–58.

Bauer, R. A., Pool, I., and Dexter, L. A. (1972), *American Business and Public Policy*, 2nd edn. (Chicago: Aldine Atherton).

Bayoumi, T. (1990), 'Savings-Investment Correlations', *IMF Staff Papers*, 37: 360–87.

—— (1997), *Financial Integration and Real Activity* (Manchester: Manchester University Press).

—— and Rose, A. D. (1993), 'Domestic Savings and Intra-national Capital Flows', *European Economic Review*, 37/2: 1197–202.

Beck, U. (1992), *The Risk Society* (London: Sage).

Beason, R., and Weinstein, D. E. (1993), 'Growth, Economies of Scale, and Targeting in Japan, 1955–90', Harvard Institute for Economic Research Discussion Paper No. 1644 (Cambridge, Mass.: Harvard University).

Beeson, M. (2000), 'Mahathir and the Markets: Globalisation and the Pursuit of Economic Autonomy in Malaysia', *Pacific Affairs*, 73/3: 35–51.

Bello, W. (1997), 'Fast Track Capitalism, Geo-economic Competition, and the Sustainable Development Debate in East Asia', in C. Thomas and P. Wilkin (eds.), *Globalization and the South* (Basingstoke: Macmillan).

—— Bullard, N., and Malhotra, K. (eds.) (2000), *Global Finance: New Thinking on Regulating Speculative Capital Markets* (London: Zed Press).

Benton, T., and Craib, I. (2001), *Philosophy of Social Science* (London: Routledge).

Berger, S., and Dore, R. (eds.) (1996), *National Diversity and Global Capitalism* (Ithaca, NY: Cornell University Press).

Bergsten, C. F. (1997), 'The Dollar and the Euro', *Foreign Affairs*, 76/4: 83–95.

—— (1999), 'America and Europe: Clash of the Titans', *Foreign Affairs*, 78/2: 20–34.

Bernard, M., and Ravenhill, J. (1995), 'Beyond Product Cycles and Flying Geese: Regionalization, Hierarchy, and the Industrialization of East Asia', *World Politics*, 45/2: 179–210.

Bernhard, W., and Leblang, D. (1999), 'Democratic Institutions and Exchange Rate Commitments', *International Organization*, 53/1: 71–97.

Besley, T. (2002), 'Globalization and the Quality of Government' (London: Economics Department, London School of Economics), March.

—— and Burgess, R. (2002), 'Halving World Poverty' (London: Economics Department, London School of Economics), August.

Bhagwati, J. (1988), *Protectionism* (Cambridge, Mass.: MIT Press).

—— (1991), *The World Trading System at Risk* (New York: Harvester Wheatsheaf).

—— (1995), 'U.S. Trade Policy: The Infatuation with Free Trade Areas', in J. N. Bhagwati and A. O. Krueger (eds.), *The Dangerous Drift to Preferential Trade Agreements* (Washington DC: AEI Press).

—— and Ruggie, J. G. (eds.) (1984), *Power, Passions, and Purpose: Prospects for North–South Negotiations* (Cambridge, Mass.: MIT Press).

—— Brecher, R., Dinopoulos, E., and Srinivasan, T. N. (1987), 'Quid Pro Quo Foreign Investment and Welfare: A Political-Economy-Theoretic Model', *Journal of Development Economics*, 27/1–2: 127–138.

Bhattarai, M., and Hammig, M. (2001), 'Institutions and the Environmental Kuznets Curve for Deforestation: A Crosscountry Analysis for Latin America, Africa and Asia', *World Development*, 29/6: 995–1010.

BIS (Bank for International Settlements) (2003), *International Banking and Financial Market Developments* (Geneva: BIS).

BIS Quarterly Review (2001) (Geneva: Bank for International Settlements).

Blackhurst, R. (1998), 'The Capacity of the WTO to Fulfill its Mandate', in A. O. Krueger (ed.), *The WTO as an International Organization* (Chicago: University of Chicago Press).

Blonigen, B., and Feenstra, R. (1996), 'Protectionist Threats and Foreign Direct Investment', NBER Working Paper 5475 (Cambridge, Mass.: National Bureau of Economic Research).

Blustein, P. (2001), *The Chastening* (New York: Public Affairs).

Blyth, M. (2003), 'Same As It Never Was: Temporality and Typology in the Varieties of Capitalism', *Comparative European Politics*, 1/2: 215–26.

Bomberg, E. E., and Stubb, A. C. G. (2003), *The European Union: How Does It Work?* (Oxford: Oxford University Press).

Bordo, M., and Eichengreen, B. (2002), 'Crises Now and Then: What Lessons from the Last Era of Financial Globalization', NBER Working Paper Series, W8716 (Cambridge, Mass.: National Bureau of Economic Research).

—— and Helbling, T. (2003), 'Have National Business Cycles Become More Synchronized?', NBER Working Paper 10130 (Cambridge, Mass.: National Bureau of Economic Research).

—— Eichengreen, B., and Irwin, D. A. (1999), 'Is Globalization Today Really Different than Globalization a Hundred Years Ago?', NBER Working Paper 7195 (Cambridge, Mass.: National Bureau of Economic Research).

Borjas, G. J. (1999), 'The Economic Analysis of Immigration', in O. Ashenfelter and D. Card (eds.), *Handbook of Labor Economics* (Amsterdam: North-Holland).

—— Freeman, R., and Katz, L. (1996), 'Searching for the Effect of Immigration on the Labor Market', *American Economic Review*, 86/2: 247–51.

Boughton, J. (2001), *Silent Revolution: The International Monetary Fund, 1979–1989* (Washington DC: International Monetary Fund).

Bovard, J. (1991), *The Fair Trade Fraud* (New York: St Martin's Press).

Boyer, R., and Drache, D. (eds.) (1996), *States against Markets* (London: Routledge).

Brack, D., Calder, F., and Dolun, M. (2001), 'From Rio to Johannesburg: The Earth Summit and Rio + 10', Royal

Institute of International Affairs Briefing Paper New Series No. 19, available at **www.riia.org/briefingpapers/ BP%2019.pdf**

Brander, J. A. (1987) 'Shaping Comparative Advantage: Trade Policy, Industrial Policy, and Economic Performance', in R. G. Lipsey and W. Dobson (eds.), *Shaping Comparative Advantage* (Toronto: C. D. Howe Institute).

Brenner, N. (1999), 'Beyond State-Centrism? Space, Territoriality and Geographic Scale in Globalization Studies', *Theory and Society*, 28/1: 39–78.

Brewer, T. L., and Young, S. (1998), *The Multilateral Investment System and Multinational Enterprises* (Oxford: Oxford University Press).

Broadbent, J. (1998), *Environmental Politics in Japan: Networks of Power and Protest* (Cambridge: Cambridge University Press).

Broz, J. L., and Frieden, J. A. (2001), 'The Political Economy of International Monetary Relations', *Annual Review of Political Science*, 4/1: 317–43.

Bryant, R. C. (2003), *Turbulent Waters: Cross-Border Finance and International Governance* (Washington DC: Brookings Institution).

Bryant, R. L., and Bailey, S. (1997), *Third World Political Ecology* (London: Routledge).

Bullard, N., Bello, W., and Malhotra, K. (1998), 'Taming the Tigers: The IMF and the Asian Crisis', *Third World Quarterly*, 19/3: 505–55.

Burch, K., and Denemark, R. A. (1997), *Constituting International Political Economy* (Boulder, Colo.: Lynne Rienner).

Burg, J. (2003), 'The World Summit on Sustainable Development: Empty Talk or Call to Action?', *Journal of Environment and Development*, 12/1: 111–20.

Burtless, G., Lawrence, R. Z., Litan, R. E., and Shapiro, R. J. (1998), *Globaphobia: Confronting Fears about Free Trade* (Washington DC: Brookings Institution).

Busch, A. (2000), 'Unpacking the Globalization Debate: Approaches, Evidence and Data', in C. Hay and D. Marsh (eds.), *Demystifying Globalization* (Basingstoke: Palgrave).

Buzan, B., Held, D., and McGrew, A. (1998), 'Realism Versus Cosmopolitanism: A Debate', *Review of International Studies*, 24/3: 387–98.

CAFOD, Christian Aid, Eurodad and Jubilee Research (2003), *Debt and the Millennium Development Goals: A new deal for low-income countries: financing development through debt cancellation and aid*, **www.oxfam.org.uk/what_we_do/issues/debt_aid/ debt_mdgs.htm_**. Accessed March 2004.

Calleo, D. (1976), 'The Historiography of the Interwar Period: Reconsiderations', in B. Rowland (ed.), *Balance of Power or Hegemony: The Interwar Monetary System* (New York: New York University Press).

—— (1987), *Beyond American Hegemony* (New York: Basic Books).

Callinicos, A. (2003), *An Anti-Capitalist Manifesto* (Cambridge: Polity Press).

Cameron, D. R. (1978), 'The Expansion of the Public Economy: A Comparative Analysis', *American Political Science Review*, 72/4: 1243–61.

Cardoso, F. H. (1977), 'The Consumption of Dependency Theory in the United States', *Latin American Research Review*, 12/3: 7–24.

—— and Faletto, E. (1979), *Dependency and Development in Latin America* (Berkeley and Los Angeles: University of California Press).

Carson, R. (1962), *Silent Spring* (Boston: Houghton Mifflin).

Carver, T., and Thomas, P. (1995), *Rational Choice Marxism* (Houndmills: Macmillan).

Castells, M. (1996), *The Rise of the Network Society* (Oxford: Blackwells).

—— (1997), *The Power of Identity* (Oxford: Blackwells).

—— (1998), *End of the Millennium* (Oxford: Blackwells).

—— (2000), *The Rise of the Network Society* (Oxford: Blackwells).

Castles, S., and Miller, M. (2002), *The Age of Global Migration* (London: Palgrave).

Caves, R. E. (1982), *Multinational Enterprises and Economic Analysis* (Cambridge, Mass.: Harvard University Press).

Cerny, P. G. (1994), 'The Dynamics of Financial Globalization: Technology, Market Structure, and Policy Response', *Policy Sciences*, 27/4: 319–42.

—— (1995), 'Globalization and the Changing Logic of Collective Action', *International Organization*, 49/4: 595–625.

—— (1997), 'Paradoxes of the Competition State: The Dynamics of Political Globalization', *Government and Opposition*, 32/2: 251–74.

Chase, K. A. (2003), 'Economic Interests and Regional Trading Arrangements: The Case of AFTA', *International Organization*, 57/1: 137–74.

Chatterjee, P., and Finger, M. (1994), *The Earth Brokers: Power, Politics and World Development* (London: Routledge).

Chenery, H. et al. (1974), *Redistribution with Growth: Policies to Improve Income Distribution in Developing Countries in the Context of Economic Growth*, a joint study [commissioned] by the World Bank's Development Research Center and the Institute of Development Studies, University of Sussex (London: Oxford University Press).

Cheru, F. (2001), 'Foot Dragging on Foreign Debt', **www.southcentre.org/info/southbulletin/ bulletin10/bulletin10web-03.htm**. Accessed Mar. 2004.

Chiswick, B. R., and Hatton, T. J. (2003), 'International Migration and Integration of Labor Markets', in M. D. Bordo, A. M. Taylor, and J. G. Williamson (eds.),

Globalization in Historical Perspective (Chicago: Chicago University Press).

Citrin, J., Green, D., Muste, C., and Wong, C. (1997), 'Public Opinion toward Immigration Reform: The Role of Economic Motivations', *Journal of Politics*, 59/3: 858–81.

Clapp, J. (2001), *Toxic Exports: The Transfer of Hazardous Wastes from Rich to Poor Countries* (Ithaca, NY: Cornell University Press).

—— (2002), 'What the Pollution Havens Debate Overlooks', *Global Environmental Politics*, 2/2: 11–19.

Clark, A. M., Friedman, E. J., and Hochstetler, K. (1998), 'The Sovereign Limits of Global Civil Society: A Comparison of NGO Participation in UN World Conferences on the Environment, Human Rights and Women', *World Politics*, 51/1: 1–35.

Clark, J. (2001), 'Ethical Globalization: The Dilemmas and Challenges of Internationalizing Civil Society', in M. Edwards and J. Gaventa (eds.), *Global Citizen Action* (Boulder, Colo.: Lynne Rienner).

Clark, W. R., and Hallerberg, M. (2000), 'Strategic Interaction between Monetary and Fiscal Actors under Full Capital Mobility', *American Political Science Review*, 94/2: 323–46.

—— and Reichert, U. N. (1998), 'International and Domestic Constraints on Political Business Cycles in OECD Economies', *International Organization*, 52/1: 87–120.

Cleaver, H. M., Jr. (1998), 'The Zapatista Effect: The Internet and the Rise of an Alternative Political Fabric', *Journal of International Affairs*, 51/2: 621–40.

Cline, W. R. (ed.) (1983), *Trade Policy in the 1980s* (Washington DC: Institute for International Economics).

Club of Rome (authors D. H. Meadows, D. L. Meadows, W. W. Behrens, and J. Randers) (1972), *The Limits to Growth* (New York: Universe Books).

Coase, R. H. (1960), 'The Problem of Social Cost', *Journal of Law and Economics*, 3: 1–44.

Coe, D. T., Subramanian, A., Tamirisa, N. T., and Bhavnani, R. (2002), 'The Missing Globalization Puzzle', IMF Working Paper No. 02/171.

Cohen, B. (1998), *The Geography of Money* (Ithaca, NY: Cornell University Press).

—— (2002), 'US Policy on Dollarization: A Political Analysis', *Geopolitics*, 7/1: 63–84.

—— (2003), 'Can the Euro Ever Challenge the Dollar?', *Journal of Common Market Studies*, 41/4: 575–95.

Coleman, W., and Porter, T. (2000), 'International Institutions, Globalization and Democracy: Assessing the Challenges', *Global Society*, 14/3: 377–98.

Commission on Global Governance (1995), *Our Global Neighbourhood: The Report of the Commission on Global Governance* (Oxford: Oxford University Press).

Condliffe, J. B. (1950), *The Commerce of Nations* (New York: W. W. Norton).

Connor, T. (2001), *Still Waiting for Nike To Do It* (San Francisco: Global Exchange).

Conybeare, J. A. C. (1980), 'International Organization and the Theory of Property Rights', *International Organization*, 34/3: 307–34.

—— (1984), 'Public Goods, Prisoners' Dilemma and the International Political Economy', *International Studies Quarterly*, 28/1: 5–22.

Cooke, W. N., and Noble, D. S. (1998), 'Industrial Relations Systems and US Foreign Direct Investment Abroad', *British Journal of Industrial Relations*, 36/4: 581–609.

Cooper, R. N. (1968), *The Economics of Interdependence* (New York: McGraw-Hill).

—— (1972), 'Economic Interdependence and Foreign Policy in the Seventies', *World Politics*, 24/2: 159–81.

—— (1975), 'Prolegomena to the Choice of an International Monetary System', *International Organization*, 29/1: 63–97.

Coote, B. (1992), *The Trade Trap: Poverty and Global Commodity Markets* (Oxford: Oxfam).

Cornes, R., and Sandler, T. (1996), *The Theory of Externalities, Public Goods, and Club Goods*, 2nd edn. (New York: Cambridge University Press).

Cornia, A., Jolly, R., and Stewart, F./UNICEF (eds.) (1987), *Adjustment with a Human Face* (Oxford: Oxford University Press).

Cox, R. W. (1987), *Production, Power, and World Order: Social Forces in the Making of History* (New York: Columbia University Press).

—— (2000), 'Explaining Business Support for Regional Trade Agreements', in J. A. Frieden and D. A. Lake (eds.), *International Political Economy: Perspectives on Global Wealth and Power*, 4th edn. (New York: St Martins), 366–76.

Crafts, N., and Venables, A. J. (2003), 'Globalization in History: A Geographical Perspective', in M. D. Bordo, A. M. Taylor, and J. G. Williamson (eds.), *Globalization in Historical Perspective* (Chicago: Chicago University Press).

Croome, J. (1995), *Reshaping the World Trading System: A History of the Uruguay Round* (Geneva: World Trade Organization).

Crystal, J. (1994), 'The Politics of Capital Flight: Exit and Exchange Rates in Latin America', *Review of International Studies*, 20/2: 131–47.

—— (2003), *Unwanted Company: Foreign Investment in American Industries* (Ithaca, NY: Cornell University Press).

Cutler, A. C. (2003), *Private Power and Global Authority* (Cambridge: Cambridge University Press).

—— Haufler, V., and Porter, T. (eds.) (1999), *Private Authority and International Affairs* (Albany, NY: State University of New York Press).

Dahl, R. A. (1963), *Modern Political Analysis* (Englewood Cliffs, NJ: Prentice-Hall).

Daly, H. (1993), 'The Perils of Free Trade', *Scientific American* (Nov.): 50–7.

—— (1996), *Beyond Growth: The Economics of Sustainable Development* (Boston: Beacon Press).

—— (2002), 'Uneconomic Growth and Globalization in a Full World', *Natur and Kultur*, available at **www.puaf.umd.edu/faculty/papers/daly/unecon.pdf**

Dam, K. W. (1970), *The GATT: Law and International Economic Organization* (Chicago: University of Chicago Press).

Dauvergne, P. (1997), *Shadows in the Forest: Japan and the Politics of Timber in Southeast Asia* (Cambridge, Mass.: MIT Press).

—— (1999), 'Asia's Environment after the 1997 Financial Meltdown: The Need of a Regional Response', *Asian Perspective: A Journal of Regional and International Affairs*, 23/3: 53–77.

—— (2001), *Loggers and Degradation in the Asia-Pacific: Corporations and Environmental Management* (Cambridge: Cambridge University Press).

—— (forthcoming), 'The Environmental Challenge to Loggers in the Asia-Pacific: Corporate Practices in Informal Regimes of Governance', in D. L. Levy and P. J. Newell (eds.), *The Business of Global Environmental Governance* (Cambridge, Mass.: MIT Press).

Davey, W. J. (2000), 'The WTO Dispute Settlement System', *Journal of International Economic Law*, 3: 15–18.

Davis, M. (2002), *The Origins of the Third World: Markets, States and Climate*, Corner House Briefing No. 27 (Dorset: Corner House), **www.thecornerhouse.org.uk/briefing/27origins.html**

Deaton, A. (2001), 'Counting the World's Poor: Problems and Possible Solutions', *World Bank Research Observer*, 16/2: 125–47.

—— (2002), 'Is World Poverty Falling?', *Finance and Development*, 39/2: 4–7.

—— (2003), 'Measuring Poverty in a Growing World (or Measuring Growth in a Poor World)', Working Paper 9822 (Cambridge, Mass.: National Bureau of Economic Research).

De Goede, M. (2000), 'Mastering Lady Credit: Discourses of Financial Crisis in Historical Perspective', *International Feminist Journal of Politics*, 2/1: 58–81.

De Gregorio, J. (2001), 'Something for Everyone: Chilean Exchange Rate Policy Since 1960', in J. Frieden, P. Ghezzi, and E. Stein (eds.), *The Currency Game: Exchange Rate Politics in Latin America* (New York: Inter-American Development Bank).

Deibert, R. (1997), *Parchment, Printing and Hypermedia* (Ithaca, NY: Cornell University Press).

Desai, P. (2003), *Financial Crisis, Contagion, and Containment* (Princeton: Princeton University Press).

Destler, I. M. (1995), *American Trade Politics*, 3rd edn. (Washington DC: Institute for International Economics).

—— and Balint, P. (1999), *The New Politics of American Trade: Trade, Labor, and the Environment* (Washington DC: Institute for International Economics).

—— and Henning, R. C. (1989), *Dollar Politics: Exchange Rate Policymaking in the U.S.* (Washington DC: Institute for International Economics).

Dicken, P. (2003), *Global Shift: Transforming the World Economy*, 4th edn. (London: Sage).

Diebold, W. (1952), *The End of the GATT* (Princeton: Princeton University Press).

Dikhanov, Y., and Ward, M. (2003), 'Evolution of the Global Distribution of Income in 1970–99', Proceedings of the Global Poverty Workshop, Initiative for Policy Dialogue, Columbia University, available at **www-1.gsb.Columbia.edu/ipd/povertywk.html**

Dormael, A. van (1978), *Bretton Woods: Birth of a Monetary System* (London: Macmillan).

Dosi, G., Pavitt, K., and Soete, L. (1990), *The Economics of Technical Change and International Trade* (New York: Harvester Wheatsheaf).

dos Santos, T. (1970), 'The Structure of Dependence', *American Economic Review*, 60/2: 231–6.

Downs, G. W., and Rocke, D. M. (1995), *Optimal Imperfection? Domestic Uncertainty and Institutions in International Relations* (Princeton: Princeton University Press).

Dowrick, S., and Akmal, M. (2002), 'Contradictory Trends in Global Income Inequality: A Tale of Two Biases', Discussion Paper 355 (Hong Kong: University of Hong Kong, School of Economics and Finance).

—— and DeLong, J. B. (2003), 'Globalization and Convergence', in M. D. Bordo, A. M. Taylor, and J. G. Williamson (eds.), *Globalization in Historical Perspective* (Chicago: Chicago University Press).

Drahos, P. (2002), 'Negotiating Intellectual Property Rights: Between Coercion and Dialogue', in P. Drahos and R. Mayne (eds.), *Global Intellectual Property Rights* (Basingstoke: Palgrave Macmillan).

Dryzek, J. (1997), *The Politics of the Earth: Environmental Discourses* (Oxford: Oxford University Press).

Duchacek, I. D. (1990), 'Perforated Sovereignties: Towards a Typology of New Actors in International Relations', in H. J. Michelman and P. Soldatos (eds.), *Federalism and International Relations* (Oxford: Oxford University Press).

Dunning, J. H. (1981), *International Production and the Multinational Enterprise* (London: Allen & Unwin).

—— (1988), 'The Eclectic Paradigm of International Production: An Update and Some Possible Extensions', *Journal of International Business Studies*, 19/1: 1–32.

—— (1993), *Multinational Enterprises and the Global Economy* (Wokingham: Addison-Wesley).

—— (2000), 'The New Geography of Foreign Direct Investment', in N. Woods (ed.), *The Political Economy of Globalization* (Basingstoke: Palgrave).

Durbin, A., and Welch, C. (2002), 'The Environmental Movement and Global Finance', in J. A. Scholte (ed.), *Civil Society and Global Finance* (London: Routledge).

Easterbrook, G. (1995), *A Moment on the Earth: The Coming Age of Environmental Optimism* (New York: Penguin).

ECLA (2001), *Panorama Social De America Latina 2000–01* (Santiago: ECLA (CEPAL)).

—— (2002), *Globalization and Development* (Santiago: ECLA (CEPAL)).

Edwards, M. (2001), 'Introduction', in M. Edwards and J. Gaventa (eds.), *Global Citizen Action* (Boulder, Colo.: Lynne Rienner).

Ehrlich, P. (1968), *The Population Bomb* (New York: Sierra Club-Ballantine).

Eichengreen, B. J. (ed.) (1985), *The Gold Standard in Theory and History* (New York: Methuen).

—— (1992), *Golden Fetters: The Gold Standard and the Great Depression: 1919–1939* (New York: Oxford University Press).

—— (1996), *Globalizing Capital: A History of the International Monetary System* (Princeton: Princeton University Press).

—— (2000) 'The International Monetary Fund in the Wake of the Asian Crisis', in G. W. Noble and J. Ravenhill (eds.), *The Asian Financial Crisis and the Architecture of Global Finance* (Cambridge: Cambridge University Press).

—— (2002), *Financial Crises and What to Do about Them* (Oxford: Oxford University Press).

—— (2003), *Capital Flows and Crises* (Cambridge, Mass.: MIT Press).

Elias, J., and Kuttner, S. (2001), '2000 BISA Gender and International Relations Working Group Workshop: Methodologies in Feminist Research', *International Feminist Journal of Politics*, 3/2: 284–7.

Elliott, L. (1998), *The Global Politics of the Environment* (New York: New York University Press).

Elshtain, J. B. (1987), *Women and War* (New York: Basic Books).

Energy Information Administration, Department of Energy, US Government (2001), 'Indonesia: Environmental Issues', Energy Information Administration October 2001. Accessed 23 Jan. 2004, available at **www.eia.doe.gov/emeu/cabs/indoe.html**

Enloe, C. H. (1990), *Bananas, Beaches & Bases: Making Feminist Sense of International Politics*, 1st US edn. (Berkeley and Los Angeles: University of California Press).

Epstein, G. (1996), 'International Capital Mobility and the Scope for National Economic Management', in R. Boyer and D. Drache (eds.), *States against Market: The Limits of Globalization* (London: Routledge).

Espenshade, T. J., and Calhoun, C. A. (1993), 'An Analysis of Public Opinion toward Undocumented Immigration', *Population Research and Policy Review*, 12: 189–224.

Esping-Andersen, G. (1996*a*), 'After the Golden Age? Welfare State Dilemmas in a Global Economy?', in

G. Esping-Andersen (ed.), *Welfare States in Transition: National Adaptations in Global Economies* (London: Sage).

—— (1996*b*), 'Positive-Sum Solutions in a World of Trade-Offs', in G. Esping-Andersen (ed.), *Welfare States in Transition: National Adaptations in Global Economies* (London: Sage).

Esty, D. (1994), *Greening the GATT: Trade, Environment and the Future* (Washington DC: Institute for International Economics).

European Commission (1990), 'One Market, One Money', *European Economy*, 44.

Evans, G., Goodman, J., and Landsbury, N. (eds.) (2001), *Moving Mountains: Communities Confront Mining and Globalisation* (Sydney, NSW: Mineral Policy Institute and Otford Press).

Evans, J. W. (1971), *The Kennedy Round in American Trade Policy: The Twilight of the GATT* (Cambridge, Mass.: Harvard University Press).

Evans, P. (1985), 'After Dependency: Recent Studies of Class, State, and Industrialization', *Latin American Research Review*, 20/2: 149–60.

—— (1995), *Embedded Autonomy: States and Industrial Transformation* (Princeton: Princeton University Press).

Evans, P. B. (1979), *Dependent Development: The Alliance of Multinational, State, and Local Capital in Brazil* (Princeton: Princeton University Press).

—— Jacobson, H. K., and Putnam, R. D. (eds.) (1993), *Double-Edged Diplomacy: International Bargaining and Domestic Politics* (Berkeley and Los Angeles: University of California Press).

Fajnzylber, P., Lederman, D., and Loayza, N. (1998), 'What Causes Violent Crime?' (Washington DC: The World Bank, Office of the Chief Economist, Latin America and the Caribbean Region).

Feldstein, M. (1983), 'Domestic Savings and International Capital Movements in the Long Run and the Short Run', *European Economic Review*, 21: 139–51.

—— and Bacchetta, P. (1991), 'National Saving and International Investment', in D. B. Bernheim and J. B. Shoven (eds.), *National Saving and Economic Performance* (Chicago: Chicago University Press).

—— and Horioka, C. (1980), 'Domestic Savings and International Capital Flows', *Economic Journal*, 90/358: 314–29.

Fernandez, R., and Portes, J. (1998), 'Returns to Regionalism: An Analysis of Nontraditional Gains from Regional Trade Agreements', *World Bank Economic Review*, 12/2: 197–220.

Ferrantino, M. (1997), 'International Trade, Environmental Quality and Public Policy', *World Economy*, 20/1: 43–72.

Finnegan, W. (2003), 'The Economics of Empire: Notes on the Washington Consensus', *Harpers Magazine* (May), **www.mindfully.org/WTO/2003/Economics-Of-EmpireMay03.htm**

Firebaugh, G. (1999), 'Empirics of World Income Inequality', *American Journal of Sociology*, 104/6: 1597–630.

—— (2003), *The New Geography of Global Income Inequality* (Cambridge, Mass.: Harvard University Press).

Fischer, S. (2000), *On the Need for an International Lender of Last Resort* (Princeton: International Economics Section, Department of Economics, Princeton University).

Foroutan, F. (1998), 'Does Membership in a Regional Prefrential Trade Arrangement Make a Country More or Less Protectionist?' *World Economy*, 21/3: 305–36.

Frank, A. G. (1967), *Capitalism and Underdevelopment in Latin America: Historical Studies of Chile and Brazil* (New York: Monthly Review Press).

—— (1971), *Capitalism and Underdevelopment in Latin America: Historical Studies of Chile and Brazil* (Harmondsworth: Penguin).

Frankel, J. A. (1991), 'Quantifying International Capital Mobility in the 1980s', in D. Bernheim and J. Shoven (eds.), *National Saving and Economic Performance* (Chicago: Chicago University Press).

—— (1997), *Regional Trading Blocs in the World Economic System* (Washington DC: Institute for International Economics).

—— (ed.) (1998), *The Regionalisation of the World Economy* (Cambridge, Mass.: National Bureau of Economic Research).

Frey, B. S. (1984), 'The Public Choice View of International Political Economy', *International Organization*, 38/1: 199–223.

Frey, R. S. (1998), 'The Export of Hazardous Industries to the Peripheral Zones of the World System', *Journal of Developing Societies*, 14/1: 66–81.

Frieden, J. A. (1991), 'Invested Interests: The Politics of National Economic Policies in a World of Global Finance', *International Organization*, 45/4: 425–51.

—— (1994), 'Exchange Rate Politics', *Review of International Political Economy*, 1/1: 81–98.

—— (1997), 'Monetary Populism in Nineteenth-Century America: An Open Economy Interpretation', *Journal of Economic History*, 57/2: 367–95.

—— Ghezzi, P., and Stein, E. (eds.) (2001), *The Currency Game: Exchange Rate Politics in Latin America* (New York: Inter-American Development Bank).

Friedman, M. (1953), 'The Case for Flexible Exchange Rates', in M. Freidman, *Essays in Positive Economics* (Chicago: University of Chicago Press).

Friedman, T. (2000), *The Lexus and the Olive Tree* (New York: Anchor Books).

—— (2002), 'Techno Logic', in 'States of Discord: A Debate between Thomas Friedman and Robert Kaplan', *Foreign Policy*, 129/Mar.–Apr.: 64–5.

Fujii, E., and Chinn, M. (2001), 'Fin de Siecle Real Interest Parity', *Journal of International Financial Markets, Institutions and Money*, 11/3–4: 289–308.

Funabashi, Y. (1988), *Managing the Dollar: From the Plaza to the Louvre* (Washington DC: Institute for International Economics).

Galbraith, J. R. (2002), 'A Perfect Crime: Inequality in an Age of Globalization', *Daedalus*, 131/1: 11–25.

Gamble, A., and Payne, A. (eds.) (1996), *Regionalism and World Order* (New York: St Martin's Press).

Garcia-Johnson, R. (2000), *Exporting Environmentalism: US Multinational Chemical Corporations in Brazil and Mexico* (Cambridge, Mass.: MIT Press).

Gardner, R. N. (1969), *Sterling-Dollar Diplomacy: The Origins and the Prospects of Our International Economic Order*, 2nd edn. (New York: McGraw-Hill).

—— (1980), *Sterling-Dollar Diplomacy in Current Perspective: The Origins and the Prospects of Our International Economic Order* (New York: Columbia University Press).

Garrett, G. (1995), 'Capital Mobility, Trade, and the Domestic Politics of Economic Policy', *International Organization*, 49/4: 657–87.

—— (1998a), 'Global Markets and National Politics: Collision Course or Virtuous Circle?', *International Organization*, 52/4: 787–824.

—— (1998b), *Partisan Politics in the Global Economy* (Cambridge: Cambridge University Press).

—— (2000a), 'The Causes of Globalization', *Comparative Political Studies*, 33/6: 945–91.

—— (2000b), 'Shrinking States? Globalization and National Autonomy', in N. Woods (ed.), *The Political Economy of Globalization* (Basingstoke: Palgrave).

—— and Lange, P. (1996) 'Internationalization, Institutions and Political Change', in R. O. Keohane and H. V. Milner (eds.), *Internationalization and Domestic Politics* (Cambridge: Cambridge University Press).

—— and Weingast, B. R. (1993), 'Ideas, Interests, and Institutions: Constructing the European Community's Internal Market', in J. Goldstein and R. O. Keohane (eds.), *Ideas and Foreign Policy: Beliefs, Institutions and Political Change* (Ithaca, NY: Cornell University Press).

Gautam, M. (2003), *Debt Relief for the Poorest: An OED Review of the HIPC Initiative* (Washington DC: Operations Evaluation Department, World Bank).

Gedicks, A. (2001), *Resource Rebels: Native Challenges to Mining and Oil Corporations* (Boston: South End Press).

Germain, R. (1997), *The International Organization of Credit* (Cambridge: Cambridge University Press).

—— and Kenny, M. (1998), 'Engaging Gramsci: International Relations Theory and the New Gramscians', *Review of International Studies*, 24/1: 3–21.

Geyer, M., and Bright, C. (1995), 'World History in a Global Age', *American Historical Review*, 100/4: 1034–60.

Ghosh, A. R. (1995), 'International Capital Mobility amongst the Major Industrialised Countries: Too Little or Too Much?', *Economic Journal*, 105/1: 173–80.

Giavazzi, F., and Pagano, M. (1988), 'The Advantage of Tying One's Hands: EMS Discipline and Central Bank Credibility', *European Economic Review*, 32/5: 1055–75.

Giddens, A. (1984), *The Constitution of Society* (Cambridge: Polity Press).

—— (1990), *The Consequences of Modernity* (Cambridge: Polity Press).

—— (2002) *Where Now for New Labour?* (Cambridge: Polity Press).

Gill, S. (1990), *American Hegemony and the Trilateral Commission* (Cambridge: Cambridge University Press).

—— (1995), 'Globalization, Market Civilization, and Disciplinary Neoliberalism', *Millennium*, 24/3: 399–424.

—— (1998), 'European Governance and New Constitutionalism: Economic and Monetary Union and Alternatives to Disciplinary Neoliberalism in Europe', *New Political Economy*, 3/1: 5–26.

—— (2003), *Power and Resistance in the New World Order* (Basingstoke: Palgrave).

—— and Law, D. (1989), 'Global Hegemony and the Structural Power of Capital', *International Studies Quarterly*, 33/4: 475–99.

Gilligan, M. (1997), *Empowering Exporters; Reciprocity and Collective Action in Twentieth Century American Trade Policy* (Ann Arbor: University of Michigan Press).

Gilpin, R. (1975), *US Power and the Multinational Corporation* (New York: Basic Books).

—— (1981), *War and Change in World Politics* (Cambridge: Cambridge University Press).

—— (1987), *The Political Economy of International Relations* (Princeton: Princeton University Press).

—— (2000), *The Challenge of Global Capitalism* (Princeton: Princeton University Press).

—— (2001), *Global Political Economy: Understanding the International Economic Order* (Princeton: Princeton University Press).

Goldberg, L. G., Lothian, J. R., and Kunev, J. (2003), 'Has International Financial Integration Increased?', *Open Economies Review*, 14/3: 299–317.

Goldin, C. (1994), 'The Political Economy of Immigration Restriction in the United States, 1890 to 1921', in C. Goldin and G. Libecap (eds.), *The Regulated Economy: A Historical Approach to Political Economy* (Chicago: University of Chicago Press).

Goldstein, J. (1993), *Ideas, Interests, and American Trade Policy* (Ithaca, NY: Cornell University Press).

—— and Keohane, R. O. (eds.) (1993), *Ideas and Foreign Policy: Beliefs, Institutions and Political Change* (Ithaca, NY: Cornell University Press).

Goodhart, C., and Illing, G. (eds.) (2002), *Financial Crises, Contagion, and the Lender of Last Resort* (Oxford: Oxford University Press).

Goodin, R. E. (2003), 'Choose Your Capitalism?', *Comparative European Politics*, 1/2: 203–14.

Goodman, J. (2002), 'Defeating the OECD's Multilateral Agreement on Investment', in J. Goodman (ed.), *Protest and Globalisation: Prospects for Transnational Solidarity* (Annandale, NSW: Pluto Press).

—— and Pauly, L. (1993), 'The Obsolescence of Capital Controls?: Economic Management in an Age of Global Markets', *World Politics*, 46/1: 50–82.

—— and Ranald, P. (eds.) (2000), *Stopping the Juggernaut: Public Interest versus the Multilateral Agreement on Investment* (Annandale, NSW: Pluto Press).

Gordenker, L., and Weiss, T. G. (1996), 'Pluralizing Global Governance: Analytical Approaches', in T. G. Weiss and L. Gordenker (eds.), *NGOs, the UN and Global Governance* (Boulder, Colo.: Lynne Rienner).

Gordon, D. (1988), 'The Global Economy: New Edifice or Crumbling Foundations?', *New Left Review*, 168: 24–64.

Gowa, J. (1983), *Closing the Gold Window* (Ithaca, NY: Cornell University Press).

—— (1994), *Allies, Adversaries, and International Trade* (Princeton: Princeton University Press).

Graham, E., and Krugman, P. R. (1995), *Foreign Direct Investment in the United States* (Washington DC: Institute for International Economics).

Gray, J. (1998), *False Dawn: The Delusions of Global Capitalism* (London: Granta).

Green, D. (1995), *Silent Revolution: The Rise of Market Economics in Latin America* (London: Frank Cassell with the Latin American Bureau).

Green, D. P., and Shapiro, I. (1994), *Pathologies of Rational Choice Theory. A Critique of Applications in Political Science* (New Haven: Yale University Press).

Greene, O. (1997), 'Environmental Issues', in J. Baylis and S. Smith (eds.), *The Globalization of World Politics: An Introduction to International Relations* (Oxford: Oxford University Press).

Greider, W. (1997), *One World, Ready or Not: The Manic Logic of Global Capitalism* (New York: Simon Schuster).

Grieco, J. M., and Ikenberry, G. J. (2002), *State Power and World Markets* (New York: Norton).

Grimes, W. (2003), 'Internationalization of the Yen and the New Politics of Monetary Insulation', in J. Kirshner (ed.), *Monetary Orders: Ambiguous Economics, Ubiquitous Politics* (Ithaca, NY: Cornell University Press).

Grossman, G. M., and Helpman, E. (1991), *Innovation and Growth in the Global Economy* (Cambridge, Mass.: MIT Press).

—— —— (1994), 'Protection for Sale', *American Economic Review*, 84/4: 833–50.

—— —— (1995). 'The Politics of Free-Trade Agreements', *American Economic Review* 85: 667–690.

—— and Krueger, A. (1995), 'Economic Growth and the Environment', *Quarterly Journal of Economics*, 110/May: 353–77.

Grundmann, R. (2001), *Transnational Environmental Policy: Reconstructing Ozone* (London: Routledge).

GUFPC (Grow up Free from Poverty Coalition) (2003), *Eighty Million Lives: Meeting the MDGs in Child and Maternal Survival* (London: Grow up Free from Poverty Coalition), September, **www.worldvision.org.uk/ resources/80+million+lives+report.pdf_** Accessed Mar. 2004.

Haas, E. B. (1958), *The Uniting of Europe: Political, Social and Economic Forces, 1950–1957* (Stanford, Calif.: Stanford University Press).

—— (1975), *The Obsolescence of Regional Integration Theory* (Berkeley: Institute of International Studies, University of California).

—— (1980), 'Why Collaborate? Issue-Linkage and International Regimes', *World Politics*, 32/3: 357–405.

Haas, P. M. (1992), 'Introduction: Epistemic Communities and International Policy Coordination', *International Organization*, 46/1: 1–35.

Haggard, S. (1990), *Pathways from the Periphery: The Politics of Growth in the Newly Industrializing Economies* (Ithaca, NY: Cornell University Press).

—— (1997), 'Regionalism in Asia and the Americas', in E. D. Mansfield and H. V. Milner (eds.), *The Political Economy of Regionalism* (New York: Columbia University Press), 20–49.

—— (2000), *The Political Economy of the Asian Financial Crisis* (Washington DC: Institute for International Economics).

—— and MacIntyre, A. (2000), 'The Political Economy of the Asian Financial Crisis: Korea and Thailand Compared', in G. Noble and J. Ravenhill (eds.), *The Asian Financial Crises and the Global Financial Architecture* (Cambridge: Cambridge University Press).

Hajnal, P. I. (2002), 'Civil Society Encounters the G7/G8', in P. I. Hajnal (ed.), *Civil Society in the Information Age* (Aldershot: Ashgate).

Halifax Initiative (2002), 'Green Band-Aid Won't Save the Environment', Press Release 29 August, **www.halifaxinitiative.org/index.php?article= ART3e9f13c05f3d1**

Hall, D. (2002), 'Environmental Change, Protest and Havens of Environmental Degradation: Evidence from Asia', *Global Environmental Politics*, 2/2: 20–8.

Hall, P. A. (ed.) (1989), *The Political Power of Economic Ideas* (Princeton: Princeton University Press).

—— and Soskice, D. (eds.) (2001), *Varieties of Capitalism* (Oxford: Oxford University Press).

Hamilton, A. (1913), *Report on Manufactures* (Washington DC: Government Printing Office).

Hansen, R. D. (1979), *Beyond the North–South Stalemate* (New York: McGraw-Hill [for] the 1980s Project Council on Foreign Relations).

Hardin, G. (1968), 'The Tragedy of the Commons', *Science*, 162/3859: 1243–8.

Hardt, M., and Negri, A. (2000), *Empire* (Cambridge, Mass.: Harvard University Press).

Harlen, C. M. (1999), 'A Reappraisal of Classical Economic Nationalism and Economic Liberalism', *International Studies Quarterly*, 43/4: 733–44.

Harmes, A. (1998), 'Institutional Investors and the Reproduction of Neoliberalism', *Review of International Political Economy*, 5/1: 92–121.

Harsanyi, J. C. (1977), *Rational Behavior and Bargaining Equilibrium in Games and Social Situations* (Cambridge: Cambridge University Press).

Harvey, D. (1989), *The Condition of Postmodernity* (Oxford: Basil Blackwell).

Hay, C. (2000), 'Contemporary Capitalism, Globalization, Regionalization and the Persistence of National Variation', *Review of International Studies*, 26/4: 509–32.

—— (2002*a*), 'Globalization as a Problem of Political Analysis: Restoring Agents to a "Process Without a Subject" and Politics to a Logic of Economic Compulsion', *Cambridge Review of International Affairs*, 15/3: 379–92.

—— (2002*b*), *Political Analysis* (Basingstoke: Palgrave).

—— (2003), 'What's Globalization Got To Do With It?', Inaugural Lecture, University of Birmingham, **www.bham.ac.uk/POLSIS/department/staff/ publications/hay_inaugural.htm**

—— (2004), 'Common Trajectories, Variable Paces, Divergent Outcomes? Models of European Capitalism Under Conditions of Complex Economic Interdependence', *Review of International Political Economy*, 11/2:231–62.

—— and Rosamond, B. (2002), 'Globalisation, European Integration and the Discursive Construction of Economic Imperatives', *Journal of European Public Policy*, 9/2: 147–67.

—— and Watson, M. (1998), 'Rendering the Contingent Necessary: New Labour's Neo-Liberal Conversion and the Discourse of Globalisation', *Center for European Studies Working Paper* (Boston: Center for European Studies, Harvard University).

Hayek, F. A. (1976), *Choice in Currency: A Way to Stop Inflation* (London: Institute of Economic Affairs).

Held, D., and McGrew, A. (2002), *Globalization/ AntiGlobalization* (Cambridge: Polity Press).

—— —— (eds.) (2000), *The Global Transformations Reader* (Cambridge: Polity Press).

—— —— Goldblatt, D., and Perraton, J. (1999), *Global Transformations: Politics, Economics and Culture* (Cambridge: Polity Press).

Helleiner, E. (1994), *States and the Reemergence of Global Finance* (Ithaca, NY: Cornell University Press).

—— (1997), 'Braudelian Reflections on Economic Globalization: The Historian as Pioneer', in S. Gill and J. Mittleman (eds.), *Innovation and Transformation in International Studies* (Cambridge: Cambridge University Press).

—— (2002), 'Economic Nationalism as a Challenge to Economic Liberalism? Lessons from the 19th Century', *International Studies Quarterly*, 46/3: 307–30.

—— (2003), *The Making of National Money: Territorial Currencies in Historical Perspective* (Ithaca, NY: Cornell University Press).

Helleiner, G. K. (1996), 'Why Small Countries Worry: Neglected Issues in Current Analyses of the Benefits and Costs for Small Countries of Integrating with Large Ones', *The World Economy*, 19/6: 759–63.

Henning, C. R. (1987), *Macroeconomic Diplomacy in the 1980s* (London: Croom Helm).

—— (1997), *Cooperating with Europe's Monetary Union* (Washington DC: Institute for International Economics).

—— (1998), 'Systemic Conflict and Regional Monetary Integration: The Case of Europe', *International Organization*, 52/3: 537–73.

—— (2002), *East Asian Financial Cooperation*, Policy Analyses in International Economics 68 (Washington DC: Institute for International Economics).

Hines, C. (2000), *Localization: A Global Manifesto* (London: Earthscan).

Hirschman, A. O. (1945), *National Power and the Structure of Foreign Trade* (Berkeley and Los Angeles: University of California Press).

Hirst, P., and Thompson, G. (1996), *Globalization in Question*, 1st edn. (Cambridge: Polity Press).

—— —— (1999), *Globalization in Question*, 2nd edn. (Cambridge: Polity Press).

—— —— (2003), 'Globalization: A Necessary Myth?', in D. Held and A. McGrew (eds.), *The Global Transformations Reader*, 2nd edn. (Cambridge: Polity Press).

Hiscox, M. J. (1999), 'The Magic Bullet? The RTAA, Institutional Reform, and Trade Liberalization', *International Organization*, 53/4: 669–98.

—— (2002), *International Trade and Political Conflict* (Princeton: Princeton University Press).

Hobson, J. A. (1948) [1902], *Imperialism* (London: Allen & Unwin).

Hoekman, B., and Kostecki, M. (1995), *The Political Economy of the World Trading System* (Oxford: Oxford University Press).

Hoffmann, S. (1966), 'Obstinate or Obsolete? The Fate of the Nation-State in Europe', *Daedalus*, 95/3: 862–915.

—— (2002), 'The Clash of Globalizations', *Foreign Affairs*, 81/4: 104–15.

Holme, R., and Watts, P. (2000), *Corporate Social Responsibility: Making Good Business Sense* (World Business Council for Sustainable Development).

Holsti, O. R. (1996), *Public Opinion and American Foreign Policy* (Ann Arbor: University of Michigan Press).

Hood, R. (2001), *Malaysian Capital Controls*, Policy Research Working Paper No. 2536 (Washington DC: World Bank), January.

Hoogvelt, A. (2001), *Globalization and the Post-Colonial World* (Basingstoke: Palgrave).

Horta, K., Round, R., and Young, Z. (2002), *The Global Environmental Facility: The First Ten Years—Growing Pains or Inherent Flaws?*, Report for Environmental Defense and the Halifax Initiative.

Hsieh, C. C., and Pugh, M. D. (1993), 'Poverty, Income Inequality, and Violent Crime: A Meta-Analysis of Recent Aggregate Data Studies', *Criminal Justice Review*, 18/2: 182–202.

Huber, E., Ragin, C., and Stephens, J. D. (1997), *Comparative Welfare States Data Set* (Northwestern University and University of North Carolina), **www.listproject.org/publications/welfaredata/welfareaccess.htm**

Hudec, R. E. (1975), *The GATT Legal System and World Trade Diplomacy* (New York: Praeger).

Hummels, D. (2001), 'The Nature and Growth of Vertical Specialization in World Trade', *Journal of International Economics*, 54/1: 75–96.

Humphreys, D. (1999), 'The Evolving Forests Regime', *Global Environmental Change*, 9/3: 251–4.

—— (2003), 'Life Protective or Carcinogenic Challenge? Global Forests Governance under Advanced Capitalism', *Global Environmental Politics*, 3/2: 40–55.

Hymer, S. (1976), *The International Operations of National Firms* (Cambridge, Mass.: MIT Press).

Ikenberry, G. J. (2001), *After Victory* (Princeton: Princeton University Press).

—— and Kupchan, C. A. (1990), 'Socialization and Hegemonic Power', *International Organization*, 44/3: 283–315.

ILO (2002), *Export Processing Zones: Addressing the Social and Labour Issues* (Geneva: Bureau for Multinational Enterprises, ILO), **www.transnationale.org/pays/epz.htm**

IMF (International Monetary Fund) (2002), *World Economic Outlook: Trade and Finance* (Washington DC: International Monetary Fund).

—— (2003*a*), Independent Evaluation Office, 'The Role of the IMF in Argentina, 1991–2002', *Issue Paper* (Washington DC: International Monetary Fund).

—— (2003*b*), *World Economic Outlook: Trade and Finance* (Washington DC: International Monetary Fund).

—— (various years), *Financial Statistics Yearbook* (Washington DC: IMF).

Inkeles, A., and Smith, D. (1974), *Becoming Modern: Individual Change in Six Developing Countries* (Cambridge, Mass.: Harvard University Press).

IPCC (Intergovernmental Panel on Climate Change) (2001), *Climate Change 2001: The Scientific Basis*, available at **www.ipcc.ch/pub/tar/wg1/index.htm**

Irwin, D. A. (1996), *Against the Tide: An Intellectual History of Free Trade* (Princeton: Princeton University Press).

—— (2003), 'Explaining America's Surge in Manufacturing Exports, 1880–1913', *Review of Economics and Statistics*, 85/2: 364–76.

—— and Kroszner, R. S. (1997), 'Interests, Institutions and Ideology in the Republican Conversion to Trade Liberalization, 1934–45', NBER Working Paper 6112 (Cambridge, Mass.: National Bureau of Economic Research) July, **http://papers.ssrn.com/sol3/delivery.cfm/ nber_w6112.pdf?abstractid=55214**

Iversen, T., Pontusson, J., and Soskice, D. (eds.) (2000), *Unions, Employers and Central Banks: Macroeconomic Coordination and Institutional Change in Social Market Economies* (Cambridge: Cambridge University Press).

Jackson, J. H. (1969), *World Trade and the Law of the GATT* (Indianapolis: Bobbs-Merrill).

—— (1998), *The World Trade Organization: Constitution and Jurisprudence* (London: Pinter).

Jackson, R. H. (1993), 'The Weight of Ideas in Decolonization: Normative Change in International Relations', in J. Goldstein and R. O. Keohane (eds.), *Ideas and Foreign Policy: Beliefs, Institutions and Political Change* (Ithaca, NY: Cornell University Press).

James, H. (1995), 'The Historical Development of the Principle of Surveillance', *IMF Staff Papers*, No. 42, December: 762–91.

—— (1996), *International Monetary Cooperation Since Bretton Woods* (Washington DC: International Monetary Fund).

—— (2001), *The End of Globalization: Lessons from the Great Depression* (Cambridge, Mass.: Harvard University Press).

Jenkins, R. (1987), *Transnational Corporations and Uneven Development* (London: Methuen).

Jessop, B. (2002), *The Future of the Capitalist State* (Cambridge: Polity Press).

Jetin, B., and de Brunhof, S. (2000), 'The Tobin Tax and the Regulation of Capital Movements', in W. Bello, N. Bullard, and K. Malhotra (eds.), *Global Finance* (London: Zed Press).

Jha, R. (2000), 'Reducing Poverty and Inequality in India: Has Liberalization Helped?', available at **www.wider.unu.edu/ research/1998–1999–3.1.publications.htm**

Johannesburg Declaration on Sustainable Development (2002), Official Document of the 2002 World Summit on Sustainable Development, 4 September.

Johnson, C. (1982), *MITI and the Japanese Miracle* (Stanford, Calif.: Stanford University Press).

Johnston, J. (2002), 'Consuming Global Justice: Fair Trade Shopping and Alternative Development', in J. Goodman (ed.), *Protest and Globalisation: Prospects for Transnational Solidarity* (Annandale, NSW: Pluto Press).

Joint Statement by NGOs (2001), 'International Civil Society Rejects WTO Doha Outcome and WTO's Manipulative Process', *Third World Resurgence*, No. 135–6: 15–17.

Jones, C. I. (1997), 'On the Evolution of the World Income Distribution', *Journal of Economic Perspectives*, 11/3: 19–36.

Jones, R. (1971), 'A Three-Factor Model in Theory, Trade, and History', in B. Jagdish, R. Jones, R. A. Mundell, and J. Vanek (eds.), *Trade, Balance of Payments, and Growth* (Amsterdam: North-Holland).

Josselin, D. (2001), 'Trade Unions for EMU: Sectorial Preferences and Political Opportunities', *West European Politics*, 24/1: 55–74.

Jubilee South, Focus on the Global South-Bangkok, AWEPON (Kampala) and Centro de Estudos Internacionales (Managua) (2002), *The World Bank and the PRSP: Flawed Thinking and Failed Experience*, Jan., **www.focusweb.org/ publications/2001/THE-WORLD-BANK-AND-THE-PRSP.html_** Accessed Mar. 2004.

Kahler, M. (1992), 'Multilateralism with Small and Large Numbers', *International Organization*, 46/3: 681–708.

Kaldor, M. (1999), 'The Ideas of 1989: The Origins of the Concept of Global Civil Society', *Transnational Law and Contemporary Problems*, 9/2: 475–88.

—— (2003), 'The Idea of Global Civil Society', *International Affairs*, 79/3: 583–93.

Kaltenthaler, K. (1998), *Germany and the Politics of Europe's Money* (Durham, NC: Duke University Press).

Kanbur, R. (2002), 'Conceptual Challenges in Poverty and Inequality: One Development Economist's Perspective', Working Paper WP2002–09 (Ithaca, NY: Department of Applied Economics, Cornell University).

Kaplan, E., and Rodrik, D. (2002), 'Did the Malaysian Capital Control Work?', in S. Edwards and J. A. Frankel (eds.) (2002), *Preventing Currency Crises in Emerging Markets* (Chicago: University of Chicago Press).

Kapstein, E. B. (1994), *Governing the Global Economy: International Finance and the State* (Cambridge, Mass.: Harvard University Press).

—— (2000), 'Winners and Losers in the Global Economy', *International Organization*, 54/2: 359–84.

Kapur, D. (2002), 'The Changing Anatomy of Governance of the World Bank', in J. Pincus and J. A. Winters (eds.), *Reinventing the World Bank* (Ithaca, NY: Cornell University Press).

Karliner, J. (1997), *The Corporate Planet, Ecology and Politics in the Age of Globalization* (San Francisco: Sierra Club).

Kasman, B., and Pigott, C. (1988), 'Interest Rate Divergences amongst the Major Industrial Nations', *Federal Reserve Bank of New York Quarterly Review*, 13/3: 28–44.

Katzenstein, P. J. (1985), *Small States in World Markets: Industrial Policy in Europe* (Ithaca, NY: Cornell University Press).

Keane, J. (2001), 'Global Civil Society?', in H. Anheier, M. Glasius, and M. Kaldor (eds.), *Global Civil Society 2001* (Oxford: Oxford University Press).

Kearney, A. T./Foreign Policy Magazine Globalization Index (2003), 'Measuring Globalization: Who's Up, Who's Down?', *Foreign Policy*, 134: 60–72.

Keck, M. E., and Sikkink, K. (1998), *Activists beyond Borders: Advocacy Networks in International Politics* (Ithaca, NY: Cornell University Press).

Keegan, J. (1998), *The First World War* (London: Random House).

Keohane, R. O. (1984), *After Hegemony: Cooperation and Discord in the World Political Economy* (Princeton: Princeton University Press).

—— (1997), 'Problematic Lucidity: Stephen Krasner's "State Power and the Structure of International Trade" ', *World Politics*, 50/1: 150–70.

—— and Nye, J. S. (eds.) (1972), *Transnational Relations and World Politics* (Cambridge, Mass.: Harvard University Press).

—— —— (1977), *Power and Interdependence* (Boston: Little, Brown).

—— —— (2003), 'Globalization: What's New? What's Not? (And So What?)', in D. Held and A. McGrew (eds.), *The Global Transformations Reader* (Cambridge: Polity Press).

Keynes, J. M. (1925), *The Economic Consequences of Mr. Churchill* (London: L. and V. Woolf).

—— (1933), 'National Self-Sufficiency', *Yale Review*, 22: 755–69.

—— (1936), *General Theory of Employment, Interest and Money* (New York: Harcourt, Brace Inc.).

—— (1980), *The Collected Writings of J. M. Keynes Volume 25, Activities, 1940–44: Shaping the Post-War World, the Clearing Union*, ed. Donald Moggridge (Cambridge: Cambridge University Press).

Khor, M. (1999), 'Letter Sent by 11 Countries to WTO Chair Criticising Green Room Process', 15 Nov., **www.globalpolicy.org/socecon/bwi-wto/wto99/letter.htm**

—— (2001), 'Manipulation by Tactics and Conquest by Drafts: How the WTO Produced its Anti-development Agenda at Doha', *Third World Resurgence*, 135–6: 11–14.

Kindleberger, C. P. (1951), 'Group Behavior and International Trade', *Journal of Political Economy*, 59: 30–46.

—— (1969), *American Business Abroad: Six Lectures on Direct Investment* (New Haven: Yale University Press).

—— (1973), *The World in Depression, 1929–1939* (Berkeley and Los Angeles: University of California Press).

—— (1975), 'The Rise of Free Trade in Western Europe', *Journal of Economic History*, 35/1: 20–55.

—— (1978), *Manias, Panics, and Crashes: A History of Financial Crises* (New York: Basic Books).

—— and Laffargue, J-P. (eds.) (1982), *Financial Crises: Theory, History, and Policy* (Cambridge: Cambridge University Press).

Kirshner, J. (1995), *Currency and Coercion: The Political Economy of International Monetary Power* (Princeton: Princeton University Press).

—— (ed.) (2003), *Monetary Orders: Ambiguous Economics, Ubiquitous Politics* (Ithaca, NY: Cornell University Press).

Kiser, E., and Laing, A. M. (2001), 'Have We Overestimated the Effects of Neoliberalism and Globalization? Some Speculations on the Anomalous Stability of Taxes on Business', in J. L. Campbell and O. K. Pedersen (eds.), *The Rise of Neoliberalism and Institutional Analysis* (Princeton: Princeton University Press).

Kitschelt, H., Lange, P., Marks, G., and Stephens, J. D. (1999), *Continuity and Change in Contemporary Capitalism* (Cambridge: Cambridge University Press).

Klein, N. (2002), *No Logo* (New York: Picador).

Kleinknecht, A., and ter Wengel, J. (1998), 'The Myth of Economic Globalization', *Cambridge Journal of Economics*, 22/5: 637–47.

Knight, J. (1992), *Institutions and Social Conflict* (Cambridge: Cambridge University Press).

Koffman, J. (1990), 'How to Define Economic Nationalism? A Critical Review of Some Old and New Standpoints', in H. Szlajfer (ed.), *Economic Nationalism in East-Central Europe and South America: 1918–1939* (Geneva: Librairie Droz).

Kohler, H. (2002), 'Working for a Better Globalization', 28 Jan., **www.imf.org/external/np/speeches/2002/012802.htm**. Accessed Mar. 2004.

Korten, D. C. (1995), *When Corporations Rule the World* (West Hartford and San Francisco: Berrett-Koehler Publishers and Kumarian Press).

Korzeniewicz, R., and Moran, T. (1997), 'World-Economic Trends in the Distribution of Income, 1965–1992', *American Journal of Sociology*, 102/4: 1000–39.

—— (2000), 'Measuring World Income Inequalities', *American Journal of Sociology*, 106/1: 209–14.

Krasner, S. D. (1976), 'State Power and the Structure of International Trade', *World Politics*, 28/3: 317–47.

—— (ed.) (1983), *International Regimes* (Ithaca, NY: Cornell University Press).

—— (1985), *Structural Conflict: The Third World against Global Liberalism* (Berkeley and Los Angeles: University of California Press).

—— (1991), 'Global Communications and National Power: Life on the Pareto Frontier', *World Politics*, 43/3: 336–66.

—— (1999), *Sovereignty: Organized Hypocrisy* (Princeton: Princeton University Press).

Krueger, A. O. (1995) *Trade Policies and Developing Nations* (Washington DC: Brookings Institution).

—— (1999), 'Are Preferential Trading Arrangements Trade-Liberalizing or Protectionist?' *Journal of Economic Perspectives*, 13/4: 105–24.

—— (2002), 'A New Approach to Sovereign Debt Restructuring', Pamphlet Series (Washington DC: International Monetary Fund).

Krugman, P. R. (ed.) (1986), *Strategic Trade Policy and the New International Economics* (Cambridge, Mass.: MIT Press).

—— (1990), 'Import Protection as Export Promotion: International Competition in the Presence of Oligopoly and Economies of Scale', in P. R. Krugman (ed.), *Rethinking International Trade* (Cambridge, Mass.: MIT Press), 185–98.

—— (1994), 'Does Third World Growth Hurt First World Prosperity?', *Harvard Business Review* (July), 113–21.

—— (1996), 'The Gold Bug Variations: The Gold Standard—and the Men Who Love It', *Slate* (22 Nov.). Available at **http://web.mit.edu/krugman/www/goldbug.html**

Kurzer, P. (1993), *Business and Banking: Political Change and Economic Integration in Western Europe* (Ithaca, NY: Cornell University Press).

Kymlicka, W. (2000), 'Citizenship in an Era of Globalization: Commentary on Held', in I. Shapiro and C. Hacker-Cordon (eds.), *Democracy's Edges* (Cambridge: Cambridge University Press).

Lamfalussy, A. (2000), *Financial Crises in Emerging Markets* (New Haven: Yale University Press).

Lasswell, H. D. (1936), *Politics: Who Gets What, When, How* (New York: Whittlesey house, McGraw-Hill Book Company).

Lawrence, R. Z. (1996*a*), *Regionalism, Multilateralism, and Deeper Integration* (Washington DC: Brookings Institution).

—— (1996*b*), *Single World, Divided Nations? International Trade and OECD Labor Markets* (Washington DC: Brookings Institution).

Leamer, E., and Levinsohn, J. (1995), 'International Trade Theory: The Evidence', in G. Grossman and K. Rogoff (eds.), *Handbook of International Economics*, vol. iii (Amsterdam: North-Holland).

Lee, M. R., and Bankston, W. B. (1999), 'Political Structure, Economic Inequality, and Homicide: A Cross-National Analysis', *Deviant Behavior*, 19/1: 27–55.

Lenin, V. I. (1967), [1916], *Imperialism: The Highest Stage of Capitalism*, reprinted in D. K. Fieldhouse (ed.), *The Theory of Capitalist Imperialism* (London: Longmans).

Levi-Faur, D. (1997), 'Economic Nationalism: From Friedrich List to Robert Reich', *Review of International Studies*, 23: 359–70.

Lewis, A. (1981), 'The Rate of Growth of World Trade, 1830–1973', in S. Grassman and E. Lundberg (eds.), *The World Economic Order: Past and Prospects* (Basingstoke: Macmillan).

Leys, C. (2001), *Market-Driven Politics: Neoliberal Democracy and the Public Interest* (London: Verso).

Lindberg, L. N. (1963), *The Political Dynamics of European Economic Integration* (Stanford, Calif.: Stanford University Press).

Lindert, P. H., and Williamson, J. G. (2001), 'Does Globalization Make the World More Unequal?' NBER Working Paper W8228 (Cambridge, Mass.: National Bureau of Economic Research) available at **http://papers.nber.org/papers/W8228**

—— —— (2003), 'Does Globalization Make the World More Unequal?', in M. D. Bordo, A. M. Taylor, and J. G. Williamson (eds.), *Globalization in Historical Perspective* (Chicago: Chicago University Press).

Lipschutz, R. D. (1992), 'Reconstructing World Politics: The Emergence of Global Civil Society', *Millennium*, 21/3: 389–420.

Lissakers, K. (1991), *Banks, Borrowers and the Establishment* (New York: Basic Books).

List, F. (1966), *The National System of Political Economy* (New York: A. M. Kelley).

Locke, R., and Kochan, T. (1985), 'The Transformation of Industrial Relations? A Cross-National Review of the Evidence', in R. Locke, T. Kochan, and M. Piore (eds.), *Employment Relations in a Changing World* (Cambridge, Mass.: MIT Press).

Lohmann, L. (1993), 'Resisting Green Globalism', in W. Sachs (ed.), *Global Ecology: A New Arena of Political Conflict* (London: Zed Press).

Lohmann, S. (1997), 'Linkage Politics', *Journal of Conflict Resolution*, 41/1: 38–67.

—— and O'Halloran, S. (1994), 'Divided Government and US Trade Policy', *International Organization*, 48/4: 595–632.

Lomborg, B. (2001), *The Skeptical Environmentalist* (Cambridge: Cambridge University Press).

Loriaux, M. (1991), *France after Hegemony* (Ithaca, NY: Cornell University Press).

Luce, R. D., and Raiffa, H. (1957), *Games and Decisions* (New York: Wiley).

Lukauskas, A. J., and Rivera-Batiz, L. F. (eds.) (2001), *The Political Economy of the East Asian Crisis and its Aftermath* (Cheltenham: Edward Elgar).

Lukes, S. (1974), *Power: A Radical View* (London: Macmillan).

McCord, N., (1958), *The Anti-Corn Law League 1838–1846* (London: George Allen & Unwin).

McCullagh, C. B. (1998), *The Truth of History* (London: Routledge).

Macdonald, L. (1994), 'Globalising Civil Society: Interpreting International NGOs in Central America', *Millennium*, 23/2: 267–86.

McDowell, L. (1997), *Capital Culture: Gender at Work in the City* (Oxford: Blackwell).

McGillivray, F. (1997), 'Party Discipline as a Determinant of the Endogenous Formation of Tariffs', *American Journal of Political Science*, 41/2: 584–607.

McGinnis, M. D. (1986), 'Issue Linkage and the Evolution of International Cooperation', *Journal of Conflict Resolution*, 30/1: 141–70.

McGrew, A. (2002), 'Liberal Internationalism: Between Realism and Cosmpolitanism', in D. Held and A. McGrew (eds.), *Governing Globalization: Power, Authority, and Global Governance* (Cambridge: Polity Press).

McKean, M. A. (1981), *Environmental Protest and Citizen Politics in Japan* (Berkeley and Los Angeles: University of California Press).

MacKenzie, D. (2002), 'Fresh Evidence on Bhopal Disaster', *New Scientist* (4 Dec.).

McKenzie, R., and Lee, D. (1991), *Quicksilver Capital: How the Rapid Movement of Wealth Has Changed the World* (New York: Free Press).

McLaren, L. (2001), 'Immigration and the New Politics of Inclusion and Exclusion in the European Union: The Effect of Elites and the EU on Individual-Level Opinions Regarding European and Non-European Immigrants', *European Journal of Political Research*, 39/1: 81–108.

McNamara, K. (1998), *The Currency of Ideas: Monetary Politics in the European Union* (Ithaca, NY: Cornell University Press).

MacNeill, J., Winsemius, P., and Yakushiji, T. (1991), *Beyond Interdependence: The Meshing of the World's Economy and the Earth's Ecology* (New York: Oxford University Press).

Maddison, A. (1987), 'Growth and Slowdown in Advanced Capitalist Economies: Techniques of Quantitative Assessment', *Journal of Economic Literature*, 25/2: 649–98.

—— (1989), *The World Economy in the 20th Century* (Paris: Development Centre of the Organisation for Economic Cooperation and Development).

—— (2001), *The World Economy: A Millennial Perspective* (Paris: Development Centre of the Organisation for Economic Cooperation and Development).

Magee, S. P. (1980), 'Three Simple Tests of the Stopler–Samuelson Theorem', in P. Oppenheimer (ed.), *Issues in International Economics* (London: Oriel Press).

—— Brock, W. A. and Young, L. (1989), *Black Hole Tariffs and Endogenous Policy Theory* (Cambridge: Cambridge University Press).

Maggi, G. (1999), 'The Role of Multilateral Institutions in International Trade Cooperation', *American Economic Review*, 89/1: 190–214.

Magnus, P. (1964), *Gladstone: A Biography* (London: Murray).

Malthus, T. R., (1798), *Essay on the Principle of Population*, 1st edn., available at **www.econlib.org/library/Malthus/malPop.html**

Manheim, J. M. (1991), *All of the People All of the Time: Strategic Communication and American Politics* (Armonk, NY: M. E. Sharpe, Inc.).

Mann, M. (2003), *Incoherent Empire* (London: Verso).

Marchak, M. P. (1995), *Logging the Globe* (Montreal: McGill-Queen's University Press).

Marchand, M. H., and Runyan, A. S. (2000), *Gender and Global Restructuring: Sightings, Sites, and Resistances* (London: Routledge).

Marden, P. (1997), 'Geographies of Dissent: Globalization, Identity and the Nation', *Political Geography*, 16/1: 37–64.

Marland, G., Boden, T. A., and Andres, R. J. (2001), 'Global, Regional, and National CO_2 Emissions', in *Trends: A Compendium of Data on Global Change* (Oak Ridge, TN: Carbon Dioxide Information Analysis Center, Oak Ridge National Laboratory, US Department of Energy).

Martin, L. L. (1992), 'Interests, Power, and Multilateralism', *International Organization*, 46/4: 765–92.

—— (2000), *Democratic Commitments: Legislatures and International Cooperation* (Princeton: Princeton University Press).

—— (2002) 'International Political Economy: From Paradigmatic Debates to Productive Disagreements', in M. Brecher and F. P. Harvey (eds.), *Conflict, Security, Foreign Policy, and International Political Economy: Past Paths and Future Directions in International Studies* (Ann Arbor: University of Michigan Press).

Maskus, K. E. (2000), *Intellectual Property Rights in the Global Economy* (Washington DC: Institute for International Economics).

Mazur, J. (2000), 'Labor's New Internationalism', *Foreign Affairs*, 79/1: 79–93.

Mearsheimer, J. J. (1990), 'Back to the Future: Instability in Europe after the Cold War', *International Security*, 15/1: 5–56.

Mehta, S. (2003), 'The Johannesburg Summit from the Depths', *Journal of Environment and Development*, 12/1: 121–8.

Mellor, D. H. (1995), *The Facts of Causation* (London: Routledge).

Meltzer, A. (2001), 'The World Bank One Year after the Commission's Report to Congress', *Hearings before the Joint Economic Committee, US Congress*, 8 Mar.

Meltzer Commission (United States Congressional Advisory Commission on International Financial Institutions) (2000), 'Report to the US Congress on the International Financial Institutions', available at **www.house.gov/jec/imf/meltzer.htm**

Michael, M. (2001), 'Jubilee 2000: Drop the Debt, Not the Campaign', *Dollars and Sense*, Mar.: 11.

Milanovic, B. (2002*a*), 'Can We Discern the Effect of Globalization on Income Distribution? Evidence from Household Budget Surveys', Policy Research Working Paper 2876 (Washington DC: World Bank). See **http://econ.worldbank.org/working_papers/17877/** (accessed Mar. 2004).

—— (2002*b*), 'True World Income Distribution, 1988 and 1993', *Economic Journal*, 112/476: 51–92.

—— (2003), 'The Two Faces of Globalization: Against Globalization as we Know It', *World Development*, 31/4: 667–83.

Mill, J. S. (1970), *Principles of Political Economy, with Some of Their Applications to Social Philosophy* (Harmondsworth: Penguin).

Milner, H. V. (1997a), *Interests, Institutions, and Information: Domestic Politics and International Relation* (Princeton: Princeton University Press).

—— (1997b), 'Industries, Governments, and the Creation of Regional Trading Blocs', in E. D. Mansfield and H. V. Milner (eds.), *The Political Economy of Regionalism* (New York: Columbia University Press), 77–106.

Milward, A. S. (1984), *The Reconstruction of Western Europe 1945–51* (London: Routledge).

—— (1992), *The European Rescue of the Nation-State* (London: Routledge).

Ministry of Economy, Trade and Industry, Government of Japan (2000), 'The Economic Foundations of Japanese Trade Policy—Promoting a Multi-Layered Trade Policy', Ministry of Economy, Trade and Industry, Accessed 24 Feb. 2002. Available at **www.meti.go.jp/english/ information/data/cJ-SFTA4e.pdf**

Mitchell, B. R. (1992), *International Historical Statistics: Europe 1750–1988*, 3rd edn. (London: Macmillan).

—— (1993), *International Historical Statistics: The Americas 1750–1988*, 2nd edn. (Basingstoke: Macmillan).

Molina, M. J., and Rowland, F. S. (1974), 'Stratospheric Sink for Chlorofluoro-methanes: Chlorine Atom Catalyzed Destruction of Ozone', *Nature*, 249: 810–14.

Moravcsik, A. (1998), *The Choice for Europe: Social Purpose and State Power from Messina to Maastricht* (Ithaca, NY: Cornell University Press).

Morse, E. L. (1976), *Modernization and the Transformation of International Relations* (New York: Free Press).

Mosley, L. (2003), *Global Capital and National Governments* (Cambridge: Cambridge University Press).

Mosley, P., and Eeckhout, M. J. (2000), 'From Project Aid to Programme Assistance', in F. Tarp (ed.), *Foreign Aid and Development: Lessons Learnt and Directions for the Future* (London: Routledge).

Motta, M., and Norman, G. (1996), 'Does Economic Integration Cause Foreign Direct Investment?' *International Economic Review*, 37/4: 757–83.

Multilateral Trade Negotiations: Evaluations and Further Recommendations Arising Therefrom (1979), UNCTAD V (UN Doc. TD/227).

Munck, R. (2002), *Globalisation and Labour* (London: Zed Press).

Mundell, R. (1961), 'A Theory of Optimum Currency Areas', *American Economic Review*, 51/3: 657–65.

—— (1963), 'Capital Mobility and Stabilization Policy under Fixed and Flexible Exchange Rates', *Canadian Journal of Economics and Political Science*, 29/4: 475–85.

Mussa, M. (1974), 'Tariffs and the Distribution of Income: The Importance of Factor Specificity, Substitutability, and Intensity in the Short and Long Run', *Journal of Political Economy*, 82/6: 1191-203.

—— (2002), *Argentina and the Fund: From Triumph to Tragedy* (Washington DC: Institute for International Economics).

Myers, N. (1997), 'Consumption in Relation to Population, Environment and Development', *The Environmentalist*, 17: 33–44.

Myers, R., and Worm, B. (2003), 'Rapid Worldwide Depletion of Predatory Fish Communities', *Nature*, 423/6937: 280–3.

Naím, M. (2002), 'Post-Terror Suprises', *Foreign Policy*, 132: 96 and 95.

Neumayer, E. (2001), *Greening Trade and Investment: Environmental Protection without Protectionism* (London: Earthscan).

Newell, P. (2000), *Climate for Change: Non-State Actors and the Global Politics of the Greenhouse* (Cambridge: Cambridge University Press).

NGO Coalition (2002), 'NGOs Call on Trade Ministers to Reject Exclusive Mini-Ministerials and Green Room Meetings in the Run-Up to, and at, the 5th WTO Ministerial', **www.ciel.org/Tae/WTO_5Min_112002.html**

Notermans, T. (2000), *Money, Markets, and the State: Social Democratic Economic Policies Since 1918* (Cambridge: Cambridge University Press).

—— (2001), *Social Democracy and Monetary Union* (New York: Berghahn).

Nye, J. S. Jr. (1990), 'Soft Power', *Foreign Policy*, 80: 153–71.

Oatley, T. (1997), *Monetary Politics: Exchange Rate Cooperation in the European Union* (Ann Arbor: University of Michigan Press).

O'Brien, R. (1992), *The End of Geography: Global Financial Integration* (London: Pinter).

—— Goetz, A. M., Scholte, J. A., and Williams, M. (2000), *Contesting Global Governance: Multilateral Economic Institutions and Global Social Movements* (Cambridge: Cambridge University Press).

Obstfeld, M. (1993), 'International Capital Mobility in the 1990s', NBER Working Paper 4534 (Cambridge, Mass.: National Bureau of Economic Research).

—— and Rogoff, K. (1996), *Foundations of International Macroeconomics* (Cambridge, Mass.: MIT Press).

—— and Taylor, A. M. (1998), 'The Great Depression as a Watershed: International Capital Mobility in the Long Run', in M. D. Bordo, C. Goldin, and E. N. White (eds.), *The Defining Moment: The Great Depression and the American Economy in the Twentieth Century* (Chicago: Chicago University Press).

—— —— (2003), 'Globalization and Capital Markets', in M. D. Bordo, A. M. Taylor, and J. G. Williamson (eds.), *Globalization in Historical Perspective* (Chicago: University of Chicago Press).

Odell, J. S. (1982), *US International Monetary Policy: Markets, Power, and Ideas as Sources of Change* (Princeton: Princeton University Press).

—— (2002), 'Making and Breaking Impasses in International Regimes: The WTO, Seattle and Doha', Paper prepared for the Conference on Gaining Leverage in International Negotiations, Yonsei University.

OECD (Organisation for Economic Cooperation and Development) (2002), 'Regional Trade Agreements and the Multilateral Trading System: Consolidated Report', Organisation for Economic Cooperation and Development 20 Nov. Accessed 18 Aug. 2003, Available at **www.olis.oecd.org/olis/2002doc.nsf/43bb6130e5e86e 5fc12569fa005d004c/db1bbc3ddbadceeec1256c77004 2bc1b/$FILE/JT00135547.PDF**

Offer, A. (1989), *The First World War: An Agrarian Interpretation* (Oxford: Clarendon Press).

Officer, L. H. (2001), 'Gold Standard', EH.Net Encyclopedia 1 Oct. Accessed 14 Mar. 2004, available at **www.eh.net/encyclopedia/contents/officer.gold. standard.php**

Ofreneo, R. (1993), 'Japan and the Environmental Degradation of the Philippines', in M. Howard (ed.), *Asia's Environmental Crisis* (Boulder, Colo.: Westview Press).

Ohmae, K. (1990), *The Borderless World* (London: Collins).

—— (1995), *The End of the Nation State* (New York: Free Press).

Okimoto, D. I. (1988), 'Political Inclusivity: The Domestic Structure of Trade', in T. Inoguchi and D. I. Okimoto (eds.), *The Political Economy of Japan*, ii: *The Changing International Context* (Stanford, Calif.: Stanford University Press).

Olson, M. (1965), *The Logic of Collective Action: Public Goods and the Theory of Groups* (Cambridge, Mass.: Harvard University Press).

Orbinski, J. (2002), 'AIDS, Médecins Sans Frontières, and Access to Essential Medicines', in P. I. Hajnal (ed.), *Civil Society in the Information Age* (Aldershot: Ashgate).

O'Rourke, K. H., and Williamson, J. G. (2000), *Globalization and History* (Boston: MIT Press).

Osherenko, G., and Young, O. R. (1993), 'The Formation of International Regimes: Hypotheses and Cases', in O. R. Young and G. Osherenko (eds.), *Polar Politics: Creating International Environmental Regimes* (Ithaca, NY: Cornell University Press), 1–21.

Osler, C. L. (1991), 'Explaining the Absence of International Factor-Price Convergence', *Journal of Money and Finance*, 10/1: 89–107.

Ottaway, M. (2001), 'Corporatism Goes Global: International Organizations, Nongovernmental Organization Networks, and Transnational Business', *Global Governance*, 7/3: 265–92.

Otto, D. (1996), 'Nongovernmental Organizations in the United Nations System: The Emerging Role of International Civil Society', *Human Rights Quarterly*, 18/1: 107–41.

Oxfam International (2002*a*), 'Last Chance in Monterrey: Meeting the Challenge of Poverty Reduction', Oxfam Briefing Paper No. 17, Mar. **www.oxfam.org/eng/ pdfs/pp020313_Monterrey_final.doc**

—— (2002*b*), *Rigged Rules and Double Standards: Trade, Globalisation, and the Fight against Poverty*, **www.maketradefair.com/assets/english/ report_english.pdf**

Oye, K. A. (1985), 'Explaining Cooperation under Anarchy: Hypotheses and Strategies', *World Politics*, 38/1: 1–24.

—— (1992), *Economic Discrimination and Political Exchange: World Political Economy in the 1930s and 1980s* (Princeton: Princeton University Press).

Paarlberg, R. L. (1997), 'Agricultural Policy Reform and the Uruguay Round: Synergistic Linkage in a Two-Level Game', *International Organization*, 51/3: 413–44.

Pace, W. R., and Panganiban, R. (2002), 'The Power of Global Activist Networks: The Campaign for an International Criminal Court', in P. I. Hajnal (ed.), *Civil Society in the Information Age* (Aldershot: Ashgate).

Palan, R. (2003), *The Offshore World: Sovereign Markets, Virtual Places and Nomad Millionaires* (Ithaca, NY: Cornell University Press).

Palmeter, D. N., and Mavroidis, P. C. (1999), *Dispute Settlement in the World Trade Organization: Practice and Procedure* (The Hague: Kluwer).

Panagariya, A. (2002), 'Developing Countries at Doha: A Political Economy Analysis', *World Economy*, 26/9: 1205–33.

Pangestu, M. (2000), 'Special and Differential Treatment in the Millennium: Special for Whom and How Different?', *World Economy*, 23/9: 1285–1302.

Parker, B. (1998), *Globalization and Business Practice: Managing across Boundaries* (London: Sage).

Parson, E. A. (2003), *Protecting the Ozone Layer: Science and Strategy* (Oxford: Oxford University Press).

Pastor, R. (1980), *Congress and the Politics of US Foreign Economic Policy, 1929–1976* (Berkeley and Los Angeles: University of California Press).

Paterson, M. (1996), *Global Warming and Global Politics* (London: Routledge).

—— (2001), 'Risky Business: Insurance Companies in Global Warming Politics', *Global Environmental Politics*, 1/4: 18–42.

Pauly, L. W. (1992), 'The Politics of European Monetary Union: National Strategies, International Implications', *International Journal*, 47: 93–111.

—— (1997), *Who Elected the Bankers: Surveillance and Control in the World Economy* (Ithaca, NY: Cornell University Press).

Perraton, J., Goldblatt, D., Held, D., and McGrew, A. (1997), 'The Globalization of Economic Activity', *New Political Economy*, 2/2: 257–78.

Perroni, C., and Whalley, J. (1994), 'The New Regionalism: Trade Liberalization or Insurance?' Working Paper 4626

(Cambridge, Mass.: National Bureau of Economic Research).

Petras, J., and Veltmeyer, H. (2001), *Globalization Unmasked: Imperialism in the 21st Century* (London: Zed Press).

Petrella, R. (1996), 'Globalization and Internationalisation: The Dynamics of the Emerging World Order', in R. Boyer and D. Drache (eds.), *States against Market: The Limits of Globalization* (London: Routledge).

Pettman, J. (1996), *Worlding Women: A Feminist International Politics* (St Leonards, NSW: Allen & Unwin).

Pharr, S. J., and Putnam, R. D. (eds.) (2000) *Disaffected Democracies: What's Troubling the Trilateral Countries?* (Princeton: Princeton University Press).

Pierson, P. (1994), *Dismantling the Welfare State? Reagan, Thatcher and the Politics of Retrenchment* (Cambridge: Cambridge University Press).

—— (1996), 'The New Politics of the Welfare State', *World Politics*, 48/2: 143–79.

Pinto, P. M. (2003), 'Tying Hands vs. Exchanging Hostages: Domestic Coalitions, Political Constraints, and FDI', Paper presented at the Annual Meeting of the American Political Science Association, Philadelphia, PA.

Piore, M., and Sabel, C. (1984), *The Second Industrial Divide: Possibilities for Prosperity* (New York: Basic Books).

Pogge, T. W., and Reddy, S. G. (2003), 'Unknown: The Extent, Distribution, and Trend of Global Income Poverty', **www.socialanalysis.org** 26 July, available at **www.columbia.edu/~sr793/povpop.pdf**

Poku, N. (2001), 'The Crisis of AIDS in Africa and the Politics of Response', in N. Poku (ed.), *Security and Development in Southern Africa* (Westport, Conn.: Praeger).

Polanyi, K. (1944), *The Great Transformation* (New York: Rinehart).

Population Reference Bureau (2002), '2002 World Population Data Sheet of the Population Reference Bureau: Demographic Data and Estimates for the Countries and Regions of the World', available at **www.prb.org/pdf/ WorldPopulationDS02_Eng.pdf**

Porter, G. (1999), 'Trade Competition and Pollution Standards: "Race to the Bottom" or "Stuck at the Bottom"?', *Journal of Environment and Development*, 8/2: 133–51.

—— Brown, J. W., and Chasek, P. (2000), *Global Environmental Politics*, 3rd edn. (Boulder, Colo.: Westview Press).

Porter, M. (1980), *Competitive Strategy* (New York: Free Press/Macmillan).

—— (1990), *The Competitive Advantage of Nations* (New York: Free Press/Macmillan).

Porter, R., and Judson, R. (1996), 'The Location of US Currency: How Much is Abroad?', *Federal Reserve Bulletin*, 82/10: 883–903.

Porter, T. (2002), 'Institutional Learning and International Financial Regimes', in M. S. Gertler and D. Wolfe (eds.),

Innovation and Social Learning (Basingstoke: Palgrave Macmillan).

Prebisch, R. (1963), *Towards a Dynamic Development Policy for Latin America* (New York: United Nations).

—— (1970), *Change and Development: Latin America's Great Task* (Washington DC: Inter-American Development Bank).

Preeg, E. H. (1970), *Traders and Diplomats: An Analysis of the Kennedy Round under the General Agreement on Tariffs and Trade* (Washington DC: Brookings).

—— (1995), *Traders in a Brave New World: The Uruguay Round and the Future of the International Trading System* (Chicago: University of Chicago Press).

Price, R. (1998), 'Reversing the Gun Sights: Transnational Civil Society Targets Land Mines', *International Organization*, 52/3: 613–44.

Princen, T. (1997), 'The Shading and Distancing of Commerce: When Internalization is not Enough', *Ecological Economics*, 20/3: 235–53.

Pritchett, L. (1997), 'Divergence Big Time', *Journal of Economic Perspectives*, 11/3: 3–18.

Putnam, R. D. (1988), 'Diplomacy and Domestic Politics: The Logic of Two-Level Games', *International Organization*, 42/3: 427–60.

—— and Bayne, N. (1987), *Hanging Together: Cooperation and Conflict in the Seven-Power Summits* (Cambridge, Mass.: Harvard University Press).

Quah, D. T. (1997), 'Empirics for Growth and Distribution: Stratification, Polarization and Convergence Clubs', *Journal of Economic Growth*, 2/1: 27–59.

Raffer, K., and Singer, H. (2001), *The Economic North–South Divide: Six Decades of Unequal Development* (Cheltenham: Edward Elgar Publishing).

Rahnema, M., and Bawtree, V. (eds.) (1997), *The Post Development Reader* (London: Zed Press).

Rapley, J. (1996), *Understanding Development* (Boulder, Colo.: Lynne Rienner).

Ravallion, M. (2002), 'How Not to Count the Poor? A Reply to Reddy and Pogge', **www.socialanalysis.org** available at **www.columbia.edu/~sr793/wbreply.pdf**

Ravenhill, J. (2001), *APEC and the Construction of Asia-Pacific Regionalism* (Cambridge: Cambridge University Press).

—— (2003), 'The New Bilateralism in the Asia-Pacific', *Third World Quarterly*, 24/2: 299–317.

Rawski, T. (2002), 'Measuring China's Recent GDP Growth: Where Do We Stand?', available at **www.pitt.edu/ ~tgrawski/papers2002/measuring.pdf**

Reddy, S. G., and Pogge, T. W. (2002), 'How *Not* to Count the Poor!—a Reply to Ravallion', **www.socialanalysis.org** 15 Aug., available at **www.columbia.edu/~sr793/ poggereddyreply.pdf**

—— —— (2003), 'How *Not* to Count the Poor', **www.socialanalysis.org** 26 Mar., available at **www.columbia.edu/~sr793/count.pdf**

Rees, W. E. (2002), 'Globalization and Sustainability: Conflict or Convergence?', *Bulletin of Science, Technology & Society*, 22/4: 249–68.

—— and Westra, L. (2003), 'When Consumption Does Violence: Can There be Sustainability and Environmental Justice in a Resource-limited World?', in J. Agyeman, R. Bullard, and B. Evans (eds.) *Just Sustainabilities: Development in an Unequal World* (London: Earthscan).

Reich, R. (1992), *The Work of Nations* (New York: Vintage Books).

Reinke, L. (2002), 'Utopias in Chiapas? Questioning Disembodied Politics', in J. Goodman (ed.), *Protest and Globalisation: Prospects for Transnational Solidarity* (Annandale, NSW: Pluto Press).

Rhodes, M. (1996), 'Globalization and West European Welfare States: A Critical Review of Recent Debates', *Journal of European Social Policy*, 6/4: 305–27.

—— (1997), 'The Welfare State: Internal Challenges, External Constraints', in M. Rhodes, P. Heywood, and V. Wright (eds.), *Developments in West European Politics* (Basingstoke: Macmillan).

Rich, B. (1994), *Mortgaging the Earth: The World Bank, Environmental Impoverishment, and the Crisis of Development* (London: Earthscan).

Rieger, E., and Leibfried, S. (2003), *Limits to Globalization: Welfare states and World Economy* (Cambridge: Polity Press).

Robbins, R. H. (2002), *Global Problems and the Culture of Capitalism*, 2nd edn (Boston: Allyn & Bacon).

Robertson, R. (2003), *The Three Waves of Globalization: A History of Developing Global Consciousness* (London: Zed Press).

Rodrik, D. (1989), 'Promises, Promises: Credible Policy Reform via Signalling', *Economic Journal*, 99/397: 756–72.

—— (1995), 'Political Economy of Trade Policy', in G. Grossman and K. Rogoff (eds.), *Handbook of International Economics*, vol. iii (Amsterdam: Elsevier).

—— (1996), 'Why Do More Open Economies Have Bigger Governments?', NBER Working Paper 5537 (Cambridge, Mass.: National Bureau of Economic Research).

—— (1997), *Has Globalization Gone Too Far?* (Washington DC: Institute for International Economics).

—— (1999), *The New Global Economy and Developing Countries: Making Openness Work* (Baltimore, MD: Johns Hopkins University Press for the Overseas Development Council).

—— (2001), 'Trading in Illusions', *Foreign Policy*, 123: 55–62.

Rødseth, A. (2000), *Open Economy Macroeconomics* (Cambridge: Cambridge University Press).

Roemer, J. E. (1988), *Free to Lose: An Introduction to Marxist Economic Philosophy* (London: Radius).

Rogers, A. (1993), *The Earth Summit: A Planetary Reckoning* (Los Angeles: Global View Press).

Rogowski, R., (1987), 'Trade and the Variety of Democratic Institutions', *International Organization*, 41/2: 203–23.

—— (1989), *Commerce and Coalitions* (Princeton: Princeton University Press).

Romer, P. M. (1986), 'Increasing Returns and Long-Run Growth', *Journal of Political Economy*, 94/5: 1002–37.

Rosamond, B. (2001), 'Discourses of Globalization and European Identities', in T. Christiansen, K. Jorgensen, and A. Wiener (eds.), *The Social Construction of Europe* (London: Sage).

Rosecrance, R. (1986), *The Rise of the Trading State: Commerce and Conquest in the Modern World* (New York: Basic Books).

—— (1999), *The Rise of the Virtual State* (New York: Basic Books).

Rosenberg, A. (1995), *Philosophy of Social Science* (Boulder, Colo.: Westview).

Rosenberg, J. (2000), *The Follies of Globalization Theory* (London: Verso).

Rostow, W. (1960), *The Stages of Economic Growth* (New York: Cambridge University Press).

Rothstein, R. L. (1979), *Global Bargaining: UNCTAD and the Quest for a New International Economic Order* (Princeton: Princeton University Press).

Rowthorn, R., and Wells, J. (1987), *De-Industrialization and Foreign Trade* (Cambridge: Cambridge University Press).

Ruggie, J. G. (1982), 'International Regimes, Transactions, and Change: Embedded Liberalism in the Postwar Economic Order', *International Organization*, 36/2: 379–415.

—— (1992), 'Multilateralism: The Anatomy of an Institution', *International Organization*, 46/3: 561–98.

—— (1998), *Constructing the World Polity* (London: Routledge).

Rugman, A. (1981), *Inside the Multinationals: The Economics of Internal Markets* (New York: Columbia University Press).

—— (2000), *The End of Globalization* (London: Random House; New York, NY: Amacom-McGraw Hill).

—— (2003), 'Regional Strategies for Service Sector Multinationals', *European Business Journal*, 15/1: 1–9.

—— (2005), *The Regional Multinationals* (Cambridge: Cambridge University Press).

—— and Girod, S. (2003), 'Retail Multinationals and Globalization: The Evidence is Regional', *European Management Journal*, 21/1: 24–37.

—— and Hodgetts, R. (2003), *International Business* (London: Prentice Hall/Financial Times).

Ruigrok, W., and Tulder, R. V. (1995), *The Logic of International Restructuring* (London: Routledge).

Sandholtz, W. (1993), 'Choosing Union: Monetary Politics and Maastricht', *International Organization*, 47/1: 1–39.

—— and Stone Sweet, A. (eds.) (1998), *European Integration and Supranational Governance* (Oxford: Oxford University Press).

—— and Zysman, J. (1989), '1992: Recasting the European Bargain', *World Politics*, 42/1: 95–128.

Sandler, T. (1992), *Collective Action: Theory and Applications* (Ann Arbor: University of Michigan Press).

Save the Children (2001), *The Bitterest Pill of All: The Collapse of Africa's Health Systems* (London: Save the Children), 21 May, **www.savethechildren.org.uk/temp/scuk/cache/cmsattach/614_bitterpill.pdf_**. Accessed Mar. 2004.

Sayer, A. (2000), *Realism and Social Science* (London: Sage).

Schelling, T. C. (1960), *The Strategy of Conflict* (Cambridge, Mass.: Harvard University Press).

Schiff, M. W., and Winters, L. A. (2003), *Regional Integration and Development* (New York: Oxford University Press for the World Bank).

Schiller, R. J. (2001), *Irrational Exuberance* (Princeton: Princeton University Press).

Schirato, T., and Webb, J. (2003), *Understanding Globalization* (London: Sage).

Schirm, S. A. (2002), *Globalization and the New Regionalism* (Cambridge: Polity Press).

Schmidheiny, S. (with World Business Council for Sustainable Development) (1992), *Changing Course: A Global Business Perspective on Development and the Environment* (Cambridge, Mass.: MIT Press).

—— and Zorraquin, F. (1996), *Financing Change: The Financial Community, Eco-efficiency, and Sustainable Development* (Cambridge, Mass.: MIT Press).

Schmidt, V. (2002), *The Futures of European Capitalism* (Oxford: Oxford University Press).

Schnietz, K. (1994), 'To Delegate or Not to Delegate: Congressional Institutional Choice in the Regulation of Foreign Trade, 1916–1934'. Ph.D. dissertation (Berkeley, University of California).

Scholte, J. A. (1997), 'The Globalization of World Politics', in J. Baylis and S. Smith (eds.), *The Globalization of World Politics: An Introduction to International Relations* (Oxford: Oxford University Press).

—— (2000a), 'Global Civil Society', in N. Woods (ed.), *The Political Economy of Globalization* (Houndmills: Macmillan).

—— (2000b), *Globalization: A Critical Introduction* (Basingstoke: Palgrave).

—— O'Brien, R., and Williams, M. (1999), 'The World Trade Organization and Civil Society', *Journal of World Trade*, 33/1: 107–24.

Schrank, A. (2002), 'Ready-to-Wear Development? Foreign Investment, Technology Transfer, and Learning-by-Watching in the Apparel Trade', Sociology Department, Yale University, available at **www.yale.edu/ccr/schrank.pdf**

Schreurs, M. A. (2002), *Environmental Politics in Japan, Germany, and the United States* (Cambridge: Cambridge University Press).

Schubert, A. (1992), *The Credit-Anstalt Crisis of 1931* (Cambridge: Cambridge University Press).

Schumacher, E. F. (1973), *Small is Beautiful: Economics as if People Mattered* (New York: Harper & Row).

Schwartz, H. (2001), 'Round up the Usual Suspects: Globalization, Domestic Politics, and Welfare State Change', in P. Pierson (ed.), *The New Politics of the Welfare State* (Oxford: Oxford University Press).

Scollay, R., and Gilbert, J. (2001), *New Regional Trading Arrangements in the Asia Pacific?* (Washington DC: Institute for International Economics).

Seligson, M., and Passe-Smith, J. (eds.) (1993), *Development and Underdevelopment: The Political Economy of Global Inequality* (Boulder, Colo.: Lynne Rienner).

Sell, S. (2000), 'Structures, Agents and Institutions: Private Corporate Power and the Globalisation of Intellectual Property Rights', in R. A. Higgott, G. R. D. Underhill, and A. S. Bieler (eds.), *Non-State Actors and Authority in the Global System* (London: Routledge).

Shaw, M. (1994), 'Civil Society and Global Politics: Beyond a Social Movements Approach', *Millennium*, 23/3: 647–68.

Shaw, R. (2001), *Reclaiming America* (Berkeley and Los Angeles: University of California Press).

Shiva, V. (1993), 'The Greening of the Global Reach', in W. Sachs (ed.), *Global Ecology: A New Arena of Political Conflict* (London: Zed Press).

Shonfield, A. (ed.) (1976), *International Economic Relations of the Western World 1959–1971*, i: *Politics and Trade* (London: Oxford University Press).

Silver, B. J. (2003), *Forces of Labor: Workers' Movements and Globalization Since 1870* (Cambridge: Cambridge University Press).

Simmons, B. A. (1994), *Who Adjusts? Domestic Sources of Foreign Economic Policy During the Interwar Years* (Princeton: Princeton University Press).

—— (1999), 'The Internationalisation of Capital', in H. Kitschelt, P. Lange, G. Marks, and J. D. Stephens (eds.), *Continuity and Change in Contemporary Capitalism* (Cambridge: Cambridge University Press).

Simon, J. L. (1996), *The Ultimate Resource 2* (Princeton: Princeton University Press).

Sinclair, T. (1994), 'Between State and Market', *Policy Sciences*, 27/4: 447–66.

Singer, H., and Roy, S. (1993), *Economic Progress and Prospects in the Third World* (Aldershot: Edward Elgar).

Singh, A., and Zammit, A. (2000), 'International Capital Flows: Identifying the Gender Dimension', *World Development*, 28/7: 1249–68.

Skidelsky, R. (2003), 'Keynes's Road to Bretton Woods: An Essay in Interpretation', in M. Flandreau, C.-L. Holtfrerich, and H. James (eds.), *International Financial History in the Twentieth Century* (Cambridge: Cambridge University Press).

Sklair, L. (2001), *The Transnational Capitalist Class* (Blackwell: London).

—— (2002), *Globalization: Capitalism and its Alternatives* (Oxford: Oxford University Press).

Smith, A. (1776/1976), *An Inquiry into the Nature and Causes of the Wealth of Nations* (Oxford: Oxford University Press). See also, **www.econlib.org/library/Smith/smWN.html**

Smith, P., and Smythe, L. (1999), 'Globalization, Citizenship and Technology: The MAI Meets the Internet', *Canadian Foreign Policy*, 7/2: 83–106.

Snidal, D. (1985*a*), 'Coordination versus Prisoners' Dilemma: Implications for International Cooperation and Regimes', *American Political Science Review*, 79/4: 923–42.

—— (1985*b*), 'The Limits of Hegemonic Stability Theory', *International Organization*, 39/4: 579–614.

Soederberg, S. (2002), 'A Historical Materialist Account of the Chilean Capital Controls: Prototype for Whom?', *Review of International Political Economy*, 9/3: 490–512.

Solomon, M. (2002), 'International NGOs: Towards a Global Cacophonous Democracy', in J. Goodman (ed.), *Protest and Globalisation: Prospects for Transnational Solidarity* (Annandale, NSW: Pluto Press).

Solomon, R. (1991), *Partners in Prosperity* (New York: Priority Press).

Soroos, M. S. (1997), *The Endangered Atmosphere* (Columbia, SC: University of South Carolina Press).

Soros, G. (1998), *The Crisis of Global Capitalism* (New York: Public Affairs).

—— (1997*a*), 'The Capitalist Threat', *Atlantic Monthly* (Feb.)

—— (1997*b*), Letter to the Editor, *Atlantic Monthly* (May).

South Commission (1990), *The Challenge to the South* (Oxford: Oxford University Press).

Spero, J. (1977), *The Politics of International Economic Relations* (London: George Allen & Unwin).

—— (1980), *The Failure of the Franklin National Bank* (New York: Columbia University Press).

Spiro, D. (1999), *The Hidden Hand of American Hegemony: Petrodollar Recycling and International Markets* (Ithaca, NY: Cornell University Press).

Srinivasan, T. N. (1999), 'Developing Countries in the World Trading System: From GATT, 1947, to the Third Ministerial Meeting of WTO, 1999', *World Economy*, 22/8: 1047–64.

Stasavage, D. (2003), 'When Do States Abandon Monetary Discretion? Lessons from the Evolution of the CFA Franc Zone', in J. Kirshner (ed.), *Monetary Orders: Ambiguous Economics, Ubiquitous Politics* (Ithaca, NY: Cornell University Press).

Steans, J. (1998), *Gender and International Relations: An Introduction* (New Brunswick, NJ: Rutgers University Press).

—— and Marchand, M. (forthcoming), *Gender and Global Political Economy* (Houndmills: Palgrave).

Stein, A. A. (1982), 'Coordination and Collaboration: Regimes in an Anarchic World', *International Organization*, 36/2: 294–324.

Steinmo, S. (2003), 'The Evolution of Policy Ideas: Tax Policy in the Twentieth Century', *British Journal of Politics and International Relations*, 5/2: 206–36.

Stiglitz, J. E. (2000), 'The Insider: What I Learned at the World Economic Crisis', *The New Republic*, (17 Apr.), **www.tnr.com/041700/stiglitz041700.html**

—— (2002), *Globalization and its Discontents* (New York: W. W. Norton & Co.).

Stolper, W., and Samuelson, P. A. (1941), 'Protection and Real Wages', *Review of Economic Studies*, 9: 58–73.

Strange, S. (1986), *Casino Capitalism* (Oxford: Basil Blackwell).

—— (1988), *States and Markets* (London: Pinter).

—— (1998), *Mad Money* (Manchester: Manchester University Press).

Streck, C. (2001), 'The Global Environment Facility—a Role Model for International Governance?', *Global Environmental Politics*, 1/2: 71–94.

Strong, M. (2000), *Where on Earth are We Going?* (Toronto: Knopf).

Subbarao, K. et al. (1997), *Safety Net Programs and Poverty Reduction: Lessons from Cross-Country Experience* (Washington DC: World Bank).

Swank, D. (2002), *Global Capital, Political Institutions and Policy Change in Developed Welfare States* (Cambridge: Cambridge University Press).

Swenson, P. (2000), *Capitalists against Markets* (Oxford: Oxford University Press).

Switzer, J. V. (2004), *Environmental Politics: Domestic and Global Dimensions*, 4th edn. (Belmont, Calif.: Thomson/Wadsworth).

Tasca, H. J. (1938), *The Reciprocal Trade Policy of the United States* (New York, NY: Russell & Russell).

Taylor, A. M. (1996), 'Domestic Saving and International Capital Flows Reconsidered', NBER Working Paper 4892 (Cambridge, Mass.: National Bureau of Economic Research).

—— (2002), 'Globalization, Trade and Development: Some Lessons from History', NBER Working Paper 9326 (Cambridge, Mass.: National Bureau of Economic Research).

Taylor, M. (1987), *The Possibility of Cooperation* (Cambridge: Cambridge University Press).

Teeple, G. (1995), *Globalization and the Decline of Social Reform* (Toronto: Garamond Press).

Teivainen, T. (2002), *Enter Economism, Exit Politics* (London: Zed Press).

Tesar, L. L. (1991), 'Saving, Investment and International Capital Flows', *Journal of International Economics*, 31/1: 55–78.

Thomas, C. (1985), *New States, Sovereignty and Intervention* (London: Gower).

—— (1987), *In Search of Security: The Third World in International Relations* (Brighton: Wheatsheaf and Boulder, Colo.: Lynne Rienner).

—— (2000), *Global Governance, Development and Human Security* (London: Pluto Press).

—— (2002), 'Trade Policy and the Politics of Access to Drugs', *Third World Quarterly*, 23/2: 251–64.

—— (2004), 'The International Financial Institutions' Relations with Sub-Saharan Africa: Insights from the Issue of Representation and Voice', in P. Williams and I. Taylor (eds.), *Into Africa: External Involvement in the African Continent after the Cold War* (London: Routledge).

—— and Weber, M. (2004), 'Whatever Happened to "Health for All" by the Year 2000?', *Global Governance*, forthcoming.

Thomas, G. D. (1998), 'Civil Society: Historical Uses Versus Global Context', *International Politics*, 35/2: 49–64.

Tichenor, D. J. (2002), *Dividing Lines: The Politics of Immigration Control in America* (Princeton: Princeton University Press).

Tirole, J. (2002), *Financial Crises, Liquidity, and the International Monetary System* (Princeton: Princeton University Press).

Tisdell, C. (2001), 'Globalization and Sustainability: Environmental Kuznets Curve and the WTO', *Ecological Economics*, 39/2: 185–96.

Transnational Corporations in World Development: A Re-Examination (1978), UN Commission on Transnational Corporations (New York: UN Publications).

Tran Van Hoa (ed.) (2002), *Economic Crisis Management* (Cheltenham: Edward Elgar).

Traxler, F., and Woitech, B. (2000), 'Transnational Investment and National Labour Market Regimes: A Case of "Regime Shopping"?', *European Journal of Industrial Relations*, 6/2: 141–59.

Triffin, R. (1960), *Gold and the Dollar Crisis* (New Haven: Yale University Press).

Tullock, G. (1983), *The Economics of Income Distribution* (Boston: Kluwer-Nijhoff).

Turner, P. (1981), 'Capital Flows in the 1980s: A Survey of Major Trends', *BIS Economic Papers*, No. 30 (Geneva: Bank for International Settlements).

Turner, S. (1998), 'Global Civil Society, Anarchy and Governance: Assessing an Emerging Paradigm', *Journal of Peace Research*, 35/1: 25–42.

Tussie, D. (1987), *The Less Developed Countries and the World Trading System: A Challenge to the GATT* (London: Frances Pinter).

Tyers, R., and Anderson, R. K. (1992), *Disarray in World Food Markets* (Cambridge: Cambridge University Press).

Ugur, M. (ed.), (2001), *Open Economy Macroeconomics: A Reader* (London: Routledge).

UN (United Nations) (1992), *Agenda 21: The United Nations Programme of Action from Rio* (New York: United Nations).

—— (2002), 'Report of the International Conference on Financing for Development (or the Monterrey Report)', A/Conf.198/11, at: **www.un.org/esa/ffd/ aconf198-11.pdf**. Accessed Mar. 2004.

UNAIDS (2002), 'The Impact of HIV/AIDS', *Fact Sheet 2002* (UNAIDS).

UNCTAD (2001), *World Investment Report: Promoting Linkages* (Geneva: UNCTAD).

—— (2002a), *The Least Developed Countries Report* (Geneva: UNCTAD), **www.rrojasdatabank.org/ldc02toc.htm**; also available at **www.unctad.org/Templates/ Webflyer.asp?docid=2026&intitemID51397&lang5_** Accessed Mar. 2004.

—— (2002b), *Trade and Development Report 2002: Developing Countries in World Trade* (Geneva: United Nations Conference on Trade and Development).

—— (2002c), *World Investment Report 2002: Transnational Corporations and Export Competitiveness* (Geneva: UNCTAD).

—— (2003), *World Investment Report 2003: FDI Policies for Development: National and International Perspectives* (Geneva: UNCTAD).

UNDP (United Nations Development Programme) (1998), 'Consumption in a Global Village—Unequal and Unbalanced', in *Human Development Report 1998* (Oxford: Oxford University Press).

—— (1999), *Globalization with a Human Face: Human Development Report 1999* (New York: Human Development Report Office, United Nations Development Programme).

—— (2002), *Human Development Report 2002: Deepening Democracy in a Fragmented World*.

—— (2003a), *Human Development Report 2003: Millennium Development Goals: A Compact among Nations to End Human Poverty*, **www.undp.org**

—— (2003b), *Making Global Trade Work for People* (London: Earthscan).

—— Heinrich Boll Foundation, Rockefeller Brothers Fund, Rockefeller Foundation and Wallace Global Fund (2003), *Making Global Trade Work for People* (London: Earthscan).

UNEP (United Nations Environment Programme) (2000a), *Action on Ozone* (Geneva: UNEP), available at **www.unep.ch/ozone/pdf/ozone-action-en.pdf**

—— (2000b), *Global Environmental Outlook 2000* (London: Earthscan).

—— (2002), *Global Environment Outlook 3* (London: Earthscan).

—— (2003), 'Backgrounder: Basic Facts and Data on the Science and Politics of Ozone Protection', available at **www.unep.org/ozone/pdf/Press-Backgrounder.pdf**

UNFPA (United Nations Fund for Population Activities) (2001), *The State of the World Population 2001. Footprints and Milestones: Population and Environmental Change* (New York: United Nations Fund for Population Activities), available at **www.unfpa.org/publications/swp.htm**

Van Dormael, A. (1978), *Bretton Woods: The Birth of a Monetary System* (London: Macmillan).

van Staveren, I. (2002), 'Global Finance and Gender', in J. A. Scholte (ed.), *Civil Society and Global Finance* (London: Routledge).

Vaubel, R. (1986), 'A Public Choice Approach to International Organization', *Public Choice*, 51/1: 39–57.

Vaubel, R. (1991) 'The Political Economy of the International Monetary Fund', in R. Vaubel and T. D. Willett (eds.), *The Political Economy of International Organizations: A Public Choice Approach* (Boulder, Colo.: Westview Press).

Verdier, D. (1994), *Democracy and International Trade: Britain, France, and the United States, 1860–1990* (Princeton: Princeton University Press).

Vernon, R. (1995), 'The World Trade Organization: A New Stage in International Trade and Development', *Harvard International Law Journal*, 36: 329–40.

Victor, D., Raustiala, K., and Skolnikoff, E. (1998), *The Implementation and Effectiveness of International Environmental Commitments: Theory and Practice* (Cambridge, Mass.: MIT Press).

Viner, J. (1948), 'Power Versus Plenty', *World Politics*, 1/1: 1–29.

—— (1950), *The Customs Union Issue* (New York: Carnegie Endowment for International Peace).

Vivian, J. (ed.) (1995), *Adjustment and Social Sector Restructuring* (Geneva: UNRISD).

Vogel, D. (1995), *Trading Up: Consumer and Environmental Regulation in a Global Economy* (Cambridge, Mass.: Harvard University Press).

Vogler, J. (2000), *The Global Commons: Environmental and Technological Governance*, 2nd edn. (Chichester: John Wiley & Sons).

—— (2003), 'Taking Institutions Seriously: How Regime Analysis can be Relevant to Multilevel Environmental Governance', *Global Environmental Politics*, 3/2: 25–39.

Wabl, M. G. (2002), 'A "Monterrey Consensus" might replace the Washington Consensus', *UN Chronicle*, XXXIX/1.

Wackernagel, M., and Rees, W. (1996), *Our Ecological Footprint: Reducing Human Impact on the Earth* (Gabriola Island: New Society Publishers).

Wade, R. (1990), *Governing the Market: Economic Theory and the Role of Government in East Asian Industrialization* (Princeton: Princeton University Press).

—— (1992), 'East Asia's Economic Success: Conflicting Perspectives, Partial Insights, Shaky Evidence', *World Politics*, 44/2: 270–320.

—— (2002), 'US Hegemony and the World Bank: The Fight over People and Ideas', *Review of International Political Economy*, 9/2: 201–29.

—— (2003a), *Governing the Market: Economic Theory and the Role of Government in East Asian Industrialization*, 2nd edn. (Princeton: Princeton University Press).

—— (2003b), 'What Strategies Are Viable for Developing Countries Today? The WTO and the Shrinkage of Development Space', *Review of International Political Economy*, 10/4: 621–44.

—— (2003c), 'The Invisible Hand of the American Empire', *Ethics and International Affairs*, 17/2: 77–88.

—— (2004), 'On the Causes of Increasing World Poverty and Inequality, or Why the Matthew Effect Prevails', *New Political Economy*, forthcoming.

—— and Veneroso, F. (1998), 'The Asian Crisis: The High Debt Model Versus the Wall Street-Treasury-IMF Complex', *New Left Review*, 228: 3–23.

Wallace, H. (2000), 'The Policy Process: A Moving Pendulum', in H. Wallace and W. Wallace (eds.), *Policy-Making in the European Union*, 4th edn. (Oxford University Press).

—— and Wallace, W. (eds.) (2000), *Policy-Making in the European Union*, 4th edn. (Oxford: Oxford University Press).

Wallerstein, I. (ed.) (1975), *World Inequality: Origins and Perspectives on the World System* (Montreal: Black Rose Books).

—— (1983), *Historical Capitalism* (London: Verso).

Walton, J., and Seddon, D. (1994), *Free Markets and Food Riots: The Politics of Global Adjustment* (Oxford: Blackwell).

Waltz, K. N. (1979), *Theory of International Politics* (Reading, Mass.: Addison Wesley).

Wapner, P. (1996), *Environmental Activism and World Civic Politics* (Albany, NY: State University of New York Press).

—— (2003), 'World Summit on Sustainable Development: Toward a Post-Jo'burg Environmentalism', *Global Environmental Politics*, 3/1: 1–10.

Warkentin, C., and Mingst, K. (2000), 'International Institutions, the State and Global Civil Society in the Age of the World Wide Web', *Global Governance*, 6/2: 237–57.

Warr, P. G. (1998), 'Thailand', in R. H. McLeod and R. Garnaut (eds.), *East Asia in Crisis: From Being a Miracle to Needing One?* (London: Routledge).

Warren, B. (1980), *Imperialism: Pioneer of Capitalism* (London: Verso).

Watkins, K. (1998), *Economic Growth with Equity: Lessons from East Asia* (Oxford: Oxfam).

—— (2002), 'Is the WTO Legit?', *Foreign Policy*, 132/Sept.–Oct.: 78–9.

Watson, M. (2001), 'International Capital Mobility in an Era of Globalization: Adding a Political Dimension to the "Feldstein-Horioka Puzzle" ', *Politics*, 21/2: 81–92.

—— (2003), 'Ricardian Political Economy and the Varieties of Capitalism Approach: Specialisation, Trade and Comparative Institutional Advantage', *Comparative European Politics*, 1/2: 227–40.

WCED (World Commission on Environment and Development) (1987), *Our Common Future* (Oxford: Oxford University Press).

Webb, M. (1995), *The Political Economy of Policy Coordination: International Adjustment Since 1945* (Ithaca, NY: Cornell University Press).

Weber, M. (1958)[1913], 'The Social Psychology of the World Religions', in H. H. Gerth and C. Wright Mills (eds.), *Max Weber: Essays in Sociology* (New York: Oxford University Press).

Weingast, B., Shepsle K., and Johnsen, C. (1981), 'The Political Economy of Benefits and Costs', *Journal of Political Economy*, 89/4: 642–64.

Weiss, L. (1997), 'Globalization and the Myth of the Powerless State', *New Left Review*, 225: 3–27.

—— (1998), *The Myth of the Powerless State: Governing the Economy in a Global Era* (Cambridge: Polity Press).

Wendt, A. (1992), 'Anarchy is What States Make of It', *International Organization*, 42/2: 391–422.

—— (1995), 'Constructing International Politics', *International Security*, 20/1: 71–81.

—— (1998), 'On Constitution and Causation in International Relations', *Review of International Studies*, 24/5: 101–17.

WFS (1996), *World Food Summit: Technical Background Documents*, 13–17 Nov., Rome, available at **www.fao.org/docrep/003/w2612e/w2612e00.htm**

Whalley, J. (1999*a*), 'Special and Differential Treatment in the Millennium Round', *World Economy*, 22/8: 1065–93.

—— (1999*b*), 'Why Do Countries Seek Regional Trade Agreements?', in J. Frankel (ed.), *The Regionalization of the World Economy* (Cambridge, Mass.: National Bureau of Economic Research).

Wheeler, D. (2002), 'Beyond Pollution Havens', *Global Environmental Politics*, 2/2: 1–10.

WHO (World Health Organization) (2002), *Healthy Environments for Children: An Alliance to Shape the Future of Life* (Geneva: WHO).

Wilensky, H. L. (2002), *Rich Democracies: Political Economy, Public Policy and Performance* (Berkeley and Los Angeles: University of California Press).

Wilks, A., and Lefrancois, F. (for Bretton Woods Project and World Vision) (2002), *Blinding with Science or Encouraging Debate? How World Bank Analysis Determines PRSP Policies*, **www.brettonwoodsproject.org/article.shtml?cmd [126]=x-126-16047**

Williams, M. (1994), *International Economic Organizations and the Third World* (Hemel Hempstead: Harvester Wheatsheaf).

—— (2003), 'Social Movements and World Politics', in E. Kofman and G. Youngs (eds.), *Globalization: Theory and Practice* (London: Continuum).

Williamson, O. (1975), *Markets and Hierarchies: Analysis and Anti-Trust Implications* (New York: The Free Press).

Winham, G. R. (1986), *International Trade and the Tokyo Round Negotiation* (Princeton: Princeton University Press).

—— (1990), 'The Prenegotiation Phase of the Uruguay Round', *International Journal*, 44: 280–303.

—— (1998*a*), 'Explanations of Developing Country Behaviour in the GATT Uruguay Round Negotiation', *World Competition*, 21/3: 109–34.

—— (1998*b*), 'The World Trade Organization: Institution-Building in the Multilateral Trade System', *World Economy*, 21/3: 349–68.

—— (2000), 'The Uruguay Round and the World Economy', in R. Stubbs and G. Underhill (eds.) *Political Economy and the Changing Global Order*, 2nd edn. (Oxford: Oxford University Press).

Wintrobe, R. (1998), *The Political Economy of Dictatorship* (Cambridge: Cambridge University Press).

Wolf, D., and Zangl, B. (1996), 'The European Economic and Monetary Union: "Two-level Games" and the Formation of International Institutions', *European Journal of International Relations*, 2/3: 355–93.

Wolfensohn, J. D. (2001), 'Responding to the Challenges of Globalization—Remarks to the G-20 Finance Ministers and Central Governors', World Bank, available at **www.worldbank.org/html/extdr/extme/ jdwsp111701.htm**. Accessed Nov. 2003.

—— (2002*a*), 'Forward', *World Development Indicators 2002* (Washington DC: World Bank).

—— (2002*b*), 'World Bank President Outlines Post-Monterrey Action Plan to Development Committee', 16 Apr., **http://web.worldbank.org/WBSITE/EXTERNAL/ NEWS/0,,contentMDK:20042672~menuPK:34463 ~pagePK:64003015~piPK:64003012~theSitePK:4607,0 0.html**; and **http://web.worldbank.org/WBSITE/ EXTERNAL/NEWS/0,,contentMDK:20042672%7Emenu PK:34463%7EpagePK:64003015%7EpiPK:64003012% 7EtheSitePK:4607,00.html**>. Accessed Mar. 2004.

Wood, A. (1994), *North–South Trade, Employment and Inequality* (Oxford: Oxford University Press).

Wood, E. M. (2003), *Empire of Capital* (London: Verso).

Woods, N. (2001) 'Making the IMF and World Bank more accountable', *International Affairs*, 77/1: 83–100.

—— (2003), 'Order, Justice, the IMF and the World Bank', in R. Foot, J. L. Gaddis, and A. Hurrell (eds.), *Order and Justice in International Relations* (Oxford: Oxford University Press).

World Bank (1992), *World Development Report 1992* (New York: Oxford University Press).

—— (1999*a*), *Global Development Finance* [electronic resource] (Washington DC: International Bank for Reconstruction and Development/The World Bank), computer disks; 3 1/2 in.

—— (1999*b*), *Global Economic Prospects and the Developing Countries 1998/99: Beyond Financial Crisis* (Washington DC: World Bank).

—— (2000), *Trade Blocs* (New York: Oxford University Press).

—— (2001*a*), *Global Development Finance 2001: Building Coalitions for Effective Development Finance* [electronic resource] (Washington DC: The World Bank).

—— (2001*b*), 'World Development Indicators 2001', World Bank.

—— (2001*c*), *World Development Report, 2000/2001: Attacking Poverty* (Oxford: Oxford University Press).

—— (2002*a*), *Global Development Finance: Financing the Poorest Countries* [electronic resource] (Washington DC: World Bank), 1 CD-ROM; 4 3/4 in. + 1 insert.

World Bank (2002*b*), *Globalization, Growth, and Poverty: Building an Inclusive World Economy* (New York: Oxford University Press).

—— (2002*c*), 'World Bank Estimates Cost of Millennium Development Goals', 21 Feb., **http://web.worldbank.org/WBSITE/EXTERNAL/ NEWS/0,,contentMDK:20034427~menuPK:34463 ~pagePK:64003015~piPK:64003012~theSitePK:4607,0 0.htm**; and **http://web.worldbank.org/WBSITE/ EXTERNAL/NEWS/0,,contentMDK:20034427%7Emenu PK:34463%EpagePK:64003015%7EpiPK:64003012%7 EtheSitePK:4607,00.htm**. Accessed Mar. 2004.

—— (2002*d*), *World Development Indicators 2002* (Washington DC: World Bank).

WTO (World Trade Organization) (1999*a*), 'World Trade Growth Slower in 1998 after Unusually Strong Growth in 1997', (Geneva: World Trade Organization) 16 Apr., **www.wto.org/wto/intltrad/internat.htm**

—— (1999*b*), *WTO, Trade and Environment*, Special Studies 4 (Geneva: WTO), Press Release available at **www.wto.org/ english/tratop_e/envir_e/stud99_e.htm**

—— (2000*a*), 'Developing Countries Merchandise Exports in 1999 Expanded by 8.5%—About Twice as Fast as the Global Average' (Geneva: World Trade Organization). Accessed 10 Jan. 2004, available at **www.wto.org/english/ news_e/pres00_e/pr175_e.htm**

—— (2000*b*), 'Mapping of Regional Trade Agreements: Note by the Secretariat', Committee on Regional Trade Agreements, WT/REG/W/41 (Geneva: World Trade Organization) 11 Oct., **www.wto.org/english/ tratop_e/region_e/wtregw41_e.doc** (Chart 2: 5).

—— (2000*c*), 'Overview of the State of Play of WTO Disputes' (2000), (Geneva: WTO Informal Paper).

—— (2001*a*), *World Trade Report* (Geneva: WTO).

—— (2001*b*), 'WTO successfully concludes negotiations on China's entry', WTO Press Release (PRESS/243), 17 Sept. 2001.

—— (2002), *World Trade Report* (Geneva: WTO).

—— (2003*a*) *Annual Report* (Geneva: WTO).

—— (2003*b*), 'Decision removes final patent obstacle to cheap drug imports', WTO Press Release, PRESS/350/Rev. 1, 4 Sept. 2003.

—— (2003*c*), *World Trade Report* (Geneva: WTO). Available at **www.wto.org/english/news_e/pres03_e/ pr348_e.htm**

WWF (World Wide Fund for Nature) (2002), *Living Planet Report 2002* (Gland, Switzerland: WWF-World Wide Fund for Nature), available at **www.panda.org/downloads/general/LPR_2002.pdf**

Yandle, B. (1984), 'Intertwined Interests, Rent Seeking and Regulation', *Social Science Quarterly*, 65/4: 1002–12.

Young, B. (2002), 'On Collision Course: The European Central Bank, Monetary Policy and the Nordic Welfare Model', *International Feminist Journal of Politics*, 4/3: 295–314.

Young, O. R. (ed.) (1999), *The Effectiveness of International Environmental Regimes: Causal Connections and Behavioral Mechanisms* (Cambridge, Mass.: MIT Press).

—— (2002), *The Institutional Dimensions of Environmental Change: Fit, Interplay, and Scale* (Cambridge, Mass.: MIT Press).

Young, Z. (2003), *A New Green Order: The World Bank and the Politics of the Global Environment Facility* (London: Pluto Press).

Zaller, J. (1992), *The Nature and Origins of Mass Opinion* (New York: Cambridge University Press).

Zartman, I. W. (ed.) (1987), *Positive Sum: Improving North–South Negotiations* (New Brunswick, NJ: Transaction Books).

Zevin, R. (1992), 'Are World Financial Markets More Open? If So, Why and with What Effects?', in T. Banuri and J. B. Schor (eds.), *Financial Openness and National Autonomy: Opportunities and Constraints* (Oxford: Oxford University Press).

Zimmerman, H. (2002), *Money and Security: Troops, Monetary Policy and West Germany's Relations with the United States and Britain 1950–71* (Cambridge: Cambridge University Press).

Zolo, D. (1997), *Cosmopolis: Prospects for World Government* (Cambridge: Polity Press).

Zürn, M. (1992), *Interessen und Institutionen in der internationalen Politik. Grundlegung und Anwendung des situationsstrukturellen Ansatzes* (Opladen: Leske & Budrich).

Glossary

Absolute Advantage Where a country produces one or more goods or services at lower cost than other countries.

Adjustable Peg A form of international monetary system in which governments are permitted to change their currencies' exchange rates, which are otherwise normally fixed in value against other currencies.

Anarchy The absence of a centralized authority in the international system capable of enforcing agreements.

Autarchy When a country attempts to maximize its self-sufficiency by minimizing contacts with the global economy.

Balance of Payments An account of a country's transactions with foreign countries and international institutions in a specific period. Transactions are divided into *current account*, which consists of the *balance of trade* in goods and services plus profits and interest on overseas assets less those paid to foreign owners of domestic assets, plus net transfers such as worker remittances. The *capital account* consists of inflows and outflows of money for investment, and for grants and loans (and their repayment). The balance of payments is an accounting identity: the entries in the account should sum to zero with, for instance, any imbalances on the current account being offset by net movements of capital.

Balance of Trade *see* **Balance of Payments**

Bretton Woods New Hampshire village in which is located the Mount Washington Hotel, the site of the 1944 United Nations Monetary and Financial Conference. The birthplace of the International Monetary Fund and the World Bank. "Bretton Woods" is often used as shorthand for the post-war international financial regimes.

Capital Account *see* **Balance of Payments**

Capital Controls Restrictions placed by governments on private actors' moving funds in or out of the territories they control.

Coase Theorem The argument that economic efficiency will be optimized as long as property rights are fully allocated and completely free trade in these rights is possible.

Collaboration Games A type of game where the **Pareto-optimal** solution the players desire is not an equilibrium outcome: the pursuit of strategies that are rational for individual players produces a sub-optimal outcome, as in the Prisoner's Dilemma.

Common Market A **customs union** that also allows free movement of factors (capital, labour) within its boundaries.

Common Pool Resources Goods that cannot be withheld from those that do not pay for them, and whose consumption comes at the expense of other potential consumers.

Comparative Advantage Where a country is relatively more efficient at producing at least one product than others, even though it may lack **absolute advantage** in producing that good or service. Production according to comparative advantage enables specialization in relatively more efficient production, thereby increasing welfare.

Competitive Advantage The competitive strength of an economy that derives from the capacity of its firms in various sectors. Whether government intervention can enhance an economy's competitive advantage remains a matter of considerable controversy.

Conditionality The stipulation by lenders of conditions that borrowers must meet if they are to continue to receive instalments of their loans.

Coordination Games A type of game that typically has multiple **Nash Equilibria**, some of which are more preferred by one or more players.

Current Account *see* **Balance of Payments**

Customs Unions Agreements between two or more countries to free trade between themselves and to adopt a common tariff on imports from countries outside the customs union.

Dollarization The adoption by foreign countries of the US dollar as their national currency.

Dumping A situation where a country's exports are sold in foreign markets at a price less than that at which they are sold at home.

Ecological Footprint A measure (translated into hectares of average biologically productive land) of the resources required to sustain a person's lifestyle.

Ecological Shadow A concept that attempts to capture the environmental impact of a country in jurisdictions beyond its sovereign control.

Economic Union A **common market** that has also adopted common **monetary** and **fiscal policies**.

Economies of Scale Realized when longer production runs enable firms to produce at a lower average unit cost.

Embedded Liberalism A concept put forward by John Gerard Ruggie, following Karl Polanyi, to capture the compromise in postwar economic regimes between liberalization and the pursuit of domestic social and political objectives.

Enabling Clause formally the 1979 Decision on Differential and More Favourable Treatment, Reciprocity and Fuller Participation of Developing Countries, it legitimizes **Special and Differential Treatment** in the trade regime for less developed countries.

Environmental Kuznets Curve A graphical representation of the relationship between level of per capita income and pollution that shows that levels of pollution initially increase with economic growth but then decline once per capita income reaches high levels.

Export-Oriented Industrialization Strategy for economic development based on domestic production primarily targeted at international markets.

Exporting Environmentalism The use by TNCs in less developed economies of more environmentally-friendly technologies than are required by local laws.

Externalities Consequences for societal welfare (costs and benefits) that are not captured in the market price of a good, e.g., pollution is a negative externality if the producers do not pay the financial costs it imposes on society; innovation can be a positive externality if pricing does not capture the full benefits that flow from innovators to the broader society. Externalities are a type of **market failure**.

Factor Price Equalization the process whereby trade generates a tendency for the prices of factors (capital or labour) to be equalized (a process predicted by the **Stolper-Samuelson theorem**).

Feldstein-Horioka Puzzle In a world of unfettered capital mobility, savings will flow to those countries offering the highest interest rates while investment will be financed from the lowest cost source. Feldstein and Horioka, however, found in a 1980 study that national savings and domestic investment were highly correlated in 16 OECD countries, suggesting segmented capital markets and low capital mobility.

Financial Intermediaries Institutions that provide links between those with surplus savings and those who desire to use these funds for investment purposes.

Fiscal Policies Government budgetary policies on taxation and expenditure.

Foreign Direct Investment The establishment by domestic firms of a foreign subsidiary or their acquisition of a controlling interest in an existing foreign company.

Free Riders Actors that fail to contribute appropriately to the cost of the goods or services from which they benefit.

Free Trade Area Agreements between two or more countries to remove tariff and non-tariff barriers on trade between themselves.

General Agreement on Tariffs and Trade A 1947 agreement that became the principal component of the international trade regime following the failure of the international community to establish the **International Trade Organization**. Its provisions were incorporated in the World Trade Organization when it was established in 1995.

Generalized System of Preferences (GSP) Non-reciprocal programmes of tariff preferences on selected goods for less developed countries introduced by industrialized countries after GATT in 1971 permitted a waiver of the **MFN** requirement to facilitate special and differential treatment for LDCs.

Gini Coefficient A measure of income inequality devised by the Italian statistician, Corrado Gini. The Gini coefficient is a number between 0 and 1 where 0 represents perfect equality (everyone has the same income) and 1 represents perfect inequality (one person has all the income, all others have zero). The Gini coefficient is calculated using the Lorenz curve, which is a graph showing the relationship between the percentage of households and the percentage of the country's income they receive.

Global Environmental Facility A fund established in 1991, jointly managed by the World Bank, the United Nations Development Programme, and the United Nations Environment Programme, that finances environmental programmes in less developed economies.

Gold Exchange Standard An international monetary system in which it is possible for central banks to convert their foreign exchange holdings into gold (one or more countries must guarantee that they will permit others to convert their currencies into gold, as the US did in the period from 1945 to 1971).

Gold Standard A monetary system in which the money supply is directly linked to the country's holdings of gold; citizens are usually entitled to exchange banknotes for gold. An international gold standard is an international monetary system in which the value of all currencies is set in terms of a unit of gold, and settlement of trade imbalances occurs through the transfer of gold reserves.

Graduation The process by which less developed economies are removed from the list of countries given special trade benefits by industrialized countries once they reach a certain level of development.

Gross Domestic Product The total value of goods and services produced by an economy in a specific time period.

Gross National Product Gross Domestic Product plus the income earned by domestic residents from investment abroad less the income earned by foreigners in the domestic market.

Heckscher-Ohlin Principle Countries will export those commodities that are intensive in the factor (land, labour, capital) in which they are best endowed.

Hegemonic Stability Argument that liberal (open) international economic regimes are associated with the presence of a dominant state.

Heavily Indebted Poor Countries (HIPC) A grouping of the world's poorest countries, identified as those eligible for concessional assistance from the World Bank group's International Development Association and from the IMF's Poverty Reduction and Growth Facility that face an unsustainable debt situation after the full application of traditional debt relief mechanisms. A debt initiative for HIPC was proposed by the World Bank and the IMF in 1996. By mid-2004, debt service relief totalling $41 billions had been agreed for 26 countries.

Import-Substituting Industrialization Strategy pursued by less developed economies to promote industrialization by domestic production of goods previously imported (usually undertaken behind high levels of tariff protection).

Inclusive Club Goods Goods that can be withheld from those who do not pay for them, and whose consumption does not reduce their availability to other potential consumers.

Infant Industry Promotion Idea that recently-established industries require protection until they are able to produce efficiently and withstand import competition from more advanced economies.

Interdependence A network of relationships among actors which is costly for any actor to break.

International Bank for Reconstruction and Development The original component of the World Bank group, created at the **Bretton Woods** conference in 1944. Subsequently, two other institutions, the International Finance Corporation (1956) and the International Development Association (1960) were added to the group. Most writers today simply refer to the "World Bank".

International Financial Institutions the International Monetary Fund and the World Bank.

International Trade Organization Intended to be the third of the major postwar international economic institutions alongside the World Bank and the IMF, the ITO was stillborn when the US Congress failed to ratify the Havana Charter.

Intra-Industry Trade International trade in products from the same sector.

Keynesian Economics A branch of economic theory associated with the work of John Maynard Keynes and his followers that suggests that there is no automatic tendency for economies to reach an equilibrium position that sustains full employment, and that governments through their manipulation of **fiscal policies** can affect aggregate demand and reduce unemployment.

Least Developed Countries A UN-designated group of 49 low income countries, membership of which is defined by per capita GDP under $900, weak human assets (a composite index of health, nutrition and education indicators), and high economic vulnerability (a composite index based on instability of export earnings, dependence on a limited number of primary product exports, and overall size of the economy).

Lender of Last Resort A financial institution, usually the central bank, that is charged with the responsibility of providing loans to other financial institutions when they need an injection of cash and no other institution is willing to lend to them.

Liquidity International liquidity comprises the total gold and foreign exchange reserves and **Special Drawing Rights** (that is, all international reserves acceptable to other countries) held by all countries in the international financial system.

Logrolling The practice whereby two or more legislators agree to trade their votes so that they support legislation on which they have no particular interest in order to gain support for legislation that they regard as more important, e.g., financing of projects in their electoral districts.

Market Failure A situation where a market does not achieve the optimal allocation of resources. Causes of market failure include the presence of public goods, externalities, and imperfect information.

Marshall Plan A US post-war programme to provide grants and loans to assist in the rebuilding of the economies of Europe and some European colonies.

Minilateralism Policy coordination among a small number of states.

Monetarism A branch of macroeconomic theory that holds that changes in the money supply affect aggregate demand for goods and services, and thus the rate of inflation.

Monetary Policies Government policies on the money supply, the rate of interest, and the exchange rate.

Moral Hazard A form of **Market Failure** the creation of a situation in which individuals or institutions are encouraged to act irresponsibly because of the guarantees (implicit or explicit) that others provide to them, for instance, people with insurance may take greater risks than those without it because they know they will receive compensation if they suffer adverse consequences from their behaviour.

Most-Favoured Nation Treatment The principle of non-discrimination, enshrined in Article I. of the GATT/WTO, that members should give all other members the most favourable treatment they offer to any member.

Multifibre Arrangement (MFA) A multilateral agreement (1974–94) limiting the exports of textiles and clothing by less developed countries to industrialized countries. Industrialized countries agreed to phased out the MFA over a ten year period as part of the Uruguay Round agreement.

Multilateral Agreement on Investment (MAI) A proposal made by OECD members originally in 1995 for a multilateral agreement that would liberalize investment regimes, provide protection for foreign investors, and establish dispute settlement mechanisms. The talks on establishing an MAI collapsed in 1998 following disagreements among industrialized countries and opposition from many less developed countries and civil society groups.

Multilateralism Policy coordination by three or more states on the basis of principles that specify appropriate conduct for a class of actions.

Multinational Enterprise *see* **Transnational Corporation**

Nash Equilibrium A situation in game theory where all participants are pursuing their best possible strategy given the strategies that other players have chosen, in other words, no player can improve his/her situation by changing their own strategy.

National Treatment A GATT/WTO principle requiring members to offer foreign producers of a good or service the same treatment they give to domestic producers of the same good or service.

Newly-Industrializing Economy term originally applied to the 'Gang of Four' economies of East Asia (Hong Kong, Korea, Singapore, Taiwan) that experienced rapid economic growth from the late 1960s. Subsequently sometimes applied to selected rapidly-growing Southeast Asian and Latin American economies.

New International Economic Order A list of demands by less developed economies in the 1970s that proposed a radical restructuring of international economic regimes.

Non-Tariff Barriers (also **Non-Tariff Measures**): A wide variety of official or unofficial devices (other than tariffs) that hinder imports into an economy, e.g., quantitative restrictions, health regulations, customs procedures.

ODA Official Development Assistance, popularly referred to as foreign aid.

OEM Original Equipment Manufacturers: Originally used (primarily in the electronics industry) to describe a company that manufactured a product that was marketed under another company's brand name. Now also used (somewhat confusingly) to refer to companies that sell a final product under their own brand name that is assembled from components manufactured by others, e.g., Toyota, General Motors and other auto assemblers are often referred to as OEMs.

Oligopoly An industry dominated by a few large suppliers.

Orderly Marketing Arrangement (OMA) An agreement between an importing and one or more exporting countries whereby the latter pledge to limit their exports of particular products. Outlawed by the GATT Uruguay Round agreement.

Pareto-Optimal Outcomes where no actor can be better off without making others worse off. In Pareto deficient situations, other outcomes could increase some actors' welfare without decreasing that of others.

Plaza Accord Agreement reached by the G7 at the Plaza Hotel in New York in 1985 for concerted intervention by central banks to produce a currency re-alignment that resulted in a depreciation of the US dollar against other major currencies.

Portfolio Investment The acquisition of interest-bearing foreign securities (either government bonds or company stocks and shares) which do not in themselves give the investor management control over the foreign concern.

Private Goods Goods and services that can be withheld from those who do not pay for them, and which cannot be used by others without additional production taking place.

Property Rights The legal right of owners of resources to be paid for their usage, e.g., fees paid to patent or copyright owners.

Public Goods Goods that cannot be withheld from consumers who do not pay for them, and whose consumption does not reduce their availability to other consumers.

Purchasing Power Parity (PPP) A method of computing an appropriate exchange rate between currencies (rather than that determined by the market or fixed by governments), which rests on determining domestic purchasing power by calculating the price of a basket of goods in the two countries in local currencies. To compute the PPP exchange rate between the two currencies, one takes the ratio of the prices for the baskets of goods in local currencies. PPP exchange rates are often used as a means of presenting a more accurate comparison of standards of living across countries than those given by actual exchange rates.

Race to the Bottom The idea that in a globalized economy, some governments will attempt to increase their attractiveness to investors by offering minimal requirements on, for example, environmental and labour standards and taxation.

Reciprocity The principle in international trade that countries that benefit from trade liberalization by others should offer equivalent (but not necessarily identical) concessions in return.

Regime A set of international governing arrangements (including rules, norms, and procedures) that are intended to regularize the behaviour of state and non-state actors and control its effects.

Rules of Origin Regulations negotiated as part of free trade agreements that specify the conditions that goods must meet if they are to be considered as originating in a partner country (e.g., that a specific share of the good's value must be added locally). Intended to prevent non-partner countries from trans-shipping goods to take advantage of the lower tariffs offered within a free trade agreement.

Safeguards Provisions enabling countries with problems in specific sectors or their economy more generally to seek temporary exemptions from some of their obligations in the trade regime.

Seigniorage The profit that results from the difference between the cost of producing and distributing money and the face value of that money. Originally the difference between the face value of a coin and the cost of the metal that went into that coin.

Singapore Issues The 1996 WTO ministerial meeting in Singapore began exploratory work on co-operation on policy harmonization in four areas: investment, competition, transparency in government procurement, and trade facilitation. These subsequently became known as the "Singapore issues".

Single Undertaking The principle within the GATT/WTO that members must accept all parts of the agreement rather than signing on selectively to individual components.

Special and Differential Treatment Exemptions for less developed countries from some of the obligations in the trade regime.

Special Drawing Rights An international reserve asset created by the International Monetary Fund in 1969. Over 30 billions SDRs have been created; these were distributed by the IMF to member countries in proportion to the size of their IMF quota. The SDR is valued in terms of a basket of sixteen major currencies.

Specific Factors Model Movement of factors of production to different uses following trade liberalization may be difficult: the effects of trade, therefore, contrary to the **Stolper-Samuelson Theorem** may not benefit/harm different factors across various sectors but rather hurt/benefit *all* factors *within* the same industrial sector.

Sterilization Efforts by monetary authorities to counter the impact of international monetary flows on domestic economic activity by issuing/selling financial instruments to reduce or increase the domestic money supply.

Stolper-Samuelson Theorem Trade benefits the owners of factors of production that are relatively abundant in an economy while lowering the returns to owners of relatively scarce factors, e.g., trade for labour-rich countries such as China should benefit (their relatively-abundant) labour.

Strategic Trade Policies Efforts by governments to promote domestic companies in international industries characterized by **oligopoly** through policies (e.g., investment subsidies) intended to permit them to move strategically (e.g., enable them to become early developers of a product).

Structural Adjustment Programmes, often designed in association with the international financial institutions, pursued by countries experiencing debt problems. Usually include privatization of assets, reductions in government expenditure to reduce budgetary deficits, trade liberalization, encouragement of foreign investment, and currency devaluation.

Sunk Costs Costs that are difficult for investors to recover, e.g., investment in physical infrastructure, plant and machinery.

Supranational Institutions International institutions to which states have ceded some of their sovereignty, for example, the European Union.

Swiss formula A method of reducing tariffs based on a mathematical equation, which results in higher tariffs being reduced more than lower tariffs. It was used in the Tokyo Round of GATT negotiations.

Terms of Trade The price of a country's exports relative to the price of its imports.

Trade Creation Where a preferential trade agreement leads to the replacement of domestic production by lower-cost imports from a party to the trade agreement.

Trade Diversion Where a preferential trade agreement leads to the displacement of goods previously imported from a non-preferred trading partner by imports from a party to the preferred agreement (because these preferential imports now enter the local market at a reduced tariff).

Tragedy of the Commons Garrett Hardin, in a paper published in *Science* in 1968, first put forward the idea that individuals rationally pursuing their self interest where they have access to a freely available good (a "commons") will inevitably act in a way that is collectively irrational, e.g., through over-grazing a pasture.

Transaction Costs The costs other than the monetary price that are involved in trading goods and services, e.g., search and information costs, bargaining and decision costs, and policing and enforcement costs. High transaction costs are often viewed as a significant example of **externalities**.

Transnational Corporations (also Multinational Enterprises): Companies that engage in **Foreign Direct Investment**, that is, which own, control, and manage assets in more than one country.

Triffin Paradox Yale University economist Robert Triffin pointed out in a 1960 book that the Bretton Woods monetary system rested on the confidence of other countries in the **gold exchange** standard, that is, that they could convert their dollar holdings into gold, yet the capacity of the US to guarantee this conversion was being undermined by dollar outflows that were the principal source of new liquidity in the system. If outflows stopped, the system would have insufficient liquidity; if they continued, confidence in the system would be undermined.

TRIMs Trade Related Investment Measures—the title of a Uruguay Round WTO agreement that prohibits governments from applying measures that discriminate against foreign companies or foreign products, e.g., requirements that foreign investors must source a certain value of their inputs locally ('local content requirements) or export a certain value of their output ('trade balancing' requirements).

TRIPs Trade-Related aspects of Intellectual Property Rights—a Uruguay Round WTO agreement that establishes minimum levels of protection that governments must give to the intellectual property of fellow WTO members.

Two-Level Game Term coined by Robert Putnam to refer to negotiations in which governments must negotiate simultaneously at two levels: with domestic constituencies and with one or more foreign partners.

Voluntary Export Restraint An agreement between an exporting and importing country under which the exporting country agrees to limit the total (value or volume of) exports of particular products. Outlawed by the GATT Uruguay Round Agreements.

Washington Consensus Phrase coined by John Williamson to refer to the prevailing views held in the late 1980s and early 1990s by the international financial institutions and governments of most industrialized countries regarding the desirable policy agenda for less developed economies, e.g., liberalization of their trade regimes, privatization of state-owned enterprises, reduction of state intervention in the economy.

OTHER USEFUL SOURCES

Print

Bannock, G., R. E. Baxter and E. Davis (2003), *The Penguin Dictionary of Economics*, 7th edit. (London: Penguin).

Black, J. (2003), *A Dictionary of Economics*, 2nd edit. (Oxford: Oxford University Press).

Pearce, D. W. (1992), *The MIT Dictionary of Modern Economics*, 4th edit. (Cambridge, Mass.: MIT Press).

Online

Deardorff's Glossary of International Economics
http://www-personal.umich.edu/~alandear/glossary/

Economics—Wikipedia, the free encyclopedia
http://en.wikipedia.org/wiki/Economics

The Economist's Economics A-Z
http://economist.com/research/Economics/

Index

Italic numbers denote references to Boxes